UNDERSTANDING POETRY

AN ANTHOLOGY FOR COLLEGE STUDENTS

BY

CLEANTH BROOKS, JR.

AND

ROBERT PENN WARREN

THE LOUISIANA STATE UNIVERSITY

NEW YORK

HENRY HOLT AND COMPANY

TO

WILLIAM A. READ

The editors of this book wish to acknowledge a deep indebtedness to the following persons for encouragement and assistance: Bertrand Bronson, of the University of California; Donald Davidson, of Vanderbilt University; Edward Davison, of the University of Colorado; Robert B. Heilman, of the Louisiana State University; Walton R. Patrick, of the Louisiana State University; John Crowe Ransom, of Kenyon College; Allen Tate, of the Woman's College of the University of North Carolina; and Mark Van Doren, of Columbia University.

LETTER TO THE TEACHER

This book has been conceived on the assumption that if poetry is worth teaching at all it is worth teaching as poetry. The temptation to make a substitute for the poem as the object of study is usually overpowering. The substitutes are various, but the most common ones are:

1. Paraphrase of logical and narrative content.
2. Study of biographical and historical materials.
3. Inspirational and didactic interpretation. *explanatory*

Of course, paraphrase may be necessary as a preliminary step in the reading of a poem, and a study of the biographical and historical background may do much to clarify interpretation; but these things should be considered as means and not as ends. And though one may consider a poem as an instance of historical or ethical documentation, the poem in itself, if literature is to be studied as literature, remains finally the object for study. Moreover, even if the interest is in the poem as a historical or ethical document, there is a prior consideration: one must grasp the poem as a literary construct before it can offer any real illumination as a document.

When, as a matter of fact, an attempt is made to treat the poem as an object in itself, the result very often is, on the one hand, the vaguest sort of impressionistic comment, or on the other, the study of certain technical aspects of the poem, metrics for instance, *in isolation from other aspects and from the total intention.*

In illustration of these confused approaches to the study of poetry the editors submit the following quotations drawn almost at random from a group of current textbooks.

The sole critical comment on "Ode to a Nightingale" in one popular textbook is:

"The song of the nightingale brings sadness and exhilaration to the poet and makes him long to be lifted up and away from the limitations of life. The seventh stanza is particularly beautiful."

In the same textbook a typical exercise reads:

"What evidences of a love of beauty do you find in Keats's poems?"

But one is constrained to voice the following questions:

1. Is not the real point of importance the relation of the paradox of "exhilaration" and "sadness" to the theme of the poem? As a matter of fact, the question of the theme of the poem is never raised in this textbook.

2. The seventh stanza is referred to as "beautiful," but on what grounds is the student to take any piece of poetry as "beautiful"?

3. Even if the exercise quoted is relevant and important, there is a real danger that the suggestion to the student to look for beautiful objects in the poem will tend to make him confuse the mention of beautiful or agreeable objects in poetry with poetic excellence.

Some of the same confusions reappear in another book: "These lyrics ["Ode to the West Wind" and "To a Skylark"] are characterized by a freshness and spontaneity, beautiful figures of speech in abundance, melody, and an unusually skillful adaptation of the form and movement of the verse to the word and the idea. Their melodiousness is sometimes compared with that of Schubert's music."

But in what, for example, does a beautiful comparison consist? The implication is that the beautiful comparison is one which makes use of beautiful objects. Again, when a student has been given no concrete exposition of the "adaptation of form and movement . . . to the word and the idea" of a poem, and has received no inkling of what the "idea" of a particular poem is, what is such a statement expected to mean to him?

Or again: "To the simplicity and exquisite melodiousness of these earlier songs, Blake added mysticism and the subtlest kind of symbolism." One is moved to comment: In the first place, the student can only be made to grasp the function of symbolism in poetry by the most careful investigation of particular instances; certainly, "the subtlest kind of symbolism" should not be flung at him with no further introduction than is provided by this sentence. In the second place, what can the sentence mean on any level? Is it proper to say that any poet "adds" mysticism to anything? And what sort of simplicity is it to which subtle symbolism can be added? Does the *mélange* remain simple? And what possible connection is implied here between the "exquisite melodiousness" and the mysticism and symbolism? In any case, the approach to poetry indicated in this sentence raises more problems than it solves.

To glean from another recent textbook: "Emily [Dickinson] the seer teases us into believing that she has dived into the depths where great truths lie and has brought up new and astounding specimens. Many of her bulletins from Immortality seem oracular. Shorn of her matchless imagery they turn out to be puritan platitudes or transcendental echoes. Her definitions of weighty abstractions are unphilosophical. They are quick fancies, created out of a fleeting mood, and are therefore frequently contradictory. But when Emily failed with logic, she succeeded with imagination." It is impossible, apparently, to determine from what principles of poetic criticism these remarks can be derived. The objection that Emily Dickinson's poetry when "shorn of its matchless imagery" would turn out to be platitudes could be raised with equal justification about the most celebrated passages of Shakespeare. The passage rests on a misconception of the relation of "truth" to poetry, and on a confused notion of what constitutes poetic originality. Certainly, to clarify the issue of "truth" and poetic excellence, or of originality and poetic excellence, would be a very ambitious undertaking; but that fact scarcely justifies a complete fogging of the issue.

Occasionally the writer of a textbook will attempt to deal with poetry as a thing in itself worthy of study; and apparently hoping to avoid the sort of vagueness found in the preceding quotation, will isolate certain aspects of poetry for special investigation. In its crudest manifestation this impulse leads to statistical surveys of one kind or another. The student, for instance, is exhorted to count or to classify the figures of speech in a poem; or to define metrical forms. There is a more sophisticated manifestation of the same impulse, as for example, in the following classification of metrical effects:

"Some of the varied effects *produced by meter* are illustrated in the following stanzas:

Sweet softness—

> Swiftly walk o'er the western wave,
>   Spirit of Night!
> Out of thy misty eastern cave,
> Where all the long and lone daylight,
> Thou wovest dreams of joy and fear,
> Which makes thee terrible, and dear—
>   Swift be thy flight!
>
> —Shelley, 'To Night' "

Stark simplicity—

> Out of the night that covers me,
>   Black as the pit from pole to pole,
> I thank whatever gods may be
>   For my unconquerable soul.
>
> —Henley, 'Invictus' "

The author has said flatly concerning these quotations that the effects described are "produced by meter." The statement is completely misleading and rests upon an imperfect understanding of the relation of meter to the other factors in a poem. A clever student would immediately confute the author by pointing out that the line, "Out of thy misty eastern cave," the meter of which is supposed to communicate "soft sweetness," and the line, "Out of the night that covers me," the meter of which is supposed to communicate "stark simplicity," have *exactly* the same meter. In fact, he might point out that many metrical effects are common to selections which communicate very different emotional effects.

This is not to deny that meter is an important factor in poetry, but it is to deny that a specific emotional effect can be tied absolutely to a particular metrical instance. The selections cited do produce different emotional effects, but the basis for the effect can only be given accurately by a study of the relations existing among all the factors, of which meter is only one.

Another instance of the isolation of one technical feature without regard for the whole context and for the particular poet's method is the following observation in a recent textbook:

"Hamlet's 'take arms against a sea of troubles' is a classic instance of the poet's failure to visualize what he is saying. Longfellow's mariner, in 'A Psalm of Life' 'sailing o'er life's solemn main' and at the same time apparently examining 'footprints on the sands of time,' is another example of confused phrasing."

This passage might be taken as a classic example of the misapplication of an undigested critical principle. We frequently see in textbooks on poetry and in rhetorics the warning against the use of "mixed metaphor." But, of course, in applying this principle one must, in every case, examine the context of the instance, the psychological basis, and the poet's intention.[1] These factors are entirely ignored in the present quotation. For instance, the dramatic situation in the passage from *Hamlet* and the relation of the style to it are dismissed by the high-handed and abstract application of this principle. Incidentally this method would eliminate the following well known passages, among many, from the work of Shakespeare:

> Tomorrow and tomorrow and tomorrow
> Creeps in this petty pace from day to day
> To the last syllable. . . .   *Macbeth*

>   If the assassination
> Could trammel up the consequence and catch
> With his surcease, success . . .   *Macbeth*

[1] This matter of mixed metaphor is discussed at length on pp. 387–391.

> Was the hope drunk
> Wherein you dressed yourself? hath it slept since?
> And wakes it now, to look so green and pale . . .
>
> *Macbeth*

The critic in question would apparently be embarrassed by the imaginative agility required for reading much of Shakespeare's poetry, especially the poetry of his so-called "great period," simply because he places his reliance on the mechanical and legalistic application of a single principle without reference to context.

As a matter of ironical fact, the image involved in the speech quoted from *Hamlet* can be visualized. One has only to remember the stories of Xerxes, and Cuchulain, one who punished and one who fought the sea, to grasp the point. Furthermore, in justice to "The Psalm of Life," which is on enough counts a very bad poem, one can indicate that a little more attentive reading will reveal the fact that the mariner who sees the footprints is not actually on the high seas at the moment, but is, as the poem specifically says, a "shipwrecked brother."

The editors of the present book hold that a satisfactory method of teaching poetry should embody the following principles.

1. Emphasis should be kept on the poem as a poem.
2. The treatment should be concrete and inductive.
3. A poem should always be treated as an organic system of relationships, and the poetic quality should never be understood as inhering in one or more factors taken in isolation.

With the hope of giving these principles some vitality the editors have undertaken this book.

This book must stand or fall by the *analyses* of individual poems which it contains. These *analyses* are intended to be discussions of the poet's adaptation of his means to his ends: that is, discussions of the relations of the various aspects of a poem to each other and to the total communication intended. Obviously, the analyses presented in the early sections of this book are simple and very incomplete accounts of the problems involved. But the analyses become more difficult as the student is provided with more critical apparatus and becomes more accustomed to the method. The analyses, therefore, form parts of an ascending scale and should not be studied haphazardly.

The general organization of the book is, likewise, determined by this scale of ascending difficulty. The book has seven divisions. Section I deals with poems in which the narrative element is relatively important. Poems of this general nature appear here because the narrative interest seems to afford the broadest and most unspecialized appeal to the ordinary student. The basic question behind the analyses in this section is: *what distinguishes the poetic treatment of a story from the more usual prose treatment?* Section II deals with poems in which the narrative is merely implied or is suppressed in favor of some such interest as that in psychology or character. Section III takes up another approach, that of the poet as observer rather than as narrator. The material in this section ranges from poems which ostensibly are simple, objective descriptions to the last poems, in which description emerges with a definite symbolic force.

Section IV takes up one of the more specialized technical problems, that of the nature of rhythm and meter as means of communication. The analyses in this section naturally emphasize the technical considerations of verse, but the attempt is constantly made to indicate the relation of these considerations to the others which the student has already studied. In Section V are considered some of the ways in which tone and attitude are communicated to the reader. The poems of Section VI present some special problems in the use of imagery as a device of communication, and those of Section VII raise questions concerning the function of idea and statement.

Although the poems are arranged in these groups, it is not to be understood that the topics which determine the arrangement are treated in isolation. As a matter of fact, the analyses and questions which are appended to each poem aim at making the student aware of the organic relationship existing among these factors in poetic communication. Obviously, any poem whatsoever would, finally, raise the questions associated with all of these topics. Questions involving imagery, for example, occur even in Section I and are treated in the analyses. Pedagogical convenience, however, demands that special attention be focused on special problems; but, as has been said, it does not demand that those problems be treated in isolation. A poem, then, is placed in any given section because it may be used to emphasize a certain aspect of poetic method and offers, it is hoped, an especially teachable example. But these classifications must be understood as classifications of convenience. Indeed, it might be a fruitful exercise for the students to return to poems in early sections after they have acquired more critical apparatus.

The poems, as has been pointed out, are arranged in a scale of increasing difficulty. Usually, poems of the simplest method and of the broadest general appeal appear in the early sections. But such a scale, of course, cannot be absolute. For example, a poem like "The Ancient Mariner," which appears in Section I, is on absolute grounds more difficult than many poems appearing in later sections. But it does offer a strong narrative interest. Furthermore, the poems in each section offer a scale of ascending difficulty in regard to the particular problem under discussion. Since this is the case, if poems toward the end of each of the later sections prove too difficult in certain classes, they may be omitted without impairing the general method.

Although the arrangement of poems adopted in this book is one of convenience, it is based on two considerations: first, on aspects of poetic communication, and second, on pedagogical expediency. Therefore, it is hoped that the present arrangement stands on a ground different from the arbitrary and irrational classifications frequently found in textbooks that depart from simple chronological order—classifications such as "lyrics of meditation" and "religious lyrics" and "poems of patriotism," or "the sonnet," the "Ode," the "song," etc.

If one accepts the principle that one must teach by a constant and analytical use of concrete examples, then the nature of the *Introduction* will be readily understood. The *Introduction* does not attempt to arrive at a "definition" of poetry or to explain, for instance, the workings of imagery or meter. It attempts, instead, to dispose of a few of the basic misconceptions with which the teacher is usually confronted in the class room, and therefore to prepare the student to enter upon an unprejudiced study of the actual poems. Likewise, the *Glossary* of critical terms is based on the idea that the teaching of the book will be by concrete example. The *Glossary* does not provide a set of definitions to be memorized all at once by the student. Rather, it provides definitions and an index of cross references to concrete applications of definitions, which the student can consult as the occasion demands. Even the schematic presentation of metrical terms has been relegated to the *Glossary,* although there it is so organized that it may be studied, if desired, as a consecutive discussion. But even in the case of metrical study, the editors suggest that the general principle of the book be applied.

There are two objections to the method of the present book which may occur to a teacher at this point. It may be objected that this text by its number of analyses attempts to usurp the function of the teacher and to do by the written word what can better be done by the spoken word. Or, second, it may be objected that the judgments of literary value which are involved (and necessarily involved) in the analyses are dogmatic and perhaps often in error.

In answer to the first objection it may be urged that: first, the analyses, if they are at all effective, relieve the teacher of a certain amount of preliminary drudgery and free him for a critical and perhaps more advanced treatment of the unanalyzed poems in each section of the book; second, since no analyses here could pretend to final completeness, a certain amount of explanation and extension will be required even in treating poems which are analyzed; and third, the fact that a liberal number of analyses are in printed form gives the student an opportunity for a careful private study of the poems in question. With regard to the second objection—the objection that the judgments in the analyses are dogmatic—the editors can only say that no dogmatism is intended. Naturally, they hope that most of their judgments are reasonable, but even if a teacher disagrees with an individual analysis, an explanation of that disagreement should dramatize for the student the basic issues involved. And in fact, the editors feel that disagreement is to be encouraged rather than discouraged in so far as pure impressionism can be eliminated from the debate.

Just as the editors feel that disagreement and debate may be healthful in sharpening the critical instinct of the student, so they feel that the study and analysis of bad and uneven poems will contribute to the same end. A reasonable number of such poems have been included, and a few have been analyzed. The great majority of the poems included in the book, however represent positive achievement. The modern poems included have not been chosen at random, nor merely on the ground of current fashion. They are intended to represent some of the various lines taken in the development of poetic method in this century. In general, it is hoped that the juxtaposition of good and bad poems, and of new and old poems, will serve to place emphasis on the primary matter of critical reading and evaluation.

Although this book is based on a principle, and is not a casual anthology, and although it is organized in the light of that principle, the final effect, it is hoped, will be to liberate rather than restrict the initiative of the teacher. By positing a principle and a definite objective, the book allows the teacher a great deal of liberty in devising correlative approaches to the general end. Although the book does suggest a variety of exercises for the student, such as analyses modeled on those in the book, comparisons of the prose and poetic versions of the same material, comparisons of poems treating the same theme, etc., the possibility for development along this line is almost infinite and can be adapted to individual needs.[1]

A last word: the editors of this book do not delude themselves that they have here provided, or could elsewhere provide, solutions for any of the fundamental problems of poetic criticism. Nor, least of all, have they provided in this book neat criteria which can be applied in rule-of-thumb fashion. Rather, they hope to present to the student, in proper context and after proper preparation, some of the basic critical problems—with the aim, not of making technical critics, but merely of making competent readers of poetry. At the least, they hope that this book will find some merit in the eyes of those who agree with Louis Cazamian: "that all students of literature should be regarded as historians is an exaggerated and a pernicious assumption. More important still, and much more fruitful than the problems of origins and development, are those of content and significance. What is the human matter, what the artistic value of the work?" So much for the general aim of this book. As for the general method, to quote again from this critic: "it is rightly felt that if the . . . student of literature is to be capable of an intelligent apprecia-

---

[1] A particularly fruitful source for the development of further exercises will lie in the application of principles developed in later sections of the book to poems treated in earlier sections. For example, the teacher may wish to return, after a study of metrics and related matters, to a poem like "The Rime of the Ancient Mariner" with such exercises as the following:

Discuss the technical devices of lines 103–106, 382, and 386.

Or he may wish to return to "La Belle Dame Sans Merci" to ask:

What is the effect of the metrical situation in lines 4 and 32?

For certain classes, the fact that this book has concentrated upon the interpretation and analysis of individual poems may provide an easy and suggestive approach to matters of literary theory and history. After the book has been completed, exercises may be framed, for instance, to relate Wordsworth's theories of diction to his actual practice in "Michael." The student may be asked to discuss lines 89, 169, and 434 in connection with the principle of the "real language of men." And in this connection the tone of the entire poem may be analyzed.

tion, he must go beyond the passive enjoyment of what he reads; he must be instructed, partly at least, in the mysteries of the art. . . ."

ACKNOWLEDGMENTS

The American Review: "Lee in the Mountains", by Donald Davidson, reprinted by permission of *The American Review*.

The Atlantic Monthly: extract from "Science and Modern Life", by Robert Andrews Millikan, from *The Atlantic Monthly,* April, 1928.

Mr. Howard Baker: "Ode to the Sea".

Chatto and Windus and Mr. Aldous Huxley: extract from *Vulgarity in Literature*.

Clarendon Press: "Nightingales", by Robert Bridges, from *The Shorter Poems of Robert Bridges,* Oxford (1931), by permission of the publishers.

Doubleday, Doran, and Company, Inc.: "Trees", by Joyce Kilmer, from: *Trees and Other poems,* by Joyce Kilmer copyright 1914 by Doubleday, Doran & Co., Inc.

Harcourt Brace, and Company: "Preludes" and "The Love Song of J. Alfred Prufrock", by T. S. Eliot, from *Collected Poems* of T. S. Eliot; "Portrait", by E. E. Cummings, from *Collected Poems* of E. E. Cummings; extract from *Queen Victoria,* by Lytton Strachey; extracts from *Practical Criticism* and *On Imagination,* by I. A. Richards, reprinted by permission of Harcourt Brace and Company, Inc.

Henry Holt, and Company: "King David" and "All But Blind", by Walter De La Mare, from *Collected Poems* of Walter De La Mare; "Out, Out", "Dust of Snow", "After Apple Picking", "Desert Places", "The Death of the Hired Man", by Robert Frost; "Hell Gate", "To an Athlete Dying Young", "Epitaph on an Army of Mercenaries", "The Lads in Their Hundreds", and "1887", by A. E. Housman; "Two of You", by Mark Van Doren.

Houghton Mifflin Company: "Pear Tree", and "Heat", by

Hilda Doolittle; "Patterns", by Amy Lowell; "Frescoes for Mr. Rockefeller's City", by Archibald MacLeish.

Alfred A. Knopf, Inc.: "Winter Remembered" and "The Equilibrists", by John Crowe Ransom, reprinted by permission of and special arrangement with Alfred A. Knopf, Inc., authorized publishers.

Liveright Publishing Corporation: "In a Station of the Metro", by Ezra Pound; "At Melville's Tomb", by Hart Crane.

Little, Brown and Company: "The Soul Selects" and "After Great Pain", by Emily Dickinson, from *The Poems of Emily Dickinson,* Centenary Edition, edited by Martha Dickinson Bianchi and Alfred Leete Hampson. Reprinted by permission of Little, Brown and Co.

The Macmillan Company: "The Man He Killed", "In Tenebris, I", "Wessex Heights", "Channel Firing", by Thomas Hardy; "Flammonde", by Edwin Arlington Robinson; "The Main-Deep", by James Stephens; "After Long Silence", "A Deep-Sworn Vow", "Among School Children", "Two Songs from a Play", and extracts from *A Vision,* by William Butler Yeats. By permission of The Macmillan Company, Publishers.

W. W. Norton and Company: extracts from *English Pastoral Poetry,* by William Empson, and from *The Scientific Outlook,* by Bertrand Russell.

Oxford University Press: extract from *English Poetry and the English Language,* by F. W. Bateson.

Poetry: A Magazine of Verse: extracts from Correspondence between Harriet Monroe and Hart Crane.

Random House, Inc.: "Doom Is Dark", by W. H. Auden, reprinted by permission of Random House, Inc., New York.

Charles Scribner's Sons: "The Last Days of Alice" and "Ode to the Confederate Dead", by Allen Tate; extracts from *Pattern and Variation in Poetry,* by Chard Powers Smith, and from "The Killers", by Ernest Hemingway.

Scrutiny: extract from "Shakespeare's Sonnets", by L. C. Knights.

CONTENTS

Asterisks (*) indicate poems which are analyzed

xvii

SECTION III: OBJECTIVE DESCRIPTION

SECTION IV: METRICS

SECTION V: TONE AND ATTITUDE

CONTENTS   xxi

SECTION VI: IMAGERY

CONTENTS   xxiii

INTRODUCTION

Poetry is a form of speech, or discourse, written or spoken. To the person who is not well acquainted with poetry the differences between poetic speech and other forms may seem to be more important than the similarities, but these differences should not be allowed to obscure the fundamental resemblances, for only by an understanding of the resemblances can one appreciate the meaning of the differences. Poetry, like all discourse, is a communication—the saying of something by one person to another person. But what is that "something"? We usually identify it with information. As practical people going about our affairs, we ask directions, read road signs, order a dinner from a menu, study football scores or stock market reports. It is altogether natural, therefore, that we should tend to think the important and central matter in all discourse to be information. But, after all, we may do well to ask how much of the discourse of an average man in any given day is primarily concerned with information for the sake of information. After he has transacted his business, obeyed his road signs, ordered and eaten his dinner, and read the stock market reports, he might be surprised to reflect on the number of non-practical functions speech had fulfilled for him that day. He had told the office boy a joke; he had commented on the weather to the traffic officer, who could observe the weather as well as he; he had told an old friend that he was glad to see him again; he had chatted with his wife on some subject on which there was already full knowledge and agreement. Even when he had been at lunch with some business associates, with whom the talk ran on informational topics, the trend in the stock market, for instance, he had not intended to use the information for buying or selling. The interest in the conversation had not been finally practical. This practical man might discover that a large part of the business of discourse had been concerned with matters which are not ordinarily thought of as really "practical," but with his relations to other

I

people, that is, with such elusive matters as feelings and attitudes.

That "something," then, conveyed by discourse is not necessarily information to be used for practical purposes. But even when the man in question was concerned primarily with a matter of practical interest, his discourse was colored by other considerations. If he telephoned an associate to ask a price he probably prefaced his question by saying, "How are you?" and concluded his conversation by saying, "Thank you," and "Goodbye." For even the most practical man a large part of discourse is not prompted by purely practical considerations; another "something" is present.

Moreover, even when a man is using speech for the purpose of conveying information, it may prove surprising to see how little of such discourse is pure information, and how difficult it is to make speech deal only with pure and exact information. Almost always a speaker conveys not only the pure information but an attitude toward and a feeling about that information. For example, let us consider the case of a motorist who stops a man driving a hay wagon to ask about the condition of the road ahead. The man on the wagon says, "It's a tolerable good road, you won't have no trouble on it." The motorist drives on, encouraged. But after a mile or so, having experienced a few substantial jolts, he hails another motorist and asks the same question. This new man says, "It's a devil of a road, it'll jerk your teeth out." Both the man on the hay wagon and the man in the second automobile think that they are telling the truth. Both intend to be helpful and to give exact information. And both feel that they know the road. But each man's language reflects his own experience with the road. For the man on the hay wagon the road *was* tolerably good, but for the second motorist, anxious to make time on his trip, the road was devilishly bad.

If this seems to be a fairly obvious example of confusion about information in ordinary speech, let us consider an example in which a trained scholar is trying to make an exact statement.

For sentimental pacifism is, after all, but a return to the method of the jungle. It is in the jungle that emotionalism alone deter-

mines conduct, and wherever that is true no other than the
law of the jungle is possible. For the emotion of hate is sure
sooner or later to follow on the emotion of love, and then there
is a spring for the throat. It is altogether obvious that the only
quality which really distinguishes man from the brutes is his
reason.[1]

The author of this statement is Robert Andrews Millikan, the
internationally famous physicist and winner of the Nobel Prize.
He is making a plea for the scientific attitude in political and
international affairs, but when one inspects this statement carefully one finds some propositions about human beings that cannot
be proved by Mr. Millikan, or by anyone else, in the same way
that he can prove certain formulae of physics in his laboratory.
Furthermore, waiving this question of whether the propositions
stated and implied are really true or not, one finds that a very
important part of the statement consists not in information about
human beings but in appeals to the reader to take a certain
attitude toward the statement. The comparisons concerning the
jungle and the leap of one infuriated beast at the throat of
another represent the sort of comparison one finds in poetry;
for the comparisons are not based on scientific analogy—the resemblance is prompted by the emotional attitude of the speaker
and is calculated to incite a corresponding attitude in the reader.
But the coloring of the general statement—that is, the bringing
in of an implied interpretation of the statement—extends beyond
the mere use of a "poetic" comparison. In the first sentence,
for example, the word *pacifism* is qualified by the word *sentimental*. Presumably it is a particular sort of pacifism here defined to which Mr. Millikan's objections apply; but does the
adjective *sentimental* really set off a "bad kind of pacifism" from
a good kind? Could the reader determine from Mr. Millikan's
statement whether or not he would consider the pacifism of
Jesus Christ, the Prince of Peace, a sentimental or a non-senti-
mental sort? Since the only kind of pacifism that Mr. Millikan
sets over against his sentimental pacifism is a scientific pacifism
operating through an organization of sociologists and economists,

[1] Science and Modern Life, *The Atlantic Monthly*, April, 1928.

one might conceivably assume that Jesus Christ would fall into the former classification. Or, to state the matter otherwise: is the basic argument for peace to be found in the fact that war is unprofitable or is horrible, or in the belief that it is wrong to kill one's fellowman? As a matter of fact, the adjective *sentimental* is, on logical grounds, a bogus qualification: its real function is to set up an attitude in the reader that will forbid his inspection of the basis of the statement.

Whether or not the general statement is logically sound, Mr. Millikan has not stated it with scientific precision; in Mr. Millikan's defense it may be said that *the proposition is one that cannot be stated with scientific precision by anyone.* Mr. Millikan, a scientist trying to state the virtues of a scientific method in human relationships, is forced to resort to devices which we associate with poetry. We should never find him coloring a mathematical formula by referring to a "sentimental figure four," or describing a well known chemical reaction by saying that two ferocious atoms of hydrogen spring at the throat of one defenseless atom of oxygen.

LIMITATIONS OF SCIENTIFIC STATEMENT

The advantages of scientific statement are not to be had without the limitations of a scientific statement also. The primary advantage of the scientific statement is that of absolute precision. But we must remember that this precision is gained by using terms in special and previously defined senses. The scientist carefully cuts away from his technical terms all associations, emotional colorings and implications of judgment. He gives up, then, all attempts to influence the reader's attitude toward his statement. For this reason, only certain kinds of statement and certain kinds of meaning are possible to true science. Science tends, indeed, toward the condition of mathematics, and the really exact scientific statements can be expressed in mathematical formulae. The chemist describes water as H_2O—two atoms of hydrogen and one atom of oxygen. The formula, H_2O, differs tremendously from even the common word *water,* for the word water, neutral as it seems in connotation, still may possess all sorts of different associations—drinking, bathing, boating, the pull of the moon to create tides, the liquid from which the goddess Aphrodite rose, or, as Keats put it,

> The moving waters at their priestlike task
> Of pure ablution round earth's human shores.

As with the liquid itself, so with the word: the scientist needs a distilled product.

The language of science represents an extreme degree of specialization of language in the direction of a certain kind of precision. It is unnecessary, of course, to point out that in this specialization tremendous advantages inhere, and that the man of the twentieth century is rightly proud of this achievement. But it is more often necessary to point out that scientific precision can be brought to bear only on certain kinds of materials. Literature in general—poetry in particular—also represents a specialization of language for the purpose of precision; but it aims at treating kinds of materials different from those of science.

We have already seen that science has to forego, because of its method, matters of attitude and interpretation; or that, when it does not forego them, it is so much the less science. For better or worse, certain kinds of communication are not possible to scientific statement. To return to the question raised at the beginning of this discussion, what is the "something" which is conveyed by speech? We have already seen that it is not exclusively information in the ordinary sense, and even less exclusively information in the scientific sense. The speech of that ordinary citizen in an ordinary way conveys many things, attitudes, feelings, and interpretations, that fall outside of these restrictions. These things, though they fill a large part of the speech of that ordinary citizen, are never stated very clearly or precisely by him. The specialization of speech which we find in poetry aims at clarity and precision of statement in these matters.

That the communication of attitudes, feelings, and interpretations constitutes a real problem, and indeed, in one sense, a more difficult problem than that offered by the communication of mere information, may be clearly illustrated by such an example as the following. Suppose, for instance, that a student sitting on the front row in a class room turns to his neighbor and whispers to him the information that it is ten minutes to eleven. This information might be passed from one person to another in the same manner through a whole class to the last man on the back row, and the probability is that the last man would receive correctly the message: it is ten minutes to eleven. The communication has been a relatively easy matter. But suppose that the first man on the first row, instead of whispering a mere bit of information, had made even a relatively simple statement involving a feeling or attitude: suppose he had said, for example, "John Jones is a fine fellow, but I feel sometimes that he is a little stuck-up." In all probability the last man who received the message would get an entirely different view of John's character from that intended by the original speaker. Indeed, anyone who is familiar with the distortions which often, and as a matter of fact, usually take place in the transmission of gossip will not be surprised at whatever the version has become, by the time it has been transmitted through thirty people. One of the reasons for the error is simple. The original statement about John is an interpretation. The person who hears it, naturally, recognizes that it is an interpretation and not a statement of objective fact, and therefore, in turn, interprets the remark in his own fashion. For example, the last man makes an interpretation of an original interpretation which has been altered more or less by twenty-eight intervening interpretations. The "something" of the first piece of communication—that it is ten minutes to eleven—arrived safely at its destination. The "something" of the second piece of communication, unlike that of the first, involves feelings which each hearer has to define for himself. In ordinary life, a hearer unconsciously bases much of his definition of such pieces of communication, not on the words themselves, but on the gestures, tone of voice, and facial expression of the speaker, and on what he knows about the speaker. For instance, every one understands how difficult it is to deal with a delicate personal matter in a letter, for the letter has nothing but words—that is, symbols written on paper and divorced from the tone of the voice, gestures, and facial expression.

MATERIALS OF POETRY

The basic problem of communication in poetry is, therefore, one of a totally different character from that involved in communication of matters of fact, and we shall merely confuse ourselves about the meaning of any poetry if we do not realize this distinction. The specialization of language in poetry is an attempt to deal with this problem.

By the very nature of the human being, the ordinary citizen in the ordinary day speaks much of what we might call incipient poetry—he attempts to communicate attitudes, feelings, and interpretations. (Unfortunately, most of this poetry is bad poetry.) And poetry in this sense is not confined to the speech of the ordinary citizen. It appears also in editorials, sermons, political speeches, magazine articles, and advertisements. We have seen that Mr. Millikan's essay can be discussed as poetry rather than as science. This, of course, is not apparent to everybody. Many a person would regard as mere poetry the Biblical statement

All they that take the sword shall perish by the sword.

But such a person might, during the next minute, regard Mr. Millikan's paragraph as a sober and verifiable scientific pronouncement. Or to take another case, this person might read an avowed poem:

THE MAN HE KILLED

THOMAS HARDY (1840–1928)

Had he and I but met
By some old ancient inn,
We should have sat us down to wet
Right many a nipperkin!

But ranged as infantry,   5
And staring face to face,

> I shot at him as he at me,
>   And killed him in his place.
>
> I shot him dead because—
>   Because he was my foe,   10
> Just so: my foe of course he was;
>   That's clear enough; although
>
> He thought he'd 'list, perhaps,
>   Off-hand like—just as I—
> Was out of work—had sold his traps—   15
>   No other reason why.
>
> Yes; quaint and curious war is!
>   You shoot a fellow down
> You'd treat if met where any bar is,
>   Or help to half-a-crown.   20

He might dismiss this as mere literature, failing to see that Mr. Millikan's paragraph is "mere literature" also—and of course, infinitely poorer literature. As has been indicated, Mr. Millikan's argument is not "science." And, as a matter of fact, it is possible that Hardy has, in his poem, put the case against war on a more solid basis than Mr. Millikan has done in his argument.

Mr. Millikan might or might not have been aware that he was using some of the methods of poetry to color the attitude of his readers and bring them to his own point of view; but any writer of advertising copy is perfectly aware of the fact that he is trying to persuade his readers to adopt a certain attitude.

POETRY AS A SPECIALIZATION OF ORDINARY SPEECH

From the examples already given we have seen that both the impulse of poetry—that is, the impulse to communicate feelings, attitudes and interpretations—and some of the methods of poetry —that is, comparisons, associations with words, etc.—appear in a great deal of our discourse that is not ordinarily considered as poetic at all. It is important to remember this fact because some people think of poetry as a thing entirely separate from ordinary life and of the matters with which poetry deals as matters with which the ordinary person is not concerned. More will have to be said about the special characteristics of formal poetry—characteristics which set it off from this "stuff of poetry" appearing in ordinary life; but it is highly important to see that both the impulse and methods of poetry are rooted very deep in human experience, and that formal poetry itself represents, not a distinction from, but a specialization of, thoroughly universal habits of human thinking and feeling.

CONFUSION BETWEEN SCIENTIFIC AND POETIC COMMUNICATION

The distinction earlier mentioned between the communication of science and the communication of poetry is also an extremely important one. People, as we have seen, are constantly confusing the two sorts of communication. They will often accept as sober scientific doctrine what is essentially a poetic statement, or they will judge formal poetry as if it were aiming at scientific truth.

An example of the first type of confusion has already been indicated in the quotation from Mr. Millikan. Mr. Millikan does not rest his case on scientifically verifiable facts but also makes an emotional appeal for a certain attitude concerning those facts. Mr. Millikan is speaking, not as a professional scientist, but as a man, and he is thoroughly justified in using this kind of speech; but it is important that the reader know exactly what Mr. Millikan is doing. Even to the person who thinks that he has no interest in formal poetry an awareness of this distinction is valuable, for he cannot move through the mass of conversation, sermons, editorials, historical and sociological writings, and advertisements without encountering situations in which this distinction is fundamental to an understanding of the actual meanings involved. The case of advertising, of course, raises the question in an extreme form. Advertisers naturally are not content to rest on a statement of fact, whether such a statement is verifiable or not. They will attempt to associate the attitude toward a certain product with an attitude toward beautiful women, little children, or gray-haired mothers; they will appeal to snobbishness, vanity, patriotism, religion, and morality. In addition to these appeals to the consumer's most basic and powerful feelings, the advertiser often attempts to imply a scientific validity for his claims—a validity which may, or may not, be justified by the product—by pictures of white-robed surgeons and research experts, statements of abstruse scientific formulae, hints of recent discoveries, coy references to the research laboratories of the plant involved, and very frequent use of the phrase "science tells us." Even the man who cares nothing for "literature" will find that he constantly has to deal with literary appeals and methods while living in the hard-headed, scientific, and practical twentieth century.

The second type of confusion mentioned above—the confusion that causes people to judge formal poetry as if it were science—is the source of most of the misunderstandings of poetry and of literature in general. It is highly necessary, if one is to understand poetry, to take up some of these typical misreadings.

1. "MESSAGE-HUNTING"

"Message-hunting"—the business of looking only for the statement of an idea which the reader thinks he can apply profitably in his own conduct—is one of the most ordinary forms of this general confusion. Here is a poem by Longfellow that has been greatly admired by many people who read poetry in this fashion:

A PSALM OF LIFE

WHAT THE HEART OF THE YOUNG MAN SAID TO THE PSALMIST

HENRY WADSWORTH LONGFELLOW (1807–1882)

Tell me not, in mournful numbers,
  Life is but an empty dream!—
For the soul is dead that slumbers,
  And things are not what they seem.

Life is real! Life is earnest!   5
  And the grave is not its goal;
Dust thou art, to dust returnest,
  Was not spoken of the soul.

Not enjoyment, and not sorrow,
  Is our destined end or way;   10
But to act, that each tomorrow
  Find us farther than today.

Art is long, and Time is fleeting,
  And our hearts, though stout and brave,
Still, like muffled drums, are beating   15
  Funeral marches to the grave.

In the world's broad field of battle,
  In the bivouac of Life,
Be not like dumb, driven cattle!
  Be a hero in the strife!   20

Trust no Future, howe'er pleasant!
  Let the dead Past bury its dead!
Act,—act in the living Present!
  Heart within, and God o'erhead!

Lives of great men all remind us   25
  We can make our lives sublime,
And, departing, leave behind us
  Footprints on the sands of time;

Footprints, that perhaps another,
  Sailing o'er life's solemn main,   30
A forlorn and shipwrecked brother,
  Seeing, shall take heart again.

Let us, then, be up and doing,
  With a heart for any fate;
Still achieving, still pursuing,   35
  Learn to labor and to wait.

This poem seems to give a great deal of good advice. It tells the
reader not to waste his time but to be up and doing; not to be
discouraged by failures but to have a heart for any fate; not to
judge life by temporary standards but to look to eternal reward.
There are probably few people who would quarrel with the

moral value of these statements. But granting that the advice is good advice, we can still ask whether or not the poem is a good poem. If the advice is what the poem has to offer us, then we can ask why a short prose statement of the advice itself is not as good as, or even better than, the poem, itself. But even the people who say they like the poem because of its "message" will usually prefer the poem to a plain prose statement. If such people would reject the prose summary in favor of the poem, they would also reject certain other versions of the poetic statement. For instance, let us alter one of the stanzas of the poem, taking care in the alteration, however, to preserve the idea. The original stanza is:

> Lives of great men all remind us
>   We can make our lives sublime,
> And departing, leave behind us
>   Footprints on the sands of time.

An alteration might run:

> Lives of all sorts of great men remind us
>   That we ourselves can make our lives sublime,
> And when we die we can leave behind us
>   Noble recollections printed on the sands of time.

The fact that any admirer of the poem would unhesitatingly choose the first version proves that "something" aside from the mere value of the idea is involved in the choice.

The fact that we have just an idea in itself is not enough to make a poem, even when the idea may be a worthy one. The neglect of this principle causes frequent misunderstandings and misreadings of poems. But another type of misreading may result from the fact that the reader does not happen to agree with an idea expressed in a poem. We may treat this distinction by a concrete case: is an admirer of Longfellow's poem, even one who says that his admiration is based on the worth of the idea, disqualified from admiring the following poem, which states an idea rather opposed to some of the ideas in Longfellow's poem?

EXPOSTULATION AND REPLY

WILLIAM WORDSWORTH (1770–1850)

"Why, William, on that old gray stone,
    Thus for the length of half a day,
Why, William, sit you thus alone,
    And dream your time away?"

"Where are your books?—that light bequeathed   5
    To beings else forlorn and blind!
Up! up! and drink the spirit breathed
    From dead men to their kind.

"You look round on your Mother Earth,
    As if she for no purpose bore you;   10
As if you were her first-born birth,
    And none had lived before you."

One morning thus, by Esthwaite lake,
    When life was sweet, I knew not why,
To me my good friend Matthew spake,   15
    And thus I made reply:

"The eye—it cannot choose but see;
    We cannot bid the ear be still;
Our bodies feel, where'er they be,
    Against or with our will.   20

"Nor less I deem that there are Powers
    Which of themselves our minds impress;
That we can feed this mind of ours
    In a wise passiveness.

"Think you, 'mid all this mighty sum   25
    Of things forever speaking,
That nothing of itself will come,
    But we must still be seeking?

"—Then ask not wherefore, here, alone,
    Conversing as I may,   30
I sit upon this old gray stone,
    And dream my time away."

This poem seems to give the advice that one should neglect the "light bequeathed" by the great men of the past in favor of what one can only learn for himself; that one should not fritter away his time by being "up and doing" or by being a "hero in the strife"; and that one should learn in contemplation to cultivate that "wise passiveness" by which, only, one comes into harmony with the great powers of the universe. If the admirer of Longfellow's poem means literally what he says when he praises the poem for the "message," then he is absolutely disqualified from enjoying this poem, for its "message" is diametrically opposed to that of "The Psalm of Life." Of course, many people who describe their appreciation of poems in terms of the "messages" do not mean literally what they say; they are simply groping for some ground to justify the fact that they like poetry at all. Since they are accustomed to think of all communication as concerned with practical information, they try to put their liking on some "practical" or "scientific" basis.

As a matter of fact, the place of ideas in poetry and their relation to the goodness of a poem cannot be treated in such an over-simplified manner. We know, for example, that devout Protestants can accept the poetry of the Catholic poet Dante, or that Catholics can accept the poetry of the Protestant poet John Milton. The fact that the Protestant reader, who holds his religious beliefs seriously, may still accept the poetry of Dante does not mean that the reader regards poetry as merely trivial and unserious. This whole matter is one that cannot be dismissed in a few sentences, but requires for a satisfactory understanding the analysis of many special poems. It will suffice to say here that the "message-hunting" method of reading poetry breaks down even in the simplest cases.

2. "PURE REALIZATION"

Many readers and critics of poetry, realizing the insufficiency of the "message-hunting" approach to poetry, have adopted a view that poetry does not deal with any ideas or truths at all, but is an "expression of pure emotion," or "deals with emotion." This view is sometimes put in other terms, as when one critic says that a poem is the expression of "a moment of pure realization of being"—that is, it attempts merely to bring vividly to the reader some scene or sensation.

When a critic trying to point out the distinguishing marks of poetry says that poetry expresses an emotion or that poetry deals with emotion, exactly what does he mean? Does he mean that a poem, about grief, for instance, would "express" the grief a poet might feel, or have felt, in the same way as a burst of tears would express the emotion of grief? Or does he mean that the reading of a poem about grief would provoke in the reader an emotion of grief in the same way as would a personal bereavement? Quite obviously, the answer to both questions is "No." Certainly, writing of a poem would be no substitute for the relief of a burst of tears; nor would the response to the reading of a poem be as intense as the experience of a real bereavement. There is some difference. On the mere ground of emotional intensity the poem does not compete with the real experience. The justification of poetry as "pure realization," like its justification on the basis of "message-hunting," breaks down even in simple cases, for the pure realization of an experience is the experience at the moment it occurs. For instance, the taste or the smell of a real apple is always more intense than any poem describing the taste or smell of an apple. The following passage from "Ode to a Nightingale," by John Keats has sometimes been praised as a moment of "pure realization":

> O for a draught of vintage! that hath been
> Cooled a long age in the deep-delvèd earth,
> Tasting of Flora and the country green,
> Dance, and Provençal song, and sunburnt mirth!
> O for a beaker full of the warm South,
> Full of the true, the blushful Hippocrene,
> With beaded bubbles winking at the brim,
> And purple-stainèd mouth. . . .

Whatever "pure realization" there is here is certainly not the pure realization of wine as such. The stanza is obviously not a substitute for an actual glass of wine: not only does it fail to give the intensity of the sensation of actual wine-drinking but it gives an effect thoroughly different in kind from the experience of drinking a glass of wine. If there is a "pure realization" of anything it is of the poet's thinking about the wine as a thing which represents to him a certain kind of life—a warm, mirthful, carefree, healthy, pagan kind of life, which in the total context of the poem stands in contrast to his own troubled and fretful existence (See "Ode to a Nightingale" and analysis, p. 407). As a matter of fact, when we inspect the passage we discover that it is not so much a pictorial description of a beaker of wine, or a description of the sensation of drinking wine, as it is a cluster of associations with the wine—associations which suggest the kind of life we have mentioned. The poet is not saying, actually, that he is thirsty for a drink of wine but that he wants a certain kind of life, the qualities of which he implies.

We have seen that the attempt to conceive of poetry as the "expression of emotion" or as "pure realization" represents an attempt to get away from the "message-hunting" approach to poetry. But in the case which we have just examined we have seen that the experience which is "realized" or communicated to the reader is far different from the experience of a physical object (wine, in this instance), an emotional reaction, or a sensation. The experience, we have seen, really involves an interpretation by the poet, so that in so far as the term "realization" is used to imply an absence of interpretation it is·thoroughly inaccurate.

3. "BEAUTIFUL STATEMENT OF SOME HIGH TRUTH"

There is another confused conception of poetry arising from the attempt to combine in a mechanical fashion the two false approaches which have just been discussed. This confused conception is variously stated. For instance, it may be expressed in a definition of poetry as "fine sentiments in fine language." Or as the "beautiful statement of some high truth." Whatever the precise manner of description may be, the basic idea may be stated as follows: poetry is a "truth" with "decorations," which may either be pleasant in themselves or dispose the reader to accept the truth.

Most often victims of this general misconception have treated poetry as a kind of "sugar-coated pill." They have justified the characteristics of poetry—rhythmical language, figures of speech, stories and dramatic situations, etc.—as a kind of bait that leads the reader to expose himself to the influence of the "truth" contained in a poem. They value these characteristics only in so far as the characteristics lead to the acceptance of the "truth." The final value of a poem for such people would depend on the value of the "truth" contained—which leads us back to the mistake of the "message hunters," which we examined with reference to Longfellow's poem.

But even if the person who regards poetry as "fine sentiments in fine language" says that he values the language as much as he values the sentiments, or "truth," he is still using a mistaken approach to poetry. For he is apparently committed to saying that the language, quite apart from its relation to some central idea or "truth," is valuable. He seems to be saying that certain words, or certain objects suggested by the words, are in themselves "poetic." He would be forced to consider a poem as simply a bundle of melodious word-combinations and pretty pictures. He would probably be embarrassed if we asked him what held these things together in any given poem, making it a poem rather than simply a collection of pleasing items. And he would probably be further embarrassed if we asked him to show us by what standard he would call a particular combination of sounds or a particular set of pictures poetically fine. If he should say that he took as a standard for poetical fitness the fact that any item—let us say, for instance, a rose—was pleasing in real life, he would be making a dangerous confusion. It is certainly true that in real life various combinations of word sounds and various objects and scenes, such as the rose, the moon, the ruins of a mediaeval tower, a maiden standing on a balcony, etc., are pleasing. But poetry does not consist merely in the use of objects of this sort or in the use of agreeable word combinations. Nor does the mere presence of these things make poetry. But the falsity of this conception can quickly be demonstrated by turning to great poetry from Shakespeare or Milton where we find material that in real life would be disagreeable or mean used for poetic effect. The image of a man grunting and sweating under a burden too heavy for him is not a poetic thing if judged by the above standard, but we will find it used in a passage of great poetry that is universally admired. In Hamlet's most famous speech we find these lines:

> For who would bear the whips and scorns of time,
> The oppressor's wrong, the proud man's contumely,
> The pangs of despised love, the law's delay,
> The insolence of office, and the spurns
> That patient merit of the unworthy takes,
> When he himself might his quietus make
> With a bare bodkin? who would fardels bear,
> To grunt and sweat under a weary life,
> But that the dread of something after death,
> The undiscovered country from whose bourn
> No traveller returns, puzzles the will. . . .

In fact, none of the things used in this passage would be thought of as being pleasing in itself in actual life. The passage does not give us a set of agreeable pictures that would be considered "poetic." Indeed, the more we examine good poetry the more difficult will appear the attempt to say that certain objects or situations or even ideas are in themselves poetic. *The poetic effect depends not on the things themselves but on the kind of use the poet makes of them.*

ORGANIC NATURE OF POETRY

We have seen, then, that a poem is not to be thought of as merely a bundle of things which are "poetic" in themselves. Nor is it to be thought of, as the "message hunters" would seem to have it, as a kind of box, decorated or not, in which a "truth" or a "fine sentiment" is hidden. We avoid such difficulties *by thinking of a poem as a piece of writing which gives us a certain effect in which, we discover, the "poetry" inheres.*

This is very different from considering a poem as a group of mechanically combined elements—meter, rime, figurative language, idea, etc.—which are put together to make a poem as bricks are put together to make a wall. The question, then about any element in a poem is not whether it is in itself pleasing, or agreeable, or valuable, or "poetical," but whether it works with the other elements to create the effect intended by the poet. The relationship among the elements in a poem is there-fore all important, and it is not a mechanical relationship but one which is far more intimate and fundamental. If we should compare a poem to the make-up of some physical object it ought not to be to a wall but to something organic like a plant.

We may investigate this general principle by looking at some particular examples. The following lines could scarcely be called melodious. Indeed, they may be thought to have a sibilant, hiss-ing quality rather than that of melody.

> If it were done when 'tis done, then 'twere well
> It were done quickly: if the assassination
> Could trammel up the consequence, and catch,
> With his surcease, success, that but this blow
> Might be the be-all and the end-all here,
> But here, upon this bank and shoal of time,
> We'd jump the life to come.

This is the speech of Macbeth at the moment when he is debating the murder of Duncan; the passage has been considered to be great poetry by innumerable critics and readers. We are not to consider that the passage is great poetry *in spite* of its lack of ordinary melodious effects; but rather we are to see that the broken rhythms and the tendency to harshness of sound are essential to the communication that Shakespeare wished. For instance, the piling up of the *s* sounds in the second, third, and fourth lines helps give an impression of desperate haste and breathless excitement. The lines give the impression of a con-spiratorial whisper. The rhythm and sound effects of the passage, then, are poetic in the only sense which we have seen to be legitimate: they are poetic because of a relation to the total effect of the passage.

Or we may approach the general problem in another way. Here are two lines by Robert Burns which have been greatly admired by the poet William Butler Yeats:

> The white moon is setting behind the white wave,
> And Time is setting with me, O!

Let us suppose that the lines had been written as follows:

> The white moon is setting behind the white wave,
> And Time, O! is setting with me.

Literally considered, the two versions say exactly the same thing: they describe a scene and give an exclamation provoked by it. If one will, however, read the two versions carefully with an ear for the rhythm he will discover that the transposition of the word *O* has made a great difference in the movement.

But this difference is not finally important *merely* because the first version may be in itself more melodious than the second. The movement of the first version is superior primarily because it contributes to the total effect, or to what we might call the total interpretation, of the scene. The placing of the cry at the emphatic position of a line-end implies that the speaker had scarcely realized the full force of his own statement until he had made it. The lingering rhythm caused by the position of the exclamation at the end of the second line coincides with the fact that the poet sees in the natural scene a representation of the pathos of the passing of Time and of his own life. By placing the exclamation anywhere else we impair this relationship between the rhythm and the other elements involved—the image of the moonset and the poet's statement about the passing of Time. Yeats has summarized the general effect of the passage and the relationship of the parts as follows:

Take from them [the lines] the whiteness of the moon and of the waves, whose relation to the setting of Time is too subtle for the intellect, and you take from them their beauty. But, when all are together, moon and wave and whiteness and setting Time and the last melancholy cry, they evoke an emotion which cannot be evoked by any other arrangement of colors and sounds and forms.[1]

The remarks by Yeats here apply, as we can see, to the elements of the scene itself as well as to the rhythm. He is not praising the lines merely because the scene of the white moon setting behind the white wave gives in itself a pretty picture. As a mat-

---

[1] "The Symbolism of Poetry," *Essays,* New York: Macmillan, p. 191.

ter of fact, a white moon may not appear as beautiful as a golden moon, but if we rewrite the lines with a golden moon we have lost something from them:

> The gold moon is setting behind the gold wave,
> And Time is setting for me, O!

The "something" that has been lost obviously depends on the relationship of the color to the other elements in the general effect. The whiteness of the moon and the wave in connection with the idea of "setting" and then more specifically in connection with the idea of the irrevocable passage of Time, suggests, even though unconsciously to most readers, a connection with the paleness of something waning or dying. The connection is not a logical connection, as Yeats intimates when he says the "relation . . . is too subtle for the intellect," but it is nonetheless a powerful one. All of this merely means that Yeats is saying that the beauty—by which he means the total poetic effect—of the lines depends on the relationship of the parts to each other.

This last point may be amply proved, as we have already hinted in discussing the passage from *Hamlet,* by considering a passage of great poetry in which the pictures used, unlike that in the lines from Burns, would be considered in ordinary life as positively ugly or at least neutral.

> Time hath, my lord, a wallet at his back,
> Wherein he puts alms for oblivion,
> A great-sized monster of ingratitudes:
> Those scraps are good deeds past; which are devoured
> As fast as they are made, forgot as soon
> As done: perseverance, dear my lord,
> Keeps honor bright: to have done, is to hang
> Quite out of fashion, like a rusty mail
> In monumental mockery. . . .

> (From *Troilus and Cressida*)

This is a speech which Shakespeare puts into the mouth of a character, Ulysses, who is trying to persuade Achilles to take part again in the war against the Trojans and not to rest on the reputation for valor he has already made. The pictures given here are definitely unattractive: a beggar putting alms in his sack, a monster, scraps of food, a rusty suit of armor. The poetic effect of the passage, then, cannot depend on the intrinsic prettiness of any of the objects mentioned. If we speak of the beauty of the passage, as Yeats speaks of the beauty of the lines from Burns, we must mean the relation of the objects to each other and to the idea of the passage.

Let us try to see what these relationships are. Ulysses is saying that a reputation for good deeds is quickly forgotten. Good deeds are like alms given to an ungrateful beggar, or are like scraps of food which the beggar forgets as soon as he has satisfied his appetite. The picture is poetically good because it accurately indicates the *attitude* which Ulysses wishes Achilles to take toward his past achievements. If Ulysses had merely given Achilles the general statement that the public forgets good deeds, he could not have stirred the feelings which Achilles, the hero and aristocrat, must have felt toward beggars and broken scraps of food. He plays on this contempt and disgust. The images of the first five lines, as we have seen, are closely bound together to define a certain attitude. Then, after a general statement that perseverance is necessary to keep honor bright, the image of the coat of mail is introduced: a man who bases his claim to honor merely on a deed done in the past is like a suit of mail that, although it is hung up as a trophy of some great event, simply rusts. It is important to see that this is not a mere repetition of the general point made about perseverance, but that it also develops and adds to the idea, for it carries with it a special urgency to immediate action. There is not only the application, as it were, of the general idea in a concrete image that can be seen as a picture, but also an application appropriate to the special situation, the need for Achilles to put on his armor and return to the battle.

The use of images in this passage, then, represents not only a close-knit organization because of the relation of the images to each other and to the intention of the passage, but also a psychological development, for the images lead from one attitude and state of mind to another. One can show the closeness of the organization of the passage even in the use of a single word. For example, take the word *monumental* in the last line. A great deal of the "meaning" of the passage is concentrated in this one word. The word *monumental* literally means, of course, the quality of something that stands as a monument. The coat of rusty mail which Ulysses uses in his comparison is one hung up as a trophy or monument to past achievement. But the word *monumental* is also used to indicate something tremendous in size. The word, then, as it appears in the present context suggests two applications to the reader: the mail is hung up as a monument and the mockery is monumental, or tremendous, in size. The fact that the word suggests to the reader these two applications gives a somewhat ironical, or sarcastic, effect to the passage—which is exactly what is intended by the speaker.

The purpose in giving the passages and comments above is to illustrate the principle that in judging the various elements of a poem or of a passage of poetry—rhythm, image, diction, etc.—one must consider not the elements taken in isolation but in relation to the total organization and intention. That is, the elements must play an organic part in the poem.

DRAMATIC ASPECT OF POETRY

It may be objected that most of the examples given above are drawn from plays and do not represent poetry as we more ordinarily find it. But the principle illustrated by these examples applies to all other poetry. It applies because all poetry, including even short lyrics or descriptive pieces (p. 171), involves a dramatic organization. This is clear when we reflect that every poem implies a speaker of the poem, either the poet writing in his own person or someone into whose mouth the poem is put, and that the poem represents the reaction of such a person to a situation, a scene, or an idea. In reading poetry it is well to remember this dramatic aspect and to be sure that one sees the part it plays in any given poem.

WHAT GOOD IS POETRY?

But even if one understands the principles by which poetry is to be read, one may still ask, "What good is poetry?" The value of science we all know. But we have attempted in the preceding pages to show how different the organization of poetry is from that of science, and how different are their objectives. It is only fair to admit that what makes science valuable cannot be held to make poetry valuable also. Science gives us a certain kind of description of the world—a description which is within its own terms verifiable—and gives us a basis for more effective practical achievement. Science is, as Bertrand Russell has called it, "power-knowledge."

But scientific thought is . . . essentially power-thought—the sort of thought, that is to say, whose purpose, conscious or unconscious, is to give power to its possessor. Now power is a causal concept, and to obtain power over any given material one need only understand the causal laws to which it is subject. This is an essentially abstract matter, and the more irrelevant details we can omit from our purview, the more powerful our thoughts will become. The same sort of thing can be illustrated in the economic sphere. The cultivator, who knows every corner of his farm, has a concrete knowledge of wheat, and makes very little money; the railway which carries his wheat views it in a slightly more abstract way, and makes rather more money; the stock exchange manipulator, who knows it only in its purely abstract aspect of something which may go up or down, is, in his way, as remote from concrete reality as the physicist, and he, of all those concerned in the economic sphere, makes the most money and has the most power. So it is with science, though the power which the man of science seeks is more remote and impersonal than that which is sought on the stock exchange.[1]

But we have seen, and can see in real life every day, how much of our experience eludes the statements science can make; and how merely practical statements or statements that approximate a scientific form satisfy only a part of our interests. One does not have to look farther than the fact that this wide domain of human interests exists to find a justification for poetry. Most people are thoroughly satisfied to admit the value of any activity

[1] *The Scientific Outlook*, by Bertrand Russell, London: Allen and Unwin, p. 86

which satisfies a basic and healthy human interest. It may be well, however, to take a few moments to remind the reader that this interest exists, and to make plain that it is this interest which poetry seeks to satisfy.

We have already seen how often talk that is apparently practical really attempts to satisfy a non-practical interest. It is easy to point out many other aspects of our experience that testify to the fact that people—even people who think that they care nothing for poetry—really have interests which are the same as those satisfied by poetry. Very few people indeed depend for the satisfaction of these interests merely on their routine activities. Instead, they listen to speeches, go to church, listen to radio programs, read magazine stories or the gossip columns of newspapers. Such people do not see any relation between these activities and poetry, but poetry does concern the same impulses and the same interests. Why and how good poetry, and good literature in general, give a fuller satisfaction to these impulses and interests is a matter which can best be stated in connection with concrete examples before us, and the attempt in this book to state this matter will be gradually developed by the study of examples. But the fundamental point, namely, that poetry has a basis in common human interests, must not be forgotten at the beginning of any attempt to study poetry.

The question of the value of poetry, then, is to be answered by saying that it springs from a basic human impulse and fulfils a basic human interest. To answer the question finally, and not immediately, one would have to answer the question as to the value of those common impulses and interests. But that is a question which lies outside of the present concern. As we enter into a study of poetry it is only necessary to see that poetry is not an isolated and eccentric thing, but springs from the most fundamental interests which human beings have.

SECTION I - *narrative poems*

FOREWORD

We have said that the "stuff of poetry" is not something separate from the ordinary business of living, but itself inheres in
that business. We hear some one say that a farm boy has suffered a fatal accident while cutting wood with a buzz-saw; or
we read in the newspaper that a woman has shot her sweetheart;
or we remember that there was once an outlaw from Missouri
named Jesse James who was killed by treachery. This sort of
thing, even though it may not at first strike us as beautiful, instructive, or elevating, appeals to the interest people have in other people.
That interest, as we have indicated, is not scientific or practical
but is simply the general interest we feel in people as human
beings. Even though the account of a painful accident or a
sordid murder seems almost as far removed as possible from
poetry, it arouses the kind of interest which poetry attempts to
satisfy, and, as we have already said, comprises the "stuff of
poetry." In the case of the three incidents mentioned—the death
of a farm boy, the murder of the sweetheart, and the betrayal of
the outlaw—the "stuff of poetry" has actually been turned into
poems. That is, the "human interest" has been put in a form
that preserves it, even after the accidental and temporary curiosity has been satisfied. (The other, and more important, things
which form does will be discussed later.)

OUT, OUT

ROBERT FROST (1875–   )

The buzz-saw snarled and rattled in the yard
And made dust and dropped stove-length sticks of wood,
Sweet-scented stuff when the breeze drew across it.

27

And from there those that lifted eyes could count
Five mountain ranges one behind the other　　　　　5
Under the sunset far into Vermont.
And the saw snarled and rattled, snarled and rattled,
As it ran light, or had to bear a load.
And nothing happened: day was all but done.
Call it a day, I wish they might have said　　　　　10
To please the boy by giving him the half hour
That a boy counts so much when saved from work.
His sister stood beside them in her apron
To tell them "Supper." At the word, the saw,
As if to prove saws knew what supper meant,　　　　　15
Leaped out at the boy's hand, or seemed to leap—
He must have given the hand. However it was,
Neither refused the meeting. But the hand!
The boy's first outcry was a rueful laugh.
As he swung toward them holding up the hand　　　　　20
Half in appeal, but half as if to keep
The life from spilling. Then the boy saw all—
Since he was old enough to know, big boy
Doing a man's work, though a child at heart—
He saw all spoiled. "Don't let him cut my hand off—
The doctor, when he comes. Don't let him, sister!"　　　26
So. But the hand was gone already.
The doctor put him in the dark of ether.
He lay and puffed his lips out with his breath.
And then—the watcher at his pulse took fright.　　　　30
No one believed. They listened at his heart.
Little—less—nothing!—and that ended it.
No more to build on there. And they, since they
Were not the one dead, turned to their affairs.

FRANKIE AND JOHNNY

ANONYMOUS

Frankie and Johnny were lovers, O, how that couple could love.
Swore to be true to each other, true as the stars above.
He was her man, but he done her wrong.

Frankie she was his woman, everybody knows.
She spent one hundred dollars for a suit of Johnny's clothes.   5
He was her man, but he done her wrong.

Frankie and Johnny went walking, Johnny in his bran' new suit,
"O good Lawd," says Frankie, "but don't my Johnny look cute?"
He was her man, but he done her wrong.

Frankie went down to Memphis; she went on the evening train.
She paid one hundred dollars for Johnny a watch and chain.   11
He was her man, but he done her wrong.

Frankie went down to the corner, to buy a glass of beer;
She says to the fat bartender, "Has my loving man been here?
He was my man, but he done me wrong."   15

"Ain't going to tell you no story, ain't going to tell you no lie,
I seen your man 'bout an hour ago with a girl named Alice Fry.
If he's your man, he's doing you wrong."

Frankie went back to the hotel, she didn't go there for fun,
Under her long red kimono she toted a forty-four gun.   20
He was her man, but he done her wrong.

Frankie went down to the hotel, looked in the window so high,
There was her lovin' Johnny a-lovin' up Alice Fry;
He was her man, but he done her wrong.

Frankie threw back her kimono; took out the old forty-four;   25
Roota-toot-toot, three times she shot, right through that hotel
    door.
She shot her man, 'cause he done her wrong.

Johnny grabbed off his Stetson. "O good Lawd, Frankie, don't
    shoot."
But Frankie put her finger on the trigger, and the gun went
    roota-toot-toot.
He was her man, but she shot him down.   30

"Roll me over easy, roll me over slow,
Roll me over easy, boys, 'cause my wounds are hurting me so,
I was her man, but I done her wrong."

With the first shot Johnny staggered; with the second shot he fell;
When the third bullet hit him, there was a new man's face in
   hell.   35
He was her man, but he done her wrong.

Frankie heard a rumbling away down under the ground.
Maybe it was Johnny where she had shot him down.
He was her man, and she done him wrong.

"Oh, bring on your rubber-tired hearses, bring on your rubber-
   tired hacks,   40
They're takin' my Johnny to the buryin' groun' but they'll never
   bring him back.
He was my man, but he done me wrong."

The judge he said to the jury, "It's plain as plain can be.
This woman shot her man, so it's murder in the second degree.
He was her man, though he done her wrong."   45

Now it wasn't murder in the second degree, it wasn't murder
   in the third.
Frankie simply dropped her man, like a hunter drops a bird.
He was her man, but he done her wrong.

"Oh, put me in that dungeon. Oh, put me in that cell.
Put me where the northeast wind blows from the southeast corner
   of hell.   50
I shot my man 'cause he done me wrong."

Frankie walked up to the scaffold, as calm as a girl could be,
She turned her eyes to heaven and said, "Good Lord, I'm coming
   to thee.
He was my man, and I done him wrong."

JESSE JAMES

ANONYMOUS

It was on a Wednesday night, the moon was shining bright,
   They robbed the Danville train.
And the people they did say, for many miles away,
   'Twas the outlaws Frank and Jesse James.

Jesse had a wife to mourn him all her life, 5
  The children they are brave.
'Twas a dirty little coward shot Mister Howard,
  And laid Jesse James in his grave.

Jesse was a man was a friend to the poor,
  He never left a friend in pain. 10
And with his brother Frank he robbed the Chicago bank
  And then held up the Glendale train.

It was Robert Ford, the dirty little coward,
  I wonder how he does feel,
For he ate of Jesse's bread and he slept in Jesse's bed, 15
  Then he laid Jesse James in his grave.

It was his brother Frank that robbed the Gallatin bank,
  And carried the money from the town.
It was in this very place that they had a little race,
  For they shot Captain Sheets to the ground. 20

They went to the crossing not very far from there,
  And there they did the same;
And the agent on his knees he delivered up the keys
  To the outlaws Frank and Jesse James.

It was on a Saturday night, Jesse was at home 25
  Talking to his family brave,
When the thief and the coward, little Robert Ford,
  Laid Jesse James in his grave.

How people held their breath when they heard of Jesse's
  . death,
  And wondered how he ever came to die. 30
'Twas one of the gang, dirty Robert Ford,
  That shot Jesse James on the sly.

Jesse went to rest with his hand on his breast;
  He died with a smile on his face.
He was born one day in the county of Clay, 35
  And came from a solitary race.

  The first of these poems was written by Robert Frost, a professional poet, who felt in the fatal accident to an obscure farm

boy the pathos and horror of the unreasonable and unpredictable end that at any moment may come to life. We do not know who composed the other two poems, but certainly not professional poets. Apparently some ordinary person felt so strongly the force of an incident, the murder of Johnny or the betrayal of Jesse James, that he tried to express it in a song that would convey his own reactions to the event. And the songs did succeed in conveying something of the reactions of the unknown composers, for they have been passed down from mouth to mouth, probably being constantly altered in the process. Poems like "Frankie and Johnny" or "Jesse James," narratives to be sung that spring from unknown sources and are transmitted by word of mouth, and that may experience alteration in this process, are usually called *ballads* (*Glossary*).

The most ordinary way by which we express the interest we as human beings have in other human beings is by telling or attending to stories. Since poetry derives from this basic human interest we expect to find, and do find, many poems in which the element of story is large. As a matter of fact, the three poems we have just read, and all the poems in the present section of this book, give enough of the explicit action of a story to appeal to the usual curiosity we feel about how any situation will turn out. But this is not the only appeal the poems make to us, just as it is not the only appeal any good piece of fiction makes. We are interested not merely in getting the information about the conclusion, but in following the process by which the conclusion is reached. As a matter of fact, we do not even want all the details of the process, but just enough to make us experience the central feeling and grasp the central meaning of the events. But this is not all: we like a poem, not because it gives us satisfaction of our curiosity or because it gives us an idea we can "carry away with us," as people sometimes put it, but because the poem itself is an experience.

We can illustrate by a comparison with a football game. If a person listens to a radio report of a game, he may really have more accurate information about it than if he were present. And when the game is over, he will know the exact score. But if he has his choice he will probably take the trouble, and spend the money, to go to the game itself. He does this because the game is a richer experience. The score and the statistics of the game come to him, if he watches it, not as bare facts, but in terms of action.

This general principle is clear if we remember that the mere fact, as a fact, that a woman in the slums shot her sweetheart Johnny is of little interest to us. If we enjoy hearing "Frankie and Johnny" sung, we do so because of something more than the statistical importance of the subject. Furthermore, we do not merely enjoy it because it satisfies our curiosity about the outcome; for we enjoy the song for an indefinite length of time after we know the conclusion. It is obvious, then, that if we like it at all, we like it because of its particular nature as an experience—just as we like the football game.

The story element in a poem, then, whether it is prominent as in "Frankie and Johnny" or relatively unimportant as in "Out, Out," is only one of many elements which work together to give the total experience of the poem. We already know what some of these other elements are: rhythm, figurative language, etc. But in these poems, where the story element is prominent, we may proceed best by studying the way in which this one element is treated in concrete cases to give the effect we call poetry.

JOHNIE ARMSTRONG

ANONYMOUS

There dwelt a man in faire Westmerland,
    Johnie Armstrong men did him call,
He had nither lands nor rents coming in,
    Yet he kept eight score men in his hall.

He had horse and harness for them all,   5
    Goodly steeds were all milke-white;
O the golden bands an about their necks,
    And their weapons, they were all alike.

Newes then was brought unto the king
    That there was sicke [1] a won as hee,   10
That livèd lyke a bold out-law,
    And robbèd all the north country.

The king he writt an a letter then,
    A letter which was large and long;
He signed it with his owner hand;   15
    And he promised to doe him no wrong.

When this letter came Johnie untill,[2]
    His heart it was as blythe as birds on the tree:
"Never was I sent for before any king,
    My father, my grandfather, nor none but mee.   20

"And if wee goe the king before,
    I would we went most orderly;
Every man of you shall have his scarlet cloak,
    Lacèd with silver laces three.

"Every won of you shall have his velvett coat,   25
    Laced with silver lace so white;
O the golden bands an about your necks,
    Black hatts, white feathers, all alyke."

By the morrow morninge at ten of the clock,
    Towards Edenburough gon was hee,   30
And with him all his eight score men;
    Good Lord, it was a goodly sight for to see!

When Johnie came befower the king,
    He fell downe on his knee;
"O pardon, my soveraine leige," he said,   35
    "O pardon my eight score men and mee!"

"Thou shalt have no pardon, thou traytor strong,
    For thy eight score men nor thee;
For tomorrow morning by ten of the clock,
    Both thou and them shall hang on the gallow-tree."

[1] such   [2] unto

But Johnie looke'd over his left shoulder,   41
    Good Lord, what a grievous look looked hee!
Saying, "Asking grace of a graceles face—
    Why there is none for you nor me."

But Johnie had a bright sword by his side,   45
    And it was made of the mettle so free,
That had not the king stept his foot aside,
    He had smitten his head from his faire bodde.

Saying, "Fight on, my merry men all,
    And see that none of you be taine;   50
For rather then men shall say we were hange'd,
    Let them report how we were slaine."

Then, God wott, faire Eddenburrough rose,
    And so besett poore Johnie rounde,
That fowerscore and tenn of Johnie's best men   55
    Lay gasping all upon the ground.

Then like a mad man Johnie laid about,
    And like a mad man then fought hee,
Untill a falce Scot came Johnie behinde,
    And runn him through the faire boddee.   60

Saying, "Fight on, my merry men all,
    And see that none of you be taine;
For I will stand by and bleed but awhile,
    And then will I come and fight againe."

Newes then was brought to young Johnie Armstrong,
    As he stood by his nurse's knee,   66
Who vowed if ere he live'd for to be a man,
    On the treacherous Scots revengd hee'd be.

   This poem treats the same kind of story as that treated by
"Jesse James." In both cases there is the brave outlaw who is
killed by treachery. In neither case do we know who composed
the ballad, but both poems must have grown out of a fairly
simple and illiterate society. In the case of this ballad, it was
the society of the Scotch peasantry in the sixteenth century; in

the case of "Jesse James" the ballad appeared in a frontier society in America. But the differences in time and in place do not conceal the fundamental likeness between the two ballads and, even, between the characters of the two heroes. The fact that human nature is very much the same at all times and places, makes it possible for us to read such poems with sympathy and understanding. In both cases, that of the outlaw Johnie Armstrong and the outlaw Jesse James, some one—we do not know who—was struck by the pathos of courage betrayed and was impelled to express his feeling by putting the incident that stirred him into a poem—or more accurately, into the song-poem which we call a ballad. In so far as the unknown composer did this successfully we can now grasp the reaction he had to the incident.

The incident of Johnie Armstrong, like that of Jesse James, derives from historical fact. Johnie Armstrong was an outlaw lord of the Scotch border country, who was lured into the power of the Scotch king, James V—treacherously, according to the ballad—and was killed with his men. It is a simple story of violent action, such a story as might be expected to appeal strongly to the kind of people among whom the ballad arose.

The basic facts as given in the summary above are not in themselves interesting to us. The event described, for instance, is of no historical importance. But when the event appears to us in the form of the poem it immediately gains an interest. Perhaps we can do something toward defining the process that gives this added interest.

First, we may look at the way in which the story is organized in the ballad, a way characteristic of most ballads. The action is not presented in a straight narrative. The first two stanzas give us an identification of the hero, the *exposition* (*Glossary*), as one would say about ordinary fiction. The next two stanzas give a bit of narrative, but from that point on the action is handled by a succession of little scenes, presented much as in a play. There is the scene of Johnie Armstrong's reception of the letter, of the appearance of his company as it rides toward court, of the betrayal and the fight, and of the little son's vow of vengeance. The method, further, is dramatic in that much of the action is presented through dialogue and not indirectly by description. The characters speak up for themselves, and so we know them directly. By this selection of key scenes and by the emphasis on dialogue the reader or hearer gets an impression of speed and excitement and of nearness to the action.

In the second place, although the reader gets an impression of nearness, the story is not greatly elaborated. In a short story on the same subject one would expect a certain amount of description and detail that is absent in the poem. The only extended piece of description in the poem is that dealing with the appearance of the retainers of Armstrong as they get ready to go to court. But we can observe that this is not straight description. It is put in the mouth of Johnie Armstrong as he orders his men to make ready. And it serves a twofold purpose in the poem in addition to its value as a piece of *atmosphere* (*Glossary*) and setting. It indicates the joy the outlaw feels at the honor the king has done him, and it gives an *ironical* contrast (*Glossary*) to the betrayal that is to follow.

In ordinary prose fiction one would expect a certain amount of analysis and description of the thoughts and feelings of characters. But in this ballad there is very little of such material. For instance, only one line describes the feeling of a character:

> His heart it was as blythe as birds on the tree.

But at the climax of the situation, when Johnie Armstrong suddenly discovers that he has been betrayed, we are not told what he felt; we are given a glimpse of the way he looked, and so seize more imaginatively and directly on the meaning of the scene.

> But Johnie looked over his left shoulder,
> Good Lord, what a grievous look looked hee!
> Saying, "Asking grace of a graceless face—
> Why there is none for you nor me."

The ballad is moving as quickly as possible to its point, selecting such details as will most stimulate the imagination. With the sight of the betrayed outlaw's sudden glance over his shoulder (and notice how, to emphasize the scene and help us visualize it, the ballad specifies which shoulder), we can know as much about his reaction to the situation as a great deal of description would give us, and we know it in a way that makes us feel that our own imagination is participating in the poem. This is a detail that by the power of suggestion makes us see the whole picture and feel the effect.

The aim of this kind of treatment is to make as vivid and as *concrete* (*Glossary*) an effect as possible, in contrast with the general and purely factual summary of the event which we gave above. Poetry tries to make us see and hear a thing and therefore to have a feeling about it. For instance, we are not told that the king is treacherous, and we are told nothing of his intentions. What we learn, we learn from the behavior of the king himself. We are never told that Johnie Armstrong is a proud and courageous man who feels an obligation to his followers, but we learn it from his own conduct and from what he says: when he discovers the king's treachery he thinks of his men as well as of himself; and there is a sort of exaltation rather than despair in his admonition to all of them to die fighting rather than be taken. "Let them report how we were slain," he says. We are given a picture of Johnie Armstrong's character in action instead of a description of it. We know what his code is, even though it is not mentioned in the poem. It is a rather primitive one, a code of crude courage, and probably a very inadequate one for us, for he was a border outlaw living four hundred years ago, but he dies true to it. There is no moral given in the poem, no general statement of an idea, but an idea is suggested through the action itself: out of disaster a spiritual value that makes even disaster seem unimportant may be produced. All of these things are in the poem, but they are there by suggestion and implication of the action; we know them without being told, for we can discover them for ourselves.

What the poem does, in short, is to take some bare facts and treat them so that they have both an emotional and an intellectual interpretation. The sympathetic reader, or hearer, of the ballad might not analyze that interpretation but the effect would be there. He would react to the pathos of the betrayal of a strong, brave man, to the exaltation at Johnie Armstrong's courage and desire for an honorable death, to the ironical contrast between Johnie Armstrong's expectation as he goes to the court and his reception there, to the selection of imaginative detail, and to the suspense and speed of movement of the story. He might not analyze any of these items separately and might not try to understand the part they play in the poem; he might merely experience a certain pleasure in the poem, and simply attribute it, if asked, to the genius of the composer or composers. The genius is there, of course, but one's pleasure is enlarged by the attempt to understand as fully as possible the process by which that genius makes itself felt.

SIR PATRICK SPENCE

ANONYMOUS

The king sits in Dumferling toune,
    Drinking the blude-reid wine:
"O whar will I get guid sailor,
    To sail this schip of mine?"

Up and spak an eldern knicht,   5
    Sat at the kings richt kne:
"Sir Patrick Spence is the best sailor,
    That sails upon the se."

The king has written a braid [1] letter,
    And signd it wi his hand,   10
And sent it to Sir Patrick Spence,
    Was walking on the sand.

The first line that Sir Patrick red,
    A loud lauch lauchèd he;
The next line that Sir Patrick red,   15
    The teir blinded his ee. [2]

"O wha is this has don this deid,
    This ill deid don to me,
To send me out this time o' the yeir,
    To sail upon the se!   20

[1] broad   [2] eye

"Mak hast, mak haste, my mirry men all
    Our guid schip sails the morne:"
"O say na sae, my master deir,
    For I feir a deadlie storme.

"Late, late yestreen I saw the new moone,   25
    Wi the auld³ moone in hir arme,
And I feir, I feir, my deir master,
    That we will cum to harme."

O our Scots nobles wer richt laith⁴
    To weet their cork-heild schoone;⁵   30
Bot lang owre a' the play wer playd,
    Thair hats they swam aboone.

O lang, lang may their ladies sit,
    Wi thair fans into their hand,
Or eir they se Sir Patrick Spence   35
    Cum sailing to the land.

O lang, lang may the ladies stand,
    Wi thair gold kems⁶ in their hair,
Waiting for thar ain deir lords,
    For they'll se thame na mair.   40

Haf owre, haf owre to Aberdour,
    It's fiftie fadom deip,
And thair lies guid Sir Patrick Spence,
    Wi the Scots lords at his feit.

EXERCISE:

   1. Analyze the divisions of the action.
   2. Discuss the use of concrete detail.
   3. What are the ironical contrasts?

THE WIFE OF USHER'S WELL

ANONYMOUS

There lived a wife at Usher's Well,   5
    And a wealthy wife was she;

³ old   ⁴ loath   ⁵ shoes
⁶ combs

She had three stout and stalwart sons,
  And sent them oer the sea.

They hadna been a week from her,   5
  A week but barely ane,
Whan word came to the carline[1] wife
  That her three sons were gane.

They hadna been a week from her,
  A week but barely three,   10
Whan word came to the carlin wife
  That her sons she'd never see.

"I wish the wind may never cease,
  Nor fashes[2] in the flood,
Till my three sons come hame to me,   15
  In earthly flesh and blood."

It fell about the Martinmass,
  When nights are lang and mirk,
The carlin wife's three sons came hame,
  And their hats were o the birk.[3]   20

It neither grew in syke[4] nor ditch,
  Nor yet in ony sheugh;[5]
But at the gates o Paradise,
  That birk grew fair eneugh.

          .   .   .

"Blow up the fire, my maidens,   25
  Bring water from the well;
For a'[6] my house shall feast this night,
  Since my three sons are well."

And she has made to them a bed,
  She's made it large and wide,   30
And she's taen her mantle her about,
  Sat down at the bed-side.

---

[1] peasant   [2] troubles   [3] birch
[4] trench   [5] furrow   [6] all

Up then crew the red, red cock,
  And up and crew the gray;
The eldest to the youngest said,   35
  " 'T is time we were away."

The cock he hadna crawd but once,
  And clappd his wings at al,
When the youngest to the eldest said,
  "Brother, we must awa.   40

"The cock doth craw, the day doth daw,
  The channerin[7] worm doth chide;
Gin we be mist out o our place,
  A sair pain we maun bide.

"Fare ye weel, my mother dear!   45
  Fareweel to barn and byre![8]
And fare ye weel, the bonny lass
  That kindles my mother's fire!"

This poem, too, is a ballad. A woman loses her three sons
at sea, and in her grief, expresses the wish that she may see them
again in flesh and blood. The three sons return to the woman
one night, but since they are only ghosts, they have to leave
again before dawn. The poem uses many more words to give
this simple narrative than the two-sentence paraphrase which
we have just given. Indeed, if we judge the poem's excellence
in terms of the conciseness and the clearness with which it
states the facts which it undertakes to give, then the prose paraphrase is much superior. The difficulty which besets many
people in reading poetry resides to a great extent in the fact
that many people mistake the *intention* of poetry. Plainly in
this poem, as we noticed in "Johnie Armstrong," the facts are
in themselves unimportant. Furthermore, from one point of
view, they are much less important than in "Johnie Armstrong,"
for here they are not even historically true.

What is the intention of this poem? And, judged in the light
of the intention, in what ways is the poem superior to the prose
paraphrase? If one considers the poem carefully, he notices that
the poem, like so many ballads, breaks up into a number of little

[7] devouring   [8] cattle-shed

pictures, and that some of the detail (otherwise irrelevant) becomes justified when we realize that it has been employed to make the scenes vivid for us. The poem is not content merely to state certain things *abstractly* (*Glossary*): we must see the pictures. For example, consider the pictures given us in the seventh and eighth stanzas. The seventh conveys some sense of the bustling excitement with which the woman puts her maids to work when her sons unexpectedly arrive; the eighth conveys with a great deal of intensity the joy with which the mother receives her long-lost sons. She is anxious to make them comfortable; she has prepared the beds carefully for them. But she cannot tear herself away from them, even to let them go to sleep, and having thrown a shawl around her shoulders to keep warm as she sits up in the late chill night air, lingers for a little while by their beds. The poem does not *tell* us of her joy and relief at seeing them home again; it conveys a sense of this to us by showing the mother's joyful activity. In preferring the concrete form of statement to the abstract, "The Wife of Usher's Well" is typical of poetry in general. Consider also the last four stanzas. The poet might have merely stated that the sons regretted having to leave their home and having to go back to the grave. He wishes to do more than communicate the idea, however: he wishes us to share in their feeling of dread as well as to know that they had such a feeling. Which is the better means of doing this: to say, they dreaded leaving "very much," or "a great deal," or "bitterly,"—use whatever adverb you will; or to describe the scene itself? The latter method, the concrete method, is very properly the one chosen.

The crowing of the cocks announcing day is described, and the brief conversation between the brothers is given. Notice that the poem does not use words of great intensity in giving the conversation, but *understatement* (*Glossary*). The eldest brother merely says, " 'Tis time we were away"; the youngest brother, "Brother, we must awa." There is no shrieking of terror. And yet in this case the brief understatement conveys perhaps more of a feeling of horror and grief than exaggerated outcries would have conveyed. We can readily see why this use of understatement is particularly effective here. The poet has refrained throughout from making comments on the situation or from hinting to us what we ought to feel. The poem is *objective* (*Glossary*); the poet stands aside, and lets the poem do its work on us in its own way.

Notice too that this poem, like the previous ones considered, makes use of suggestion. People prefer suggestion to explicit statement in these matters—if for no other reason than that the person who feels the suggestion participates fully and immediately —he feels that he has made a discovery for himself, which is quite another thing than having some one tell him what he ought to feel. Moreover, suggestion is rich in that, the reader's own imagination, aroused, goes on to enrich the whole subject with feeling. We have an excellent example of this power in the last stanza. After the dialogue between the brothers to the effect that they must go back to the grave, the youngest brother says,

"Fare ye well, my mother dear!
Farewell to barn and byre!
And fare ye well, the bonny lass
That kindles my mother's fire."

Was the youngest brother in love with the bonny lass before his death? We have received no earlier hint that he was. Perhaps he has been. But it is not necessary for an appreciation of the poem to read this interpretation into the passage. The stanza gives us all we need to have if we see the bonny lass as representing the warm, beautiful life of flesh and blood which the dead men have lost and which they now must leave. If the girl does stand for this, then one may perhaps find the reason for the effect which the last line gives—

"That kindles my mother's fire."

The description in its effect on us is not merely an identification of the girl; the association of the girl with the fire makes us think of her particularly in her contrast with the cold and desolate grave to which the dead brothers must return.[1]

One may raise the question at this point as to whether the

[1] In order to accept this interpretation of the effect of the last stanza on the reader it is not necessary to assume that the effect was consciously planned by the poet. For a reference to the problem of the degree of self-consciousness in a poet's artistry see Section VI, pp. 477–482.

average reader will feel that the line means this. Is the average reader expected to be able to make this interpretation? The answer must be, no; most readers do not make this interpretation consciously; and it is not necessary for them to make it consciously in order to enjoy the poem. Many of the details of poetry affect us *unconsciously*. We can not explain just how the effect was made. But if we are to enjoy poetry to its fullest we must be alert and sensitive to such details as this. In "The Wife of Usher's Well," the suggestiveness of the images works rather simply. In some poems, especially those in Section VI and Section VII, the suggestions made by the images may have a much more complicated relationship to the general intention of the poem.

We have seen that this poem differs from the prose paraphrase in being concrete where the prose is abstract, in concerning itself with feelings as well as with mere ideas, and in making use of suggestions rather than depending merely on explicit statement. One more point may be worth making. The *structure* (*Glossary*) of the poem is based on an appeal to the reader's feelings. It is not merely logical or chronological. The poem takes advantage of a reader's natural curiosity. It employs suspense. (Though the end is foreshadowed when we are told where the birch grew which adorns the dead men's hats, we are not told that they are dead—only that the wife was told that she would never see them. The solution is held up to the end.) Furthermore, the poem builds to a climax. That climax lies in the contrast between the horrors of the grave and the warmth and friendliness of life. The channering worm is contrasted with the bonny lass in the last two stanzas, and the final crowing of the cock has been so prepared for that we feel it as a gruesome summons—we feel it as the dead men feel it. Moreover, the effectiveness is increased by an ironic contrast in the crowing itself. The scene is a farm-scene. The atmosphere of warmth and life has been developed in terms of the farmhouse setting. But the crowing of the birds, which have an integral part in this friendly setting—the crowing which is only one of the friendly noises associated with the boys' home—itself becomes the signal for departure from this comfortable and human world to the monstrous world to which the dead men must return.

HELEN OF KIRCONNELL

ANONYMOUS

I wish I were where Helen lies,
Night and day on me she cries;
O that I were where Helen lies,
   On fair Kirconnell lea!

Curst be the heart that thought the thought,   5
And curst the hand that fired the shot,
When in my arms burd [1] Helen dropt,
   And died to succour me!

O think not ye my heart was sair,[2]
When my love dropt and spoke no mair! [3]   10
There did she swoon wi' mickle care,
   On fair Kirconnell lea.

As I went down the water side,
None but my foe to be my guide,
None but my foe to be my guide,   15
   On fair Kirconnell lea;

I lighted down my sword to draw,
I hackèd him in pieces sma',[4]
I hackèd him in pieces sma',
   For her sake that died for me.   20

O Helen fair, beyond compare!
I'll make a garland of thy hair,
Shall bind my heart for evermair,
   Until the day I die!

O that I were where Helen lies!   25
Night and day on me she cries;
Out of my bed she bids me rise,
   Says, "Haste, and come to me!"

O Helen fair! O Helen chaste!
If I were with thee, I'd be blest,   30
Where thou lies low and takes thy rest,
   On fair Kirconnell lea.

---

[1] of gentle birth   [2] sore   [3] more   [4] small

> I wish my grave were growing green,
> A winding-sheet drawn o'er my e'en,
> And I in Helen's arms lying,   35
> On fair Kirconnell lea.
>
> I wish I were where Helen lies!
> Night and day on me she cries;
> And I am weary of the skies,
> For her sake that died for me.   40

Why is it not necessary in this poem for the reader to have any details of the love story?

THE DEMON LOVER

ANONYMOUS

> "O where have you been, my long, long love,
> This long seven years and mair?"
> "O I'm come to seek my former vows
> Ye granted me before."
>
> "O hold your tongue of your former vows,   5
> For they will breed sad strife;
> O hold your tongue of your former vows,
> For I am become a wife."
>
> He turned him right and round about,
> And the tear blinded his ee: 10
> "I wad never hae trodden on Irish ground,
> If it had not been for thee.
>
> "I might hae had a king's daughter,
> Far, far beyond the sea;
> I might have had a king's daughter,   15
> Had it not been for love o thee."

"If ye might have had a king's daughter,
  Yersel ye had to blame;
Ye might have had taken the king's daughter,
  For ye kend [1] that I was nane.[2]   20

"If I was to leave my husband dear,
  And my two babes also,
O what have you to take me to,
  If with you I should go?"

"I hae seven ships upon the sea—   25
  The eighth brought me to land—
With four-and-twenty bold mariners,
  And music on every hand."

She has taken up her two little babes,
  Kissd them baith [3] cheek and chin: 30
"O fair ye weel, my ain [4] two babes,
  For I'll never see you again."

She set her foot upon the ship,
  No mariners could she behold;
But the sails were o the taffetie,   35
  And the masts o the beaten gold.

She had not sailed a league, a league,
  A league but barely three,
When dismal grew his countenance,   40
  And drumlie [5] grew his ee.

They had not saild a league, a league,
  A league but barely three,
Until she espied his cloven foot,
  And she wept right bitterlie.   45

"O hold your tongue of your weeping," says he,
  "Of your weeping now let me be;
I will shew you how the lilies grow
  On the banks of Italy."

[1] knew   [2] none   [3] both   [4] own   [5] dark

    "O what hills are yon, yon pleasant hills,   50
      That the sun shines sweetly on?"
    "O yon are the hills of heaven," he said,
      "Where you will never win."

    "O whaten a mountain is yon," she said,
      "All so dreary wi frost and snow?"   55
    "O yon is the mountain of hell," he cried,
      "Where you and I will go."

    He strack the tap-mast wi his hand,
      The fore-mast wi his knee,
    And he brake that gallant ship in twain,   60
      And sank her in the sea.

EXERCISE:

  Write an analysis of this poem, using the analysis of "The Wife of Usher's Well" for a model.

THE RIME OF THE ANCIENT MARINER

IN SEVEN PARTS

SAMUEL TAYLOR COLERIDGE (1772–1834)

Part I

An ancient Mariner meeteth three Gallants bidden to a wedding-feast, and detaineth one.

It is an ancient Mariner,
And he stoppeth one of three.
"By thy long gray beard and glittering eye,
Now wherefore stopp'st thou me?

"The Bridegroom's doors are opened wide,   5
And I am next of kin;
The guests are met, the feast is set:
May'st hear the merry din."

He holds him with his skinny hand,
"There was a ship," quoth he.   10
"Hold off! unhand me, graybeard loon!"
Eftsoons his hand dropt he.

The Wedding-
Guest is spell-
bound by the eye
of the old seafar-
ing man, and con-
strained to hear
his tale.

He holds him with his glittering eye—
The wedding-guest stood still,
And listens like a three years' child: 15
The Mariner hath his will.

The wedding-guest sat on a stone:
He cannot choose but hear;
And thus spake on that ancient man,
The bright-eyed Mariner.   20

"The ship was cheered, the harbor cleared,
Merrily did we drop
Below the kirk, below the hill,
Below the lighthouse top.

The Mariner tells
how the ship
sailed southward
with a good wind
and fair weather
till it reached the
Line.

"The sun came up upon the left,   25
Out of the sea came he!
And he shone bright, and on the right
Went down into the sea.

"Higher and higher every day,
Till over the mast at noon—"   30
The wedding-guest here beat his breast,
For he heard the loud bassoon.

The Wedding-
Guest heareth the
bridal music; but
the Mariner con-
tinueth his tale.

The bride hath paced into the hall,
Red as a rose is she;
Nodding their heads before her goes   35
The merry minstrelsy.

The wedding-guest he beat his breast,
Yet he cannot choose but hear;
And thus spake on that ancient man,
The bright-eyed Mariner: 40

The ship driven
by a storm toward
the south pole

"And now the storm-blast came, and he
Was tyrannous and strong:
He struck with his o'ertaking wings,
And chased us south along.

"With sloping masts and dipping prow,   45
As who pursued with yell and blow

Still treads the shadow of his foe,
And forward bends his head,
The ship drove fast, loud roared the blast,
And southward aye we fled.   50

"And now there came both mist and snow,
And it grew wondrous cold;
And ice, mast-high, came floating by,
As green as emerald;

The land of ice, and of fearful sounds where no living thing was to be seen.

"And through the drifts the snowy clifts   55
Did send a dismal sheen:
Nor shapes of men nor beasts we ken—
The ice was all between.

"The ice was here, the ice was there,
The ice was all around: 60
It cracked and growled, and roared and howled,
Like noises in a swound!

Till a great sea-bird, called the Albatross, came through the snow-fog, and was received with great joy and hospitality.

"At length did cross an Albatross:
Thorough the fog it came:
As if it had been a Christian soul,   65
We hailed it in God's name.

"It ate the food it ne'er had eat,
And round and round it flew.
The ice did split with a thunder-fit;
The helmsman steered us through!   70

And lo! the Albatross proveth a bird of good omen, and followeth the ship as it returned northward through fog and floating ice.

"And a good south wind sprung up behind;
The Albatross did follow,
And every day, for food or play,
Came to the mariners' hollo!

"In mist or cloud, on mast or shroud,   75
It perched for vespers nine;
Whiles all the night, through fog-smoke white,
Glimmered the white moon-shine."

The ancient Mariner inhospitably killeth the pious bird of good omen.

"God save thee, ancient Mariner!
From the fiends, that plague thee thus!—   80
Why look'st thou so?"—"With my cross-bow
I shot the Albatross!

Part II

"The sun now rose upon the right:
Out of the sea came he,
Still hid in mist, and on the left   85
Went down into the sea.

"And the good south wind still blew behind,
But no sweet bird did follow,
Nor any day, for food or play,
Came to the mariners' hollo!   90

His shipmates cry
out against the an-
cient Mariner for
killing the bird of
good luck.

"And I had done a hellish thing,
And it would work 'em woe;
For all averred, I had killed the bird
That made the breeze to blow.
Ah wretch! said they, the bird to slay   95
That made the breeze to blow!

But when the fog
cleared off, they
justify the same,
and thus make
themselves accom-
plices in the crime.

"Nor dim nor red, like God's own head,
The glorious sun uprist:
Then all averred, I had killed the bird
That brought the fog and mist.   100
'Twas right, said they, such birds to slay,
That bring the fog and mist.

The fair breeze
continues; the ship
enters the Pacific
Ocean, and sails
northward, even
till it reaches the
Line.

"The fair breeze blew, the white foam flew,
The furrow followed free:
We were the first that ever burst   105
Into that silent sea.

The ship hath
been suddenly be-
calmed.

"Down dropt the breeze, the sails dropt down,
'Twas sad as sad could be;
And we did speak only to break
The silence of the sea!   110

"All in a hot and copper sky,
The bloody sun, at noon,
Right up above the mast did stand,
No bigger than the moon.

"Day after day, day after day,   115
We stuck, nor breath nor motion;

As idle as a painted ship
Upon a painted ocean.

And the Albatross
begins to be
avenged.

"Water, water, everywhere,
And all the boards did shrink;   120
Water, water, everywhere,
Nor any drop to drink.

"The very deep did rot: O Christ!
That ever this should be!
Yea, slimy things did crawl with legs   125
Upon the slimy sea.

"About, about, in reel and rout,
The death-fires danced at night;
The water, like a witch's oils,
Burnt green, and blue, and white.   130

A Spirit had fol-
lowed them; one
of the invisible in-
habitants of this
planet, neither de-
parted souls nor
angels.

"And some in dreams assurèd were
Of the spirit that plagued us so:
Nine fathom deep he had followed us,
From the land of mist and snow.

The shipmates, in
their sore distress,
would fain throw
the whole guilt on
the ancient Mari-
ner: in sign
whereof they hang
the dead seabird
round his neck.

"And every tongue, through utter drought,   135
Was withered at the root;
We could not speak, no more than if
We had been choked with soot.

"Ah! well-a-day! what evil looks
Had I from old and young!   140
Instead of the cross, the Albatross
About my neck was hung.

Part III

The ancient Mari-
ner beholdeth a
sign in the ele-
ment afar off.

"There passed a weary time. Each throat
Was parched, and glazed each eye.
A weary time! A weary time!   145
How glazed each weary eye!
When looking westward I beheld
A something in the sky.

"At first it seemed a little speck,
And then it seemed a mist: 150
It moved and moved, and took at last
A certain shape, I wist.

"A speck, a mist, a shape, I wist!
And still it neared and neared:
As if it didged a water-sprite,   155
It plunged and tacked and veered.

At its nearer ap-
proach, it seemeth
him to be a ship;
and at a dear ran-
som he freeth his
speech from the
bonds of thirst.

"With throats unslaked, with black lips baked,
We could nor laugh nor wail;
Through utter drought all dumb we stood!
I bit my arm, I sucked the blood,   160
And cried, 'A sail! a sail!'

A flash of joy;

"With throats unslaked, with black lips baked,
Agape they heard me call:
Gramercy! they for joy did grin,
And all at once their breath drew in,   165
As they were drinking all.

And horror fol-
lows. For can it be
a ship that comes
onward without
wind or tide?

" 'See! see (I cried) she tacks no more!
Hither to work us weal;
Without a breeze, without a tide,
She steadies with upright keel!'   170

"The western wave was all a-flame:
The day was well nigh done:
Almost upon the western wave
Rested the broad bright sun;
When that strange shape drove suddenly   175
Betwixt us and the sun.

It seemeth him
but the skeleton of
a ship.

"And straight the sun was flecked with bars,
(Heaven's Mother send us grace!)
As if through a dungeon grate he peered,
With broad and burning face.   180

"Alas! (thought I, and my heart beat loud)
How fast she nears and nears!
Are those her sails that glance in the sun,
Like restless gossameres?

And its ribs are seen as bars on the face of the setting sun.

"Are those her ribs through which the sun   185
Did peer, as through a grate?
And is that Woman all her crew?
Is that a Death? and are there two?
Is Death that woman's mate?

The Spectre-Woman and her Death-mate, and no other on board the skeleton-ship.

Like vessel, like crew!

"Her lips were red, her looks were free,   190
Her locks were yellow as gold:
Her skin was as white as leprosy,
The nightmare Life-in-Death was she,
Who thicks man's blood with cold.

Death and Life-in-Death have diced for the ship's crew, and she (the latter) winneth the ancient Mariner.

"The naked hulk alongside came,   195
And the twain were casting dice;
'The game is done! I've won, I've won!'
Quoth she, and whistles thrice.

No twilight within the courts of the sun.

"The sun's rim dips; the stars rush out:
At one stride comes the dark;   200
With far-heard whisper, o'er the sea,
Off shot the spectre-bark.

At the rising of the moon,

"We listened and looked sideways up!
Fear at my heart, as at a cup,
My life-blood seemed to sip!   205
The stars were dim, and thick the night,
The steersman's face by his lamp gleamed white;
From the sails the dew did drip—
Till clomb above the eastern bar
The hornéd moon, with one bright star   210
Within the nether tip.

One after another,

"One after one, by the star-dogged moon,
Too quick for groan or sigh,
Each turned his face with a ghastly pang,
And cursed me with his eye.   215

His shipmates drop down dead.

"Four times fifty living men,
(And I heard nor sigh nor groan)
With heavy thump, a lifeless lump,
They dropped down one by one.

But Life-in-Death
begins her work
on the ancient
Mariner.

"The souls did from their bodies fly,—   220
They fled to bliss or woe!
And every soul, it passed me by,
Like the whizz of my cross-bow!"

Part IV

The Wedding-
Guest feareth that
a spirit is talking
to him;

"I fear thee, ancient Mariner!
I fear thy skinny hand!   225
And thou art long, and lank, and brown,
As is the ribbed sea-sand.

But the ancient
Mariner assureth
him of his bodily
life, and proceed-
eth to relate his
horrible penance.

"I fear thee and thy glittering eye,
And thy skinny hand, so brown."—
"Fear not, fear not, thou wedding-guest!   230
This body dropt not down.

"Alone, alone, all, all alone,
Alone on a wide, wide sea!
And never a saint took pity on
My soul in agony.   235

He despiseth the
creatures of the
calm,

"The many men, so beautiful!
And they all dead did lie:
And a thousand thousand slimy things
Lived on; and so did I.

And envieth that
they should live,
and so many be
dead.

"I looked upon the rotting sea,   240
And drew my eyes away;
I looked upon the rotting deck,
And there the dead men lay.

"I looked to heaven, and tried to pray;
But or ever a prayer had gusht,   245
A wicked whisper came, and made
My heart as dry as dust.

"I closed my lids, and kept them close,
And the balls like pulses beat;
For the sky and the sea, and the sea and the
      sky,   250
Lay like a load on my weary eye,
And the dead were at my feet.

But the curse
liveth for him in
the eye of the
dead men.

"The cold sweat melted from their limbs,
Nor rot nor reek did they:
The look with which they looked on me   255
Had never passed away.

"An orphan's curse would drag to hell
A spirit from on high;
But oh! more horrible than that
Is the curse in a dead man's eye!   260
Seven days, seven nights, I saw that curse,
And yet I could not die.

In his loneliness
and fixedness he
yearneth towards
the journeying
moon, and the
stars that still so-
journ, yet still
move onward;
and everywhere
the blue sky be-
longs to them, and
is their appointed
rest, and their na-
tive country and
their natural
homes, which they
enter unan-
nounced, as lords
that are certainly
expected; and yet
there is a silent joy
at their arrival.

"The moving moon went up the sky,
And nowhere did abide:
Softly she was going up,   265
And a star or two beside—

"Her beams bemocked the sultry main,
Like April hoar-frost spread;
But where the ship's huge shadow lay,
The charmèd water burnt alway   270
A still and awful red.

"Beyond the shadow of the ship,
I watched the water-snakes:
They moved in tracks of shining white,
And when they reared, the elfish light   275
Fell off in hoary flakes.

"Within the shadow of the ship
I watched their rich attire:
Blue, glossy green, and velvet black,
They coiled and swam; and every track   280
Was a flash of golden fire.

Their beauty and
their happiness.

He blesseth them
in his heart.

"O happy living things! no tongue
Their beauty might declare:
A spring of love gushed from my heart,
And I blessed them unaware!   285
Sure my kind saint took pity on me,
And I blessed them unaware.

The spell begins to
break.
"The selfsame moment I could pray;
And from my neck so free
The Albatross fell off, and sank   290
Like lead into the sea.

Part V

"O sleep! it is a gentle thing,
Beloved from pole to pole!
To Mary Queen the praise be given!
She sent the gentle sleep from Heaven,   295
That slid into my soul.

By grace of the
Holy Mother, the
ancient Mariner is
refreshed with
rain.
"The silly buckets on the deck,
That had so long remained,
I dreamt that they were filled with dew;
And when I awoke, it rained.   300

"My lips were wet, my throat was cold,
My garments all were dank;
Sure I had drunken in my dreams,
And still my body drank.

"I moved, and could not feel my limbs: 305
I was so light—almost
I thought that I had died in sleep,
And was a blessed ghost.

He heareth sounds
and seeth strange
sights and com-
motions in the sky
and the element.
"And soon I heard a roaring wind:
It did not come anear;   310
But with its sound it shook the sails,
That were so thin and sere.

"The upper air burst into life!
And a hundred fire-flags sheen,
To and fro they were hurried about;   315
And to and fro, and in and out,
The wan stars danced between.

"And the coming wind did roar more loud,
And the sails did sigh like sedge;
And the rain poured down from one black
          cloud;   320
The moon was at its edge.

"The thick black cloud was cleft, and still
The moon was at its side:
Like waters shot from some high crag,
The lightning fell with never a jag,   325
A river steep and wide.

The bodies of the ship's crew are inspired, and the ship moves on;

"The loud wind never reached the ship,
Yet now the ship moved on!
Beneath the lightning and the moon
The dead men gave a groan.   330

"They groaned, they stirred, they all uprose,
Nor spake, nor moved their eyes;
It had been strange, even in a dream,
To have seen those dead men rise.

"The helmsman steered, the ship moved on;
Yet never a breeze up-blew;   336
The mariners all 'gan work the ropes,
Where they were wont to do:
They raised their limbs like lifeless tools—
We were a ghastly crew.   340

"The body of my brother's son
Stood by me, knee to knee:
The body and I pulled at one rope,
But he said nought to me."

But not by the souls of the men, nor by demons of earth or middle air, but by a blessed troop of angelic spirits, sent down by the invocation of the guardian saint.

"I fear thee, ancient Mariner!"   345
"Be calm, thou Wedding-Guest!
'Twas not those souls that fled in pain,
Which to their corses came again,
But a troop of spirits blest:

"For when it dawned—they dropped their arms,
And clustered round the mast;   351
Sweet sounds rose slowly through their mouths,
And from their bodies passed.

"Around, around, flew each sweet sound,
Then darted to the sun;   355
Slowly the sounds came back again,
Now mixed, now one by one.

"Sometimes a-dropping from the sky
I heard the skylark sing;
Sometimes all little birds that are,   360
How they seemed to fill the sea and air
With their sweet jargoning!

"And now 'twas like all instruments,
Now like a lonely flute;
And now it is an angel's song,   365
That makes the heavens be mute.

"It ceased; yet still the sails made on
A pleasant noise till noon,
A noise like of a hidden brook
In the leafy month of June,   370
That to the sleeping woods all night
Singeth a quiet tune.

"Till noon we quietly sailed on,
Yet never a breeze did breathe:
Slowly and smoothly went the ship,   375
Moved onward from beneath.

The lonesome
Spirit from the
south pole carries
on the ship as far
as the Line, in
obedience to the
angelic troop, but
still requireth
vengeance.

"Under the keel nine fathom deep,
From the land of mist and snow,
The spirit slid; and it was he
That made the ship to go.   380
The sails at noon left off their tune,
And the ship stood still also.

"The sun, right up above the mast,
Had fixed her to the ocean;
But in a minute she 'gan stir,   385
With a short uneasy motion—
Backwards and forwards half her length,
With a short uneasy motion.

"Then like a pawing horse let go,
She made a sudden bound: 390
It flung the blood into my head,
And I fell down in a swound.

The Polar Spirit's fellow-demons, the invisible inhabitants of the element, take part in his wrong, and two of them relate, one to the other, that penance long and heavy for the ancient Mariner hath been accorded to the Polar Spirit, who returneth southward.

"How long in that same fit I lay,
I have not to declare;
But ere my living life returned,   395
I heard, and in my soul discerned
Two voices in the air.

" 'Is it he?' quoth one, 'is this the man?
By Him who died on cross,
With his cruel bow he laid full low   400
The harmless Albatross.

" 'The spirit who bideth by himself
In the land of mist and snow,
He loved the bird that loved the man
Who shot him with his bow.'   405

"The other was a softer voice,
As soft as honey-dew:
Quoth he, 'The man hath penance done,
And penance more will do.'

Part VI

First Voice

" 'But tell me, tell me! speak again,   410
Thy soft response renewing—
What makes that ship drive on so fast?
What is the ocean doing?'

Second Voice

" 'Still as a slave before his lord,
The ocean hath no blast;   415
His great bright eye most silently
Up to the moon is cast—

" 'If he may know which way to go;
For she guides him, smooth or grim.
See, brother, see! how graciously   420
She looketh down on him.'

First Voice

<table>
<tr><td>

The Mariner hath
been cast into a
trance; for the an-
gelic power
causeth the vessel
to drive north-
ward faster than
human life could
endure.

</td><td>

" 'But why drives on that ship so fast,
Without or wave or wind?'

Second Voice

" 'The air is cut away before,
And closes from behind.   425

" 'Fly, brother, fly! more high, more high!
Or we shall be belated:
For slow and slow that ship will go,
When the Mariner's trance is abated.'

</td></tr>
</table>

The supernatural
motion is re-
tarded; the Mari-
ner awakes, and
his penance be-
gins anew.

"I woke, and we were sailing on,   430
As in a gentle weather:
'Twas night, calm night, the moon was high;
The dead men stood together.

"All stood together on the deck,
For a charnel-dungeon fitter:
All fixed on me their stony eyes,   435
That in the moon did glitter.

"The pang, the curse, with which they died,
Had never passed away:
I could not draw my eyes from theirs,   440
Nor turn them up to pray.

The curse is
finally expiated.

"And now this spell was snapt: once more
I viewed the ocean green,
And looked far forth, yet little saw
Of what had else been seen—   445

"Like one, that on a lonesome road
Doth walk in fear and dread,
And having once turned round, walks on,
And turns no more his head;
Because he knows a frightful fiend   450
Doth close behind him tread.

"But soon there breathed a wind on me,
Nor sound nor motion made:
Its path was not upon the sea,
In ripple or in shade.   455

"It raised my hair, it fanned my cheek
Like a meadow-gale of spring—
It mingled strangely with my fears,
Yet it felt like a welcoming.

"Swiftly, swiftly flew the ship,   460
Yet she sailed softly too:
Sweetly, sweetly blew the breeze—
On me alone it blew.

And the ancient
Mariner beholdeth
his native country.

"Oh! dream of joy! is this indeed
The lighthouse top I see?   465
Is this the hill? is this the kirk?
Is this mine own countree?

"We drifted o'er the harbor-bar,
And I with sobs did pray—
'O let me be awake, my God!   470
Or let me sleep alway.'

"The harbor-bay was clear as glass,
So smoothly it was strewn!
And on the bay the moonlight lay,
And the shadow of the moon.   475

"The rock shone bright, the kirk no less,
That stands above the rock:
The moonlight steeped in silentness
The steady weathercock.

The angelic spirits
leave the dead
bodies.

"And the bay was white with silent light,   480
Till rising from the same,
Full many shapes, that shadows were,
In crimson colors came.

And appear in
their own forms
of light.

"A little distance from the prow
Those crimson shadows were: 485
I turned my eyes upon the deck—
Oh, Christ! what saw I there!

"Each corse lay flat, lifeless and flat,
And, by the holy rood!
A man all light, a seraph-man, 490
On every corse there stood.

"This seraph-band, each waved his hand:
It was a heavenly sight!
They stood as signals to the land,
Each one a lovely light: 495

"This seraph-band, each waved his hand,
No voice did they impart—
No voice; but oh! the silence sank
Like music on my heart.

"But soon I heard the dash of oars, 500
I heard the pilot's cheer;
My head was turned perforce away,
And I saw a boat appear.

"The pilot, and the pilot's boy,
I heard them coming fast: 505
Dear Lord in Heaven! it was a joy
The dead men could not blast.

"I saw a third—I heard his voice:
It is the Hermit good!
He singeth loud his godly hymns 510
That he makes in the wood.
He'll shrieve my soul, he'll wash away
The Albatross's blood.

Part VII

The Hermit of the wood,

"This Hermit good lives in that wood
Which slopes down to the sea.
How loudly his sweet voice he rears! 515
He loves to talk with marineres
That come from a far countree.

"He kneels at morn, and noon, and eve—
He hath a cushion plump: 520
It is the moss that wholly hides
The rotted old oak-stump.

"The skiff-boat neared: I heard them talk,
'Why, this is strange, I trow!
Where are those lights so many and fair,   525
That signal made but now?'

Approacheth the
ship with wonder.

" 'Strange, by my faith!' the Hermit said—
'And they answered not our cheer!
The planks look warped! and see those sails,
How thin they are and sere!   530
I never saw aught like to them,
Unless perchance it were

" 'Brown skeletons of leaves that lag
My forest-brook along:
When the ivy-tod is heavy with snow,   535
And the owlet whoops to the wolf below,
That eats the she-wolf's young.'

" 'Dear Lord! it hath a fiendish look'—
(The pilot made reply)
'I am a-feared'—'Push on, push on!'   540
Said the Hermit cheerily.

"The boat came closer to the ship,
But I nor spake nor stirred;
The boat came close beneath the ship,
And straight a sound was heard.   545

The ship suddenly
sinketh.

"Under the water it rumbled on,
Still louder and more dread:
It reached the ship, it split the bay;
The ship went down like lead.

The ancient Mari-
ner is saved in the
Pilot's boat.

"Stunned by that loud and dreadful sound,   550
Which sky and ocean smote,
Like one that hath been seven days drowned,
My body lay afloat;
But swift as dreams, myself I found
Within the pilot's boat.   555

"Upon the whirl, where sank the ship,
The boat spun round and round;
And all was still, save that the hill
Was telling of the sound.

"I moved my lips—the pilot shrieked,   560
And fell down in a fit;
The Holy Hermit raised his eyes,
And prayed where he did sit.

"I took the oars: the pilot's boy,
Who now doth crazy go,   565
Laughing loud and long, and all the while
His eyes went to and fro.
'Ha! ha!' quoth he, 'full plain I see,
The Devil knows how to row.'

"And now, all in my own countree,   570
I stood on the firm land!
The Hermit stepped forth from the boat,
And scarcely he could stand.

The ancient Mariner earnestly entreateth the Hermit to shrieve him; and the penance of life falls on him.

"'O shrieve me, shrieve me, holy man!'
The Hermit crossed his brow.   575
'Say quick,' quoth he, 'I bid thee say—
What manner of man art thou?'

"Forthwith this frame of mine was wrenched
With a woeful agony,
Which forced me to begin my tale;   580
And then it left me free.

And ever and anon throughout his future life an agony constraineth him to travel from land to land,

"Since then at an uncertain hour,
That agony returns;
And till my ghastly tale is told,
This heart within me burns.   585

"I pass, like night, from land to land;
I have strange power of speech;
That moment that his face I see,
I know the man that must hear me:
To him my tale I teach.   590

"What loud uproar bursts from that door:
The wedding-guests are there;
But in the garden-bower the bride
And the bride-maids singing are;
And hark the little vesper bell,   595
Which biddeth me to prayer!

"O Wedding-Guest! this soul hath been
Alone on a wide, wide sea:
So lonely 'twas, that God himself
Scarce seemèd there to be.   600

"O sweeter than the marriage-feast,
'Tis sweeter far to me,
To walk together to the kirk
With a goodly company!—

"To walk together to the kirk,   605
And all together pray,
While each to his great Father bends,
Old men, and babes, and loving friends,
And youths and maidens gay!

And to teach, by   "Farewell, farewell! but this I tell   610
his own example,   To thee, thou Wedding-Guest!
love and reverence   He prayeth well, who loveth well
to all things that   Both man and bird and beast.
God made and
loveth.

"He prayeth best, who loveth best
All things both great and small;   615
For the dear God who loveth us,
He made and loveth all."

The Mariner, whose eye is bright,
Whose beard with age is hoar,
Is gone; and now the Wedding-Guest   620
Turned from the bidegroom's door.

He went like one that hath been stunned,
And is of sense forlorn:
A sadder and a wiser man
He rose the morrow morn.   625

EXERCISE:

The poems that we have previously considered are folk ballads (p. 32). But professional writers, admiring the dramatic simplicity of the true ballad, have sometimes written poems in which they have attempted to give something of the same effect. Such poems are called *literary ballads* in order to distinguish them from the true folk ballad. The extent to which the professional poet imitates the true ballad varies from instance to instance. In this case, some of the points of similarity are: the frequent use of the ballad *stanza* (*Glossary*); archaic *diction* (*Glossary*); simplicity of statement and conscious naïveté; repetition; use of the supernatural. But there are several points of difference. The poet, feeling that the consistent use of the ballad stanza in a poem as long as this would be monotonous, has varied the stanza form. Second, the movement of the story is not so definitely by leaps and pauses as is the case in the usual folk ballad; that is, the poem tends toward a narrative rather than a dramatic effect (p. 36). Third, the description is more elaborate. Fourth, this poem tends to give a less objective treatment than does the ordinary ballad (p. 44). For instance, the character does not only display his feelings but, in addition, describes them. In "The Demon Lover," we gather from the following stanza the feelings of the lover:

> I might hae had a king's daughter
> Far, far beyond the sea;
> I might have had a king's daughter,
> Had it not been for love o thee.

But in "The Rime of the Ancient Mariner" the speaker tries to describe his emotions:

> Forthwith this frame of mind was wrenched
> With a woeful agony,
> Which forced me to begin my tale;
> And then it left me free.

Although the relation of the literary ballad to the folk ballad is important and interesting in that it shows one of the ways in which a poet may work, it is not a fundamental consideration. The fundamental question is this: has the poet succeeded in making a good poem? If the reader does feel that the poem is successful, it may be proper, then, for him to consider some of the means the poet has employed.

1. How does the amount of description contribute to the poem's total effect?

2. Why is the subjective treatment necessary here?

3. Since the naïve statement of the "moral" at the end of the poem is obviously intended to give an impression of the simple and uncritical piety of the Middle Ages, what part should it bear in the total interpretation of the poem?

LA BELLE DAME SANS MERCI

JOHN KEATS (1795–1821)

O what can ail thee, knight-at-arms!
  Alone and palely loitering!
The sedge has withered from the lake,
  And no birds sing.

O what can ail thee, knight-at-arms!   5
  So haggard and so woe-begone?
The squirrel's granary is full,
  And the harvest's done.

I see a lily on thy brow
  With anguish moist and fever dew,   10
And on thy cheeks a fading rose
  Fast withereth too.

I met a lady in the meads,
  Full beautiful—a faery's child,
Her hair was long, her foot was light,   15
  And her eyes were wild.

I made a garland for her head,
  And bracelets too, and fragrant zone;
She looked at me as she did love,
  And made sweet moan.   20

I set her on my pacing steed,
　And nothing else saw all day long.
For sidelong would she bend, and sing
　A faery's song.

She found me roots of relish sweet,   25
　And honey wild, and manna dew,
And sure in language strange she said—
　"I love thee true."

She took me to her elfin grot,
　And there she wept, and sighed full sore,   30
And there I shut her wild wild eyes
　With kisses four.

And there she lullèd me asleep,
　And there I dreamed—Ah! woe betide!
The latest dream I ever dreamed   35
　On the cold hill's side.

I saw pale kings and princes too,
　Pale warriors, death-pale were they all;
They cried—"La Belle Dame sans Merci
　Hath thee in thrall!"   40

I saw their starved lips in the gloam,
　With horrid warning gapèd wide,
And I awoke and found me here,
　On the cold hill's side.

And this is why I sojourn here,   45
　Alone and palely loitering,
Though the sedge is withered from the lake
　And no birds sing.

EXERCISE:

1. This poem, like "The Rime of the Ancient Mariner," is a literary ballad, but one can see that it follows more closely the structure of the folk ballad. How does it resemble a poem like "The Wife of Usher's Well," and how does it differ from such a poem?

2. Like "The Wife of Usher's Well" and "The Demon Lover,"
this poem employs the supernatural. Is this poem merely a sort
of "fairy tale" or does it have some meaning that more directly
concerns ordinary human beings?

MICHAEL

A Pastoral [1] Poem

WILLIAM WORDSWORTH (1770–1850)

If from the public way you turn your steps;
Up the tumultuous brook of Green-head Ghyll,
You will suppose that with an upright path
Your feet must struggle; in such bold ascent
The pastoral mountains front you face to face.   5
But courage! for around that boisterous brook
The mountains have all opened out themselves,
And made a hidden valley of their own.
No habitation can be seen: but they
Who journey thither find themselves alone   10
With a few sheep, with rocks and stones, and kites
That overhead are sailing in the sky.
It is in truth an utter solitude;
Nor should I have made mention of this Dell
But for one object which you might pass by,   15
Might see and notice not. Beside the brook
Appears a straggling heap of unhewn stones!
And to that simple object appertains,
A story unenriched with strange events,
Yet not unfit, I deem, for the fireside,   20
Or for the summer shade. It was the first
Of those domestic tales that spake to me
Of Shepherds, dwellers in the valleys, men
Whom I already loved;—not verily
For their own sakes, but for the fields and hills   25
Where was their occupation and abode.
And hence this Tale, while I was yet a Boy

[1] (Glossary)

Careless of books, yet having felt the power
Of Nature, by the gentle agency
Of natural objects led me on to feel   30
For passions ·that were not my own, and think
(At random and imperfectly indeed)
On man, the heart of man, and human life.
Therefore, although it be a history
Homely and rude, I will relate the same   35
For the delight of a few natural hearts;
And, with yet fonder feeling, for the sake
Of youthful Poets who among these hills
Will be my second self when I am gone.

Upon the forest-side in Grasmere Vale   40
There dwelt a Shepherd, Michael was his name;
An old man, stout of heart, and strong of limb.
His bodily frame had been from youth to age
Of an unusual strength: his mind was keen,
Intense, and frugal, apt for all affairs,   45
And in his shepherd's calling he was prompt
And watchful more than ordinary men.
Hence had he learned the meaning of all winds,
Of blasts of every tone; and, oftentimes,
When others heeded not, He heard the South   50
Make subterraneous music, like the. noise
Of bagpipers on distant Highland hills.
The Shepherd, at such warning, of his flock
Bethought him, and he to himself would say,
'The winds are now devising work for me!'   55
And, truly, at all times, the storm, that drives
The traveler to a shelter, summoned him
Up to the mountains; he had been alone
Amid the heart of many thousand mists,
That came to him and left him on the heights.   60
So lived he till his eightieth year was past.
And grossly that man errs, who should suppose
That the green valleys, and the streams and rocks,
Were things indifferent to the Shepherd's thoughts.
Fields, where with cheerful spirits he had breathed   65
The common air; hills, which with vigorous step
He had so often climbed; which had impressed
So many incidents upon his mind

Of hardship, skill or courage, joy or fear;
Which like a book preserved the memory 70
Of the dumb animals, whom he had saved,
Had fed or sheltered, linking to such acts,
The certainty of honorable gain;
Those fields, those hills—what could they less?—had laid
Strong hold on his affections, were to him 75
A pleasurable feeling of blind love,
The pleasure which there is in life itself.

His days had not been passed in singleness.
His Helpmate was a comely matron, old—
Though younger than himself full twenty years. 80
She was a woman of a stirring life,
Whose heart was in her house: two wheels she had
Of antique form, this large for spinning wool,
That small for flax; and if one wheel had rest,
It was because the other was at work. 85
The Pair had but one inmate in their house,
An only Child, who had been born to them
When Michael, telling o'er his years, began
To deem that he was old,—in shepherd's phrase,
With one foot in the grave. This only Son, 90
With two brave sheep-dogs tried in many a storm,
The one of an inestimable worth,
Made all their household. I may truly say,
That they were as a proverb in the vale
For endless industry. When day was gone, 95
And from their occupations out of doors
The Son and Father were come home, even then,
Their labor did not cease; unless when all
Turned to the cleanly supper-board, and there,
Each with a mess of pottage and skimmed milk, 100
Sat round the basket piled with oaten cakes,
And their plain home-made cheese. Yet when the meal
Was ended, Luke (for so the Son was named)
And his old father both betook themselves 105
To such convenient work as might employ
Their hands by the fire-side; perhaps to card
Wool for the Housewife's spindle, or repair
Some injury done to sickle, flail, or scythe,
Or other implement of house or field. 110

Down from the ceiling by the chimney's edge
That in our ancient uncouth country style
With huge and black projection overbrowed
Large space beneath, as duly as the light
Of day grew dim the Housewife hung a lamp;   115
An aged utensil, which had performed
Service beyond all others of its kind.
Early at evening did it burn and late,
Surviving comrade of uncounted hours,
Which going by from year to year had found   120
And left the couple neither gay perhaps
Nor cheerful, yet with objects and with hopes,
Living a life of eager industry.
And now, when Luke had reached his eighteenth year
There by the light of this old lamp they sat,   125
Father and Son, while far into the night
The Housewife plied her own peculiar work,
Making the cottage through the silent hours
Murmur as with the sound of summer flies.
This light was famous in its neighborhood,   130
And was a public symbol of the life
That thrifty Pair had lived. For, as it chanced,
Their cottage on a plot of rising ground
Stood single, with large prospect, north and south,
High into Easedale, up to Dunmail-Raise   135
And westward to the village near the lake;
And from this constant light, so regular
And so far seen, the House itself, by all
Who dwelt within the limits of the vale,
Both old and young, was named The Evening Star.   140

Thus living on through such a length of years,
The shepherd, if he loved himself, must needs
Have loved his Helpmate; but to Michael's heart
This son of his old age was yet more dear—
Less from instinctive tenderness, the same   145
Fond spirit that blindly works in the blood of all—
Than that a child, more than all other gifts,
That earth can offer to declining man
Brings hope with it, and forward looking thoughts,
And stirrings of inquietude, when they   150
By tendency of nature needs must fail.

Exceeding was the love he bare to him,
His heart and his heart's joy! For oftentimes
Old Michael, while he was a babe in arms,
Had done him female service, not alone   155
For pastime and delight, as is the use
Of fathers, but with patient mind enforced
To acts of tenderness; and he had rocked
His cradle as with a woman's gentle hand.

    And, in a later time, ere yet the Boy   160
Had put on boy's attire, did Michael love,
Albeit of a stern unbending mind,
To have the Young one in his sight, when he
Wrought in the field, or on his shepherd's stool
Sat with a fettered sheep before him stretched,   165
Under the large old oak, that near his door,
Stood single, and, from matchless depth of shade,
Chosen for the Shearer's covert from the sun,
Thence in our rustic dialect was called
The Clipping Tree, a name which yet it bears.   170
There, while they two were sitting in the shade,
With others round them, earnest all and blithe,
Would Michael exercise his heart with looks
Of fond correction and reproof bestowed
Upon the Child, if he disturbed the sheep   175
By catching at their legs, or with his shouts
Scared them, while they lay still beneath the shears.

    And when by Heaven's good grace the boy grew up
A healthy Lad, and carried in his cheek
Two steady roses that were five years old.   180
Then Michael from a winter coppice cut
With his own hand a sapling, which he hooped
With iron, making it throughout in all
Due requisites a perfect shepherd's staff,
And gave it to the Boy; wherewith equipt   185
He as a watchman oftentimes was placed
At gate or gap, to stem or turn the flock;
And, to his office prematurely called,
There stood the urchin, as you will divine,
Something between a hindrance and a help;   190
And for this course not always, I believe,

Receiving from his Father hire of praise;
Though nought was left undone which staff or voice,
Or looks, or threatening gestures could perform.

But soon as Luke, full ten years old, could stand   195
Against the mountain blasts; and to the heights,
Not fearing toil, nor length of weary ways,
He with his Father daily went, and they
Were as companions, why should I relate
That objects which the Shepherd loved before   200
Were dearer now? that from the Boy there came
Feelings and emanations—things which were
Light to the sun and music to the wind;
And that the old Man's heart seemed born again.
Thus in his Father's sight the Boy grew up;   205
And now when he had reached his eighteenth year,
He was his comfort and his daily hope.

While in this sort the simple household lived
From day to day, to Michael's ear there came
Distressful tidings. Long before the time   210
Of which I speak, the Shepherd had been bound
In surety for his brother's son, a man
Of an industrious life, and ample means—
But unforeseen misfortunes suddenly
Had pressed upon him,—and old Michael now   215
Was summoned to discharge the forfeiture,
A grievous penalty, but little less
Than half his substance. This unlooked for claim
At the first hearing, for a moment took
More hope out of his life than he supposed   220
That any old man ever could have lost.
As soon as he had armed himself with strength
To look his trouble in the face, it seemed
The Shepherd's sole resource to sell at once
A portion of his patrimonial fields.   225
Such was his first resolve; he thought again,
And his heart failed him. 'Isabel,' said he,
Two evenings after he had heard the news,
'I have been toiling more than seventy years,
And in the open sunshine of God's love   230
Have we all lived; yet if these fields of ours

Should pass into a stranger's hand, I think
That I could not lie quiet in my grave.
Our lot is a hard lot; the sun himself
Has scarcely been more diligent than I;   235
And I have lived to be a fool at last
To my own family. An evil man
That was, and made an evil choice, if he
Were false to us; and if he were not false,
There are ten thousand to whom loss like this   240
Had been no sorrow. I forgive him—but
'T were better to be dumb, than to talk thus.
When I began, my purpose was to speak
Of remedies and of a cheerful hope.
Our Luke shall leave us, Isabel; the land   245
Shall not go from us, and it shall be free;
He shall possess it free as is the wind
That passes over it. We have, thou knowest,
Another kinsman—he will be our friend
In this distress. He is a prosperous man,   250
Thriving in trade—and Luke to him shall go,
And with his kinsman's help and his own thrift
He quickly will repair this loss, and then
He may return to us. If here he stay,
What can be done? Where every one is poor,   255
What can be gained?' At this the old Man paused,
And Isabel sat silent, for her mind
Was busy, looking back into past times.
There's Richard Bateman, thought she to herself,
He was a parish-boy—at the church-door   260
They made a gathering for him, shillings, pence,
And halfpennies, wherewith the neighbors bought
A basket, which they filled with pedlar's wares;
And with this basket on his arm, the lad
Went up to London, found a master there,   265
Who out of many chose the trusty boy
To go and overlook his merchandise
Beyond the seas: where he grew wondrous rich,
And left estates and monies to the poor,
And at his birthplace built a chapel floored   270
With marble, which he sent from foreign lands.
These thoughts, and many others of like sort,
Passed quickly through the mind of Isabel

And her face brightened. The old Man was glad,
And thus resumed:—'Well, Isabel! this scheme   275
These two days has been meat and drink to me.
Far more than we have lost is left us yet.
We have enough—I wish indeed that I
Were younger,—but this hope is a good hope.
Make ready Luke's best garments, of the best   280
Buy for him more, and let us send him forth
Tomorrow, or the next day, or tonight:
If he *could* go, the Boy should go tonight.'

Here Michael ceased, and to the fields went forth
With a light heart. The Housewife for five days   285
Was restless morn and night, and all day long
Wrought on with her best fingers to prepare
Things needful for the journey of her son.
But Isabel was glad when Sunday came
To stop her in her work: for, when she lay   290
By Michael's side, she through the last two nights
Heard him, how he was troubled in his sleep:
And when they rose at morning she could see
That all his hopes were gone. That day at noon
She said to Luke, while they two by themselves   295
Were sitting at the door. 'Thou must not go:
We have no other Child but thee to lose,
None to remember—do not go away,
For if thou leave thy Father he will die.'
The Youth made answer with a jocund voice;   300
And Isabel, when she had told her fears,
Recovered heart. That evening her best fare
Did she bring forth, and all together sat
Like happy people round a Christmas fire.

With daylight Isabel resumed her work;   305
And all the ensuing week the house appeared
As cheerful as a grove in Spring: at length
The expected letter from their kinsman came,
With kind assurances that he would do
His utmost for the welfare of the Boy;   310
To which, requests were added, that forthwith
He might be sent to him. Ten times or more
The letter was read over; Isabel

Went forth to show it to the neighbors round;
Nor was there at that time on English land   315
A prouder heart than Luke's. When Isabel
Had to her house returned, the old Man said,
'He shall depart tomorrow.' To this word
The Housewife answered, talking much of things
Which, if at such short notice he should go,   320
Would surely be forgotten. But at length
She gave consent, and Michael was at ease.

   Near the tumultuous brook of Green-head Ghyll,
In that deep valley, Michael had designed
To build a Sheep-fold; and, before he heard   325
The tidings of his melancholy loss,
For this same purpose he had gathered up
A heap of stones, which by the streamlet's edge
Lay thrown together, ready for the work.
With Luke that evening thitherward he walked;   330
And soon as they had reached the place he stopped,
And thus the old Man spake to him.—'My son,
Tomorrow thou wilt leave me: with full heart
I look upon thee, for thou art the same
That wert a promise to me ere thy birth,   335
And all thy life hast been my daily joy.
I will relate to thee some little part
Of our two histories; 't will do thee good
When thou art from me, even if I should touch
On things thou canst not know of.—After thou   340
First cam'st into the world—as oft befalls
To new-born infants—thou didst sleep away
Two days, and blessings from thy Father's tongue
Then fell upon thee. Day by day passed on,
And still I loved thee with increasing love.   345
Never to living ear came sweeter sounds
Than when I heard thee by our own fireside
First uttering, without words, a natural tune;
While thou, a feeding babe, didst in thy joy
Sing at thy Mother's breast. Month followed month, 350
And in the open fields my life was passed
And on the mountains, else I think that thou
Hadst been brought up upon thy Father's knees.
But we were playmates, Luke: among these hills,

As well thou know'st, in us the old and young   355
Have played together, nor with me didst thou
Lack any pleasure which a boy can know.'
Luke had a manly heart; but at these words
He sobbed aloud. The old Man grasped his hand
And said, 'Nay, do not take it so—I see   360
That these are things of which I need not speak.
Even to the utmost I have been to thee
A kind and a good Father: and herein
I but repay a gift which I myself
Received at others' hands; for, though now old   365
Beyond the common life of man, I still
Remember them who loved me in my youth.
Both of them sleep together: here they lived
As all their forefathers had done; and when
At length their time was come, they were not loath   370
To give their bodies to the family mold.
I wished that thou shouldst live the life they lived.
But 't is a long time to look back, my Son,
And see so little gain from threescore years.
These fields were burdened when they came to me;   375
Till I was forty years of age, not more
Than half of my inheritance was mine.
I toiled and toiled; God blessed me in my work,
And till these three weeks past the land was free.
It looks as if it never could endure   380
Another Master. Heaven forgive me, Luke,
If I judge ill for thee, but it seems good
That thou shouldst go.' At this the old Man paused;
Then, pointing to the stones near which they stood,
Thus, after a short silence, he resumed: 385
'This was a work for us; and now, my son,
It is a work for me. But, lay one stone—
Here, lay it for me, Luke, with thine own hands.
Nay, Boy, be of good hope;—we both may live
To see a better day. At eighty-four   390
I still am strong and hale;—do thou thy part,
I will do mine.—I will begin again
With many tasks that were resigned to thee;
Up to the heights, and in among the storms,
Will I without thee go again, and do   395
All works which I was wont to do alone,

Before I knew thy face.—Heaven bless thee, Boy!
Thy heart these two weeks has been beating fast
With many hopes; it should be so—yes—yes—
I knew that thou couldst never have a wish   400
To leave me, Luke: thou hast been bound to me
Only by links of love: when thou art gone,
What will be left to us!—But, I forget
My purposes. Lay now the corner-stone,
As I requested; and hereafter, Luke,   405
When thou art gone away, should evil men
Be thy companions, think of me, my Son,
And of this moment; hither turn thy thoughts,
And God will strengthen thee: amid all fear
And all temptation, Luke, I pray that thou   410
Mayst bear in mind the life thy Fathers lived,
Who, being innocent, did for that cause
Bestir them in good deeds. Now, fare thee well—
When thou return'st, thou in this place wilt see
A work which is not here: a covenant   415
'T will be between us—But, whatever fate
Befall thee, I shall love thee to the last,
And bear thy memory with me to the grave.'

    The Shepherd ended here; and Luke stooped down,
And, as his Father had requested, laid   420
The first stone of the Sheep-fold. At the sight
The old Man's grief broke from him; to his heart
He pressed his Son, he kissèd him and wept;
And to the house together they returned.
Hushed was that House in peace, or seeming peace, 425
Ere the night fell;—with morrow's dawn the Boy
Began his journey, and when he had reached
The public way, he put on a bold face;
And all the neighbors as he passed their doors
Came forth with wishes and with farewell prayers, 430
That followed him till he was out of sight.

    A good report did from their Kinsman come,
Of Luke and his well doing: and the Boy
Wrote loving letters, full of wondrous news,
Which, as the Housewife phrased it, were throughout 435
'The prettiest letters that were ever seen.'

Both parents read them with rejoicing hearts.
So, many months passed on: and once again
The Shepherd went about his daily work
With confident and cheerful thoughts; and now   440
Sometimes when he could find a leisure hour
He to that valley took his way, and there
Wrought at the sheep-fold. Meantime Luke began
To slacken in his duty; and at length
He in the dissolute city gave himself   445
To evil courses: ignominy and shame
Fell on him, so that he was driven at last
To seek a hiding-place beyond the seas.

        There is a comfort in the strength of love;
'T will make a thing endurable, which else   450
Would overset the brain, or break the heart:
I have conversed with more than one who well
Remember the old Man, and what he was
Years after he had heard this heavy news.
His bodily frame had been from youth to age   455
Of an unusual strength. Among the rocks
He went, and still looked up to sun and cloud
And listened to the wind; and as before
Performed all kinds of labor for his sheep,
And for the land, his small inheritance.   460
And to that hollow dell from time to time
Did he repair, to build the fold of which
His flock had need. 'T is not forgotten yet
The pity which was then in every heart
For the old Man—and 't is believed by all   465
That many and many a day he thither went,
And never lifted up a single stone.

        There, by the Sheep-fold, sometimes was he seen
Sitting alone, or with his faithful Dog,
Then old, beside him, lying at his feet.   470
The length of full seven years from time to time
He at the building of this Sheep-fold wrought,
And left the work unfinished when he died.
Three years, or little more, did Isabel
Survive her Husband: at her death the estate   475
Was sold, and went into a stranger's hand.

The cottage which was named the Evening Star
Is gone—the ploughshare has been through the ground
On which it stood; great changes have been wrought
In all the neighborhood:—yet the oak is left   480
That grew beside their door; and the remains
Of the unfinished Sheep-fold may be seen
Beside the boisterous brook of Green-head Ghyll.

This poem after the first forty lines, which serve as a sort
of introduction to the story proper, is a direct and simple narrative. The poet is apparently not aiming at an effect of condensation or at a swift dramatic effect such as is aimed at, for
example, in the ballads which have been analyzed. The effect
is rather cumulative as the details of the story, piled up in
chronological order, make their weight felt on the reader; the
method is here effective, for the story deals with the whole life
of a man and not with a single sharp, climactic incident.

Since the poem is so straightforward in its organization, the
numerous details are really necessary for an appreciation of the
story because the effect of the poem does not depend on the
sharp imaginative flashes such as we have found in the preceding
poems. It is no accident, then, that the poem is as long as it
is. In fact, the method of this poem lies very close to that of
prose fiction in its lack of condensation, just as that of the
ballads we have read lies rather close to the method of drama.

But the reader may still be disposed to ask, "Have we
not too many details? Are not some of the details really irrelevant?" For instance, he may ask, of what use in the poem is
the statement that Michael's wife had a big wheel for spinning
wool and a small one for spinning flax, and that the large oak
by the cottage door was called the "Clipping Tree"? By way
of reply, we could scarcely maintain that any specific detail is
absolutely essential to the effect of the poem; but we can maintain that the effect of the total mass of detail is highly important
if we are to understand the sort of life which Michael leads and
is attached to. In the first place, the number of intimate details
gives a sense of close observation and makes the reader feel that
the scene and the incident that occurs in it are real. But in
addition to giving an impression of *realism* (*Glossary*) this use

of detail serves a second, and perhaps more important, purpose. Since the tragedy turns on the fact of Michael's attachment to the land and the way of life on it, it is necessary that the reader have some sense of the reason for his mastering desire to hold the land and pass it on to his son. The reader is led into an easy and familiar acquaintance with those objects that represent the kind of life on the land in much the same way as Michael himself would know them. The elaboration of details, then, serves to suggest the fundamental relationship on which the poem depends.

The poet, if he is to be successful in this poem, must make the reader feel as forcefully as possible the pathos of Michael's situation. But he cannot make the reader feel this merely by telling him that the situation is pathetic. As a matter of fact, mature people have a thoroughly justifiable suspicion of people who are prompt to weep over situations of pathos. Mature people do not like to be bullied into feeling something; they want, instead, to see the justification for the reaction. The poet, unless he is writing for an audience of *sentimentalists, (Glossary)*—that is, people who enjoy any excuse for indulging their feelings—must really justify the reaction he wishes to provoke. How does Wordsworth do this? First, we can see what he does not do. He does not give sentimental comments himself. He merely presents the situation in an objective way. In the second place, he does not even have the characters themselves give way to violent grief. As a matter of fact, for Michael, who is presented as a sober and restrained person, to give violent expression to his disappointment and sorrow would seem to us false and out of character. How then is the poet to give us the impression of the depth of the grief when the character himself does not give way to it? Here the importance of the background which he has established—what Michael's life is, his attachment to the land, etc.—becomes clear. Because we have been given a vivid sense of this background through the use of detail early in the poem, the poet here can merely point out objectively the facts of the situation, and depend upon the imagination of his readers to do the rest. He does not insist on the pathos, but lets the reader discover it for himself. The old man does not die of heartbreak when the news of his son's running away comes to him. People do not often die of heart-break; the poet does not test our credulity by making us believe that this one does; and moreover, the old man resting by the unfinished sheep-fold is a more moving figure than is a person on a literal death-bed.

One further point should be mentioned in describing how the poem gets its effect. The poet has managed to find a concrete situation which stands for and concentrates the whole tragedy: it is, of course, the scene at the sheepfold, where Michael has his son lay the cornerstone so that the work may stand for the love and interest which unites them, and stand for the continuity of life which the old man is trying to preserve. The disappointment is made much more poignant by picturing the old man later at the fold, sometimes never lifting "up a single stone," than by the poet's own comment on the old man's sadness and disappointment.

One more word should be said about the general method which Wordsworth is using here. It has been pointed out that he does not concentrate his work by sudden flashes of the imagination but works by accumulation of details. Since this is so, he does not try for a strong dramatic conclusion at the end of this poem, such as we have, for example, in "The Wife of Usher's Well". Instead, he levels the poem off at the end by a description of the present appearance of Michael's farm, the cottage gone, but the oak remaining, and the ruins of the unfinished sheep-fold still to be seen. It is an ending which accords with the general effect which the poet has been working for from the first—an effect of slow-moving forcefulness.

THE DEATH OF THE HIRED MAN

ROBERT FROST (1875–   )

Mary sat musing on the lamp-flame at the table
Waiting for Warren. When she heard his step,
She ran on tip-toe down the darkened passage
To meet him in the doorway with the news

And put him on his guard. "Silas is back."   5
She pushed him outward with her through the door
And shut it after her. "Be kind," she said.
She took the market things from Warren's arms
And set them on the porch, then drew him down
To sit beside her on the wooden steps.   10

"When was I ever anything but kind to him?
But I'll not have the fellow back," he said.
"I told him so last haying, didn't I?
'If he left then,' I said, 'that ended it.'
What good is he? Who else will harbor him   15
At his age for the little he can do?
What help he is there's no depending on.
Off he goes always when I need him most.
'He thinks he ought to earn a little pay,
Enough at least to buy tobacco with,   20
So he won't have to beg and be beholden.'
'All right,' I say, 'I can't afford to pay
Any fixed wages, though I wish I could.'
'Some one else can.' 'Then some one else will have to.'
I shouldn't mind his bettering himself   25
If that was what it was. You can be certain,
When he begins like that, there's some one at him
Trying to coax him off with pocket-money,—
In haying time, when any help is scarce.
In winter he comes back to us. I'm done."   30

"Sh! not so loud: he'll hear you," Mary said.

"I want him to: he'll have to soon or late."

"He's worn out. He's asleep beside the stove.
When I came up from Rowe's I found him here,
Huddled against the barn-door fast asleep,
A miserable sight, and frightening, too—   35
You needn't smile—I didn't recognize him—
I wasn't looking for him—and he's changed.
Wait till you see."

                    "Where did you say he'd been?"

"He didn't say. I dragged him to the house,   40
And gave him tea and tried to make him smoke.
I tried to make him talk about his travels.
Nothing would do: he just kept nodding off."

"What did he say? Did he say anything?"

"But little."

                    "Anything?   Mary, confess   45
He said he'd come to ditch the meadow for me."

"Warren!"

                    "But did he? I just want to know."
"Of course he did. What would you have him say?
Surely you wouldn't grudge the poor old man
Some humble way to save his self-respect.   50
He added, if you really care to know,
He meant to clear the upper pasture, too.
That sounds like something you have heard before?
Warren, I wish you could have heard the way
He jumbled everything. I stopped to look   55
Two or three times—he made me feel so queer—
To see if he was talking in his sleep.
He ran on Harold Wilson—you remember—
The boy you had in haying four years since.
He's finished school, and teaching in his college.   60
Silas declares you'll have to get him back.
He says they two will make a team for work:
Between them they will lay this farm as smooth!
The way he mixed that in with other things.
He thinks young Wilson a likely lad, though daft   65
On education—you know how they fought
All through July under the blazing sun,
Silas up on the cart to build the load,
Harold along beside to pitch it on."

"Yes, I took care to keep well out of earshot."   70

"Well, those days trouble Silas like a dream.
You wouldn't think they would. How some things linger!

Harold's young college boy's assurance piqued him.
After so many years he still keeps finding
Good arguments he sees he might have used.   75
I sympathize. I know just how it feels
To think of the right thing to say too late.
Harold's associated in his mind with Latin.
He asked me what I thought of Harold's saying
He studied Latin like the violin   80
Because he liked it—that an argument!
He said he couldn't make the boy believe
He could find water with a hazel prong—
Which showed how much good school had ever done him.
He wanted to go over that. But most of all   85
He thinks if he could have another chance
To teach him how to build a load of hay—"

"I know, that's Silas' one accomplishment.
He bundles every forkful in its place,
And tags and numbers it for future reference,   90
So he can find and easily dislodge it
In the unloading. Silas does that well.
He takes it out in bunches like big birds' nests.
You never see him standing on the hay
He's trying to lift, straining to lift himself."   95

"He thinks if he could teach him that, he'd be
Some good perhaps to some one in the world.
He hates to see a boy the fool of books.
Poor Silas, so concerned for other folk,
And nothing to look backward to with pride,   100
And nothing to look forward to with hope,
So now and never any different."

Part of a moon was falling down the west,
Dragging the whole sky with it to the hills.
Its light poured softly in her lap. She saw   105
And spread her apron to it. She put out her hand
Among the harp-like morning-glory strings,
Taut with the dew from garden bed to eaves,
As if she played unheard the tenderness
That wrought on him beside her in the night.   110
"Warren," she said, "he has come home to die:
You needn't be afraid he'll leave you this time."

"Home," he mocked gently.

          "Yes, what else but home?
It all depends on what you mean by home.
Of course he's nothing to us, any more   115
Than was the hound that came a stranger to us
Out of the woods, worn out upon the trail."

"Home is the place where, when you have to go there,
They have to take you in."

         "I should have called it
Something you somehow haven't to deserve."   120

Warren leaned out and took a step or two,
Picked up a little stick, and brought it back
And broke it in his hand and tossed it by.
"Silas has better claim on us you think
Than on his brother? Thirteen little miles   125
As the road winds would bring him to his door.
Silas has walked that far no doubt today.
Why didn't he go there? His brother's rich,
A somebody—director in the bank."

"He never told us that."

        "We know it though."   130

"I think his brother ought to help, of course.
I'll see to that if there is need. He ought of right
To take him in, and might be willing to—
He may be better than appearances.
But have some pity on Silas. Do you think   135
If he'd had any pride in claiming kin
Or anything he looked for from his brother,
He'd keep so still about him all this time?"

"I wonder what's between them."

        "I can tell you.
Silas is what he is—we wouldn't mind him—   140
But just the kind that kinsfolk can't abide.

He never did a thing so very bad.
He don't know why he isn't quite as good
As any one. He won't be made ashamed
To please his brother, worthless though he is."   145

"I can't think Si ever hurt any one."

"No, but he hurt my heart the way he lay
And rolled his old head on that sharp-edged chair-back.
He wouldn't let me put him on the lounge.
You must go in and see what you can do.   150
I made the bed up for him there tonight.
You'll be surprised at him—how much he's broken.
His working days are done; I'm sure of it."

"I'd not be in a hurry to say that."

"I haven't been. Go, look, see for yourself.   155
But, Warren, please remember how it is:
He's come to help you ditch the meadow.
He has a plan. You mustn't laugh at him.
He may not speak of it, and then he may.
I'll sit and see if that small sailing cloud   160
Will hit or miss the moon."

                                        It hit the moon.
Then there were three there, making a dim row,
The moon, the little silver cloud, and she.
Warren returned—too soon, it seemed to her,
Slipped to her side, caught up her hand and waited.   165

"Warren," she questioned.

                              "Dead," was all he answered.

EXERCISE:

Write an analysis of this poem involving the following points:
1. Definition of the characters of the speakers.
2. The use made of realistic detail and the effect of ordinary conversation which the poet uses.
3. The way in which the poet presents the pathos.

THE REVENGE

A Ballad of the Fleet

ALFRED, LORD TENNYSON (1809–1892)

I

At Flores in the Azores Sir Richard Grenville lay,
And a pinnace, like a fluttered bird, came flying from far away;
"Spanish ships of war at sea! we have sighted fifty-three!"
Then sware Lord Thomas Howard: "'Fore God I am no coward;
But I cannot meet them here, for my ships are out of gear,   5
And the half my men are sick. I must fly but follow quick.
We are six ships of the line; can we fight with fifty-three?"

II

Then spake Sir Richard Grenville: "I know you are no coward;
You fly them for a moment to fight with them again.
But I've ninety men and more that are lying sick ashore.   10
I should count myself the coward if I left them, my Lord Howard,
To these Inquisition dogs and the devildoms of Spain."

III

So Lord Howard passed away with five ships of war that day,
Till he melted like a cloud in the silent summer heaven;
But Sir Richard bore in hand all his sick men from the land   15
Very carefully and slow,
Men of Bideford in Devon,
And we laid them on the ballast down below:
For we brought them all aboard,
And they blest him in their pain, that they were not left to Spain,   20
To the thumb-screw and the stake, for the glory of the Lord.

IV

He had only a hundred seamen to work the ship and to fight
And he sailed away from Flores till the Spaniard came in sight,
With his huge sea-castles heaving upon the weather bow.
"Shall we fight or shall we fly?

Good Sir Richard, tell us now,
For to fight is but to die!
There'll be little of us left by the time this sun be set."
And Sir Richard said again: "We be all good English men.
Let us bang these dogs of Seville, the children of the devil,   30
For I never turned my back upon Don or devil yet."

V

Sir Richard spoke and he laughed, and we roared a hurrah,
    and so
The little Revenge ran on sheer into the heart of the foe,
With her hundred fighters on deck, and her ninety sick below;
For half of their fleet to the right and half to the left were
    seen,   35
And the little Revenge ran on through the long sea-lane between.

VI

Thousands of their soldiers looked down from their decks and
    laughed,
Thousands of their seamen made mock at the mad little craft
Running on and on, till delayed
By their mountain-like San Philip that, of fifteen hundred
    tons,   40
And up-shadowing high above us with her yawning tiers of guns,
Took the breath from our sails, and we stayed.

VII

And while now the great San Philip hung above us like a cloud
Whence the thunderbolt will fall
Long and loud.   45
Four galleons drew away
From the Spanish fleet that day,
And two upon the larboard and two upon the starboard lay,
And the battle-thunder broke from them all.

VIII

But anon the great San Philip, she bethought herself and
    went,   50
Having that within her womb that had left her ill content;
And the rest they came aboard us, and they fought us hand
    to hand,

For a dozen times they came with their pikes and musqueteers,
And a dozen times we shook 'em off as a dog that shakes his ears
When he leaps from the water to the land.   55

IX

And the sun went down, and the stars came out far over the
    summer sea,
But never a moment ceased the fight of the one and the fifty-
    three.
Ship after ship, the whole night long, their high-built galleons
    came,
Ship after ship, the whole night long, with her battle-thunder
    and flame;
Ship after ship, the whole night long, drew back with her dead
    and her shame.   60
For some were sunk and many were shattered, and so could
    fight us no more—
God of battles, was ever a battle like this in the world before?

X

For he said, "Fight on! fight on!"
Though his vessel was all but a wreck;
And it chanced that, when half of the short summer night was
    gone,   65
With a grisly wound to be drest he had left the deck,
But a bullet struck him that was dressing it suddenly dead,
And himself he was wounded again in the side and the head,
And he said, "Fight on! fight on!"

XI

And the night went down, and the sun smiled out far over
    the summer sea,   70
And the Spanish fleet with broken sides lay round us all in a
    ring;
But they dared not touch us again, for they feared that we still
    could sting,
So they watched what the end would be.
And we had not fought them in vain,
But in perilous plight were we,   75
Seeing forty of our poor hundred were slain,
And half of the rest of us maimed for life

In the crash of the cannonades and the desperate strife;
And the sick men down in the hold were most of them stark
   and cold,
And the pikes were all broken or bent, and the powder was all
   of it spent;   80
And the masts and the rigging were lying over the side;
But Sir Richard cried in his English pride:
"We have fought such a fight for a day and a night
As may never be fought again!
We have won great glory, my men!   85
And a day less or more
At sea or ashore,
We die—does it matter when?
Sink me the ship, Master Gunner—sink her, split her in twain!
Fall into the hands of God, not into the hands of Spain!"   90

XII

And the gunner said, "Ay, ay," but the seamen made reply:
"We have children, we have wives,
And the Lord hath spared our lives.
We will make the Spaniard promise, if we yield, to let us go;
We shall live to fight again and to strike another blow."   95
And the lion there lay dying, and they yielded to the foe.

XIII

And the stately Spanish men to their flagship bore him then,
Where they laid him by the mast, old Sir Richard caught at last,
And they praised him to his face with their courtly foreign grace;
But he rose upon their decks, and he cried: 100
"I have fought for Queen and Faith like a valiant man and
   true;
I have only done my duty as a man is bound to do.
With a joyful spirit I Sir Richard Grenville die!"
And he fell upon their decks, and he died.

XIV

And they stared at the dead that had been so valiant and
   true,   105
And had holden the power and glory of Spain so cheap
That he dared her with one little ship and his English few;

Was he devil or man? He was devil for aught they knew,
But they sank his body with honor down into the deep,
And they manned the Revenge with a swarthier alien crew,   110
And away she sailed with her loss and longed for her own;
When a wind from the lands they had ruined awoke from sleep,
And the water began to heave and the weather to moan,
And or ever that evening ended a great gale blew,
And a wave like the wave that is raised by an earthquake
grew,   115
Till it smote on their hulls and their sails and their masts and
their flags,
And the whole sea plunged and fell on the shot-shattered navy
of Spain,
And the little Revenge herself went down by the island crags
To be lost evermore in the main.

EXERCISE:

This poem is based on the following account by Sir Walter
Ralegh of an actual battle. Compare carefully the poem with
the prose account, trying to understand the reasons for the poet's
selection of detail and management of the action. What is the
difference in effect between the two treatments?

THE LAST FIGHT OF THE REVENGE

The Lord Thomas Howard, with six of her Majesty's ships,
six victualers of London, the bark *Raleigh,* and two or three
pinnaces, riding at anchor near unto Flores, one of the westerly
islands of the Azores, the last of August in the afternoon, had
intelligence by one Captain Middleton of the approach of the
Spanish Armada. Which Middleton being in a very good sailer
had kept them company three days before, of good purpose, both
to discover their forces the more, as also to give advice to my
Lord Thomas of their approach. He had no sooner delivered
the news but the fleet was in sight.

Many of our ships' companies were on the shore in the island,
some providing ballast for their ships, others filling of water

and refreshing themselves from the land with such things as they could either for money or by force recover. By reason whereof our ships being all pestered and roomaging every thing out of order, very light for want of ballast, and that which was most to our disadvantage, the one-half part of the men of every ship sick and utterly unserviceable. For in the *Revenge* there were ninety diseased; in the *Bonaventure* not so many in health as could handle her mainsail. For had not twenty men been taken out of a bark of Sir George Cary's, his being commanded to be sunk, and those appointed to her, she had hardly ever recovered England. The rest for the most part were in little better state. The names of her Majesty's ships were these as followeth: the *Defiance,* which was admiral, the *Revenge,* vice-admiral, the *Bonaventure* commanded by Captain Cross, the *Lion* by George Fenner, the *Foresight* by Mr. Thomas Vavasour, and the *Crane* by Duffild. The *Foresight* and the *Crane* being but small ships; only the others were of the middle size; the rest, besides the bark *Raleigh* commanded by Captain Thin, were victualers and of small force or none.

The Spanish fleet having shrouded their approach by reason of the island, were now so soon at hand as our ships had scarce time to weigh their anchors, but some of them were driven to let slip their cables and set sail. Sir Richard Grenville was the last weighed, to recover the men that were upon the island, which otherwise had been lost. The Lord Thomas with the rest very hardly recovered the wind, which Sir Richard Grenville not being able to do was persuaded by the master and others to cut his mainsail and cast about, and to trust to the sailing of his ship; for the squadron of Sivil were on his weather bow. But Sir Richard utterly refused to turn from the enemy, alleging that he would rather choose to die than to dishonor himself, his country, and her Majesty's ship, persuading his company that he would pass through the two squadrons in despite of them, and enforce those of Sivil to give him way. Which he performed upon divers of the foremost, who, as the mariners term it, sprang their luff, and fell under the lee of the *Revenge*. But the other course had been the better, and might right well have been answered in so great an impossibility of prevailing. Notwithstanding, out of the greatness of his mind he could not be persuaded.

In the meanwhile as he attended those which were nearest him, the great *San Philip* being in the wind of him and coming towards him becalmed his sails in such sort as the ship could neither make way nor feel the helm, so huge and high cargoed was the Spanish ship, being of a thousand and five hundred tons. Who after laid the *Revenge* aboard. When he was thus bereft of his sails, the ships that were under his lee, luffing up, also laid him aboard; of which the next was the admiral of the Biscaines, a very mighty and puissant ship commanded by Brittandona. The said *Philip* carried three tier of ordnance on a side, and eleven pieces in every tier. She shot eight forthright out of her chase, besides those of her stern ports.

After the *Revenge* was entangled with this *Philip,* four other boarded her; two on her larboard and two on her starboard. The fight thus beginning at three of the clock in the afternoon continued very terrible all that evening. But the great *San Philip* having received the lower tier of the *Revenge,* discharged with crossbar-shot, shifted herself with all diligence from her sides, utterly misliking her first entertainment. Some say that the ship foundered, but we cannot report it for truth unless we were assured.

The Spanish ships were filled with companies of soldiers, in some two hundred besides the mariners, in some five, in others eight hundred. In ours there were none at all, beside the mariners, but the servants of the commanders and some few voluntary gentlemen only. After many interchanged volleys of great ordnance and small shot, the Spaniards deliberated to enter the *Revenge,* and made divers attempts, hoping to force her by the multitudes of their armed soldiers and musketeers, but were still repulsed again and again, and at all times beaten back into their own ships or into the seas.

In the beginning of the fight the *George Noble* of London, having received some shot through her by the armadas, fell under the lee of the *Revenge* and asked Sir Richard what he would command him, being but one of the victualers and of small force. Sir Richard bid him save himself and leave him to his fortune.

After the fight had thus without intermission continued while the day lasted and some hours of the night, many of our men were slain and hurt, and one of the great galleons of the Armada, and the admiral of the hulks both sunk, and in many of the Spanish ships great slaughter was made. Some write that Sir Richard was very dangerously hurt almost in the beginning of the fight and lay speechless for a time ere he recovered. But two of the *Revenge's* own company, brought home in a ship of lime from the islands, examined by some of the lords and others, affirmed that he was never so wounded as that he forsook the upper deck, till an hour before midnight; and then being shot into the body with a musket, as he was a-dressing was again shot into the head, and withal his chirurgeon wounded to death. . . .

But to return to the fight, the Spanish ships which attempted to board the *Revenge,* as they were wounded and beaten off, so always others came in their places, she having never less than two mighty galleons by her sides and aboard her. So that ere the morning, from three of the clock the day before, there had fifteen several armadas assailed her; and all so ill approved their entertainment as they were by the break of day far more willing to hearken to a composition than hastily to make any more assults or entries. But as the day increased, so our men decreased; and as the light grew more and more, by so much more grew our discomforts. For none appeared in sight but enemies, saving one small ship called the *Pilgrim,* commanded by Jacob Whiddon, who hovered all night to see the success, but in the morning bearing with the *Revenge,* was hunted like a hare amongst many ravenous hounds, but escaped.

All the powder of the *Revenge* to the last barrel was now spent, all her pikes broken, forty of her best men slain, and the most part of the rest hurt. In the beginning of the fight she had but one hundred free from sickness, and fourscore and ten sick, laid in hold upon the ballast. A small troop to man such a ship, and a weak garrison to resist so mighty an army. By those hundred all was sustained, the volleys, boardings, and enterings of fifteen ships of war, besides those which beat her at large. On the contrary, the Spanish were always supplied with soldiers brought from every squadron; all manner of arms and powder at will. Unto ours there remained no comfort at all, no hope, no supply either of ships, men, or weapons; the masts all beaten overboard, all her tackle cut asunder, her upper work altogether rased, and in effect evened she was with the water, but the very foundation or bottom of a ship, nothing being left overhead either for flight or defence.

Sir Richard, finding himself in this distress and unable any longer to make resistance, having endured in this fifteen hours' fight the assult of fifteen several armadas all by turns aboard him, and by estimation eight hundred shot of great artillery, besides many assults and entries; and that himself and the ship must needs be possessed by the enemy, who were now all cast in a ring round about him, the *Revenge* not able to move one way or other but as she was moved with the waves and billow of the sea; commanded the master gunner, whom he knew to be a most resolute man, to split and sink the ship; that thereby nothing might remain of glory or victory to the Spaniards, seeing in so many hours' fight and with so great a navy they were not able to take her, having had fifteen hours' time, above ten thousand men, and fifty and three sail of men-of-war to perform it withal; and persuaded the company, or as many as he could induce, to yield themselves unto God and to the mercy of none else, but as they had like valiant resolute men repulsed so many enemies they should not now shorten the honor of their nation by prolonging their own lives for a few hours or a few days.

The master gunner readily condescended, and divers others; but the captain and the master were of another opinion, and besought Sir Richard to have care of them; alleging that the Spaniard would be as ready to entertain a composition as they were willing to offer the same; and that there being divers sufficient and valiant men yet living, and whose wounds were not mortal, they might do their country and prince acceptable service hereafter. And that whereas Sir Richard had alleged that the Spaniards should never glory to have taken one ship of her Majesty, seeing that they had so long and so notably defended themselves, they answered that the ship had six foot water in hold, three shot under water which were so weakly stopped as with the first working of the sea she must needs sink, and was besides so crushed and bruised as she could never be removed out of the place.

And as the matter was thus in dispute, and Sir Richard refusing to hearken to any of those reasons, the master of the *Revenge* (while the captain wan unto him the greater party) was convoyed aboard the general, Don Alfonso Baçan. Who finding none over-hasty to enter the *Revenge* again, doubting lest Sir Richard would have blown them up and himself, and perceiving by the report of the master of the *Revenge* his dangerous disposition, yielded that all their lives should be saved, the company sent for England, and the better sort to pay such reasonable ransom as their estate would bear, and in the mean season to be free from galley or imprisonment. To this he so much the rather condescended as well, as I have said, for fear of further loss and mischief to themselves, as also for the desire he had to recover Sir Richard Grenville; whom for his notable valor he seemed greatly to honor and admire.

When this answer was returned, and that safety of life was promised, the common sort being now at the end of their peril, the most drew back from Sir Richard and the master gunner, being no hard matter to dissuade men from death to life. The master gunner, finding himself and Sir Richard thus prevented and mastered by the great number, would have slain himself with a sword, had he not been by force withheld and locked into his cabin. Then the general sent many boats aboard the *Revenge,* and divers of our men fearing Sir Richard's disposition stole away aboard the general and other ships. Sir Richard, thus overmatched, was sent unto by Alfonso Baçan to remove out of the *Revenge,* the ship being marvelous unsavory, filled with blood and bodies of dead and wounded men like a slaughterhouse. Sir Richard answered that he might do with his body what he list, for he esteemed it not, and as he was carried out of the ship he swounded, and reviving again desired the company to pray for him. The general used Sir Richard with all humanity, and left nothing unattempted that tended to his recovery, highly commending his valor and worthiness, and greatly bewailing the danger wherein he was, being unto them a rare spectacle and a resolution seldom approved, to see one ship turn toward so many enemies, to endure the charge and boarding of so many huge armadas, and to resist and repel the assults and entries of so many soldiers. All which and more is confirmed by a Spanish captain of the same Armada, and a present actor in the fight, who being severed from the rest in a storm was by the *Lion* of London, a small ship, taken, and is now prisoner in London. . . .

The admiral of the hulks and the *Ascension* of Sivil were both sunk by the side of the *Revenge;* one other recovered the road of St. Michael and sunk also there; a fourth ran herself with the shore to save her men. Sir Richard died, as it is said, the second or third day aboard the general, and was by them greatly bewailed. What became of his body, whether it were buried in the sea or on the land, we know not; the comfort that remaineth to his friends is that he hath ended his life honorably in respect of the reputation won to his nation and country, and of the same to his posterity, and that being dead he hath not outlived his own honor. . . .

A few days after the fight was ended and the English prisoners dispersed into the Spanish and Indy ships there arose so great a storm from the west and northwest that all the fleet was dispersed, as well the Indian fleet which were then come unto them as the rest of the Armada that attended their arrival, of which fourteen sail, together with the *Revenge,* and in her two hundred Spaniards, were cast away upon the isle of St. Michael. So it pleased them to honor the burial of that renowned ship the *Revenge,* not suffering her to perish alone, for the great honor she achieved in her life-time. . . . The fourth of this month of November we received letters from the Tercera affirming that there are three thousand bodies of men remaining in that island, saved out of the perished ships; and that by the Spaniards' own confession there are ten thousand cast away in this storm besides those that are perished between the islands and the main.

(From *A Report of the Truth of the Fight about the Isles of Açores this Last Summer betwixt the "Revenge" and an Armada of the King of Spain.*)

TAM O' SHANTER

A TALE

ROBERT BURNS (1759–1796)

Of Brownyis and of Bogillis full is this buke.
—GAWIN DOUGLAS.

When chapman billies [1] leave the street,
And drouthy neibors, neibors meet,
As market-days are wearing late,
And folk begin to tak the gate; [2]
While we sit bousin at the nappy   5
And gettin fou [3] and unco [4] happy,
We think na on the lang Scots miles,
The mosses, [5] waters, slaps, [6] and stiles,
That lie between us and our hame,
Whare sits our sulky, sullen dame,   10
Gathering her brows like gathering storm,
Nursing her wrath to keep it warm.

This truth fand honest Tam o' Shanter,
As he frae Ayr ae night did canter:
(Auld Ayr, wham ne'er a town surpasses,   15
For honest men and bonie lasses.)

O Tam! had'st thou but been sae wise
As taen thy ain wife Kate's advice!
She tauld thee weel thou was a skellum, [7]
A bletherin, [8] blusterin, drunken blellum; [9]   20
That frae November till October,
Ae market-day thou was na sober;
That ilka melder [10] wi' the miller,
Thou sat as lang as thou had siller; [11]
That ev'ry naig was ca'd [12] a shoe on,   25
The smith and thee gat roarin fou on;
That at the Lord's house, ev'n on Sunday,
Thou drank wi' Kirkton Jean till Monday.

[1] pedlar comrades	[2] go home	[3] full
[4] very	[5] bogs	[6] gates
[7] good-for-nothing	[8] idly talking	[9] babbler
[10] every grinding	[11] silver	[12] nailed

She prophesied, that, late or soon,
Thou would be found deep drown'd in Doon;   30
Or catch't wi' warlocks in the mirk,
By Alloway's auld haunted kirk.

Ah, gentle dames! it gars me greet,[13]
To think how mony counsels sweet,
How mony lengthened sage advices,   35
The husband frae the wife despises!

But to our tale:—Ae market night,
Tam had got planted unco right,
Fast by an ingle, bleezin finely,
Wi' reamin swats [14] that drank divinely;   40
And at his elbow, Souter [15] Johnie,
His ancient, trusty, drouthy crony:
Tam lo'ed him like a vera brither; [16]
They had been fou for weeks thegither.
The night drave on wi' sangs and clatter;   45
And ay the ale was growing better:
The landlady and Tam grew gracious
Wi' secret favors, sweet, and precious:
The souter tauld his queerest stories;
The landlord's laugh was ready chorus: 50
The storm without might rair and rustle
Tam did na mind the storm a whistle.

Care, mad to see a man sae happy,
E'en drowned himsel amang the nappy:
As bees flee hame wi' lades o' treasure,   55
The minutes winged their way wi' pleasure;
Kings may be blest, but Tam was glorious,
O'er a' the ills o' life victorious!

But pleasures are like poppies spread,
You seize the flow'r, its bloom is shed;   60
Or like the snow falls in the river,
A moment white—then melts forever;
Or like the borealis race,

[13] makes me weep   [14] foaming new ale   [15] cobbler
[16] brother

That flit ere you can point their place;
Or like the rainbow's lovely form   65
Evanishing amid the storm.
Nae man can tether time or tide:
The hour approaches Tam maun ride,—
That hour, o' night's black arch the keystane,
That dreary hour he mounts his beast in;   70
And sic a night he taks the road in,
As ne'er poor sinner was abroad in.

   The wind blew as 't wad blawn its last;
The rattling show'rs rose on the blast;
The speedy gleams the darkness swallowed;   75
Loud, deep, and lang the thunder bellowed:
That night, a child might understand,
The Deil had business on his hand.

   Weel mounted on his grey mear, Meg,—
A better never lifted leg,—   80
Tam skelpit [17] on thro' dub [18] and mire,
Despising wind and rain and fire;
Whiles holding fast his guid blue bonnet,
Whiles crooning o'er some auld Scots sonnet,
Whiles glowrin round wi' prudent cares,   85
Lest bogles [19] catch him unawares.
Kirk-Alloway was drawing nigh,
Whare ghaists and houlets nightly cry.

   By this time he was cross the ford,
Whare in the snaw the chapman smoored; [20]   90
And past the birks and meikle stane,
Whare drunken Charlie brak's neck-bane;
And thro' the whins,[21] and by the cairn,
Whare hunters fand [22] the murdered bairn;
And near the thorn, aboon the well,   95
Whare Mungo's mither hanged hersel.
Before him Doon pours all his floods;
The doubling storm roars thro' the woods;
The lightnings flash from pole to pole,

---

[17] clattered   [18] puddle   [19] hobgoblins
[20] smothered   [21] furze   [22] found

Near and more near the thunders roll;   100
When, glimmering thro' the groaning trees,
Kirk-Alloway seemed in a bleeze:
Thro' ilka bore the beams were glancing,
And loud resounded mirth and dancing.

Inspiring bold John Barleycorn!   105
What dangers thou can'st make us scorn!
Wi' tippenny[23] we fear nae evil;
Wi' usquebae[24] we'll face the devil!
The swats sae reamed[25] in Tammie's noddle,
Fair play, he cared na deils a boddle.[26]   110
But Maggie stood right sair astonished,
Till, by the heel and hand admonished,
She ventured forward on the light;
And, wow! Tam saw an unco sight!

Warlocks and witches in a dance;   115
Nae cotillon brent-new[27] frae France,
But hornpipes, jigs, strathspeys, and reels
Put life and mettle in their heels:
A winnock bunker[28] in the east,
There sat Auld Nick in shape o' beast;   120
A towzie tyke,[29] black, grim, and large,
To gie them music was his charge;
He screw'd the pipes and gart them skirl,[30]
Till roof and rafters a' did dirl.[31]—
Coffins stood round like open presses,   125
That shaw'd the dead in their last dresses;
And by some devilish cantraip[32] sleight
Each in its cauld hand held a light,
By which heroic Tam was able
To note upon the haly table   130
A murderer's banes in gibbet airns;[33]
Twa span-lang, wee, unchristened bairns;
A thief, new-cutted frae the rape—
Wi' his last gasp his gab[34] did gape;
Five tomahawks, wi' blude red-rusted;   135

[23] twopenny ale   [24] whisky   [25] foamed
[26] farthing   [27] brand-new   [28] window seat
[29] shaggy cur   [30] scream   [31] ring
[32] magic   [33] irons   [34] mouth

Five scymitars, wi' murder crusted;
A garter, which a babe had strangled;
A knife, a father's throat had mangled;
Whom his ain son o' life bereft—
The grey hairs yet stack to the heft;   140
Wi' mair o' horrible and awfu',
Which ev'n to name wad be unlawfu'.

   As Tammie glow'red, amazed and curious,
The mirth and fun grew fast and furious;
The piper loud and louder blew,   145
The dancers quick and quicker flew;
They reeled, they set, they crossed, they cleekit,[35]
Till ilka carlin swat and reekit
And coost[36] her duddies[37] to the wark
And linket[38] at it in her sark![39]   150

   Now Tam, O Tam! had thae been queans,
A' plump and strapping in their teens!
Their sarks, instead o' creeshie[40] flannen,
Been snaw-white seventeen hunder linen!—
Thir breeks o' mine, my only pair,   155
That ance were plush, o' gude blue hair,
I wad hae gien them aff my hurdies,[41]
For ae blink o' the bonie burdies![42]

                    *   *   *

   But Tam kened what was what fu' brawlie;[43]
There was ae winsom wench and walie,[44]   160
That night enlisted in the core
(Lang after ken'd on Carrick shore:
For mony a beast to dead she shot,
And perish'd mony a bonie boat,
And shook baith meikle corn and bear,[45]   165
And kept the country-side in fear);
Her cutty sark[46] o' Paisley harn,[47]

[35] caught hold of each other   [36] cast   [37] clothes
[38] went   [39] shift   [40] greasy
[41] hips   [42] lasses   [43] full well
[44] buxom   [45] wheat and barley [46] short skirt
[47] coarse linen

That while a lassie she had worn,
In longitude tho' sorely scanty,
It was her best, and she was vauntie.[48]   170
Ah! little kent thy reverend grannie,
That sark she coft [49] for her wee Nannie,
Wi' twa pund Scots ('t was a' her riches),
Wad ever graced a dance o' witches!

But here my Muse her wing maun cow'r,   175
Sic flights are far beyond her pow'r;
To sing how Nannie lap and flang,[50]
(A souple jad she was and strang,)
And how Tam stood like ane bewitched,
And thought his very een enriched;   180
Even Satan glow'red and fidged fu' fain,[51]
And hotched [52] and blew wi' might and main:
Till first ae caper, syne anither,
Tam tint [53] his reason a' thegither,
And roars out, 'Weel done, Cutty-sark!'   185
And in an instant all was dark:
And scarcely had he Maggie rallied,
When out the hellish legion sallied.
    As bees bizz out wi' angry fyke,[54]
When plundering herds assail their byke; [55]   190
As open [56] pussie's [57] mortal foes,
When pop! she starts before their nose;
As eager runs the market-crowd,
When "Catch the thief!" resounds aloud;
So Maggie runs, the witches follow,   195
Wi' mony an eldritch skriech and hollo.

Ah, Tam! ah, Tam! thou'll get thy fairin! [58]
In hell they'll roast thee like a herrin!
In vain thy Kate awaits thy comin!
Kate soon will be a woefu' woman!   200
Now, do thy speedy utmost, Meg,
And win the key-stane of the brig:
There at them thou thy tail may toss,

[48] proud	[49] bought	[50] jumped and kicked
[51] pleasure	[52] jerked	[53] lost
[54] fuss	[55] hive	[56] begin to bark
[57] the hare's	[58] reward	

A running stream they dare na cross.
But ere the key-stane she could make,   205
The fient [59] a tail she had to shake!
For Nannie, far before the rest,
Hard upon noble Maggie pressed,
And flew at Tam wi' furious ettle; [60]
But little wist she Maggie's mettle—   210
Ae spring brought aff her master hale,
But left behind her ain grey tail.

EXERCISE:

1. This poem is not merely an objective narrative. Now and then the poet puts in some comment of his own.

How do these comments help define his attitude toward Tam, his hero?

2. What is the effect intended in the poem?

MORTE D'ARTHUR

ALFRED LORD TENNYSON (1809–1892)

So all day long the noise of battle rolled
Among the mountains by the winter sea;
Until King Arthur's table, man by man,
Had fallen in Lyonnesse about their Lord,
King Arthur: then, because his wound was deep,   5
The bold Sir Bedivere uplifted him,
Sir Bedivere, the last of all his knights,
And bore him to a chapel nigh the field,
A broken chancel with a broken cross,
That stood on a dark strait of barren land.   10
On one side lay the Ocean, and on one
Lay a great water, and the moon was full.
    Then spake King Arthur to Sir Bedivere:
"The sequel of today unsolders all
The goodliest fellowship of famous knights   15
Whereof this world holds record. Such a sleep

[59] devil   [60] aim

They sleep—the men I loved. I think that we
Shall never more, at any future time,
Delight our souls with talk of knightly deeds,
Walking about the gardens and the halls   20
Of Camelot, as in the days that were.
I perish by this people which I made,—
Though Merlin sware that I should come again
To rule once more—but let what will be, be,
I am so deeply smitten through the helm   25
That without help I cannot last till morn.
Thou therefore take my brand Excalibur,
Which was my pride: for thou rememberest how
In those old days, one summer noon, an arm
Rose up from out the bosom of the lake,   30
Clothed in white samite, mystic, wonderful,
Holding the sword—and how I rowed across
And took it, and have worn it, like a king:
And, wheresoever I am sung or told
In aftertime, this also shall be known: 35
But now delay not: take Excalibur,
And fling him far into the middle mere:
Watch what thou seëst, and lightly bring me word."
   To him replied the bold Sir Bedivere:
"It is not meet, Sir King, to leave thee thus,   40
Aidless, alone, and smitten through the helm.
A little thing may harm a wounded man.
Yet I thy hest will all perform at full,
Watch what I see, and lightly bring thee word."
   So saying, from the ruined shrine he stept   45
And in the moon athwart the place of tombs,
Where lay the mighty bones of ancient men,
Old knights, and over them the sea-wind sang
Shrill, chill, with flakes of foam. He, stepping down
By zig-zag paths, and juts of pointed rock,   50
Came on the shining levels of the lake.
   There drew he forth the brand Excalibur,
And o'er him, drawing it, the winter moon,
Brightening the skirts of a long cloud, ran forth
And sparkled keen with frost against the hilt: 55
For all the haft twinkled with diamond sparks,
Myriads of topaz-lights, and jacinth-work
Of subtlest jewelry. He gazed so long

That both his eyes were dazzled, as he stood,
This way and that dividing the swift mind,   60
In act to throw: but at the last it seemed
Better to leave Excalibur concealed
There in the many-knotted waterflags,
That whistled stiff and dry about the marge.
So strode he back slow to the wounded King.   65
    Then spake King Arthur to Sir Bedivere:
"Hast thou performed my mission which I gave?
What is it thou hast seen? or what hast heard?"
    And answer made the bold Sir Bedivere:
"I heard the ripple washing in the reeds,   70
And the wild water lapping on the crag."
    To whom replied King Arthur, faint and pale:
"Thou hast betrayed thy nature and thy name,
Not rendering true answer, as beseemed
Thy fealty, nor like a noble knight: 75
For surer sign had followed, either hand,
Or voice, or else a motion of the mere.
This is a shameful thing for men to lie.
Yet now, I charge thee, quickly go again
As thou art lief and dear, and do the thing   80
I bade thee, watch, and lightly bring me word."
    Then went Sir Bedivere the second time
Across the ridge, and paced beside the mere,
Counting the dewy pebbles, fixed in thought;
But when he saw the wonder of the hilt,   85
How curiously and strangely chased, he smote
His palms together, and he cried aloud,
    "And if indeed I cast the brand away,
Surely a precious thing, one worthy note,
Should thus be lost for ever from the earth,   90
Which might have pleased the eyes of many men.
What good should follow this, if this were done?
What harm, undone? deep harm to disobey,
Seeing obedience is the bond of rule.
Were it well to obey then, if a king demand   95
An act unprofitable, against himself?
The King is sick, and knows not what he does.
What record, or what relic of my lord
Should be to aftertime, but empty breath
And rumors of a doubt? but were this kept,   100

Stored in some treasure-house of mighty kings,
Some one might show it at a joust of arms,
Saying, 'King Arthur's sword, Excalibur,
Wrought by the lonely maiden of the Lake.
Nine years she wrought it, sitting in the deeps   105
Upon the hidden bases of the hills.'
So might some old man speak in the aftertime
To all the people, winning reverence.
But now much honor and much fame were lost."

    So spake he, clouded with his own conceit,   110
And hid Excalibur the second time,
And so strode back slow to the wounded King.

    Then spoke King Arthur, breathing heavily:
"What is it thou hast seen? or what hast heard?"

    And answer made the bold Sir Bedivere: 115
"I heard the water lapping on the crag,
And the long ripple washing in the reeds."

    To whom replied King Arthur, much in wrath:
"Ah, miserable and unkind, untrue,
Unknightly, traitor-hearted! Woe is me!   120
Authority forgets a dying king,
Laid widowed of the power in his eye
That bowed the will. I see thee what thou art,
For thou, the latest-left of all my knights,
In whom should meet the offices of all,   125
Thou wouldst betray me for the precious hilt;
Either from lust of gold, or like a girl
Valuing the giddy pleasure of the eyes.
Yet, for a man may fail in duty twice,
And the third time may prosper, get thee hence: 130
But, if thou spare to fling Excalibur,
I will arise and slay thee with my hands."

    Then quickly rose Sir Bedivere, and ran,
And, leaping down the ridges lightly, plunged
Among the bulrush-beds, and clutched the sword,   135
And strongly wheeled and threw it. The great brand
Made lightnings in the splendor of the moon,
And flashing round and round, and whirled in an arch,
Shot like a streamer of the northern morn,
Seen where the moving isles of winter shock   140
By night, with noises of the northern sea.
So flashed and fell the brand Excalibur:

But ere he dipped the surface, rose an arm
Clothed in white samite, mystic, wonderful,
And caught him by the hilt, and brandished him   145
Three times, and drew him under in the mere.
And lightly went the other to the King.
   Then spoke King Arthur, drawing thicker breath:
"Now see I by thine eyes that this is done.
Speak out: what is it thou hast heard, or seen?"   150
   And answer made the bold Sir Bedivere:
"Sir King, I closed mine eyelids, lest the gems
Should blind my purpose, for I never saw,
Nor shall see, here or elsewhere, till I die,
Not though I live three lives of mortal men,   155
So great a miracle as yonder hilt.
Then with both hands I flung him, wheeling him;
But when I looked again, behold an arm,
Clothed in white samite, mystic, wonderful,
That caught him by the hilt, and brandished him   160
Three times, and drew him under in the mere."
   And answer made King Arthur, breathing hard:
"My end draws nigh; 'tis time that I were gone.
Make broad thy shoulders to receive my weight,
And bear me to the margin; yet I fear   165
My wound hath taken cold, and I shall die."
   So saying, from the pavement he half rose,
Slowly, with pain, reclining on his arm,
And looking wistfully with wide blue eyes
As in a picture. Him Sir Bedivere   170
Remorsefully regarded through his tears,
And would have spoken, but he found not words,
Then took with care, and kneeling on one knee,
O'er both his shoulders drew the languid hands,   ·
And rising bore him through the place of tombs.   175
   But, as he walked, King Arthur panted hard,
Like one that feels a nightmare on his bed
When all the house is mute. So sighed the King,
Muttering and murmuring at his ear, "Quick, quick!
I fear it is too late, and I shall die."   180
But the other swiftly strode from ridge to ridge,
Clothed with his breath, and looking, as he walked,
Larger than human on the frozen hills.
He heard the deep behind him, and a cry

Before. His own thought drove him like a goad.   185
Dry clashed his harness in the icy caves
And barren chasms, and all to left and right
The bare black cliff clanged round him, as he based
His feet on juts of slippery crag that rang
Sharp-smitten with the dint of armèd heels—   190
And on a sudden, lo! the level lake,
And the long glories of the winter moon.
    Then saw they how there hove a dusky barge,
Dark as a funeral scarf from stem to stern,
Beneath them; and descending they were ware   195
That all the decks were dense with stately forms
Black-stoled, black-hooded, like a dream—by these
Three Queens with crowns of gold—and from them rose
A cry that shivered to the tingling stars,
And, as it were one voice, an agony   200
Of lamentation, like a wind, that shrills
All night in a waste land, where no one comes,
Or hath come, since the making of the world.
    Then murmured Arthur, "Place me in the barge,"
And to the barge they came. There those three Queens
Put forth their hands, and took the King, and wept. 206
But she, that rose the tallest of them all
And fairest, laid his head upon her lap,
And loosed the shattered casque, and chafed his hands,
And called him by his name, complaining loud,   210
And dropping bitter tears against his brow
Striped with dark blood: for all his face was white
And colorless, and like the withered moon
Smote by the fresh beam of the springing east;
And all his greaves and cuisses dashed with drops 215
Of onset; and the light and lustrous curls—
That made his forehead like a rising sun
High from the dais-throne—were parched with dust;
Or, clotted into points and hanging loose,
Mixed with the knightly growth that fringed his lips. 220
So like a shattered column lay the King;
Not like that Arthur who, with lance in rest,
From spur to plume a star of tournament,
Shot through the lists at Camelot, and charged
Before the eyes of ladies and of kings.   225
    Then loudly cried the bold Sir Bedivere,

"Ah! my Lord Arthur, whither shall I go?
Where shall I hide my forehead and my eyes?
For now I see the true old times are dead,
When every morning brought a noble chance,   230
And every chance brought out a noble knight.
Such times have been not since the light that led
The holy Elders with the gift of myrrh.
But now the whole ROUND TABLE is dissolved
Which was an image of the mighty world;   235
And I, the last, go forth companionless,
And the days darken round me, and the years,
Among new men, strange faces, other minds."
    And slowly answered Arthur from the barge:
"The old order changeth, yielding place to new,   240
And God fulfills Himself in many ways,
Lest one good custom should corrupt the world.
Comfort thyself: what comfort is in me?
I have lived my life, and that which I have done
May He within Himself make pure! but thou,   245
If thou shouldst never see my face again,
Pray for my soul. (More things are wrought by prayer
Than this world dreams of.) Wherefore, let thy voice
Rise like a fountain for me night and day.
For what are men better than sheep or goats   250
That nourish a blind life within the brain,
If, knowing God, they lift not hands of prayer
Both for themselves and those who call them friend?
For so the whole round earth is every way
Bound by gold chains about the feet of God.   255
But now farewell. I am going a long way
With these thou seëst—if indeed I go—
(For all my mind is clouded with a doubt)
To the island-valley of Avilion;
Where falls not hail, or rain, or any snow,   260
Nor ever wind blows loudly; but it lies
Deep-meadowed, happy, fair with orchard-lawns
And bowery hollows crowned with summer sea,
Where I will heal me of my grievous wound."
    So said he, and the barge with oar and sail   265
Moved from the brink, like some full-breasted swan
That, fluting a wild carol ere her death,
Ruffles her pure cold plume, and takes the flood

With swarthy webs. Long stood Sir Bedivere
Revolving many memories, till the hull   270
Looked one black dot against the verge of dawn,
And on the mere the wailing died away.

EXERCISE:

1. The attitude expressed in "Tam O' Shanter" is one of humorous tolerance for the failings of human nature. What is the attitude toward the characters in this poem?

2. There is a great deal of description in this poem. Does it merely impede the action or does it contribute to the total effect of the poem?

3. How does the poet indicate the basic interpretation of the story?

consice

concise

FOREWORD

All of the poems in the previous section give consecutive stories. The poetic effect derives to a large degree from the way in which the story element is managed. But the poems in the present section do not give such consecutive stories. There is a story obviously implied in each case, and we shall be able in each case to make out from the scene or situation or character something of the story that lies behind the poem; but in these cases the poet's purpose requires only the implication of the story. It will be easy, however, for one to pass from the poems of the first group to those of the second, for we have already seen that in the case of the poems of the first group the poet practices a very considerable degree of selectivity in comparison with the ordinary treatment one would find in prose fiction, because he is aiming, not at full information about the events, but at telling the story in such a way as to give the reader the tragic or pathetic or comic effect which he himself has found in the material. That is, the poet has given merely enough of the consecutive story to support his interpretation. Naturally, this amount would vary from instance to instance.

In the poems that follow, the poet's purpose is such that only a little of the story itself appears on the surface of the poem. To appreciate fully one of these poems the reader should try to see how the little that is given and the suggestions made concerning the implied part of the story are related to the effect of the poem.

THE THREE RAVENS

ANONYMOUS

There were three ravens sat on a tree,
  Downe a downe, hay downe, hay downe
There were three ravens sat on a tree,
  With a downe
There were three ravens sat on a tree,   5
They were as blacke as they might be.
  With a downe derrie, derrie, derrie,
    downe, downe.

The one of them said to his mate,
"Where shall we our breakefast take?"

"Downe in yonder greene field,   10
There lies a knight slain under his shield.

"His hounds they lie downe at his feete,
So well they can their master keepe.

"His haukes they flie so eagerly,
There's no fowle dare him come nie."   15

Downe there comes a fallow doe,
As great with yong as she might goe.

She lift up his bloudy hed,
And kist his wounds that were so red.

She got him up upon her backe,   20
And carried him to earthen lake.[1]

She buried him before the prime,
She was dead herselfe ere even-song time.

God send every gentleman,
Such haukes, such hounds, and such a leman.[2]   25

The story which is implied by this ballad may be stated as
follows: A knight has been killed, but his hounds guard the

[1] pit   [2] loved one: wife or sweetheart

body, and his hawks, waiting by their master, keep away the crows that would prey upon it. The knight's leman comes and with her own hands buries him, and then dies herself. But we know nothing more about the "story" as such. We do not know how the knight was killed, or why, or by whom. We simply have the scene by the body, and as elements of the scene, the picture of the ravens gathered in the tree, the picture of the knight with the hounds at his feet and his hawks flying above him. The only thing that happens is the coming of the woman and her death. The poet is not so much interested, then, in giving the reader the consecutive facts of the story as he is in creating a certain feeling about the scene.

What is the feeling which the poet is interested in giving the reader? What does he want the poem to mean to us? We can best answer these questions by examining the manner in which the poet has used the elements of the poem.

As we can quickly see, the details are chosen, not haphazardly, but for a particular effect. The hounds on guard are a type of loyalty, and so also are the vigilant hawks. And these two references prepare for the mention of the third and most important of those who are loyal to the dead knight, the woman herself. She forms a sort of *climax* (*Glossary*) to the examples of loyalty.

Why, then, does the poet mention the ravens? They have no affection for the dead man whatsoever; they consider him only as so much food. The answer is that they form an effective contrast to what follows. They represent the cruelly impersonal background against which the various acts of loyalty are described. There is an ironic shock in passing from the ravens to the hounds, for we pass from a consideration of the knight as so much carrion to a consideration of him as master and friend, even in death, master and friend still.

We may observe the cunning with which the poem presents this material. The poet does not depend on the kind of general statement which we have given in our prose paraphrase. The material is arranged so that we feel the effect intended without the direct statement. The mere fact that the poet allows the ravens themselves to describe the scene accomplishes two things

that would otherwise be impossible. First, what would otherwise be flat description of a scene becomes dramatic action. The
reader comes more directly to the central fact of the poem.
Second, the ironic contrast is more pointed when the ravens
themselves, examples of mere brute appetite, comment on the
hawk and the hounds, examples of a fidelity that reaches beyond
such appetite. Thus, the material is arranged in such a manner
that a comment on the meaning of the situation is unnecessary:
we grasp it immediately, even when we do not take the trouble
to put it in the form of a general statement.

After the poet has set the scene directly and dramatically, the
development of the action is given in terms of narrative. We
are told how the "doe" comes down to the dead knight. But
why is the leman of the dead knight called a doe? [1] The poet
gains again a sort of dramatic shock by characterizing the woman
as a deer. But we see that the characterization is "right," after
all. The shyness and timidity of the deer provides a fitting
description for the gentleness of the woman. But that is not all.
A real doe would not come down among the hounds; she is the
hunted animal, they are the hunters. Therefore the fact that
the woman is described as a doe coming to the scene defines
for us subtly but emphatically the strength of her fidelity, and
courage. In other words, the poet has made the comparison
really tell us something that is essential for the meaning of the
poem. Furthermore, the comparison is the most concentrated
way of giving us the meaning. But the comparison does not
merely give us meaning in the sense of information about the
situation; by appealing to our attitude toward the timidity and
shyness of the doe, it creates our attitude toward the woman
herself.

The line,

As great with yong as she might goe

emphasizes further the pathos of the situation and the strength
of the fidelity that brings the "doe" to the scene. It tells us that

[1] For origin of this comparison see Wimberly: *Folklore in English and
Scottish Ballads,* p. 55.

her action in burying her lover was most difficult, and helps account for her death. It has another effect. She is evidently great with the knight's child. The love has been consummated, and her grief is therefore all the more poignant.

In the body of the poem are given the various examples of loyalty in action. The poet himself refrains from any comment until the last stanza:

> God send every gentleman,
> Such haukes, such hounds, and such a leman.

But notice the form the comment takes. It does not insist on the loyalty. It does not exaggerate. It is, indeed, an understatement. But as such it employs a contrast which is more emphatic than fulsome praise would be. The form of the statement implies that there are few enough knights who have such hawks and hounds and such a lover. This implication is a clue to what might be called the *theme* (*Glossary*) of the poem. We may state the theme more largely somewhat as follows. The poem, taken as a whole, makes a contrast between two ways of looking at life. The ravens represent one way, the hawks, hounds, and "doe" the other. One view regards life in a purely materialistic way; the other finds an importance in life beyond mere material circumstance. The same theme appears in "Johnie Armstrong." Even though he knows he is going to be killed, he feels that the way in which he meets death is important. He says to his men,

> Let them report how ye were slain.

And a similar theme is found in "Sir Patrick Spence."

The statement of the theme of a poem must not be taken as equivalent to the poem itself. It is not to be taken as a "message." But the definition of the theme of a poem may help us to a fuller understanding of the entire poem, if we are careful never to think of it as a little moral comment or platitude which the poem has been written in order to give. We may put the matter in this way: the theme does not give the poem its force; the poem gives the theme its force.

LORD RANDAL

ANONYMOUS

"O where hae ye been, Lord Randal, my son?
O where hae ye been, my handsome young man?"
"I hae been to the wild wood; mother, make my bed soon,
For I'm weary wi hunting, and fain wald lie down."

"Where gat ye your dinner, Lord Randal, my son?   5
Where gat ye your dinner, my handsome young man?"
"I dined wi my true-love; mother, make my bed soon,
For I'm weary wi hunting, and fain wald lie down."

"What gat ye to your dinner, Lord Randal, my son?
What gat ye to your dinner, my handsome young man?"   10
"I gat eels boiled in broo; [1] mother, make my bed soon,
For I'm weary wi hunting, and fain wald lie down."

"What became of your bloodhounds, Lord Randal, my son?
What became of your bloodhounds, my handsome young man?"
"O they swelld and they died; mother, make my bed soon, 15
For I'm weary wi hunting, and fain wald lie down."

"O I fear ye are poisond, Lord Randal, my son!
O I fear ye are poisond, my handsome young man!"
"O yes! I am poisond; mother, make my bed soon,
For I'm sick at the heart, and I fain wald lie down."   20

This ballad shows some devices that are not found in "Johnie
Armstrong," for instance, but are characteristic of many folk
ballads—dialogue, as the only vehicle for narration, and repetition.
The poem does not give a consecutive narrative, as does "Johnie
Armstrong," but merely takes a single dramatic moment in an
action and presents that in five questions and answers that are
framed in the repetition. That is, the movement is defined by a
series of leaps and pauses.

The action proper is suppressed, or only hinted at. But the
treatment is extremely effective, moving, as it does, with increasing
suspense from a simple question and apparently innocent answer

[1] broth

in the first stanza to the tragic discovery in the last. In each stanza the refrain serves to focus this growing intensity, for with its recurrence the reader begins to realize that more and more is implied, until he discovers in the end that not healthy weariness from the hunt, but death makes the young man fain to lie down.

The treatment is not the treatment of narrative. A more rigid selectivity has been brought to bear on the material than would apply in direct narrative. Just such details are used as will be essential and will suggest the rest of the story. The reader is not provided with the kind of information on which a newspaper account or even an ordinary piece of fiction would thrive. We know nothing about the relation between Lord Randal and his true-love except the fact that she poisoned him. The motivation is entirely lacking. Nor do we know anything about the relation between the mother and her son's true-love, although by reason of the mother's quick suspicion we may venture the surmise that the relation was not one of untroubled confidence, perhaps one of mutual jealousy. Just enough information is given to stimulate the imagination, to give the reader a sudden glimpse into the depth of the tragic and ironical situation in the lives of these three people. This sudden glimpse, if the details are properly chosen, may be more effective in provoking the emotional response of the reader than a careful elaboration of facts that might satisfy the full curiosity. Poetry frequently employs this kind of suggestiveness to gain its effects rather than a method of detailed analysis.

A further word might be said about the use of repetition here. We have said that the repetition frames the questions and answers on which the movement of the action depends. In Section IV we shall discuss the function of meter, rime, and stanza—that is, the effect of rhythmical patterns. It is enough for our purpose here to notice the effect of a regular pattern in the form of the questions and answers—that is, the use of repetition and refrain. Repetition and refrain are devices a poet may use to bring the material of a poem under control. The repetition and refrain, like meter, rime, and stanza, help give the poem a *form (Glossary)*.

If the material is deprived of a poetic form, we merely

have left something like this: A young man named Lord
Randal, on returning home from a hunt and a dinner with
his true-love, asks his mother to make his bed because he is
weary. After several questions about the meal and the dis-
appearance of the son's dogs, which the son says died with
mysterious suddenness, the mother comes to the conclusion that
her son has been poisoned. The son, now desperately ill, says
that this is true and that he must lie down. This account is
flatter and less moving than the poem, not because it does not
give the essential facts, but because it lacks the organization, the
form, of the poem.

Perhaps it cannot finally be said why we are affected as we
are by artistic and other forms. For the present, it is enough
that the reader should be aware of the part certain things like
meter or repetition, things he may have regarded merely as
mechanical decorations, are playing in his total response. In this
poem, the repetition, for instance, serves as a kind of binder for
each stanza, the fixed item to which the new material is tied each
time. But it serves a further purpose, as well. The request to
make the bed soon because he is weary with hunting begins to
affect us with a secondary and symbolic meaning which is
gradually developed: he is going to die, he is weary of life
not merely because of his sickness from the poison but because
his own true-love has betrayed him, life has disappointed him
and he returns to his mother as when a child, etc. All of this
becomes involved in the repetition as the poem progresses, yet
not explicitly; here again suggestiveness plays an important part.
The poem does not state all that it has to say. It employs understatement.

One may notice, in addition, the effect of the change from strict
repetition in the last stanza of the poem. Instead of

For I'm weary wi hunting, and fain wald lie down

there appears

For I'm sick at the heart, and I fain wald lie down.

The reader has come to expect the strict repetition, and when
this variation comes, it comes with an effect of emphasis and

climax. This is an example of expressive *variation* (*Glossary*)
from a form that has been established in the poem. A reader
should, in studying a poem, watch for variations of metrical and
other patterns and should try to determine whether such variations are truly expressive or are arbitrary and accidental.

EDWARD

ANONYMOUS

'Why dois your brand sae drap wi bluid,
        Edward, Edward,
Why dois your brand sae drap wi bluid,
   And why sae sad gang yee O?'
'O I hae killed my hauke sae guid,   5
        Mither, mither,
O I hae killed my hauke sae guid,
   And I had nae mair bot hee O.'

'Your haukis bluid was nevir sae reid,
        Edward, Edward,   10
Your haukis bluid was nevir sae reid,
   My deir son I tell thee O.'
'O I hae killed my reid-roan steid,
        Mither, mither,
O I hae killed my reid-roan steid,   15
   That erst was sae fair and frie O.'

'Your steid was auld, and ye hae got mair,
        Edward, Edward,
Your steid was auld, and ye hae got mair,
   Sum other dule¹ ye drie² O.'   20
'O I hae killed my fadir deir,
        Mither, mither,
O I hae killed my fadir deir,
   Alas, and wae is mee O!'

'And whatten penance wul ye drie for that,   25
        Edward, Edward,

¹ grief   ² suffer

And whatten penance will ye drie for that?
   My deir son, now tell me O.'
'Ile set my feit in yonder boat,
         Mither, mither,   30
Ile set my feit in yonder boat,
   And Ile fare ovir the sea O.'

'And what wul ye doe wi your towirs and your ha,
         Edward, Edward?
And what wul ye doe wi your towirs and your ha, 35
   That were sae fair to see O?'
'Ile let thame stand tul they doun fa,
         Mither, mither,
Ile let thame stand tul they down fa,
   For here nevir mair maun [3] I bee O.'   40

'And what wul ye leive to your bairns and your wife,
         Edward, Edward?
And what wul ye leive to your bairns and your wife,
   Whan ye gang ovir the sea O?'
'The warldis room, late them beg thrae [4] life,   45
         Mither, mither,
The warldis room, late them beg thrae life,
   For thame nevir mair wul I see O.'

'And what wul ye leive to your ain mither deir,
         Edward, Edward?   50
And what wul ye leive to your ain mither deir?
   My deir son, now tell me O.'
'The curse of hell frae me sall ye beir,
         Mither, mither,
The curse of hell frae me sall ye beir,   55
   Sic counseils ye gave to me O.'

EXERCISE:

1. The action of this poem is given, for the most part, by indirect rather than direct means. How do we know that Edward is a knight? What is the relation of the mother and father? What is the character of the mother?

2. How does this indirect method contribute to the suspense? How is it related to other effects of the poem?

[3] must   [4] through

PROUD MAISIE

SIR WALTER SCOTT (1771–1832)

Proud Maisie is in the wood,
  Walking so early;
Sweet Robin sits on the bush,
  Singing so rarely.

"Tell me, thou bonny bird,   5
  When shall I marry me?"
"When six braw [1] gentlemen,
  Kirkward shall carry ye."

"Who makes the bridal bed,
  Birdie, say truly?"—   10
"The gray-headed sexton
  Who delves the grave duly.

"The glow-worm o'er grave and stone
  Shall light thee steady.
The owl from the steeple sing,   15
  'Welcome, proud lady.'"

EXERCISE:

Compare the method used in this poem with that employed in
"The Three Ravens."

KING DAVID

WALTER DE LA MARE (1873–   )

King David was a sorrowful man:
  No cause for his sorrow had he;
And he called for the music of a hundred harps,
  To ease his melancholy.

They played till they all fell silent: 5
  Played—and play sweet did they;
But the sorrow that haunted the heart of King David
  They could not charm away.

[1] brave

He rose; and in his garden
  Walked by the moon alone,   10
A nightingale hidden in a cypress-tree
  Jargoned on and on.

King David lifted his sad eyes
  Into the dark-boughed tree—
"Tell me, thou little bird that singest,   15
  Who taught my grief to thee?"

But the bird in no wise heeded;
  And the king in the cool of the moon
Harkened to the nightingale's sorrowfulness,
  Till all his own was gone.   20

EXERCISE:

State the theme of this poem.

Monday

ULYSSES

ALFRED, LORD TENNYSON (1809–1892)

It little profits that an idle king,
By this still hearth, among these barren crags,
Matched with an agèd wife, I mete and dole
Unequal laws unto a savage race,
That hoard, and sleep, and feed, and know not me.   5
I cannot rest from travel; I will drink
Life to the lees. All times I have enjoyed
Greatly, have suffered greatly, both with those
That loved me, and alone; on shore, and when
Through scudding drifts the rainy Hyades   10
Vext the dim sea. I am become a name;
For always roaming with a hungry heart
Much have I seen and known,—cities of men
And manners, climates, councils, governments,
Myself not least, but honored of them all;   15
And drunk delight of battle with my peers,
Far on the ringing plains of windy Troy.
I am a part of all that I have met;

Yet all experience is an arch wherethro'
Gleams that untraveled world whose margin fades   20
For ever and for ever when I move.
How dull it is to pause, to make an end,
To rust unburnished, not to shine in use!
As though to breathe were life! Life piled on life
Were all too little, and of one to me   25
Little remains; but every hour is saved
From that eternal silence, something more.
A bringer of new things; and vile it were
For some three suns to store and hoard myself,
And this gray spirit yearning in desire   30
To follow knowledge like a sinking star,
Beyond the utmost bound of human thought.

This is my son, mine own Telemachus,
To whom I leave the scepter and the isle—
Well-loved of me, discerning to fulfil   35
This labor, by slow prudence to make mild
A rugged people, and through soft degrees
Subdue them to the useful and the good.
Most blameless is he, centered in the sphere
Of common duties, decent not to fail   40
In offices of tenderness, and pay
Meet adoration to my household gods,
When I am gone. He works his work, I mine.

There lies the port; the vessel puffs her sail:
There gloom the dark, broad seas. My mariners,   45
Souls that have toiled and wrought, and thought with
    me—
That ever with a frolic welcome took
The thunder and the sunshine, and opposed
Free hearts, free foreheads—you and I are old;
Old age hath yet his honor and his toil.   50
Death closes all; but something ere the end,
Some work of noble note, may yet be done,
Not unbecoming men that strove with Gods.
The lights begin to twinkle from the rocks;
The long day wanes; the slow moon climbs; the deep 55
Moans round with many voices. Come, my friends,
'T is not too late to seek a newer world.

Push off, and sitting well in order smite
The sounding furrows; for my purpose holds
To sail beyond the sunset, and the baths   60
Of all the western stars, until I die.
It may be that the gulfs will wash us down;
It may be we shall touch the Happy Isles,
And see the great Achilles, whom we knew.
Though much is taken, much abides; and though   65
We are not now that strength which in old days
Moved earth and heaven, that which we are, we are;
One equal temper of heroic hearts,
Made weak by time and fate, but strong in will
To strive, to seek, to find, and not to yield.   70

EXERCISE:

1. Ulysses, the hero of Homer's *Odyssey,* has returned home
from the siege of Troy after ten years of wandering and adventure. (Consult the library for a full account.) He is here
picturing the prospect of old age. The poet uses this situation
for dramatizing what general attitude and feeling?

2. Compare the mood of this poem with that established in
"Michael."

TWO OF YOU

MARK VAN DOREN (1894–   )

I know you after sixty years;
They have not changed, she said—
Those incombustible black stones
High in your ashen head;
Those coals that, as our passion blew,   5
Outlasted my poor dread.

Those eyes that I so lowly feared
For their unstopping gaze—
I may not fancy even now
That on my snow it stays;   10
This level whiteness of my life;
These warm, forgotten ways.

I have come back to look at you,
I have come back to find
The incorruptible straight stalk,   15
The rod within the rind.
And I can wonder if time erred,
Proving so rigid-kind.

He has made two of you, I say.
Does either of them hear?   20
That dark one rising inwardly?
This other one—this sere,
This whiter one that snows have singed,
Piling the faggot year?

But not the first, the ageless man—   25
I see him where he stands,
Stiff prisoner inside the glass,
Contented with smooth hands;
Condemned, erect, and total-deaf
To the sweet run of sands.   30

From the swift song of change, my love,
You long ago were locked;
A young man in an old man's hide,
And both of them are mocked;
Unless you listened, one of you,   35
When my crisp knuckles knocked.

EXERCISE: *Monday*

1. Compare the attitude toward age in this poem, with that in
"Ulysses."
2. How is the attitude dramatized in this poem?

iambic tetrameter
aa b b cc dd
form

FLAMMONDE

EDWIN ARLINGTON ROBINSON (1869–1935)

The man Flammonde, from God knows where,
With firm address and foreign air,
With news of nations in his talk

And something royal in his walk,
With glint of iron in his eyes,   5
But never doubt, nor yet surprise,
Appeared, and stayed, and held his head
As one by kings accredited.

Erect, with his alert repose
About him, and about his clothes,   10
He pictured all tradition hears
Of what we owe to fifty years.
His cleansing heritage of taste
Paraded neither want nor waste;
And what he needed for his fee   15
To live, he borrowed graciously.

He never told us what he was,
Or what mischance, or other cause,
Had banished him from better days
To play the Prince of Castaways.   20
Meanwhile he played surpassing well
A part, for most, unplayable;
In fine, one pauses, half afraid
To say for certain that he played.

For that, one may as well forego   25
Conviction as to yes or no;
Nor can I say just how intense
Would then have been the difference
To several, who, having striven
In vain to get what he was given,   30
Would see the stranger taken on
By friends not easy to be won.

Moreover, many a malcontent
He soothed and found munificent;
His courtesy beguiled and foiled   35
Suspicion that his years were soiled;
His mien distinguished any crowd,
His credit strengthened when he bowed;
And women, young and old, were fond
Of looking at the man Flammonde.   40

There was a woman in our town
On whom the fashion was to frown;

But while our talk renewed the tinge
Of a long-faded scarlet fringe,
The man Flammonde saw none of that,   45
And what he saw we wondered at—
That none of us, in her distress,
Could hide or find our littleness.

There was a boy that all agreed
Had shut within him the rare seed   50
Of learning. We could understand,
But none of us could lift a hand.
The man Flammonde appraised the youth,
And told a few of us the truth;
And thereby, for a little gold,   55
A flowered future was unrolled.

There were two citizens who fought
For years and years, and over nought;
They made life awkward for their friends,
And shortened their own dividends.   60
The man Flammonde said what was wrong
Should be made right; nor was it long
Before they were again in line,
And had each other in to dine.

And these I mention are but four   65
Of many out of many more.
So much for them. But what of him—
So firm in every look and limb?
What small satanic sort of kink
Was in his brain? What broken link   70
Withheld him from the destinies
That came so near to being his?

What was he, when we came to sift
His meaning, and to note the drift
Of incommunicable ways   75
That make us ponder while we praise?
Why was it that his charm revealed
Somehow the surface of a shield?
What was it that we never caught?
What was he, and what was he not?   80

How much it was of him we met
We cannot ever know; nor yet
Shall all he gave us quite atone
For what was his, and his alone;
Nor need we now, since he knew best,   85
Nourish an ethical unrest:
Rarely at once will nature give
The power to be Flammonde and live.

We cannot know how much we learn
From those who never will return,   90
Until a flash of unforeseen
Remembrance falls on what has been
We've each a darkening hill to climb;
And this is why, from time to time
In Tilbury Town, we look beyond   95
Horizons for the man Flammonde.

EXERCISE:

1. What is Flammonde's character? How does the poet develop this in terms of his experiences in the little town?
2. Is Flammonde represented as an entire hero?
3. What is the basic irony in this poem?

LUCY GRAY; OR, SOLITUDE

WILLIAM WORDSWORTH (1770–1850)

Oft I had heard of Lucy Gray:
And, when I crossed the wild,
I chanced to see at break of day
The solitary child.

No mate, no comrade Lucy knew;   5
She dwelt on a wide moor,
—The sweetest thing that ever grew
Beside a human door!

You yet may spy the fawn at play,
The hare upon the green;   10
But the sweet face of Lucy Gray
Will never more be seen.

"To-night will be a stormy night—
You to the town must go;
And take a lantern, Child, to light   15
Your mother through the snow."

"That, Father! will I gladly do:
'Tis scarcely afternoon—
The minster-clock has just struck two,
And yonder is the moon!"   20

At this the father raised his hook,
And snapped a faggot-band;
He plied his work;—and Lucy took
The lantern in her hand.

Not blither is the mountain roe: 25
With many a wanton stroke
Her feet disperse the powdery snow,
That rises up like smoke.

The storm came on before its time:
She wandered up and down;   30
And many a hill did Lucy climb:
But never reached the town.

The wretched parents all that night
Went shouting far and wide;
But there was neither sound nor sight   35
To serve them for a guide.

At daybreak on a hill they stood
That overlooked the moor;
And thence they saw the bridge of wood,
A furlong from their door.   40

They wept—and, turning homeward, cried,
"In heaven we all shall meet";
—When in the snow the mother spied
The print of Lucy's feet.

Then downwards from the steep hill's edge   45
They tracked the footmarks small;
And through the broken hawthorn hedge,
And by the long stone-wall;

And then an open field they crossed:
The marks were still the same;   50
They tracked them on, nor ever lost;
And to the bridge they came.

They followed from the snowy bank
Those footmarks, one by one,
Into the middle of the plank;   55
And further there were none!

—Yet some maintain that to this day
She is a living child;
That you may see sweet Lucy Gray
Upon the lonesome wild.   60

O'er rough and smooth she trips along,
And never looks behind;
And sings a solitary song
That whistles in the wind.

EXERCISE:

What does the poet gain by the use of the frame into which
the incident itself is cast?

PATTERNS

AMY LOWELL (1874–1925)

I walk down the garden paths,
And all the daffodils
Are blowing, and the bright blue squills.
I walk down the patterned garden paths

In my stiff, brocaded gown.   5
With my powdered hair and jewelled fan,
I too am a rare
Pattern. As I wander down
The garden paths.

My dress is richly figured,   10
And the train
Makes a pink and silver stain
On the gravel, and the thrift
Of the borders.
Just a plate of current fashion,   15
Tripping by in high-heeled, ribboned shoes.
Not a softness anywhere about me,
Only whale-bone and brocade.
And I sink on a seat in the shade
Of a lime tree. For my passion   20
Wars against the stiff brocade.
The daffodils and squills
Flutter in the breeze
As they please.
And I weep;   25
For the lime tree is in blossom
And one small flower has dropped upon my bosom.

And the plashing of waterdrops
In the marble fountain
Comes down the garden paths.   30
The dripping never stops.
Underneath my stiffened gown
Is the softness of a woman bathing in a marble basin,
A basin in the midst of hedges grown
So thick, she cannot see her lover hiding,   35
But she guesses he is near,
And the sliding of the water
Seems the stroking of a dear
Hand upon her.
What is Summer in a fine brocaded gown!   40
I should like to see it lying in a heap upon the ground,
All the pink and silver crumpled up on the ground.

I would be the pink and silver as I ran along the paths
And he would stumble after,

Bewildered by my laughter.   45
I should see the sun flashing from his sword hilt and the
   buckles on his shoes.
I would choose
To lead him in a maze along the patterned paths,
A bright and laughing maze for my heavy-booted lover,
Till he caught me in the shade,   50
And the buttons of his waistcoat bruised my body as he
   clasped me,
Aching, melting, unafraid,
With the shadows of the leaves and the sundrops,
And the plopping of the waterdrops,
All about us in the open afternoon—   55
I am very like to swoon
With the weight of this brocade,
For the sun sifts through the shade.

Underneath the fallen blossom
In my bosom,   60
Is a letter I have hid.
It was brought to me this morning by a rider from the
   Duke.
"Madam, we regret to inform you that Lord Hartwell
Died in action Thursday se'n night."
As I read it in the white, morning sunlight,   65
The letters squirmed like snakes.
"Any answer, Madam," said my footman.
"No," I told him.
"See that the messenger takes some refreshment.
No, no answer."   70
And I walked into the garden,
Up and down the patterned paths,
In my stiff, correct brocade.
The blue and yellow flowers stood up proudly in the sun,
Each one.   75
I stood upright too,
Held rigid to the pattern
By the stiffness of my gown.
Up and down I walked,
Up and down.   80

In a month he would have been my husband.
In a month, here, underneath this lime,

We would have broke the pattern;
He for me, and I for him,
He as Colonel, I as Lady,   85
On this shady seat.
He had a whim
That sunlight carried blessing.
And I answered, "It shall be as you have said."
Now he is dead.   90

In Summer and in Winter I shall walk
Up and down
The patterned garden paths
In my stiff, brocaded gown.
The squills and daffodils   95
Will give place to pillared roses, and to asters, and to snow.
I shall go
Up and down,
In my gown.
Gorgeously arrayed,   100
Boned and stayed.
And the softness of my body will be guarded from embrace
By each button, hook, and lace.
For the man who should loose me is dead,
Fighting with the Duke in Flanders,   105
In a pattern called a war.
Christ! What are patterns for?

The narrative, as such, does not compose the greater part of "Patterns," for it only takes a definite form in the second and third sections from the end of the poem. The content of the narrative is very simple. The heroine of the poem, of whose mind the poem is given as an expression, has been engaged to be married to a certain Lord Hartwell. On the morning of the action of the poem, she receives a letter from the Duke (whom, because of the eighteenth-century background and the line, "Fighting with the Duke in Flanders," we may take to be the Duke of Marlborough) to the effect that her lover has been killed in battle. On learning the news she orders that the messenger be given some refreshment, and goes out to walk in the garden. There she thinks of her courtship and her present situation.

At least in one respect, then, this poem differs from those in the previous section. Like the other poems in this section, "Patterns" in only small part deals with direct narrative. Just enough narrative is given to make clear the present situation, to explain to the reader the basis in fact for the woman's state of mind: that is, to provide a dramatic context for the mood of the poem. The reader is concerned with the reaction of the woman after the narrative proper is over. In fact, the poem pretends to be a soliloquy, a monologue that the woman is carrying on alone in the garden. The fact that the course of the poem follows the workings of the mind of the grief-stricken woman accounts for the apparently illogical construction as compared with the rather straight chronological narrative of a poem like "Johnie Armstrong." In the present poem, for instance, we do not discover the cause of the situation, the death of Lord Hartwell, until the poem is two thirds over.

We have said that the method used to present the material of the poem is apparently illogical because it departs from the strict chronological order of events. But the poet is not merely interested in telling the story in as clear a way as possible; he has, in fact, a real intention quite different from that of telling a story. Giving the outline of the story in a quickly comprehensible form could, in any case, be done better in a prose summary, even in the summary in the first paragraph of this analysis. The reader must be in possession of the facts of the narrative before he can properly appreciate the poem, but he will quickly realize that a presentation of the facts of the narrative is not the aim of the poem; for, if it were, then the prose summary would be logically superior to the poem. The poem has another object, and understanding that object will probably make clear the method the poet has used.

We have seen from previous analyses that the poet has attempted not merely to give the facts of a story, but to give facts so selected and arranged and so expressed that the reader will adopt a certain attitude toward, and experience a certain emotion concerning, the story. Now, in "Patterns" the poet has decided that this kind of interest is best served by emphasizing the character and condition of the woman rather than the chain of events leading up to the scene in the garden on the morning when she receives news of the death of her lover. To accomplish this the poet has plunged us into the mind of the woman at the moment when she sees her past life and her future life in contrast, at the moment when she discovers that her life has definitely changed its course and will never be the same. We are not given this information all at once, but bit by bit, the poem following, as it were, the gradual growth of the conviction in the woman's mind to the climax when she cries out in protest. In other words, the poet has taken for the model of the organization of the poem, not the order in which a series of events occurred, historically speaking (the courtship, the death of Hartwell, etc.), but the sequence of thoughts and feelings the woman experiences as a result of those events.

But this cannot mean that the poet has organized the poem loosely and at random. First, the reader must feel that the progression from one thing to another is justified psychologically. He must feel that the woman in this condition might notice the beauty of the garden and her costume, and be aware of the ironical fact that these things now have no meaning for her since her lover is dead; that her mind trying to escape from its grief might indulge in the fantasy of her lover's return to discover her bathing in the garden; that the stiffness of her dress and her suffocation might recall her to the miserable reality and to the letter in her bosom; that she might have a glimpse of what her future will be; and that as she cries out in protest, she might see herself and others as victims of the "patterns."

There is another aspect, however, of the organization of the poem, the organization of the parts in relation to a general idea, or what we have called a *theme*. "Patterns" is the title of the poem and indicates the theme, which we may state in its simplest and loosest terms as a contrast between the natural and the artificial. The theme appears almost casually in the first section with the observation that the garden has been patterned and that the woman is a pattern. In the second this is further developed:

> Not a softness anywhere about me,
> Only whalebone and brocade.

Then the theme, having been hinted at, is given a more dramatic turn:

>   For my passion
> Wars against the stiff brocade.

And again in the third section:

>   What is summer in a fine brocaded gown!

In the fourth section the woman's self-control on receiving the letter means that she is conforming to another kind of pattern; then she goes out to walk along "the patterned paths" in her "stiff, correct brocade," being held rigid to the pattern. And in the last stanza the poem comes to its climax of theme as it comes to its psychological climax in the cry of protest. Not only are the gown, the paths, the whalebone and stays, patterns, but a thing like war is a pattern too, something man has systematized to cut across the natural and happier development of life. Then, in the last cry of protest, the reader realizes that the "patterns" are all the systems and conventions that repress human development.

Two general principles will appear from the preceding discussion of the theme of "Patterns." First, one can see how the poem is held together, given *unity* (*Glossary*) by the fact that the various parts are connected, not only by reason of their reference to the workings of the mind of the grief-stricken woman, but by their reference to the theme of the poem. There is a *thematic development* (*Glossary*) of the poem and a psychological development, both working together. Second, one comes to realize, as the poem progresses, that the different things, such as the flower beds, the paths, the whalebone and stays, the brocade, buttons, and lace that appear again and again in the poem come to stand in the woman's mind for the idea of the patterns, the systems, and the restrictions against which she is protesting. In other words, they come to have the meaning of *symbols* (*Glossary*) in so far as they represent, not only themselves as particular objects, but an idea. Third, one may realize that the whole poem is a dramatization, the presentation of an idea, not abstractly, but concretely in a particular situation; the

woman is like all people who are victims of the systems man has
built up that sometimes react painfully on individual men just as
the "pattern called a war" has robbed the woman of her lover,
who was for her the one hope of full and happy development;
and we therefore may feel that the poem has put in its special
case an idea or theme that has at least a certain degree of general
meaning. (At this point it may be added, however, that the
bare statement in the form of a prose summary of the idea
would not be equivalent to the poem, for the reader would not
usually give much response to a general statement; the feeling
is evoked only when one sympathizes with the pathos of the
particular situation.)

THE LAST RIDE TOGETHER

ROBERT BROWNING (1812–1889)

I

I said—Then, dearest, since 't is so,
Since now at length my fate I know,
Since nothing all my love avails,
Since all, my life seemed meant for, fails,
  Since this was written and needs must be—   5
My whole heart rises up to bless
Your name in pride and thankfulness!
Take back the hope you gave,—I claim
Only a memory of the same,
—And this beside, if you will not blame,   10
  Your leave for one more last ride with me.

II

My mistress bent that brow of hers;
Those deep dark eyes where pride demurs
When pity would be softening through,
Fixed me a breathing-while or two   15
  With life or death in the balance: right!
The blood replenished me again;
My last thought was at least not vain:

I and my mistress, side by side
Shall be together, breathe and ride,   20
So, one day more am I deified.
  Who knows but the world may end tonight?

III

Hush! if you saw some western cloud
All billowy-bosomed, over-bowed
By many benedictions—sun's   25
And moon's and evening-star's at once—
  And so, you, looking and loving best,
Conscious grew, your passion drew
Cloud, sunset, moonrise, star-shine too,
Down on you, near and yet more near,   30
Till flesh must fade for heaven was here!—
Thus leant she and lingered—joy and fear!
  Thus lay she a moment on my breast.

IV

Then we began to ride. My soul
Smoothed itself out, a long-cramped scroll   35
Freshening and fluttering in the wind.
Past hopes already lay behind.
  What need to strive with a life awry?
Had I said that, had I done this,
So might I gain, so might I miss.   40
Might she have loved me? just as well
She might have hated, who can tell!
Where had I been now if the worst befell?
  And here we are riding, she and I.

V

Fail I alone, in words and deeds?   45
Why, all men strive, and who succeeds?
We rode; it seemed my spirit flew,
Saw other regions, cities new,
  As the world rushed by on either side.
I thought,—All labor, yet no less   50
Bear up beneath their unsuccess.
Look at the end of work, contrast
The petty done, the undone vast,

This present of theirs with the hopeful past!
I hoped she would love me; here we ride.   55

VI

What hand and brain went ever paired?
What heart alike conceived and dared?
What act proved all its thought had been?
What will but felt the fleshly screen?
　　We ride and I see her bosom heave.   60
There's many a crown for who can reach.
Ten lines, a statesman's life in each!
The flag stuck on a heap of bones,
A soldier's doing! what atones?
They scratch his name on the Abbeystones.   65
　　My riding is better, by their leave.

VII

What does it all mean, poet? Well,
Your brains beat into rhythm, you tell
What we felt only; you expressed
You hold things beautiful the best,   70
　　And pace them in rhyme so, side by side.
'T is something, nay 't is much: but then,
Have you yourself what's best for men?
Are you—poor, sick, old ere your time—
Nearer one whit your own sublime   75
Than we who never have turned a rhyme?
　　Sing, riding's a joy! For me, I ride.

VIII

And you, great sculptor—so, you gave
A score of years to Art, her slave,
And that's your Venus, whence we turn   80
To yonder girl that fords the burn!
　　You acquiesce, and shall I repine?
What, man of music, you grown gray
With notes and nothing else to say,
Is this your sole praise from a friend,   85
"Greatly his opera's strains intend,
But in music we know how fashions end!"
　　I gave my youth; but we ride, in fine.

IX

Who knows what's fit for us?   Had fate
Proposed bliss here should sublimate   90
My being—had I signed the bond—
Still one must lead some life beyond,
    Have a bliss to die with, dim-descried.
This foot once planted on the goal,
This glory-garland round my soul,   95
Could I descry such?   Try and test!
I sink back shuddering from the quest.
Earth being so good, would heaven seem best?
    Now, heaven and she are beyond this ride.

X

And yet—she has not spoke so long!   100
What if heaven be that, fair and strong
At life's best, with our eyes upturned
Whither life's flower is first discerned,
    We, fixed so, ever should so abide?
What if we still ride on, we two,   105
With life for ever old yet new,
Changed not in kind but in degree,
The instant made eternity,—
And heaven just prove that I and she
    Ride, ride together, for ever ride?   110

EXERCISE:

    1. What is the narrative implied here?
    2. To what paradox (*Glossary*) does this narrative give dramatic form?

HELL GATE

A. E. HOUSMAN (1859–1936)

Onward led the road again
Through the sad uncolored plain
Under twilight brooding dim,

And along the utmost rim
Wall and rampart risen to sight   5
Cast a shadow not of night,
And beyond them seemed to glow
Bonfires lighted long ago.
And my dark conductor spoke,
Saying, "You conjectured well: 10
Yonder is the gate of hell."

    Ill as yet the eye could see
The eternal masonry,
But beneath it on the dark
To and fro there stirred a spark.   15
And again the sombre guide
Knew my question and replied:
"At hell gate the damned in turn
Pace for sentinel and burn."

    Dully at the leaden sky   20
Staring, and with idle eye
Measuring the listless plain,
I began to think again.
Many things I thought of then,
Battle, and the loves of men,   25
Cities entered, oceans crossed,
Knowledge gained and virtue lost,
Cureless folly done and said,
And the lovely way that led
To the slimepit and the mire   30
And the everlasting fire.
And against a smoulder dun
And a dawn without a sun
Did the nearing bastion loom,
And across the gate of gloom   35
Still one saw the sentry go,
Trim and burning, to and fro,
One for women to admire
In his finery of fire.
Something, as I watched him pace,   40
Minded me of time and place,
Soldiers of another corps
And a sentry known before.

Ever darker hell on high
Reared its strength upon the sky,   45
And our footfall on the track
Fetched the daunting echo back.
But the soldier pacing still
The insuperable sill,
Nursing his tormented pride,   50
Turned his head to neither side,
Sunk into himself apart
And the hell-fire of his heart.
But against our entering in
From the drawbridge Death and Sin   55
Rose to render key and sword
To their father and their lord.
And the portress foul to see
Lifted up her eyes on me
Smiling, and I made reply: 60
"Met again, my lass," said I.
Then the sentry turned his head,
Looked, and knew me, and was Ned.

Once he looked, and halted straight,
Set his back against the gate,   65
Caught his musket to his chin,
While the hive of hell within
Sent abroad a seething hum
As of towns whose king is come
Leading conquest home from far   70
And the captives of his war,
And the car of triumph waits,
And they open wide the gates.
But across the entry barred
Straddled the revolted guard,   75
Weaponed and accoutred well
From the arsenals of hell;
And beside him, sick and white,
Sin to left and Death to right
Turned a countenance of fear   80
On the flaming mutineer.
Over us the darkness bowed,
And the anger in the cloud
Clenched the lightning for the stroke;
But the traitor musket spoke.   85

And the hollowness of hell
Sounded as its master fell,
And the mourning echo rolled
Ruin through his kingdom old.
Tyranny and terror flown   90
Left a pair of friends alone,
And beneath the nether sky
All that stirred was he and I.

Silent, nothing found to say,
We began the backward way;   95
And the ebbing lustre died
From the soldier at my side,
As in all his spruce attire
Failed the everlasting fire.
Midmost of the homeward track   100
Once we listened, and looked back;
But the city, dusk, and mute,
Slept, and there was no pursuit.

EXERCISE:

1. What is the implied relation between the speaker and the sentry?
2. Since the poem is a fantasy, what is the intention of the narrative?

WALSINGHAME

SIR WALTER RALEGH (1552–1618)

"As you came from the holy land
    Of Walsinghame,
Met you not with my true love
    By the way as you came?"

"How shall I know your true love,   5
    That have met many a one
As I went to the holy land,
    That have come, that have gone?"

"She is neither white nor brown,
    But as the heavens fair,   10
There is none hath a form so divine
    In the earth or the air."

"Such an one did I meet, good Sir,
    Such an angelic face,
Who like a queen, like a nymph did appear   15
    By her gait, by her grace."

"She hath left me here alone,
    All alone as unknown,
Who sometimes did me lead with herself,
    And me loved as her own."   20

"What's the cause that she leaves you alone
    And a new way doth take,
Who loved you once as her own
    And her joy did you make?"

"I have loved her all my youth,   25
    But now old as you see,
Love likes not the falling fruit
    From the withered tree.

"Know that Love is a careless child,
    And forgets promise past;   30
He is blind, he is deaf when he list
    And in faith never fast.

"His desire is a dureless content
    And a trustless joy;
He is won with a world of despair   35
    And is lost with a toy.

"Of womenkind such indeed is the love
    Or the word love abused,
Under which many childish desires
    And conceits are excused.   40

> "But love is a durable fire
>   In the mind ever burning;
> Never sick, never old, never dead,
>   From itself never turning."

EXERCISE:

Compare this poem in content and form with "La Belle Dame sans Merci."

THE EVE OF ST. AGNES

JOHN KEATS (1795–1821)

Spenserian Stanza

St. Agnes' Eve—Ah, bitter chill it was!
The owl, for all his feathers, was a-cold;
The hare limped trembling through the frozen grass,
And silent was the flock in woolly fold:
Numb were the Beadsman's fingers, while he told   5
His rosary, and while his frosted breath,
Like pious incense from a censer old,
Seemed taking flight for heaven, without a death,
Past the sweet Virgin's picture, while his prayer he saith.

His prayer he saith, this patient, holy man; *a*   10
Then takes his lamp, and riseth from his knees, *b*
And back returneth, meager, barefoot, wan, *a*
Along the chapel aisle by slow degrees: *b*
The sculptured dead, on each side, seem to freeze, *b*
Emprisoned in black, purgatorial rails: *c*   15
Knights, ladies, praying in dumb orat'ries, *b*
He passeth by; and his weak spirit fails *c*
To think how they may ache in icy hoods and mails. *c*

Northward he turneth through a little door,
And scarce three steps, ere Music's golden tongue   20
Flattered to tears this aged man and poor;
But no—already had his deathbell rung;
The joys of all his life were said and sung:
His was harsh penance on St. Agnes' Eve:
Another way he went, and soon among   25
Rough ashes sat he for his soul's reprieve,
And all night kept awake, for sinners' sake to grieve.

That ancient Beadsman heard the prelude soft;
And so it chanced, for many a door was wide,
From hurry to and fro. Soon, up aloft,   30
The silver, snarling trumpets 'gan to chide:
The level chambers, ready with their pride,
Were glowing to receive a thousand guests:
The carvèd angels, ever eager-eyed,
Stared, where upon their heads the cornice rests,   35
With hair blown back, and wings put crosswise on their breasts.

At length burst in the argent revelry,
With plume, tiara, and all rich array,
Numerous as shadows haunting fairily
The brain, new stuffed, in youth, with triumphs gay   40
Of old romance. These let us wish away,
And turn, sole-thoughted, to one Lady there,
Whose heart had brooded, all that wintry day,
On love, and winged St. Agnes' saintly care,
As she had heard old dames full many times declare.   45

They told her how, upon St. Agnes' Eve,
Young virgins might have visions of delight,
And soft adorings from their loves receive
Upon the honeyed middle of the night,
If ceremonies due they did aright: 50
As, supperless to bed they must retire,
And couch supine their beauties, lily white;
Nor look behind, nor sideways, but require
Of Heaven with upward eyes for all that they desire.

Full of this whim was thoughtful Madeline: 55
The music, yearning like a God in pain,
She scarcely heard: her maiden eyes divine,
Fixed on the floor, saw many a sweeping train
Pass by—she heeded not at all: in vain
Came many a tiptoe, amorous cavalier,   60
And back retired; not cooled by high disdain,
But she saw not: her heart was otherwhere:
She sighed for Agnes' dreams, the sweetest of the year.

She danced along with vague, regardless eyes,
Anxious her lips, her breathing quick and short: 65

The hallowed hour was near at hand: she sighs
Amid the timbrels, and the thronged resort
Of whisperers in anger, or in sport;
'Mid looks of love, defiance, hate, and scorn,
Hoodwinked with faery fancy; all amort,   70
Save to St. Agnes and her lambs unshorn,
And all the bliss to be before tomorrow morn.

So, purposing each moment to retire,
She lingered still.   Meantime, across the moors,
Had come young Porphyro, with heart on fire   75
For Madeline.   Beside the portal doors,
Buttressed from moonlight, stands he, and implores
All saints to give him sight of Madeline,
But for one moment in the tedious hours,
That he might gaze and worship all unseen;   80
Perchance speak, kneel, touch, kiss—in sooth such things have
    been.

He ventures in: let no buzzed whisper tell:
All eyes be muffled, or a hundred swords
Will storm his heart, Love's fev'rous citadel:
For him, those chambers held barbarian hordes,   85
Hyena foemen, and hot-blooded lords,
Whose very dogs would execrations howl
Against his lineage: not one breast affords
Him any mercy, in that mansion foul,
Save one old beldame, weak in body and in soul.   90

Ah, happy chance! the aged creature came,
Shuffling along with ivory-headed wand,
To where he stood, hid from the torch's flame,
Behind a broad hall-pillar, far beyond
The sound of merriment and chorus bland: 95
He startled her; but soon she knew his face,
And grasped his fingers in her palsied hand,
Saying, "Mercy, Porphyro! hie thee from this place;
They are all here tonight, the whole blood-thirsty race!

"Get hence! get hence! there's dwarfish Hildebrand;   100
He had a fever late, and in the fit
He cursèd thee and thine, both house and land:

Then there's that old Lord Maurice, not a whit
More tame for his gray hairs—Alas me! flit!
Flit like a ghost away."—"Ah, Gossip dear,   105
We're safe enough; here in this armchair sit,
And tell me how"—"Good Saints! not here, not here;
Follow me, child, or else these stones will be thy bier."

He followed through a lowly archèd way,
Brushing the cobwebs with his lofty plume;   110
And as she muttered "Well-a-day!"
He found him in a little moonlight room,
Pale, latticed, chill, and silent as a tomb.
"Now tell me where is Madeline," said he,
"O tell me, Angela, by the holy loom   115
Which none but secret sisterhood may see,
When they St. Agnes' wool are weaving piously."

"St. Agnes!   Ah! it is St. Agnes' Eve—
Yet men will murder upon holy days:
Thou must hold water in a witch's sieve,   120
And be liege-lord of all the Elves and Fays,
To venture so; it fills me with amaze
To see thee, Porphyro!—St. Agnes' Eve!
God's help! my lady fair the conjurer plays
This very night: good angels her deceive!   125
But let me laugh awhile, I've mickle time to grieve."

Feebly she laugheth in the languid moon,
While Porphyro upon her face doth look,
Like puzzled urchin on an aged crone
Who keepeth closed a wond'rous riddle-book,   130
As spectacled she sits in chimney nook.
But soon his eyes grew brilliant, when she told
His lady's purpose; and he scarce could brook
Tears, at the thought of those enchantments cold,
And Madeline asleep in lap of legends old.   135

Sudden a thought came like a full-blown rose,
Flushing his brow, and in his painèd heart
Made purple riot: then doth he propose
A stratagem, that makes the beldame start:
"A cruel man and impious thou art: 140

Sweet lady, let her pray, and sleep, and dream
Alone with her good angels, far apart
From wicked men like thee. Go, go!—I deem
Thou canst not surely be the same that thou didst seem."

"I will not harm her, by all saints I swear,"   145
Quoth Porphyro: "O may I ne'er find grace
When my weak voice shall whisper its last prayer,
If one of her soft ringlets I displace,
Or look with ruffian passion in her face:
Good Angela, believe me by these tears;   150
Or I will, even in a moment's space,
Awake, with horrid shout, my foemen's ears,
And beard them, though they be more fanged than wolves and
        bears."

"Ah! why wilt thou affright a feeble soul?
A poor, weak, palsy-stricken, churchyard thing,—   155
Whose passing-bell may ere the midnight toll;
Whose prayers for thee, each morn and evening,
Were never missed."—Thus plaining, doth she bring
A gentler speech from burning Porphyro;
So woeful, and of such deep sorrowing,   160
That Angela gives promise she will do
Whatever he shall wish, betide her weal or woe.

Which was, to lead him, in close secrecy,
Even to Madeline's chamber, and there hide
Him in a closet, of such privacy   165
That he might see her beauty unespied,
And win perhaps that night a peerless bride,
While legioned fairies paced the coverlet,
And pale enchantment held her sleepy-eyed.
Never on such a night have lovers met,   170
Since Merlin paid his Demon all the monstrous debt.

"It shall be as thou wishest," said the dame:
"All cates and dainties shall be storèd there
Quickly on this feast-night: by the tambour frame
Her own lute thou wilt see: no time to spare,   175
For I am slow and feeble, and scarce dare
On such a catering trust my dizzy head.

Wait here, my child, with patience; kneel in prayer
The while. Ah! thou must needs the lady wed,
Or may I never leave my grave among the dead."   180

So saying, she hobbled off with busy fear.
The lover's endless minutes slowly passed;
The dame returned, and whispered in his ear
To follow her; with agèd eyes aghast
From fright of dim espial. Safe at last,   185
Through many a dusky gallery, they gain
The maiden's chamber, silken, hushed, and chaste;
Where Porphyro took covert, pleased amain.
His poor guide hurried back with agues in her brain.

Her falt'ring hand upon the balustrade,   190
Old Angela was feeling for the stair,
When Madeline, St. Agnes' charmèd maid,
Rose, like a missioned spirit, unaware:
With silver taper's light, and pious care,
She turned, and down the agèd gossip led   195
To a safe level matting. Now prepare,
Young Porphyro, for gazing on that bed;
She comes, she comes again, like ring-dove frayed and fled.

Out went the taper as she hurried in;
Its little smoke, in pallid moonshine, died: 200
She closed the door, she panted, all akin
To spirits of the air, and visions wide:
No uttered syllable, or, woe betide!
But to her heart, her heart was voluble,
Paining with eloquence her balmy side;   205
As though a tonguless nightingale should swell
Her throat in vain, and die, heart-stifled, in her dell.

A casement high and triple-arched there was,
All garlanded with carven imag'ries
Of fruits, and flowers, and bunches of knot-grass,   210
And diamonded with panes of quaint device,
Innumerable of stains and splendid dyes,
As are the tiger-moth's deep-damasked wings;
And in the midst, 'mong thousand heraldries,
And twilight saints, and dim emblazonings,   215
A shielded scutcheon blushed with blood of queens and kings.

Full on this casement shone the wintry moon,
And threw warm gules on Madeline's fair breast,
As down she knelt for heaven's grace and boon;
Rose-bloom fell on her hands, together pressed,   220
And on her silver cross soft amethyst,
And on her hair a glory, like a saint:
She seemed a splendid angel, newly dressed,
Save wings, for heaven:—Porphyro grew faint:
She knelt, so pure a thing, so free from mortal taint.   225

Anon his heart revives: her vespers done,
Of all its wreathèd pearls her hair she frees;
Unclasps her warmèd jewels one by one;
Loosens her fragrant bodice; by degrees
Her rich attire creeps rustling to her knees: 230
Half-hidden, like a mermaid in seaweed,
Pensive awhile she dreams awake, and sees,
In fancy, fair St. Agnes in her bed,
But dares not look behind, or all the charm is fled.

Soon, trembling in her soft and chilly nest,   235
In sort of wakeful swoon, perplexed she lay,
Until the poppied warmth of sleep oppressed
Her soothèd limbs, and soul fatigued away;
Flown, like a thought, until the morrow-day;
Blissfully havened both from joy and pain;   240
Clasped like a missal where swart Paynims pray;
Blinded alike from sunshine and from rain,
As though a rose should shut, and be a bud again.

Stol'n to this paradise, and so entranced,
Porphyro gazed upon her empty dress,   245
And listened to her breathing, if it chanced
To wake into a slumberous tenderness;
Which when he heard, that minute did he bless,
And breathed himself: then from the closet crept,
Noiseless as fear in a wide wilderness,   250
And over the hushed carpet, silent, stepped,
And 'tween the curtains peeped, where, lo!—how fast she slept.

Then by the bedside, where the faded moon
Made a dim, silver twilight, soft he set

A table, and, half anguished, threw thereon   255
A cloth of woven crimson, gold, and jet:—
O for some drowsy Morphean amulet!
The boisterous, midnight, festive clarion,
The kettle-drum, and far-heard clarionet,
Affray his ears, though but in dying tone:—   260
The hall door shuts again, and all the noise is gone.

And still she slept an azure-lidded sleep,
In blanchèd linen, smooth, and lavendered,
While he from forth the closet brought a heap
Of candied apple, quince, and plum, and gourd;   265
With jellies soother than the creamy curd,
And lucent syrups, tinct with cinnamon;
Manna and dates, in argosy transferred
From Fez; and spicèd dainties, every one,
From silken Samarcand to cedared Lebanon.   270

These delicates he heaped with glowing hand
On golden dishes and in baskets bright
Of wreathèd silver: sumptuous they stand
In the retired quiet of the night,
Filling the chilly room with perfume light.—   275
"And now, my love, my seraph fair, awake!
Thou art my heaven, and I thine eremite:
Open thine eyes, for meek St. Agnes' sake,
Or I shall drowse beside thee, so my soul doth ache."

Thus whispering, his warm, unnervèd arm   280
Sank in her pillow. Shaded was her dream
By the dusk curtains:—'twas a midnight charm
Impossible to melt as icèd stream:
The lustrous salvers in the moonlight gleam;
Broad golden fringe upon the carpet lies: 285
It seemed he never, never could redeem
From such a steadfast spell his lady's eyes;
So mused awhile, entoiled in woofèd phantasies.

Awakening up, he took her hollow lute,—
Tumultuous,—and, in chords that tenderest be,   290
He played an ancient ditty, long since mute,
In Provence called, "La belle dame sans merci,"

Close to her ear touching the melody;—
Wherewith disturbed she uttered a soft moan:
He ceased—she panted quick—and suddenly   295
Her blue affrayèd eyes wide open shone:
Upon his knees he sank, pale as smooth-sculptured stone.

Her eyes were open, but she still beheld,
Now wide awake, the vision of her sleep:
There was a painful change, that nigh expelled   300
The blisses of her dream so pure and deep,
At which fair Madeline began to weep,
And moan forth witless words with many a sigh;
While still her gaze on Porphyro would keep;
Who knelt, with joinèd hands and piteous eye,   305
Fearing to move or speak, she looked so dreamingly.

"Ah, Porphyro!" said she, "but even now
Thy voice was at sweet tremble in mine ear,
Made tunable with every sweetest vow;
And those sad eyes were spiritual and clear: 310
How changed thou art! how pallid, chill, and drear!
Give me that voice again, my Porphyro,
Those looks immortal, those complainings dear!
Oh, leave me not in this eternal woe,
For if thou diest, my Love, I know not where to go."   315

Beyond a mortal man impassioned far
At these voluptuous accents, he arose,
Ethereal, flushed, and like a throbbing star
Seen 'mid the sapphire heaven's deep repose;
Into her dream he melted, as the rose   320
Blendeth its odor with the violet,—
Solution sweet: meantime the frostwind blows
Like Love's alarum, pattering the sharp sleet
Against the window-panes; St. Agnes' moon hath set.

'Tis dark: quick pattereth the flaw-blown sleet: 325
"This is no dream, my bride, my Madeline!"
'Tis dark: the icèd gusts still rave and beat:
"No dream, alas! alas! and woe is mine!
Porphyro will leave me here to fade and pine.—
Cruel! what traitor could thee hither bring?   330

I curse not, for my heart is lost in thine,
  Though thou forsakest a deceivèd thing;—
A dove forlorn and lost with sick unprunèd wing."

  "My Madeline! sweet dreamer! lovely bride!
  Say, may I be for aye thy vassal blest?   335
  Thy beauty's shield, heart-shaped and vermeil dyed?
  Ah, silver shrine, here will I take my rest
  After so many hours of toil and quest,
    A famished pilgrim,—saved by miracle.
  Though I have found, I will not rob thy nest   340
    Saving of thy sweet self; if thou think'st well
To trust, fair Madeline, to no rude infidel.

  "Hark! 'tis an elfin-storm from faery land,
  Of haggard seeming, but a boon indeed:
  Arise—arise! the morning is at hand;—   345
  The bloated wassailers will never heed:—
  Let us away, my love, with happy speed;
  There are no ears to hear, or eyes to see,—
    Drowned all in Rhenish and the sleepy mead:
  Awake! arise! my love, and fearless be,   350
For o'er the southern moors I have a home for thee."

  She hurried at his words, beset with fears,
  For there were sleeping dragons all around,
  At glaring watch, perhaps, with ready spears—
  Down the wide stairs a darkling way they found.—   355
  In all the house was heard no human sound.
  A chain-drooped lamp was flickering by each door;
    The arras, rich with horseman, hawk, and hound,
  Fluttered in the besieging wind's uproar;
And the long carpets rose along the gusty floor.   360

  They glide, like phantoms, into the wide hall;
  Like phantoms, to the iron porch they glide;
  Where lay the Porter, in uneasy sprawl,
  With a huge empty flagon by his side:
  The wakeful bloodhound rose, and shook his hide,   365
  But his sagacious eye an inmate owns:
    By one, and one, the bolts full easy slide:—
  The chains lie silent on the footworn stones;—
The key turns, and the door upon its hinges groans.

And they are gone: aye, ages long ago   370
These lovers fled away into the storm.
That night the Baron dreamt of many a woe,
And all his warrior-guests, with shade and form
Of witch, and demon, and large coffin-worm,
Were long be-nightmared. Angela the old   375
Died palsy-twitched, with meager face deform;
The Beadsman, after thousand avès told,
For aye unsought for slept among his ashes cold.

EXERCISE:

This poem does give a fully presented narrative, but the emphasis is not finally on the narrative. Where does the emphasis
lie? In answering this question consider the use of description
in the poem, the general mood, and the function of the last
stanza.

LOVE AMONG THE RUINS

ROBERT BROWNING (1812–1889)

Where the quiet-colored end of evening smiles
    Miles and miles
On the solitary pastures where our sheep
    Half-asleep
Tinkle homeward through the twilight, stray or stop   5
    As they crop—
Was the site once of a city great and gay
    (So they say),
Of our country's very capital, its prince
    Ages since   10
Held his court in, gathered councils, wielding far
    Peace or war.

Now,—the country does not even boast a tree,
    As you see,
To distinguish slopes of verdure, certain rills   15
    From the hills
Intersect and give a name to (else they run
    Into one),

Where the domed and daring palace shot its spires
  Up like fires   20
O'er the hundred-gated circuit of a wall
  Bounding all,
Made of marble, men might march on nor be pressed,
  Twelve abreast.

And such plenty and perfection, see, of grass   25
  Never was!
Such a carpet as, this summer-time, o'er-spreads
  And embeds
Every vestige of the city, guessed alone,
  Stock or stone—   30
Where a multitude of men breathed joy and woe
  Long ago;
Lust of glory pricked their hearts up, dread of shame
  Struck them tame;
And that glory and that shame alike, the gold   35
  Bought and sold.

Now,—the single little turret that remains
  On the plains,
By the caper overrooted, by the gourd
  Overscored,   40
While the patching houseleek's head of blossom winks
  Through the chinks—
Marks the basement whence a tower in ancient time
  Sprang sublime,
And a burning ring, all round, the chariots traced   45
  As they raced,
And the monarch and his minions and his dames
  Viewed the games.

And I know—while thus the quiet-colored eve
  Smiles to leave   50
To their folding, all our many tinkling fleece
  In such peace,
And the slopes and rills in undistinguished gray
  Melt away—
That a girl with eager eyes and yellow hair   55
  Waits me there
In the turret whence the charioteers caught soul
  For the goal,

When the king looked, where she looks now, breathless,
    dumb
    Till I come.   60

But he looked upon the city, every side,
    Far and wide,
All the mountains topped with temples, all the glades'
    Colonnades,
All the causeys, bridges, aqueducts,—and then,   65
    All the men!
When I do come, she will speak not, she will stand,
    Either hand
On my shoulder, give her eyes the first embrace
    Of my face,   70
Ere we rush, ere we extinguish sight and speech
    Each on each.

In one year they sent a million fighters forth
    South and North,
And they built their gods a brazen pillar high   75
    As the sky,
Yet reserved a thousand chariots in full force—
    Gold, of course.
Oh heart! oh blood that freezes, blood that burns!
    Earth's returns   80
For whole centuries of folly, noise and sin!
    Shut them in,
With their triumphs and their glories and the rest!
    Love is best.

EXERCISE:

What is the relation of the last statement of the poem to the
entire body of the poem?

CORINNA'S GOING A-MAYING

ROBERT HERRICK (1591–1674)

Get up, get up for shame, the blooming morn
Upon her wings presents the god unshorn.

See how Aurora throws her fair
Fresh-quilted colors through the air:
Get up, sweet slug-a-bed, and see   5
The dew bespangling herb and tree.
Each flower has wept and bowèd toward the east
Above an hour since: yet you not dressed;
    Nay; not so much as out of bed?
    When all the birds have matins said   10
    And sung their thankful hymns, 't is sin,
    Nay, profanation, to keep in,
Whenas a thousand virgins on this day
Spring, sooner than the lark, to fetch in May.

Rise, and put on your foliage, and be seen   15
To come forth, like the spring-time, fresh and green,
    And sweet as Flora. Take no care
    For jewels for your gown or hair:
    Fear not; the leaves will strew
    Gems in abundance upon you: 20
Besides, the childhood of the day has kept,
Against you come, some orient pearls unwept;
    Come and receive them while the light
    Hangs on the dew-locks of the night:
    And Titan on the eastern hill   25
    Retires himself, or else stands still
Till you come forth. Wash, dress, be brief in praying:
Few beads are best when once we go a-Maying.

Come, my Corinna, come; and, coming mark
How each field turns a street, each street a park   30
    Made green and trimmed with trees; see how
    Devotion gives each house a bough
    Or branch: each porch, each door ere this
    An ark, a tabernacle is,
Made up of white-thorn, neatly interwove;   35
As if here were those cooler shades of love.
    Can such delights be in the street
    And open fields and we not see't?
    Come, we'll abroad; and let's obey
    The proclamation made for May: 40
And sin no more, as we have done, by staying;
But, my Corinna, come, let's go a-Maying.

There's not a budding boy or girl this day
But is got up, and gone to bring in May.
    A deal of youth, ere this, is come   45
    Back, and with white-thorn laden home.
    Some have despatched their cakes and cream
    Before that we have left to dream:
And some have wept, and wooed, and plighted troth,
And chose their priest, ere we can cast off sloth: 50
    Many a green-gown has been given;
    Many a kiss, both odd and even:
    Many a glance too has been sent
    From out the eye, love's firmament;
Many a jest told of the keys betraying   55
This night, and locks picked, yet we're not a-Maying.

Come, let us go while we are in our prime;
And take the harmless folly of the time.
    We shall grow old apace, and die
    Before we know our liberty.   60
    Our life is short, and our days run
    As fast away as does the sun;
And, as a vapor or a drop of rain,
Once lost, can ne'er be found again,
    So when or you or I are made   65
    A fable, song, or fleeting shade,
    All love, all liking, all delight
    Lies drowned with us in endless night.
Then while time serves, and we are but decaying,
Come, my Corinna, come let's go a-Maying.   70

EXERCISE:

Write a comparison of the interpretation of this poem with that
of "Love among the Ruins."

THE PULLEY

GEORGE HERBERT (1593–1633)

    When God at first made man,
Having a glass of blessing standing by;
    'Let us,' said he, 'pour on him all we can:

Let the world's riches, which dispersèd lie,
   Contract into a span.'   5

  So Strength first made a way;
Then Beauty flowed; then Wisdom, Honor, Pleasure.
  When almost all was out, God made a stay,
Perceiving that alone, of all his treasure,
   Rest in the bottom lay.   10

  'For if I should,' said he,
'Bestow this jewel also on my creature,
  He would adore my gifts instead of me,
And rest in Nature, not the God of Nature;
   So both should losers be.   15

  'Yet let him keep the rest,
But keep them with repining restlessness;
  Let him be rich and weary, that at least,
If goodness lead him not, yet weariness
   May toss him to my breast.'   20

EXERCISE:

The method of this poem is *allegorical* (*Glossary*). What advantages does the poet gain by such a method in this poem?

AFTERWORD

In the two sections just completed we have been considering
poems in which the narrative element is relatively prominent.
In opening Section I, we decided to use our interest in narrative
as a device for leading into the study of poetry, because narrative
presents the most obvious form which our interest in the stuff
of literature takes. As we pointed out there, however, and as
the analyses of various poems have indicated, narrative is only
one element among several which the poet may use to gain his
effect. The poet is not content with the narrative as such, even
in the poems of the first group, which have a direct and promi-

nent use of narrative. He is primarily interested in provoking a certain reaction toward the narrative. He wants to present the material of the narrative so that the reader will have a certain feeling toward it and will grasp a certain interpretation of it.

But this is also true of the writers of novels or short stories in prose, for such writers, like the poet, are more than reporters giving us a bare statement of facts and events. Indeed, it is not easy, except in regard to the use of verse, to make an absolute distinction between poetry and prose fiction, but it is possible on the basis of the poems we have already analyzed to state a difference in the following terms. Poetry *tends* toward *concentration* (*Glossary*). A poem treating, let us say, the story of Johnie Armstrong is a great deal shorter than a piece of prose fiction on the same subject would be. In general, it may be said that the writer of prose fiction tries to convince his reader by the accumulation of detail, and that the poet tries to convince his reader by the sharpness of selected detail. The distinction, as we have suggested, is not absolute, but the analyses which have already been studied will provide instances of the use which poetry makes of details. The poet tries to make a direct appeal to the imagination. The suggestiveness, which we have already commented on in several analyses, is an example of this. This method may be described as a short cut to the effect desired, as compared with the more round-about method which prose fiction is forced to use. In the poems that follow we shall discover other methods whereby the poet can condense his material far more than the writer of prose fiction is able to do.

The effect of this condensation in poetry is a sense of greater *intensity* (*Glossary*) than is usually found in prose fiction. If poetry employs fewer details than prose fiction, then it stands to reason that to gain a comparable result the details must (1) be more effective in themselves than those in prose fiction—that is, they must be very carefully selected—and/or (2) they must be so arranged that they will have the greatest effect on the reader. The arrangement or *form* (*Glossary*) of a poem, then, is a most important matter and is directly connected with the concentration and intensity of poetry. In the analyses previously presented we have touched on certain aspects of the form of various poems, for the form of a poem must obviously differ from case to case according to the effect intended. It is enough at this point however, if we see that the form of poetry in general as contrasted with the form of prose fiction is more closely organized. For instance, in poetry even the rhythms themselves are put into more definite form—into a pattern which we call meter. In Section IV we shall discuss this matter at length, but for the present it is only necessary to be aware of the contribution meter makes to the concentration and intensity of poetry.

SECTION III - *objective description*

FOREWORD

Most of the poems in this section would be called descriptive. For example, the poems, "The Main-Deep," "Pear Tree," and "Heat," which will be presented early in this section, apparently give, as accurately as the poet could manage, a direct impression received through the poet's senses. In the poems of Section I and Section II the element of narrative is relatively prominent, but, as we have seen, the final intention of these poems is not merely to tell a story. In the same way, the final intention of the poems in the present section is not merely to give a picture or a description. But what is the final intention, the meaning, of such a poem as "The Main-Deep," which appears merely to give an impression of the sea?

THE MAIN-DEEP

JAMES STEPHENS (1882–   )

The long, rolling,
Steady-pouring,
Deep-trenchèd
Green billow:

The wide-topped,   5
Unbroken,
Green-glacid,
Slow-sliding,

Cold-flushing,
On—on—on—   10
Chill-rushing,
Hush-hushing,

Hush—hushing . . .

When we read this poem, although our imagination may call up a picture of the sea, we are having an experience different from the experience of looking at the real sea. In other words the poem does not attempt to provide us with a substitute for a trip to the seashore. If providing such a substitute were the purpose of a poem, then the poem would have very slight justification for being, for it can provide only a very inferior substitute for the real object in nature. The interest and pleasure one takes in the poem is of a different kind from the interest and pleasure one would take in the real object in nature. This can easily be proved if a reader studies his reaction to a poetic treatment of an object that in real nature would be unpleasant to look at. A pair of bloody hands would, in reality, be a disgusting rather than a pleasant sight. Let us take a passage from Shakespeare's *Macbeth,* however, that treats such a sight. Macbeth has just killed the king, Duncan, and is shocked at the sight of the blood on his hands:

> What hands are here! Ha! they pluck out mine eyes.
> Will all great Neptune's ocean wash this blood
> Clean from my hand? No, this my hand will rather
> The multitudinous seas incarnadine,
> Making the green one red.

The passage does not disgust us. Rather, it stirs our imagination so that we really grasp Macbeth's own feeling that nothing in the world can remove the guilt from him. The blood has become an expression of a psychological fact.

But one might argue that a poem like "The Main-Deep" is different, because the passage from *Macbeth* comes in a play which provides us with a situation giving a basis for the interpretation of the expressive quality of the passage. This is true to a certain extent. We know nothing about the situation of "The Main-Deep" except that a human being, the poet, is looking at the sea. We know nothing about the circumstances leading up to the event and nothing about the spectator except what we can read by implication from the poem. Indeed the presence of a human being is not even mentioned in the poem, but we feel, nevertheless, that the poem is an expression of a human being; it involves an ordering and therefore an *interpretation* (*Glossary*).

How is this true?

First, we know that the poet has assumed a particular view of the sea to the exclusion of other possible views. For instance, the sea in "The Main-Deep" is not a stormy one. The poet, then, has selected the particular view that will suit his purpose.

Second, his selectivity has been exercised further in regard to the details from the particular view. We know that it is obviously impossible for the poet to put into a poem the enormous body of real detail in his view of the sea. He must select details to build up the poem. But the selection is not performed at random. It must be directed by some principle if the finished poem is to appear coherent in its organization and unified in its effect. Both types of selection mentioned show that the poem is expressive of the action of a human mind contemplating the sea. The sea that comes over to our imagination from the poem is not the sea that we might chance upon in a walk along the coast. Such a chance view might provoke any of a number of different feelings and reactions in us, or perhaps none at all; but the sea in the poem has been arranged by the poet so as to cause the reaction he wished to communicate. That reaction communicated by the poet is his interpretation of the material—the material being in this case a view of the sea. The selection, then, has been governed by the intended interpretation.

Let us try to analyze the way in which the present poem, which seems at first glance so purely descriptive and *objective* (*Glossary*), embodies, after all, an interpretation.

The poet has chosen, as it were, one billow on which the attention can be directed and which can give a kind of focus for the poem. The concentration on the single billow has another advantage, for while the sea as a whole, though agitated, does not progress, the single billow does seem to move forward. The eyes of the reader seem to be directed to a single billow advancing toward him, as though he were on a ship at sea. Only those qualities of the billow are singled out for comment that will not distract him from a concentrated gaze at the billow itself; the poet does not comment on the general scene. There is no direct reference, even, to the fact that the billow approaches the spectator but we gather this from the nature of the billow's movement. In the third stanza with the line

On—on—on—

we get an impression of increased speed, an impression not only from the words but from the additional accent in the line (no other line has more than two accents) that implies the hurry and piling up as the billow approaches. Further, this stanza gives a reference to the temperature of the billow, "cold-flushing," and "chill-rushing," as though on its nearer approach the spectator could almost tell the coldness of the water, something one could not think of in connection with a distant wave. Then with the last rush the billow passes and there is only the thin line of receding foam. This effect is supported by the repetition of the line

Hush—hushing . . .

We have here a process working itself out to a natural fulfilment. Out of the beautiful and splendid tumult of the billow comes the moment of poise when the process is completed. The idea is not stated, that is, the poem seems objective and descriptive, but the poem has been so arranged that the effect is communicated to the reader. Even less does the poet present an application of his idea, as is the case in some poems; he does not moralize. He does not say, for instance, that the billow is like man's life, or that the billow shows us the process of struggle and fulfilment, or that nature always holds out a promise of peace, or anything of that sort. It might be possible to write a poem about the sea along those lines that would not necessarily be better or worse than "The Main-Deep," but it would be a different kind of poem. James Stephens, however, leaves the reader, apparently, as close to the simple experience of looking at the sea as possible; but he has given an interpretation because, by his management of the materials, he has made the sea give the reader one feeling, the feeling of peace and fulfilment, and not any of the almost innumerable other feelings which the sea might be used by a poet to communicate. The reader may or may not take the step himself of attributing a specific application to the poem. The poem may be richer and more exciting if the reader does not fix on one specific application of the feeling and idea; for if he does leave it so, the poem has potential in it an attitude one might take toward many different experiences of life.

The following poems obviously bear a close resemblance to "The Main-Deep" in their objective and descriptive quality.

PEAR TREE

H. D. (1886–   )

Silver dust
lifted from the earth,
higher than my arms reach,
you have mounted.
O silver,   5
higher than my arms reach
you front us with great mass;
no flower ever opened
so staunch a white leaf,
no flower ever parted silver   10
from such rare silver;

O white pear,
your flower-tufts,
thick on the branch,
bring summer and ripe fruits   15
in their purple hearts.

HEAT

H. D. (1886–   )

O wind, rend open the heat,
cut apart the heat,
rend it to tatters.

Fruit cannot drop
through this thick air—   5
fruit cannot fall into heat
that presses up and blunts
the points of pears
and rounds the grapes.

Cut through the heat—   10
plow through it,
turning it on either side
of your path.

IN A STATION OF THE METRO

EZRA POUND (1885–   )

The apparition of these faces in the crowd;
Petals on a wet, black bough.

These poems by H. D. (Hilda Doolittle) and Ezra Pound
obviously bear a close resemblance to "The Main-Deep" in their
objective and descriptive quality. But, as we have said, no poem
is ever purely objective, for the fact of the poem involves an
observer who necessarily has some attitude toward the material,
since, otherwise, he would not write the poem at all. And further,
the selection of details of the material for a poem means in itself
that the poet is controlling the effect on the reader; if the reader
himself should see a pear tree in bloom the chances are that
he would have a reaction somewhat different from that of H.D.
That is, the poem, like all poems, embodies an interpretation.
Both H. D. and Ezra Pound belonged at one time to a group
of poets who called themselves "Imagists" (*Glossary*), a group
that also included Amy Lowell and John Gould Fletcher. One
of the theories of this group was that poetry should concern
itself with presenting to the reader a very sharp, clear picture,
or image, and should not attempt to discuss ideas or give applications of the meanings of the images presented. The poems
here are very good examples of "imagist poetry," but as we have

seen, they involve interpretation on the part of the poet. Let us take Pound's poem describing the faces of people in a subway station.

> The apparition of these faces in the crowd;
> Petals on a wet, black bough.

Suppose he had written:

> The apparition of these faces in the crowd;
> Dead leaves caught in the gutter's stream.

Or:

> The apparition of these faces in the crowd;
> Dry leaves blown down the dry gutter.

The revised versions and the original version communicate to the reader very different interpretations of exactly the same sight, the faces in the subway. In the original version the reader catches a glimpse of something beautiful and fresh in the most unlikely place, and therefore grasps an interpretation that is potentially applicable to a great deal of experience. The poem is similar in this respect to the one which follows.

DUST OF SNOW

ROBERT FROST (1875–   )

> The way a crow
> Shook down on me
> The dust of snow
> From a hemlock tree
>
> Has given my heart   5
> A change of mood
> And saved some part
> Of a day I had rued.

But Frost makes his poem much more explicit than does Pound in that he presents his poem in the form of a little incident and also defines the effect of the incident on the poet himself.

But to return to the comparison of the revised versions with the original version of Pound's poem. The comparison of the faces to leaves caught on the water in a gutter or blown down a dry gutter by a gust of wind has just as much basis in common sense or logic as does the comparison to white petals on a bough. The subway station does bear a certain resemblance to a gutter; the stream of people hurrying down bears likewise a resemblance to a stream of water, as the ordinary use of the word "stream" in such a connection in ordinary speech indicates; or we might say that the roar of the subway train and the gust of its passing reminds one of the wind; and the comparison of faces to leaves is probably as valid as the comparison to petals. As we inspect the different implications of the sets of comparisons, however, we see that the interpretations are different. The revised versions give an impression of the confusion of the crowd, the people seem lost and dead, going from one place to another driven by forces over which they have no control. Even if a reader does not analyze a poem at all he is affected by the poem; we usually say that one poem has a certain mood, and another poem has another mood. But this mood that an apparently objective poem gives is the thing the poet communicates; it is what he has used the material of the poem for, and it is the result of the way he has handled the material.

But poems that merely give us one or a few "images" or aim at a single mood are usually short, for such poems have no narrative, no incident, no presentation of character, and no progression of interpretation, that is, no thinking about the various different ways in which an idea or interpretation might be applied to life. Such poems, therefore, have a more limited range of interest. (It is quite significant that most of the poets in the Imagist group soon gave up the writing of poetry that would strictly fit their theory. The theory of Imagism limited them too much. For instance, "Patterns," by Amy Lowell, which has already been studied, is not an Imagist poem, although Amy Lowell, was very prominent among that group of poets.

And James Stephens, who was not a member of the Imagist group, has written a very few poems similar to his "The Main-Deep.")

The sharp presentation of images and description that appeals clearly to the imagination are important factors, however, in all good poetry, in poetry that aims at creating mood, and in poetry that offers very complicated interpretations.

SPRING

WILLIAM SHAKESPEARE (1564–1616)

I.

When daisies pied and violets blue
   And lady-smocks all silver-white
And cuckoo-buds of yellow hue
   Do paint the meadows with delight,
The cuckoo then, on every tree,   5
Mocks married men; for thus sings he,
               "Cuckoo;
Cuckoo, cuckoo": O, word of fear,
Unpleasing to a married ear!

II.

When shepherds pipe on oaten straws,   10
   And merry larks are ploughmen's clocks,
When turtles tread, and rooks, and daws,
   And maidens bleach their summer smocks,
The cuckoo then, on every tree,
Mocks married men; for thus sings he,   15
               "Cuckoo;
Cuckoo, cuckoo": O, word of fear,
Unpleasing to a married ear!

WINTER

When icicles hang by the wall,
  And Dick the shepherd blows his nail,
And Tom bears logs into the hall,
  And milk come frozen home in pail,
When blood is nipped and ways be foul,   5
Then nightly sings the staring owl,
"Tu-whit, tu-who!" a merry note,
While greasy Joan doth keel the pot.

When all aloud the wind doth blow,
  And coughing drowns the parson's saw,   10
And birds sit brooding in the snow,
  And Marian's nose looks red and raw,
When roasted crabs hiss in the bowl,
Then nightly sings the staring owl,
"Tu-whit, tu-who!" a merry note,   15
While greasy Joan doth keel the pot.

            (From *Love's Labor's Lost*)

EXERCISE:

   1. On what principle has the poet selected the details which
he gives in these two songs?
   2. How do these details contribute to the mood of each?

TO SPRING

WILLIAM BLAKE (1757–1827)

O thou with dewy locks, who lookest down
Through the clear windows of the morning, turn
Thine angel eyes upon our western isle,
Which in full choir hails thy approach, O Spring!

The hills tell each other, and the listening   5
Valleys hear; all our longing eyes are turned
Up to thy bright pavilions: issue forth,
And let thy holy feet visit our clime.

Come o'er the eastern hills, and let our winds
Kiss thy perfumèd garments; let us taste   10
Thy morn and evening breath; scatter thy pearls
Upon our love-sick land that mourns for thee.

O deck her forth with thy fair fingers; pour
Thy soft kisses on her bosom; and put
Thy golden crown upon her languished head,   15
Whose modest tresses were bound up for thee.

EXERCISE:

Compare the mood of this poem with that of "Spring," by
Shakespeare and try to define some of the factors that account
for any difference.

WINTER WINDS

JAMES THOMSON (1700–1748)

Nature! great parent! whose unceasing hand
Rolls round the seasons of the changeful year,
How mighty, how majestic, are thy works!
With what a pleasing dread they swell the soul,
That sees astonished! and astonished sings!   5
Ye too, ye Winds! that now begin to blow
With boisterous sweep, I raise my voice to you.
Where are your stores, ye powerful beings! say,
Where your aerial magazines, reserved
To swell the brooding terrors of the storm?   10
In what far-distant region of the sky,
Hushed in deep silence, sleep ye when 'tis calm?
    When from the pallid sky the sun descends,
With many a spot, that o'er his glaring orb
Uncertain wanders, stained; red fiery streaks   15
Begin to flush around. The reeling clouds
Stagger with dizzy poise, as doubting yet
Which master to obey; while, rising slow,
Blank in the leaden-colored east, the moon

Wears a wan circle round her blunted horns.   20
Seen through the turbid, fluctuating air,
The stars obtuse emit a shivering ray;
Or frequent seem to shoot athwart the gloom,
And long behind them trail the whitening blaze.
Snatched in short eddies, plays the withered leaf;   25
And on the flood the dancing feather floats.
With broadened nostrils to the sky upturned,
The conscious heifer snuffs the stormy gale.
E'en as the matron, at her nightly task,
With pensive labor draws the flaxen thread,   30
The wasted taper and the crackling flame
Foretell the blast.   But chief the plumy race,
The tenants of the sky, its changes speak.
Retiring from the downs, where all day long
They picked their scanty fare, a blackening train   35
Of clamorous rooks thick-urge their weary flight,
And seek the closing shelter of the grove.
Assiduous, in his bower, the wailing owl
Plies his sad song. The cormorant on high
Wheels from the deep, and screams along the land.   40
Loud shrieks the soaring hern; and with wild wing
The circling sea-fowl cleave the flaky clouds.
Ocean, unequal pressed, with broken tide
And blind commotion heaves; while from the shore,
Ate into caverns by the restless wave,   45
And forest-rustling mountains, comes a voice
That, solemn-sounding, bids the world prepare.
Then issues forth the storm with sudden burst,
And hurls the whole precipitated air
Down, in a torrent. On the passive main   50
Descends the ethereal force, and with strong gust
Turns from its bottom the discolored deep.
Through the black night that sits immense around,
Lashed into foam, the fierce conflicting brine
Seems o'er a thousand raging waves to burn: 55
Meantime the mountain-billows, to the clouds
In dreadful tumult swelled, surge above surge,
Burst into chaos with tremendous roar,
And anchored navies from their stations drive,
Wild as the winds, across the howling waste   60
Of mighty waters: now the inflated wave

Straining they scale, and now impetuous shoot
Into the secret chambers of the deep,
The wintry Baltic thundering o'er their head.
Emerging thence again, before the breath   65
Of full-exerted heaven they wing their course,
And dart on distant coasts; if some sharp rock,
Or shoal insidious, break not their career,
And in loose fragments fling them floating round.

(From *The Seasons*)

EXERCISE:

Compare the mood of this selection with that of "To Spring,"
by Blake.

form — 1st 10 3 5 3 5 3 5 / remainder iambic tetrameter

IL PENSEROSO

JOHN MILTON (1608–1674)

Hence, vain deluding joys,
The brood of Folly, without father bred!
How little you bested,
Or fill the fixèd mind with all your toys!
Dwell in some idle brain,   5
And fancies fond with gaudy shapes possess
As thick and numberless
As the gay motes that people the sun beams,
Or likest hovering dreams,
The fickle pensioners of Morpheus' train.   10
But, hail! thou goddess sage and holy,
Hail, divinest Melancholy,
Whose saintly visage is too bright
To hit the sense of human sight,
And, therefore, to our weaker view,   15
O'erlaid with black, staid Wisdom's hue;
Black, but such as in esteem
Prince Memnon's sister might beseem,
Or that starred Ethiop queen that strove
To set her beauty's praise above   20

The sea-nymphs, and their powers offended.
Yet thou art higher far descended;
Thee bright-haired Vesta, long of yore,
To solitary Saturn bore;
His daughter she; in Saturn's reign   25
Such mixture was not held a stain.
Oft in glimmering bowers and glades
He met her, and in secret shades
Of woody Ida's inmost grove,
Whilst yet there was no fear of Jove.   30
  Come, pensive nun, devout and pure,
Sober, steadfast, and demure,
All in a robe of darkest grain
Flowing with majestic train,
And sable stole of cypress lawn   35
Over thy decent shoulders drawn.
Come, but keep thy wonted state,
With even step, and musing gait,
And looks commércing with the skies,
Thy rapt soul sitting in thine eyes: 40
There, held in holy passion still,
Forget thyself to marble, till,
With a sad leaden downward cast,
Thou fix them on the earth as fast.
And join with thee calm Peace and Quiet,   45
Spare Fast, that oft with gods doth diet,
And hears the Muses, in a ring,
Aye round about Jove's altar sing.
And add to these retirèd Leisure,
That in trim gardens takes his pleasure.   50
But first, and chiefest, with thee bring,
Him that yon soars on golden wing,
Guiding the fiery-wheelèd throne,
The cherub Contemplation;
And the mute silence hist along,   55
'Less Philomel will deign a song,
In her sweetest saddest plight,
Smoothing the rugged brow of Night,
While Cynthia checks her dragon yoke
Gently o'er the accustomed oak.   60
Sweet bird, that shunn'st the noise of folly,
Most musical, most melancholy!

Thee, chantress, oft, the woods among,
I woo, to hear thy even-song;
And, missing thee, I walk unseen   65
On the dry smooth-shaven green,
To behold the wandering moon
Riding near her highest noon,
Like one that had been led astray
Through the heaven's wide pathless way,   70
And oft, as if her head she bowed,
Stooping through a fleecy cloud.
   Oft, on a plat of rising ground,
I hear the far-off curfew sound
Over some wide watered shore,   75
Swinging slow with sullen roar;
Or, if the air will not permit,
Some still, removèd place will fit,
Where glowing embers through the room
Teach light to counterfeit a gloom;   80
Far from all resort of mirth,
Save the cricket on the hearth,
Or the bellman's drowsy charm
To bless the doors from nightly harm.
   Or let my lamp, at midnight hour,   85
Be seen in some high lonely tower
Where I may oft outwatch the Bear
With thrice great Hermes, or unsphere
The spirit of Plato, to unfold
What worlds or what vast regions hold   90
The immortal mind that hath forsook
Her mansion in this fleshly nook,
And of those demons that are found
In fire, air, flood, or underground,
Whose power hath a true consent,   95
With planet or with element.
Sometime let gorgeous Tragedy,
In sceptered pall, come sweeping by,
Presenting Thebes, or Pelops' line,
Or the tale of Troy divine,   100
Or what (though rare) of later age
Ennobled hath the buskined stage.
   But, O, sad virgin! that thy power
Might raise Musæus from his bower;

Or bid the soul of Orpheus sing   105
Such notes as, warbled to the string,
Drew iron tears down Pluto's cheek,
And made hell grant what love did seek;
Or call up him that left half told
The story of Cambuscan bold,   110
Of Camball, and of Algarsife,
And who had Canacé to wife
That owned the virtuous ring and glass,
And of the wondrous horse of brass,
On which the Tartar king did ride;   115
And if aught else great bards beside
In sage and solemn tunes have sung,
Of tourneys, and of trophies hung,
Of forests, and enchantments drear,
Where more is meant than meets the ear.   120
    Thus, Night, oft see me in thy pale career,
Till civil-suited Morn appear,
Not tricked and frounced as she was wont
With the Attic boy to hunt,
But kerchieft in a comely cloud,   125
While rocking winds are piping loud;
Or ushered with a shower still,
When the gust hath blown his fill,
Ending on the rustling leaves,
With minute drops from off the eaves.   130
And, when the sun begins to fling
His flaring beams, me, goddess, bring
To archèd walks of twilight groves,
And shadows brown, that Sylvan loves,
Of pine, or monumental oak,   135
Where the rude axe with heavèd stroke
Was never heard the nymphs to daunt
Or fright them from their hallowed haunt.
There in close covert by some brook,
Where no profaner eye may look,   140
Hide me from day's garish eye,
While the bee, with honied thigh,
That at her flowery work doth sing,
And the waters murmuring,
With such concert as they keep,   145
Entice the dewy-feathered sleep;

And let some strange mysterious dream
Wave at his wings, in airy stream
Of lively portraiture displayed,
Softly on my eyelids laid.   150
And, as I wake, sweet music breathe
Above, about, or underneath,
Sent by some spirit to mortals good,
Or the unseen genius of the wood.
  But let my due feet never fail   155
To walk the studious cloister's pale,
And love the high embowèd roof,
With antique pillars massy proof,
And storied windows richly dight,
Casting a dim religious light: 160
There let the pealing organ blow
To the full-voiced choir below
In service high and anthems clear
As may with sweetness, through mine ear,
Dissolve me into ecstasies,   165
And bring all heaven before mine eyes.
  And may at last my weary age
Find out the peaceful hermitage,
The hairy gown and mossy cell,
Where I may sit and rightly spell   170
Of every star that heaven doth shew,
And every herb that sips the dew,
Till old experience do attain
To something like prophetic strain.
  These pleasures, Melancholy, give,   175
And I with thee will choose to live.

EXERCISE:

  How are the various details of this description related to each
other?

AFTER APPLE-PICKING

ROBERT FROST (1875–   )

My long two-pointed ladder's sticking through a tree
Toward heaven still,

And there's a barrel that I didn't fill
Beside it, and there may be two or three
Apples I didn't pick upon some bough.   5
But I am done with apple-picking now.
Essence of winter sleep is on the night,
The scent of apples: I am drowsing off.
I cannot rub the strangeness from my sight
I got from looking through a pane of glass   10
I skimmed this morning from the drinking trough
And held against the world of hoary grass.
It melted, and I let it fall and break.

But I was well
Upon my way to sleep before it fell,   15
And I could tell
What form my dreaming was about to take.
Magnified apples appear and disappear,
Stem-end and blossom-end,
And every fleck of russet showing clear.   20
My instep arch not only keeps the ache,
It keeps the pressure of a ladder-round.
I feel the ladder sway as the boughs bend.
And I keep hearing from the cellar bin
The rumbling sound   25
Of load on load of apples coming in.
For I have had too much
Of apple-picking: I am overtired
Of the great harvest I myself desired.
There were ten thousand fruit to touch,   30
Cherish in hand, lift down, and not let fall.
For all
That struck the earth,
No matter if not bruised or spiked with stubble,
Went surely to the cider-apple heap   35
As of no worth.
One can see what will trouble
This sleep of mine, whatever sleep it is.
Were he not gone,
The woodchuck could say whether it's like his   40
Long sleep, as I describe its coming on,
Or just some human sleep.

Exercise:

1. What means does the poet use to give a sense of autumn in New England?

2. How important for this poem, as contrasted with previous poems in this section, which do not define an observer, is the personal focus of the material?

3. The poet makes a much more specific interpretation of the material in this poem than is the case in previous poems in this section. Define this interpretation.

[handwritten annotations: 9 line stanza / 8 iambic pentameter / final line hexameter / a b a b c b c c / Spenserian stanza]

OCEAN

GEORGE GORDON, LORD BYRON (1788–1824)

Roll on, thou deep and dark blue Ocean—roll!
Ten thousand fleets sweep over thee in vain;
Man marks the earth with ruin—his control
Stops with the shore;—upon the watery plain
The wrecks are all thy deed, nor doth remain   5
A shadow of man's ravage, save his own,
When for a moment, like a drop of rain,
He sinks into thy depths with bubbling groan,
Without a grave, unknelled, uncoffined and unknown.

His steps are not upon thy paths—thy fields   10
Are not a spoil for him—thou dost arise
And shake him from thee; the vile strength he wields
For earth's destruction thou dost all despise
Spurning him from thy bosom to the skies,
And send'st him, shivering in thy playful spray,   15
And howling, to his Gods, where haply lies
His petty hope in some near port or bay,
And dashest him again to earth—there let him lay.

The armaments which thunderstrike the walls
Of rock-built cities, bidding nations quake,   20
And monarchs tremble in their capitals,
The oak leviathans, whose huge ribs make

Their clay creator the vain title take
Of lord of thee, and arbiter of war;
These are thy toys, and, as the snowy flake,   25
They melt into thy yeast of waves, which mar
Alike the Armada's pride, or spoils of Trafalgar.

Thy shores are empires, changed in all save thee—
Assyria, Greece, Rome, Carthage, what are they?
Thy waters washed them power while they were free,
And many a tyrant since; their shores obey   31
The stranger, slave or savage; their decay
Has dried up realms to deserts:—not so thou,
Unchangeable save to thy wild waves' play—
Time writes no wrinkle on thine azure brow—   35
Such as creation's dawn beheld, thou rollest now.

Thou glorious mirror, where the Almighty's form
Glasses itself in tempests: in all time,
Calm or convulsed—in breeze, or gale, or storm,
Icing the pole, or in the torrid clime   40
Dark-heaving;—boundless, endless, and sublime—
The image of Eternity—the throne
Of the Invisible; even from out thy slime
The monsters of the deep are made; each zone
Obeys thee; thou goest forth, dread, fathomless, alone. 45

(From *Childe Harold*)

EXERCISE:

Compare and contrast the method used in this poem for in-
terpreting the material with that employed in "The Main-Deep."

THE ROBIN

GEORGE DANIEL (1616–1657)

Poor bird! I do not envy thee;
Pleased in the gentle melody
    Of thy own song.
Let crabbèd winter silence all

The wingèd choir; he never shall   5
    Chain up thy tongue:
      Poor innocent:
When I would please myself, I look on thee;
And guess some sparks of that felicity,
      That self-content.   10

When the bleak face of winter spreads
The earth, and violates the meads
    Of all their pride;
When sapless trees and flowers are fled,
Back to their causes, and lie dead   15
    To all beside:
      I see thee set
Bidding defiance to the bitter air,
Upon a withered spray; by cold made bare,
      And drooping yet.   20

There, full in notes, to ravish all
My earth, I wonder what to call
    My dullness; when
I hear thee, pretty creature, bring
Thy better odes of praise, and sing,   25
    To puzzle men:
      Poor pious elf!
I am instructed by thy harmony,
To sing the time's uncertainty,
      Safe in myself.   30

Poor redbreast, carol out thy lay,
And teach us mortals what to say.
    Here cease the choir
Of airy choristers; no more
Mingle your notes; but catch a store   35
    From her sweet lyre;
      You are but weak,
Mere summer chanters; you have neither wing
Nor voice, in winter. Pretty redbreast, sing,
      What I would speak.   40

EXERCISE:

State the implications of the relationship of the man and the
bird.

TO A WATERFOWL

WILLIAM CULLEN BRYANT (1794–1878)

3553
a ba b

Whither, midst falling dew,
While glow the heavens with the last steps of day,
Far, through their rosy depths, dost thou pursue
    Thy solitary way?

Vainly the fowler's eye   5
Might mark thy distant flight to do thee wrong,
As, darkly seen against the crimson sky,
    Thy figure floats along.

Seek'st thou the plashy brink
Of weedy lake, or marge of river wide,   10
Or where the rocking billows rise and sink
    On the chafed ocean-side?

There is a Power whose care
Teaches thy way along that pathless coast—
The desert and illimitable air—   15
    Lone wandering, but not lost.

All day thy wings have fanned,
At that far height, the cold thin atmosphere,
Yet stoop not, weary, to the welcome land,
    Though the dark night is near.   20

And soon that toil shall end;
Soon shall thou find a summer home, and rest,
And scream among thy fellows; reeds shall bend,
    Soon, o'er thy sheltered nest.

Thou'rt gone, the abyss of heaven   25
Hath swallowed up thy form; yet, on my heart
Deeply hath sunk the lesson thou hast given,
    And shall not soon depart.

He, who, from zone to zone,
Guides through the boundless sky thy certain flight,   30
In the long way that I must tread alone,
    Will lead my steps aright.

Exercise:

Compare the statement of the relation of man and bird in this
poem with that made in "The Robin," p. 189. Is the application
made too directly in this poem? How much of the force of the
poem depends on the success of the description in the first six
stanzas?

POOR WAT

WILLIAM SHAKESPEARE (1564–1616)

And when thou hast on foot the purblind hare,
Mark the poor wretch, to overshoot his troubles
How he outruns the winds, and with what care
He cranks and crosses with a thousand doubles:
 The many musits [1] through the which he goes   5
 Are like a labyrinth to amaze his foes.

Sometime he runs among a flock of sheep,
To make the cunning hounds mistake their smell,
And sometime where earth-delving conies keep,
To stop the loud pursuers in their yell,   10
 And sometime sorteth with a herd of deer;
 Danger deviseth shifts; wit waits on fear:

For there his smell with others being mingled,
The hot scent-snuffing hounds are driven to doubt,
Ceasing their clamorous cry till they have singled 15
With much ado the cold fault cleanly out;
 Then do they spend their mouths: Echo replies,
 As if another chase were in the skies.

By this, poor Wat, far off upon a hill,
Stands on his hinder legs with listening ear,   20
To hearken if his foes pursue him still:
Anon their loud alarums he doth hear;
 And now his grief may be compared well
 To one sore sick that hears the passing-bell.

[1] hedge-gaps

Then shalt thou see the dew-bedabbled wretch   25
Turn, and return, indenting with the way;
Each envious briar his weary legs doth scratch,
Each shadow makes him stop, each murmur stay:
   For misery is trodden on by many,
    And being low never relieved by any.   30

                 (From *Venus and Adonis*)

EXERCISE:

   1. Does the poet succeed in giving a realistic picture?
   2. Is the expansion of the hare's plight to an application to human relationships justified by the realistic picture?

DESERT PLACES

ROBERT FROST (1875–   )

Snow falling and night falling fast oh fast
In a field I looked into going past,
And the ground almost covered smooth in snow,
But a few weeds and stubble showing last.

The woods around it have it—it is theirs.   5
All animals are smothered in their lairs.
I am too absent-spirited to count;
The loneliness includes me unawares.

And lonely as it is that loneliness
Will be more lonely ere it will be less—   10
A blanker whiteness of benighted snow
With no expression, nothing to express.

They cannot scare me with their empty spaces
Between stars—on stars void of human races.
I have it in me so much nearer home   15
To scare myself with my own desert places.

This poem differs from most of the preceding ones in this section in one important respect: the interest is, in the last stanza, swung specifically to the observer in the poem. That is, it abandons the objective method of treating the theme for the subjective, and the interpretation becomes definite.

Let us assume that the poem had been written without the last stanza. It would still be a poem, and a good one, but a very different one from the poem we know. Such a poem would differ from "The Main-Deep," for instance, in several particulars. In the first place, the reader knows who the observer is. A man, at dusk, is passing an open field where snow is falling. The poem is quickly defined as *his* observation. In the second place, the man, in the second stanza, indicates a relation between himself and the empty field on which the snow falls, although he does not definitely state it. The field, with its desolation, stands as a kind of symbol for the man's own loneliness. And since this relation is established for us in the second stanza, what follows in the third, though it is stated only in application to the field, comes to us as having application to the loneliness of the man who is observing. Then follow the lines:

> A blanker whiteness of benighted snow
> With no expression, nothing to express.

As implied here, it does not matter what happens to the man now or what he does, for nothing can have any further meaning.

If the poem be taken as ending there, the process used by the poet to give his effect is very easily defined: the observer describes a natural scene which becomes for the reader a *symbol* (*Glossary*) of the observer's own despairing state of mind. The scene in nature has been presented so that it serves to communicate a human meaning.

But the poem in reality does not end with the third stanza, and the last stanza introduces a new element into the poem, that is, the poet's own analysis and statement, an element that is almost wholly lacking from previous poems in this section.

The last stanza is not introduced with a transition from the earlier part; the observer does not say that, after looking at the

empty field he lifted his eyes to the sky and remembered what
he had been told about the great emptiness of the stars and the
interstellar spaces. But the reader understands that, and by the
very abruptness of the shift gets a more dramatic effect, as though
the man had jerked himself from his musing on the field to look
at the sky and then make his comment. This comment, in
summary, says this: a man who has known the desolation possible
to human experience cannot be frightened or depressed by mere
desolation in nature. And though this comment emphasizes the
loneliness of the man, it gives us a different impression of him
and gives a different total impression of the poem. It is not an
impression of mere despair, for the man, we feel, has not been
overcome by his own "desert places," but has mastered them.

He does not make this statement in so many words, but his
attitude is implied. A reader analyzing the poem can almost
base this implication of the man's attitude on the use of the
single words *scare*. The man says,

> They cannot scare me with their empty spaces.

He does not use *terrify,* or *horrify,* or *astound*—any word that
would indicate the full significance of human loneliness and despair. Instead, he uses the word *scare,* which is an understatement,
a common, colloquial word. One "scares" children by telling them
ghost stories, by jumping at them from behind corners, etc. But
by the use of the word in the poem the man is made to imply that
he is not a child to be so easily affected. Knowledge of the
infinite emptiness of space, which astronomers may give him,
cannot affect him, for he knows, being a grown man, that the
loneliness of spirit can be greater than the loneliness of external
nature. But in the last line the word *scare* is repeated, and its
connotations (*Glossary*) are brought into play in the new connection:

> To scare myself with my own desert places.

That is, the man has had so much experience of life, is so truly
mature, that even that greater loneliness of the spirit cannot make
him behave like a child who is afraid of the dark or of ghost
stories. Even in his loneliness of spirit he can still find strength
enough in himself.

ALL BUT BLIND

WALTER DE LA MARE (1873–   )

All but blind
   In his chambered hole
Gropes for worms
   The four-clawed Mole.

All but blind   5
   In the evening sky,
The hooded Bat
   Twirls softly by.

All but blind
   In the burning day   10
The Barn-Owl blunders
   On her way.

And blind as are
   These three to me,
So, blind to Someone   15
   I must be.

EXERCISE:

   What function do the following words fulfil in the poem: *four-clawed, twirls,* and *blunders?*

AUTUMNUS

JOSHUA SYLVESTER (1563–1618)

When the leaves in autumn wither,
   With a tawny tannèd face,
   Warped and wrinkled-up together,
The year's late beauty to disgrace:

There thy life's glass may'st thou find thee,   5
   Green now, gray now, gone anon;
   Leaving (worldling) of thine own,
Neither fruit, nor leaf behind thee.

SIC VITA

HENRY KING (1592–1669)

Like to the falling of a star;
Or as the flights of eagles are;
Or like the fresh spring's gaudy hue;
Or silver drops of morning dew;
Or like a wind that chafes the flood;   5
Or bubbles which on water stood;
Even such is man, whose borrowed light
Is straight called in, and paid tonight.

The wind blows out; the bubble dies;
The spring entombed in autumn lies;   10
The dew dries up; the star is shot;
The flight is past; and man forgot.

EXERCISE:

The organization of this poem might give an impression of
mechanical monotony to some readers. Why?

MARGARITAE SORORI

WILLIAM ERNEST HENLEY (1849–1903)

A late lark twitters from the quiet skies;
And from the west,
Where the sun, his day's work ended,
Lingers as in content,
There falls on the old, gray city   5
An influence luminous and serene,
A shining peace.

The smoke ascends
In a rosy-and-golden haze. The spires
Shine, and are changed. In the valley   10
Shadows rise. The lark sings on. The sun,
Closing his benediction,

            Sinks, and the darkening air
            Thrills with a sense of the triumphing night—
            Night with her train of stars   15
            And her great gift of sleep.

            So be my passing!
            My task accomplished and the long day done,
            My wages taken, and in my heart
            Some late lark singing,   20
            Let me be gathered to the quiet west,
            The sundown splendid and serene,
            Death.

EXERCISE:

   1. What is the mood evoked in this description of evening?
   2. What is the relation between the last lines of the second
stanza and the last lines of the third?

A DIRGE

JOHN WEBSTER (1580?–1625?)

Call for the robin-redbreast and the wren,
Since o'er shady groves they hover,
And with leaves and flowers do cover
The friendless bodies of unburied men.
  Call unto his funeral dole   5
  The ant, the field-mouse, and the mole,
To rear him hillocks that shall keep him warm,
And, when gay tombs are robbed, sustain no harm;
But keep the wolf far thence, that's foe to men,
For with his nails he'll dig them up again.   10

EXERCISE:

   What does the poet here imply about man's relationship to
nature?

NIGHTINGALES

ROBERT BRIDGES (1844–1930)

Beautiful must be the mountains whence ye come,
And bright in the fruitful valleys the streams wherefrom
    Ye learn your song:
Where are those starry woods?   O might I wander there,
   Among the flowers, which in that heavenly air   5
    Bloom the year long!

Nay, barren are those mountains and spent the streams:
Our song is the voice of desire, that haunts our dreams,
    A throe of the heart,
Whose pining visions dim, forbidden hopes profound, 10
   No dying cadence nor long sigh can sound,
    For all our art.

Alone, aloud in the raptured ear of men
We pour our dark nocturnal secret; and then,
    As night is withdrawn   15
From these sweet-springing meads and bursting boughs of
    May,
   Dream, while the innumerable choir of day
    Welcome the dawn.

    The idea of this poem might be stated somewhat crudely as
follows: the greatest beauty does not spring from pleasure but
from pain, not from happiness but from sorrow, not from satisfaction, but from desire.   It is, we might say, a kind of conquest of
pain and sorrow and desire.   But how does the idea become
incorporated into a poem?   The poet does not say in so many
words that this is his idea, or theme; instead, he has put it in a
form that appeals to our imagination.
    First, we observe that the poem is composed of two parts, a
statement to the nightingales by the poet (the first stanza) and
the reply of the nightingales (the second and third stanzas).
Given as a prose paraphrase the poem might be stated in this way:
The poet says that, since the song of the nightingales is so
beautiful, they must come from a place where the beauty of the

mountains and the music of streams in the fruitful valleys instructs them; and that he, who lives in a far less beautiful place, longs to wander where the flowers in that heavenly air never wither and where there is no change from perfect beauty. But the birds reply to him that the land from which they come is a harsh place with spent streams, and that the beauty of their song comes, not from satisfaction, but from desire which is so great and so hopeless that it can never be fully expressed even in their song. At night, they add, they pour their song into the ears of men, and then with the coming of dawn on the spring landscape, dream while the birds of the day sing with pleasure.

Obviously, this paraphrase does not exhaust even the meaning of the poem that can be reduced to statement. (It is entirely lacking, of course, in the kind of meaning that comes to us from the nature of the poetic form. See "Afterword" to Section II). One might even add to this paraphrase a statement of the theme of the poem, and the description would remain incomplete. It may repay us in understanding the method a poet uses in communicating his meaning to try to define some of the things that are absent from the paraphrase and the general statement of the idea.

First, this poem, like many poems, carries with it an allusion to a special piece of information, the Greek myth concerning the woman who, after a tragic experience, was turned into the nightingale. The poem would still make sense to a person who was unacquainted with the suppressed reference to the myth, but a knowledge of the myth does support the meaning of the poem.

But dismissing the implied allusion, we can strike on other implications in the poem that are necessary to a full appreciation. In the first stanza an important instance is involved. Why does the poet in addressing the nightingales express a wish to wander in the beautiful land from which he assumes they have come? There is the answer that anyone likes agreeable surroundings. Then we realize that this land is a kind of mythical paradise where there is no decay or change, a static perfection, such a place as men in a world of change, struggle, and decay dream of. This land of the nightingales implies, then, all men's longing for a kind of other-worldly peace and happiness. But something more is implied here. The speaker is a poet and in the present world is compelled to create his imperfect beauty by effort; he feels that if he inhabited that other land his poems might be as perfect and as spontaneous as the song of the nightingales.

The implications of the second stanza depend on these of the first, and merely involve a correction of the mistaken beliefs implied in the first stanza. But the third stanza raises some new issues, and becomes richer as we contemplate it. First, what is the "dark nocturnal secret"? It is of course the song of the nightingales. The bird sings at night and the use of "dark" seems merely to support and emphasize the use of "nocturnal." The bird also sings from some hidden, or secret place, and not in the open. So far the phrase seems only a very good poetic statement about the song. But it carries further a truth about life, that beauty comes from desire, struggle, and pain and not from easy perfection. It is a dark truth, a truth usually hidden, and it may be a depressing truth. But—and this takes us back to the "raptured ear" of the previous line—it is a paradoxical fact that the statement of this dark secret does not depress but exalts the hearer more than the merely pleasant songs of the "innumerable choir of day" can do.

The poet, then, has made the nightingales serve as a symbol to express his idea. He has developed the implications of the image so that it is unnecessary for him to argue his point; we seize on it in seizing on the image itself. The poet is not merely describing his own pleasure in the song of nightingales, or merely trying to make the reader who has no acquaintance with nightingales appreciate the poem fully; he is, instead, using the image of the nightingale to make us respond, emotionally and intellectually, to an interpretation of human experience.

PHILOMELA

MATTHEW ARNOLD (1822–1888)

Hark! ah, the nightingale—
The tawny-throated!

Hark, from that moonlit cedar what a burst!
What triumph! hark!—what pain!
O wanderer from a Grecian shore,   5
Still, after many years, in distant lands,
Still nourishing in thy bewildered brain
That wild, unquenched, deep-sunken, old-world pain—
    Say, will it never heal?
And can this fragrant lawn   10
With its cool trees, and night,
And the sweet, tranquil Thames,
And moonshine, and the dew,
To thy racked heart and brain
    Afford no balm?   15

    Dost thou to-night behold
Here, through the moonlight on this English grass,
The unfriendly palace in the Thracian wild?
    Dost thou again peruse
With hot cheeks and seared eyes   20
The too clear web, and thy dumb sister's shame?

    Dost thou once more assay
Thy flight, and feel come over thee,
Poor fugitive, the feathery change
Once more, and once more seem to make resound   25
With love and hate, triumph and agony,
Lone Daulis, and the high Cephissian vale?
    Listen, Eugenia—
How thick the bursts come crowding through the leaves!
    Again—thou hearest?   30
Eternal passion!
Eternal pain!

EXERCISE:

Compare the symbolic use of the nightingale here with that in
the poem by Bridges.

COMPOSED UPON WESTMINSTER
BRIDGE SEPT. 3 1802

WILLIAM WORDSWORTH (1770–1850)

Earth has not anything to show more fair:
Dull would he be of soul who could pass by
A sight so touching in its majesty:
This city now doth like a garment wear
The beauty of the morning; silent, bare,   5
Ships, towers, domes, theaters, and temples lie
Open unto the fields, and to the sky;
All bright and glittering in the smokeless air.
Never did sun more beautifully steep
In his first splendor valley, rock, or hill;   10
Ne'er saw I, never felt, a calm so deep!
The river glideth at his own sweet will:
Dear God! the very houses seem asleep;
And all that mighty heart is lying still!

EXERCISE:

Wordsworth here is describing a sunrise over the same city
which Henley describes at sunset in "Margaritae Sorori." Compare the moods of the two descriptions and attempt to relate the
use of descriptive detail to mood and to the idea of each poem.

PRELUDES

T. S. ELIOT (1888–   )

I

The winter evening settles down
With smells of steaks in passageways.
Six o'clock.
The burnt-out ends of smoky days.
And now a gusty shower wraps   5
The grimy scraps
Of withered leaves about his feet

And newspapers from vacant lots;
The showers beat
On broken blinds and chimney pots,   10
And at the corner of the street
A lonely cab-horse steams and stamps.
And then the lighting of the lamps.

II

The morning comes to consciousness
Of faint stale smells of beer   15
From the sawdust-trampled street
With all its muddy feet that press
To early coffee-stands.
With the other masquerades
That time resumes,   20
One thinks of all the hands
That are raising dingy shades
In a thousand furnished rooms.

III

You tossed a blanket from the bed,
You lay upon your back, and waited;   25
You dozed, and watched the night revealing
The thousand sordid images
Of which your soul was constituted;
They flickered against the ceiling.
And when all the world came back   30
And the light crept up between the shutters,
And you heard the sparrows in the gutters,
You had such a vision of the street
As the street hardly understands;
Sitting along the bed's edge, where   35
You curled the papers from your hair,
Or clasped the yellow soles of feet
In the palms of both soiled hands.

IV

His soul stretched tight across the skies
That fade behind a city block,   40
Or trampled by insistent feet
At four and five and six o'clock;

And short square fingers stuffing pipes,
And evening newspapers, and eyes
Assured of certain certainties,   45
The conscience of a blackened street
Impatient to assume the world.

I am moved by fancies that are curled
Around these images, and cling:
The notion of some infinitely gentle   50
Infinitely suffering thing.

Wipe your hand across your mouth, and laugh;
The worlds revolve like ancient women
Gathering fuel in vacant lots.

EXERCISE:

1. The first two sections of this poem describe a winter evening and a winter morning in a city. The description in these sections is objective, but it establishes a mood and attitude. Discuss the mood and attitude. What effect do the last three lines of the second section give?

2. In the third section, one of the people whose hand will raise dingy shades is addressed. Out of her own misery she has "a vision of the street"—an awareness of the general loneliness and defeat. Why does the poet say that the street hardly understands this vision?

3. In the fourth section another character is referred to, a man who is sensitive enough to be constantly affected by the life he sees around him—a life which appears to be dominated by a meaningless routine of satisfying animal requirements, the "certain certainties." Ironically, the poet calls this assurance of these certainties the only "conscience" that the street has; and the street seems to impose its own standards on the entire world. Then the poet announces himself as a commentator on the scenes he has presented. What attitude does he take? Whom is he addressing in the last three lines? How do the last two lines serve as a symbolic summary of the poem? How in the body of the poem is this general conclusion prepared for?

ON A DROP OF DEW

ANDREW MARVELL (1621–1678)

See how the orient dew,
   Shed from the bosom of the morn
   Into the blowing roses,
Yet careless of its mansion new;
For the clear region where 'twas born   5
   Round in itself encloses:
   And in its little globe's extent,
Frames as it can its native element.
   How it the purple flower does slight,
     Scarce touching where it lies,   10
   But gazing back upon the skies,
     Shines with a mournful light;
      Like its own tear,
Because so long divided from the sphere.
   Restless it rolls and unsecure,   15
     Trembling lest it grow impure:
   Till the warm sun pity its pain,
And to the skies exhale it back again.
     So the soul, that drop, that ray
Of the clear fountain of eternal day,   20
Could it within the human flower be seen,
   Rememb'ring still its former height,
   Shuns the sweet leaves and blossoms green;
   And, recollecting its own light,
Does, in its pure and circling thoughts express   25
The greater heaven in a heaven less.
   In how coy a figure wound,
   Every way it turns away:
   So the world excluding round,
   Yet receiving in the day.   30
   Dark beneath, but bright above:
   Here disdaining, there in love.
  How loose and easy hence to go:
  How girt and ready to ascend.
  Moving but on a point below,   35
  It all about does upwards bend.
Such did the manna's sacred dew distill;

White, and entire, though congealed and chill.
Congealed on earth: but does, dissolving, run
Into the glories of the almighty sun.   40

EXERCISE:

1. Analyze carefully the points of resemblance which the poet establishes between the dew drop and the soul.

2. What is the general effect given by the poet's elaborate development of the comparison?

3. How do the last four lines summarize the poem's intention?

ODE TO THE WEST WIND

PERCY BYSSHE SHELLEY (1792–1822)

I

O, wild West Wind, thou breath of Autumn's being, *a*
Thou, from whose unseen presence the leaves dead *b*
Are driven, like ghosts from an enchanter fleeing, *a*

Yellow, and black, and pale, and hectic red, *b*
Pestilence-stricken multitudes: O, thou, *c*   5
Who chariotest to their dark wintry bed *b*

The wingèd seeds, where they lie cold and low, *c*
Each like a corpse within its grave, until *d*
Thine azure sister of the spring shall blow *c*

Her clarion o'er the dreaming earth, and fill *d*   10
(Driving sweet buds like flocks to feed in air) *e*
With living hues and odors plain and hill: *d*

Wild Spirit, which art moving everywhere; *e*
Destroyer and preserver; hear, O, hear!

II

Thou on whose stream, 'mid the steep sky's commotion,
Loose clouds like earth's decaying leaves are shed,   16
Shook from the tangled boughs of Heaven and Ocean,

iambic pentameter

a b a
b c b
c d c
d e d
etc.

Angels of rain and lightning: there are spread
On the blue surface of thine airy surge,
Like the bright hair uplifted from the head   20

Of some fierce Mænad, even from the dim verge
Of the horizon to the zenith's height
The locks of the approaching storm. Thou dirge

Of the dying year, to which this closing night
Will be the dome of a vast sepulcher,   25
Vaulted with all thy congregated might

Of vapors, from whose solid atmosphere
Black rain, and fire, and hail will burst: O hear!

III

Thou who didst waken from his summer dreams
The blue Mediterranean, where he lay,   30
Lulled by the coil of his crystalline streams,

Beside a pumice isle in Baiæ's bay,
And saw in sleep old palaces and towers
Quivering within the wave's intenser day,

All overgrown with azure moss and flowers   35
So sweet, the sense faints picturing them! Thou
For whose path the Atlantic's level powers

Cleave themselves into chasms, while far below
The sea-blooms and the oozy woods which wear
The sapless foliage of the ocean, know   40

Thy voice, and suddenly grow gray with fear,
And tremble and despoil themselves: O hear!

IV

If I were a dead leaf thou mightest bear;
If I were a swift cloud to fly with thee;
A wave to pant beneath thy power, and share   45

The impulse of thy strength, only less free
Than thou, O, uncontrollable! If even
I were as in my boyhood, and could be

The comrade of thy wanderings over heaven,
As then, when to outstrip thy skiey speed   50
Scarce seemed a vision; I would ne'er have striven

As thus with thee in prayer in my sore need.
Oh! lift me as a wave, a leaf, a cloud!
I fall upon the thorns of life! I bleed!

A heavy weight of hours has chained and bowed   55
One too like thee: tameless, and swift, and proud.

                         v

Make me thy lyre, even as the forest is:
What if my leaves are falling like its own!
The tumult of thy mighty harmonies

Will take from both a deep, autumnal tone,   60
Sweet though in sadness. Be thou, spirit fierce,
My spirit! Be thou me, impetuous one!

Drive my dead thoughts over the universe
Like withered leaves to quicken a new birth!
And, by the incantation of this verse,   65

Scatter, as from an unextinguished hearth
Ashes and sparks, my words among mankind!
Be through my lips to unawakened earth

The trumpet of a prophecy! O, wind,
If Winter comes, can Spring be far behind?   70

EXERCISE:

  Write an analysis of the method and an interpretation of this
poem.

SECTION IV - *metrics*

FOREWORD

We have said ("Afterword," Section II, p. 167) that concentration and intensity are two of the qualities that tend to distinguish the poetic treatment of a subject from the prose treatment; and we related these qualities to the emphasis on form in poetry. The form of poetry, we said, is more closely organized than is the form of prose. As an example of this principle we indicated the greater selectivity in use of detail, the emphasis on suggestiveness, and the importance in the placing of details in relation to the central intention of a poem. For example, we indicated the importance of the line, "That kindles my mother's fire" in "The Wife of Usher's Well" (p. 44); the accumulation of descriptive detail in "Michael" as a basis for the final presentation of the pathos of the poem (p. 84); and the implications of the phrase "their dark nocturnal secret" in "The Nightingales" (p. 200). All of these things indicate the close-knit organization of various elements which one finds in poetry. Some of the same types of organization are to be found in prose as well as in poetry; but we have pointed out that poetry *tends* toward a higher degree of organization than does prose. For example, the poor choice of words on the basis of connotation is much less damaging to a novel than to a poem. The damaged novel may still give some satisfaction, but the poem in which the writer has given little attention to connotation would certainly be a complete failure.

This tendency toward a high degree of organization in poetry is most obvious in the use of *rhythmical* language (*Glossary*). Some people, in fact, are accustomed to think that the use of rhythmical language is what chiefly distinguishes poetry from prose. But the distinction made on this basis can in the end only be one of degree and not of kind. This is obviously true when we reflect that any use of language in prose or poetry involves rhythm. In any prose whatsoever we feel a rise and fall of emphasis: we do not pronounce each syllable with precisely the same emphasis. We may say, however, that even if there is not an absolute difference between prose and poetry on the basis of rhythm, there is still a very important relative difference. A consideration of the following extracts from essays, stories, and poems may make clear what the relative difference is:

(1)

As a sample of popular interest it may be noted that a single talk last spring by Professor MacMurry on psychology brought 17,000 requests for the supplementary aid-to-study pamphlet, and one by Professor Burt on the study of the mind brought 26,000.

("The Level of Thirteen-Year-Olds," William Orton)

(2)

But verse, you say, circumscribes a quick and luxuriant fancy, which would extend itself too far on every subject, did not the labor which is required to well-turned and polished rime, set bounds to it. Yet this argument, if granted, would only prove that we may write better in verse, but not more naturally.

("An Essay of Dramatic Poesy," John Dryden)

(3)

If there be any truth in astrology, I may outlive a jubilee; as yet I have not seen one revolution of Saturn, nor hath my pulse beat thirty years, and yet, excepting one, have seen the ashes of, and left underground, all the kings of Europe; have been contemporary to three emperors, four grand signiors, and as many popes: methinks I have outlived myself, and begin to be weary of the sun; I have shaken hands with delight in my warm blood and canicular days; I perceive I do anticipate the vices of age; the world to me is but a dream or mock-show, and we all therein but pantaloons and antics, to my severer contemplations.

(*Religio Medici,* Sir Thomas Browne)

(4)

These and all else were to me the same as they are to you,
I loved well those cities, loved well the stately and rapid river,
The men and women I saw were all near to me,
Others the same—others who look back on me because I looked
    forward to them

(The time will come, though I stop here today and tonight).
("Crossing Brooklyn Ferry," Walt Whitman)

(5)

These our actors,

As I foretold you, were all spirits, and
Are melted into air, into thin air:
And, like the baseless fabric of this vision,
The cloud-capped towers, the gorgeous palaces,   5
The solemn temples, the great globe itself,
Yea, all which it inherit, shall dissolve,
And, like this insubstantial pageant faded,
Leave not a wrack behind.

(*The Tempest,* William Shakespeare)

(6)

The gale, it plies the saplings double,
It blows so hard 'twill soon be gone.
Today the Roman and his trouble
Are ashes under Uricon.

("On Wenlock Edge," A. E. Housman)

If one will read, preferably aloud, the specimens given above, it will be clear that all of them possess the quality of rhythm—even the first one with its dull, flat, matter-of-fact statement. Indeed, if we read carefully we can see that the specimens form, roughly speaking, a sort of ascending scale in regard to the regularity of the rhythm. If one hears specimen 1 and 6 read aloud he can easily detect the difference in the regularity and emphasis of the rhythm. In the case of specimen 1 the rhythm is almost completely unsystematized and chaotic; in the case of specimen 6 the rhythm is systematized and regularized—that is, it takes the form of *verse* (*Glossary*).

But if specimens 1 and 6 represent extremes of regularity and irregularity, what of a comparison between specimens 3 and 4 or between 4 and 5? Specimen 3 is taken from a work in *prose,* specimen 4 from a *poem;* yet a person hearing the two read aloud might not very easily distinguish them on this basis. Evidently there are degrees, as we have said, of regularization of rhythm, and the distinction between verse (regularized rhythm) and prose (unregularized rhythm) is not an absolute one. Indeed, we can make this point concretely by printing part of specimen 3, an example of highly rhythmical prose, as if it were verse and by indicating the accented syllables.

> . . . . methínks I have outlíved mysélf,
> And begín to be weáry of the sún; I have sháken hánds
> With delíght in my wárm blóod and canícular dáys;
> I percéive I do antícipáte the víces of áge;
> The world, to mé is bút a dreám or móck-show,
> And we all therein but pantaloóns and ántics,
> To mý sevérer contemplátions.

The manner in which we have just rearranged specimen 3 as verse is obviously a somewhat arbitrary one; but when compared with specimen 4, which is professedly verse, the pattern which we have just printed above will indicate clearly enough that prose and verse shade off into each other and that there are cases in which the rhythms of prose become regularized almost to the point of verse, and cases of verse in which the pattern is so vague that one might maintain that, strictly speaking, there is no verse at all. This type of writing is usually called *free verse* (*Glossary*.) We may easily illustrate how vague is the borderline between free verse and rhythmical prose by taking a poem by H. D. and putting it into prose:

PEAR TREE

Silver dust lifted from the earth, higher than my arms reach, you have mounted. O silver, higher than my arms reach you front us with great mass; no flower ever opened so staunch a white leaf, no flower ever parted silver from such rare silver; O white pear, your flower-tufts, thick on the branch, bring summer and ripe fruits in their purple hearts.

H. D. actually wrote the poem in the following form:

PEAR TREE

Silver dust
lifted from the earth,
higher than my arms reach,
you have mounted.
O silver,
higher than my arms reach
you front us with great mass;
no flower ever opened
so staunch a white leaf,
no flower ever parted silver
from such rare silver;

O white pear,
your flower-tufts,
thick on the branch,
bring summer and ripe fruits
in their purple hearts.

There is not as much of a rhythmical pattern in this poem by H. D. as there is in the prose passage from Sir Thomas Browne given as Specimen 3. This means that there is certainly as much difference on the basis of rhythmical regularity between the ordinary verse we find in Specimen 6, for example, and the free verse by H. D., as there is between the poem by H. D. and Specimen 3. There are, then, degrees in the regularization of rhythm. As we have already noted (p. 209), one aspect of the greater emphasis on form in poetry as compared with prose is found in the regularizing of rhythm. But verse is not a thing in absolute contrast to prose. Instead, it is a specialization of that quality of rhythm which is found in all discourse. We have pointed out before (*Introduction,* p. 8) that other aspects of poetry are likewise special adaptations of elements found in all discourse; for instance, figurative language.

The systematic ordering of rhythm we call verse. Verse is so obvious in most poetry that a body of special terms has been developed to describe its various elements. For instance, by the term *meter* we mean the measure of the verse according to the line. The unit of measure is called the *foot,* a unit composed in English verse of one accented syllable and one or more unaccented syllables. And we have given names to the various types of foot. (For full discussion of the general subject see *Glossary*). For instance, the most common foot in English poetry is called the *iambic foot;* it is composed of one unaccented and one accented syllable. The following line is composed of iambic feet:

Is this the face that launched a thousand ships

We can mark the divisions into feet and the accents as follows:

Is thís / the fáce / that laúnched / a thóu / sand shíps

The line may be described as *iambic pentameter;* that is, it is composed of five iambic feet (*Glossary*).

Because of the prominence of rhythmical system in poetry and perhaps because of the amount of attention which is usually given to the technique of *versification* (*Glossary*), people sometimes tend to confuse verse with poetry, forgetting that *verse is only one of the instruments which the poet uses to gain his effect* (*Introduction* pp. 18–19). This confusion is immediately avoided if we realize that one can have verse without having a poetic effect. To illustrate the fact that verse, as such, does not give the poetic effect and is not to be confused with poetry, we can point to the following line, which provides an example of iambic pentameter:

A Mr. Wilkerson, a clergyman

We can scan it as follows:

A Míst / -er Wílk / -er -són / a clérg / -y mán

Or it would be possible to construct a pattern of pure nonsense that could be accurately scanned.

> Investigation sad or verbally
> Reveal unvision here this house no cat
> Divests warm compromise imperially
> What yes untold unwicked hiss nor that.

These lines are in regular iambic pentameter. They are arranged, furthermore, in the form of a simple stanza, the quatrain (*Glossary* under *stanza*). No one would care to maintain that the mere fact that these unrelated words are put into a rhythmical pattern creates poetry. To have poetry the words must be related in other ways as well. Verse is simply one instrument which to produce poetry is used in conjunction with other instruments, narrative, dramatic incident, figurative language, logical sense of words, associations of words, etc. Our present interest is, then, to see some of the ways in which this element of verse works in making its contribution to the poetic effect, and to see some of its relations to the other elements which the poet has at his disposal; for one must always remember that poetry is the result of a combination of relationships among the elements and does not inhere specially in any one of them (*Introduction*, p. 18).

We have said that verse represents a specialization of rhythm in language, and that it is one aspect of the greater formality, or of the closer organization, of poetry as contrasted with other literary modes. Form in poetry, as in anything else, is simply the arrangement of various factors for a given purpose. Verse is a means for controlling the use of language. One of the purposes of this control is to focus attention. The pattern of accents, once we have grasped it as a pattern, sets up the unconscious expectation in us that the pattern will continue. That is, we give closer attention than is usual in order to verify our expectation. This lies at the basis of what has been called the hypnotic power of verse.

People think of hypnosis as a condition of sluggishness or sleep artificially induced. But the fundamental characteristic of the hypnoidal state is not—it must be remembered—sluggishness or dullness but the vastly increased concentration of attention and suggestibility. The person who is in such a condition hangs upon every word of the hypnotist and attends to and accepts even the slightest suggestion. In a similar fashion, by the regularity of the meter, the reader of poetry may be put into a state of greater susceptibility to the suggestions of ideas, attitudes, feelings, and images contained in the poem. The meter, then, tends to put the reader in such a condition that his imagination can work with greater freedom; it helps create in the reader what has been called the "willing suspension of disbelief." Meter tends, as Coleridge has said, "to increase the vivacity and susceptibility both of the general feelings and of the attention. . . . As a medicated atmosphere, or as a wine during animated con-

versation, they [the anticipations set up by the meter] act power-
fully, though themselves unnoticed." [1]

We have been talking about an effect of meter on the reader or
hearer. But if we approach the subject of meter from the stand-
point of the genesis of meter we shall find that the same general
characteristics emerge. On the one hand, as a result of meter,
we get increased susceptibility; on the other hand, as a source of
meter, we find that intense states of emotion, quite naturally and
instinctively, tend toward a rhythmical expression. Investigations
of the life of primitive peoples or of the habits of children or
considerations of religious rituals—all testify to this psychological
fact. And we know how the moans of a person in great grief or
pain tend to assume a rhythmical pattern. Consideration of such
examples will indicate to us why verse has become associated with
poetry—for poetry, as we have seen, tries to evoke the reader's
feelings as one of the factors in his response. This is not to say,
of course, that poetry is *merely* emotional, or is to be defined as
the "expression of pure emotion" or the "pure realization of
being." (*Introduction*, pp. 14–16). But poetry, which attempts
to do justice to the emotional factors in experience in addition to
the other factors, and which does often treat experiences of great
intensity, tends to use verse as a characteristic instrument.

Verse is a characteristic instrument of poetry, but it is an
instrument which is used variously for various specific purposes.
There obviously should be some appropriate relation between
the verse form used in a given poem and the general effect
intended by the poet. We all know that different rhythms tend
to stimulate different feelings. Verse, as we have already said
(p. 215), is a means for controlling the use of language, but
the control in a successful poem is exercised in conjunction with
a variety of factors. This principle is true in prose as well as in
verse. For instance, notice the difference in effect in the rhythms
of the following passages of prose:

(1)

Outside it was getting dark. The street-light came on outside
the window. The two men at the counter read the menu. From

[1] *Biographia Literaria*, Ch. XVIII

the other end of the counter Nick Adams watched them. He
had been talking to George when they came in.

("The Killers," Ernest Hemingway)

(2)

The place was worthy of such a trial. It was the great hall of
William Rufus, the hall which had resounded with acclamations
at the inauguration of thirty kings, the hall which had witnessed
the just sentence of Bacon and the just absolution of Somers,
the hall where the eloquence of Strafford had for a moment
awed and melted a victorious party inflamed with just resent-
ment, the hall where Charles had confronted the High Court
of Justice with the placid courage which has half redeemed his
fame. Neither military nor civil pomp was wanting. The
avenues were lined with grenadiers. The streets were kept clear
by cavalry. The peers, robed in gold and ermine, were mar-
shalled by the heralds under Garter-King-at-Arms. The judges
in their vestments of state attended to give advice on points of
law.

(*Essay on Warren Hastings,* Thomas Babington, Lord Macaulay)

(3)

Yet, perhaps, in the secret chambers of consciousness, she had her
thoughts, too. Perhaps her fading mind called up once more
the shadows of the past to float before it, and retraced, for the
last time, the vanished visions of that long history—passing back
and back, through the cloud of years, to older and ever older
memories—to the spring woods at Osborne, so full of primroses
for Lord Beaconsfield—to Lord Palmerston's queer clothes and
high demeanor, and Albert's face under the green lamp, and
Albert's first stag at Balmoral, and Albert in his blue and silver
uniform, and the Baron coming in through a doorway, and Lord
M. dreaming at Windsor with the rooks cawing in the elm-trees,
and the Archbishop of Canterbury on his knees in the dawn, and
the old King's turkey-cock ejaculations, and Uncle Leopold's
soft voice at Claremont, and Lehzen with the globes, and her
mother's feathers sweeping down towards her, and a great old
repeater-watch of her father's in its tortoise-shell case, and a
yellow rug, and some friendly flounces of sprigged muslin, and
the trees and the grass at Kensington.

(*Queen Victoria,* Lytton Strachey)

The first example is part of a description of a scene in a lunch room in the early evening. The rather flat, unemphatic, and broken rhythms of the passage are appropriate to the author's intention: these rhythms, after the story develops and we discover that "the two men" are killers, take on the ironical quality of understatement. The apparent casualness and simplicity of the rhythms in this passage (and in the story as a whole) come not from the writer's lack of control but from his complete control of his style as related to other factors of his story.

But when we consider the writer's attitude toward his material in the second example, we see that the style used by Hemingway in the first example would here be thoroughly inappropriate. Macaulay wants the reader to feel the pomp and solemnity of the occasion he is describing and to feel this as one more important incident in the history of the great historic hall; we can notice in the second sentence the long, swelling rhythms. Then, when we come to the third sentence which describes the details of the present scene, we notice the contrast of shorter, more rapid, and less emphatic rhythms.[1] Furthermore, we can notice in the third example, which deals with the death of Queen Victoria, that the writer has made the rhythm emphasize the structure of thought in the passage; each of the items of memory which Strachey imagines to have passed through the dying queen's mind is given in a little rhythmical unit, and the whole passage has a gently flowing, almost monotonous quality appropriate to the reverie.

If the expressive quality of rhythm in prose, however, is important, the treatment of rhythm is obviously much more important in poetry because of the more highly organized treatment of rhythm. And if, as we have said, different rhythms tend to stimulate different feelings, a poem on a serious subject will not give us the intended effect if the poet has chosen a light, tripping rhythm—that is, if he has chosen the wrong kind of verse to be combined with the other elements of the poem. The following

---

[1] We can also notice a contrast on the basis of the sonority between the second sentence and the following sentences. For example, notice how often long vowels, and especially long back vowels—the sounds *oo, oh, ah,* and *aw* —occur in positions of emphasis, in the second sentence (*Glossary* under *verse texture*).

poem, especially the first two stanzas, is often used to illustrate the choice of a wrong type of rhythm for a subject:

DEATH

PERCY BYSSHE SHELLEY (1792–1822)

Death is here, and death is there,
Death is busy everywhere,
All around, within, beneath,
Above, is death—and we are death.

Death has set his mark and seal   5
On all we are and all we feel,
On all we know and all we fear,

  *   *   *   *   *   *

First our pleasures die—and then
Our hopes, and then our fears—and when
These are dead, the debt is due,   10
Dust claims dust—and we die too.

All things that we love and cherish,
Like ourselves must fade and perish;
Such is our rude mortal lot—
Love itself would, did they not.   15

The student, however, might object at this point by saying that, if verse exercises a hypnotic effect and makes the reader more susceptible to suggestion, then the strongly marked rhythms of the present poem should make the reader extremely susceptible to what the poet wishes him to feel. But, as we have said, different rhythms tend to stimulate different general states of feeling, as well as to heighten suggestibility. Here, in "Death," then, we have a case in which the specific feeling stimulated by the jigging rhythm, tends to contradict the response suggested by the ideas, images, etc. of the poem. The poem is an unsuccessful poem because the parts do not work together—they

are not properly related. The general conditioning effect of verse
—by that we mean its power to heighten suggestibility and to
focus attention—comes into play only in the case of poems which
are highly unified, and this means, among other things, that the
expressive quality of the rhythm itself partakes of the general
unity.

Let us examine, then, a somewhat longer poem on the grounds
of this general principle.

THE BELLS OF SHANDON

FRANCIS MAHONY (1805–1866)

With deep affection,
And recollection,
I often think of
   Those Shandon bells,
Whose sounds so wild would,   5
In the days of childhood,
Fling around my cradle
   Their magic spells:
On this I ponder
Where'er I wander,   10
And thus grow fonder,
   Sweet Cork, of thee;
With thy bells of Shandon,
That sound so grand on
The pleasant waters   15
   Of the River Lee.

I've heard bells chiming
Full many a clime in,
Tolling sublime in
   Cathedral shrine,   20
While at a glib rate
Brass tongues would vibrate—
But all their music
   Spoke naught like thine;

For memory, dwelling   25
On each proud swelling
Of the belfry knelling
      Its bold notes free,
Made the bells of Shandon
Sound far more grand on   30
The pleasant waters
      Of the River Lee.

I've heard bells tolling
Old Adrian's Mole in,
Their thunder rolling   35
      From the Vatican,
And cymbals glorious
Swinging uproarious
In the gorgeous turrets
      Of Notre Dame;   40
But thy sounds were sweeter
Than the dome of Peter
Flings o'er the Tiber,
      Pealing solemnly—
O, the bells of Shandon   45
Sound far more grand on
The pleasant waters
      Of the River Lee.

There's a bell in Moscow,
While on tower and kiosk O   50
In Saint Sophia
      The Turkman gets,
And loud in air
Calls men to prayer
From the tapering summits   55
      Of tall minarets.
Such empty phantom
I freely grant them;
But there's an anthem
      More dear to me,—   60
'Tis the bells of Shandon,
That sound so grand on
The pleasant waters
      Of the River Lee.

This poem is apparently a serious attempt to communicate to the reader with increased feeling and concentration an experience which is familiar enough in every day life: the superior beauty possessed by things which are endeared to us by memory or some personal tie. The bells of Shandon, because they were heard by the poet in his childhood always sound sweeter to him than any other bells which he has ever heard.

The first two stanzas make the statement just discussed. The rest of the poem is taken up with naming the various famous bells which the poet has heard and which have less meaning for him than do the bells of Shandon. The experience in its general terms, we have already said, is one which people often have, and it might form the basis of a fine poem. Has the poet made "The Bells of Shandon" a fine poem? An adverse criticism of the poem does not *question* the fact that in actuality the bells of Shandon may have had a very profound meaning for Francis Mahony, the man. The criticism to follow is occupied rather with this question: has Francis Mahony, the artist, succeeded in constructing a poem which will really suggest to us the quality and meaning of such an experience?

A really thoughtful consideration of the poem will reveal that we can take the experience only on our faith in the sincerity of Mahony, the man. He does not recreate the experience for us at all. Perhaps the most obvious reason for the failure of the poem is the lack of any real dramatic quality (*Introduction,* p. 23). Notice how little development there is. The poem gives nothing more than the statement that the bells have such and such effect, and a statement of their superiority to a whole list of other bells. The statement is mere repetition, the list of bells merely a catalogue which lengthens the poem without developing the experience. The whole experience is vague and undramatic, and the statement of it is rambling and monotonous. This deficiency in structure is matched by a comparable deficiency in the monotonous and inexpressive meter.

One notices that the meter (which is elaborate and emphatic enough to call attention to itself) is mechanical and inflexible. We continue at the same trot whether the subject is the bells of Shandon or those of Notre Dame or—not bells at all—the cry of

the muezzin. If the meter were a little more self-effacing, the
lack of appropriateness in the movement of the verse in various
parts of the poem would not be so sharply indicated as it is. But
in spite of some few variations, the tripping speed of the rhythm
sweeps away any effect of contrast or development. Instead of
being co-ordinated with the other elements in the poem, the meter
is broken loose from the other elements and dominates the poem;
the jog-trot metrical pattern is emphasized, apparently, as an end
in itself.

But the domination by the meter goes to even greater extremes.
The inversions of grammar which occur in the poem can hardly
be defended as intended to give force or emphasis, or for any
other rhetorical reason: they are rather plainly evidences of the
fact that this poet could not control his meter. The meter in
this poem—far from being one of the instruments used by the
poet to get intended effects—actually twists the sense into distor-
tion.

An examination of the riming will corroborate this judgment.
The poet establishes a pattern of *feminine rimes* (*Glossary*)—
perhaps from some vague notion of achieving melodious effects
suitable to a poem on the music of the bells. But very soon we
see that the feminine rimes have become as merciless a taskmaster
to the poet as the meter. The poet gives us such rimes as: *wild
would*, with *childhood; Shandon*, with *grand on; Mole in*, with
tolling; and finally such an absurdity as *Moscow*, with *kiosk O*.
Such rimes as these which have the effect of having been consciously striven for and violently forced tend to give a comic
effect. But such an effect is not intended here. It is the effect
which is shown by the rimes in Byron's *Don Juan* (pp. 266–7)
or in many of the plays of Gilbert and Sullivan; but the effect in
such a work as the present is entirely inappropriate. In this
poem the ludicrous effect is completely at variance with the solemnity of tone which the poet apparently wants to secure.

Why is it that more people have not been aware of these comic
effects? Why should the poem have been so popular as it has
been? (It is included in the *Oxford Book of Victorian Verse*.)
One may best explain perhaps in this way: many people in reading a poem lay aside the critical habit of mind, doing so out

of deference to the poet, though of course this is a very poor compliment to the poet. Such a person, however, seizing on the statement about fond recollection and the beauty of the bells so recollected, might easily be seduced into feeling that the poem was good. He would probably consider the elaborate metrics as contributing beauty to the poem, for he would hardly inspect it closely enough to see the discrepancies between the effect of the meter and the intended effect of the poem. But as we have already seen, meter is only one of several means which the poet may use and must use in securing certain effects. The meter and these other means must pull together—not apart, as in this poem. As a matter of fact, monotony of meter is one of the surest symptoms of the fact that the materials of a poem have not been focused sharply and clearly by the poet. The poet has not mastered his subject. The impulse behind the poem is apparently weak, and the elaborate metrics and riming have probably been used to disguise this very fact. In "The Bells of Shandon" this failure to master the subject is indicated by the dependence on mere prosy statement and by the failure to develop dramatically the quality of the feelings actually referred to the bells.

AFTER LONG SILENCE

w. b. yeats (1865–   )

Speech after long silence; it is right,
All other lovers being estranged or dead,
Unfriendly lamplight hid under its shade,
The curtains drawn upon unfriendly night,
That we descant and yet again descant   5
Upon the supreme theme of Art and Song:
Bodily decrepitude is wisdom; young
We loved each other and were ignorant.

The dramatic situation implied by the poem is easily defined. The two lovers are in a shadowed room alone, the lamplight being almost hidden by the shade. One of the lovers is speaking to the other, and before we comment on what he says, several points may be rehearsed. The lovers are evidently old. The relationship has not been a constant one, for we are told that all other lovers are "estranged or dead." The first line suggests that there has been a long silence after they have "descanted" on the "supreme theme of Art and Song." (The nature of this theme will be discussed later.) This silence has been broken by more talk on the same subject, apparently now the only subject left to them, and one of the lovers makes the comment which constitutes the poem itself.

The speaker says, in effect, this: one lover can no longer take pleasure in the physical beauty of the other (for the lamplight, which would reveal the decay of age, is described as "unfriendly"). Furthermore, the outside world has no more use for them (for the world outside their drawn curtains is likewise "unfriendly"). It is right that, having passed other phases of their lives, they should talk of the "theme of Art and Song," which is "supreme" because it involves the interpretation of their own previous experience. Wisdom, the power to reach an interpretation, comes only as the body decays. The poet sees the wisdom as a positive gain, but at the same time he can regret the time of beauty and youth when the lovers could dispense with wisdom. The basic point of the poem is the recognition, with its attendant pathos, of the fact that man cannot ever be complete—cannot, that is, possess beauty and wisdom together.

Why is the poem so much richer and more moving than the bare statement in our summary? The reader would say immediately that the poet has dramatized the general statement—that is, he has made us feel that the idea as given through the incident has the weight of experience belonging to real people. The reader would also point out the suggestiveness of the images used in the first four lines. Such comments would be incomplete as an account of any poem, but would be particularly incomplete for a poem like the present one. For it will be possible in this poem to show how the use made of the verse is especially important in making the poem achieve its intended effect. But this will require a detailed examination of the versification.

Speech after long silence; it is right,
All other lovers being estranged or dead,
Unfriendly lamplight hid under its shade,
The curtains drawn upon unfriendly night,
That we descant and yet again descant   5
Upon the supreme theme of Art and Song:
Bodily decrepitude is wisdom; young
We loved each other and were ignorant.

The reader will observe that the basic metrical pattern is that of
iambic pentameter. He will also observe, however, that there are
a number of variations from the basic pattern. What are they,
and do they play any part in giving the poem its effect?

Consider the first line. The line does not set the regular metrical pattern of the poem. The irregularity here supports, with
dramatic appropriateness, the effect of informal conversation.
This is the general effect of the line, but let us analyze the particular details. Instead of the normal iambic opening, we find
an accent falling on the first syllable, *speech*. The second foot,
after long, may be regarded as an anapest, in which the syllable
added to the iambic norm is a compensation for the defect in
the first foot.[1] The foot, *silence,* represents a trochaic *substitution*
(*Glossary*) for the normal iambic foot. Let us pause here
to see what effect these variations have on the movement of the
line. *Speech* is accented emphatically, as it should be for dramatic reasons: the abrupt start is appropriate to the idea of speech
suddenly breaking upon silence. The fact that the reader must
hurry over the two unaccented syllables of *after* before he can
rest on the accent of *long* makes the emphasis on *long* greater
than it would otherwise be; and this heavy emphasis on *long*
fortifies the meaning of the word. This emphasis is further increased by the fact that the accented syllable *si-* of the trochaic
foot *silence* follows the accented *long* without an intervening
unaccented syllable. But when two accented syllables are thrust
together in this way, the reader is forced to take a slight pause
between them. The effect of such a condition is to increase the

[1] Some students may prefer to regard the first foot of the first line as
trochaic and the second as iambic. Even if one takes such a view, the
system of accents and pauses is not altered. One's experience of the particular
verse remains the same.

emphasis on the accented syllables, because the reader has lingered at that point in the verse.

To proceed with the analysis of the line, we may say that the word *it* is an imperfect foot, with the pause dictated by the end of the previous phrase (marked by the semicolon) standing as the missing unaccented syllable. This is followed by a regular iambic foot. The heavy pause after *silence* (a pause dictated by rhetorical construction) gives the effect of the speaker's meditating a moment after making his initial statement as though in order to explore its full meaning before he commits himself to a conclusion. The words that follow, then, come to us with the weight of this meditation. But in addition to this there is a more special effect. The word *it* receives, by reason of the weak syllable (the second syllable of *silence*) and the pause which precede it, an especially heavy emphasis. This heavy emphasis, again, is dramatically right, for the word *it,* usually a fairly unimportant word and lightly stressed, in this context is important. When the word occurs we do not yet know what the *it* refers to; and what it does refer to—what the speaker says is "right"—constitutes the basic statement of the poem. Explaining the *it* gives us the body of the poem.

To summarize, we can say that the first line is characterized by several daring departures from what we discover to be the metrical norm of the poem as a whole; and yet each of these variations, as we have seen, operates to support the intention of the line. (The division into feet used here may seem to some readers arbitrary. There are perhaps other possible interpretations. But in any case, the accented syllables and the pauses are definitely fixed. The important matter is to understand the function of the variations in making the line expressive.)

After the very irregular first line, the basic pattern is asserted in the second line with only one slight and usual variation (the fourth foot, *-ing estranged,* is anapestic rather than iambic, and tends to accelerate the line and emphasize the word *estranged*).

The third line offers two slight variations from the norm. There is a strong *secondary accent* (*Glossary*) on the syllable *-light,* for in the compound word *lamplight,* as is true of most such compounds (*midnight, bookcase*), there is a marked sec-

ondary accent. (Contrast, for example, *lamplight* with *truly* on
this basis.) The result is to give the accent in the foot *-light hid* a
hovering effect rather than that of a decisive fixing on one of
the two syllables. The use of a hovering accent gives a lingering
rhythm—a dwelling on the statement of the central idea of light
being hidden. After this retardation, the trochaic substitution of *under* again accelerates the line to its conclusion, because
of the grouping together of the weak syllables (*-der its*), so that
the reader hastens to the accented syllable at the end.

The next metrical variation occurs in line 6. The second foot,
the supreme, is anapaestic; this means that the syllable *-preme* receives a more than normally emphatic pronunciation. The next
foot is imperfect, containing only the syllable *theme;* a lingering
on the syllable *-preme* and a pause compensate for the missing
syllable in the next foot. This situation, as we have already seen
from line 1, gives unusual emphasis. The emphasis at this point
is further increased by the unusual device of the rime of the two
accented syllables.

Early in line 7 we have the rather unusual situation of three
unaccented syllables in succession between two accented syllables,
the first of the line, *Bod-* and the fifth *crep-*. (This situation may
be described as a dactylic followed by an iambic foot.) [1] The
reader is forced, as it were, to accelerate the pace to reach the
second accent. In this part of the line he is somewhat like a
man running off balance. When he reaches the pause after
wisdom, the metrical structure of the line is still undefined, even
though an iambic movement has set in. After the pause, therefore, the reader is forced to stress, and linger on, the syllable *young,*
for only by this accent does the line achieve any metrical system.
So much for the metrical stress on *young.* But how does this
relate to the meaning intended? *Young* is, obviously, a very important word here. It is set in contrast against everything that
has come before it in the poem, for the preceding part of the
poem gives the picture of age. Indeed, the single adjective *young*
serves as a condensation for some such statement as, "But when
we were young, etc." The word serves, therefore, as a kind of

[1] Or the opening of this line may be scanned as a trochaic foot followed
by an anapaestic foot.

pivot for the poem. The unusual emphasis forced on it by the metrical arrangement of the line fortifies the whole meaning of the word in the poem.

Before discussing the last line, which completes the contrast suggested in the word *young,* it may be well to summarize the general metrical situation in the first seven lines of the poem. We have seen that these seven lines are characterized by a great deal of variation, only lines 4 and 5 being perfectly systematic. The poet has used variation, sometimes extreme variation, to focus certain particular words and to give to the whole poem a flexible movement suggestive of conversation. The reader unconsciously has been waiting for an emphatic assertion of the pattern, which is built toward in lines 1, 2, and 3, and finally stated in lines 4 and 5, but which is rather violently broken again in lines 6 and 7. Consequently, when the pattern is strongly and regularly re-affirmed in the last line, the reader has a sense of a statement uttered with positiveness and finality. This is the general effect of the line, but there is a special effect in the line which is worthy of some comment. We observe that the conjunction *and,* which ordinarily is an unimportant word, receives an accent. But here *and* is a highly important word, for it serves as more than a mere casual connective. We have said earlier that the point of the poem—the theme on which the lovers descant—is that man cannot be complete, cannot possess beauty and wisdom at the same time; and the emphatic connective here condenses and asserts this meaning.[1] The metrical accent falling on *and* gives a clue to, and a reenforcement of, the interpretation of the line and of the poem.

We began the discussion of the meter of this poem by asking why it is so much more rich and moving than the bare statement of content which we had given; and we had just pointed out that, whereas in part this is due to the dramatization and the use of imagery, the meter is largely responsible for the richness and concreteness which the poem has. More specifically, this

---

[1] Readers familiar with Yeats' other work or with his general system of beliefs will recognize in this theme one of the basic parodoxes which occupy his attention. In this connection, "Sailing to Byzantium" may be specially indicated.

richness and concreteness is gained in three ways: (1) The handling of the meter is flexible enough to give the dramatic impression of speech without violating the impression of a metrical pattern. (The poet, of course, does not undertake to give a transcript of conversation; he merely gives, as we have said, an impression, by moving away from a fixed pattern.) (2) The metrical variations are never arbitrary but are used to secure the proper degree of emphasis on words where the meaning is focussed. (3) The development of the idea of the poem is made alive and significant by being underscored by the metrical contrast between lines 7 and 8.

People sometimes make the mistake of supposing that very particular effects are attached to particular metrical situations. They will identify a special emotion or idea with a special movement of verse, and perhaps assume the movement of the verse to be *the* cause. That is, they assume that a particular metrical situation would convey the effect even to a person who did not understand the language in which the poem was written. In opposition to this view I. A. Richards writes as follows:

. . . if the meaning of the words is irrelevant to the form of the verse, and if this independent form possesses aesthetic virtue [can transmit the effect without regard to actual meaning of the words involved], as not a few have maintained, it should be possible to take some recognized masterpiece of poetic rhythm and compose, with nonsense syllables, a double or dummy which at least comes recognizably near to possessing the same virtue.

> J. Drootan-Sussting Benn
> Mill-down Leduren N.
>   Telamba-taras oderwainto weiring
> Awersey zet bidreen
> Ownd istellester sween
>   Lithabian tweet ablissood owdswown stiering
> Apleven aswetsen sestinal
> Yintomen I adaits afurf I gallas Ball.

If the reader has any difficulty in scanning these verses, reference to Milton, *On the Morning of Christ's Nativity,* xv, [p. 458] will prove of assistance, and the attempt to divine the movement of the original before looking it up will at least show how much the sense, syntax, and feeling of verse may serve as an introduction to its form. But the illustration will also support a subtler argument against anyone who affirms that the mere sound of verse has *independently* any considerable aesthetic virtue. For he will either have to say that this verse is valuable (when he may be implored to take up his pen at once and enrich the world with many more such verses, for nothing could be easier), *or* he will have to say that it is the differences *in sound* between this purified dummy and the original which deprive the dummy of poetic merit. In which case he will have to account for the curious fact that just those transformations which redeem it as sound, should also give it the sense and feeling we find in Milton. A staggering coincidence, unless the meaning were highly relevant to the effect of the form.

Such arguments (which might be elaborated) do not tend to diminish the power of the sound (the inherent rhythm) *when it works in conjunction with sense and feeling.* . . . In fact the close co-operation of the form with the meaning—modifying it and being modified by it in ways that though subtle are, in general, perfectly intelligible—is the chief secret of Style in poetry. But so much mystery and obscurity has been raised around this relation by talk about the *identity* of Form and Content, or about the extirpation of the Matter in the Form, that we are in danger of forgetting how natural and inevitable their co-operation must be.[1]

The real point is this: the meter, no more than any other single element in a poem, gives absolute effects; that is, the particular poetic effect in any case does not inhere in the meter alone. But the meter, as our analysis of "After Long Silence" has shown, can be used by the poet as a highly important element to combine with the other elements in order to give the total result which is the poem.

Therefore it is well to remember that metrical analysis is never valuable as an end in itself. The impression that metrical analysis is valuable as an end in itself is sometimes given in hand books on poetry, and may have been suggested by the relative length of the preceding analyses of poems in this Section. A confusion of length of discussion with importance is to be avoided, however.

[1] *Practical Criticism,* New York: Harcourt, Brace, & Co., pp. 232–233.

Metrical analysis, in the very nature of the case, requires detailed and consistent study of specific instances. The question of meter is, of course, extremely important; but, as has been said repeatedly in this section, it is but one contributing element among many, and finally should be considered only in its relation to other elements.

ABSENT YET PRESENT

EDWARD BULWER-LYTTON, LORD LYTTON (1803–1873)

As the flight of a river
    That flows to the sea
My soul rushes ever
    In tumult to thee.

A twofold existence   5
    I am where thou art;
My heart in the distance
    Beats close to thy heart.

Look up, I am near thee,
    I gaze on thy face;   10
I see thee, I hear thee,
    I feel thine embrace.

As a magnet's control on
    The steel it draws to it,
Is the charm of thy soul on   15
    The thoughts that pursue it.

And absence but brightens
    The eyes that I miss,
And custom but heightens
    The spell of thy kiss.   20

It is not from duty,
    Though that may be owed,—
It is not from beauty,
    Though that be bestowed;

But all that I care for,   25
  And all that I know,
Is that, without wherefore,
  I worship thee so.

Through granite it breaketh
  A tree to the ray;   30
As a dreamer forsaketh
  The grief of the day,

My soul in its fever
  Escapes unto thee;
O dream to the griever!   35
  O light to the tree!

A twofold existence
  I am where thou art;
Hark, hear in the distance
  The beat of my heart!   40

EXERCISE:

With the analysis of "The Bells of Shandon" as a model, write a discussion of this poem.

ABSENCE

JOHN HOSKINS (1566–1638)

Absence, hear my protestation
  Against thy strength,
  Distance and length,
Do what thou canst for alteration:
  For hearts of truest metal   5
  Absence doth join, and time doth settle.

Who loves a mistress of right quality,
  His mind hath found
  Affection's ground
Beyond time, place, and all mortality: 10
  To hearts that cannot vary
  Absence is present, time doth tarry.

My senses want their outward motion
   Which now within
   Reason doth win,   15
Redoubled by her secret notion:
   Like rich men that take pleasure
   In hiding more than handling treasure.

By absence this good means I gain
   That I can catch her   20
   Where none can watch her
In some close corner of my brain:
   There I embrace and kiss her,
   And so enjoy her, and so miss her.

EXERCISE:

   Does the movement of this poem contribute to the total effect
of the poem? Compare "Absence" with "Absent, yet Present"
(p. 232) on this basis.

FAIR INES

THOMAS HOOD (1798–1845)

O saw ye not fair Ines?
   She's gone into the West,
To dazzle when the sun is down,
   And rob the world of rest:
She took our daylight with her,   5
   The smiles that we love best,
With morning blushes on her cheek,
   And pearls upon her breast.

O turn again, fair Ines,
   Before the fall of night,   10
For fear the Moon should shine alone,
   And stars unrivalled bright;
And blessèd will the lover be
   That walks beneath their light,

And breathes the love against thy cheek   15
  I dare not even write!

Would I had been, fair Ines,
  That gallant cavalier,
Who rode so gaily by thy side,
  And whispered thee so near!   20
Were there no bonny dames at home,
  Or no true lovers here,
That he should cross the seas to win
  The dearest of the dear?

I saw thee, lovely Ines,   25
  Descend along the shore,
With bands of noble gentlemen,
  And banners waved before;
And gentle youth and maidens gay,
  And snowy plumes they wore: 30
It would have been a beauteous dream,—
  If it had been no more!

Alas, alas! fair Ines!
  She went away with song,
With Music waiting on her steps,   35
  And shoutings of the throng;
But some were sad, and felt no mirth,
  But only Music's wrong,
In sounds that sang Farewell, farewell,
  To her you've loved so long.   40

Farewell, farewell, fair Ines!
  That vessel never bore
So fair a lady on its deck,
  Nor danced so light before,—
Alas for pleasure on the sea,   45
  And sorrow on the shore!
The smile that blessed one lover's heart
  Has broken many more!

EXERCISE:

The general technical competence displayed in this poem is considerably higher than that displayed in "Absent, yet Present" (p. 232). Try to justify this statement, using specific illustrations.

TO HEAVEN

BEN JONSON (1573–1637)

Good and great God! can I not think of thee,
But it must straight my melancholy be?
Is it interpreted in me disease,
That, laden with my sins, I seek for ease?
O be thou witness, that the reins dost know   5
And hearts of all, if I be sad for show;
And judge me after, if I dare pretend
To aught but grace, or aim at other end.
As thou art all, so be thou all to me,
First, midst, and last, converted One and Three!   10
My faith, my hope, my love; and, in this state,
My judge, my witness, and my advocate!
Where have I been this while exiled from thee,
And whither rapt, now thou but stoop'st to me?
Dwell, dwell here still! O, being everywhere,   15
How can I doubt to find thee ever here?
I know my state, both full of shame and scorn,
Conceived in sin, and unto labor born,
Standing with fear, and must with horror fall,
And destined unto judgment, after all.   20
I feel my griefs too, and there scarce is ground
Upon my flesh t' inflict another wound;
Yet dare I not complain or wish for death
With holy Paul, lest it be thought the breath
Of discontent; or that these prayers be   25
For weariness of life, not love of thee.

EXERCISE:

Discuss the metrical situation in the first four lines and in line 15.

AH, SUNFLOWER

WILLIAM BLAKE (1757–1827)

Ah, Sunflower, weary of time,
    Who countest the steps of the sun;
Seeking after that sweet golden clime
    Where the traveller's journey is done;

Where the Youth pined away with desire,   5
And the pale virgin shrouded in snow,
Arise from their graves, and aspire
Where my Sunflower wishes to go!

EXERCISE:

This poem is prevailingly anapaestic in meter. Such poems often tend to give a mechanical rhythm. But this poem does not give such an effect, and, as a matter of fact, is characterized by its delicate and lingering rhythm. We can notice that the first foot in lines 1, 2, and 7 constitute iambic substitutions. Relate these substitutions to the context. But the most important factor in securing the characteristic rhythm of this poem lies in the use of what might be called the secondary accent on the first syllable of the anapaest. For example, the following line might be scanned:

Seeking aft / -er that sweet / golden clime

The first and the third feet are obviously different in effect from the second foot, which is a normal anapaest. The effect of this situation in the anapaest corresponds to that hovering effect given by the secondary accent in an iambic foot. Work out the scansion of the entire poem.

A CHRISTMAS CAROL

GEORGE WITHER (1588–1677)

So, now is come our joyful feast;
Let every man be jolly.
Each room with ivy leaves is dressed,
And every post with holly.
    Though some churls at our mirth repine,   5
    Round your foreheads garlands twine,
    Drown sorrow in a cup of wine.
And let us all be merry.

Now, all our neighbors' chimneys smoke,
And Christmas blocks are burning;   10
Their ovens, they with baked-meats choke,
And all their spits are turning.
  Without the door, let sorrow lie:
   And, if for cold, it hap to die,
   We'll bury 't in a Christmas pie.   15
And evermore be merry.

Rank misers now, do sparing shun:
Their hall of music soundeth:
And, dogs, thence with whole shoulders run,
So, all things there aboundeth.   20
  The country-folk themselves advance;
   For *Crowdy-Mutton's* come out of *France:*
   And *Jack* shall pipe, and *Jill* shall dance,
And all the town be merry.

Ned Swash hath fetched his bands from pawn,   25
And all his best apparel.
Brisk *Nell* hath brought a ruff of lawn,
With droppings of the barrel.
  And those that hardly all the year
   Had bread to eat, or rags to wear,   30
   Will have both clothes, and dainty fare:
And all the day be merry.

Now poor men to the Justices,
With capons make their arrants,
And if they hap to fail of these,   35
They plague them with their warrants.
  But now they feed them with good cheer,
   And what they want, they take in beer:
   For, Christmas *comes but once a year:*
And then they shall be merry.   40

The client now his suit forbears,
The prisoner's heart is eased,
The debtor drinks away his cares,
And, for the time, is pleased.

> Though others' purses be more fat,   45
> Why should we pine or grieve at that?
> *Hang sorrow, care will kill a cat.*
And therefore let's be merry.

> Then wherefore in these merry days,
> Should we, I pray, be duller?   50
> No; let us sing some roundelays,
> To make our mirth the fuller.
>> And, whilest thus inspired we sing,
>> Let all the streets with echoes ring:
>> Woods, and hills, and every thing,   55
> Bear witness we are merry.

EXERCISE:

How is the general rhythm of this poem related to the subject?
Discuss this question in terms of meter.

RHETORICAL VARIATION

It has probably already occurred to the careful reader of poetry
that the rhythm of any individual line, as actually experienced by
the reader, is determined by other factors than the formal metrical
scheme or shifts of metrical accent in that scheme. It should be
clear to anyone that no line of verse, however accurately it can be
scanned, has a purely mechanical regularity—such a regularity,
for instance, as is given by the beat of a metronome. Let us look
at the following line:

Not marble, nor the gilded monuments

(Shakespeare, Sonnet 55)

This line can be scanned as iambic pentameter with absolute
metrical regularity;

Not mar / -ble nor / the gild / -ed mon / -u- ments

The meter would seem to demand an equal accent on each of the
syllables indicated. This might be graphed as follows:

Not mar / ble nor / the gild / -ed mon / -u- ments

But obviously some accented syllables are more important than others, and no one would ever read the line as a purely mechanical sing-song. In earlier comments on meter the student has undoubtedly realized that the marking of accents did not mean the same stress, in practice, would be given to each syllable so indicated. The degree of emphasis dictated by the *sense* would also have to be taken into account. For instance, in the line given above, the word *nor* as a conjunction would not receive as much emphasis as some other syllables. Or, to take another case, *-ments* in the word *monuments,* cannot receive an emphasis equal to that on *mon-* because the word *monuments* is, as a matter of fact, accented on the first syllable. To sum up, any but a purely mechanical reading of the line must take into account such variations as these we have described. On this basis the emphatic syllables in the line are *mar-, gild-,* and *mon-.* Variation from a fixed degree of emphasis for the accented syllables because of the requirements of sense may be called *rhetorical variation.* Thus:

Not mar / -ble nor / the gild / -ed mon / -u- ments

This factor of rhetorical variation appears in all verse, because it exists by the very nature of language; and this factor is one which the competent poet attempts to control. Francis Mahoney in "Shandon Bells" has so neglected the relation of this factor to the metrical factor that one has to read certain parts of the poem as mechanical singsong, distorting the sense, or has to read them according to sense, distorting the metrical pattern past recognition. For instance:

> There's a bell in Moscow,
>
> While on tower and kiosk O!
>
> In Saint Sophia
>
> The Turkman gets,

And loud in air

Calls men to prayer

From tapering summits

Of tall minarets

Here we may see that the exclamation *O* in the second line, which by all sense, or rhetorical, requirements should be heavily accented, is treated according to the metrical pattern as a weak syllable. For an example of very effective co-ordination of metrical and rhetorical factors we may return to "After Long Silence" (p. 224). Let us inspect the relation of the pause which marks the rhetorical units in line 1 to the meaning.

Speech after long silence; // it is right

Such a pause is usually called a *caesura* (*Glossary*). The caesura in line 1 falls after the word *silence*. That is, one word group is completed at that point and another word group is begun. The pause here contributes to the weight of the accent on *it,* and we also have a metrical situation which, as we have said in our previous discussion (p. 227), is dramatically right. Or for another example, let us look at line 6. The line may be scanned and the caesura marked as follows:

Upon the supreme theme//of Art and Song

The sense division gives us two word groups which are marked by the caesura. But we see the significant metrical pause between *supreme* and *theme,* which we have discussed earlier (p. 228). The caesura and the metrical pause before *theme* isolate, as it were, and emphasize that word; and the rime with *supreme* also contributes to the emphasis. And it can be easily observed that *theme* also takes the greatest rhetorical emphasis, with *supreme,* which is also emphasized heavily on metrical grounds, next in importance. A general consideration of this poem in contrast with

"The Bells of Shandon" will show that the meter, the rhetorical variations, and the other factors such as imagery, supplement and corroborate each other. That is, we have a real coherence and unity.

We have been discussing the relation of the various aspects of meter and variations from strict metrical regularity to what is being said in a given poem. Here is a famous passage of verse written to illustrate some of the principles which we have been discussing. The student should attempt to see how fully the poet justifies his statement that the sound should echo the sense, and to ascertain the means which he employs.

SOUND AND SENSE

ALEXANDER POPE (1688–1744)

True ease in writing comes from art, not chance,
As those move easiest who have learned to dance.
'T is not enough no harshness gives offense,
The sound must seem an echo to the sense:
Soft is the strain when Zephyr gently blows,   5
And the smooth stream in smoother numbers flows;
But when loud surges lash the sounding shore,
The hoarse, rough verse should like the torrent roar:
When Ajax strives some rock's vast weight to throw,   10
The line too labors, and the words move slow;
Not so, when swift Camilla scours the plain,
Flies o'er the unbending corn, and skims along the main.
Hear how Timotheus' varied lays surprise,
And bid alternate passions fall and rise!   15
(From "An Essay on Criticism")

QUANTITATIVE VARIATION AND ONOMATOPOEIA

There remains to be considered one more important kind of variation from the regularity that would be dictated by meter. This variation involves the question of time. Some syllables require a relatively longer time than others for pronunciation.

Syllables containing long vowels or syllables containing several consonants, for example, require a longer time than other syllables. This means that, for example, one iambic foot may be really longer than another iambic foot, or one iambic pentameter line longer than another. For instance, both of the following lines are iambic pentameter:

'Mid hushed, cool-rooted flowers fragrant-eyed
             ("Ode to Psyche," John Keats)
How soon they find fit instruments of ill
             ("Rape of the Lock," Alexander Pope)

By the very nature of language what we may call the *quantitative aspect* (*Glossary*) will vary from line to line. From syllable to syllable different lengths of time are required for pronunciation. This factor is constantly interplaying with the strictly metrical factor. For instance, a syllable that is long in quantity may or may not receive a metrical accent. In the line by Keats given above, the foot, *cool-rooted,* is composed of two very long syllables; there is a hovering effect in the accentuation, but the foot fits the iambic pattern. The mere fact of the inter-play of the quantitative with the strictly metrical factor gives a vitality to verse. But, further, the quantitative factor may sometimes be adjusted to special effects, as in the line by Keats which is quoted above.

In regard to the relation of verse effects to the meaning, it may be well to comment on the special relation which is called *onomatopoeia.* (*Glossary*). The word means properly *name-making.* Words that are imitative of their own literal meanings are *onomatopoeic.* For example: *bang, fizz, hiss, crackle, murmur, moan, whisper, roar.* We may observe that all of the words listed here denote special sounds. *The sound of a word can only be truly imitative of a sound, and only to such words can the term onomatopoeia be strictly applied.* Obviously, onomatopoeia can only be occasional in poetry. An example often given is found in the following lines from Tennyson's "Princess":

The moan of doves in immemorial elms,
And murmuring of innumerable bees.

We have two strictly onomatopoeic words in these lines, *moan* and *murmuring*. The poet, in each line, supports and extends the particular onomatopoeic effect by repeating the sounds found in the onomatopoeic word. For instance, in the first line, the *m* and *o* are repeated in "*imme*m*o*rial el*ms*." Since the particular sound association has been already established by the denotation of *moan,* the repetitions of the sounds become part of the onomatopoeic effect. The same principle is at work in the next line. But if, for example, the line were not introduced by the specific meaning of *moan* it is highly improbable that anyone would discover onomatopoeia in the line.

It is important to insist upon at least a relatively strict interpretation of the term onomatopoeia and of onomatopoeic effects, for it is very easy for an unwary critic to attribute to onomatopoeia effects which arise from other causes. Such critics attribute a particular imitative meaning to the sound of a word, when at best only a general suitability, usually arising from causes which we have been discussing in this section, can actually be observed. For example here is what one critic has written of a certain line of Edna St. Vincent Millay's poetry:

"But she gets many different effects with clusters of unaccented syllables. With the many *f*'s and *r*'s and *th*'s a fine feeling of fluffiness is given to one line by the many unaccented syllables:

      /   /   /   /

    Comfort, softer than the feathers of its breast,

sounds as soft as the bird's downy breast feels."

But another critic challenges this interpretation, as follows: ". . . the effect [is said to be] a fine feeling of fluffiness and a softness as of the bird's downy breast, while the cause is said to be the many unaccented syllables, assisted by the many *f*'s, *r*'s and *th*'s. But I will substitute a line which preserves all these factors and departs from the given line mainly by rearrangement:

    Crumpets for the foster-fathers of the brats.

Here I miss both fluffiness and downiness." [1]

[1] John Crowe Ransom, "The Poet as Woman," *The Southern Review,* Vol. 2, number 4, pp. 796–97.

In the same way, one might imagine a critic stating that the following line by Keats is onomatopoeic, and identifying the suggestion of coolness and repose with the presence of certain vowel and consonant sounds:

'Mid hushed, cool-rooted flowers fragrant-eyed.

The line does give an effect of coolness and repose, *but the effect is not to be identified with specific vowels or consonants, nor are specific vowels and consonants to be defined as the cause of the impression.* What one can say of the sound effect of the line is this. The hovering accent on the foot, *cool-rooted,* and the length and sonority of the vowels repeated in the foot, emphasize these words, which with the accented word *hushed* just preceding, set the whole impression of coolness and repose; but they set it primarily by their literal meanings. The lingering rhythm of the line, caused largely by the length of the dominant syllables may be said furthermore to be appropriate here to the effect— it suggests a place where one would like to linger. But a lingering rhythm might be used in another context with a very different intention. The function of the verse as such is highly important, but important in supporting and stressing the meaning. Close analysis of the elements of verse is extremely valuable for any reader of poetry. But such analysis runs into absurdity when the reader begins to forget the cardinal principle which has already been stated several times: poetry is a result of a relationship among various elements and does not ever inhere specially in any single element. In the following poems the students should try to analyze the verse in relation to the other factors.

SLOW, SLOW, FRESH FOUNT

BEN JONSON (1573–1637)

Slow, slow, fresh fount, keep time with my salt tears;
   Yet slower, yet, O faintly gentle springs:
List to the heavy part the music bears,
   Woe weeps out her division, when she sings.

Droop herbs, and flowers;   5
Fall grief in showers;
Our beauties are not ours:
    O, I could still
(Like melting snow upon some craggy hill,)
        Drop, drop, drop, drop,   10
Since nature's pride is, now, a withered daffodil.
                        (From *Cynthia's Revels*)

EXERCISE:

Discuss this poem in regard to questions of quantity, onomatopoeia, and hovering accent as related to the intention of the poem.

TO AUTUMN

JOHN KEATS (1795–1821)

Season of mists and mellow fruitfulness,
    Close bosom friend of the maturing sun:
Conspiring with him how to load and bless
    With fruit the vines that round the thatch-eaves run;
To bend with apples the mossed cottage-trees,   5
    And fill all fruit with ripeness to the core;
        To swell the gourd, and plump the hazel shells
With a sweet kernel; to set budding more,
    And still more, later flowers for the bees,
    Until they think warm days will never cease,   10
        For Summer has o'er-brimmed their clammy cells.

Who hath not seen thee oft amid thy store?
    Sometimes whoever seeks abroad may find
Thee sitting careless on a granary floor,   15
    Thy hair soft-lifted by the winnowing wind;
Or on a half-reaped furrow sound asleep,
    Drowsed with the fume of poppies, while thy hook
        Spares the next swath and all its twinèd flowers:
And sometimes like a gleaner thou dost keep,   20
    Steady thy laden head across a brook;
    Or by a cider-press, with patient look,
        Thou watchest the last oozings hours by hours.

Where are the songs of Spring?   Ay, where are they?
　　Think not of them, thou hast thy music too,—   25
While barrèd clouds bloom the soft-dying day,
　　And touch the stubble-plains with rosy hue;
Then in a wailful choir the small gnats mourn
　　Among the river sallows, borne aloft
　　　　Or sinking as the light wind lives or dies;   30
And full-grown lambs loud bleat from hilly bourn;
　　Hedge-crickets sing: and now with treble soft
　　The red-breast whistles from a garden-croft;
　　　　And gathering swallows twitter in the skies.

EXERCISE:

Discuss this poem in regard to questions of metrical variation,
onomatopoeia, quantity, and hovering accent as related to the
intention of the poem.

THE BLINDNESS OF SAMSON

JOHN MILTON (1608–1674)

O loss of sight, of thee I most complain!
Blind among enemies, O worse than chains,
Dungeon, or beggary, or decrepit age!
Light, the prime work of God, to me is extinct,
And all her various objects of delight   5
Annulled, which might in part my grief have eased,
Inferior to the vilest now become
Of man or worm; the vilest here excel me,
They creep, yet see, I dark in light exposed
To daily fraud, contempt, abuse and wrong,   10
Within doors, or without, still as a fool,
In power of others, never in my own;
Scarce half I seem to live, dead more than half.
O dark, dark, dark, amid the blaze of noon,
Irrevocably dark, total eclipse   15
Without all hope of day!
O first created beam, and thou great Word,

Let there be light, and light was over all;
Why am I thus bereaved Thy prime decree?
The sun to me is dark   20
And silent as the moon,
When she deserts the night
Hid in her vacant interlunar cave.
Since light so necessary is to life,
And almost life itself, if it be true   25
That light is in the soul,
She all in every part; why was the sight
To such a tender ball as th' eye confined?
So obvious and so easy to be quenched,
And not as feeling through all parts diffused,   30
That she might look at will through every pore?
Then had I not been thus exiled from light;
As in the land of darkness yet in light,
To live a life half dead, a living death,
And buried; but O yet more miserable!   35
Myself, my sepulcher, a moving grave.
                              (From *Samson Agonistes*)

EXERCISE:

1. Discuss metrical variation in the first five lines of this
passage and in line 14.

2. What is the reason for the unusual grammatical construction
in lines 17 and 18?

3. Why, in lines 20 and 21, does Samson say that the sun is
silent as the moon? Since the sun is, of course, silent, what is
served by this statement?

FUNERAL SONG

JOHN FLETCHER (1579–1625)

Urns and odors, bring away,
Vapors, sighs, darken the day;
Our dole more deadly looks than dying
Balms, and gums, and heavy cheers,

　　　　Sacred vials filled with tears,   5
　　　　And clamors, through the wild air flying:

　　　　Come all sad and solemn shows,
　　　　That are quick-eyed pleasure's foes;
　　　　We convent nought else but woes.
　　　　　　We convent nought else but woes.   10
　　　　　　(From *The Two Noble Kinsmen*)

EXERCISE:

Write an analysis of technical factors involved in this poem.

RIME AND STANZA

All of our previous discussion in this section of the book has been concerned with aspects of rhythm. We have pointed out that rhythm is a constant factor in all use of language, and that its use in verse is a special adaptation. But there are other factors that tend to shape and bind poetry that are not ever-present in the use of language. These factors are *alliteration, assonance, consonance,* and *rime.* (*Glossary*) All of these involve the element of repetition of identical or of related sounds; and it is this repetition that gives the impression of a binding of the words together.

In poetry written during the Old English period the device of alliteration was used regularly for the purpose of defining a poetic scheme. The following lines illustrate, in modern English, the way alliteration was used to give lines unity, just as meter tends to unify a line:

　　　　Now *B*eowulf *b*ode in the *b*urg of the Scyldings,
　　　　*l*eader be*l*ovèd, and *l*ong he ruled
　　　　in *f*ame with all *f*olk, since his *f*ather had gone
　　　　a*w*ay from the *w*orld, till a*w*oke an heir . . ..
　　　　　　(From *Beowulf,* translated by Francis B. Gummere.)

But now alliteration is not used in verse according to any regular scheme. Where is occurs frequently, as in the work of Swinburne (p. 290), it often impresses the reader as a mechanical and monotonous mannerism or a too gaudy decoration. Most poets use it with discretion to give a line or a group of lines a greater unity or to emphasize the words alliterated. In the following lines we can see how alliteration is used to emphasize and support the contrast in the second line and to relate the contrast to the word, *forgot:*

> Hast thou *forgot* me then, and do I seem
> Now in thine eye so *foul*, once deemed so *fair*
>   (From *Paradise Lost,* Book II, John Milton)

Assonance may sometimes serve the same purposes of binding or emphasis. In the following line from Keats, one already given for other illustration, we can see a good example of assonance used for emphasis:

> 'Mid hushed, *cool-root*ed flowers fragrant-eyed

We have already pointed out the effect of the hovering accent in the foot *cool-root*—and of the length and sonority of the vowel sound. (p. 245). The repetition of this vowel sound, that is, the assonance, lends even greater emphasis. Let us examine another example:

> Or alum styptics with contracting power
> Shrink his thin essence like a shriveled flower;
> Or, as Ixion fixed, the wretch shall feel
> The giddy motion of the whirling mill . . .
>   (From *The Rape of the Lock,* Canto II, by
>   Alexander Pope)

Here the most obvious result of the sustained assonance, involving both accented and unaccented syllables, is the high degree of unification. In the second place we can see how emphasis is secured by repetition in new combinations of the vowel sounds of the most important syllables.

Consonance occurs much more rarely than assonance, but is sometimes used much more systematically. In the following lines we see consonance serving to link lines in the same way as rime:

> You are the one whose part it is to *lean,*
> For whom it is not good to be *alone.*
> Laugh warmly turning shyly in the *hall*
> Or climb with bare knees the volcanic *hill*
> (From "III," *Poems,* by W. H. Auden)

Consonance is not confined, however, to such cases, but may occur internally in a single line or in several lines to serve the same general function as assonance. This use, however, is much rarer than the use of mere alliteration or assonance.

Rime is the most emphatic binder used in English verse. Alliteration, assonance, and consonance may be regarded as types of rime; that is, they derive from sound resemblances. But it is customary to confine the use of the term *rime* to instances of end-rime. There are several types of rime, *masculine, feminine, weak,* etc. (*Glossary*). Instances of these will appear in the poems of this section.

Rime serves usually, as we have already said, to bind lines together into larger units of composition. We have already seen that the metrical scheme of a single line does its work by setting up in the mind of the hearer or reader an anticipation of regular recurrence. In the same way a fixed pattern of riming, a *rime scheme,* will, in conjunction with a fixed pattern of line lengths, a *stanza* (*Glossary*), define a group of lines as a unit. In stanzas where rime is employed the rime emphasizes the nature of the stanza pattern by marking the end of each line unit. But rime is sometimes used irregularly; in such cases, it still exerts a binding and unifying effect, though much less forcefully. In addition, irregular rime may appear as a device of emphasis, in so far as it has not been used consistently in the poem or passage. The basic function of rime, however, has already been described: the unifying and "forming" function, which is most positively exhibited in the reinforcing of the line pattern of stanzas.[1]

There are a number of different stanza forms in use in English

[1] Although the function of rime as a structural factor is emphasized here, there is, of course a pleasure intrinsic in rime itself. Children, for example, delight even in nonsense rimes. But the functional use of rime is much more important than the "decorative" use. (*Glossary* under *rime*).

poetry.   A student may consult the *Glossary* for systematic definitions of them.   A knowledge of the stanza types is important, of
course; but *any given type of stanza must be regarded as an
instrument at the poet's disposal and not as a thing important in
itself.*   The same instrument may be used for widely different purposes.   Any given type of stanza is used in conjunction with
so many other poetic factors that a reader must be very wary of
attributing special effects to special stanza forms.   Only the most
general principles may be arrived at concerning stanza forms
considered in isolation from other poetic factors.   For instance, it
is fair to say that complicated stanza forms such as the *Spenserian
stanza* (*Glossary*) are not primarily suitable to long narrative
poems because the involved form may become monotonous and
may impede the movement of the action (p. 265).   But the
folly of asserting, as many people have, that the *sonnet* (*Glossary*)
is especially adapted for love poetry will be demonstrated by the
following pair of sonnets:

HOW DO I LOVE THEE

ELIZABETH BARRETT BROWNING (1809–1861)

How do I love thee?   Let me count the ways.
I love thee to the depth and breadth and height
My soul can reach, when feeling out of sight
For the ends of Being and ideal Grace.
I love thee to the level of everyday's   5
Most quiet need, by sun and candle-light.
I love thee freely, as men strive for Right;
I love thee purely, as they turn from Praise.
I love thee with the passion put to use
In my old griefs, and with my childhood's faith.   10
I love thee with a love I seemed to lose
With my lost saints,—I love thee with the breath,
Smiles, tears, of all my life!—and, if God choose,
I shall but love thee better after death.
                                        (From *Sonnets from the Portuguese*)

ON THE LATE MASSACRE IN PIEDMONT

JOHN MILTON (1608–1674)

Avenge, O Lord, thy slaughtered saints, whose bones
Lie scattered on the Alpine mountains cold;
Even them who kept thy truth so pure of old,
When all our fathers worshipped stocks and stones,
Forget not: in thy book record their groans   5
Who were thy sheep, and in their ancient fold
Slain by the bloody Piedmontese, that rolled
Mother with infant down the rocks. Their moans
The vales redoubled to the hills, and they
To heaven. Their martyred blood and ashes sow   10
O'er all the Italian fields, where still doth sway
The triple Tyrant that from these may grow
A hundredfold, who, having learnt thy way,
Early may fly the Babylonian woe.

These sonnets have precisely the same rime scheme, both being
examples of what is called the *Italian sonnet* (*Glossary*). But
the difference in subject matter and treatment is obvious, and
this simple example should indicate why one should be extremely
cautious in assuming that any effect or subject matter is absolutely
associated with a particular stanza form. The proper approach
to the study of the significance of stanza form may be through
this question: *how does the poet use his stanza form in any given
poem to produce the special effect of that poem?*

   In answering this question in any instance, one must bring into
play all the principles which have been previously discussed
in this section. But there are still other principles which must
be taken into consideration in answering this question. In particular, there is the consideration of the relation of the rhetorical
structure, not only to the metrical pattern within the line, which we
have already discussed (pp. 239–42) but also to the stanza pattern
itself. Obviously the distribution of pauses within the lines (p.
241) and of pauses at the ends of lines will have an important
bearing on the general effect of any stanza form. Stanzas that
have a large number of marked pauses at the ends of lines tend

to be strongly defined; stanzas that have many run-over lines, or *enjambments* (*Glossary*) tend to give an impression of fluidity and speed. But the effects of the distribution of pauses at the ends of lines are constantly conditioned by the rhythms used within the lines themselves and by the distribution and emphasis of pauses within the lines.

Among the following poems will be found examples of many of the patterns of lines which usually appear in English poetry.[1] The student should try to investigate, in each case, the basis for the poet's choice of a particular form and the relation the form bears to the total effect of the poem; he should try to investigate the particular way in which a given form has been used; and he should compare each selection with other items using the same form for a different intention.

CONFESSION OF FAITH

JOHN DRYDEN (1631–1700)

But, gracious God, how well dost Thou provide
For erring judgments an unerring guide!
Thy throne is darkness in th' abyss of light,
A blaze of glory that forbids the sight;
O teach me to believe Thee thus concealed,   5
And search no farther than Thyself revealed;
But her alone for my director take
Whom Thou hast promised never to forsake!
My thoughtless youth was winged with vain desires,
My manhood, long misled with wand'ring fires,   10
Followed false lights; and when their glimpse was gone,
My pride struck out new sparkles of her own.
Such was I, such by nature still I am,
Be Thine the glory and be mine the shame.

[1] In the *Glossary* under *stanza* will be found definitions of the standard forms used in English, and an index of the forms appears in this book. The index can be used as a guide for preparing additional exercises involving a consideration of the various uses made of stanza forms.

Good life be now my task: my doubts are done,   15
(What more could fright my faith, than Three in One?)

(From *The Hind and the Panther*)

MY LAST DUCHESS

ROBERT BROWNING (1812–1889)

That's my last Duchess painted on the wall,
Looking as if she were alive; I call
That piece a wonder, now: Fra Pandolf's hands
Worked busily a day, and there she stands.
Will't please you sit and look at her? I said   5
"Fra Pandolf" by design, for never read
Strangers like you that pictured countenance,
The depth and passion of its earnest glance,
But to myself they turned (since none puts by
The curtain I have drawn for you, but I)   10
And seemed as they would ask me, if they durst,
How such a glance came there; so, not the first
Are you to turn and ask thus. Sir, 'twas not
Her husband's presence only, called that spot
Of joy into the Duchess' cheek: perhaps   15
Fra Pandolf chanced to say "Her mantle laps
Over my Lady's wrist too much," or "Paint
Must never hope to reproduce the faint
Half-flush that dies along her throat"; such stuff
Was courtesy, she thought, and cause enough   20
For calling up that spot of joy. She had
A heart . . . how shall I say? . . . too soon made glad,
Too easily impressed; she liked whate'er
She looked on, and her looks went everywhere.
Sir, 'twas all one! My favor at her breast,   25
The dropping of the daylight in the West,
The bough of cherries some officious fool
Broke in the orchard for her, the white mule
She rode with round the terrace—all and each
Would draw from her alike the approving speech,   30
Or blush, at least. She thanked men,—good; but thanked

Somehow . . . I know not how . . . as if she ranked
My gift of a nine-hundred-years-old name
With anybody's gift. Who'd stoop to blame
This sort of trifling? Even had you skill   35
In speech—(which I have not)—to make your will
Quite clear to such an one, and say "Just this
Or that in you disgusts me; here you miss
Or there exceed the mark"—and if she let
Herself be lessoned so, nor plainly set   40
Her wits to yours, forsooth, and made excuse,
—E'en then would be some stooping, and I choose
Never to stoop. Oh, Sir, she smiled, no doubt,
Whene'er I passed her; but who passed without
Much the same smile? This grew; I gave commands;   45
Then all smiles stopped together. There she stands
As if alive. Will't please you rise? We'll meet
The company below, then. I repeat,
The Count your Master's known munificence
Is ample warrant that no just pretence   50
Of mine for dowry will be disallowed;
Though his fair daughter's self, as I avowed
At starting, is my object. Nay, we'll go
Together down, Sir! Notice Neptune, though,
Taming a sea-horse, thought a rarity,   55
Which Claus of Innsbruck cast in bronze for me.

PREPARATION OF THE PYRE FOR PATROCLUS

ALEXANDER POPE (1688–1744)

But Agamemnon, as the rites demand,
With mules and wagons sends a chosen band
To load the timber and the pile to rear,
A charge consigned to Merion's faithful care.
With proper instruments they take the road,   5
Axes to cut, and ropes to sling the load.
First march the heavy mules, securely slow,
O'er hills, o'er dales, o'er crags, o'er rocks, they go:
Jumping high o'er the shrubs of the rough ground,

Rattle the clatt'ring cars, and the shocked axle bound. 10
But when arrived at Ida's spreading woods
(Fair Ida, watered with descending floods),
Loud sounds the axe, redoubling strokes on strokes;
On all sides round the forest hurls her oaks
Headlong. Deep-echoing groan the thickets brown;   15
Then rustling, crackling, crashing, thunder down.

(From *The Iliad*)

EXERCISE:

1. All these selections are in iambic pentameter couplets, and
yet the effect of each is very different. For instance, contrast the
poem by Browning, and "The Confession of Faith," by Dryden.
The first exhibits frequent enjambment, many heavy pauses within
the lines, and a certain degree of metrical irregularity. The intention has been to give a flavor of conversation; the reader is
scarcely aware, at times, of the rime. In the second example
there is little enjambment, the rimes are emphasized, there are
few heavy pauses within the line, and the general temper of the
piece is one of positive though reverent statement. The metrical
factors in each case support the intended effect.

2. Compare and contrast the use of the couplet in "Atticus"
(p. 353) with the use in these two pieces.

3. Discuss "Patroclus" on the basis of onomatopoeia.

THE RETREAT

HENRY VAUGHAN (1622–1695)

Happy those early days, when I
Shined in my angel-infancy!
Before I understood this place
Appointed for my second race,
Or taught my soul to fancy aught   5
But a white celestial thought:
When yet I had not walk'd above
A mile or two from my first Love,
And looking back—at that short space—

Could see a glimpse of His bright face: 10
When on some gilded cloud, or flow'r,
My gazing soul would dwell an hour,
And in those weaker glories spy
Some shadows of eternity:
Before I taught my tongue to wound   15
My conscience with a sinful sound,
Or had the black art to dispense
A several sin to ev'ry sense,
But felt through all this fleshly dress
Bright shoots of everlastingness.   20
    O how I long to travel back,
And tread again that ancient track!
That I might once more reach that plain
Where first I left my glorious train;
From whence th' enlightened spirit sees   25
That shady City of Palm-trees.
But ah! my soul with too much stay
Is drunk, and staggers in the way!
Some men a forward motion love,
But I by backward steps would move;   30
And when this dust falls to the urn,
In that state I came, return.

EXERCISE:

This poem is written in a tetrameter couplet. Contrast this
poem with the portrait of Hudibras (p. 351), which also employs
the tetrameter couplet. Try to define as many factors as possible
that contribute to the difference of effect.

A THANKSGIVING TO GOD, FOR HIS HOUSE

ROBERT HERRICK (1591–1674)

Lord, Thou hast given me a cell
        Wherein to dwell,
A little house, whose humble roof
        Is weather-proof;

Under the spars of which I lie   5
    Both soft, and dry;
Where Thou my chamber for to ward
    Hast set a guard
Of harmless thoughts, to watch and keep
    Me, while I sleep.   10
Low is my porch, as is my fate,
    Both void of state;
And yet the threshold of my door
    Is worn by th' poor,
Who thither come, and freely get   15
    Good words, or meat;
Like as my parlor, so my hall
    And kitchen's small:
A little buttery, and therein
    A little bin,   20
Which keeps my little loaf of bread
    Unchipped, unflead: [1]
Some brittle sticks of thorn or briar
    Make me a fire,
Close by whose living coal I sit,   25
    I glow like it.
Lord, I confess too, when I dine,
    The pulse is Thine,
And all those other bits, that be
    There placed by Thee;   30
The worts, the purslain, and the mess
    Of water cress,
Which of Thy kindness Thou hast sent;
    And my content
Make those, and my beloved beet,   35
    To be more sweet.
'Tis Thou that crown'st my glittering hearth
    With guiltless mirth;
And giv'st me wassail bowls to drink,
    Spiced to the brink.   40
Lord, 'tis Thy plenty-dropping hand,
    That soils my land;
And giv'st me, for my bushel sown,
    Twice ten for one:
Thou mak'st my teeming hen to lay   45
    Her egg each day:

[1] Unflayed, whole

Besides my healthful ewes to bear
  Me twins each year:
The while the conduits of my kine
  Run cream (for wine).   50
All these, and better Thou dost send
  Me, to this end,
That I should render, for my part,
  A thankful heart;
Which, fired with incense, I resign,   55
  As wholly Thine;
But the acceptance, that must be,
  My Christ, by Thee.

EXERCISE:

1. Try to compare the effect of this poem in mixed couplet form with the imagined effect of such a poem in regular tetrameter couplet form.

2. This form might easily become very monotonous. Discuss some of the means employed by Herrick to avoid this defect.

THE ADDRESS OF RICHARD III TO HIS ARMY

WILLIAM SHAKESPEARE (1564–1616)

What shall I say more than I have inferred?
Remember whom you are to cope withal:
A sort of vagabonds, rascals, and run-aways,
A scum of Bretons and base lackey peasants,
Whom their o'er-cloyed country vomits forth   5
To desperate adventures and assured destruction.
You sleeping safe, they bring you to unrest;
You having lands, and blessed with beauteous wives,
They would restrain the one, distain the other.
And who doth lead them but a paltry fellow,   10
Long kept in Britain at our mother's cost?
A milksop, one that never in his life
Felt so much cold as over shoes in snow?
Let's whip these stragglers o'er the sea again;

Lash hence these overweening rags of France,   15
These famished beggars, weary of their lives;
Who, but for dreaming on this fond exploit,
For want of means, poor rats, had hanged themselves:
If we be conquered, let men conquer us,
And not these bastard Bretons; whom our fathers   20
Have in their own land beaten, bobbed, and thumped,
And, on record, left them the heirs of shame.
Shall these enjoy our lands? lie with our wives?
Ravish our daughters?   [*Drum afar off*.
                    Hark! I hear their drum.   25
Fight, gentlemen of England! fight, bold yeomen!
Draw, archers, draw your arrows to the head!
Spur your proud horses hard, and ride in blood;
Amaze the welkin with your broken staves!

(From *Richard III*)

DISCOVERY OF PITY

WILLIAM SHAKESPEARE (1564–1616)

Poor naked wretches, wheresoe'er you are,
That bide the pelting of this pitiless storm,
How shall your houseless heads and unfed sides,
Your looped and windowed raggedness, defend you
From seasons such as these? O! I have ta'en   5
Too little care of this. Take physic, pomp;
Expose thyself to feel what wretches feel,
That thou mayst shake the superflux to them,
And show the heavens more just.

(From *King Lear*)

FLOWERS

WILLIAM SHAKESPEARE (1564–1616)

Perdita   Out, alas!
You'd be so lean, that blasts of January
Would blow you through and through. Now my fair'st
    friend,

I would I had some flowers o' the spring that might
Become your time of day; and yours, and yours,   5
That wear upon your virgin branches yet
Your maidenheads growing: O Proserpina!
For the flowers now that frighted thou let'st fall
From Dis's waggon! daffodils,
That come before the swallow dares, and take   10
The winds of March with beauty; violets dim,
But sweeter than the lids of Juno's eyes
Or Cytherea's breath; pale prime-roses,
That die unmarried, ere they can behold
Bright Phœbus in his strength, a malady   15
Most incident to maids; bold oxlips and
The crown imperial; lilies of all kinds,
The flower-de-luce being one. O! these I lack
To make you garlands of, and my sweet friend,
To strew him o'er and o'er!   20
    Florizel   What! like a corse?
    Perdita   No, like a bank for love to lie and play on;
Not like a corse; or if,—not to be buried,
But quick and in mine arms. Come, take your flowers:
Methinks I play as I have seen them do   25
In Whitsun pastorals: sure this robe of mine
Does change my disposition.
    Florizel   What you do
Still betters what is done. When you speak, sweet,
I'd have you do it ever. . . .   30
                    (From *The Winter's Tale*)

BEËLZEBUB RISES TO SPEAK

JOHN MILTON (1608–1674)

He scarce had finished, when such murmur filled
The assembly, as when hollow rocks retain
The sound of blustering winds, which all night long
Had roused the sea, now with hoarse cadence lull
Seafaring men o'erwatched, whose bark by chance,   5
Or pinnace, anchors in a craggy bay
After the tempest: such applause was heard

As Mammon ended, and his sentence pleased,
Advising peace; for such another field
They dreaded worse than Hell; so much the fear   10
Of thunder and the sword of Michael
Wrought still within them; and no less desire
To found this nether empire, which might rise,
By policy, and long process of time,
In emulation opposite to Heaven.   15
Which when Beëlzebub perceived—than whom,
Satan except, none higher sat—with grave
Aspect he rose, and in his rising seemed
A pillar of state. Deep on his front engraven
Deliberation sat and public care;   20
And princely counsel in his face yet shone,
Majestic, though in ruin. Sage he stood,
With Atlantean shoulders fit to bear
The weight of mightiest monarchies; his look
Drew audience and attention still as night   25
Or summer's noontide air, while thus he spake:—
                              (From *Paradise Lost*)

EXERCISE:

In addition to the foregoing passages of blank verse reread
"Michael" (p. 71) and "The Death of the Hired Man" (p. 85).
Make a comparative study of the use of blank verse in these
various selections, with especial attention to enjambment, placing
of the caesura, metrical variation, and other technical factors.
Try to relate these factors to the general intention of each passage.

THE HOUSE OF MORPHEUS

EDMUND SPENSER (1552–1599)

He making speedy way through spersèd air,
And through the world of waters wide and deep,
To Morpheus' house doth hastily repair.
Amid the bowels of the earth full steep,

And low, where dawning day doth never peep,   5
His dwelling is; there Tethys [1] his wet bed
Doth ever wash, and Cynthia [2] still doth steep
In silver dew his ever-drooping head,
Whiles sad Night over him her mantle black doth spread.

Whose double gates he findeth lockèd fast,   10
The one fair framed of burnished ivory,
The other all with silver overcast;
And wakeful dogs before them far do lie,
Watching to banish Care their enemy,
Who oft is wont to trouble gentle Sleep.   15
By them the sprite doth pass in quietly,
And unto Morpheus comes, whom drownèd deep
In drowsy fit he finds: of nothing he takes keep.

And more to lull him in his slumber soft,
A trickling stream from high rock tumbling down   20
And ever-drizzling rain upon the loft,
Mixed with a murmuring wind, much like the sound
Of swarming bees, did cast him in a swoon:
No other noise, nor people's troublous cries,
As still are wont t'annoy the wallèd town,   25
Might there be heard: but careless Quiet lies,
Wrapped in eternal silence far from enemies.

(From *The Faerie Queene, Book I.*)

NOVEMBER EVENING

ROBERT BURNS (1759–1796)

November chill blaws loud wi' angry sugh,[1]
    The short'ning winter day is near a close;
The miry beasts retreating frae the pleugh,
    The black'ning trains o' craws to their repose;
    The toil-worn cotter frae his labor goes,—   5

[1] ocean   [2] moon   [1] moan

This night his weekly moil is at an end,—
   Collects his spades, his mattocks, and his hoes,
Hoping the morn in ease and rest to spend,
And weary, o'er the moor, his course does hameward bend.

At length his lonely cot appears in view,   10
   Beneath the shelter of an agèd tree;
Th' expectant wee-things, toddlin, stacher [2] through
   To meet their dad, wi' flichterin [3] noise an' glee.
His wee bit ingle,[4] blinkin bonilie,
His clean hearth-stane, his thrifty wifie's smile,   15
   The lisping infant prattling on his knee,
Does a' his weary kiaugh [5] and care beguile,
An' makes him quite forget his labor an' his toil.

               (From "The Cotter's Saturday Night")

EXERCISE:

1. In connection with these two examples of the Spenserian stanza reread "Ocean" (p. 187), by Byron. The Spenserian stanza was invented by Edmund Spenser, who used it in his *epic* (*Glossary*) poem, *The Faerie Queene* (p. 263). Compare and contrast these various examples, noting the function in each of various technical factors.

2. Discuss the selection from Spenser in regard to onomatopoeic effects.

3. Investigate the appropriateness for narrative of the Spenserian stanza, using "The Eve of Saint Agnes" (p. 151) by Keats as an example. In this connection take into account the statement on p. 252.

THE BEGINNING OF LOVE

JOHN KEATS (1795–1821)

Fair Isabel, poor simple Isabel!
Lorenzo, a young palmer in Love's eye!

---

[2] stagger   [3] fluttering   [4] fire-place   [5] anxiety

They could not in the self-same mansion dwell
Without some stir of heart, some malady;
They could not sit at meals but feel how well   5
It soothed each to be the other by;
They could not, sure, beneath the same roof sleep,
But to each other dream, and nightly weep.

With every morn their love grew tenderer,
With every eve deeper and tenderer still;   10
He might not in house, field, or garden stir,
But her full shape would all his seeing fill;
And his continual voice was pleasanter
To her, than noise of trees or hidden rill;
Her lute-string gave an echo of his name,   15
She spoilt her half-done broidery with the same.

He knew whose gentle hand was at the latch
Before the door had given her to his eyes;
And from her chamber-window he would catch
Her beauty farther than the falcon spies;   20
And constant as her vespers would he watch,
Because her face was turned to the same skies;
And with sick longing all the night outwear,
To hear her morning-step upon the stair.

                                        (From *Isabella*)

THE LAKE POETS

GEORGE GORDON, LORD BYRON (1788–1824)

All are not moralists, like Southey, when
    He prated to the world of "Pantisocracy";
Or Wordsworth, unexcised, unhired, who then
    Seasoned his peddler poems with democracy:
Or Coleridge, long before his flighty pen   5
    Let to the *Morning Post* its aristocracy;
When he and Southey, following the same path,
Espoused two partners [1] (milliners of Bath).

[1] Coleridge and Southey married sisters

Such names at present cut a convict figure,
 The very Botany Bay² in moral geography;   10
Their loyal treason, renegado rigor,
 Are good manure for their more bare biography.
Wordsworth's last quarto, by the way, is bigger
 Than any since the birthday of typography;
A drowsy, frowsy poem called *The Excursion,*   15
Writ in a manner which is my aversion. . . .

But let me to my story: I must own,
 If I have any fault, it is digression—
Leaving my people to proceed alone,
 While I soliloquize beyond expression;   20
But these are my addresses from the throne,
 Which put off business to the ensuing session,
Forgetting each omission is a loss to
The world, not quite so great as Ariosto.

I know that what our neighbors called *longueurs*   25
 (We've not so good a *word,* but have the *thing,*
In that complete perfection which ensures
 An epic from Bob Southey every spring—)
Form not the true temptation which allures
 The reader; but 'twould not be hard to bring   30
Some fine examples of the *épopée*³
To prove its grand ingredient is *ennui.*⁴

(From *Don Juan*)

EXERCISE:

1. Both of these selections make use of the ottava rima stanza.
But observe what different intentions appear in the two passages.
The passage by Byron is a satirical attack on Coleridge, Words-
worth, and Southey, who are sometimes known as "the Lake
poets." We have already studied poems in this collection by
Coleridge and Wordsworth. Southey at this time was Poet
Laureate, and was the author of a number of rather heavy and
dull works. (Consult the library for information concerning

---

² an English penal settlement in Australia, established 1787
³ epic   ⁴ tediousness

"Pantisocracy" and for information to explain the statement that
Wordsworth "seasoned his peddler poems with democracy.")

2. Observe closely the type of rimes which Byron uses now
and then in his selection. What is it in these rimes that supports a comic effect?

OZYMANDIAS

PERCY BYSSHE SHELLEY (1792–1822)

I met a traveler from an antique land
Who said: Two vast and trunkless legs of stone
Stand in the desert. Near them, on the sand,
Half sunk, a shattered visage lies, whose frown,
And wrinkled lip, and sneer of cold command,   5
Tell that its sculptor well those passions read
Which yet survive, (stamped on these lifeless things,)
The hand that mocked them and the heart that fed;
And on the pedestal these words appear:
"My name is Ozymandias, king of kings;   10
Look on my works, ye Mighty, and despair!"
Nothing beside remains. Round ·the decay
Of that colossal wreck, boundless and bare
The lone and level sands stretch far away.

EXERCISE:

In connection with this poem reread "Composed upon West-
minster Bridge," (p. 202), "How Do I Love Thee" (p. 252),
and "On the Late Massacre in Piedmont" (p. 253), and read
several of the sonnets by Shakespeare which appear in this collection (pp. 325, 395, 397, 434, 454, 473). Consult the *Glossary*
for a definition and discussion of the sonnet form. How does this
sonnet differ in form and method from the Shakespearian sonnet
on the one hand and the Italian on the other?

THREE SONGS

WILLIAM SHAKESPEARE (1564–1616)

I

Blow, blow, thou winter wind!
Thou art not so unkind
    As man's ingratitude;
Thy tooth is not so keen,
Because thou art not seen,   5
    Although thy breath be rude.

Heigh ho! sing, heigh ho! unto the green holly:
Most friendship is feigning, most loving mere folly:
    Then, heigh ho, the· holly!
    This life is most jolly.   10

    Freeze, freeze, thou bitter sky!
    That dost not bite so nigh
        As benefits forgot;
    Though thou the waters warp,
    Thy sting is not so sharp   15
        As friend remembered not.

Heigh ho! sing, heigh ho! etc.
                        (From *As You Like It*)

II

Take, O, take those lips away,
    That so sweetly were forsworn;
And those eyes, the break of day,
    Lights that do mislead the morn:
But my kisses bring again,   5
                        Bring again;
Seals of love, but sealed in vain,
                        Sealed in vain!
                (From *Measure for Measure*)

III

Hark, hark! the lark at heaven's gate sings
    And Phœbus 'gins arise,
His steeds to water at those springs

On chaliced flowers that lies;
And winking Mary-buds begin   5
To ope their golden eyes:
With every thing that pretty is,
My lady sweet, arise!
Arise, arise!

(From *Cymbeline*)

EXERCISE:

1. None of these songs uses a commonly accepted stanza form. Can one justify the line patterns used here?

2. Write an analysis on technical grounds of Song II. Compare it with "Slow, Slow, Fresh Fount" (p. 245).

3. Discuss *euphony* (*Glossary*) in all of these songs.

ROSE AYLMER

WALTER SAVAGE LANDOR (1775–1864)

Ah, what avails the sceptred race,
Ah, what the form divine!
What every virtue, every grace!
Rose Aylmer, all were thine.

Rose Aylmer, whom these wakeful eyes   5
May weep, but never see,
A night of memories and of sighs
I consecrate to thee.

Like "After Long Silence," this poem is perfectly straightforward in its statement. But the statement alone does not give us the poem—that is, other factors are required to make the statement come alive for us. One thing that serves very obviously to convert the bare statement into poetry is the use made of the various elements which we have previously discussed in this general section. As a preliminary to analysis we may mark the accents:

Ah, whát aváils the scéptrẹd ráce,
   Ah, whát the fórm divíne!
What évery vírtue, évery gráce!
   Rosé Aýlmer, áll were thíne.

Rosé Aýlmer, whóm these wákeful éyes
   May wéep, but néver sée,
A níght of mémories ánd of síghs
   I cónsecráte to thée.

   In the first stanza, we may note, in the first foot of every line
the hovering accent, and the length of the first syllable of the
foot. These factors tend to give an unusual emphasis to those
feet, especially since the remainder of each line is characterized
by a very positive difference between accented and unaccented
syllables; and those feet, by the repetitions, set the basic attitude
of questioning. The marked regularity of the metrical pattern
of each line, the definite stop at the end of each line, and the
repetition involved in the first three lines—all of these factors
contribute to a formal and elevated tone. (We can notice the
formal tone supported, further, by the repetitive balance of the
first and second lines, which is repeated by the balance within
the third line. "What every virtue" is balanced against "[what]
every grace." And we can notice how the distinction between
the first and second parts of the line is marked by the pause,
which tends to cause greater emphasis to fall on the first syllable
of *every*.)
   The first line of the second stanza, with the repetition of the
name *Rose Aylmer,* picks up the metrical pattern characteristic
of the first stanza, providing a kind of transition between the
rhythm characteristic of the first stanza and that characteristic
of the second. The difference in the rhythm of the second stanza
is caused chiefly by the run-on lines, the absence of the hovering
accents on the initial syllables of the last three lines, and the
metrical accenting of syllables not usually accented. We may
try to relate some of these special details to the meaning of the
poem.
   The first run-on line serves to emphasize the word *weep:*
since the sense unit is so radically divided by the line end, when

we do pick up the rest of the clause at the beginning of the second line, it comes with a feeling of emphatic fulfilment, which is further supported by the marked pause after the word *weep*. The emphasis on the word *weep* is, of course, rhetorically right because it is set over in contrast with the word *see* at the end of the second line. And we may also observe how the alliteration of the word *weep* with the word *wakeful* in the preceding line helps to mark the association of the two ideas: it is not merely weeping which is to be contrasted with seeing, but the lonely weeping at night when the sense of loss becomes most acute.

The third line is also a run-on line, giving a kind of balance to the structure of the stanza, which functions as do the various balances of structure in the first stanza. Although neither the first line nor the third line of the second stanza is punctuated at the end, we can see that the tendency to run on into the next line is not so strong in the third line as in the first; we can see that the phrase "whom these wakeful eyes" strikes us with a more marked sense of incompleteness than does the phrase "A night of memories and of sighs." This is especially true because the first of the two phrases, coming early in the stanza, is less supported by a context, by the sense of things preceding it. But, even though the tendency to run on is not so strong in the third line as in the first, the tendency is still marked; and such a tendency to enjambment fixes our attention on the clause, "I consecrate," which begins the last line, and forces a pause after that clause.

The word *consecrate,* which is thereby emphasized, is very important. We can see how important it is, and how effective it is in avoiding a sentimental or stereotyped effect, by substituting other words which convey approximately the same meaning. For instance, the lines might be re-written:

> A night of memories and sighs
> I now will give to thee.

We immediately see a great difference. The re-written passage tends toward sentimentality. The word *consecrate* means "to set apart perpetually for sacred uses"; it implies the formality and impersonality of a ceremony. This implication in conjunction with the formality of tone, which has already been discussed in connection with the technique of the first stanza, helps to prevent any suggestion of self-pity.

Another technical feature appears in the use of the word *consecrate,* which does not appear in the re-written line

> I now will give to thee.

The word *consecrate* is accented in ordinary usage on the first syllable. But when the word is used in this poem, meter dictates an additional accent on the last syllable, for the line is to be scanned as follows:

> I cón/ -secráte/ to thée.

Thus the metrical situation tends to give the word an emphasis which it would not possess in ordinary prose usage; and this is appropriate because of the importance of the word in the poem.

EXERCISE:

1. What would have been the difference in effect if the poet had written, in the next to the last line, "an age" instead of "a night"?

2. Discuss the effect of the accent on the ordinarily unimportant word *and* in the same line.

A DEEP-SWORN VOW

WILLIAM BUTLER YEATS (1865–   )

Others because you did not keep
That deep-sworn vow have been friends of mine;
Yet always when I look death in the face,
When I clamber to the heights of sleep,
Or when I grow excited with wine,   5
Suddenly I meet your face.

The theme of this poem is the lasting impression made by a love-affair which has been broken off, apparently long ago, and which has been superseded by other friendships. On the conscious level of the mind, the loved one has been forgotten, but the image is still carried indelibly imprinted on the deeper, unconscious mind.

When we come to consider how this theme is made concrete and forceful in its statement in the poem, we must consider of course such matters as tone, imagery, structure of incidents, etc. For example, there is the contrast of the almost casual tone of the opening of the poem and the tone of excitement with which the poem ends. One notices also the arrangement of the three instances which the lover gives of the moments when the face suddenly appears to him: at moments of great danger, in sleep when the subconscious is released, and in moments of intoxication. The last item balances the first: the poet does not intend to falsify the experience by saying "Only when I look death in the face, I remember you." The memory comes also when the occasion is one of no seriousness at all—merely one of conviviality. And yet the three classes of occasions, though they contrast with each other in their associations, all reinforce one particular idea: the face appears when concern for the immediate, self-conscious every-day existence has been let down—for whatever reason.

One needs to inspect the imagery too, though this poem is relatively bare of imagery. One notices, however, that the image in the line

When I clamber to the heights of sleep

supports the theme. Sleep, we usually think of as completely passive, yet the image is one of difficult action, and of attainment after such action—as if her face lay over a mountain ridge and as if sleep were a sort of search in which the poet managed (the implication is, "with difficulty and not often") to reach the top and be granted the vision.

Yet important as are all the details of this sort which have been mentioned, we shall have to examine the metrical arrange-

ment and rime scheme of this poem before we can account for
its effectiveness.

The poem may be scanned as follows:

> Óthers/becaúse/you díd/not kéep/
> That déep/-swórn vów/have been fríends/of míne;/
> Yet ál/-wáys whén/I loók/déath/in the fáce,/
> When I clám/-ber tó/the heíghts/of sléep,/
> Or whén/I gów/excí/-ted with wíne,/   5
> Súddenly/I méet/your fáce./

The poem is highly irregular: There is a considerable variation in the kinds of lines, trimeter, tetrameter, and pentameter;
though the basic foot is of two syllables, some feet are defective
and others have three syllables—that is, are anapaestic or dactylic.
Moreover, there are, one notices, a number of hovering accents.
But the irregularity in this poem is far from a haphazard matter.
If we examine the poem carefully we shall see that the irregularity
supports the poem's intended effect.

The tone of the first lines, we have already pointed out, is that
of calm, unexcited statement. There is no anger or bitterness
toward the woman who did not keep her vow. And this tone is
supported by the casual rhythm of the line (p. 642). Notice
that the poet does not emphasize the word, *you,* but the word,
others. The accent is thrown on the first syllable of *others,* and
the word, *you,* does not receive a metrical accent at all, though
rhetorical considerations throw some emphasis on it, and there
is, because of the competition here between rhetoric and meter,
a slight hover on the foot, *you did,* and on the foot, *not keep.*
This hovering accent in each case retards the movement; and
the substitution of the trochaic foot, *others,* for the normal iamb
forces a slight pause before the word, *because*—a pause which is
justified by the rhetorical emphasis: there is a contrast between
the conduct of the "others" and that of the loved one.

The second line is highly irregular. There is a decided hovering accent on the foot, *sworn vow,* and the long syllables here,
plus the foregoing accented long syllable, *deep,* urge the reader
to give all three syllables decided emphasis, and force him to
pause, before going on with the rest of the line. One notices,

also, that the sense unit does not terminate with the end of the first line but runs on rapidly to the second. The important phrase, "deep-sworn vow," is thus isolated, as it were, for emphasis.

The attempt to reassert the metrical pattern at the end of the second line causes a rather heavy accent to be placed on the words, *friends* and *mine*. This is proper, for the word, *friends,* is important. The speaker has carefully chosen this word rather than some other word, such as, say, *lovers*. The quieter, more guarded word is important for the tone which the poet wishes to establish in the opening lines of the poem. The word, *friends,* stands as a correlative of the word, *others*.

The next three lines of the poem are more regular, and in the three instances of memory which the poet gives, the basic pattern is more clearly affirmed and established in the reader's mind. One notices, however, that in the third line, the syllable, *-ways,* receives a rather definite secondary accent. The word, *always,* is, thus, emphasized and dwelt upon—quite properly, for it is the important word here. In this same line there is also a rather marked pause between the words, *look* and *death,* because both words are accented.[1] The defect in the foot, *death,* is compensated for by the substitution of an anapaest for an iamb in the following foot, and by the pause after the word, *look*.

The fourth line, with the exception of one detail, the substitution of an anapaest for an iamb in the first foot, is regular, and asserts the pattern which has been obscured to some extent by the variations of lines two and three.

The fifth line has a rapid movement which is consonant with the sense of the line and with the effect of rapid, casual, even careless excitement. The movement may be accounted for in its metrical aspect as follows: The last foot of the line represents an anapaestic substitution for the expected iamb, and the extra syllable speeds up the end of the line. This added speed results from the following special situation. The fact that the first syllable of the last foot, *-ted,* is an integral part of the word, *excited,* demands that the anapaest be given unusual speed if

[1] In connection with this pause, see also the Exercise on "In Tenebris, I," p. 280.

the syllable, *-ted,* is to be drawn into the last foot at all. (Contrast the situation in this anapaest with the situation in the anapaest at the beginning of the fourth line. See Exercise on "The Sunflower," p. 236).

Moreover, this last substitution helps to bring into sharper focus the substitution made in the last line of the poem, where a dactyl is substituted for the iamb in the first foot. The abrupt shock given by this substitution (the accent on the syllable, *sud-,* follows immediately after the heavy accent on the word, *wine*), and the pause after *suddenly* prepare us for the climax of the poem, which appears in the phrase, "I meet your face." Other factors in the last line tend to underscore the climax. The line has only three accents, two less than line three, and one less than any other line. The reader, conditioned to the longer line, is prompted to take this line more slowly. The reader is further encouraged to do this by the fact that the word, *your,* from rhetorical considerations, demands a rather strong accent. This provides a hovering effect on the last foot. The pause after *suddenly,* the strong accent on *meet,* and the definite hover on the phrase, *your face,* give an effect of reserved and solemn statement.

One observes that the rime scheme is a, b, c, a, b, c. But *c* is a repetition, and not a rime. The repetition suggests that death's face, at moment of crisis when the speaker meets it, is somehow equated for him with the face of the lost love. The reader expects the rime, and the repetition, therefore, comes with an appropriate shock. The face is, as it were, echoed, and echoed at the climactic point of the poem, where the meter has helped to prepare us to receive the whole implication.

SABRINA

JOHN MILTON (1608–1674)

Sabrina fair,
   Listen where thou art sitting
Under the glassie, cool, translucent wave,
   In twisted braids of lillies knitting

The loose train of thy amber-dropping hair;   5
    Listen for dear honor's sake,
    Goddess of the silver lake,
        Listen and save!

Listen, and appear to us,
In name of great Oceanus,   10
By the earth-shaking Neptune's mace,
And Tethys' grave majestic pace;
By hoary Nereus' wrinkled look,
And the Carpathian wizard's hook;
By scaly Triton's winding shell,   15
And old sooth-saying Glaucus' spell;
By Leucothea's lovely hands,
And her son that rules the strands;
By Thetis' tinsel-slippered feet,
And the songs of Sirens sweet;   20
By dead Parthenopè's dear tomb,
And fair Ligea's golden comb,
Wherewith she sits on diamond rocks
Sleeking her soft alluring locks;
By all the nymphs that nightly dance   25
Upon thy streams with wily glance;
Rise, rise, and heave thy rosie head
From thy coral-paven bed,
And bridle in thy headlong wave,
Till thou our summons answered have.   30
                        Listen and save!
                             (From *Comus*)

EXERCISE:

1. Discuss the following topics: euphony, alliteration, assonance, and quantitative variation.

2. Discuss the metrical situation in line 27.

THE COLLAR

GEORGE HERBERT (1593–1633)

I struck the board, and cried, No more.
    I will abroad.

What? shall I ever sigh and pine?
My lines and life are free; free as the road,
   Loose as the wind, as large as store.   5
      Shall I be still in suit?
Have I no harvest but a thorn
To let me blood, and not restore
What I have lost with cordial fruit?
      Sure there was wine   10
   Before my sighs did dry it: there was corn
   Before my tears did drown it.
   Is the year only lost to me?
     Have I no bays to crown it?
No flowers, no garlands gay? all blasted?   15
   All wasted?
   Not so, my heart: but there is fruit,
    And thou hast hands.
   Recover all thy sigh-blown age
On double pleasures: leave thy cold dispute   20
Of what is fit, and not; forsake thy cage,
    Thy rope of sands,
Which petty thoughts have made, and made to thee
   Good cable, to enforce and draw,
     And be thy law,   25
   While thou didst wink and wouldst not see.
    Away; take heed:
    I will abroad.
Call in thy death's head there: tie up thy fears.
    He that forbears   30
   To suit and serve his need,
    Deserves his load.
But as I raved and grew more fierce and wild
    At every word,
   Me thought I heard one calling, *Child:*   35
   And I replied, *My Lord.*

EXERCISE:

This poem employs an unusual line arrangement. Try to define the effect gained here by the interplay of the long and short lines.

IN TENEBRIS, I

THOMAS HARDY (1840–1928)

Wintertime nighs;
But my bereavement pain
It cannot bring again:
    Twice no one dies.

Flower-petals flee;   5
But since it once hath been,
No more that severing scene
    Can harrow me.

Birds faint in dread:
I shall not lose old strength   10
In the lone frost's black length:
    Strength long since fled!

Leaves freeze to dun;
But friends cannot turn cold
This season as of old   15
    For him with none.

Tempests may scath;
But love cannot make smart
Again this year his heart
    Who no heart hath.   20

Black is night's cope;
But death will not appall
One who, past doubtings all,
    Waits in unhope.

EXERCISE:

   This poem, unlike "Sabrina," would not be regarded as euphonious. As a matter of fact, there are a number of pauses
forced by *cacophonous combinations* (*Glossary*). Are such pauses
functional in this poem or are they an indication of inferior
craftsmanship? Write a complete analysis of the poem which
will involve this problem.

ODE ON THE DEATH OF THE DUKE
OF WELLINGTON

ALFRED, LORD TENNYSON (1809–1892)

Bury the Great Duke
 With an empire's lamentation;
Let us bury the Great Duke
 To the noise of the mourning of a mighty nation;
Mourning when their leaders fall,   5
Warriors carry the warrior's pall,
And sorrow darkens hamlet and hall.

Where shall we lay the man whom we deplore?
Here, in streaming London's central roar.
Let the sound of those he wrought for,   10
And the feet of those he fought for,
Echo round his bones for evermore.
Lead out the pageant; sad and slow,
As fits an universal woe,
Let the long, long procession go,   15
And let the sorrowing crowd about it grow,
And let the mournful martial music blow;
The last great Englishman is low.

Mourn, for to us he seems the last,
Remembering all his greatness in the past.   20
No more in soldier fashion will he greet
With lifted hand the gazer in the street.
O friends, our chief state-oracle is mute!
Mourn for the man of long-enduring blood,
The statesman-warrior, moderate, resolute,   25
Whole in himself, a common good.
Mourn for the man of amplest influence,
Yet clearest of ambitious crime,
Our greatest yet with least pretense,
Great in council and great in war.   30
Foremost captain of his time,
Rich in saving common-sense,
And, as the greatest only are,
In his simplicity sublime.
O good gray head which all men knew,   35

O voice from which their omens all men drew,
O iron nerve to true occasion true,
O fallen at length that tower of strength
Which stood four-square to all the winds that blew!
Such was he whom we deplore.   40
The long self-sacrifice of life is o'er.
The great World-victor's victor will be seen no more.

All is over and done.
Render thanks to the Giver,
England, for thy son.   45
Let the bell be tolled.
Render thanks to the Giver,
And render him to the mould.
Under the cross of gold
That shines over city and river,   50
There he shall rest forever
Among the wise and the bold.
Let the bell be tolled,
And a reverent people behold
The towering car, the sable steeds.   55
Bright let it be with his blazoned deeds,
Dark in its funeral fold.
Let the bell be tolled,
And a deeper knell in the heart be knolled;
And the sound of the sorrowing anthem rolled   60
Through the dome of the golden cross;
And the volleying cannon thunder his loss;
He knew their voices of old.
For many a time in many a clime
His captain's-ear has heard them boom,   65
Bellowing victory, bellowing doom.
When he with those deep voices wrought
Guarding realms and kings from shame,
With those deep voices our dead captain taught
The tyrant, and asserts his claim   70
In that dread sound to the great name
Which he had worn so pure of blame,
In praise and in dispraise the same,
A man of well-attempered frame.
O civic muse, to such a name,   75
To such a name for ages long,

To such a name,
Preserve a broad approach of fame,
And ever-echoing avenues of song!

"Who is he that cometh, like an honored guest,   80
With banner and with music, with soldier and with priest,
With a nation weeping, and breaking on my rest?"—
Mighty Seaman, this is he
Was great by land as thou by sea.
Thine island loves thee well, thou famous man,   85
The greatest sailor since our world began.
Now, to the roll of muffled drums,
To thee the greatest soldier comes;
For this is he
Was great by land as thou by sea.   90
His foes were thine; he kept us free;
Oh, give him welcome, this is he
Worthy of our gorgeous rites,
And worthy to be laid by thee;
For this is England's greatest son,   95
He that gained a hundred fights,
Nor ever lost an English gun;
This is he that far away
Against the myriads of Assaye
Clashed with his fiery few and won;   100
And underneath another sun,
Warring on a later day,
Round affrighted Lisbon drew
The treble works, the vast designs
Of his labored rampart-lines,   105
Where he greatly stood at bay,
Whence he issued forth anew,
And ever great and greater grew,
Beating from the wasted vines
Back to France her banded swarms,   110
Back to France with countless blows,
Till o'er the hills her eagles flew
Beyond the Pyrenean pines,
Followed up in valley and glen
With blare of bugle, clamour of men,   115
Roll of cannon and clash of arms,
And England pouring on her foes,

Such a war had such a close.
Again their ravening eagle rose
In anger, wheeled on Europe-shadowing wings,   120
And barking for the throne of kings;
Till one that sought but Duty's iron crown
On that loud Sabbath shook the spoiler down;
A day of onsets of despair!
Dashed on every rocky square,   125
Their surging charges foamed themselves away;
Last, the Prussian trumpet blew;
Through the long-tormented air
Heaven flashed a sudden jubilant ray,
And down we swept and charged and overthrew.   130
So great a soldier taught us there
What long-enduring hearts could do
In that world-earthquake, Waterloo!
Mighty Seaman, tender and true,
And pure as he from taint of craven guile,   135
O savior of the silver-coasted isle,
O shaker of the Baltic and the Nile,
If aught of things that here befall
Touch a spirit among things divine,
If love of country move thee there at all,   140
Be glad because his bones are laid by thine!
And through the centuries let a people's voice
In full acclaim,
A people's voice,
The proof and echo of all human fame,   145
A people's voice, when they rejoice
At civic revel and pomp and game,
Attest their great commander's claim
With honor, honor, honor, honor to him,
Eternal honor to his name.   150

A people's voice! we are a people yet.
Though all men else their nobler dreams forget,
Confused by brainless mobs and lawless Powers,
Thank Him who isled us here, and roughly set
His Briton in blown seas and storming showers,   155
We have a voice with which to pay the debt
Of boundless love and reverence and regret
To those great men who fought, and kept it ours.

And keep it ours, O God, from brute control!
O statesmen, guard us, guard the eye, the soul   160
Of Europe, keep our noble England whole,
And save the one true seed of freedom sown
Betwixt a people and their ancient throne,
That sober freedom out of which there springs
Our loyal passion for our temperate kings!   165
For, saving that, ye help to save mankind
Till public wrong be crumbled into dust,
And drill the raw world for the march of mind,
Till crowds at length be sane and crowns be just.
But wink no more in slothful overtrust.   170
Remember him who led your hosts;
He bade you guard the sacred coasts.
Your cannons moulder on the seaward wall;
His voice is silent in your council-hall
Forever; and whatever tempests lour   175
Forever silent; even if they broke
In thunder, silent; yet remember all
He spoke among you, and the Man who spoke;
Who never sold the truth to serve the hour,
Nor paltered with Eternal God for power;   180
Who let the turbid streams of rumor flow
Through either babbling world of high and low;
Whose life was work, whose language rife
With rugged maxims hewn from life;
Who never spoke against a foe;   185
Whose eighty winters freeze with one rebuke
All great self-seekers trampling on the right.
Truth-teller was our England's Alfred named;
Truth-lover was our English Duke!
Whatever record leap to light   190
He never shall be shamed.

Lo! the leader in these glorious wars
Now to glorious burial slowly borne,
Followed by the brave of other lands,
He, on whom from both her open hands   195
Lavish Honor showered all her stars,
And affluent Fortune emptied all her horn.
Yea, let all good things await
Him who cares not to be great

But as he saves or serves the state.   200
Not once or twice in our rough island-story
The path of duty was the way to glory.
He that walks it, only thirsting
For the right, and learns to deaden
Love of self, before his journey closes,   205
He shall find the stubborn thistle bursting
Into glossy purples, which out-redden
All voluptuous garden-roses.
Not once or twice in our fair island-story
The path of duty was the way to glory.   210
He, that ever following her commands,
On with toil of heart and knees and hands,
Through the long gorge to the far light has won
His path upward, and prevailed
Shall find the toppling crags of Duty scaled   215
Are close upon the shining table lands
To which our God Himself is moon and sun.
Such was he; his work is done.
But while the races of mankind endure
Let his great example stand   220
Colossal, seen of every land,
And keep the soldier firm, the statesman pure;
Till in all lands and through all human story
The path of duty be the way to glory.
And let the land whose hearths he saved from shame   225
For many and many an age proclaim
At civic revel and pomp and game,
And when the long-illumined cities flame,
· Their ever-loyal iron leader's fame,
With honor, honor, honor, honor to him,   230
Eternal honor to his name.

Peace, his triumph will be sung
By some yet unmoulded tongue
Far on in summers that we shall not see.
Peace, it is a day of pain   235
For one about whose patriarchal knee
Late the little children clung.
O peace, it is a day of pain
For one upon whose hand and heart and brain

Once the weight and fate of Europe hung.   240
Ours the pain, be his the gain!
More than is of man's degree
Must be with us, watching here
At this, our great solemnity.
Whom we see not we revere;   245
We revere, and we refrain
From talk of battles loud and vain,   .
And brawling memories all too free
For such a wise humility
As befits a solemn fane.   250
We revere, and while we hear
The tides of Music's golden sea
Setting toward eternity,
Uplifted high in heart and hope are we,
Until we doubt not that for one so true   255
There must be other nobler work to do
Than when he fought at Waterloo,
And victor he must ever be.
For though the Giant Ages heave the hill
And break the shore, and evermore   260
Make and break, and work their will,
Though world on world in myriad myriads roll
Round us, each with different powers,
And other forms of life than ours,
What know we greater than the soul?   265
On God and Godlike men we build our trust.
Hush, the Dead March wails in the people's ears;
The dark crowd moves, and there are sobs and tears;
The black earth yawns; the mortal disappears;
Ashes to ashes, dust to dust;   270
He is gone who seemed so great.—
Gone, but nothing can bereave him
Of the force he made his own
Being here, and we believe him
Something far advanced in state,   275
And that he wears a truer crown
Than any wreath that man can weave him.
Speak no more of his renown,
Lay your earthly fancies down,
And in the vast cathedral leave him,   280
God accept him, Christ receive him!

Exercise:

1. This poem is irregular in form. Try to determine the principle on which the poet proceeds. Compare and contrast this poem with the selection given from *Samson Agonistes* (p. 247) and with "Patterns" (p. 136).

2. Much of this poem is peculiarly bare of imagery. Discuss onomatopoeia, alliteration, repetition, and assonance in making the poem forceful and vivid. Does the poem become too thin and prosy in any part? In this connection read "The Horatian Ode" (p. 531), which, like this poem, is a tribute to a great public figure. (Consult the library for information concerning the historical background of both poems.)

SHE WALKS IN BEAUTY

GEORGE GORDON, LORD BYRON (1788–1824)

She walks in beauty, like the night
   Of cloudless climes and starry skies;
And all that's best of dark and bright
   Meet in her aspect and her eyes:
Thus mellowed to that tender light   5
   Which heaven to gaudy day denies.

One shade the more, one ray the less,
   Had half impaired the nameless grace
Which waves in every raven tress,
   Or softly lightens o'er her face;   10
Where thoughts serenely sweet express
   How pure, how dear, their dwelling-place.

And on that cheek, and o'er that brow,
   So soft, so calm, so eloquent,
The smiles that win, the tints that glow,   15
   But tell of days in goodness spent,
A mind at peace with all below,
   A heart whose love is innocent!

EXERCISE:

1. Investigate the factors of alliteration and assonance in this poem.

2. Why might it be said that the last stanza is inferior to the previous two in management of both end and internal pauses?

THE NIGHTINGALE

SIR PHILIP SIDNEY (1554–1586)

The nightingale, as soon as April bringeth
  Unto her rested sense a perfect waking,
While late bare earth, proud of new clothing, springeth,
  Sings out her woes, a thorn her song-book making;
    And mournfully bewailing,   5
Her throat in tunes expresseth
What grief her breast oppresseth
  For Tereus' force on her chaste will prevailing.
O Philomela fair, O take some gladness,
That here is juster cause of plaintful sadness.   10
    Thine earth now springs, mine fadeth;
    Thy thorn without, my thorn my heart invadeth.

Alas, she hath no other cause of anguish
  But Tereus' love, on her by strong hand wroken,
Wherein she suffering, all her spirits languish;   15
  Full womanlike complains her will was broken.
    But I, who daily craving,
Cannot have to content me,
Have more cause to lament me,
  Since wanting is more woe than too much having.   20
O Philomela fair, O take some gladness,
That here is juster cause of plaintful sadness.
    Thine earth now springs, mine fadeth;
    Thy thorn without, my thorn my heart invadeth.

EXERCISE:

1. This poem employs a very elaborate and unusual stanza form. Is it one that works effectively here?

2. For what effect are feminine endings used here?

WILT THOU YET TAKE ALL

ALGERNON CHARLES SWINBURNE (1837–1909)

Wilt thou yet take all, Galilean? but these thou shalt not take,
The laurel, the palms and the paean, the breasts of the nymphs
  in the brake;
Breasts more soft than a dove's, that tremble with tenderer breath;
And all the wings of the Loves, and all the joy before death;
All the feet of the hours that sound as a single lyre,   5
Dropped and deep in the flowers, with strings that flicker like fire.
More than these wilt thou give, things fairer than all these things?
Nay, for a little we live, and life hath mutable wings.
A little while and we die; shall life not thrive as it may?
For no man under the sky lives twice, outliving his day.   10
And grief is a grievous thing, and a man hath enough of his
  tears:
Why should he labor, and bring fresh grief to blacken his years?
Thou hast conquered, O pale Galilean; the world has grown
  gray from thy breath;
We have drunken of things Lethean, and fed on the fullness
  of death.
Laurel is green for a season, and love is sweet for a day;   15
But love grows bitter with treason, and laurel outlives not May.
Sleep, shall we sleep after all? for the world is not sweet in the
  end;
For the old faiths loosen and fall, the new years ruin and rend.

(From "Hymn to Proserpine")

EXERCISE:

1. This section is in hexameter couplets with cross rimes within
the lines; it could, as a matter of fact, be printed as trimeter,
riming a, b, a, b. We can observe, however, that the rimes
within the lines are rarely emphasized, for they rarely come at
positions where they are followed by a heavy pause. What is
the function of the rimes within the lines? Discuss the meter.

2. What is the effect of the use of alliteration here? Compare
it with the use of alliteration in "The Nightingale," by Sidney.

FAREWELL

SIR THOMAS WYATT (1503–1542)

What should I say,
  Since faith is dead,
And truth away
  From you is fled?
  Should I be led   5
    With doubleness?
    Nay, nay, mistress!

I promised you,
  And you promised me,
To be as true,   10
  As I would be.
  But since I see
    Your double heart,
    Farewell my part!

Though for to take   15
  It is not my mind,
But to forsake
  One so unkind,
  And as I find
    So will I trust,   20
    Farewell, unjust!

Can ye say nay,
  But that you said
That I alway
  Should be obeyed?   25
  And thus betrayed,
    Or that I wist,
    Farewell, unkissed!

EXERCISE:

Can you define the general contribution this stanza form makes
to the effect of the poem? In this connection compare the poem
with "The Nightingale," another poem of unhappy love, or with
the second song in "Three Songs" (p. 269).

NO MORE BE GRIEVED

WILLIAM SHAKESPEARE (1564–1616)

No more be grieved at that which thou hast done,
Roses have thorns, and silver fountains mud,
Clouds and eclipses stain both Moon and Sun,
And loathsome canker lives in sweetest bud.
All men make faults, and even I in this,
Authorizing thy trespass with compare,
My self corrupting salving thy amiss,
Excusing thy sins more than thy sins are:
For to thy sensual fault I bring in sense,
Thy adverse party is thy Advocate,
And gainst myself a lawful plea commence,
Such civil war is in my love and hate,
That I an accessory needs must be,
To that sweet thief which sourly robs from me.

The following analysis of this poem has been made by a modern critic:

The first four lines we may say, both in movement and imagery, are . . . straightforward. The fifth line begins by continuing the excuses, 'All men make faults,' but with an abrupt change of rhythm Shakespeare turns the generalization against himself: 'All men make faults, and even I in this,' i.e. in wasting my time finding romantic parallels for your sins, as though intellectual analogies ('sense') were relevant to your sensual fault. The painful complexity of feeling (Shakespeare is at the same time tender towards the sinner and infuriated by his own tenderness) is evident in the seventh line which means both, 'I corrupt myself when I find excuses for you' (or 'when I comfort myself in this way'), and, 'I'm afraid I myself make you worse by excusing your faults'; and although there is a fresh change of tone towards the end (The twelfth line is virtually a sigh as he gives up hope of resolving the conflict), the equivocal 'needs must' and the sweet-sour opposition show the continued civil war of the emotions.

Some such comment as this was unavoidable, but it is upon the simplest and most obvious of technical devices that I wish to direct attention. In the first quatrain the play upon the letters *s* and *l* is mainly musical and decorative, but with the change of tone and direction the alliterative *s* becomes a hiss of half-impotent venom:

> All men make faults, and even I in this,
> Authorizing thy trespass with compare,
> My self corrupting salving thy amiss,
> Excusing thy sins more than thy sins are:
> For to thy sensual fault I bring in sense . . .

The scorn is moderated here, but it is still heard in the slightly rasping note of the last line,

> To that sweet thief which sourly robs from me.

From the fifth line, then, the alliteration is functional: by playing off against the comparative regularity of the rhythm it expresses an important part of the meaning, and helps to carry the experience alive into the mind of the reader.[1]

[1] L. C. Knights "Shakespeare's Sonnets," *Scrutiny*, Vol. 3, number 2, pp. 142–143.

SECTION V *tone + attitude*

FOREWORD

The *tone* of a poem indicates the poet's *attitude* toward his subject and toward his audience. In conversation we often imply our attitude by the tone of voice which we use. We are respectful or contemptuous, mocking or reverent. In a poem the poet must of course indicate this tone by his treatment of the material itself; he must so choose and arrange his words that the proper tone will be dictated to the reader of the poem by the poem itself.

Obviously, tone is very important. As we have emphasized again and again, in poetry the important thing is not the intrinsic value of the facts as such; it is rather the value of the poem as an experience, and since this is true, so important an element of the experience as the attitude of the writer toward subject and audience needs careful examination. We praise a poet for being able to set and sustain a tone without breaking it by ineptitude, or we praise him for his ability to shift effectively from one tone to another.

In some of the poems already analyzed, particularly in poems which have a strong dramatic element, such as "Patterns" (p. 136) or "After Long Silence" (p. 224), we have really considered without using the term many questions of tone. In poems with a marked dramatic framework, the tone is usually more easily grasped than in other poems, because the identity of the speaker and his attitude toward the listener (who in cases, like "After Long Silence" or "Rose Aylmer" is usually, as it were, a kind of silent character in the little drama) is rather clearly implied or even stated. But all poems involve questions of tone, for all poems, as we have said (*Introduction,* p. 23), are fundamentally dramatic.

In taking up the question of tone, therefore, the student is not approaching a new element. But the poems that follow in this section allow him to inspect more closely the relationship of tone

to other elements that go to create the poetic effect. Furthermore, the student can see in these poems illustrations of certain
technical devices whereby a poet may define his tone.

PORTRAIT

E. E. CUMMINGS (1894–   )

Buffalo Bill's
defunct
      who used to
      ride a watersmooth-silver
                    stallion
and break onetwothreefourfive pigeonsjustlikethat
                                 Jesus
he was a handsome man
                  and what i want to know is
how do you like your blueeyed boy
Mister Death

This poem essentially deals with a very usual theme and
treats that theme simply. Death claims all men, even the strong-
est and most glamorous. How does the poet in treating such
a common theme manage to give a fresh and strong impression
of it? He might have achieved this effect of course in a number
of different ways, and as a matter of fact, the general device
which he employs is not simply one device: it is complex. In
this case however, the most prominent element is the unconven-
tional attitude which he takes toward a conventional subject, and
in this particular poem, the matter of tone is isolated sufficiently
for us to examine it rather easily (though we must not forget
either that there are other matters to be examined in this poem
or that tone is a factor in every poem).

In the first place, what is the difference between writing

                  Buffalo Bill's
                  Defunct

and

                  Buffalo Bill's
                  Dead?

The first carries something of a tone of conscious irreverence. The poet here does not approach the idea of death with the usual and expected respect for the dead. He is matter-of-fact, unawed, and even somewhat flippant and joking. But the things which he picks out to comment on in Buffalo Bill make a strong contrast with the idea of death. The picture called up is one of tremendous vitality and speed: for example, the stallion is mentioned and is described as "watersmooth-silver." The adjective contains not only a visual description of the horse which Buffalo Bill rode but a kinetic description is implied too. How was the horse "watersmooth"? Smooth, graceful, in action. (The poet by running the words together in the next line is perhaps telling us how to read the line, running the words together to give the effect of speed. The way the poem is printed on the page is designed probably to serve the same purpose, the line divisions being intended as a kind of arrangement for punctuation and emphasis. But the odd typography is not of fundamental importance.) The "portrait" of Buffalo Bill given here after the statement that he is "defunct" is a glimpse of him in action breaking five claypigeons in rapid succession as he flashes by on his stallion—the sort of glimpse which one might remember from the performance of the Wild West show in which Buffalo Bill used to star. The exclamation which follows is exactly the sort of burst of boyish approval which might be struck from a boy seeing him in action or remembering him as he saw him. And the quality of "handsome" applies, one feels, not merely to his face but to his whole figure in action.

The next lines carry on the tone of unabashed, unawed, slangy irreverence toward death. Death becomes "Mister Death." The implied figure of the spectator at a performance of the Wild West show helps justify the language and manner of expression used here, making us feel that it is in character. But the question as asked here strikes us on another level. It is a question which no boy would ask; it is indeed one of the old unanswerable questions. But here it is transformed by the tone into something fresh and startling. Moreover, the dashing, glamorous character of the old Indian fighter gets a sharp emphasis. The question may be paraphrased like this: death, you don't get lads like him every day, do you? The way the question is put implies several things. First, it implies the pathos at the fact that even a man who had such enormous vitality and unfailing youthfulness, had to die. But this pathos is not insisted upon; rather, it is presented indirectly and ironically because of the bantering and flippant attitude given in the question, especially in the phrases, "Mister Death" and "blueeyed boy." And in the question, which sums up the whole poem, we also are given the impression that death is not terrible for Buffalo Bill—it is "Mister Death" who stands in some sort of fatherly and prideful relation to the "blueeyed boy."

In attempting to state what the tone is here we have perhaps distorted it somewhat in trying to state it specifically. There are perhaps additional aspects of interpretation of the tone used in this poem. But what has been said above is perhaps nearly enough complete to let us see how important an element the tone of the poem is. In this case—a case as we have already noted in which it is easy to deal with the tone in some isolation —it is the *tone* which transforms what might be easily a hackneyed and dead poem into something fresh and startling.

AN EPITAPH ON SALATHIEL PAVY

BEN JONSON (1573–1637)

Weep with me all you that read
   This little story;
And know, for whom a tear you shed
   Death's self is sorry.
'Twas a child that so did thrive   5
   In grace and feature,
As heaven and nature seemed to strive
   Which owned the creature.
Years he numbered scarce thirteen
   When fates turned cruel,   10
Yet three filled zodiacs had he been
   The stage's jewel;
And did act, what now we moan,

     Old men so duly,
   As, sooth, the Parcae thought him one,   15
     He played so truly.
   So, by error, to his fate
     They all consented,
   But viewing him since, alas, too late!
     They have repented;   20
   And have sought, to give new birth,
     In baths to steep him;
   But being so much too good for earth,
     Heaven vows to keep him.

EXERCISE:

 1. This poem, by one of the leading dramatists of his age, is on the death of a child-actor. What is the poet's attitude toward the child?

 2. How is this attitude indicated?

ADDRESS TO THE DEIL

ROBERT BURNS (1759–1796)

  O thou! whatever title suit thee,—
  Auld Hornie, Satan, Nick, or Clootie! [1]
  Wha in yon cavern, grim an' sootie,
    Clos'd under hatches,
  Spairges [2] about the brunstane cootie [3] 5
    To scaud [4] poor wretches!

  Hear me, auld Hangie, for a wee,
  An' let poor damnèd bodies be;
  I'm sure sma' pleasure it can gie,
    E'en to a deil.   10
  To skelp [5] an' scaud poor dogs like me,
    An' hear us squeel!

[1] little hoof   [2] splashes   [3] brimstone foot-tub
[4] scold   [5] slap

Great is thy pow'r, an' great thy fame;
Far kenned an' noted is thy name;
An though yon lowin heugh's [6] thy hame,   15
    Thou travels far;
An' faith! thou's neither lag [7] nor lame,
    Nor blate nor scaur.[8]

Whyles, rangin like a roarin lion,
For prey a' holes an' corners tryin;   20
Whyles, on the strong-winged tempest flyin,
    Tirlin' [9] the kirks;
Whyles, in the human bosom pryin,
    Unseen thou lurks.

I've heard my rev'rend grannie say,   25
In lanely glens ye like to stray;
Or whare auld ruined castles gray
    Nod to the moon,
Ye fright the nightly wand'rer's way
    Wi' eldritch croon.[10]   30

When twilight did my grannie summon
To say her pray'rs, douce [11] honest woman!
Aft yont [12] the dike she's heard you bummin,
    Wi eerie drone;
Or, rustlin, through the boortrees [13] comin,   35
    Wi' heavy groan.

Ae dreary, windy, winter night,
The stars shot down wi' sklentin [14] light,
Wi' you mysel I gat a fright
    Ayont the lough; [15]   40
Ye like a rash-buss [16] stood in sight
    Wi' waving sough.

The cudgel in my nieve did shake,
Each bristl'd hair stood like a stake,

---

[6] flaming cavern   [7] slow   [8] shy nor timid
[9] unroofing   [10] unearthly moan   [11] sober
[12] often beyond   [13] elder bushes   [14] slanting
[15] lake   [16] clump of rushes

When wi' an eldritch, stoor [17] 'Quaick, quaick,'   45
    Amang the springs,
Awa ye squatter'd like a drake,
    On whistlin wings.

Let warlocks grim an' wither'd hags
Tell how wi' you on ragweed nags   50
They skim the muirs an' dizzy crags
    Wi' wicked speed;
And in kirk-yards renew their leagues,
    Owre howket [18] dead.

Thence, countra wives wi' toil an' pain   55
May plunge an' plunge the kirn [19] in vain;
For oh! the yellow treasure's taen
    By witchin skill;
An' dawtet,[20] twal-pint hawkie's [21] gaen
    As yell's [22] the bill.[23]   60

Thence, mystic knots mak great abuse,
On young guidmen, fond, keen, an' crouse; [24]
When the best wark-lume [25] i' the house,
    By cantrip [26] wit,
Is instant made no worth a louse,   65
    Just at the bit.

When thowes dissolve the snawy hoord,
An' float the jinglin icy-boord [27]
Then water-kelpies [28] haunt the foord
    By your direction,   70
An' nighted trav'lers are allured
    To their destruction.

And aft your moss-traversing spunkies [29]
Decoy the wight that late and drunk is:
The bleezin,[30] curst, mischievous monkeys   75

[17] harsh	[18] dug-up	[19] churn
[20] petted	[21] white-face	[22] dry
[23] bull	[24] bold	[25] work loom
[26] magic	[27] ice-surface	[28] demons
[29] will-o-the-wisps	[30] blazing	

Delude his eyes,
Till in some miry slough he sunk is,
    Ne'er mair to rise.

When masons' mystic word and grip
In storms an' tempests raise you up,   80
Some cock or cat your rage maun stop,
    Or, strange to tell,
The youngest brither ye wad whip
    Aff straught to hell!

Lang syne, in Eden's bonie yard,   85
When youthfu' lovers first were paired,
And all the soul of love they shared,
    The raptur'd hour,
Sweet on the fragrant flow'ry swaird,
    In shady bow'r;   90

Then you, ye auld sneck-drawin [31] dog!
Ye cam to Paradise incog,
And played on man a cursed brogue,[32]
    (Black be your fa'!)
And gied the infant warld a shog,[33]   95
    Maist ruin'd a'.

D'ye mind that day, when in a bizz,[34]
Wi' reeket [35] duds and reestet gizz,[36]
Ye did present your smoutie phiz
    Mang better folk,   100
An' sklented [37] on the man of Uz
    Your spitefu' joke?

An' how ye gat him i' your thrall,
An' brak' him out o' house and hal',
While scabs and blotches did him gall,   105
    Wi' bitter claw,
An' lowsed [38] his ill-tongued, wicked scaul,[39]
    Was warst ava? [40]

[31] latch-lifting   [32] trick   [33] shock
[34] flurry   [35] smoky   [36] singed wig
[37] turned   [38] let loose   [39] scold
[40] worst of all

> But a' your doings to rehearse,
> Your wily snares an' fechtin [41] fierce,   110
> Sin' that day Michael did you pierce,
>   Down to this time,
> Wad ding [42] a Lallan [43] tongue, or Erse,
>   In prose or rhyme.

> An' now, auld Cloots, I ken ye 're thinkin   115
> A certain Bardie's rantin, drinkin,
> Some luckless hour will send him linkin,[44]
>   To your black pit;
> But faith! he'll turn a corner jinkin,[45]
>   An' cheat you yet.   120

> But fare you weel, auld Nickie-ben!
> O wad ye tak a thought an' men'!
> Ye aiblins [46] might—I dinna ken—
>   Still hae a stake:
> I'm wae [47] to think upo' yon den,   125
>   Ev'n for your sake!

EXERCISE:

How does the first stanza set the tone?

A SONG OF ALE

ANONYMOUS

> Back and side go bare, go bare,
>   Both hand and foot go cold,
> But belly, God send thee good ale enough
>   Whether it be new or old!

> But if that I may have truly   5
>   Good ale my belly full,
> I shall look like one, by sweet Saint John,
>   Were shorn against the wool.

---

[41] fighting   [42] out do   [43] Lowland
[44] skipping   [45] dodging   [46] perhaps
[47] sad

Though I go bare, take you no care,
  I am nothing a-cold,   10
I stuff my skin so full within
  Of jolly good ale and old.

I cannot eat but little meat,
  My stomach is not good;
But sure I think that I could drink   15
  With him that weareth an hood.
Drink is my life; although my wife
  Some time do chide and scold,
Yet spare I not to ply the pot
  Of jolly good ale and old.   20

I love no roast but a brown toast,
  Or a crab in the fire;
A little bread shall do me stead;
  Much bread I never desire.
Nor frost, nor snow, nor wind I trow,   25
  Can hurt me if it would,
I am so wrapped within and lapped
  With jolly good ale and old.

I care right nought, I take no thought
  For clothes to keep me warm;   30
Have I good drink, I surely think
  Nothing can do me harm:
For truly than I fear no man,
  Be he never so bold,
When I am armed and throughly warmed   35
  With jolly good ale and old.

But now and than I curse and ban,
  They make their ale so small;
God give them care and evil to fare!
  They stry the malt and all.   40
Such peevish pew, I tell you true,
  Not for a crown of gold,
There cometh one sip within my lip,
  Whether it be new or old.

Good ale and strong maketh me among   45
  Full jocund and full light,
That oft I sleep and take no keep
  From morning until night.
Then start I up and flee to the cup;
  The right way on I hold;   50
My thirst to staunch, I fill my paunch
  With jolly good ale and old.

And Kit my wife, that as her life
  Loveth well good ale to seek,
Full oft drinketh she, that ye may see   55
  The tears run down her cheek.
Then doth she troll to me the bowl,
  As a good malt-worm should,
And say "Sweet-heart, I have take my part
  Of jolly good ale and old."   60

They that do drink till they nod and wink,
  Even as good fellows should do,
They shall not miss to have the bliss,
  That good ale hath brought them to.
And all poor souls that scour black bowls,   65
  And them hath lustily trolled,
God save the lives of them and their wives,
  Whether they be young or old!

EXERCISE:

How do the rhythms and the use of internal rime help define the tone of the poem?

AN EPITAPH

THOMAS CAREW (1598?–1639?)

This little vault, this narrow room,
Of love and beauty is the tomb;
The dawning beam, that 'gan to clear
Our clouded sky, lies darkened here,

For ever set to us, by death   5
Sent to inflame the world beneath.
   'Twas but a bud, yet did contain
More sweetness than shall spring again;
A budding star, that might have grown
Into a sun when it had blown.   10
This hopeful beauty did create
New life in love's declining state;
But now his empire ends, and we
From fire and wounding darts are free;
   His brand, his bow, let no man fear: 15
   The flames, the arrows, all lie here.

EXERCISE:

   Compare this poem with "An Epitaph on Salathiel Pavy."
What is the difference in tone and what elements contribute to
this difference?

HIS PRAYER TO BEN JONSON

ROBERT HERRICK (1591–1674)

When I a verse shall make,
Know I have prayed thee,
For old religion's sake,
Saint Ben, to aid me.

Make the way smooth for me,   5
When I, thy Herrick,
Honoring thee, on my knee
Offer my lyric.

Candles I'll give to thee,
And a new altar;   10
And thou, Saint Ben, shalt be
Writ in my psalter.

AN ODE FOR BEN JONSON

ROBERT HERRICK (1591–1674)

Ah, Ben!
Say how or when

> Shall we, thy guests,
> Meet at those lyric feasts,
> Made at the Sun,   5
> The Dog, the Triple Tun;
> Where we such clusters had,
> As made us nobly wild, not mad?
> And yet each verse of thine
> Out-did the meat, out-did the frolic wine.   10
>
> My Ben!
> Or come again,
> Or send to us
> Thy wit's great overplus;
> But teach us yet   15
> Wisely to husband it,
> Lest we that talent spend;
> And having once brought to an end
> That precious stock, the store
> Of such a wit the world should have no more.   20

EXERCISE:

Both "His Prayer to Ben Jonson" and "Ode for Ben Jonson" were written by Herrick to the poet whom he regarded as his friend and master. (Consult the library for information concerning the relationship between the two poets.) In one of these poems the poet adopts a half-playful attitude and in the other an attitude of serious tribute. Attempt to define this difference more closely and more fully; and relate the difference to metrical and other technical factors.

CHANNEL FIRING

THOMAS HARDY (1840–1928)

That night your great guns unawares,
Shook all our coffins as we lay,
And broke the chancel window squares,
We thought it was the Judgment-day

And sat upright. While drearisome   5
Arose the howl of wakened hounds:
The mouse let fall the altar-crumb,
The worms drew back into the mounds,

The glebe cow drooled. Till God called, "No;
It's gunnery practice out at sea   10
Just as before you went below;
The world is as it used to be:

"All nations striving strong to make
Red war yet redder. Mad as hatters
They do no more for Christés sake   15
Than you who are helpless in such matters.

"That this is not the judgment-hour
For some of them's a blessed thing,
For if it were they'd have to scour
Hell's floor for so much threatening . . .   20

"Ha, ha. It will be warmer when
I blow the trumpet (if indeed
I ever do; for you are men,
And rest eternal sorely need)."

So down we lay again. "I wonder,   25
Will the world ever saner be,"
Said one, "than when He sent us under
In our indifferent century!"

And many a skeleton shook his head.
"Instead of preaching forty year,"   30
My neighbor Parson Thirdly said,
"I wish I had stuck to pipes and beer."

Again the guns disturbed the hour,
Roaring their readiness to avenge,
As far inland as Stourton Tower,   35
And Camelot, and starlit Stonehenge.

The situation in this poem is a fantastic one. The practice firing of battleships at night in the English Channel (and ironically enough this poem is dated by Hardy in April, 1914) disturbs the sleep of the dead at a church near the coast, and even frightens the church mouse that has been stealing crumbs left from the sacrament, and the worms that have crept out of the mounds. Then God speaks to the dead, telling them that the noise isn't the clap of doom, as they had thought, that it's just the world going about the same old business, with the same old disregard for the teachings of Christ. Then a preacher buried there, thinking how little good his forty years of work had accomplished, says that he regrets not having spent his time in worldly pleasure. Meanwhile the guns continue the firing. To make the situation even more fantastic, the person who speaks the poem is one of the skeletons of the churchyard.

If the situation is fantastic, at what sort of reality is the poet aiming? He is aiming to dramatize a theme, a certain view of human life, a fatalistic and somewhat ironical view of the persistence of evil in human life. The situation, then, is a little fable, or parable.

But what attitude does the poet expect us to take to the unreality of the situation? And how does he define the attitude that he does desire? He approaches the whole matter very casually, playing down rather than up the weird and ghostly element of the situation. A poorer poet, or even a good poet with a very different intention from that of Hardy, might have emphasized the horror of the scene. But Hardy domesticates that horror, as it were, for he puts the poem in the mouth of one of the skeletons; to the skeleton there is naturally nothing unusual and shocking in the surroundings. A poor poet would have emphasized the conventional devices for giving a weird effect, for instance, the dolorous howling of the hounds and the crawling of the grave worms, things that are the stage-properties of horror. Hardy uses these things, but he mixes them with the hungry little church mouse and the cow that is drooling over its cud in the meadow. There is, then, a casual, and perhaps slightly ironical approach to the horror.

This casual tone is emphasized by the conversational quality.

For instance, observe the effect of the running over of the first stanza into the second, and of the second into the third. This spilling over of a stanza to a full pause in the middle of the first line of the next stanza, breaks up the regular and stately movement of the verse, with a kind of tag. The content of each of these tags that spills over supports the same impression. In the first instance, we would get a much more serious effect if the statement should end with the line

We thought it was the Judgment-day.

But, no. Hardy makes the spill-over tag a kind of anti-climax, almost comic in its effect. The dead do not rise to the sound of the Judgment, filled with hope and terror. They merely sit up in their coffins, a little irritated at being bothered, like people who have been disturbed in their beds at night. The same kind of effect is attained in the tag that spills over into the third stanza,

The glebe cow drooled.

The effect here again is that of a kind of anti-climax, and ironical contrast, for the drooling cow follows the grave worms, conventional creatures of horror.

When God speaks the effect is still conversational and simple. He says: "The world is as it used to be"—a line that might be spoken by any one in ordinary talk. And He uses such a phrase as "Mad as hatters." He even makes a kind of sardonic joke about scouring the floors of hell, and another one, at which He himself laughs, about the time when the trumpet will be blown. And the same tone is held in the following stanzas of dialogue among the skeletons. The whole effect, thus far, is a mixture of the grotesque and the horrible with the comic and of the serious with the ironical.

But the tone of the last stanza changes abruptly. The movement becomes emphatic and stately,[1] and the imagination is presented with a sudden panoramic vision of the whole English

---

[1] How do the devices of alliteration, assonance, quantitative emphasis, and hovering accents function in this stanza?

countryside at night with the sound of the great guns dying inland. All of this elevated poetic effect is more emphatic because of the contrast in abrupt juxtaposition with the earlier section of the poem.

Perhaps further details are worthy of some comment. In the first section of the poem there is no such use of conventional poetic suggestiveness as in the second with "Camelot" and "Stonehenge." The effectiveness of this suggestion is increased by the contrast. But we may ask ourselves how the aura of poetic suggestion about these names really works in the poem. Is it merely decoration, as it were, or does it have a direct reference to the meaning of the poem? On the slightest reflection, we see that the use of these place names, with their poetic associations, is really necessary and functional. The meaning is this: even though the sound of modern heavy guns is contrasted with the medieval associations of Arthurian chivalry, with Camelot and the prehistoric Stonehenge, man's nature does not change. The starlit scene with the guns roaring in the distance becomes a kind of symbolic conclusion for the poem.

PIONEERS! O PIONEERS!

WALT WHITMAN (1819–1892)

Come my tan-faced children,
Follow well in order, get your weapons ready,
Have you your pistols? have you your sharp-edged axes?
    Pioneers! O pioneers!

For we cannot tarry here,   5
We must march my darlings, we must bear the brunt of danger,
We the youthful sinewy races, all the rest on us depend,
    Pioneers! O pioneers!

O you youths, Western youths,
So impatient, full of action, full of manly pride and friend-
    ship,   10
Plain I see you Western youths, see you tramping with the
    foremost,
    Pioneers! O pioneers!

Have the elder races halted?
Do they droop and end their lesson, wearied over there beyond
    the seas?
We take up the task eternal, and the burden and the lesson,   15
        Pioneers! O pioneers!

All the past we leave behind,
We debouch upon a newer mightier world, varied world,
Fresh and strong the world we seize, world of labor and the
    march,
        Pioneers! O pioneers!   20

We detachments steady throwing,
Down the edges, through the passes, up the mountains steep,
Conquering, holding, daring, venturing as we go the unknown
    ways,
        Pioneers! O pioneers!

We primeval forests felling,   25
We the rivers stemming, vexing we and piercing deep the mines
    within,
We the surface broad surveying, we the virgin soil upheaving,
        Pioneers! O pioneers!

Colorado men are we,
From the peaks gigantic, from the great sierras and the high
    plateaus,   30
From the mine and from the gulley, from the hunting trail we
    come,
        Pioneers! O pioneers!

From Nebraska, from Arkansas,
Central inland race are we, from Missouri, with the continental
    blood interveined,
All the hands of comrades clasping, all the Southern, all the
    Northern,   35
        Pioneers! O pioneers!

O resistless restless race!
O beloved race in all! O my breast aches with tender love for all!
O I mourn and yet exult, I am rapt with love for all,
        Pioneers! O pioneers!   40

Raise the mighty mother mistress,
Waving high the delicate mistress, over all the starry mistress
(bend your heads all),
Raise the fanged and warlike mistress, stern, impassive, weaponed
mistress,
Pioneers! O pioneers!

See my children, resolute children,   45
By those swarms upon our rear we must never yield or falter,
Ages back in ghostly millions frowning there behind us urging,
Pioneers! O pioneers!

On and on the compact ranks,
With accessions ever waiting, with the places of the dead quickly
filled,   50
Through the battle, through defeat, moving yet and never
stopping,
Pioneers! O pioneers!

O to die advancing on!
Are there some of us to droop and die? has the hour come?
Then upon the march we fittest die, soon and sure the gap is
filled,   55
Pioneers! O pioneers!

All the pulses of the world,
Falling in they beat for us, with the Western movement beat,
Holding single or together, steady moving to the front, all for us,
Pioneers! O pioneers!   60

Life's involved and varied pageants,
All the forms and shows, all the workmen at their work,
All the seamen and the landsmen, all the masters with their
slaves,
Pioneers! O pioneers!

All the hapless silent lovers,   65
All the prisoners in the prisons, all the righteous and the wicked,
All the joyous, all the sorrowing, all the living, all the dying,
Pioneers! O pioneers!

I too with my soul and body,
We, a curious trio, picking, wandering on our way,   70
Through these shores amid the shadows, with the apparitions
   pressing,
      Pioneers! O pioneers!

Lo, the darting bowling orb!
Lo, the brother orbs around, all the clustering suns and planets,
All the dazzling days, all the mystic nights with dreams,   75
      Pioneers! O pioneers!

These are of us, they are with us,
All for primal needed work, while the followers there in embryo
   wait behind,
We today's procession heading, we the route for travel clearing,
      Pioneers! O pioneers!   80

O you daughters of the West!
O you young and elder daughters! O you mothers and you wives!
Never must you be divided, in our ranks you move united,
      Pioneers! O pioneers!

Minstrels latent on the prairies!   85
(Shrouded bards of other lands, you may rest, you have done
   your work,)
Soon I hear you coming warbling, soon you rise and tramp amid
   us,
      Pioneers! O pioneers!

Not for delectations sweet,
Not the cushion and the slipper, not the peaceful and the
   studious,   90
Not the riches safe and palling, not for us the tame enjoyment,
      Pioneers! O pioneers!

Do the feasters gluttonous feast?
Do the corpulent sleepers sleep? have they locked and bolted
   doors?
Still be ours the diet hard, and the blanket on the ground,   95
      Pioneers! O pioneers!

Has the night descended?
Was the road of late so toilsome? did we stop discouraged nodding
　　on our way?
Yet a passing hour I yield you in your tracks to pause oblivious,
　　Pioneers! O pioneers!   100

　　Till with sound of trumpet,
Far, far off the daybreak call—hark! how loud and clear I hear
　　it wind,
Swift! to the head of the army!—swift! spring to your places,
　　Pioneers! O pioneers!

EXERCISE:

Define the tone of this poem in relation to metrical and other
technical factors.

SOLILOQUY OF THE SPANISH CLOISTER

ROBERT BROWNING (1812–1889)

Gr-r-r—there go, my heart's abhorrence!
　　Water your damned flower-pots, do!
If hate killed men, Brother Lawrence,
　　God's blood, would not mine kill you!
What? your myrtle-bush wants trimming?   5
　　Oh, that rose has prior claims—
Needs its leaden vase filled brimming?
　　Hell dry you up with its flames!

At the meal we sit together:
　　Salve tibi! I must hear   10
Wise talk of the kind of weather,
　　Sort of season, time of year:
Not a plenteous cork-crop: scarcely
　　Dare we hope oak-galls, I doubt:
What's the Latin name for "parsley"?   15
　　What's the Greek name for Swine's Snout?

Whew! We'll have our platter burnished,
  Laid with care on our own shelf!
With a fire-new spoon we're furnished,
  And a goblet for ourself,   20
Rinsed like something sacrificial
  Ere 'tis fit to touch our chaps—
Marked with L for our initial!
  (He-he! There his lily snaps!)

Saint, forsooth! While brown Dolores   25
  Squats outside the Convent bank
With Sanchicha, telling stories,
  Steeping tresses in the tank,
Blue-black lustrous, thick like horse-hairs,
  —Can't I see his dead eye glow,   30
Bright as 'twere a Barbary corsair's?
  (That is, if he'd let it show!)

When he finishes refection,
  Knife and fork he never lays
Cross-wise, to my recollection,   35
  As do I, in Jesu's praise.
I the Trinity illustrate,
  Drinking watered orange-pulp
In three sips the Arian frustrate;
  While he drains his at one gulp.   40

Oh, those melons! If he's able
  We're to have a feast! so nice!
One goes to the Abbot's table,
  All of us get each a slice.
How go on your flowers? None double?   45
  Not one fruit-sort can you spy?
Strange!—And I, too, at such trouble
  Keep them close-nipped on the sly!

There's a great text in Galatians,
  Once you trip on it, entails   50
Twenty-nine distinct damnations,
  One sure, if another fails:

If I trip him just a-dying,
   Sure of heaven as sure can be,
Spin him round and send him flying   55
   Off to hell, a Manichee!

Or, my scrofulous French novel
   On gray paper with blunt type!
Simply glance at it, you grovel
Hand and foot in Belial's gripe: 60
If I double down its pages
   At the woeful sixteenth print,
When he gathers his greengages,
   Ope a sieve and slip it in't?

Or, there's Satan! one might venture   65
   Pledge one's soul to him, yet leave
Such a flaw in the indenture
   As he'd miss till, past retrieve,
Blasted lay that rose-acacia
   We're so proud of! *Hy, Zy, Hine* . . .   70
'St, there's Vespers! *Plena gratiâ,*
   Ave, Virgo! Gr-r-r—you swine!

EXERCISE:

   1. Discuss the characters of the two men.
   2. The attitude of the speaker toward the other monk is obvious. What is the attitude of the poet toward the speaker?

PAST RUINED ILION

WALTER SAVAGE LANDOR (1775–1864)

Past ruined Ilion Helen lives,
   Alcestis rises from the shades;
Verse calls them forth; 't is verse that gives
   Immortal youth to mortal maids.

Soon shall Oblivion's deepening veil   5
  Hide all the peopled hills you see,
The gay, the proud, while lovers hail
  These many summers you and me.

EXERCISE:

1. Using the analysis of "Rose Aylmer" (pp. 270–3) for suggestions, write a discussion of the metrical and other technical
factors which help to define the tone of this poem.

2. Write a short definition of the tone of "Rose Aylmer" in
relation to the analysis already given.

THE SOUL SELECTS

EMILY DICKINSON (1830–1886)

The soul selects her own society,
Then shuts the door;
On her divine majority
Obtrude no more.

Unmoved, she notes the chariots pausing   5
At her low gate;
Unmoved, an emperor is kneeling
Upon her mat.

I've known her from an ample nation
Choose one;   10
Then close the valves of her attention
Like stone.

EXERCISE:

1. Define the tone of this poem.
2. How is the stanza form related to the tone?

TO LUCASTA GOING TO THE WARS

RICHARD LOVELACE (1618–1658)

Tell me not, Sweet, I am unkind,
   That from the nunnery
Of thy chaste breast and quiet mind
   To war and arms I fly.

True, a new mistress now I chase,   5
   The first foe in the field;
And with a stronger faith embrace
   A sword, a horse, a shield.

Yet this inconstancy is such
   As thou too shalt adore;   10
I could not love thee, Dear, so much,
   Loved I not Honor more.

EXERCISE:

1. How does the poet use his paradox to support the tone of the poem?

2. Discuss metrical variations in this poem in relation to the tone.

THE INDIAN SERENADE

PERCY BYSSHE SHELLEY (1792–1822)

I arise from dreams of thee
In the first sweet sleep of night,
When the winds are breathing low,
And the stars are shining bright:
I arise from dreams of thee,   5
And a spirit in my feet
Hath led me—who knows how?
To thy chamber window, Sweet!

The wandering airs they faint
On the dark, the silent stream—　　　　　　10
The Champak odors fail
Like sweet thoughts in a dream;
The nightingale's complaint,
It dies upon her heart;—
As I must on thine,　　　　　　　　　　15
Oh! beloved as thou art!

Oh lift me from the grass!
I die! I faint! I fail!
Let thy love in kisses rain
On my lips and eyelids pale.　　　　　　20
My cheek is cold and white, alas!
My heart beats loud and fast;—
Oh! press it to thine own again,
Where it will break at last.

The lover is speaking to his mistress. He has been dreaming of her, and awaking, finds himself at her window. He describes the night scene. The winds are lulled, the stars shining brightly overhead, and the air perfumed faintly with the odor of the champak tree. The nightingale has just ceased her singing. Quite overcome by his passion, he half swoons away, and appeals to his mistress to revive him, or at least (though the poem is not too clear here) to allow him to die upon her breast.

The *atmosphere* (*Glossary*) of the poem is that of the love swoon: the hushed, perfumed air, starlight, and the dying echoes of the nightingale. Her song and the breezes themselves seem to faint in sympathy with the lover.

The poet is attempting then to convey to the reader the experience of a very intense love, and love in a very remote and romantic setting. Moreover his method is a direct method. He might conceivably have conveyed the intensity of his love to the reader by hints and implications merely, allowing the reader to infer for himself the intensity. Or he might have given emphasis by understatement. But he has chosen to state the intensity directly and to the full. The poet using the method of understatement runs the risk of falling into dullness and flatness; the characteristic danger of the method Shelley has chosen, on the other hand, is that the reader may feel that the statements are overstatements—merely absurd exaggerations.

Is the method chosen successful? Perhaps we can answer this question more clearly by approaching the matter in this way. The poet tells us outright that his love is so intense that he is dying of it. But some people die very easily—they are always dying over this or that—always thinking that they are dying. Has the poet taken his lover out of this class? Has he made his audience feel that the lover's statement that he is dying is meant literally and is justified by the intensity of his love? The statement, "I die," comes with very different effect when wrung from the lips of a man of few words, cautious and well balanced, than it does when shrieked out by a flighty, hysterical sentimentalist. In the first case, it comes with tremendous effect; in the second, it merely provokes amusement or disgust.

What is implied then about the character ·of the lover in the poem? There is little to keep us from feeling that he is a confirmed sentimentalist, ready to faint and fail whenever the proper stimulus is applied. We know nothing of the lover except that he has lost control over himself. If he is usually poised and restrained, overpowered here only because of tremendous emotions, we have no hint of it. We see him in this poem only at the moment of romantic ecstasy. The poet, as a matter of fact, makes no attempt to supply a context which would give a background for this particular experience. Instead, he merely tries to give an exotic and remote atmosphere to the scene by assembling the conventional exhibits of a "prettified" love affair, and by removing it to a far-off and romantic scene.

The student should notice that the question at issue here is not whether Shelley felt "sincere" when he wrote the poem, or whether Shelley ever had such an experience. Even if Shelley had had in real life just the experience described, that fact would have no relevance for the problem before us here. For what we have to determine is this question: are the statements made by the lover in this poem convincing to the reader? They are unconvincing and the poem, for the mature reader, is a sentimental one. Sentimentality we may define as the display of more emotion than the situation warrants. The poet has not in this case properly prepared for the outburst of emotion. We also use the term *sentimentalist* occasionally to indicate a person whose emotions are on hairtrigger. And we also use it to indicate a person who likes to indulge in emotion for its own sake. The last two meanings are obviously closely related to the first one. And this poem will, as a matter of fact, illustrate all three meanings. For the lover in this poem seems to the reader to go into an ecstasy under very little stimulus indeed, and, furthermore, he certainly seems to revel in the emotions without much concern for their occasion or for their specific quality or for anything else than their thrilling sweetness.

An almost inevitable accompaniment of sentimentality is this obsession with one's own emotions—an exclusive interest which blinds the person involved to everything except the sweet intensity of the emotion in question. It is symptomatic of this sentimental attitude that there is nowhere in this poem a sharp and definite image. The poet apparently does not perceive anything sharply and compellingly and he does not cause the reader to perceive anything very compellingly. This obsession with the sweet thrill is so strong here that the mistress herself is not described—even by implication. But the poet does describe himself and his own feelings—in detail. The whole of the last stanza is devoted to a description of his "symptoms."

And having seen that this blindness to the context is characteristic of the sentimental attitude, we are better able to understand the reason for the remote, vague, exotic setting of the poem. Sentimentality, since it is an emotional one-sidedness, has to be posed in a special light. Under anything like critical inspection it is seen to be one-sided. It is this critical inspection which the poet wishes to avoid—or rather it does not occur to him to inspect his experience critically. Hence, the vague, romantic setting. If the reader can be induced to yield himself to the dreamy sweetness of the setting, and if his intellect can be lulled to sleep, he feels that the poem is fine. Good love poetry, on the other hand, does not need to resort to such devices. The poet achieves an effect of intensity without violating our sense of reality and without asking us to stop thinking so that we can exclusively and uninterruptedly "emote." Compare with this poem such love poems as "A Litany," by Philip Sidney (p. 341), "Rose Aylmer," by Walter Savage Landor (p. 270).

SUMMER NIGHT

ALFRED LORD TENNYSON (1809–1892)

Now sleeps the crimson petal, now the white;
    Nor waves the cypress in the palace walk;
Nor winks the gold fin in the porphyry font:—
    The firefly wakens: waken thou with me.

Now droops the milk-white peacock like a ghost, 5
    And like a ghost she glimmers on to me.

Now lies the Earth all Danaë to the stars,
    And all thy heart lies open unto me.

Now slides the silent meteor on, and leaves
    A shining furrow, as thy thought in me.   10

Now folds the lily all her sweetness up,
    And slips into the bosom of the lake:
So fold thyself, my dearest, thou, and slip
    Into my bosom and be lost in me.

EXERCISE:

Using the analysis of "The Indian Serenade," write a full analysis of this poem.

CUPID AND CAMPASPE

JOHN LYLY (1554–1606)

Cupid and my Campaspe played
At cards for kisses; Cupid paid.
He stakes his quiver, bow, and arrows,
His mother's doves and team of sparrows;

Loses them too; then down he throws   5
The coral of his lip, the rose
Growing on's cheek (but none knows how);
With these the crystal of his brow,
And then the dimple of his chin;
All these did my Campaspe win.   10
At last he set her both his eyes;
She won, and Cupid blind did rise.
O Love, has she done this to thee?
What shall, alas! become of me?

EXERCISE:

1. Here the poet presents a fanciful picture of a game at cards
between Cupid and the poet's mistress, Campaspe; at the end
Cupid has wagered ("set") and lost even his eyes. How does
this incident define the tone of the compliment? (See *Glossary*
under *vers de société*.)

BLAME NOT MY CHEEKS

THOMAS CAMPION (1567–1620)

Blame not my cheeks, though pale with love they be;
The kindly heat unto my heart is flown,
To cherish it that is dismaid by thee,
Who art so cruel and unsteadfast grown:
For nature, called for by distressed hearts,
Neglects and quite forsakes the outward parts.   5

But they whose cheeks with careless blood are stained,
Nurse not one spark of love within their hearts,
And, when they woo, they speak with passion feigned,
For their fat love lies in their outward parts: 10
But in their breasts, where love his ccurt should hold,
Poor Cupid sits and blows his nails for cold.

EXERCISE:

1. Contrast the tone and attitude of this poem with the sentimentality of "The Indian Serenade" on one hand, and the play-
fulness of "Cupid and Campaspe" on the other.

2. In relation to the previous exercise discuss the following factors: the metrical situation in the fourth line of the first stanza; the phrases "careless blood" and "fat love" in the first and fourth lines respectively of the second stanza; and the use of the figure of Cupid in the last line of the second stanza.

LET ME NOT TO THE MARRIAGE OF TRUE MINDS

WILLIAM SHAKESPEARE (1564–1616)

Let me not to the marriage of true minds
Admit impediments. Love is not love
Which alters when it alteration finds,
Or bends with the remover to remove:
O, no! it is an ever-fixèd mark   5
That looks on tempests and is never shaken;
It is the star to every wandering bark,
Whose worth's unknown, although his height be taken.
Love's not Time's fool, though rosy lips and cheeks
Within his bending sickle's compass come;   10
Love alters not with his brief hours and weeks,
But bears it out even to the edge of doom.
If this be error and upon me proved,
I never writ, nor no man ever loved.

EXERCISE:

1. Compare the tone of this poem with that of "The Indian Serenade."

2. Write a full analysis of the metrical and other technical factors of this poem in relation to tone.

THE PASSIONATE SHEPHERD TO HIS LOVE

CHRISTOPHER MARLOWE (1564–1593)

Come live with me and be my love,
And we will all the pleasures prove,
That valleys, groves, hills, and fields,
Woods, or steepy mountains, yields.

iambic tetrameter
a a b b

And we will sit upon the rocks,   5
Seeing the shepherds feed their flocks,
By shallow rivers, to whose falls
Melodious birds sing madrigals.

And I will make thee beds of roses,
And a thousand fragrant posies,   10
A cap of flowers and a kirtle
Embroidered all with leaves of myrtle:

A gown made of the finest wool,
Which from our pretty lambs we pull;
Fair linèd slippers for the cold,   15
With buckles of the purest gold;

A belt of straw and ivy buds,
With coral clasps and amber studs;
And if these pleasures may thee move,
Come live with me and be my love.   20

The shepherd swains shall dance and sing
For thy delights each May morning;
If these delights thy mind may move,
Then live with me and be my love.

ANSWER TO MARLOWE

SIR WALTER RALEGH (1552–1618)

If all the world and love were young,
And truth in every shepherd's tongue,
These pretty pleasures might me move
To live with thee and be thy love.

But time drives flocks from field to fold,   5
When rivers rage and rocks grow cold,
And Philomel becometh dumb;
The rest complain of cares to come.

The flowers do fade, and wanton fields
To wayward Winter reckoning yields;   10
A honey tongue, a heart of gall,
Is fancy's spring, but sorrow's fall.

Thy gowns, thy shoes, thy beds of roses,
Thy cap, thy kirtle, and thy posies
Soon break, soon wither, soon forgotten,   15
In folly ripe, in reason rotten.

Thy belt of straw and ivy buds,
Thy coral clasps and amber studs,
All these in me no means can move
To come to thee and be thy love.   20

But could youth last and love still breed,
Had joys no date nor age no need,
Then these delights my mind might move
To live with thee and be thy love.

EXERCISE:

1. Both "The Passionate Shepherd to his Love" and Ralegh's reply make use of the *pastoral machinery* (*Glossary*). How is the difference in the use of the pastoral machinery in the two poems related to the difference in tone?

DELIGHT IN DISORDER

ROBERT HERRICK (1591–1674)

A sweet disorder in the dress
Kindles in clothes a wantonness:
A lawn about the shoulders thrown
Into a fine distraction:
An erring lace, which here and there   5
Enthralls the crimson stomacher:
A cuff neglectful, and thereby
Ribbands to flow confusedly:

A winning wave (deserving note)
In the tempestuous petticoat: 10,
A careless shoe-string, in whose tie
I see a wild civility:
Do more bewitch me, than when art
Is too precise in every part.

EXERCISE:

F. W. Bateson has analysed as follows the attitudes implicit in this poem:—"The impression of a surprising richness, and almost grandeur (as of a painting by Titian), with a certain tantalizing quality, that Herrick's poem leaves, is primarily due to the skill with which he has exploited the ambiguous associations of the epithets. On the surface his subject is the "Delight in the Disorder" of the title—a disorder, that is, of costume. But a second subject is hinted at, though not protruded: a delight in disorder, not of costume but of manners and morals. It is not only the clothes but their wearers too whom he would have *sweet, wanton, distracted, erring, neglectful, winning, tempestuous, wild,* and *bewitching* rather than *precise.* The poem, in fact, instead of being the mere *jeu d'esprit* that it would seem to be, is essentially a plea for paganism. There are three themes: (1) untidiness is becoming; (2) the clothes are the woman; (3) anti-Puritanism. But the success of the poem depends upon the fact that the themes are not isolated and contrasted but grow out of and into each other. The suspension between the various meanings produces a range of reference that none of them would have alone."[1]

Indicate other words and phrases in the poem which would support Bateson's view.

[1] *English Poetry and the English Language,* Oxford: Oxford University Press, pp. 42–43.

PROTHALAMION

EDMUND SPENSER (1552–1599)

Calm was the day, and through the trembling air
Sweet breathing Zephyrus did softly play,

A gentle spirit, that lightly did delay
Hot Titan's beams, which then did glister fair;
When I (whom sullen care,   5
Through discontent of my long fruitless stay
In princes' court, and expectation vain
Of idle hopes, which still do fly away,
Like empty shadows, did afflict my brain)
Walked forth to ease my pain   10
Along the shore of silver streaming Thames;
Whose rutty bank, the which his river hems,
Was painted all with variable flowers,
And all the meads adorned with dainty gems
Fit to deck maidens' bowers,   15
And crown their paramours,
Against the bridal day, which is not long.
   Sweet Thames, run softly, till I end my song.

There, in a meadow, by the river's side,
A flock of nymphs I chancëd to espy,   20
All lovely daughters of the flood thereby,
With goodly greenish locks, all loose untied,
As each had been a bride;
And each one had a little wicker basket,
Made of fine twigs entrailëd curiously,   25
In which they gathered flowers to fill their flasket,
And with fine fingers cropped full feateously
The tender stalks on high.
Of every sort which in that meadow grew
They gathered some; the violet pallid blue,   30
The little daisy, that at evening closes,
The virgin lily, and the primrose true,
With store of vermeil roses,
To deck their bridegroom's posies
Against the bridal day, which was not long.   35
   Sweet Thames, run softly, till I end my song.

With that I saw two swans of goodly hue
Come softly swimming down alóng the Lee.
Two fairer birds I yet did never see;
The snow which doth the top of Pindus strew   40
Did never whiter shew,
Nor Jove himself, when he a swan would be

For love of Leda, whiter did appear;
Yet Leda was, they say, as white as he,
Yet not so white as these, nor nothing near;   45
So purely white they were
That even the gentle stream, the which them bare,
Seemed foul to them, and bade his billows spare
To wet their silken feathers, lest they might
Soil their fair plumes with water not so fair,   50
And mar their beauties bright,
That shone as heaven's light,
Against their bridal day, which was not long.
  Sweet Thames, run softly, till I end my song.

Eftsoons the nymphs, which now had flowers their fill,   55
Ran all in haste to see that silver brood,
As they came floating on the crystal flood;
Whom when they saw, they stood amazèd still,
Their wondering eyes to fill;
Them seemed they never saw a sight so fair   60
Of fowls so lovely, that they sure did deem
Them heavenly born, or to be that same pair
Which through the sky draw Venus' silver team;
For sure they did not seem
To be begot of any earthly seed,   65
But rather angels, or of angels' breed;
Yet were they bred of summer's heat, they say,
In sweetest season, when each flower and weed
The earth did fresh array;
So fresh they seemed as day,   70
Even as their bridal day, which was not long.
  Sweet Thames, run softly, till I end my song.

Then forth they all out of their baskets drew
Great store of flowers, the honor of the field,
That to the sense did fragrant odors yield,   75
All which upon those goodly birds they threw,
And all the waves did strew,
That like old Peneus' waters they did seem,
When down along by pleasant Tempe's shore,
Scatt'rèd with flowers, through Thessaly they stream,   80
That they appear, through lilies' plenteous store,
Like a bride's chamber floor.

Two of those nymphs meanwhile two garlands bound
Of freshest flowers which in that mead they found,
The which presenting all in trim array,   85
Their snowy foreheads therewithal they crowned,
Whilst one did sing this lay,
Prepared against that day,
Against their bridal day, which was not long:
   Sweet Thames, run softly, till I end my song.   90

"Ye gentle birds, the world's fair ornament,
And heaven's glory, whom this happy hour
Doth lead unto your lovers' blissful bower,
Joy may you have, and gentle hearts' content
Of your love's couplement;   95
And let fair Venus, that is queen of love,
With her heart-quelling son, upon you smile,
Whose smile, they say, hath virtue to remove
All love's dislike, and friendship's faulty guile
For ever to assoil.   100
Let endless peace your steadfast hearts accord,
And blessëd plenty wait upon your board;
And let your bed with pleasures chaste abound,
That fruitful issue may to you afford,
Which may your foes confound,   105
And make your joys redound
Upon your bridal day, which is not long."
   Sweet Thames, run softly, till I end my song.

So ended she; and all the rest around
To her redoubled that her undersong,   110
Which said their bridal day should not be long;
And gentle Echo from the neighbor ground
Their accents did resound.
So forth those joyous birds did pass along,
Adown the Lee, that to them murmured low,   115
As he would speak, but that he lacked a tongue,
Yet did by signs his glad affection show,
Making his stream run slow.
And all the fowl which in his flood did dwell
Gan flock about these twain, that did excel   120
The rest, so far as Cynthia doth shend
The lesser stars. So they, enrangëd well,

Did on those two attend,
And their best service lend,
Against their wedding day, which was not long.   125
  Sweet Thames, run softly, till I end my song.

At length they all to merry London came,
To merry London, my most kindly nurse,
That to me gave this life's first native source,
Though from another place I take my name,   130
An house of ancient fame.
There when they came, whereas those bricky towers
The which on Thames' broad, agèd back do ride,
Where now the studious lawyers have their bowers,
There whilom wont the Templar Knights to bide,   135
Till they decayed through pride;
Next whereunto there stands a stately place,
Where oft I gainèd gifts and goodly grace
Of that great lord which therein wont to dwell,
Whose want too well now feels my friendless case— 140
But ah! here fits not well
Old woes, but joys, to tell,
Against the bridal day, which is not long.
  Sweet Thames, run softly, till I end my song.

Yet therein now doth lodge a noble peer,   145
Great England's glory, and the world's wide wonder,
Whose dreadful name late through all Spain did thunder,
And Hercules' two pillars standing near
Did make to quake and fear.
Fair branch of honor, flower of chivalry,   150
That fillest England with thy triumph's fame,
Joy have thou of thy noble victory,
And endless happiness of thine own name,
That promiseth the same;
That through thy prowess and victorious arms   155
Thy country may be freed from foreign harms;
And great Eliza's glorious name may ring
Through all the world, filled with thy wide alarms,
Which some brave muse may sing
To ages following,   160
Upon the bridal day, which is not long.
  Sweet Thames, run softly, till I end my song.

From those high towers this noble lord issuing,
Like radiant Hesper, when his golden hair
In the ocean billows he hath bathèd fair,   165
Descended to the river's open viewing,
With a great train ensuing.
Above the rest were goodly to be seen
Two gentle knights of lovely face and feature,
Beseeming well the bower of any queen,   170
With gifts of wit, and ornaments of nature,
Fit for so goodly stature,
That like the twins of Jove they seemed in sight,
Which deck the baldrick of the heavens bright.
They two, forth pacing to the river's side   175
Received those two fair brides, their love's delight;
Which, at the appointed tide,
Each one did make his bride,
Against their bridal day, which is not long.
    Sweet Thames, run softly, till I end my song.   180

EXERCISE:

1. Compare the tone of this poem with that of "The Indian Serenade," by Shelley (p. 319).
2. How is the tone achieved in this poem?

THE PILGRIMS

ADELAIDE ANNE PROCTOR (1825–1864)

The way is long and dreary,
The path is bleak and bare;
Our feet are worn and weary,
But we will not despair;
More heavy was Thy burden,   5
More desolate Thy way;—
O Lamb of God who takest
The sin of the world away,
    Have mercy on us.

The snows lie thick around us   10
In the dark and gloomy night;

And the tempest wails above us,
And the stars have hid their light;
But blacker was the darkness
Round Calvary's Cross that day:—   15
O Lamb of God who takest
The sin of the world away,
    Have mercy on us.

Our hearts are faint with sorrow,
Heavy and hard to bear;   20
For we dread the bitter morrow,
But we will not despair:
Thou knowest all our anguish,
And Thou wilt bid it cease,—
O Lamb of God who takest   25
The sin of the world away,
    Give us Thy peace!

Even though the work of Adelaide Proctor, who is known now only as the author of "The Lost Chord," was once greatly admired by Charles Dickens, most modern readers of poetry would find this poem bad. Most readers who admire it probably do so because they approve of the pious sentiment expressed in it. Such readers go to poetry merely to have their own beliefs and feelings flattered or to find what they would call "great truths" or "worthwhile ideas" expressed in an agreeable form. Such readers do not go to poetry for anything that poetry, as poetry, can give them, but for something that they might get, though in not so compact and pleasant a form, in a sermon or a collection of adages.

"The Pilgrims" can be appreciated only because of something the reader may bring to it (an uncritical and sentimental piety) and not because of anything it brings to the reader. A truly pious person who was also an experienced reader of poetry might, as a matter of fact, have his piety offended rather than sustained by this poem. He might feel it as stupid, trivial, and not worthy of the subject.

He might feel this because the business of a poem is to sharpen and renew the experience of the subject. But the present poem does nothing to accomplish that purpose. It is composed of worn-out materials, stereotyped images and phrases. The trouble is not that the basic idea of salvation through the Christ has been used in poetry before. Basic ideas, or themes, of poetry are relatively limited in number and occur again and again. Numerous fine poems (two in this collection) have been written on this theme, and others in all probability will be written. But if a poem is successful, the reader feels it as a new experience; it is again proved, as it were, by the fact that the poem provokes a new response to it, by new devices of dramatization, new images and combinations of images, new shades of feeling in expression, new phrasing, new combinations of rhythm.

"The Pilgrims" has a serious theme and one about which a body of emotional response might easily gather. But if that response is stereotyped, if the theme merely appeals to what is called the *stock response* (*Glossary*) the seriousness or interest of the theme loses all value. Now Adelaide Proctor, apparently, responded to her theme in a perfectly stereotyped way. The attitude developed in the poem is *conventional* (*Glossary*) in a bad sense.

This failure to bring any freshness to the theme, to make it into something the reader could experience as new, is indicated by the numerous *clichés* (*Glossary*) in the poem. A *cliché* is a trite expression, an expression that has become so worn-out that it no longer can impress the reader with a fresh and sharp perception. The poem is built up of such phrases: the way is *long and dreary;* the path *bleak and bare;* the snows *lie thick;* the tempest *wails;* the stars hide their light; hearts are *faint with sorrow,* etc. In every instance the poet has used a phrase that dulls the reader's perception of the scene rather than stimulates it. In other words, the poet has made no real attempt to visualize, or make the reader visualize, the objects. Nothing strikes the reader with the force of a new perception, and the total effect is vague. (By the very nature of language every poem must employ certain stereotyped expressions; the poet may even deliberately use clichés to set a certain tone (see "A Litany," p. 341). The question is to see how the clichés relate to the general intention in each case.)

This defect in the use of detail is paralleled by a similar defect

in the general dramatic framework of the poem. Life is presented as a journey over difficult country in bad weather. This
basic comparison has been used innumerable times, and does
not in itself bring any poetic or dramatic freshness to the theme.
It could only be effective if the detail work were adequate. But
that is not the case. The clichés, the poorly visualized imagery,
and the dull and mechanical rhythms all help to dull the reader's
response.

HIS LITANY, TO THE HOLY SPIRIT

ROBERT HERRICK (1591–1674)

In the hour of my distress,
When temptations me oppress,
And when I my sins confess,
    Sweet Spirit comfort me!

When I lie within my bed,   5
Sick in heart, and sick in head,
And with doubts discomforted,
    Sweet Spirit comfort me!

When the house doth sigh and weep,
And the world is drowned in sleep,   10
Yet mine eyes the watch do keep;
    Sweet Spirit comfort me!

When the artless doctor sees
No one hope, but of his fees,
And his skill runs on the lees;   15
    Sweet Spirit comfort me!

When his potion and his pill,
Has, or none, or little skill,
Meet for nothing, but to kill;
    Sweet Spirit comfort me!   20

When the passing-bell doth toll,
And the Furies in a shoal
Come to fright a parting soul;
    Sweet Spirit comfort me!

When the tapers now burn blue,   25
And the comforters are few,
And that number more than true;
    Sweet Spirit comfort me!

When the priest his last hath prayed,
And I nod to what is said,   30
'Cause my speech is now decayed;
    Sweet Spirit comfort me!

When (God knows) I'm tossed about,
Either with despair, or doubt;
Yet before the glass be out,   35
    Sweet Spirit comfort me!

When the Tempter me pursu'th
With the sins of all my youth,
And half damns me with untruth;
    Sweet Spirit comfort me!   40

When the flames and hellish cries
Fright mine ears, and fright mine eyes,
And all terrors me surprise;
    Sweet Spirit comfort me!

When the Judgment is revealed,   45
And that opened which was sealed,
When to Thee I have appealed;
    Sweet Spirit comfort me!

EXERCISE:

This, like "The Pilgrims," is a religious poem. How does the
poet prevent it from falling into the same sentimentality?

AFTER THE BURIAL

JAMES RUSSELL LOWELL (1819–1891)

Yes, faith is a goodly anchor;
  When skies are sweet as a psalm,
At the bows it lolls so stalwart,
  In its bluff, broad-shouldered calm.

And when over breakers to leeward   5
    The tattered surges are hurled,
It may keep our head to the tempest,
    With its grip ·on the base of the world.

But, after the shipwreck, tell me
    What help in its iron thews,   10
Still true to the broken hawser,
    Deep down, among sea-weed and ooze?

In the breaking gulfs of sorrow,
    When the helpless feet stretch out
And find in the deeps of darkness   15
    No footing so solid as doubt,

Then better one spar of Memory,
    One broken plank of the Past,
That our human heart may cling to,
    Though hopeless of shore at last!   20

To the spirit its splendid conjectures,
    To the flesh its sweet despair,
Its tears o'er the thin-worn locket
    With its anguish of deathless hair!

Immortal?   I feel it and know it,   25
    Who doubts it of such as she?
But that is the pang's very awe
    Immortal away from me.

There's a narrow ridge in the graveyard
    Would scarce stay a child in his race,   30
But to me and my thought it is wider
    Than the star-sown vague of Space.

Your logic, my friend, is perfect,
    Your moral most drearily true;
But, since the earth clashed on *her* coffin,   35
    I keep hearing that, and not you.

Console if you will, I can bear it;
    'T is a well-meant alms of breath;
But not all the preaching since Adam
    Has made Death other than Death.   40

It is pagan; but wait till you feel it,—
 That jar of our earth, that dull shock
When the ploughshare of deeper passion
 Tears down to our primitive rock.

Communion in spirit! Forgive me,   45
 But I, who am earthly and weak,
Would give all my incomes from dreamland
 For a touch of her hand on my cheek.

That little shoe in the corner,
 So worn and wrinkled and brown,   50
With its emptiness confutes you,
 And argues your wisdom down.

EXERCISE:

 1. We know that this poem was written by Lowell as an expression of personal grief. But this does not mean that the poem is necessarily a good one. Why are the third and eleventh stanzas better than the rest of the poem? Why are stanzas ten and twelve especially poor?

 2. This poem, like "The Sunflower" (p. 236), employs an anapaestic meter. Try to determine why the rhythm of this poem is mechanical and monotonous and that of "The Sunflower" flexible.

ON HIS BLINDNESS

JOHN MILTON (1608–1674)

When I consider how my light is spent
Ere half my days in this dark world and wide,
And that one talent which is death to hide
Lodged with me useless, though my soul more bent
To serve therewith my Maker, and present   5
My true account, lest he returning chide,
"Doth God exact day-labor, light denied?"
I fondly ask. But Patience, to prevent

That murmur, soon replies, "God doth not need
Either man's work or his own gifts. Who best   10
Bear his mild yoke, they serve him best. His state
Is kingly: thousands at his bidding speed,
And post o'er land and ocean without rest;
They also serve who only stand and wait."

EXERCISE:

Here Milton takes quite as direct an approach to the subject
of his own blindness as Lowell does to the subject of his own
grief in "After the Burial." Try to define the difference in
attitude and tone. Why is one poem sentimental and the other
not?

WHEN LOVE MEETS LOVE

THOMAS EDWARD BROWN (1830–1897)

When love meets love, breast urged to breast,
God interposes,
An unacknowledged guest,
And leaves a little child among our roses.

We love, God makes: in our sweet mirth   5
God spies occasion for a birth.
Then is it His, or is it ours?
I know not—He is fond of flowers.

EXERCISE:

Write an analysis of this poem, using the analysis of "Pilgrims"
as a model.

ON LUCRETIA BORGIA'S HAIR

WALTER SAVAGE LANDOR (1775–1864)

Borgia, thou once wert almost too august
And high for adoration; now thou'rt dust;

> All that remains of thee these plaits unfold,
> Calm hair meandering in pellucid gold.

EXERCISE:

This poem has a subject that often appears in poetry. Consider the metrical and other technical factors in relation to the tone of the poem. Does the tone keep this poem from being sentimental or trite?

A LITANY

SIR PHILIP SIDNEY (1554–1586)

> Ring out your bells, let mourning shows be spread;
> For Love is dead.
>   All Love is dead, infected
> With plague of deep disdain;
>   Worth, as nought worth, rejected,   5
> And Faith fair scorn doth gain.
>   From so ungrateful fancy,
>   From such a female franzy,
>   From them that use men thus,
>   Good Lord, deliver us!   10
>
> Weep, neighbors, weep! do you not hear it said
> That Love is dead?
>   His death-bed, peacock's folly;
> His winding-sheet is shame;
>   His will, false-seeming holy;   15
> His sole executor, blame.
>   From so ungrateful fancy,
>   From such a female franzy,
>   From them that use men thus,
>   Good Lord, deliver us!   20
>
> Let dirge be sung and trentals rightly read,
> For Love is dead.
>   Sir Wrong his tomb ordaineth

My mistress Marble-heart,
  Which epitaph containeth,   25
"Her eyes were once his dart."
  From so ungrateful fancy,
  From such a female franzy,
    From them that use men thus,
    Good Lord, deliver us!   30

Alas! I lie, rage hath this error bred;
Love is not dead.
  Love is not dead, but sleepeth
In her unmatchèd mind,
  Where she his counsel keepeth,   35
Till due desert she find.
  Therefore from so vile fancy,
  To call such wit a franzy,
    Who Love can temper thus,
    Good Lord, deliver us!   40

What is the tone of the first stanza of this poem? The title
tells us that the poem is a litany, that is, a prayer connected
with religious ritual; and we find that the last line of the refrain
is actually taken from the liturgy of the Church. Moreover,
the poet asks that the bells be rung. The death of love is described as if it were the death of a person, a person who has died
of the plague. Disdain, like a disease, has infected the love of
the lady for the speaker, and that love is now dead, altogether
dead.

By describing the death of love in terms of a funeral, the poet
achieves a certain solemnity. He refrains from comment on
the situation, or rather he defers his comment on the situation
until the last line, and this last line of comment is not mere bold
comment—it is part of the imagery of the church service already
prepared for above.

The first stanza has then the tone of a solemn announcement.
The word *fancy,* by the way, means "love." It is used here in the
sense which it has still in our phrase "fancy free"—a meaning
which is otherwise obsolete today.

But the tone of the poem, already shifted a little in the refrain
with the phrase "female franzy," alters radically in the second

stanza. The change is indicated in the very first line in calling
on the neighbors to weep. It is as if the poet querulously and
in self-mockery should nudge the people next to him and say,
Why don't you do something about it? The movement of
the first two lines helps to convey this sense of mocking impa-
tience. In the first stanza there is a heavy pause after the long
first line, so that the short line

   For Love is dead

comes as a solemn announcement. In the second stanza, in the
first line, a heavy pause occurs after the second *weep* so that we
hurry on rapidly through the sense-unit: "do you not hear it
said that Love is dead?"

But in his self-mockery the poet does not abandon his original
figure. He retains it, for ironical effect, exaggerating it somewhat, for the purpose of making it a vehicle for his bitter scorn.
The little allegory of the death of love is thus made a piece of
conscious frippery for the poet to exhibit ironically for laughter.
He pictures love on a death bed made of peacock feathers and
the gorgeousness of the bed itself increases the irony. The peacock, incidentally, is a stock figure of overweening pride. It is
appropriate therefore that its feathers should furnish forth love's
death bed. The poet goes on to elaborate for the purposes of
mockery all the other appurtenances of a human death—the
winding-sheet, the will, the executor.

The third stanza, which carries on this elaboration, contains
several elliptical constructions which the reader must be aware
of if he is to understand the grammar: "Sir Wrong ordaineth
(that is, solemnly proclaims) my mistress's Marble-heart as his
(love's) tomb which containeth (the) epitaph 'Her (the mistress's) eyes were once his (love's) dart.' " The irony of this
last clause would be more apparent to a reader of Sidney's own
time than perhaps to a modern reader, for in Elizabethan time
certain mannerisms of love poetry were flourishing. These mannerisms grew from the tradition of Petrarch, the Italian poet of
the fourteenth century who first popularized the love sonnet. In
what came to be known as the Petrarchan tradition, the lover's
mistress was often ridiculously idolized; her beauty was superla-
tive; her eyes gave death-dealing glances, etc; the devotion of the

lover could only be described in extravagant terms. The imagery, used here in the description of Love's tomb, is Petrarchan; princely tombs were made of marble, and the hardness of the lady's heart, its marblelike quality, makes it appropriate that it should be Love's tomb. She once furnished Love with his darts, supplying him with the bright beams of her eyes (with an allusion to the belief that love flashed from a beautiful woman's eyes). But the imagery here is plainly *mock-heroic* (*Glossary*). Sidney has used these clichés ironically, expecting the reader to recognize their stereotyped quality. They help define the appropriate tone. (See "The Pilgrims," p. 333)

But with the fourth stanza the tone is abruptly changed again. The poet suddenly tells us in the first line that he has been lying. The meter of the first four lines of this stanza reflects the change in tone. Consider the system of pauses. There is a definite pause after *lie*. The sense demands it, but in addition the meter supports it. Sidney has substituted a trochee for the expected iamb in the third foot. Compare for example

> Alás! I lié, ráge hath this érror bréd

with

> Alás! I lié, for ráge this érror bréd.

The first demands more than usual stress on *rage* and it demands a heavy pause after *I lie*. (See analysis of "After Long Silence," pp. 224–30)

There is, of course, a heavy pause after *bred*, but the poet has done something else to throw emphasis on the statement that "Love is not dead." In the three earlier stanzas the second line reads, "For Love is dead," "That love is dead," and "For Love is dead." All of these are regular iambic lines, and we have become accustomed to expect that pattern at this point in each stanza. But in this stanza the poet makes a trochaic substitution in the first foot and writes:

> Love is not dead.

The result is a slight shock—the other pattern having been established in our minds—and a slowing down of the line: this is appropriate because the poem turns here. The poet has used still another device. He repeats in the next line, "Love is not dead" and the statement is emphasized only to be swept along with the full line: "Love is not dead, but sleepeth."

The flow of the verse through this part of the stanza with the run-on line and the volume given to *unmatched* by pronouncing it as a dissyllable, give a sense of triumphant assurance after the halting pauses of the first part of the stanza.

The tone is that which a man might use who has come to himself and finds that the precious thing which he has believed lost is not lost at all. This tone is supported not only by the movement of the verse but also by the contrast of the imagery of the last stanza with the Petrarchan frippery of the two preceding stanzas.

Moreover, the refrain which has been used to castigate his mistress is now turned on himself and the belief to which he has been previously giving expression. We have already pointed out that the word *fancy* as used earlier in the poem means "love" though it also bears the meaning of "whim" associated as it is with "female franzy." But in this last stanza its meaning is clearly defined. It is merely an imagination and it is a vile imagination "To call such wit a franzy."

The poem then shows several changes of tone: the solemn pronouncement of the first lines, the mock-heroic ironic tone of the middle section, and the tone of the last section just described. The changes of tone correspond to a very definite psychological structure. It is as if a lover stated to himself the fact that his love was dead; then went on to parade his grief in scorn of it and revulsion; and finally, having vented his irony—his anger having spent itself and cleared the air—turned suddenly to see that love was not dead at all, and that his mistress, far from being whimsical and cruel was justified, his temporary revulsion having the effect of letting him see her real nature better. We do not of course have to read this dramatic interpretation into the poem. But the development of tone in a poem always conforms, in so far as the work is successful, to a psychological structure; for, as we have said, every poem is a little drama (*Introduction,* p. 23). It is easy to isolate, in a poem like "A Litany," the matter of tone for discussion, but it must be remembered that tone is a factor in all poetry.

THE FAIRIES' FAREWELL

RICHARD CORBET (1582–1635)

"Farewell rewards and fairies,"
    Good housewives now may say,
For now foul sluts in dairies
    Do fare as well as they.
And though they sweep their hearths no less   5
    Than maids were wont to do,
Yet who of late for cleanliness,
    Finds sixpence in her shoe?

Lament, lament, old abbeys,
    The fairies lost command;   10
They did but change priests' babies,
    But some have changed your land;
And all your children stol'n from thence
    Are now grown Puritanes;
Who live as changelings ever since   15
    For love of your domains.

At morning and at evening both
    You merry were and glad,
So little care of sleep and sloth
    These pretty ladies had;   20
When Tom came home from labor,
    Or Cisse to milking rose,
Then merrily, merrily went their tabor,
    And nimbly went their toes.

Witness those rings and roundelays   25
    Of theirs, which yet remain,
Were footed in Queen Mary's days
    On many a grassy plain;
But since of late, Elizabeth,
    And later, James came in,   30
They never danced on any heath
    As when the time hath been.

By which we note the fairies
    Were of the old profession;
Their songs were Ave-Marys,   35

Their dances were procession:
But now, alas! they all are dead
    Or gone beyond the seas,
Or farther for religion fled,   40
    Or else they take their ease.

EXERCISE:

This is a poem by an Anglican bishop in reference to the victory
of Protestantism over Catholicism in the Reformation. In
commenting on the situation the poet interprets it as a victory
of a narrow rationalism and common sense over an imaginative
attitude, and of the commercial spirit over the "Merry England"
of the past. What is the tone of the poem? What is the attitude toward the change? What is the attitude toward the Puritans? Why does the poem focus attention on the fairies?

THE BAD SEASON MAKES THE POET SAD

ROBERT HERRICK (1591–1674)

Dull to myself, and almost dead to these
My many fresh and fragrant mistresses:
Lost to all music now, since everything
Puts on the semblance here of sorrowing.
Sick is the land to th' heart, and doth endure   5
More dangerous faintings by her desp'rate cure.
But if that golden age would come again,
And Charles here rule, as he before did reign;
If smooth and unperplexed the seasons were,
As when the sweet Maria livèd here;   10
I should delight to have my curls half drowned
In Tyrian dews, and head with roses crowned;
And once more yet, ere I am laid out dead,
Knock at a star with my exalted head.

EXERCISE:

1. This poem refers to the victory of the Puritans in the Civil
War of the seventeenth century, a development of the same

general conflict as that to which "The Fairies' Farewell" refers. Write a comparison of the two poems on the basis of tone and attitude.

2. How does the last line give a kind of symbolic summary of the poem?

CYNARA

ERNEST DOWSON (1867-1900)

Last night, ah, yesternight, betwixt her lips and mine
There fell thy shadow, Cynara! thy breath was shed
Upon my soul between the kisses and the wine;
And I was desolate and sick of an old passion,
    Yea, I was desolate and bowed my head: 5
I have been faithful to thee, Cynara! in my fashion.

All night upon mine heart I felt her warm heart beat,
Night-long within mine arms in love and sleep she lay;
Surely the kisses of her bought red mouth were sweet;
But I was desolate and sick of an old passion,   10
    When I awoke and found the dawn was gray:
I have been faithful to thee, Cynara! in my fashion.

I have forgot much, Cynara! gone with the wind,
Flung roses, roses riotously with the throng,
Dancing, to put thy pale, lost lilies out of mind;   15
But I was desolate and sick of an old passion,
    Yea, all the time, because the dance was long:
I have been faithful to thee, Cynara! in my fashion.

I cried for madder music and for stronger wine,
But when the feast is finished and the lamps expire,   20
Then falls thy shadow, Cynara! the night is thine;
And I am desolate and sick of an old passion,
    Yea, hungry for the lips of my desire:
I have been faithful to thee, Cynara! in my fashion.

EXERCISE:

This poem, like "A Litany," by Sidney, (p. 341), deals with the subject of lost love. Try to define differences in attitude and tone. Discuss the question of sentimentality. Dowson centers his poem on a paradox: "I have been faithful to thee, Cynara! in my fashion." Presumably, he felt that the use of this paradox would lend a sharpness, a sense of precise statement, and a toughness that would help him to avoid the sentimental and trite in treating his subject. But does the paradox succeed in this? Will the paradox really stand any inspection? Compare and contrast with the use of paradox in "To Lucasta" (p. 319) and "Nightingales" (p. 198).

WINTER REMEMBERED

JOHN CROWE RANSOM (1888–   )

Two evils, monstrous either one apart,
Possessed me, and were long and loath at going:
A cry of Absence, Absence, in the heart,
And in the wood the furious winter blowing.

Think not, when fire was bright upon my bricks,   5
And past the tight boards hardly a wind could enter,
I glowed like them, the simple burning sticks,
Far from my cause, my proper heat and center.

Better to walk forth in the murderous air
And wash my wound in the snows; that would be healing;
Because my heart would throb less painful there,   11
Being caked with cold, and past the smart of feeling.

And where I went, the hugest winter blast
Would have this body bowed, these eyeballs streaming,
And though I think this heart's blood froze not fast,   15
It ran too small to spare one drop for dreaming.

Dear love, these fingers that had known your touch,
And tied our separate forces first together,
Were ten poor idiot fingers not worth much,
Ten frozen parsnips hanging in the weather.   20

EXERCISE:

Write an analysis of this poem, using that of "A Litany," by Sidney as a model. Consider the means in this poem whereby the poet indicates a shift of tone. Compare the conclusion of this poem with the conclusion of "Blame not my Cheeks," by Campion (p. 324).

TO THE MEMORY OF MR. OLDHAM

JOHN DRYDEN (1631–1700)

Farewell, too little and too lately known,
Whom I began to think and call my own:
For sure our souls were near allied, and thine
Cast in the same poetic mold with mine.
One common note on either lyre did strike,   5
And knaves and fools we both abhorred alike.
To the same goal did both our studies drive:
The last set out the soonest did arrive.
Thus Nisus fell upon the slippery place,
Whilst his young friend performed and won the race.
O early ripe! to thy abundant store   11
What could advancing age have added more?
It might (what nature never gives the young)
Have taught the numbers of thy native tongue.
But satire needs not those, and wit will shine   15
Through the harsh cadence of a rugged line.
A noble error, and but seldom made,
When poets are by too much force betray'd.
Thy generous fruits, though gathered ere their prime,
Still showed a quickness; and maturing time   20
But mellows what we write to the dull sweets of rhyme.
Once more, hail, and farewell! farewell, thou young,
But ah! too short, Marcellus of our tongue!
Thy brows with ivy and with laurels bound;
But Fate and gloomy night encompass thee around.   25

EXERCISE:

John Oldham was a brilliant young satirist of Dryden's time who died at the age of thirty (1653–1683). Dryden, the most

famous poet of the period, here pays a tribute to the younger man
and compares him to a young poet of the Augustan period of
Rome, Marcellus, who also died before his promise was fulfilled.
Compare and contrast the tone of this poem with that of "His
Prayer to Ben Jonson" (p. 306) and "An Ode to Ben Jonson"
(p. 306), both by Herrick.

SIR HUDIBRAS

SAMUEL BUTLER (1612–1680)

He could raise scruples dark and nice,
And after solve 'em in a trice:
As if Divinity had catched
The itch, of purpose to be scratched;
Or, like a mountebank, did wound   5
And stab herself with doubts profound,
Only to show with how small pain
The sores of faith are cured again;
Although by woeful proof we find,   10
They always leave a scar behind.
He knew the seat of Paradise,
Could tell in what degree it lies:
And as he was disposed, could prove it,
Below the moon, or else above it.   15
What Adam dreampt of when his bride
Came from her closet in his side:
Whether the Devil tempted her
By a High Dutch interpreter:
If either of them had a navel;   20
Who first made music malleable:
Whether the Serpent at the fall
Had cloven feet, or none at all.
All this without a gloss or comment,
He would unriddle in a moment: 25
In proper terms, such as men smatter
When they throw out and miss the matter.
For his religion it was fit
To match his learning and his wit:

'Twas Presbyterian true blue,   30
For he was of that stubborn crew
Of errant saints, whom all men grant
To be the true Church *Militant:*
Such as do build their faith upon
The holy text of pike and gun;   35
Decide all controversies by
Infallible artillery;
And prove their doctrine orthodox
By apostolic blows and knocks;
Call fire and sword and desolation,   40
A "godly thorough reformation,"
Which always must be carried on,
And still be doing, never done:
As if religion were intended
For nothing else but to be mended.   45
A sect, whose chief devotion lies
In odd perverse antipathies;
In falling out with that or this,
And finding somewhat still amiss:
More peevish, cross, and splenetic,   50
Than dog-distract, or monkey-sick.
That with more care keep holy-day
The wrong, than others the right way:
Compound for sins they are inclined to;
By damning those they have no mind to;   55
Still so perverse and opposite,
As if they worshipped God for spite,
The self-same thing they will abhor
One way, and long another for.

(From *Hudibras*)

EXERCISE:

This is a section from a long satirical poem of the seventeenth
century attacking the Puritans. The passage given here is a
portrait of the Puritan knight, Sir Hudibras.

Both "The Fairies' Farewell" (p. 346) and "The Bad Season
Makes the Poet Sad" (p. 347) make reference to the triumph
of the Puritans over the Royalists in the Civil War of England.
All of these poems are favorable to the Royalist party. Try to
define differences of attitude and tone.

PORTRAIT OF ATTICUS

ALEXANDER POPE (1688–1744)

heroic couplet

Peace to all such! but were there one whose fires
True genius kindles, and fair fame inspires;
Blessed with each talent and each art to please,
And born to write, converse, and live with ease:
Should such a man, too fond to rule alone,   5
Bear, like the Turk, no brother near the throne,
View him with scornful, yet with jealous eyes,
And hate for arts that caused himself to rise;
Damn with faint praise, assent with civil leer,
And without sneering, teach the rest to sneer;   10
Willing to wound, and yet afraid to strike,
Just hint a fault, and hesitate dislike;
Alike reserved to blame, or to commend,
A timorous foe, and a suspicious friend;
Dreading e'en fools, by flatterers besieged,   15
And so obliging, that he ne'er obliged;
Like Cato, give his little senate laws,
And sit attentive to his own applause;
While wits and Templars every sentence raise,
And wonder with a foolish face of praise—   20
Who but must laugh, if such a man there be?
Who would not weep, if Atticus were he!

(From "Epistle to Dr. Arbuthnot")

EXERCISE:

1. This is a portrait of Joseph Addison, at the time when he
was literary dictator of England and Pope's was the rising reputation. Compare and contrast the tone of this satirical portrait
with that by Butler in "Hudibras" (p. 351).

2. In both of these satirical portraits relate the metrical and
other technical factors to the general attitude and tone.

3. Compare the use of the heroic couplet in "Portrait of Atticus"
with the use in "Confession of Faith" (p. 254), "My Last Duchess"
(p. 255), and "Preparation of the Pyre for Patroclus" (p. 256).
In this connection reread the Exercise on page 257.

4. Discuss the use of the caesura in this passage, particularly as
a device for emphasizing antitheses.

TO A MOUNTAIN DAISY

ON TURNING ONE DOWN WITH THE
PLOW IN APRIL, 1786

ROBERT BURNS (1759–1796)

Wee, modest, crimson-tippèd flow'r,
Thou's met me in an evil hour;
For I maun crush amang the stoure [1]
    Thy slender stem:
To spare thee now is past my pow'r,   5
    Thou bonie gem.

Alas! it's no thy neebor sweet,
The bonie lark, companion meet,
Bending thee 'mang the dewy weet
    Wi' spreckled breast,   10
When upward-springing, blythe, to greet
    The purpling east.

Cauld blew the bitter-biting north
Upon thy early, humble birth;
Yet cheerfully thou glinted forth   15
    Amid the storm,
Scarce reared above the parent-earth
    Thy tender form.

The flaunting flowers our gardens yield
High sheltering woods an' was' [2] maun shield: 20
But thou, beneath the random bield [3]
    O' clod or stane,
Adorns the histie [4] stibble-field
    Unseen, alane.

There, in thy scanty mantle clad,   25
Thy snawie bosom sun-ward spread,
Thou lifts thy unassuming head
    In humble guise;
But now the share uptears thy bed,
    And low thou lies!   30

[1] dust   [2] walls   [3] shelter
[4] dry

Such is the fate of artless maid,
Sweet flow'ret of the rural shade!
By love's simplicity betrayed
              And guileless trust;
Till she, like thee, all soiled, is laid   35
              Low i' the dust.

Such is the fate of simple bard,
On life's rough ocean luckless starred!
Unskilful he to note the card
              Of prudent lore,   40
Till billows rage and gales blow hard,
              And whelm him o'er!

Such fate to suffering worth is giv'n,
Who long with wants and woes has striv'n,
By human pride or cunning driv'n   45
              To misery's brink;
Till, wrenched of ev'ry stay but Heav'n,
              He ruined sink!

Ev'n thou who mourn'st the daisy's fate,
That fate is thine—no distant date;   50
Stern Ruin's ploughshare drives elate,
              Full on thy bloom,
Till crushed beneath the furrow's weight
              Shall be thy doom.

EXERCISE:

Does the poet succeed in avoiding sentimentality in this poem?

ULALUME—A BALLAD

EDGAR ALLAN POE (1809–1849)

The skies they were ashen and sober;
    The leaves they were crispéd and sere—
    The leaves they were withering and sere.
It was night, in the lonesome October

Of my most immemorial year: 5
It was hard by the dim lake of Auber,
    In the misty mid region of Weir:
It was down by the dank tarn of Auber,
    In the ghoul-haunted woodland of Weir.

Here once, through an alley Titanic,   10
    Of cypress, I roamed with my Soul—
    Of cypress, with Psyche, my Soul.
These were days when my heart was volcanic
    As the scoriac rivers that roll—
    As the lavas that restlessly roll   15
Their sulphurous currents down Yaanek
    In the realms of the Boreal Pole.

Our talk had been serious and sober,
    But our thoughts they were palsied and sere—
    Our memories were treacherous and sere;   20
For we knew not the month was October,
    And we marked not the night of the year
    (Ah, night of all nights in the year!)
We noted not the dim lake of Auber
    (Though once we had journeyed down here)—   25
We remembered not the dank tarn of Auber,
    Nor the ghoul-haunted woodland of Weir.

And now, as the night was senescent
    And star-dials pointed to morn—
    As the star-dials hinted of morn—   30
At the end of our path a liquescent
    And nebulous lustre was born,
Out of which a miraculous crescent
    Arose with a duplicate horn—
Astarte's bediamonded crescent   35
    Distinct with its duplicate horn.

And I said—"She is, warmer than Dian;
    She rolls through an ether of sighs—
    She revels in a region of sighs.
She has seen that the tears are not dry on   40
    These cheeks, where the worm never dies,
And has come past the stars of the Lion,

To point us the path to the skies—
   To the Lethean peace of the skies—
Come up, in despite of the Lion,   45
   To shine on us with her bright eyes—
Come up through the lair of the Lion,
   With love in her luminous eyes."

But Psyche, uplifting her finger,
   Said—"Sadly this star I mistrust—   50
   Her pallor I strangely mistrust:
Ah, hasten!—ah, let us not linger!
   Ah, fly!—let us fly!—for we must."
In terror she spoke, letting sink her
   Wings till they trailed in the dust—   55
In agony sobbed, letting sink her
   Plumes till they trailed in the dust—
   Till they sorrowfully trailed in the dust.

I replied—"This is nothing but dreaming:
   Let us on by this tremulous light!   60
   Let us bathe in this crystalline light!
Its Sibyllic splendor is beaming
   With Hope and in Beauty to-night:—
   See!—it flickers up the sky through the night!
Ah, we safely may trust to its gleaming,   65
   And be sure it will lead as aright—
We surely may trust to a gleaming,
   That cannot but guide us aright,
   Since it flickers up to Heaven through the night."

Thus I pacified Psyche and kissed her,   70
   And tempted her out of her gloom—
   And conquered her scruples and gloom;
And we passed to the end of the vista,
   But were stopped by the door of a tomb—
   By the door of a legended tomb: 75
And I said—"What is written, sweet sister,
   On the door of this legended tomb?"
   She replied—"Ulalume—Ulalume!—
   'Tis the vault of thy lost Ulalume!"

Then my heart it grew ashen and sober   80
   As the leaves that were crisped and sere—

      As the leaves that were withering and sere;
    And I cried—"It was surely October
      On *this* very night of last year
      That I journeyed—I journeyed down here!—   85
      That I brought a dread burden down here—
      On this night of all nights in the year,
      Ah, what demon hath tempted me here?
    Well I know, now, this dim lake of Auber—
      This misty mid region of Weir—   90
    Well I know, now, this dank tarn of Auber,
      This ghoul-haunted woodland of Weir."

    Said we, then—the two, then—"Ah, can it
      Have been that the woodlandish ghouls—
      The pitiful, the merciful ghouls—   95
    To bar up our way and to ban it
      From the secret that lies in these wolds
      From the thing that lies hidden in the wolds
    Have drawn up the specter of a planet
      From the limbo of lunary souls—   100
    This sinfully scintillant planet
      From the Hell of the planetary souls?"

"Ulalume," by Edgar Allan Poe, raises some questions about suggestiveness, and atmosphere in poetry. Poe is sometimes praised because of an ability to create a mood, an atmosphere, by suggestion and association. All poetry in one sense shares this quality with the work of Poe. But why do admirers of Poe usually connect these things especially with him? Perhaps the best way to approach this particular matter will be to try to analyze the poem as a whole.[1]

What is it about? The element of incident may be summarized as follows: A man, engaged in conversation with Psyche, his soul, walks through a mysterious landscape. He and his soul are so preoccupied that they do not notice the setting nor

---

[1] In connection with this analysis the student may be interested in reading some remarks and a parody on this poem, by Aldous Huxley, which appear in the *Glossary* at the end of the section on *verse*. As a matter of fact, a good parody may often serve a real critical purpose by displaying in an accentuated form an author's characteristic mannerisms.

do they even know what month of the year it is, even though, as it is pointed out, they have been here before and this night marks a mysterious and important anniversary. Then a light appears, which the man takes to be Astarte, and not Diana, that is, love and not chastity. Psyche is terrified by this and wishes to flee, but the man overcomes her scruples and persuades her to follow the light. They stumble upon a tomb, which, Psyche tells the man, is the tomb of his lost love, Ulalume. Then the man remembers that, precisely a year before, he had brought the body to the tomb. This discovery being made, both the man and Psyche simultaneously say that the sight of Astarte's crescent has been conjured up, perhaps, by the merciful ghouls to prevent them from stumbling on the tomb. But they had failed to heed the warning.

This is, apparently, an *allegorical* (*Glossary*) way of saying that love (or the semblance of love, for the crescent is defined as "the spectre of a planet") only leads him to the door of the tomb where Ulalume is buried.

But all of this leaves a great many questions, even questions that should have factual answers, without answer. For instance, what significance, if any, is possessed by the following lines:

> It was hard by the dim lake of Auber,
> In the misty mid region of Weir:
> It was down by the dank tarn of Auber,
> In the ghoul-haunted woodland of Weir.

The poet returns to similar descriptions during the course of the poem and evidently attaches considerable importance to them. He is trying to give an unreal, mysterious atmosphere to the poem. These places have no historical or geographical existence; the reference to them is supposed to tease the reader with mysterious implications in the same way as do the later references to Mount Yaanek and "the stars of the Lion." The details of the first description are directed to the same end: "the ghoul-haunted woodland." It is the kind of suggestiveness used in romantic ghost stories, a kind of atmosphere that we can accept only if we do not inspect its occasion too closely—for dank tarns and ghoul-haunted woodlands are stage-sets, we might say, that are merely good for frightening children. We accept them only if we happen to be willing to forego our maturity and make a temporary concession. The process whereby the poet has created his atmosphere is too transparent, too obvious; we feel that we humor him by accepting it. The process whereby the atmosphere of mystery and foreboding is created here is similar to that whereby the atmosphere of exotic romance is created in "The Indian Serenade," by Shelley (p. 319).

One might justify the general atmosphere of the poem, perhaps, by saying that the whole poem is unrealistic, is a kind of fable (though this justification would not necessarily excuse the poet for the particular manner by which the atmosphere is given, the stale devices of mystification). But even in such a poem as this the reader can expect that the parts all contribute something directly to the poem, that they be consistent among themselves, and that the devices of mystification bear some relation to the business of the poem and do more than indicate a love of mystification merely for its own sake (See "Channel Firing," p. 307). What, then, about the ghouls that haunt the woodland of Weir? A ghoul, according to the dictionary, is a "demon who robs graves and feeds on corpses." But these are pitiful ghouls that summon up ghosts of planets from "the Hell of planetary souls," in order to savè the man from finding the tomb. The situation might be something like this: The poet could not let the planet of Astarte appear as a fact in itself; it was a ghost of a planet. He felt that he had to account for its presence. Arbitrarily he chose ghouls to serve this purpose. He had used the word *ghoulhaunted* earlier in the poem and so had some preparation for the reference; ghouls may provoke in the reader a kind of shudder of supernatural mystery and horror. But the reader feels that this has little or no real reference to the meaning of the poem. It may be said to contribute to the atmosphere of the poem, but otherwise it does not connect with the meaning of the poem; it simply does not pull its weight in the boat.

One might compare this rather disorderly use of suggestion in "Ulalume," the use of the place names, the ghouls, etc., with the use made in other poems in this collection. For instance, one can see how the suggestions of the names Camelot, Stourton

Tower, and Stonehenge in "Channel Firing," by Hardy, directly contribute to the meaning of the poem itself. (See p. 311) Or one can see how, in a similar fashion, suggestion is employed in poems like "Ode on a Grecian Urn" (p. 526) and "Ode to a Nightingale," (p. 407) by Keats, to develop and present the actual theme of a poem as well as to create an atmosphere. We feel that in the poems by Hardy and Keats, who are poets with great differences between them, the atmosphere is not only appropriate to the poem in question, but that the suggestion actually helps us to the meaning of the experience in the poem; the devices used by the poet will stand a logical definition and inspection. It is no surprise, after studying "Ulalume" in this respect, to discover that Poe could make the following remark about poetry in general: "Poetry, above all things, is a beautiful painting whose tints, to minute inspection, are confusion worse confounded, but start boldly out to the cursory glance of the connoisseur." (Letter to Mr. Elam Bliss, Preface to the *Poems* of 1831.) That is, Poe expected poetry to stand little analysis, and to affect only the person who gave it a "cursory glance," a superficial reading. It is no wonder, then, that much of Poe's work is very vague and confused, for he said that poetry has for its "object an *indefinite* instead of a *definite* pleasure." But really good poetry will stand a great deal of close inspection, even poetry that is simple and unambitious. We feel that the parts all contribute definitely to the total meaning of the poem.

We may apply the same line of reasoning to another feature of "Ulalume," the rhythm. In this connection we may quote again from Poe: ". . . presenting perceptible images with definite, poetry with *indefinite* sensations, to which music is an *essential,* since the comprehension of sweet sound is our most indefinite conception." Poe, then, holds that the function of the rhythms of poetry is to lull the reader; to increase the indefiniteness of the impression; to prevent him, in fact, from having the impulse to analyze the poem closely; to contribute to the general atmosphere; to have a hypnotic effect on the reader. One may notice that in "Ulalume," by consequence, there is an emphatic beat of rhythm that becomes monotonous, that there is a lack of variation in the rhythmic effects of the poem. This

fact will become quite clear if one compares "Ulalume" with
the poems by Keats already mentioned, or with "A Litany" (p.
341). This monotonous and unexpressive quality of the rhythm
is also found in the elaborate use of repetition. We have seen
that in some poems, for instance, "Lord Randal" (See p. 123),
repetition can contribute to a sense of form, but here it seems
only to make the poem diffuse and vague.

TO NIGHT

PERCY BYSSHE SHELLEY (1792–1822)

Swiftly walk o'er the western wave,
    Spirit of Night!
  Out of the misty eastern cave,
Where all the long and lone daylight,
Thou wovest dreams of joy and fear,   5
Which make thee terrible and dear,—
    Swift be thy flight!

Wrap thy form in a mantle gray,
    Star in-wrought!
Blind with thine hair the eyes of Day;   10
Kiss her until she be wearied out;
Then wander o'er city, and sea, and land,
Touching all with thine opiate wand—
    Come, long sought!

When I arose and saw the dawn,   15
    I sighed for thee;
When light rode high, and the dew was gone,
And noon lay heavy on flower and tree,
And the weary Day turned to his rest,
Lingering like an unloved guest,   20
    I sighed for thee.

Thy brother Death came, and cried,
    Wouldst thou me?
Thy sweet child Sleep, the filmy-eyed,

Murmured like a noon-tide bee,
Shall I nestle near thy side?   25
Wouldst thou me?—And I replied,
    No, not thee!

Death will come when thou art dead,
        Soon, too soon—
Sleep will come when thou art fled;   30
Of neither would I ask the boon
I ask of thee, belovèd Night
Swift be thine approaching flight,
        Come soon, soon!

EXERCISE:

1. What is the poet's attitude toward the subject of his poem?
2. Does the poet succeed in avoiding sentimentality?

THE SLEEPER

EDGAR ALLAN POE (1809–1849)

At midnight in the month of June,
I stand beneath the mystic moon.
An opiate vapor, dewy, dim,
Exhales from out her golden rim,
And, softly dripping, drop by drop,   5
Upon the quiet mountain top,
Steals drowsily and musically
Into the universal valley.
The rosemary nods upon the grave;
The lily lolls upon the wave;   10
Wrapping the fog about its breast,
The ruin moulders into rest;
Looking like Lethe, see! the lake
A conscious slumber seems to take,
And would not, for the world, awake.   15
All Beauty sleeps!—and lo! where lies
Irene, with her Destinies!

Oh, lady bright! can it be right—
This window open to the night?
The wanton airs, from the tree-top,   20
Laughingly through the lattice drop—
The bodiless airs, a wizard rout,
Flit through thy chamber in and out,
And wave the curtain canopy
So fitfully—so fearfully—   25
Above the closed and fringed lid
'Neath which thy slumb'ring soul lies hid,
That, o'er the floor and down the wall,
Like ghosts the shadows rise and fall!
Oh, lady dear, hast thou no fear?   30
Why and what art thou dreaming here?
Sure thou art come o'er far-off seas,
A wonder to these garden trees!
Strange is thy pallor! strange thy dress!
Strange, above all, thy length of tress,   35
And this all solemn silentness!

The lady sleeps! Oh, may her sleep,
Which is enduring, so be deep!
Heaven have her in its sacred keep!
This chamber changed for one more holy,   40
This bed for one more melancholy,
I pray to God that she may lie
Forever with unopened eye,
While the pale sheeted ghosts go by!

My love, she sleeps! Oh, may her sleep,   45
As it is lasting, so be deep!
Soft may the worms about her creep!
Far in the forest, dim and old,
For her may some tall vault unfold—
Some vault that oft hath flung its black   50
And winged panels fluttering back,
Triumphant, o'er the crested palls,
Of her grand family funerals—
Some sepulchre, remote, alone,
Against whose portal she hath thrown,   55
In childhood, many an idle stone—
Some tomb from out whose sounding door

> She ne'er shall force an echo more,
> Thrilling to think, poor child of sin!
> It was the dead who groaned within.   60

EXERCISE:

Write a full analysis with the analysis of "Ulalume" as a model.

TEARS, IDLE TEARS

ALFRED, LORD TENNYSON (1809–1892)

> Tears, idle tears, I know not what they mean,
> Tears from the depth of some divine despair
> Rise in the heart, and gather to the eyes,
> In looking on the happy Autumn-fields,
> And thinking of the days that are no more.   5
>
> Fresh as the first beam glittering on a sail,
> That brings our friends up from the underworld,
> Sad as the last which reddens over one
> That sinks with all we love below the verge;
> So sad, so fresh, the days that are no more.   10
>
> Ah, sad and strange as in dark summer dawns
> The earliest pipe of half-awakened birds
> To dying ears, when unto dying eyes
> The casement slowly grows a glimmering square;
> So sad, so strange, the days that are no more.   15
>
> Dear as remembered kisses after death,
> And sweet as those by hopeless fancy feigned
> On lips that are for others; deep as love,
> Deep as first love, and wild with all regret;
> O Death in Life, the days that are no more!   20

(From *The Princess*)

EXERCISE:

This poem is far more successful than is "Ulalume," even though its subject is vague. How does Tennyson achieve his success?

WESSEX HEIGHTS

THOMAS HARDY (1840–1928)

There are some heights in Wessex, shaped as if by a kindly hand
For thinking, dreaming, dying on, and at crises when I stand,
Say, on Ingpen Beacon eastward, or on Wylls-Neck westwardly,
I seem where I was before my birth, and after death may be.

In the lowlands I have no comrade, not even the lone man's
    friend—   5
He who suffereth long and is kind; accepts what he is too weak
    to mend:
Down there they are dubious and askance; there nobody thinks
    as I,
But mind-chains do not clank where one's next neighbor is the
    sky.

In the towns I am tracked by phantoms having weird detective
    ways—
Shadows of beings who fellowed with myself of earlier days: 10
They hang about at places, and they say harsh heavy things—
Men with a wintry sneer, and women with tart disparagings.

Down there I seem to be false to myself, my simple self that was,
And is not now, and I see him watching, wondering what crass
    cause
Can have merged him into such a strange continuator as this,   15
Who yet has something in common with himself, my chrysalis.

I cannot go to the great gray Plain; there's a figure against the
    moon,
Nobody sees it but I, and it makes my breast beat out of tune;
I cannot go to the tall-spired town, being barred by the forms
    now passed
For everybody but me, in whose long vision they stand there
    fast.   20

There's a ghost at Yell'ham Bottom chiding loud at the fall
    of the night,
There's a ghost in Froom-side Vale, thin lipped and vague, in
    a shroud of white,
There is one in the railway train whenever I do not want it near,
I see its profile against the pane, saying what I would not hear.

As for one rare fair woman, I am now but a thought of hers,   25
I enter her mind and another thought succeeds me that she
    prefers;
Yet my love for her in its fulness she herself even did not know;
Well, time cures hearts of tenderness, and now I can let her go.

So I am found on Ingpen Beacon, or on Wylls-Neck to the west,
Or else on homely Bulbarrow, or little Pilsdon Crest,   30
Where men have never cared to haunt, nor women have walked
    with me,
And ghosts then keep their distance; and I know some liberty.

EXERCISE:

1. This poem, like "Tears, Idle Tears," deals with the feeling
about the past. Define the difference in attitude and tone.

2. Discuss the following factors in relation to the effect of the
poem: the phrases "weird detective ways," and "my chrysalis";
the contrast in the sixth stanza between the ghost "in a shroud
of white" and the ghost in "the railway train"; the general
metrical scheme of the poem and the special questions raised in
the fourth stanza.

TO BLOSSOMS

ROBERT HERRICK (1591–1674)

Fair pledges of a fruitful tree,
    Why do ye fall so fast?
    Your date is not so past;
But you may stay yet here a while,
    To blush and gently smile;   5
        And go at last.

What, were ye born to be
    An hour or half's delight;
    And so to bid goodnight?
'Twas pity Nature brought ye forth   10
    Merely to show your worth,
        And lose you quite.

But you are lovely leaves, where we
    May read how soon things have
        Their end, though ne'er so brave: 15
And after they have shown their pride,
    Like you a while: they glide
        Into the grave.

THE BLOSSOM

JOHN DONNE (1573–1631)

Little think'st thou, poor flower,
Whom I have watched six or seven days,
And seen thy birth, and seen what every hour
Gave to thy growth, thee to this height to raise,
And now dost laugh and triumph on this bough,   5
    Little think'st thou
That it will freeze anon, and that I shall
To morrow find thee fallen, or not at all.

Little think'st thou poor heart
That labor'st yet to nestle thee,
And think'st by hovering here to get a part   10
In a forbidden or forbidding tree,
And hop'st her stiffness by long siege to bow:
    Little think'st thou,
That thou tomorrow, ere that sun doth wake,   15
Must with this sun, and me a journey take.

  Here are two poems which are similar in title and similar
moreover in other regards. Both poems make use of an object
drawn from nature as a symbol for the fragility of all life and
of all earthly beauty. The generalization, as such, is a conventional one, and the symbol used is also a conventional one.
What raises the poem from a commonplace utterance is the *tone*
of the poem. The tone of a poem, as we have already seen, is
one indication of the poet's attitude toward his subject and
toward his audience. What is Herrick's attitude toward the
blossoms? And how does he indicate the attitude to his readers?

Herrick's attitude is one of tenderness and regret. He establishes this, in part, by dramatizing the scene and personifying the flowers, speaking to them first in a tone of surprise that they are already falling. He pretends that they are leaving of their own will and might be persuaded to stay. With the beginning of the second stanza, he implies that not until this moment has he realized that the flowers have no power to remain. The point is made dramatic by the exclamation of surprise, "What, were ye born to be," at the beginning of the second stanza. And this dramatic device gives renewed emphasis to what would otherwise be a merely commonplace generalization. The reader feels with something of renewed surprise what he has known on the level of abstract generalization all along.

This renewed sense of the fragility of all temporal beauty prepares for and justifies the application to the universal which he makes in the last stanza. The flowers he says are leaves, and we see in a moment that he means not merely leaves of a plant but leaves of a book, wherein one may read what is true of all that lives.

It is most important to notice, however, that the poet does not overemphasize his personification nor does he unduly insist on the beauty of the flowers. He uses hint and implication instead. For example, the blossoms are addressed first as "Fair pledges of a fruitful tree." The poets of Herrick's time and later often refer to children as fair pledges and this much of personification is implied at once. Notice that the poet also merely implies the beauty of the blossoms. One gathers that they are beautiful from the effect on the poet. He does not dilate on this point. His references to the flowers are altogether in terms of their innocence and brevity of life: "To blush and gently smile." But the sense of their beauty is stronger because of the fact that it is merely to be inferred from what the poet says; and the point of the poem is enforced from the fact that all of the references are directed to this one end.

The use of the word *glide* at the end of the last stanza is effective and gives just the amount of emphasis required at the end of the poem. It is the exact word to describe the easy descent of blossoms falling through the air, and so supports the actual picture; but it also implies the easy, quiet descent into the grave which the poet is considering in the poem. It is therefore thoroughly appropriate to the tone and atmosphere of the poem.

Here one may well call attention to the stanza form. The pattern of the stanza, one notices, is of lines of four feet, three, three, four, three, and *two*. The pattern is not quite symmetrical: the last line has one less foot than we might expect, and this fact gives the line an especial emphasis. We read it more slowly than the others. We can notice how at the end of each stanza the idea of finality and loss appears in this line of retarded movement.

When we look at the first stanzas of Donne's "The Blossom" we find that the first stanza has a tone very similar to that which Herrick's poem possesses. If we analyze carefully, of course, we shall see that it is not exactly the same. It could hardly be exactly the same any more than the personalities of two different people could be exactly the same or the features of two men, even men who resembled each other strongly. But there is in Donne's poem something of the same tenderness and regret which we find in Herrick's, though Donne's attitude toward the flower has in it a more prominent note of patronage: he speaks out of a knowledge which the flower cannot have. He knows the fate which is in store for it. The patronage is far from a supercilious one, however. He is tender in his attitude toward the blossom, and we feel already that what he says about the fate of the blossom is, no more than the general fate which he knows is in store for everything, including himself. We sense even in this first stanza the application to his own heart which he is going to make in the second stanza.

Even the second stanza does not depart altogether from the tone of Herrick's poem. The application of the flowers' innocence and ignorance to his heart parallels Herrick's application of the transient beauty of the blossoms to all temporal beauty. Donne, of course, is making the comparison for a different effect: he is telling his heart, pretending that it is as ignorantly innocent as the blossom, that it little realizes how soon he must leave his mistress and that its freezing time (lack of love) will soon be upon it. On the basis of tone, as well as the basis of the imagery of flowers, the poems, although they treat different themes, are quite similar.

But, in actuality, we have only quoted the first section of Donne's poem.

> Little think'st thou, poor flower,
>   Whom I have watch'd six or seven dayes,
> And seen thy birth, and seen what every hour
> Gave to thy growth, thee to this height to raise,   20
> And now dost laugh and triumph on this bough,
>   Little think'st thou   .
> That it will freeze anon, and that I shall
> Tomorrow finde thee fallen, or not at all.
>   Little think'st thou poor heart   25
>   That labor'st yet to nestle thee,
> And think'st by hovering here to get a part
> In a forbidden or forbidding tree,
> And hop'st her stiffness by long siege to bow:
>   Little think'st thou,   30
> That thou tomorrow, ere that sun doth wake,
> Must with this sun, and me a journey take.
>
>   But thou which lov'st to be
>   Subtle to plague thy self, wilt say,
> Alas, if you must go, what's that to me?   35
> Here lies my business, and here I will stay:
> You go to friends, whose love and means present
>   Various content
> To your eyes, ears, and tongue, and every part.
> If then your body go, what need you a heart?   40
>
>   Well then, stay here; but know,
>   When thou hast stayed and done thy most;
> A naked thinking heart, that makes no show,
> Is to a woman, but a kind of Ghost;
> How shall she know my heart; or having none,   45
>   Know thee for one?
> Practise may make her know some other part,
> But take my word, she doth not know a Heart.
>
>   Meet me at London, then,
>   Twenty days hence, and thou shalt see   50
> Me fresher, and more fat, by being with men,

> Than if I had stayed still with her and thee.
> For God's sake, if you can, be you so too:
>   I would give you
> There, to another friend, whom we shall find   55
> As glad to have my body, as my mind.

One can easily see that the third stanza initiates a new section of the poem. A new attitude is taken toward the subject, and the poem exhibits a change of tone. The poet no longer considers the heart a passive thing like the blossom but lets it state its own reply to him; or rather he himself states what the heart's reply will be, for he implies that he knows the arguments of old. The attitude changes, therefore, from pitying tenderness to amused tolerance such as one might have for a stubborn but charming child who argues brightly but unreasonably for something on which it has set its heart.

The turn at the beginning of the third stanza is supported by a metrical shift, one may notice. The first line of the first stanza may be analyzed as follows:

Líttle thínk'st thóu, póór flówer

In both the second and third foot of the line we have an instance of a hovering accent; and in the third foot with the syllable *poor* we have the hovering effect further supported by the quantitative factor. The differences between non-accented and accented syllables tend to be reduced. The whole line gives a lingering, retarded effect. The same is true of the first line of the second stanza. But the first line of the third stanza is sharply defined metrically, with positive differences between non-accented and accented syllables, and furthermore, falls into a precise iambic pattern:

But thóu which lóv'st to bé

The change in tone is supported by the change from the characteristic rhythm of the initial lines of the two preceding stanzas.

With the fourth stanza the poet abruptly changes his tone, a shift which again reflects itself in the meter, and the poet turns suddenly and says to his heart, "Well then, stay here." He accepts the heart's argument at face value, and so tells it, since it is bent on such a course, to go ahead; but he assures it, using the same type of argument which the heart employs, that it is remaining in vain. A heart deprived of a body cannot express itself. Women are too sensual to be able to perceive a "naked thinking heart"—something of pure spirit.

And in the last stanza the poet, accepting the heart's decision and addressing it as if it were another man, a friend, tells it to meet him in London "twenty days hence," and prophesies that it will find him "fresher and more fat, by being with men." The poet advises the heart to be so too, if it can. He does not wish it ill: he merely knows, and knows positively, that there is no chance that the heart will prosper.

The poem ends with an explicit statement of the point up to which the whole poem has been moving: a protest against an absurd idealizing of love:

> I would give you
> There, to another friend, whom we shall find
> As glad to have my body as my mind.

The absurd idealizing of love which ignores its realistic elements, and ignores the fact that the human being is made of many elements, body and soul, flesh and spirit, etc., is in this particular case the idealizing attitude of the Petrarchan tradition, to which we have already referred in our discussion of "A Litany," by Philip Sidney (pp. 343-4). But the poet here, especially in the third stanza and after, employs many of the devices of the Petrarchan tradition in order to upset them. He makes use of all the Petrarchan machinery—the heart speaking as a separate person, for example—in his protest; and he has his own heart maintain the Petrarchan argument. In answering the heart, the attitude, as we have indicated, is ironical, but the irony is not bitter or heavily sarcastic; there is a certain tolerance and understanding mixed with the irony. The poem on the surface seems almost as artificial and as trifling as the kind of poetry which it really attacks; but this is only true superficially, because the reader who gets a sense of the whole poem se
the trifling, which is conscious and ironical here.

presenting the positive theme of the poem: love (or any other experience) that is to be real and meaningful must involve the entire nature of man.

The shifts in tone in the poem, as we have seen, are brilliant and complex, and a close comparison of Donne's poem with Herrick's will readily illustrate the degree of this complexity. For the first two stanzas of Donne's poem form the only part that is as consistent in tone as the one by Herrick. Had Donne cared to end his poem at this point he would have given us a poem remarkably similar to Herrick's (though we can observe that the tone of Donne's poem, even in the first two stanzas, is more conversational and informal). Instead, Donne is merely using his first two stanzas as an introduction, and with the third stanza begins to develop his real theme and to turn the imagery, which in Herrick is direct, into a kind of teasing travesty of the Petrarchan tradition.

One more point needs to be made. Are we to conclude that Donne's poem is better than Herrick's? Not at all. Herrick's poem, within its limits (which are narrower than Donne's) is splendid. But the study of the two poems in conjunction with one another may illustrate for us the relation of a good poem which is rather simple to a good poem which is more complex.

TO PERILLA

ROBERT HERRICK (1591–1674)

Ah my Perilla! dost thou grieve to see
Me, day by day, to steal away from thee?
Age calls me hence, and my gray hairs bid come,
And haste away to mine eternal home;
'Twill not be long (Perilla) after this   5
That I must give thee the supremest kiss;
Dead when I am, first cast in salt, and bring
Part of the cream from that religious spring;
With which (Perilla) wash my hands and feet;
    done, then wind me in that very sheet   10

Which wrapped thy smooth limbs (when thou didst im-
    plore
The gods' protection, but the night before),
Follow me weeping to my turf, and there
Let fall a primrose, and with it a tear;
Then lastly, let some weekly strewings be   15
Devoted to the memory of me:
Then shall my ghost not walk about, but keep
Still in the cool, and silent shades of sleep.

EXERCISE:

1. Discuss the complications of tone in this poem, taking into
account such matters as the contrast between the first four lines
and lines eleven and twelve, the use of the word *supremest,* and
the metrical situation in line six.

2. In connection with this poem read Bateson's remarks on
"Disorder in Dress," and examine the use here of ambiguous
associations.

UPON A DEAD MAN'S HEAD

JOHN SKELTON (1460?–1529)

Sent to him from an honorable gentlewoman for a token, he
devised this ghostly meditation in English covenable, in sentence
commendable, lamentable, lacrimable, profitable for a soul.

Your ugly token
My mind hath broken
From worldly lust:
For I have discussed
We are but dust,   5
And die we must.
    It is general
To be mortal:
I have well espied
No man may him hide   10
From Death hollow-eyed,
With sinews witherèd,

With bonès shiverèd,
With his worm-eaten maw,
And his ghastly jaw   15
Gasping aside,
Naked of hide,
Neither flesh nor fell.[1]
    Then, by my counsel,
Look that ye spell   20
Well this gospel:
For whereso we dwell
Death will us quell,
And with us mell.[2]
    For all our pampered paunches   25
There may no fraunchis,
Nor worldly bliss,
Redeem us from this:
Our days be dated
To be check-mated   30
With draughtès of death
Stopping our breath:
Our eyen sinking,
Our bodies stinking,
Our gummès grinning,   35
Our soulès brinning.[3]
To Whom, then, shall we sue,
For to have rescue,
But to sweet Jesu
On us then for to rue?   40
    O goodly Child
Of Mary mild,
Then be our shield!
That we be not exiled
To the dun dale   45
Of bootless bale,[4]
Nor to the lake
Of fiendès blake.[5]
    But grant us grace
To see thy Face,   50
And to purchase
Thine heavenly place,

---

[1] skin   [2] meddle   [3] burning
[4] sorrow   [5] black

> And thy palace
> Full of solace
> Above the sky   55
> That is so high,
> Eternally
> To behold and see
> The Trinitie!
>   Amen   60
> *Myrres vous y*

EXERCISE:

   This poem may be thought to deal rather straightforwardly with a trite subject. What factors in the poem prevent it from being trite?

ODE TO EVENING

WILLIAM COLLINS (1721–1759)

If aught of oaten stop, or pastoral song,
May hope, chaste Eve, to sooth thy modest ear.
  Like thy own solemn springs,
  Thy springs and dying gales,

O nymph reserved, while now the bright-hair'd sun   5
Sits in yon western tent, whose cloudy skirts,
  With brede ethereal wove,
  O'erhang his wavy bed:

Now air is hushed, save where the weak-eyed bat,
With short shrill shriek, flits by on leathern wing,   10
  Or where the beetle winds
  His small but sullen horn,

As oft he rises 'midst the twilight path,
Against the pilgrim borne in heedless hum.
  Now teach me, maid composed,   15
  To breathe some softened strain,

Whose numbers, stealing through thy dark'ning vale
May not unseemly with its stillness suit,
    As, musing slow, I hail
    Thy genial lov'd return!   20

For when thy folding-star arising shews
His paly circlet, at his warning lamp
    The fragrant Hours, the elves
    Who slept in flow'rs the day,

And many a nymph who wreaths her brows with sedge,
And sheds the fresh'ning dew, and, lovelier still   26
    The pensive Pleasures sweet,
    Prepare thy shadowy car.

Then lead, calm vot'ress, where some sheety lake
Cheers the lone heath, or some time-hallowed pile   30
    Or upland fallows grey
    Reflect its last cool gleam.

But when chill blust'ring winds, or driving rain,
Forbid my willing feet, be mine the hut
    That from the mountain's side   35
    Views wilds, and swelling floods,

And hamlets brown, and dim-discover'd spires,
And hears their simple bell, and marks o'er all
    Thy dewy fingers draw
    The gradual dusky veil.   40

While Spring shall pour his show'rs, as oft he wont,
And bathe thy breathing tresses, meekest Eve;
    While Summer loves to sport
    Beneath thy ling'ring light;

While sallow Autumn fills thy lap with leaves;   45
Or Winter, yelling through the troublous air,
    Affrights thy shrinking train,
    And rudely rends thy robes;

So long, sure-found beneath the sylvan shed,
Shall Fancy, Friendship, Science, rose-lipp'd Health,   50
    Thy gentlest influence own,
    And hymn thy fav'rite name!

The "Ode to Evening," by Warton, and "To Spring," by
Roscoe, which immediately follow, are obviously similar to the
"Ode to Evening," by Collins, and attempt to give something
of the same tone. Make a careful comparison of the poems by
Warton and Roscoe with that by Collins, and attempt to indi-
cate the reasons for their inferiority.

ODE TO EVENING

JOSEPH WARTON (1722–1800)

Hail, meek-eyed maiden, clad in sober gray,
Whose soft approach the weary woodman loves
As, homeward bent to kiss his prattling babes,
He jocund whistles through the twilight groves.

When Phoebus sinks beneath the gilded hills,   5
You lightly o'er the misty meadows walk,
The drooping daisies bathe in dulcet dews,
And nurse the nodding violet's slender stalk.

The panting dryads, that in day's fierce heat
To inmost bowers and cooling caverns ran,   10
Return to trip in wanton evening dance,
Old Sylvan too returns, and laughing Pan.

To the deep woods the clamorous rooks repair,
Light skims the swallow o'er the wat'ry scene,
And from the sheep-cotes, and fresh-furrowed field,   15
Stout plowmen meet to wrestle on the green.

The swain that artless sings on yonder rock,
His nibbling sheep and length'ning shadow spies,
Pleased with the cool, the calm, refreshful hour,
And with hoarse hummings of unnumbered flies.   20

Now every passion sleeps; desponding love,
And pining envy, ever-restless pride;
An holy calm creeps o'er my peaceful soul,
Anger and mad ambition's storms subside.

O modest Evening, oft let me appear 25
A wandering votary in thy pensive train,
List'ning to every wildly warbling throat
That fills with farewell notes the dark'ning plain.

TO SPRING

WILLIAM STANLEY ROSCOE (1782–1841)

O thou that from the green vales of the West
Com'st in thy tender robes with bashful feet,
And to the gathering clouds
Liftest thy soft blue eye:

I woo thee, Spring!—though thy dishevelled hair 5
In misty ringlets sweep thy snowy breast,
And thy young lips deplore
Stern Boreas' ruthless rage:

While morn is steeped in dews, and the dank show'r
Drops from the green boughs of the budding trees; 10
And the thrush tunes his song
Warbling with unripe throat:

Through the deep wood where spreads the sylvan oak
I follow thee, and see thy hands unfold
The love-sick primrose pale 15
And moist-eyed violet:

While in the central grove, at thy soft voice,
The Dryads start forth from their wintry cells,
And from their oozy waves
The Naiads lift their heads 20

In sedgy bonnets trimmed with rushy leaves
And water-blossoms from the forest stream,
To pay their vows to thee,
Their thrice adorèd queen!

The stripling shepherd wand'ring through the wood 25
Startles the linnet from her downy nest,
Or wreathes his crook with flowers,
The sweetest of the fields.

From the gray branches of the ivied ash
The stock-dove pours her vernal elegy,   30
While further down the vale
Echoes the cuckoo's note.

Beneath this trellised arbour's antique roof,
When the wild laurel rustles in the breeze,
By Cam's slow murmuring stream   35
I waste the live-long day;

And bid thee, Spring, rule fair the infant year,
Till my loved Maid in russet stole approach:
O yield her to my arms,
Her red lips breathing love!   40

So shall the sweet May drink thy falling tears,
And on thy blue eyes pour a beam of joy;
And float thy azure locks
Upon the western wind.

So shall the nightingale rejoice thy woods,   45
And Hesper early light his dewy star;
And oft at eventide
Beneath the rising moon,

May lovers' whispers soothe thy list'ning ear,
And as they steal the soft impassioned kiss,   50
Confess thy genial reign,
O love-inspiring Spring!

FOREWORD

In many instances we have already commented on various functions of imagery in poetry, and we have seen how important these are. The poems in this section raise no new principles concerning the fundamental nature of poetic imagery, but they have been chosen because they offer the student an opportunity for further analysis. Some poems rely more than others on imagery for conveying their meanings. The following analysis of two lines from Shakespeare's *Venus and Adonis* is made by Samuel Taylor Coleridge, the poet and critic, and has been further expanded by I. A. Richards, a psychologist and critic. This analysis indicates some of the ways in which imagery does its work.

> Look! how a bright star shooteth from the sky
> So glides he in the night from Venus' eye.

How many images and feelings are here brought together without effort and without discord—the beauty of Adonis—the rapidity of his flight—the yearning yet helplessness of the enamoured gazer—and a shadowy ideal character thrown over the whole (Raysor, I, 213).

Here, in contrast to the other case, the more the image is followed up, the more links of relevance between the units are discovered. As Adonis to Venus, so these lines to the reader seem to linger in the eye like the after-images that make the trail of the meteor. Here Shakespeare is realizing, and making the reader realize—not by any intensity of effort, but by the fulness and self-completing growth of the response—Adonis' flight as it was to Venus, and the sense of loss, of increased darkness, that invades her. The separable meanings of each word, *Look!* (our surprise at the meteor, hers at his flight), *star* (a light-giver, an influence, a remote and uncontrollable thing) *shooteth* (the sudden, irremediable, portentous fall or death of what had been a guide, a destiny), *the sky* (the source of light and now of ruin), *glides* (not rapidity only, but fatal ease too), *in the night* (the darkness of the scene and of Venus' world now)—all these separable meanings are here brought into one. And as they come together, as the reader's mind finds cross-connexion after cross-connexion between them, he seems, in becoming more aware of them, to be discovering not only Shakespeare's meaning, but something which he, the reader, is himself making. His understanding of Shakespeare is sanctioned by his own activity in it. As Coleridge says: "You feel him to be a poet, inasmuch as for a time he has made you one—an active creative being."[1]

The reader should be on the alert for the implications the imagery in any poem may have and for the relation of imagery to the full intention.

TO AN ATHLETE DYING YOUNG

A. E. HOUSMAN (1859–1936)

The time you won your town the race
We chaired you through the market-place;
Man and boy stood cheering by,
And home we brought you shoulder-high.

Today, the road all runners come,   5
Shoulder-high we bring you home,
And set you at your threshold down,
Townsman of a stiller town.

Smart lad, to slip betimes away
From fields where glory does not stay,   10
And early though the laurel grows
It withers quicker than the rose.

Eyes the shady night has shut
Cannot see the record cut,
And silence sounds no worse than cheers   15
After earth has stopped the ears:

Now you will not swell the rout
Of lads that wore their honors out,
Runners whom renown outran
And the name died before the man.   20

[1] *Coleridge on the Imagination*, New York: Harcourt-Brace, pp. 82–84.

So set, before its echoes fade,
The fleet foot on the sill of shade,
And hold to the low lintel up
The still-defended challenge-cup.

And round that early-laureled head   25
Will flock to gaze the strengthless dead,
And find unwithered on its curls
The garland briefer than a girl's.

In this poem the poet states a paradox: namely, that the early
death of the young athlete is a matter for congratulation rather
than for sorrow. This is the real theme of the poem. But we
should hardly be impressed with the bare statement that it is
better to die young rather than old, and even the startling quality of the statement would awaken interest for only a moment.
The poet has known better than to state the matter baldly, therefore. He has arranged a little dramatic framework for the
statement. In a familiar, almost conversational tone—"Smart
lad"—he addresses his congratulations to the young man who
is dead; and more than that, he uses the images which are associated with the young man's athletic achievements to describe
his death. Indeed, the statement implied by the imagery of
the poem is that the young runner has, in dying, won his race
again—he has beaten his competitors to the final goal of all of
them, death.

Notice, for example, that the funeral is treated exactly as if
it were a triumph for the young runner celebrated by his friends.
On the day on which he won the race for his town, his friends
made a chair for him of their hands and carried him home
shoulder-high in triumph. Now on the day of his funeral,
they carry him "shoulder-high" again, and they bring him
"home." "Smart lad," the poet then calls him, as if he had just
finished running a heady race.

The reasons for saying this follow: it is better to die at the
prime than to witness one's records broken by some one else.
But the poet does not relax his hold on concrete details in making
this statement. The laurel, symbol of fame, withers even quicker
than does the rose, emblem of beauty. Eyes closed in death

cannot see the record broken; to ears stopped with earth, the silence rings as loud as the air filled with cheering. And now the poet returns to the dominant figure of the race. Fame has a habit of outrunning the fastest runner and leaving him behind; the young athlete has not been outrun by his renown.

The figure is developed further in the sixth stanza. The brink of the grave is "the sill of shade" on which the young man has just placed his fleet foot, and the edge of the grave is the "low lintel" up to which the boy holds the "still defended challenge cup." The paradoxes here are especially rich. We think of death as being opposed in every regard to fleetness, and its inertia as incapable of defending anything. Yet by the reasoning which has preceded this stanza, the foot of the dead youth *is* fleet in death—only in death can he hold his challenge-cup still defended. Others will not be able to wrest it from him. The passage is a fine example of the poet's ability to put things which we ordinarily think of as quite unrelated, or even opposed to each other, into a pattern which gives a meaningful relation where one had not been seen before.

The last stanza exhibits also a fine effect which the poet has prepared for. The stanza catches up the contrast between the laurel and the rose already made in the third stanza. The connection is hinted at in the phrase "early-laureled head." Fame perishes even more quickly than beauty—the garland of laurel withers even faster than the garland of roses which a girl might be supposed to wear. We think of a young girl dead in the first flush of her beauty as an object of pathos, and at the same time think of her as having achieved a sort of triumph at having brought all her beauty untarnished with her into the grave. The poet wishes to get, and does get, something of the same effect for the athlete, and he gets it by suggesting the comparison.

Does he overplay his hand? Does he appear to be trying to extract the last degree of pathos from the situation? The mature reader will feel that the effect of pathos has been secured legitimately, and that the poet is not guilty of sentimentality; that is, that the emotion evoked in the poem is really inherent in the situation and has been developed by the poet for the reader by no unfair means. The pathos is a clean pathos therefore, revealed by a sudden insight but not lingered over for its own sake. One may observe how the firmness of the rhythm of the poem, and the familiar tone of the opening stanzas help to avoid a sentimental effect.

The use of paradox in this poem is also important in this regard, for a paradox tends to provoke a certain mental alertness, a certain awareness which in this case prevents the tone of the poem from becoming too soft. In the same way, and important for the same effect, is the use of symbol (laurel and rose), the use of the particular detail and image, and the use of suggestion rather than flat statement. All of these means are *indirect* as opposed to the direct prose statement; and this means that the reader must to some extent discover the meaning and the pathos for himself. The reader responds to the situation with force, but legitimately, because he feels that he has been merely helped by the poet to see the real character of the experience.

TREES

JOYCE KILMER (1886–1918)

I think that I shall never see
A poem lovely as a tree.

A tree whose hungry mouth is pressed
Against the sweet earth's flowing breast;

A tree that looks at God all day,   5
And lifts her leafy arms to pray;

A tree that may in summer wear
A nest of robins in her hair;

Upon whose bosom snow has lain;
Who intimately lives with rain.   10

Poems are made by fools like me,
But only God can make a tree.

This poem has been very greatly admired by a large number of people. The fact that it has been popular does not necessarily condemn it as a bad poem. But it is a bad poem.

First, let us look at it merely on the technical side, especially in regard to the use Kilmer makes of his imagery. Now the poet, in a poem of twelve lines, only makes one fundamental comparison on which the other comparisons are based; this is the same method used by Housman in "To an Athlete Dying Young." In "Trees" this fundamental comparison is not definitely stated but is constantly implied. The comparison is that of the tree to a human being. If the tree is compared to a human being, the reader has a right to expect a consistent use to be made of the aspects of the human being which appear in the poem. But look at stanza two:

> A tree whose hungry mouth is pressed
> Against the sweet earth's flowing breast;

Here the tree is *metaphorically* (*Glossary*) treated as a sucking babe and the earth, therefore, as the mother—a perfectly good comparison that has been made for centuries—the earth as the "great mother," the "giver of life," etc.

But the third stanza introduces a confusion:

> A tree that looks at God all day,
> And lifts her leafy arms to pray;

Here the tree is no longer a sucking babe, but, without warning, is old enough to indulge in religious devotions. But that is not the worst part of the confusion. Remember that the tree is a human being and that in the first stanza the *mouth* of that human being was the *root* of the tree. But now, if the branches are "leafy arms" the tree is a strangely deformed human being.

The fourth and fifth stanzas maintain the same anatomical arrangement for the tree as does the third, but they make other unexpected changes: the tree that wears a "nest of robins in her hair" must be a grown-up person, a girl with jewels in her hair; the tree with snow on its bosom is a chaste and pure girl, for so the *associations* of snow with purity and chastity tell the reader; and the tree that "lives with rain" is a chaste and pure young woman who, although vain enough to wear jewels, is yet withdrawn from the complications of human relationships and

lives alone with "nature," i.e., rain, or might be said to be nun-
like, an implication made by the religious tone of the poem.

Now it would be quite legitimate for the poet to use any one
of the thoughts he wishes to convey about the tree (1. the tree
as a babe nursed by mother earth, 2. the tree as a devout person
praying all day, 3. the tree as a girl with jewels in her hair, or
4. the tree as a chaste woman alone with nature and God) and
to create a metaphor for it, but the trouble is that he tries to convey
all of these features by a single basic comparison to a person,
and therefore presents a picture thoroughly confused. The poet
confuses his reader if the reader tries actually to *see* the images
the poet uses or tries to think about their *implications;* and that
is exactly what a good poet wants his readers to do, to *visualize*
or *feel* or *hear* his images (for there are images of sight, touch,
sound, etc.) and then to understand what those images imply,
for that is one of the chief ways a poet *communicates* his meaning, a way more important in the long run to most poets than
that of the actual flat prose statement of idea.

All of this does not mean of course that a poet *must* take a
single comparison and develop it *fully* and *consistently,* or that
there must be a strict *transition* from one comparison or image to
the next. For instance:

> O my love is like a red, red rose,
>   That's newly sprung in June;
> O my love is like the melody
>   That's sweetly played in tune.

Although this stanza seems to have in it the same abrupt change
in the comparison, there is really a very important difference.
Burns does not say that his love is like a rose in the same way
that Kilmer says that the tree is like a person; Burns merely implies that his love is beautiful, fragrant, etc. like a rose, or affects
him like a rose, but he does not insist on a consistent development
of the comparison; he merely wanted to point out the effective
part of the comparison, not even thinking, for instance, of the
thorns which are not pretty and are painful and which would
have caused trouble if he had started a consistent development
of the image, as Kilmer does. But without warning Burns

then jumps to a melody. Now Kilmer jumps from a sucking babe to a grown person without warning and thereby creates a confusion in the reader's mind. Burns creates no confusion. Why? Because Burns makes an absolute leap from rose to melody with reference to "his love" as the only connecting link, while Kilmer is maintaining a false consistency by a continued reference to a human being. Poets are constantly jumping from one comparison to another quite successfully because they treat each comparison in terms of its own special contribution to the poet's intention.

But in "Trees" there are other difficulties on the technical side. The rhythm is not well chosen. It is monotonous. Each stanza has the same rhythm, with a full pause at the end of a couplet and no pauses within the lines. The effect is sharp and pert, with no impression of thoughtfulness or of competent control on the part of the poet. This is especially inappropriate for a poem which pretends to treat a serious subject. Compare the rhythm, the variety of pauses, etc. of "Trees" with this passage from another poem in the same meter and rime scheme:

> Accept, thou shrine of my dead Saint,
> Instead of dirges this complaint;
> And for sweet flowers to crown thy hearse,
> Receive a strew of weeping verse
> From thy grieved friend, whom thou might'st see
> Quite melted into tears for thee.

> (From "The Exequy," by Henry King)

But how seriously does Kilmer treat his "serious subject"?

The rhythm does not contribute to a serious approach; nor does the confusion of the treatment of imagery. But let us try to consider his *meaning* or *thought* as such.

The poet is expressing a highly romantic mood in which he pretends that the works of man's mind are not comparable in "loveliness" to the works of Nature. What he wants to say is that he is tired of the works of man and takes refuge in the works of nature, which is quite different from comparing the two things on the basis of "loveliness." (See "The Garden," by Marvell, p. 451 or "Expostulation and Reply," by Wordsworth p.

13). But the two kinds of loveliness, that of art and that of nature, are not comparable; and in the second place "loveliness" is not the word to apply to *Hamlet* by Shakespeare, "Lycidas," by Milton, "The Canterbury Tales," by Chaucer, etc. And the tree, as opposed to the poem, is lacking in *meaning* and *expressiveness;* it has those things only in so far as a man can give them to it. Kilmer writes:

> Poems are made by fools like me
> But only God can make a tree.

That is perfectly true, but by the same line of reasoning God makes the poems too, through his agency in man. Or reversing the argument: Bad poems are made by bad poets like Kilmer and good poems are made by good poets like Yeats, Shakespeare, Landor, Milton, etc. Furthermore the paradox created by Kilmer breaks down, because it isn't justified in terms given in the poem; it will not stand inspection. Housman uses a paradox successfully in "To an Athlete Dying Young," because in the poem he limits the application and illustrates the precise ways in which it contains a truth.

But why has the poem been popular, if so bad? It appeals, as does "The Pilgrims" (p. 335), to a stock response which has nothing to do, as such, with poetry. It praises God and appeals to a religious sentiment. Therefore people who do not stop to look at the poem itself or to study the images in the poem and think about what the poem really says, are inclined to accept the poem because of the pious sentiment, the prettified little pictures (which in themselves appeal to stock responses), and the mechanical rhythm.

CROSSING THE BAR

ALFRED, LORD TENNYSON (1809–1892)

Sunset and evening star,
    And one clear call for me!
And may there be no moaning of the bar,
    When I put out to sea,

But such a tide as moving seems asleep,   5
    Too full for sound and foam,
When that which drew from out the boundless deep
    Turns again home.

Twilight and evening bell,
    And after that the dark!   10
And may there be no sadness of farewell,
    When I embark;

For though from out our bourne of Time and Place
    The flood may bear me far,
I hope to see my Pilot face to face   15
    When I have crossed the bar.

EXERCISE:

This poem involves a confusion of imagery such as that found in "Trees." Define it. Can it be justified?

MY STAR

ROBERT BROWNING (1812–1889)

All that I know
    Of a certain star
Is, it can throw
    (Like the angled spar)
Now a dart of red,   5
    Now a dart of blue;
Till my friends have said
    They would fain see, too,
My star that dartles the red and the blue!
Then it stops like a bird; like a flower, hangs furled: 10
    They must solace themselves with the Saturn above it.
What matter to me if their star is a world?
    Mine has opened its soul to me; therefore I love it.

EXERCISE:

Write a full analysis of this poem, emphasizing the problem of imagery.

ON THE COUNTESS DOWAGER OF PEMBROKE

WILLIAM BROWNE (1592–1643)

Underneath this sable hearse
Lies the subject of all verse:
Sidney's sister, Pembroke's mother:
Death, ere thou hast slain another
Fair and learned and good as she,   5
Time shall throw a dart at thee.

Marble piles let no man raise
To her name: for after days
Some kind woman, born as she,
Reading this, like Niobe   10
Shall turn marble, and become
Both her mourner and her tomb.

EXERCISE:

This epitaph is written with regard to the woman who was the
sister of Sir Philip Sidney and the mother of the Earl of Pembroke.
She herself was greatly interested in literature. Niobe, who is
alluded to the second stanza, was fabled to have been turned
into stone after the death of her children. Analyze the function
of the comparison in the second stanza.

THE SOLITARY REAPER

WILLIAM WORDSWORTH (1770–1850)

Behold her, single in the field,
Yon solitary Highland Lass!
Reaping and singing by herself;
Stop here, or gently pass!
Alone she cuts and binds the grain,   5
And sings a melancholy strain;
O listen! for the Vale profound
Is overflowing with the sound.

No Nightingale did ever chaunt
More welcome notes to weary bands   10
Of travelers in some shady haunt,
Among Arabian sands:
A voice so thrilling ne'er was heard
In spring-time from the Cuckoo-bird,
Breaking the silence of the seas   15
Among the farthest Hebrides.

Will no one tell me what she sings?—
Perhaps the plaintive numbers flow
For old, unhappy, far-off things,
And battles long ago: 20
Or is it some more humble lay,
Familiar matter of today?
Some natural sorrow, loss, or pain,
That has been, and may be again?

Whate'er the theme, the Maiden sang   25
As if her song could have no ending;
I saw her singing at her work,
And o'er the sickle bending;—
I listened, motionless and still;
And, as I mounted up the hill,   30
The music in my heart I bore,
Long after it was heard no more.

EXERCISE:

How do the images, especially in the second stanza, support
the poet's general intention?

LUCIFER

JOHN MILTON (1608–1674)

. . . . as when the sun new-risen
Looks through the horizontal misty air
Shorn of his beams, or from behind the moon,
In dim eclipse, disastrous twilight sheds
On half the nations, and with fear of change   5
Perplexes monarchs. Darkened so, yet shone

Above them all the Archangel; but his face
Deep scars of thunder had intrenched, and care
Sat on his faded cheek, but under brows
Of dauntless courage, and considerate pride   10
Waiting revenge.   Cruel his eye, but cast
Signs of remorse and passion, to behold
The fellows of his crime, the followers rather
(Far other once beheld in bliss), condemned
Forever now to have their lot in pain;   15
Millions of Spirits for his fault amerced
Of Heaven, and from eternal splendors flung
For his revolt; yet faithful how they stood,
Their glory withered: as, when Heaven's fire
Hath scathed the forest oaks or mountain pines,   20
With singèd top their stately growth, though bare,
Stands on the blasted heath.

(From *Paradise Lost,* Book I)

EXERCISE:

1. What is the tone of this passage?
2. How is the tone defined by metrical and other technical factors, and by the imagery?

SINCE BRASS NOR STONE

WILLIAM SHAKESPEARE (1564–1616)

Since brass, nor stone, nor earth, nor boundless sea,
But sad mortality o'er-sways their power,
How with this rage shall beauty hold a plea,
Whose action is no stronger than a flower?
O, how shall summer's honey breath hold out   5
Against the wreckful siege of battering days,
When rocks impregnable are not so stout,
Nor gates of steel so strong, but Time decays?
O fearful meditation! where, alack,
Shall Time's best jewel from Time's chest lie hid?   10
Or what strong hand can hold his swift foot back?

Or who his spoil of beauty can forbid?
O, none, unless this miracle have might,
That in black ink my love may still shine bright.

EXERCISE:

The first eight lines of this sonnet merely say, in terms of general statement, that since time destroys all things, beauty cannot survive. What justification is there for the poet's elaboration of this statement?

I WANDERED LONELY AS A CLOUD

WILLIAM WORDSWORTH (1770–1850)

I wandered lonely as a cloud
That floats on high o'er vales and hills,
When all at once I saw a crowd,
A host of golden daffodils;
Beside the lake, beneath the trees,   5
Fluttering and dancing in the breeze.

Continuous as the stars that shine
And twinkle on the milky way,
They stretched in never-ending line
Along the margin of a bay: 10
Ten thousand saw I at a glance,
Tossing their heads in sprightly dance.

The waves beside them danced, but they
Outdid the sparkling waves in glee:—
A poet could not but be gay   15
In such a jocund company:
I gazed—and gazed—but little thought
What wealth the show to me had brought.

For oft when on my couch I lie
In vacant or in pensive mood,   20
They flash upon that inward eye
Which is the bliss of solitude,
And then my heart with pleasure fills,
And dances with the daffodils.

Exercise:

Compare this poem on the grounds of meaning and method
with "The Solitary Reaper" (p. 393).

FULL MANY A GLORIOUS MORNING

WILLIAM SHAKESPEARE (1564–1616)

Full many a glorious morning have I seen
Flatter the mountain-tops with sovereign eye,
Kissing with golden face the meadows green,
Gilding pale streams with heavenly alchemy;
Anon permit the basest clouds to ride   5
With ugly rack on his celestial face,
And from the forlorn world his visage hide,
Stealing unseen to west with this disgrace:
Even so my sun one early morn did shine
With all-triumphant splendor on my brow;   10
But out, alack! he was but one hour mine;
The region cloud hath masked him from me now.
Yet him for this my love no whit disdaineth;
Suns of the world may stain when heaven's sun staineth.

Exercise:

The general comparisons involved in this sonnet are obvious;
but consider the function of such comparisons as those implied
in the words *flatter* and *alchemy*.

LIKE AS THE WAVES

WILLIAM SHAKESPEARE (1564–1616)

Like as the waves make towards the pebbled shore,
So do our minutes hasten to their end;
Each changing place with that which goes before,
In sequent toil all forwards do contend.
Nativity, once in the main of light,   5
Crawls to maturity, wherewith being crowned,

Crookèd eclipses 'gainst his glory fight,
And Time that gave doth now his gift confound.
Time doth transfix the flourish set on youth
And delves the parallels in beauty's brow,   10
Feeds on the rarities of nature's truth,
And nothing stands but for his scythe to mow:
And yet to times in hope my verse shall stand,
Praising thy worth, despite his cruel hand.

EXERCISE:

Write a full analysis of this poem in terms of metrical and other technical factors, tone, and imagery.

THUS, PITEOUSLY LOVE CLOSED

GEORGE MEREDITH (1828–1909)

Thus piteously Love closed what he begat:
The union of this ever-diverse pair!
These two were rapid falcons in a snare,
Condemned to do the flitting of the bat.
Lovers beneath the singing sky of May,   5
They wandered once; clear as the dew on flowers:
But they fed not on the advancing hours:
Their hearts held cravings for the buried day.
Then each applied to each that fatal knife,
Deep questioning, which probes to endless dole.   10
Ah, what a dusty answer gets the soul
When hot for certainties in this our life!—
In tragic hints here see what evermore
Moves dark as yonder midnight ocean's force,
Thundering like ramping hosts of warrior horse,   15
To throw that faint thin line upon the shore!

                          (From *Modern Love*)

EXERCISE:

Compare the logical structure of this poem with that of the two preceding ones. Discuss any differences in the use of imagery in the three sonnets, especially in the conclusion.

TO HELEN

EDGAR ALLAN POE (1809–1849)

Helen, thy beauty is to me
   Like those Nicèan barks of yore
That gently, o'er a perfumed sea,
   The weary way-worn wanderer bore
   To his own native shore.   5

On desperate seas long wont to roam,
   Thy hyacinth hair, thy classic face,
Thy Naiad airs have brought me home
   To the glory that was Greece,
And the grandeur that was Rome.   10

Lo, in yon brilliant window-niche
   How statue-like I see thee stand,
   The agate lamp within thy hand,
Ah! Psyche, from the regions which
   Are holy land!   15

EXERCISE:

1. The poet says that the woman addressed has a "classic face."
How does the imagery support this statement?

2. Another poem by Poe, "Ulalume" (p. 355), has been un-
favorably analyzed. Try to define the reasons why "To Helen"
is more successful.

DAYS

RALPH WALDO EMERSON (1803–1882)

Daughters of Time, the hypocritic Days,
Muffled and dumb like barefoot dervishes,
And marching single in an endless file,
Bring diadems and faggots in their hands.
To each they offer gifts after his will,   5

Bread, kingdoms, stars, and sky that holds them all.
I, in my pleached garden, watched the pomp.
Forgot my morning wishes, hastily
Took a few herbs and apples, and the Day
Turned and departed silent. I, too late,   10
Under her solemn fillet saw the scorn.

EXERCISE:

State the general idea of this poem.

PEACE

HENRY VAUGHAN (1622–1695)

My soul, there is a country
   Afar beyond the stars,
Where stands a wingèd sentry
   All skilful in the wars.
There, above noise and danger,   5
   Sweet Peace sits crowned with smiles,
And one born in a manger
   Commands the beauteous files.
He is thy gracious friend,
   And—O my soul, awake!—   10
Did in pure love descend
   To die here for thy sake.
If thou canst get but thither,
   There grows the flower of peace,
The rose that can not wither,   15
   Thy fortress and thy ease.

Leave then thy foolish ranges,
   For none can thee secure
But one who never changes,
   Thy God, thy life, thy cure.   20

EXERCISE:

Some of the images in this poem, for instance, that in the first
two lines, would appear as clichés if taken alone. (In this
connection read the analysis of "The Pilgrims," pp. 334–36.) But
does the poem appear stereotyped?

THE CHAMBERED NAUTILUS

OLIVER WENDELL HOLMES (1809–1894)

This is the ship of pearl, which, poets feign,
  Sails the unshadowed main,—
  The venturous bark that flings
On the sweet summer wind its purpled wings
In gulfs enchanted, where the Siren sings,   5
  And coral reefs lie bare,
Where the cold sea-maids rise to sun their streaming hair.

Its webs of living gauze no more unfurl;
  Wrecked is the ship of pearl!   10
  And every chambered cell,
Where its dim dreaming life was wont to dwell,
As the frail tenant shaped his growing shell,
  Before thee lies revealed,—
Its irised ceiling rent, its sunless crypt unsealed!   15

Year after year beheld the silent toil
  That spread his lustrous coil;
  Still, as the spiral grew,
He left the past year's dwelling for the new,
Stole with soft step its shining archway through,   20
  Built up its idle door,
Stretched in his last-found home, and knew the old no
    more.

Thanks for the heavenly message brought by thee,
  Child of the wandering sea,   25
  Cast from her lap, forlorn!
From thy dead lips a clearer note is born
Than ever Triton blew from wreathèd horn!
  While on mine ear it rings,
Through the deep caves of thought I hear a voice that
    sings:—   30

Build thee more stately mansions, O my soul,
  As the swift seasons roll!
  Leave thy low-vaulted past!
Let each new temple, nobler than the last,   35

Shut thee from heaven with a dome more vast
    Till thou at length art free,
Leaving thine outgrown shell by life's unresting sea!

EXERCISE:

1. After the very fine presentation of the subject in the first three stanzas, does the fourth really add to the effectiveness of the poem? Is the shift in tone successful? Does the comparison with Triton's horn provide an adequate transition to the last stanza?

2. Is there a confusion involved in the imagery of the last stanza? Analyze the function of the imagery there in order to discuss this question.

THE HOUND OF HEAVEN

FRANCIS THOMPSON (1859–1907)

I fled Him, down the nights and down the days;
    I fled Him, down the arches of the years;
I fled Him, down the labyrinthine ways
    Of my own mind; and in the mist of tears
I hid from Him, and under running laughter.   5
            Up vistaed hopes, I sped;
            And shot, precipitated,
Adown Titanic glooms of chasmèd fears,
    From those strong Feet that followed, followed after.

            But with unhurrying chase,   10
            And unperturbèd pace,
Deliberate speed, majestic instancy,
            They beat—and a Voice beat
            More instant than the Feet—
    "All things betray thee, who betrayest Me."   15

            I pleaded, outlaw-wise,
By many a hearted casement, curtained red,
    Trellised with intertwining charities;

(For, though I knew His love Who followèd,
          Yet was I sore adread   20
Lest, having Him, I must have naught beside.)
But, if one little casement parted wide,
     The gust of His approach would clash it to.
Fear wist not to evade as Love wist to pursue.
Across the margent of the world I fled,   25
     And troubled the gold gateways of the stars,
     Smiting for shelter on their clangèd bars;
               Fretted to dulcet jars
And silvern chatter the pale ports o' the moon.
I said to dawn: Be sudden; to eve: Be soon—   30
     With thy young skyey blossoms heap me over
          From this tremendous Lover!
Float thy vague veil about me, lest He see!
     I tempted all His servitors, but to find
My own betrayal in their constancy,   35
In faith to Him their fickleness to me,
     Their traitorous trueness, and their loyal deceit.
To all swift things for swiftness did I sue;
     Clung to the whistling mane of every wind.
               But whether they swept, smoothly fleet,   40
          The long savannahs of the blue;
          Or whether, Thunder-driven,
          They clanged His chariot 'thwart a heaven,
Plashy with flying lightnings round the spurn o' their
               feet:—
     Fear wist not to evade as Love wist to pursue.   45

               Still with unhurrying chase,
               And unperturbèd pace,
     Deliberate speed, majestic instancy,
               Came on the following Feet,
               And a Voice above their beat—   50
     "Naught shelters thee, who wilt not shelter Me."

I sought no more that after which I strayed
          In face of man or maid;
But still within the little children's eyes
     Seems something, something that replies,   55
They at least are for me, surely for me!
I turned me to them very wistfully;

But just as their young eyes grew sudden fair
    With dawning answers there,
Their angel plucked them from me by the hair.   60
"Come then, ye other children, Nature's—share
With me" (said I) "your delicate fellowship;
    Let me greet you lip to lip,
    Let me twine with you caresses,
        Wantoning   65
    With our Lady-Mother's vagrant tresses,
        Banqueting
    With her in her wind-walled palace,
    Underneath her azured daïs,
    Quaffing, as your taintless way is,   70
        From a chalice
Lucent-weeping out of the dayspring."
        So it was done:
I in their delicate fellowship was one—
Drew the bolt of Nature's secrecies.   75
    I knew all the swift importings
    On the wilful face of skies;
    I knew how the clouds arise,
    Spumèd of the wild sea-snortings;
        All that's born or dies   80
    Rose and drooped with; made them shapers
Of mine own moods, or wailful or divine—
    With them joyed and was bereaven.
    I was heavy with the even,
    When she lit her glimmering tapers   85
    Round the day's dead sanctities.
    I laughed in the morning's eyes.
I triumphed and I saddened with all weather,
    Heaven and I wept together,
And its sweet tears were salt with mortal mine;   90
Against the red throb of its sunset-heart
    I laid my own to beat,
    And share commingling heat;
But not by that, by that, was eased my human smart.
In vain my tears were wet on Heaven's gray cheek.   95
For ah! we know not what each other says,
    These things and I; in sound *I* speak—
Their sound is but their stir, they speak by silences.
Nature, poor stepdame, cannot slake my drouth;

> Let her, if she would owe me,   100
> Drop yon blue bosom-veil of sky, and show me
>   The breasts o' her tenderness:
> Never did any milk of hers once bless
>   My thirsting mouth.
>   Nigh and nigh draws the chase,   105
>   With unperturbèd pace,
>   Deliberate speed, majestic instancy,
>   And past those noisèd Feet
>   A Voice comes yet more fleet—
> "Lo! naught contents thee, who content'st not Me."

> Naked I wait Thy love's uplifted stroke!   111
> My harness piece by piece Thou hast hewn from me,
>   And smitten me to my knee;
>   I am defenseless utterly.
>   I slept, methinks, and woke,   115
> And, slowly gazing, find me stripped in sleep.
> In the rash lustihead of my young powers,
>   I shook the pillaring hours
> And pulled my life upon me; grimed with smears,
> I stand amid the dust o' the mounded years—   120
> My mangled youth lies dead beneath the heap.
> My days have crackled and gone up in smoke,
> Have puffed and burst as sun-starts on a stream.
>   Yea, faileth now even dream
> The dreamer, and the lute the lutanist;   125
> Even the linked fantasies, in whose blossomy twist
> I swung the earth a trinket at my wrist,
> Are yielding; cords of all too weak account
> For earth, with heavy griefs so overplussed.
>   Ah! is Thy love indeed   130
> A weed, albeit an amaranthine weed,
> Suffering no flowers except its own to mount?
>   Ah! must—
>   Designer infinite!—
> Ah! must Thou char the wood ere Thou canst limn
>   with it?   135
> My freshness spent its wavering shower i' the dust;
> And now my heart is as a broken fount,
> Wherein tear-drippings stagnate, spilt down ever
>   From the dank thoughts that shiver

Upon the sighful branches of my mind.   140
    Such is; what is to be?
The pulp so bitter, how shall taste the rind?
I dimly guess what Time in mists confounds;
Yet ever and anon a trumpet sounds
From the hid battlements of Eternity: 145
Those shaken mists a space unsettle, then
Round the half-glimpsèd turrets slowly wash again;
    But not ere him who summoneth
    I first have seen, enwound
With glooming robes purpureal, cypress-crowned;   150
His name I know, and what his trumpet saith.
Whether man's heart or life it be which yields
    Thee harvest, must Thy harvest fields
    Be dunged with rotten death?

    Now of that long pursuit   155
    Comes on at hand the bruit;
That Voice is round me like a bursting sea:
    "And is thy earth so marred,
    Shattered in shard on shard?
Lo, all things fly thee, for thou fliest Me!   160
    Strange, piteous, futile thing!
Wherefore should any set thee love apart?
Seeing none but I makes much of naught"
      (He said),
"And human love needs human meriting:
    How hast thou merited—   165
Of all man's clotted clay the dingiest clot?
    Alack, thou knowest not
How little worthy of any love thou art!
Whom wilt thou find to love ignoble thee,
    Save Me, save only Me?   170
All which I took from thee I did but take,
    Not for thy harms,

But just that thou might'st seek it in My arms,
    All which thy child's mistake
Fancies as lost, I have stored for thee at home: 175
    Rise, clasp My hand, and come!"

    Halts by me that footfall:
    Is my gloom, after all,

Shade of His hand, outstretched caressingly?
"Ah, fondest, blindest, weakest,   180
I am He Whom thou seekest!
Thou dravest love from thee, who dravest Me."

EXERCISE:

1. Make a careful study of the imagery in this poem, especially
in the section from line 111 to line 154. How much variety is
presented in the imagery? How does this affect the tone of the
poem? How much does the poet depend upon his use of
imagery for the communication of his idea as such?

2. Study the metrical and other technical factors involved in
this poem in relation to particular effects. Consider especially
the section from line 1 to line 15 and from line 122 to line 140.

ODE TO A NIGHTINGALE

JOHN KEATS (1795–1821)

My heart aches, and a drowsy numbness pains
    My sense, as though of hemlock I had drunk,
Or emptied some dull opiate to the drains
    One minute past, and Lethe-wards had sunk:
'Tis not through envy of thy happy lot,   5
    But being too happy in thine happiness,—
        That thou, light-wingèd Dryad of the trees,
            In some melodious plot
Of beechen green, and shadows numberless,
    Singest of summer in full-throated ease.   10

O for a draught of vintage! that hath been
    Cooled a long age in the deep-delvèd earth,
Tasting of Flora and the country green,
    Dance, and Provençal song, and sunburnt mirth!
O for a beaker full of the warm South,   15
    Full of the true, the blushful Hippocrene,
        With beaded bubbles winking at the brim,
            And purple-stainèd mouth;

That I might drink, and leave the world unseen,
    And with thee fade away into the forest dim: 20
Fade far away, dissolve, and quite forget
    What thou among the leaves has never known,
The weariness, the fever, and the fret
    Here, where men sit and hear each other groan;
Where palsy shakes a few, sad, last gray hairs,   25
    Where youth grows pale, and spectre-thin, and dies;
        Where but to think is to be full of sorrow
            And leaden-eyed despairs,
    Where Beauty cannot keep her lustrous eyes,
        Or new Love pine at them beyond tomorrow.   30

    Away! away! for I will fly to thee,
      Not charioted by Bacchus and his pards,
But on the viewless wings of Poesy,
    Though the dull brain perplexes and retards:
Already with thee! tender is the night,   35
    And haply the Queen-Moon is on her throne,
      Clustered around by all her starry Fays;
        But here there is no light,
Save what from heaven is with the breezes blown
    Through verdurous glooms and winding mossy ways.

I cannot see what flowers are at my feet,   41
    Nor what soft incense hangs upon the boughs,
But, in embalmèd darkness, guess each sweet
    Wherewith the seasonable month endows
The grass, the thicket, and the fruit-tree wild;   45
    White hawthorn, and the pastoral eglantine;
      Fast fading violets covered up in leaves;
        And mid-May's eldest child,
    The coming musk-rose, full of dewy wine,
      The murmurous haunt of flies on summer eves.   50

Darkling I listen; and, for many a time
    I have been half in love with easeful Death,
Called him soft names in many a musèd rhyme,
    To take into the air my quiet breath;
Now more than ever seems it rich to die,   55
    To cease upon the midnight with no pain,
      While thou art pouring forth thy soul abroad

                    In such an ecstasy!
            Still wouldst thou sing, and I have ears in vain—
                To thy high requiem become a sod.   60

            Thou wast not born for death, immortal Bird!
                No hungry generations tread thee down;
            The voice I hear this passing night was heard
                In ancient days by emperor and clown:
            Perhaps the self-same song that found a path   65
                Through the sad heart of Ruth, when, sick for home,
                    She stood in tears amid the alien corn;
                        The same that oft-times hath
                Charmed magic casements, opening on the foam
                    Of perilous seas, in faery lands forlorn.   70

            Forlorn! the very word is like a bell
                To toll me back from thee to my sole self!
            Adieu! the fancy cannot cheat so well
                As she is famed to do, deceiving elf.
            Adieu! adieu! thy plaintive anthem fades   75
                Past the near meadows, over the still stream,
                Up the hill-side; and now 'tis buried deep
                    In the next valley-glades:
            Was it a vision, or a waking dream?
            Fled is that music:—Do I wake or sleep?   80

   This poem is essentially a reverie induced by the poet's listening to the song of the nightingale. In the first stanza the poet
is just sinking into the reverie; in the last stanza, he comes out
of the reverie and back to a consciousness of the actual world
in which he and all other human beings live. The first lines of
the poem and the last, therefore, constitute a sort of frame for the
reverie proper.
   The dominating idea in the reverie is the contrast between the
world of the imagination (to which the song of the bird carries
the poet and for which the life of the bird becomes a sort of
symbol) and the world of actuality in which beauty is merely
transient and in which life is beset by sorrow.
   The poet has chosen to present his reverie largely in terms of
imagery—imagery drawn from nature, the flowers and leaves, etc.

actually associated with the bird physically, and imagery drawn
from myth and literature which has been associated with the
nightingale imaginatively. The images are elaborate and decorative and the poet dwells upon them lovingly and leisurely,
developing them in some detail as pictures. It is not the sort of
method which would suit a poem exhibiting a rapid and dramatic
play of thought such as one finds in the passages from Shakespeare's *Measure for Measure* (p. 527). But one remembers the
general character of the poem. The loving elaboration and
slowed movement resembles the slowed movement of meditative
trance, or dream, and therefore is appropriate to the general tone
of this poem. The imagery, then, in its elaboration is not merely
beautifully decorative but has a relation to the general temper of
the whole poem.

In the first stanza the poet is slipping off into the trance under
the influence of the bird's song. But he does not represent the
act as a merely facile and joyous release from the burden of
actuality into the completely beautiful realm of the imagination.
He is conscious of pain and numbness. The reverie, filled with
beautiful images as it is, is not merely an escape from life, therefore. And if it enables him to appreciate beauty more keenly, it
also causes him to appreciate the sorrow of life more keenly too.

The progression of thought in the reverie—for there is a
progression—is as follows. The poet, with his desire to escape
from the world of actuality, calls for a drink of wine

> That I might drink, and leave the world unseen.

But the wish for the draught of wine is half fancy. The poet
lingers over the description of the wine, making it an idealized
and lovingly elaborated thing too. We know that it is not a
serious and compelling request. The grammar of the passage
itself tells us this: after "O for a draught of vintage" the poet
interposes seven lines of rich description identifying the wine
with the spirit of summer and pastoral joys and with the romantic
associations of Provençe, and finally gives a concrete picture of a
bubbling glass of the wine itself before he goes on to tell us why he
wishes the draught of wine. (*Introduction*, p. 15)

The third stanza amplifies the desire to get away from the

world of actuality. The word *fade* in the last line of the second stanza is echoed in the next stanza in "Fade far away, dissolve . . ." The implication is that the poet wishes for a dissolution of himself; a wish which later in the poem becomes an explicit pondering on death as something attractive and desirable. The principal aspects of the actual world which the poet would like to escape are just those aspects of it which seem opposed to the world conjured up by the bird's song: its feverish hurry, the fact that in it youth dies and beauty fades. The world which the nightingale seems to inhabit is one of deathless youth and beauty. This idea too is to be developed explicitly by the poet in the seventh stanza.

In the fourth stanza the poet apparently makes a sudden decision to attempt to leave actual life and penetrate to the world of the imagination. The apparent suddenness of the decision is reflected in the movement of the first line of the stanza,

> Away! away! for I will fly to thee.

But he will fly to it by exciting his mind, not with wine, but with poetry. And in line 5 of the stanza the poet has apparently been successful: "Already with thee," he says. There follows down to the opening of the sixth stanza a very rich description of the flowery, darkened thicket in which the nightingale is singing.

But stanzas six and seven imply that the poet, even though he has said "already with thee," has not really been able to win to the world which he imagines the nightingale to inhabit, for in these stanzas he is again occupied with the problem already dealt with earlier in the poem: the apparent antithesis between the transience of beauty in the actual world and the permanence of beauty in the imagination. His wish for dissolution, which he expresses in the third stanza, becomes in the sixth almost a wish for death itself, an utter dissolution. But the idea as repeated receives an additional twist. Earlier, his wish to fade away was a desire to escape the sorrow and sordidness of the real world. Now even death itself seems to the poet an easy and attractive thing; and, more than that, it seems even a sort of positive fulfillment to die to the sound of the nightingale's high requiem.

But the nightingale at the height of its singing seems not to be

subject to death at all. Not only does it seem the antithesis of
the sorrowful world of actuality, but it actually seems to possess
immortality.   The poet goes on to describe the effect of the
nightingale's song by two incidents drawn from the remote past
as if he believed that the nightingale which he now hears had
literally lived forever.   The two incidents are chosen also to
illustrate two different aspects of the bird's song.   The first, the
song as heard by Ruth, is an incident taken from biblical literature, and gives the effect of the song as it reminded the home-sick
girl of her native land.   The second, hinting at some unnamed
romance of the Middle Ages, gives the unearthly magic of the
song.

  With the first word of the last stanza, the poet returns to himself. It is as if it had suddenly occurred to him that the word
forlorn, which closes the previous stanza, applies to himself. He
so applies it, and he gives up the attempt to escape from the world
of actuality:

> . . . the fancy cannot cheat so well.

He cannot escape. And as the song of the bird dies away, he is
back where he began when the poem opened, and is asking himself whether the reverie out of which he has just come is a dream.

  The structure of the poem, one may see, is not a logical one.
Image leads on to image, or idea to idea, in a seemingly illogical
sequence.   As a matter of fact, the association of ideas in this
poem is really very close in principle to that which one finds in
"stream of consciousness" (*Glossary* and analysis of "Patterns,"
pp. 139–43) writing—though it may be somewhat startling at first
glance to associate this modern term with a poet like Keats. Here
we come on the essential weakness of the poem (and it is a
higher compliment to Keats to examine his poetry closely enough
to find such a weakness than to rest our praise on those parts
which are completely praiseworthy, the elaboration of the particular details).   The weakness is that Keats has not made a virtue
out of the abruptness of the shifts and contrasts—which do
exist in the poem—by calling our attention to them, and by en-
forcing the irony inherent in the whole situation: the contrast
between the world as it is and the world of ideal beauty which

the poet longs for. A certain irony does inhere in the poem. As a matter of fact, the poet attempts a mildly ironical ending in the last stanza. He catches up the word "forlorn" which he has used in describing one of the imagined settings, and suddenly finds that the word accurately describes himself. The psychological situation is that of a man who, trying to forget his pain and isolation and succeeding in forgetting it for the moment by weaving splendid descriptive tapestries, is carried suddenly back to his own case by his chance employment of a word which describes only too accurately his own plight. But the effect of irony here is not corroborated by what follows. He does not maintain this attitude in looking back at his reverie. Instead, he attacks it directly:

> . . . the fancy cannot cheat so well
> As she is famed to do, deceiving elf.

The poem as a whole lives obviously in terms of its imagery, but the emphasis on the imagery is on the decorative side. The imagery is not welded sufficiently to the theme; the ironical effect of the experience as a whole is not achieved through the imagery. Indeed, this imagery, superb as it is, lies closer to surface description than does, for example, the highly functional imagery of, say, Shakespeare. But admitting this defect, we can consider the imagery of this ode as carrying almost as far as is humanly possible beautiful description rich in association. Consider, for example, in the second stanza the description of the wine. The poet uses the term *vintage* rather than *wine* because of the associations of vintage with age and excellence. It tastes of Flora (goddess of flowers) and the country green (a land predominantly fruitful and rich) and of dance and Provençal song (associations with the merry country of the Troubadours and associations with the period of the troubadours) and sunburnt mirth. Mirth cannot in fact, of course, be sunburnt, but the sensitive reader will not be troubled by this. The phrase is a condensation of the fuller phrase: mirth of hearty folk who live close to nature and to the earth and whose sunburnt faces and arms indicate that they live close to nature. These associations of the wine with Provençe and with all that Provençe implies are caught up and corroborated by another bold and condensed phrase: "full of the warm South." For the word, *South,* not only carries its associations of warmth but also of the particular South which the poet has just been describing: the south of France, Provençe. Thus, the form of the statement carries with it a sort of shock and surprise such as we often find in great imaginative poetry. Then having built up the associations with the wine, the poet presents us with a very vivid concrete picture of the wine itself sparkling in its glass.

This for a rather inadequate account of only one item of the sort of description which fills the poem. The student might attempt to analyze in the same way certain other passages. In making such an examination, he will notice that Keats does not sacrifice sharpness of perception to mere prettiness. Again and again it is the sharp and accurate observation which gives the richness a validity. For example,

> The coming musk-rose, full of dewy wine,
> The murmurous haunt of flies on summer eves.

The passage is not merely beautiful and rich. It embodies an item of observation which the poet has made. We feel that he knows what he is talking about. A poorer poet would try only for the decorative effect and would fail. Moreover, much of the suggestiveness resides also in the choice of precise details. Many a poet feels that, because the stimulus to the imagination makes for an indefinite richness of association, this indefiniteness is aroused by vague, general description. On the contrary, the force of association is greatest when it is aroused by precise detail. For example, consider the passage most famous for its suggestiveness.

> Charmed magic casements, opening on the foam
> Of perilous seas, in faery lands forlorn.

After all, the item is a scene precisely visualized. If the casements opening on the seas and framing the scene were omitted, the general, vague words, *perilous, faery,* and *forlorn* would not be sufficient to give the effect actually transmitted by this part of the poem.

This poem, then, will furnish the student with a very illuminating exercise in imagery. For on one side—what we may call the picturesque or decorative or surface side—the imagery is about as fine as it is possible for it to be; but on the functional side, in which idea is transmitted and developed through images, Keats' images are not so closely knit and so coherent as the images which one finds, to take a minor poem, in Marvell's "The Definition of Love" or, to take a major poem, in Shakespeare's *Macbeth*. We do not need to disparage a fine poem, however, in order to make this point. Moreover, we are allowed to do justice to Keats the critic as well as Keats the poet. For Keats himself realized that his weakness lay in general structure and in the occasional lack of positive relation between meaning and imagery in his work.

WHEN THE LAMP IS SHATTERED

PERCY BYSSHE SHELLEY (1792–1822)

When the lamp is shattered
The light in the dust lies dead—
    When the cloud is scattered
The rainbow's glory is shed.
    When the lute is broken,   5
Sweet tones are remembered not;
    When the lips have spoken,
Loved accents are soon forgot.

    As music and splendor
Survive not the lamp and the lute,   10
    The heart's echoes render
No song when the spirit is mute:—
    No song but sad dirges,
Like the wind through a ruined cell,
    Or the mournful surges   15
That ring the dead seaman's knell.

When hearts have once mingled
Love first leaves the well-built nest,
  The weak one is singled
To endure what it once possessed.   20
  O Love! who bewailest
The frailty of all things here,
  Why choose you the frailest
For your cradle, your home, and your bier?

  Its passions will rock thee   25
As the storms rock the ravens on high:
  Bright reason will mock thee,
Like the sun from a wintry sky.
  From thy nest every rafter
Will rot, and thine eagle home   30
  Leave thee naked to laughter,
When leaves fall and cold winds come.

EXERCISE:

What is the principle upon which the various images have
been selected? Are the images bound together on any consistent
principle?

EPITAPH ON AN ARMY OF MERCENARIES

A. E. HOUSMAN (1859–1936)

These, in the day when heaven was falling,
  The hour when earth's foundations fled,
Followed their mercenary calling
  And took their wages and are dead.

Their shoulders held the sky suspended;   5
  They stood, and earth's foundations stay;
What God abandoned, these defended,
  And saved the sum of things for pay.

EXERCISE:

What do the "mercenaries" symbolize?

ON FIRST LOOKING INTO CHAPMAN'S HOMER

JOHN KEATS (1795–1821)

Much have I traveled in the realms of gold,
And many goodly states and kingdoms seen;
Round many western islands have I been
Which bards in fealty to Apollo hold.
Oft of one wide expanse had I been told   5
That deep-browed Homer ruled as his demesne;
Yet did I never breathe its pure serene
Till I heard Chapman speak out loud and bold:
Then felt I like some watcher of the skies
When a new planet swims into his ken;   10
Or like stout Cortez when with eagle eyes
He stared at the Pacific—and all his men
Looked at each other with a wild surmise—
Silent, upon a peak in Darien.

EXERCISE:

The poet is here attempting to describe the effect made upon
him by his first reading of the translation of Homer by Chapman,
the Elizabethan poet and dramatist. May it be said that the
real statement of the poem is not made except by the last two
images? Analyze as carefully as possible the appropriateness of
these two images.

on death of Keats

ADONAIS

PERCY BYSSHE SHELLEY (1792–1822)

I weep for Adonais—he is dead!
O, weep for Adonais! though our tears
Thaw not the frost which binds so dear a head!
And thou, sad Hour, selected from all years
To mourn our loss, rouse thy obscure compeers,   5
And teach them thine own sorrow! Say: "With me
Died Adonais; till the Future dares
Forget the Past, his fate and fame shall be
An echo and a light unto eternity!"

Where wert thou, mighty Mother, when he lay,   10
When thy Son lay, pierced by the shaft which flies
In darkness? where was lorn Urania
When Adonais died?   With veilèd eyes,
'Mid listening Echoes, in her Paradise
She sate, while one, with soft enamored breath,   15
Rekindled all the fading melodies,
With which, like flowers that mock the corse beneath,
He had adorned and hid the coming bulk of death.

O, weep for Adonais—he is dead!
Wake, melancholy Mother, wake and weep!   20
Yet wherefore?   Quench within their burning bed
Thy fiery tears, and let thy loud heart keep
Like his, a mute and uncomplaining sleep;
For he is gone, where all things wise and fair
Descend;—oh, dream not that the amorous Deep   25
Will yet restore him to the vital air;
Death feeds on his mute voice, and laughs at our despair.

Most musical of mourners, weep again!
Lament anew, Urania!—He died,—
Who was the Sire of an immortal strain,   30
Blind, old, and lonely, when his country's pride,
The priest, the slave, and the liberticide,
Trampled and mocked with many a loathèd rite
Of lust and blood; he went, unterrified,
Into the gulf of death; but his clear Sprite   35
Yet reigns o'er earth; the third among the sons of light.

Most musical of mourners, weep anew!
Not all to that bright station dared to climb;
And happier they their happiness who knew,
Whose tapers yet burn through that night of time   40
In which suns perished; others more sublime,
Struck by the envious wrath of man or God,
Have sunk, extinct in their refulgent prime;
And some yet live, treading the thorny road,
Which leads, through toil and hate, to Fame's serene abode.

But now, thy youngest, dearest one has perished.   46
The nursling of thy widowhood, who grew,
Like a pale flower by some sad maiden cherished,

And fed with true love tears, instead of dew;
Most musical of mourners, weep anew! 50
Thy extreme hope, the loveliest and the last,
The bloom, whose petals, nipped before they blew,
Died on the promise of the fruit, is waste;
The broken lily lies—the storm is over-past.

To that high Capital, where kingly Death 55
Keeps his pale court in beauty and decay,
He came; and bought, with price of purest breath,
A grave among the eternal.—Come away!
Haste, while the vault of blue Italian day
Is yet his fitting charnel-roof! while still 60
He lies, as if in dewy sleep he lay;
Awake him not! surely he takes his fill
Of deep and liquid rest, forgetful of all ill.

He will awake no more, oh, never more!—
Within the twilight chamber spreads apace, 65
The shadow of white Death, and at the door
Invisible Corruption waits to trace
His extreme way to her dim dwelling-place;
The eternal Hunger sits, but pity and awe
Soothe her pale rage, nor dares she to deface 70
So fair a prey, till darkness, and the law
Of change, shall o'er his sleep the mortal curtain draw.

O, weep for Adonais!—The quick Dreams,
The passion-wingèd Ministers of thought,
Who were his flocks, whom near the living streams 75
Of his young spirit he fed, and whom he taught
The love which was its music, wander not,—
Wander no more, from kindling brain to brain,
But droop there, whence they sprung; and mourn their lot
Round the cold heart, where, after their sweet pain, 80
They ne'er will gather strength, or find a home again.

And one with trembling hands clasps his cold head,
And fans him with her moonlight wings, and cries:
"Our love, our hope, our sorrow, is not dead;
See, on the silken fringe of his faint eyes, 85
Like dew upon a sleeping flower, there lies

A tear some Dream has loosened from his brain."
Lost Angel of a ruined Paradise!
She knew not 't was her own; as with no stain
She faded, like a cloud which had outwept its rain.   90

One from a lucid urn of starry dew
Washed his light limbs as if embalming them;
Another clipped her profuse locks, and threw
The wreath upon him, like an anadem,
Which frozen tears instead of pearls begem;   95
Another in her wilful grief would break
Her bow and wingèd reeds, as if to stem
A greater loss with one which was more weak;
And dull the barbèd fire against his frozen cheek.

Another Splendor on his mouth alit,   100
That mouth, whence it was wont to draw the breath
Which gave it strength to pierce the guarded wit,
And pass into the panting heart beneath
With lightning and with music: the damp death
Quenched its caress upon his icy lips;   105
And, as a dying meteor stains a wreath
Of moonlight vapor, which the cold night clips,
It flushed through his pale limbs, and passed to its eclipse.

And others came . . . Desires and Adorations,
Wingèd Persuasions and veiled Destinies,   110
Splendors, and Glooms, and glimmering Incarnations
Of hopes and fears, and twilight Phantasies;
And Sorrow, with her family of Sighs,
And Pleasure, blind with tears, led by the gleam
Of her own dying smile instead of eyes,   115
Came in slow pomp;—the moving pomp might seem
Like pageantry of mist on an autumnal stream.

All he had loved, and molded into thought,
From shape, and hue, and odor, and sweet sound,
Lamented Adonais.   Morning sought   120
Her eastern watch-tower, and her hair unbound.
Wet with the tears which should adorn the ground,
Dimmed the aërial eyes that kindle day;
Afar the melancholy thunder moaned,

    Pale Ocean in unquiet slumber lay,   125
And the wild winds flew round, sobbing in their dismay.

    Lost Echo sits amid the voiceless mountains,
    And feeds her grief with his remembered lay,
    And will no more reply to winds or fountains,
    Or amorous birds perched on the young green spray,   130
    Or herdsman's horn, or bell at closing day;
    Since she can mimic not his lips, more dear
    Than those for whose disdain she pined away
    Into a shadow of all sounds;—a drear
Murmur, between their songs, is all the woodmen hear.   135

    Grief made the young Spring wild, and she threw down
    Her kindling buds, as if she Autumn were,
    Or they dead leaves; since her delight is flown,
    For whom should she have waked the sullen year?
    To Phœbus was not Hyacinth so dear   140
    Nor to himself Narcissus, as to both
    Thou, Adonais: wan they stand and sere
    Amid the faint companions of their youth,
With dew all turned to tears; odor, to sighing ruth.

    Thy spirit's sister, the lorn nightingale,   145
    Mourns not her mate with such melodious pain;
    Not so the eagle, who like thee could scale
    Heaven, and could nourish in the sun's domain
    Her mighty youth with morning, doth complain,
    Soaring and screaming round her empty nest,   150
    As Albion wails for thee: the curse of Cain
    Light on his head who pierced thy innocent breast,
And scared the angel soul that was its earthly guest!

    Ah, woe is me! Winter is come and gone,
    But grief returns with the revolving year;   155
    The airs and streams renew their joyous tone;
    The ants, the bees, the swallows reappear;
    Fresh leaves and flowers deck the dead Seasons' bier;
    The amorous birds now pair in every brake,
    And build their mossy homes in field and brere;   160
    And the green lizard, and the golden snake,
Like unimprisoned flames, out of their trance awake.

Through wood and stream and field and hill and Ocean
A quickening life from the Earth's heart has burst,
As it has ever done, with change and motion   165
From the great morning of the world when first
God dawned on Chaos; in its stream immersed
The lamps of Heaven flash with a softer light;
All baser things pant with life's sacred thirst;
Diffuse themselves; and spend in love's delight   170
The beauty and the joy of their renewèd might.

The leprous corpse touched by this spirit tender
Exhales itself in flowers of gentle breath;
Like incarnations of the stars, when splendor
Is changed to fragrance, they illumine death   175
And mock the merry worm that wakes beneath;
Naught we know, dies. Shall that alone which knows
Be as a sword consumed before the sheath
By sightless lightning?—the intense atom glows
A moment, then is quenched in a most cold repose.   180

Alas! that all we loved of him should be,
But for our grief, as if it had not been
And grief itself be mortal! Woe is me!
Whence are we, and why are we? of what scene
The actors or spectators? Great and mean   185
Meet massed in death, who lends what life must borrow.
As long as skies are blue, and fields are green,
Evening must usher night, night urge the morrow,
Month follow month with woe, and year wake year to sor-
row.

He will awake no more, oh, never more!   190
"Wake thou," cried Misery, "childless Mother, rise
Out of thy sleep, and slake, in thy heart's core,
A wound more fierce than his with tears and sighs."
And all the Dreams that watched Urania's eyes,
And all the Echoes whom their sister's song   195
Had held in holy silence, cried: "Arise!"
Swift as a Thought by the snake Memory stung,
From her ambrosial rest the fading Splendor sprung.

She rose like an autumnal Night, that springs
Out of the East, and follows wild and drear   200

The golden Day, which, on eternal wings,
Even as a ghost abandoning a bier,
Had left the Earth a corpse. Sorrow and fear
So struck, so roused, so rapt Urania;
So saddened round her like an atmosphere   205
Of stormy mist; so swept her on her way
Even to the mournful place where Adonais lay.

Out of her secret Paradise she sped,
Through camps and cities rough with stone and steel,
And human hearts, which to her aëry tread   210
Yielding not, wounded the invisible
Palms of her tender feet where'er they fell:
And barbèd tongues, and thoughts more sharp than they,
Rent the soft Form they never could repel,
Whose sacred blood, like the young tears of May,   215
Paved with eternal flowers that undeserving way.

In the death chamber for a moment Death,
Shamed by the presence of that living Might,
Blushed to annihilation, and the breath
Revisited those lips, and life's pale light   220
Flashed through those limbs, so late her dear delight.
"Leave me not wild and drear and comfortless,
As silent lightning leaves the starless night!
Leave me not!" cried Urania: her distress
Roused Death: Death rose and smiled, and met her vain
    caress.   225

"Stay yet awhile! speak to me once again;
Kiss me, so long but as a kiss may live;
And in my heartless breast and burning brain
That word, that kiss shall all thoughts else survive,
With food of saddest memory kept alive,   230
Now thou art dead, as if it were a part
Of thee, my Adonais! I would give
All that I am to be as thou now art!
But I am chained to Time, and cannot thence depart!

"Oh gentle child, beautiful as thou wert,   235
Why didst thou leave the trodden paths of men
Too soon, and with weak hands though mighty heart

Dare the unpastured dragon in his den?
Defenceless as thou wert, oh, where was then
Wisdom the mirrored shield, or scorn the spear?   240
Or hadst thou waited the full cycle, when
Thy spirit should have filled its crescent sphere,
The monsters of life's waste had fled from thee like deer.

"The herded wolves, bold only to pursue;
The obscene ravens, clamorous o'er the dead;   245
The vultures to the conqueror's banner true,
Who feed where Desolation first has fed
And whose wings rain contagion;—how they fled,
When like Apollo, from his golden bow,
The Pythian of the age one arrow sped   250
And smiled!—The spoilers tempt no second blow;
They fawn on the proud feet that spurn them lying low.

"The sun comes forth, and many reptiles spawn;
He sets, and each ephemeral insect then
Is gathered into death without a dawn,   255
And the immortal stars awake again;
So is it in the world of living men:
A godlike mind soars forth, in its delight
Making earth bare and veiling heaven, and when
It sinks, the swarms that dimmed or shared its light 260
Leave to its kindred lamps the spirit's awful night."

Thus ceased she: and the mountain shepherds came,
Their garlands sere, their magic mantles rent;
The Pilgrim of Eternity, whose fame   265
Over his living head like Heaven is bent,
An early but enduring monument,
Came, veiling all the lightnings of his song
In sorrow: from her wilds Ierne sent
The sweetest lyrist of her saddest wrong,
And love taught grief to fall like music from his tongue. 270

Midst others of less note, came one frail Form,
A phantom among men, companionless
As the last cloud of an expiring storm
Whose thunder is its knell; he, as I guess,
Had gazed on Nature's naked loveliness,   275

Actæon-like, and now he fled astray
With feeble steps o'er the world's wilderness,
And his own thoughts, along that rugged way,
Pursued, like raging hounds, their father and their prey.

A pardlike Spirit beautiful and swift—   280
A Love in desolation masked;—a Power
Girt round with weakness—it can scarce uplift
The weight of the superincumbent hour;
It is a dying lamp, a falling shower,
A breaking billow;—even whilst we speak   285
Is it not broken? On the withering flower
The killing sun smiles brightly; on a cheek
The life can burn in blood, even while the heart may break.

His head was bound with pansies overblown,
And faded violets, white, and pied, and blue;   290
And a light spear topped with a cypress cone,
Round whose rude shaft dark ivy tresses grew
Yet dripping with the forest's noonday dew,
Vibrated, as the ever-beating heart
Shook the weak hand that grasped it; of that crew   295
He came the last, neglected and apart;
A herd-abandoned deer, struck by the hunter's dart.

All stood aloof, and at his partial moan
Smiled through their tears; well knew that gentle band
Who in another's fate now wept his own;   300
As, in the accents of an unknown land,
He sung new sorrow; sad Urania scanned
The Stranger's mien, and murmured: "Who art thou?"
He answered not, but with a sudden hand
Made bare his branded and ensanguined brow,   305
Which was like Cain's or Christ's—Oh! that it should be so!

What softer voice is hushed over the dead?
Athwart what brow is that dark mantle thrown?
What form leans sadly o'er the white death-bed,
In mockery of monumental stone,   310
The heavy heart heaving without a moan?
If it be He, who, gentlest of the wise,
Taught, soothed, loved, honored the departed one,

Let me not vex with inharmonious sighs
The silence of that heart's accepted sacrifice.   315

Our Adonais has drunk poison—oh!
What deaf and viperous murderer could crown
Life's early cup with such a draught of woe?
The nameless worm would now itself disown:
It felt yet could escape the magic tone   320
Whose prelude held all envy, hate, and wrong,
But what was howling in one breast alone,
Silent with expectation of the song,
Whose master's hand is cold, whose silver lyre unstrung.

Live thou, whose infamy is not thy fame!   325
Live! fear no heavier chastisement from me,
Thou noteless blot on a remembered name!
But be thyself, and know thyself to be!
And ever at thy season be thou free
To spill the venom when thy fangs o'erflow: 330
Remorse and Self-contempt shall cling to thee;
Hot Shame shall burn upon thy secret brow,
And like a beaten hound tremble thou shalt—as now.

Nor let us weep that our delight is fled
Far from these carrion kites that scream below;   335
He wakes or sleeps with the enduring dead;
Thou canst not soar where he is sitting now.—
Dust to the dust! but the pure spirit shall flow
Back to the burning fountain whence it came,
A portion of the Eternal, which must glow   340
Through time and change, unquenchably the same,
Whilst thy cold embers choke the sordid hearth of shame.

Peace, peace! he is not dead, he doth not sleep—
He hath awakened from the dream of life—
'T is we who, lost in stormy visions, keep   345
With phantoms an unprofitable strife,
And in mad trance strike with our spirit's knife
Invulnerable nothings.—*We* decay
Like corpses in a charnel; fear and grief
Convulse us and consume us day by day,   350
And cold hopes swarm like worms within our living clay.

He has outsoared the shadow of our night;
Envy and calumny and hate and pain,
And that unrest which men miscall delight,
Can touch him not and torture not again;   355
From the contagion of the world's slow stain
He is secure, and now can never mourn
A heart grown cold, a head grown gray in vain;
Nor, when the spirit's self has ceased to burn,
With sparkless ashes load an unlamented urn.   360

He lives, he wakes—'t is Death is dead, not he;
Mourn not for Adonais.—Thou young Dawn,
Turn all thy dew to splendor, for from thee
The spirit thou lamentest is not gone;
Ye caverns and ye forests, cease to moan!   365
Cease, ye faint flowers and fountains, and thou Air,
Which like a mourning veil thy scarf hadst thrown
O'er the abandoned Earth, now leave it bare
Even to the joyous stars which smile on its despair!

He is made one with Nature: there is heard   370
His voice in all her music, from the moan
Of thunder, to the song of night's sweet bird;
He is a presence to be felt and known
In darkness and in light, from herb and stone,
Spreading itself where'er that Power may move   375
Which has withdrawn his being to its own;
Which wields the world with never wearied love,
Sustains it from beneath, and kindles it above.

He is a portion of the loveliness
Which once he made more lovely: he doth bear   380
His part, while the one Spirit's plastic stress
Sweeps through the dull dense world, compelling there
All new successions to the forms they wear;
Torturing the unwilling dross that checks its flight
To its own likeness, as each mass may bear;   385
And bursting in its beauty and its might
From trees and beasts and men into the Heaven's light.

The splendors of the firmament of time
May be eclipsed, but are extinguished not;

Like stars to their appointed height they climb   390
And death is a low mist which cannot blot
The brightness it may veil. When lofty thought
Lifts a young heart above its mortal lair,
And love and life contend in it, for what
Shall be its earthly doom, the dead live there   395

And move like winds of light on dark and stormy air.
   The inheritors of unfulfilled renown
   Rose from their thrones, built beyond mortal thought,
   Far in the Unapparent. Chatterton
   Rose pale, his solemn agony had not   400
   Yet faded from him; Sidney, as he fought
   And as he fell and as he lived and loved,
   Sublimely mild, a Spirit without spot,
   Arose; and Lucan, by his death approved:
Oblivion, as they rose, shrank like a thing reproved.   405

   And many more, whose names on Earth are dark
   But whose transmitted effluence cannot die
   So long as fire outlives the parent spark,
   Rose, robed in dazzling immortality.
   "Thou art become as one of us," they cry,   410
   "It was for thee yon kingless sphere has long
   Swung blind in unascended majesty,
   Silent alone amid an Heaven of Song.
Assume thy wingèd throne, thou Vesper of our throng!"

   Who mourns for Adonais? oh, come forth,   415
   Fond wretch! and know thyself and him aright.
   Clasp with thy panting soul the pendulous Earth;
   As from a center, dart thy spirit's light
   Beyond all worlds, until its spacious might
   Satiate the void circumference: then shrink   420
   Even to a point within our day and night;
   And keep thy heart light, lest it make thee sink,
When hope has kindled hope, and lured thee to the brink.

   Or go to Rome, which is the sepulcher,
   O, not of him, but of our joy: 't is naught   425
   That ages, empires, and religions there
   Lie buried in the ravage they have wrought;
   For such as he can lend,—they borrow not

Glory from those who made the world their prey;
And he is gathered to the kings of thought 430
Who waged contention with their time's decay,
And of the past are all that cannot pass away.

Go thou to Rome,—at once the Paradise,
The grave, the city, and the wilderness;
And where its wrecks like shattered mountains rise 435
And flowering weeds and fragrant copses dress
The bones of Desolation's nakedness
Pass, till the Spirit of the spot shall lead
Thy footsteps to a slope of green access
Where, like an infant's smile, over the dead, 440
A light of laughing flowers along the grass is spread.

And gray walls moulder round, on which dull Time
Feeds, like slow fire upon a hoary brand;
And one keen pyramid with wedge sublime,
Pavilioning the dust of him who planned 445
This refuge for his memory, doth stand
Like flame transformed to marble; and beneath,
A field is spread, on which a newer band
Have pitched in Heaven's smile their camp of death,
Welcoming him we lose with scarce extinguished breath.

Here pause: these graves are all too young as yet 451
To have outgrown the sorrow which consigned
Its charge to each; and if the seal is set,
Here, on one fountain of a mourning mind,
Break it not thou! too surely shalt thou find 455
Thine own well full, if thou returnest home,
Of tears and gall. From the world's bitter wind
Seek shelter in the shadow of the tomb.
What Adonais is, why fear we to become?

The One remains, the many change and pass; 460
Heaven's light forever shines, Earth's shadows fly;
Life, like a dome of many-colored glass,
Stains the white radiance of Eternity,
Until Death tramples it to fragments.—Die,
If thou wouldst be with that which thou dost seek! 465
Follow where all is fled!—Rome's azure sky,

Flowers, ruins, statues, music, words, are weak
The glory they transfuse with fitting truth to speak.

Why linger? why turn back, why shrink, my Heart?
Thy hopes are gone before: from all things here   470
They have departed; thou shouldst now depart!
A light is past from the revolving year,
And man, and woman; and what still is dear
Attracts to crush, repels to make thee wither.
The soft sky smiles,—the low wind whispers near;   475
'T is Adonais calls! oh, hasten thither,
No more let Life divide what Death can join together.

That Light whose smile kindles the Universe,
That Beauty in which all things work and move,
That Benediction which the eclipsing Curse   480
Of birth can quench not, that sustaining Love
Which, through the web of being blindly wove
By man and beast and earth and air and sea,
Burns bright or dim, as each are mirrors of
The fire for which all thirst, now beams on me,   485
Consuming the last clouds of cold mortality.

The breath whose might I have invoked in song
Descends on me; my spirit's bark is driven,
Far from the shore, far from the trembling throng
Whose sails were never to the tempest given;   490
The massy earth and spherèd skies are riven!
I am borne darkly, fearfully, afar:
Whilst burning through the inmost veil of Heaven,
The soul of Adonais, like a star,
Beacons from the abode where the Eternal are.   495

EXERCISE:

1. This is a *pastoral elegy* (*Glossary*) written on the death of
John Keats. In the course of the poem various other poets, living
and dead, are mentioned: Milton (line 28), Byron (line 264),
Thomas Moore (line 269), Shelley himself (line 271), Leigh
Hunt (line 307), Chatterton, another poet who had died young
(line 399), Philip Sidney (line 401), and the young Latin poet,
Lucan (line 404). Shelley also refers (line 244 and, later, line

319) to the critics who had attacked the work of Keats, and whom Shelley considered responsible for the death of Keats. (Consult the library on this general question.)   What is gained by presenting these persons under the guises used by Shelley?

2. What is Shelley's attitude toward Keats?   Toward himself? How can one account for the selection of the imagery in these terms?

3. Does the poem possess unity?   What part does the imagery play in unifying the poem?

4. What changes of tone occur in the poem?

5. Try to analyze carefully the imagery in the section from line 460 to line 465.   Does the imagery of the last stanza serve to summarize the effect of the poem?

VIRTUE

GEORGE HERBERT (1593–1633)

Sweet day, so cool, so calm, so bright,
    The bridal of the earth and sky!
The dew shall weep thy fall to-night;
    For thou must die.

Sweet rose, whose hue, angry and brave,   5
    Bids the rash gazer wipe his eye,
Thy root is ever in its grave,
    And thou must die.

Sweet spring, full of sweet days and roses,
    A box where sweets compacted lie,   10
My music shows ye have your closes,
    And all must die.

Only a sweet and virtuous soul,
    Like seasoned timber, never gives;
But though the whole world turn to coal,   15
    Then chiefly lives.

EXERCISE:

1. The use of the imagery in the first and second stanzas is perfectly obvious and, indeed, might be considered trite (compare "To Blossoms," p. 367 and "The Blossom," p. 368). How is the imagery developed in the third and fourth stanzas?

2. What use does the poet make of the stanza form? Notice especially the function of the short last line of each stanza.

3. Investigate the quantitative effects in the poem.

4. Comment on the implications of the following words: *angry, brave, rash,* and *compacted*. (Notice that the word *brave* is used in two senses. Consult the library for the meaning of the word *brave* in the seventeenth century.)

THE NIGHT

John 3: 2

HENRY VAUGHAN (1622–1695)

Through that pure virgin-shrine,
That sacred veil drawn o'er thy glorious noon
That men might look and live as glow-worms shine,
    And face the moon:
  Wise Nicodemus saw such light   5
  As made him know his God by night.

  Most blest believer he!
Who in that land of darkness and blind eyes
Thy long-expected healing wings could see,
    When thou didst rise,   10
  And what can never more be done,
  Did at midnight speak with the Sun!

  O who will tell me, where
He found thee at that dead and silent hour!
What hallowed solitary ground did bear   15
    So rare a flower,
  Within whose sacred leaves did lie
  The fullness of the Deity.

No mercy-seat of .gold,
No dead and dusty cherub, nor carved stone,   20
But his own living works did my Lord hold
   And lodge alone;
  Where trees and herbs did watch and peep
  And wonder, while the Jews did sleep.

  Dear night! this world's defeat;   25
The stop to busy fools; care's check and curb;
The day of spirits; my soul's calm retreat
   Which none disturb!
  Christ's progress, and his prayer time;
  The hours to which high heaven doth chime.   30

  God's silent, searching flight:
When my Lord's head is filled with dew, and all
His locks are wet with the clear drops of night;
   His still, soft call;
  His knocking time; the soul's dumb watch,   35
  Where spirits their fair kindred catch.

  Were all my loud, evil days
Calm and unhaunted as is thy dark tent,
Whose peace but by some angel's wing or voice
   Is seldom rent;   40
  Then I in heaven all the long year
  Would keep, and never wander here.

  But living where the sun
Doth all things wake, and where all mix and tire
Themselves and others, I consent and run   45
   To every mire,
  And by this world's ill-guiding light,
  Err more than I can do by night.

  There is in God (some say)
A deep, but dazzling darkness; as men here   50
Say it is late and dusky, because they
   See not all clear;
  O for that night! where I in Him
  Might live invisible and dim.

Exercise:

Write a full analysis, considering among other things the following aspects of the poem:

1. The extension of the paradox involving the image of night throughout the poem.

2. The use made of the short fourth line and the concluding couplet of the stanza form.

3. An account of the metrical situation in line 20, and of the use of enjambment in stanzas 3, 8, and 9.

4. The shifts of tone in stanzas 8 and 9.

5. The use of alliteration in the last stanza in emphasizing the paradox and in focusing the attention on the climactic word *dim,* which also involves that paradox.

SWEET LOVE, RENEW THY FORCE

WILLIAM SHAKESPEARE (1564–1616)

Sweet love, renew thy force; be it not said
Thy edge should blunter be than appetite,
Which but today by feeding is allayed,
Tomorrow sharpened in his former might
So, love, be thou; although today thou fill   5
Thy hungry eyes, even till they wink with fulness,
Tomorrow see again, and do not kill
The spirit of love with a perpetual dulness.
Let this sad interim like the ocean be
Which parts the shore, where two contracted new   10
Come daily to the banks, that, when they see
Return of love, more blessed may be the view;
　　Or call it winter, which, being full of care,
　　Makes summer's welcome thrice more wished, more rare.

Exercise:

Observe how the poet uses comparisons involving the edge of an instrument and appetite in order to define the structure of the poem.

ASIA'S SONG

PERCY BYSSHE SHELLEY (1792–1822)

My soul is an enchanted boat,
Which, like a sleeping swan, doth float
Upon the silver waves of thy sweet singing;
And thine doth like an angel sit
Beside a helm conducting it,   5
Whilst all the winds with melody are ringing.
It seems to float ever, for ever,
Upon that many-winding river,
Between mountains, woods, abysses,
A paradise of wildernesses!   10
Till, like one in slumber bound,
Borne to the ocean, I float down, around,
Into a sea profound, of ever-spreading sound:

Meanwhile thy spirit lifts its pinions
In music's most serene dominions;   15
Catching the winds that fan that happy heaven.
And we sail on, away, afar,
Without a course, without a star,
But, by the instinct of sweet music driven;
Till through Elysian garden islets   20
By thee, most beautiful of pilots,
Where never mortal pinnace glided,
The boat of my desire is guided:
Realms where the air we breathe is love,
Which in the winds and on the waves doth move,   25
Harmonizing this earth with what we feel above.

We have passed Age's icy caves,
And Manhood's dark and tossing waves,
And Youth's smooth ocean, smiling to betray:
Beyond the glassy gulfs we flee   30
Of shadow-peopled Infancy,
Through Death and Birth, to a diviner day;
A paradise of vaulted bowers,
Lit by downward-gazing flowers,
And watery paths that wind between   35
Wilderness calm and green,

Peopled by shapes too bright to see,
And rest, having beheld; somewhat like thee;
Which walk upon the sea, and chant melodiously!

(From *Prometheus Unbound*)

EXERCISE:

Compare the unification of imagery here with that in "The Night" (p. 432).

THE DEFINITION OF LOVE

ANDREW MARVELL (1621–1678)

*a b a b
iambic tetrameter*

My love is of a birth as rare
As 'tis for object strange and high:
It was begotten by Despair
Upon Impossibility.

Magnanimous Despair alone   5
Could show me so divine a thing,
Where feeble Hope could ne'er have flown
But vainly flapped its tinsel wing.

And yet I quickly might arrive
Where my extended soul is fixed,   10
But Fate does iron wedges drive,
And always crowds itself betwixt.

For Fate with jealous eye does see
Two perfect loves, nor lets them close:
Their union would her ruin be,   15
And her tyrannic power depose.

And therefore her decrees of steel
Us as the distant poles have placed,
(Though love's whole world on us doth wheel)
Not by themselves to be embraced,   20

Unless the giddy heaven fall,
And earth some new convulsion tear,
And, us to join, the world should all
Be cramped into a planisphere.

> As lines, so loves oblique may well   25
> Themselves in every angle greet;
> But ours, so truly parallel,
> Though infinite, can never meet.
>
> Therefore the love which us doth bind,
> But fate so enviously debars,   30
> Is the conjunction of the mind,
> And opposition of the stars.

This poem deals with a subject which may seem at first glance too narrow to afford very much scope, and which would seem to afford little opportunity to say anything very fresh and new. The intensity of one's love is surely a conventional enough theme. The poet might easily, in handling such a subject, fail to convey the sense of the intensity, or, in attempting to convey it, might easily overwrite his poem and find himself betrayed into hollow sounding exaggeration or embarrassing sentimentality, as in the case of "The Indian Serenade" (p. 319). This is the problem which the poet faces here. The solution which he makes is not the only solution, of course. It is only one of the many possible solutions, as the great number of fine poems on the same theme will indicate, but a close examination of it may tell us a great deal about the use of imagery. For it is largely in terms of his imagery that this poet presents the complex and rich experience which the poem embodies.

The poet begins by stating the matter in terms of a paradox, and the shock of this paradox—the sharp break which it makes with the stale and conventional in general—allows him to state with no sense of overfacile, glib exaggeration that

> My love is of a birth as rare
> As 'tis for object strange and high:

The first word of the second stanza enforces the paradox. It lets us know that the poet is going to stand by his paradox. Despair is not *grim* or *harsh* or *cruel,* as one would anticipate, but *magnanimous.* His love is too divine to have been hoped for—it could only have been shown to him by Despair itself.

Already the paradox has done something more than startle us out of an accustomed attitude; but the startling paradox is only a device to lead one to grasp the poet's attitude which is an attitude complex enough to perceive a magnanimity in the very hopelessness of attaining his love since only that hopelessness allows him to see the true and ideal character of his love.

The poet now proceeds to develop this paradox through the remainder of the poem. The development is made largely in terms of images.

It is nothing less than fate that separates him from his love—but again the poet provides us with a concrete image: Fate drives iron wedges between them. And the poet, having personified fate—having turned it into a person, provides the person with a motive. Fate itself would cease to exist if any complete perfection might be attained. Their love is so perfect that its consummation would be incompatible with a world ruled over by fate. That this should be prevented from happening is therefore not the result of one of fate's malicious caprices—the character of the love itself determines the "fate."

Notice at this point that the poet's attitude toward fate is not that of hysterical outrage. There is a calm reasoned tone here such as we have already found in the ability to see despair as "magnanimous." And yet this sense of reasonableness has been achieved *in the process* of making statements which ordinarily would seem the most outrageous exaggerations! His love is the highest possible; his love is too divine to be even hoped for. The result is that the statements are felt, not as outrageous statements to be immediately discounted, but as having the weight of reasoned truth.

In the fifth stanza the major paradox is given a particularly rich statement by means of the use of an unusually fine figure. Fate has placed the two lovers as far apart as the poles. "As far apart as the poles" seems at first merely the conventional expression which we use to indicate great distance apart. But the poet immediately seizes on the implied figure and develops it for us. The two lovers are, like the poles of the earth, unable to touch each other; but though they are separated by the distance of the entire globe, they are the focal points in determining the rotation of the earth. Thus, the lovers, though separated, define the ideal nature of love. The world of love, like a globe, turns on the axis of their relationship. The exactness of the comparison gives force to his statement, and Marvell further stresses the exactness of the relationship between his own situation and the figure which he uses to illustrate it, by going on to state the only condition on which the poles might be united. The poles might be united only if the earth were suddenly compressed into a two dimensional disc which would have no thickness at all— that is, into a *planisphere*. The associations of a technical word again support the sense of exact, calculated statement in the poem. The poet continues to expound the incredible nature of his love with the poise of a mathematician. Therefore we are more readily inclined to accept the statement.

The technical word also prepares somewhat perhaps for the figure which the poet uses in the seventh stanza. Loves "oblique," the loves of those who are not in perfect accord, are like lines which cross each other at an angle. Their very lack of parallelism forms the possibility of their meeting. His own love and that of his mistress accord with each other so perfectly that, though stretched to infinity, they could draw no nearer together. In this image, then, the poet finds exactly the illustration of the paradoxical relationship of which he is writing. The application of this image is made easier by the ordinary association of the idea of infinity with the idea of love; it is a conventional association in love poetry. But Marvell has taken the conventional association and, by developing it, has derived a renewed life and freshness.

The poem closes with another paradox, this time drawn from astrology. We say that stars are in *conjunction* when they are seen in the sky very close together; that they are in *opposition* when they are situated in opposite parts of the sky. According to astrology, moreover, planets in conjunction unite their influences. In opposition they fight against each other. Here the lovers' minds are in conjunction. They are united, but their stars (fate) are against them. This concluding comparison, then, combines the idea of the third and fourth stanza with that of the fifth and sixth. In a way, it epitomizes the whole poem.

Is the poem merely an ingenious bundle of paradoxes? Some
readers may dislike the very active play of the mind here, and
will dislike also the exactness of the diction, and the imagery
drawn from mathematics and kindred subjects. But does this
ingenuity and exactness make the poem insincere? Does it
not have indeed the opposite effect? The lover protesting his
love is too often vague and rhetorical. He gives a sense of glib-
ness and effusiveness. The effect of Marvell's imagery is not
only one of freshness as opposed to stale conventionality—it is
also one of calculation as opposed to one of unthinking excitement.

MY SPRINGS

SIDNEY LANIER (1842–1881)

In the heart of the Hills of Life, I know
Two springs that with unbroken flow
Forever pour their lucent streams
Into my soul's far Lake of Dreams.

Not larger than two eyes, they lie   5
Beneath the many-changing sky
And mirror all of life and time,
—Serene and dainty pantomime.

Shot through with lights of stars and dawns,
And shadowed sweet by ferns and fawns,   10
—Thus heaven and earth together vie
Their shining depths to sanctify.

Always when the large Form of Love
Is hid by storms that rage above,
I gaze in my two springs and see   15
Love in his verity.

Always when Faith with stifling stress
Of grief hath died in bitterness,
I gaze in my two springs and see
A faith that smiles immortally.   20

Always when Charity and Hope,
In darkness bounden, feebly grope,
I gaze in my two springs and see
A Light that sets my captives free.

Always when Art on perverse wing   25
Flies where I cannot hear him sing,
I gaze in my two springs and see
A charm that brings him back to me.

When Labor faints, and Glory fails,
And coy Reward in sighs exhales,   30
I gaze in my two springs and see
Attainment full and heavenly.

O Love, O Wife, thine eyes are they,
—My springs from out whose shining gray
Issue the sweet celestial streams   35
That feed my life's bright Lake of Dreams.

Oval and large and passion-pure
And gray and wise and honor-sure;
Soft as a dying violet-breath
Yet calmly unafraid of death;   40

Thronged, like two dove-cotes of gray doves,
With wife's and mother's and poor-folk's loves,
And home-loves and high glory-loves
And science-loves and story-loves,

And loves for all that God and man   45
In art and nature make or plan,
And lady-loves for spidery lace
And broideries and supple grace

And diamonds and the whole sweet round
Of littles that large life compound,   50
And loves for God and God's bare truth,
And loves for Magdalen and Ruth,

Dear eyes, dear eyes and rare complete—
Being heavenly-sweet and earthly-sweet,
—I marvel that God made you mine,   55
For when He frowns, 'tis then ye shine!

This poem by Sidney Lanier would probably be regarded as a sentimental poem by most experienced readers of poetry. It appears sentimental because it insists on more response than the reader feels is justified by the occasion as presented in the poem. The poem is, therefore, extravagant. We know that, as a matter of fact, a very great devotion existed between Sidney Lanier and his wife, and that she was a constant source of comfort to him in his struggles against poverty and illness. *But the mere fact that we know of this relationship between the poet and his wife does not necessarily redeem the poem from the charge of sentimentality, for a poem must be able to achieve its effect without reference to the biographical facts behind its composition.*

Sentimentality often makes itself felt as a kind of strain, a strain on the part of the writer to convince the reader that he should respond in such and such a way. In this poem the strain most clearly manifests itself in the use the poet makes of imagery. In the discussion of "The Pilgrims" (p. 334), it was said that the clichés of phrase and idea indicate a sentimental approach, the lack of any attempt on the part of the poet to investigate the real possibilities of the subject, the poet's unconscious dependence on some sort of stock response in the reader. Both of these defects may indicate sentimentality, for both imply an attempt to get a response not justified in the poem itself. But let us try to study the nature of the imagery in Lanier's poem.

The first nine stanzas are constructed about one basic image, that of the springs, and the next four about another, that of the doves in a dove-cote. Now the image of the eyes as springs is given a kind of geographical location on an imaginary landscape. The springs (the eyes) are located, says the poet, in the midst of the Hills of Life, and by their overflow keep full the Lake of Dreams of the poet's soul. Is there any basis for what we might call the construction of this little piece of poetic landscape? Does anything really bind its parts together? The poet apparently means by the Hills of Life the difficulties that beset him. He has taken an abstraction, the general idea of difficulties, and has in his poem made it equivalent to the concrete objects, hills. This is really a cliché, but the poet has tried to save the comparison by giving it a relationship to the Springs.

The comparison of eyes to pools or springs, however, is another cliché, equally dull. These two worn-out images could be given new strength only if the relationship established between them were really expressive and imaginatively justifiable. (We have seen how Marvell succeeded in such an attempt in "The Definition of Love.")

But first we may observe that the two images are not arrived at by the same process. That of the hills is an identification of an abstraction (difficulties) with a concrete object (hills); that of the springs is an identification of one concrete object (eyes) with another concrete object (springs). The image of the Lake of Dreams is arrived at by the former process. Yet all of these three images are parts of the same landscape: the springs in the hills overflow into the lake. The reader feels that the poet has arbitrarily put these things together and that they do not really represent an imaginative insight.

There is no particular reason why, for instance, the Dreams should be represented by a lake rather than by any of a dozen other objects except that a lake fits the landscape better. As a matter of fact, as the poem goes on, we discover that the Lake of Dreams is not at all what we presume the poet to mean. In plain prose, the eyes of his wife encourage him in Love, Faith, Charity, Hope, Art, and Ambition. Yet we know that the poet does not mean to say that the things by which he lives, for instance, love, faith, and art, are illusions; he would maintain that they are realities. Or perhaps the poet does not mean the image in this sense; he may mean that the eyes of his wife encourage him to dream of worthwhile things. This is more consistent with the general temper of the poem, but it bears no specific connection with the image itself.

Further, the poet was not really willing to stand by his identification of the eyes with springs, and he proceeds without dealing at all with one important inconsistency implied in the image. The springs, we remember, overflow. The springs are eyes. The most emphatic implication here is that of weeping, which is inconsistent with the meaning the poet has in mind. The poet should have solved this difficulty of implication for the reader or should have abandoned the image. Instead, he ignored the matter, which seems to argue that he himself really was not paying much attention to the full implication of what he was doing. In other words, there is a kind of vagueness here, and a kind of strain.

The personifications, the "Form of Love," "Faith," "Charity," and "Hope," bear no real relation to the scene in which they are put. For instance, how much close investigation can the relation between Charity and the basic scene of the springs, etc. be made to bear. In what darkness are Charity and Hope, personified as real persons, bound? Is there a dungeon or a cave near by? No provision has been made for this in the scene. And how can the Light that the poet sees in the spring set the "captives free?" It would have been perfectly possible for the poet to leap from one image to another in pursuit of his idea, *if he had not insisted on the formal connection between the two images.* For example, in the following passage by Shakespeare there is no attempt to make the series of images logically consistent with each other, and yet the reader's imagination can make the leap from one to the next because each in itself is appropriate:

> To be, or not to be: that is the question:
> Whether 'tis nobler in the mind to suffer
> The slings and arrows of outrageous fortune,
> Or to take arms against a sea of troubles,
> And by opposing end them? To die: to sleep;
> No more; and by a sleep to say we end
> The heart-ache and the thousand natural shocks
> That flesh is heir to. 'Tis a consummation
> Devoutly to be wished.

(From *Hamlet*)

But Lanier does insist on the consistency between the image of Charity and Hope as captives in darkness and that of the springs, etc., because the latter provides the location, as it were, of the former. Therefore, since this consistency is not really inherent in the images employed, we have an effect of strain and artificiality.

The basic image of the eleventh, twelfth, and thirteenth stanzas, the image of the dove-cote and doves, shares the same quality of strain and artificiality. On what basis can we conceive of the love of science ("science-loves") or the love of fine lace ("lady-loves for spidery lace") or the love of fiction and poetry ("story-loves") as gray doves? It is a purely arbitrary equating of the two things. And the image becomes even more arbitrary and more complicated when we conceive, or try to conceive, of those doves in two dove-cotes which are a lady's eyes. If a reader will compare the imagery of this poem with the imagery in most other poems in this collection, he will see that the present poem lacks imagery that is truly functional and expressive, and that the poet by his use of imagery is trying to force a reaction on the reader that is not justified by the material.

SHADOWS IN THE WATER

THOMAS TRAHERNE (1637?–1674)

In unexperienced infancy
Many a sweet mistake doth lie:
Mistake though false, intending true;
A seeming somewhat more than view,
    That doth instruct the mind   5
    In things that lie behind,
And many secrets to us show
Which afterwards we come to know.

Thus did I by the water's brink
Another world beneath me think;   10
And while the lofty spacious skies
Reversèd there abused mine eyes,
    I fancied other feet
    Came mine to touch or meet;
As by some puddle I did play   15
Another world within it lay.

Beneath the water people drowned,
Yet with another heaven crowned,

In spacious regions seemed to go
As freely moving to and fro: 20
  In bright and open space
  I saw their very face;
Eyes, hands, and feet they had like mine;
Another sun did with them shine.

'Twas strange that people there should walk,   25
And yet I could not hear them talk:
That through a little wat'ry chink,
Which one dry ox or horse might drink,
  We other worlds should see,
  Yet not admitted be;   30
And other confines there behold
Of light and darkness, heat and cold.

I called them oft, but called in vain;
No speeches we could entertain:
Yet did I there expect to find   35
Some other world, to please my mind.
  I plainly saw by these
  A new Antipodes,
Whom, though they were so plainly seen,
A film kept off that stood between.   40

By walking men's reversèd feet
I chanced another world to meet;
Though it did not to view exceed
A phantasm, 'tis a world indeed,
  Where skies beneath us shine,   45
  And earth by art divine
Another face presents below,
Where people's feet against ours go.

Within the regions of the air,
Compassed about with heavens fair,   50
Great tracts of land there may be found
Enriched with fields and fertile ground;
  Where many numerous hosts,
  In those far distant coasts,
For other great and glorious ends,   55
Inhabit, my yet unknown friends.

O ye that stand upon the brink,
Whom I so near me, through the chink,
With wonder see: what faces there,
Whose feet, whose bodies, do ye wear?   60
   I my companions see
   In you, another me.
They seemed others, but are we;
Our second selves those shadows be.

Look how far off those lower skies   65
Extend themselves! scarce with mine eyes
I can them reach, O ye my friends,
What secret borders on those ends?
   Are lofty heavens hurled
   'Bout your inferior world?   70
Are ye the representatives
Of other people's distant lives?

Of all the playmates which I knew
That here I do the image view
In other selves; what can it mean   75
But that below the purling stream
   Some unknown joys there be
   Laid up in store for me;
To which I shall, when that thin skin
Is broken, be admitted in.   80

EXERCISE:

Is the elaboration of the incident from childhood successful or
does it grow monotonous? Discuss this question in relation to
the tone of the poem.

THE TEAR

RICHARD CRASHAW (1613?–1649)

What bright soft thing is this,
   Sweet Mary, thy fair eyes' expense?
A moist spark it is,

A wat'ry diamond; from whence
The very term, I think, was found,   5
The water of a diamond.

Oh! 'tis not a tear,
  'Tis a star about to drop
From thine eye, its sphere;
  The Sun will stoop and take it up.   10
Proud will his sister be to wear
This thine eye's jewel in her ear.

Oh! 'tis a tear,
  Too true a tear; for no sad eyne,[1]
How sad soe'er,   15
  Rain so true a tear as thine;
Each drop, leaving a place so dear,
Weeps for itself, is its own tear.

Such a pearl as this is,
  (Slipped from Aurora's dewy breast)   20
The rose-bud's sweet lip kisses;
  And such the rose itself, when vexed
With ungentle flames, does shed,
Sweating in too warm a bed.

Such the maiden gem   25
  By the wanton Spring put on,
Peeps from her parent stem,
  And blushes on the wat'ry Sun:
This wat'ry blossom of thy eyne,
Ripe, will make the richer wine.   30

Fair drop, why quak'st thou so?
  'Cause thou straight must lay thy head
In the dust? Oh no;
  The dust shall never be thy bed:
A pillow for thee will I bring,   35
Stuffed with down of angel's wing.

Thus carried up on high,
  (For to heaven thou must go)

[1] eyes

Sweetly shalt thou lie,
  And in soft slumbers bathe thy woe;   40
Till the singing orbs awake thee,
And one of their bright chorus make thee.

There thyself shalt be
  An eye, but not a weeping one;
Yet I doubt of thee,   45
  Whither thou'dst rather there have shone
An eye of Heaven; or still shine here
In th' Heaven of Mary's eye, a tear.

EXERCISE:

  Criticize the imagery in this poem. Is it too far-fetched?
Does it create an impression of sentimentality? Compare the
imagery of this poem with that of "The Definition of Love."

COME INTO THE GARDEN, MAUD

ALFRED, LORD TENNYSON (1809–1892)

Come into the garden, Maud,
  For the black bat, Night, has flown,
Come into the garden Maud,
  I am here at the gate alone;
And the woodbine spices are wafted abroad,   5
  And the musk of the rose is blown.

For a breeze of morning moves,
  And the planet of Love is on high,
Beginning to faint in the light that she loves
  On a bed of daffodil sky,   10
To faint in the light of the sun she loves,
  To faint in his light and to die.

All night have the roses heard
  The flute, violin, bassoon;
All night has the casement jessamine stirred   15

To the dancers dancing in tune;
Till a silence fell with the waking bird,
And a hush with the setting moon.

I said to the lily, "There is but one
    With whom she has heart to be gay.   20
When will the dancers leave her alone?
    She is weary of dance and play."
Now half to the setting moon are gone,
    And half to the rising day;
Low on the sand and loud on the stone   25
    The last wheel echoes away.

I said to the rose, "The brief night goes
    In babble and revel and wine.
O young lord-lover, what sighs are those
    For one that will never be thine?   30
But mine, but mine," so I sware to the rose,
    "For ever and ever, mine."

And the soul of the rose went into my blood,
    As the music clashed in the hall;
And long by the garden lake I stood,   35
For I heard your rivulet fall
From the lake to the meadow and on to the wood,
    Our wood, that is dearer than all;

From the meadow your walks have left so sweet
    That whenever a March-wind sighs   40
He sets the jewel-print of your feet
    In violets blue as your eyes,
To the woody hollows in which we meet
    And the valleys of Paradise.

The slender acacia would not shake   45
    One long milk-bloom on the tree;
The white lake-blossom fell into the lake,
    As the pimpernel dozed on the lea;
But the rose was awake all night for your sake,
    Knowing your promise to me;   50
The lilies and roses were all awake,
    They sigh'd for the dawn and thee.

Queen rose of the rosebud garden of girls,
    Come hither, the dances are done,
In gloss of satin and glimmer of pearls,   55
    Queen lily and rose in one;
Shine out, little head, sunning over with curls,
    To the flowers, and be their sun.

There has fallen a splendid tear
    From the passion-flower at the gate.   60
She is coming, my dove, my dear;
    She is coming, my life, my fate;
The red rose cries, "She is near, she is near;"
    And the white rose weeps, "She is late;"
The larkspur listens, "I hear, I hear;"   65
    And the lily whispers, "I wait."

She is coming, my own, my sweet;
    Were it ever so airy a tread,
My heart would hear her and beat,
    Were it earth in an earthy bed;   70
My dust would hear her and beat,
    Had I lain for a century dead;
Would start and tremble under her feet,
    And blossom in purple and red.

                                              (From *Maud*)

EXERCISE:

    1. Is there any real content to the comparison in line 33?
    2. In the passage from line 45 to line 52 is there any basis
for the behavior attributed to the various flowers?
    3. Compare this poem with "Indian Serenade" (p. 319) and
"Ode to a Nightingale" (p. 407).

THE GARDEN

ANDREW MARVELL (1621–1678)

How vainly men themselves amaze,
    To win the palm, the oak, or bays,

And their incessant labors see
Crowned from some single herb or tree
Whose short and narrow-vergèd shade   5
Does prudently their toils upbraid,
While all the flowers and trees do close
To weave the garlands of repose!

Fair Quiet, have I found thee here,
And Innocence, thy sister dear?   10
Mistaken long, I sought you then
In busy companies of men.
Your sacred plants, if here below,
Only among the plants will grow;
Society is all but rude   15
To this delicious solitude.

No white nor red was ever seen
So amorous as this lovely green.
Fond lovers, cruel as their flame,
Cut in these trees their mistress' name.   20
Little, alas! they know or heed,
How far these beauties hers exceed!
Fair trees! wheres'e'r your barks I wound
No name shall but your own be found.

When we have run our passion's heat,   25
Love hither makes his best retreat.
The gods, that mortal beauty chase,
Still in a tree did end their race;
Apollo hunted Daphne so,
Only that she might laurel grow;   30
And Pan did after Syrinx speed,
Not as a nymph, but for a reed.

What wondrous life is this I lead!
Ripe apples drop about my head;
The luscious clusters of the vine   35
Upon my mouth do crush their wine;
The nectarine, and curious peach,
Into my hands themselves do reach;
Stumbling on melons, as I pass,
Insnared with flowers, I fall on grass.   40

Meanwhile the mind, from pleasure less,
Withdraws into its happiness;—
The mind, that ocean where each kind
Does straight its own resemblance find;
Yet it creates, transcending these, 45
Far other worlds, and other seas,
Annihilating all that's made
To a green thought in a green shade.

Here at the fountain's sliding foot,
Or at some fruit-tree's mossy root, 50
Casting the body's vest aside,
My soul into the boughs does glide:
There, like a bird, it sits and sings,
Then whets and combs its silver wings,
And, till prepared for longer flight, 55
Waves in its plumes the various light.

Such was that happy garden-state,
While man there walked without a mate
After a place so pure and sweet.
What other help could yet be meet! 60
But 't was beyond a mortal's share
To wander solitary there:
Two paradises 't were in one,
To live in paradise alone.

How well the skilful gardener drew 65
Of flowers, and herbs, this dial new;
Where, from above, the milder sun
Does through a fragrant zodiac run,
And, as it works, the industrious bee
Computes its time as well as we! 70
How could such sweet and wholesome hours
Be reckoned but with herbs and flowers?

EXERCISE:

1. This poem appears to be primarily a description of a garden.
But what interpretation derives from this description?
2. Discuss the meaning of the section from line 46 to line 48.
3. Indicate and define the shifts of tone in the poem.

THUS IS HIS CHEEK THE MAP

WILLIAM SHAKESPEARE (1564–1616)

Thus is his cheek the map of days outworn,
When beauty lived and died as flowers do now,
Before these bastard signs of fair were born,
Or durst inhabit on a living brow;
Before the golden tresses of the dead,   5
The right of sepulchres, were shorn away,
To live a second life on second head;
Ere beauty's dead fleece made another gay:
In him those holy antique hours are seen,
Without all ornament, itself and true,   10
Making no summer of another's green,
Robbing no old to dress his beauty new;
    And him as for a map doth Nature store,
    To show false Art what beauty was of yore.

EXERCISE:

In this poem a number of comparisons are stated or implied.
Is the use of imagery confused?

LIKE AS TO MAKE OUR APPETITES

WILLIAM SHAKESPEARE (1564–1616)

Like as, to make our appetites more keen,
With eager compounds we our palate urge;
As, to prevent our maladies unseen,
We sicken to shun sickness when we purge;
Even so, being full of your ne'er-cloying sweetness,   5
To bitter sauces did I frame my feeding;
And, sick of welfare, found a kind of meetness
To be diseased, ere that there was true needing.
Thus policy in love, to anticipate
The ills that were not, grew to faults assured,   10
And brought to medicine a healthful state,
Which, rank of goodness, would by ill be cured;

But thence I learn, and find the lesson true,
Drugs poison him that so fell sick of you.

EXERCISE:

Some of the comparisons involved here would be regarded,
taken in isolation, as unpleasant. What is the relation of this
fact to the general intention of the poem? Discuss the tone of
the poem in this connection.

IN THE HOLY NATIVITY OF OUR LORD GOD

A HYMN SUNG AS BY THE SHEPHERDS

RICHARD CRASHAW (1613?–1649)

CHORUS

Come, we shepherds, whose blest sight
Hath met Love's noon in Nature's night;
Come, lift we up our loftier song
And wake the sun that lies too long.

To all our world of well-stol'n joy   5
He slept, and dreamt of no such thing;
While we found out heaven's fairer eye
And kissed the cradle of our King.
Tell him he rises now, too late
To show us aught worth looking at.   10

Tell him we now can show him more
Than he e'er showed to mortal sight;
Than he himself e'er saw before;
Which to be seen needs not his light.
Tell him, Tityrus, where th' hast been   15
Tell him, Thyrsis, what th' hast seen.

TITYRUS. Gloomy night embraced the place
    Where the noble infant lay,
        The babe looked up and showed his face;

In spite of darkness, it was day.   20
   It was thy day, sweet! and did rise
Not from the east, but from thine eyes.

CHORUS. It was thy day, sweet, etc.

THYRSIS. Winter chid aloud; and sent
   The angry North to wage his wars.   25
     The North forgot his fierce intent;
And left perfumes instead of scars.
     By those sweet eyes' persuasive powers,
Where he meant frost he scattered flowers.

CHO. By those sweet eyes', etc.   30

BOTH. We saw thee in thy balmy nest,
   Young dawn of our Eternal Day!
     We saw thine eyes break from their east
And chase the trembling shades away.
     We saw thee, and we blest the sight,   35
We saw thee by thine own sweet light.

TIT. Poor World, said I, what wilt thou do
   To entertain this starry stranger?
     Is this the best thou canst bestow?
A cold, and not too cleanly, manger?   40
     Contend, ye powers of heaven and earth,
To fit a bed for this huge birth!

CHO. Contend ye powers, etc.

THYR. Proud World, said I; cease your contest
   And let the mighty babe alone;   45
     The phœnix builds the phœnix' nest,
Love's architecture is his own;
     The babe whose birth embraves this morn,
Made his own bed e'er he was born.

CHO. The babe whose, etc.   50

TIT. I saw the curled drops, soft and slow,
   Come hovering o'er the place's head;

Off'ring their whitest sheets of snow
To furnish the fair infant's bed.
    Forbear, said I; be not too bold.   55
Your fleece is white, but 't is too cold.

CHO.   Forbear, said I, etc.

THYR.   I saw the obsequious seraphim
    Their rosy fleece of fire bestow,
      For well they now can spare their wings,   60
Since heaven itself lies here below.
    Well done, said I; but are you sure
Your down so warm, will pass for pure?

CHO.   Well done, said I, etc.

TIT.   No, no, your king's not yet to seek   65
    Where to repose his royal head;
      See, see how soon his new-bloomed cheek
'Twixt's mother's breasts is gone to bed!
    Sweet choice, said we! no way but so
Not to lie cold, yet sleep in snow.   70

CHO.   Sweet choice, said we, etc.

BOTH.   We saw thee in thy balmy nest,
    Bright dawn of our Eternal Day!
      We saw thine eyes break from their east
And chase the trembling shades away.   75
    We saw thee, and we blessed the sight,
We saw thee by thine own sweet light.

CHO.   We saw thee, etc.

FULL CHORUS

Welcome all wonders in one sight!
Eternity shut in a span,   80
  Summer in winter, day in night,
Heaven in earth, and God in man.
  Great Little One, whose all-embracing birth
Lifts earth to heaven, stoops heaven to earth!

Welcome, though nor to gold nor silk,   85
To more than Cæsar's birthright is;
 Two sister-seas of virgin-milk
With many a rarely-tempered kiss
 That breathes at once both maid and mother,
Warms in the one, cools in the other.   90

Welcome, though not to those gay flies
Gilded i' the beams of earthly kings,
 Slippery souls in smiling eyes,
But to poor shepherds, homespun things,
 Whose wealth's their flock, whose wit's to be   95
Well read in their simplicity.

Yet when young April's husband showers
Shall bless the fruitful Maia's bed,
 We'll bring the first-born of her flowers
To kiss thy feet and crown thy head.   100
 To thee, dread Lamb! Whose love must keep
The shepherds, more than they the sheep.

To Thee, meek Majesty! soft King
Of simple graces and sweet loves!
 Each of us his lamb will bring,   105
Each his pair of silver doves!
 Till burnt at last in fire of thy fair eyes,
Ourselves become our own best sacrifice!

EXERCISE:

This poem is built on a succession of paradoxes. Which ones
do you regard as appropriate? Compare the poem on this basis
with "The Night" (p. 432).

ON THE MORNING OF CHRIST'S NATIVITY

JOHN MILTON (1608–1674)

This is the month, and this the happy morn,
Wherein the Son of Heaven's eternal King,
Of wedded maid and virgin mother born,

Our great redemption from above did bring;
For so the holy sages once did sing,   5
    That he our deadly forfeit should release,
And with his Father work us a perpetual peace.

That glorious form, that light unsufferable,
And that far-beaming blaze of majesty,
Wherewith he wont at Heaven's high council-table   10
To sit the midst of Trinal Unity,
He laid aside, and, here with us to be,
    Forsook the courts of everlasting day,
And chose with us a darksome house of mortal clay.

Say, Heavenly Muse, shall not thy sacred vein   15
Afford a present to the Infant God?
Hast thou no verse, no hymn, or solemn strain,
To welcome him to this his new abode,
Now while the heaven, by the Sun's team untrod,
    Hath took no print of the approaching light,   20
And all the spangled host keep watch in squadrons bright?

See how from far upon the eastern road
The star-led wizards haste with odors sweet!
Oh! run; prevent them with thy humble ode,
And lay it lowly at his blessèd feet;   25
Have thou the honor first thy Lord to greet,
    And join thy voice unto the Angel Quire,
From out his secret altar touched with hallowed fire.

THE HYMN

It was the winter wild,
    While the heaven-born child
All meanly wrapt in the rude manger lies;
    Nature, in awe to him,
    Had doffed her gaudy trim,   5
With her great Master so to sympathize:
It was no season then for her
To wanton with the Sun, her lusty paramour.

Only with speeches fair
She woos the gentle air   10
To hide her guilty front with innocent snow,
    And on her naked shame,
    Pollute with sinful blame,
The saintly veil of maiden white to throw;
Confounded, that her Maker's eyes   15
Should look so near upon her foul deformities.

    But he, her fears to cease,
    Sent down the meek-eyed Peace:
She, crowned with olive green, came softly sliding
    Down through the turning sphere,   20
    His ready harbinger,
With turtle wing the amorous clouds dividing;
And, waving wide her myrtle wand,
She strikes a universal peace through sea and land.

    No war, or battle's sound,   25
    Was heard the world around;
The idle spear and shield were high uphung;
    The hooked chariot stood,
    Unstained with hostile blood;
The trumpet spake not to the armèd throng;   30
And kings sat still with awful eye,
As if they surely knew their sovran Lord was by.

    But peaceful was the night
    Wherein the Prince of Light
His reign of peace upon the earth began.   35
    The winds, with wonder whist,
    Smoothly the waters kissed,
Whispering new joys to the mild Ocean,
Who now hath quite forgot to rave,
While birds of calm sit brooding on the charmèd wave. 40

    The stars, with deep amaze,
    Stand fixed in steadfast gaze,
Bending one way their precious influence,
    And will not take their flight,
    For all the morning light,   45
Or Lucifer that often warned them thence;

But in their glimmering orbs did glow,
Until their Lord himself bespake, and bid them go.

    And, though the shady gloom
      Had given day her room,   50
The Sun himself withheld his wonted speed,
    And hid his head for shame,
    As his inferior flame
The new-enlightened world no more should need:
He saw a greater Sun appear   55
Than his bright throne or burning axletree could bear.

    The shepherds on the lawn,
      Or ere the point of dawn,
Sat simply chatting in a rustic row;
    Full little thought they than   60
    That the mighty Pan
Was kindly come to live with them below:
Perhaps their loves, or else their sheep,
Was all that did their silly thoughts so busy keep.

    When such music sweet   65
      Their hearts and ears did greet
As never was by mortal finger strook,
    Divinely-warbled voice
    Answering the stringed noise,
As all their souls in blissful rapture took: 70
The air, such pleasure loth to lose,
With thousand echoes still prolongs each heavenly close.

    Nature, that heard such sound
      Beneath the hollow round
Of Cynthia's seat the airy region thrilling,   75
    Now was almost won
    To think her part was done,
And that her reign had here its last fulfilling:
She knew such harmony alone
Could hold all Heaven and Earth in happier union.   80

    At last surrounds their sight
    A globe of circular light,

That with long beams the shamefaced Night arrayed;
    The helmèd cherubim
    And sworded seraphim   85
Are seen in glittering ranks with wings displayed,
Harping in loud and solemn quire,
With unexpressive notes, to Heaven's new-born Heir.

    Such music (as 'tis said)
    Before was never made,   90
But when of old the Sons of Morning·sung,
    While the Creator great
    His constellations set,
And the well-balanced World on hinges hung,
And cast the dark foundations deep,   95
And bid the weltering waves their oozy channel keep.

    Ring out, ye crystal spheres!
    Once bless our human ears,
If ye have power to touch our senses so;
    And let your silver chime   100
    Move in melodious time;
And let the bass of heaven's deep organ blow;
And with your ninefold harmony
Make up full consort to the angelic symphony.

    For, if such holy song   105
    Enwrap our fancy long,
Time will run back and fetch the Age of Gold;
    And speckled Vanity
    Will sicken soon and die,
And leprous Sin will melt from earthly mould;   110
And Hell itself will pass away,
And leave her dolorous mansions to the peering day.

    Yea, Truth and Justice then
    Will down return to men,
Orbed in a rainbow; and, like glories wearing,   115
    Mercy will sit between,
    Throned in celestial sheen,
With radiant feet the tissued clouds down steering;
And Heaven, as at some festival,
Will open wide the gates of her high palace-hall.   120

But wisest Fate says No,
This must not yet be so;
The Babe lies yet in smiling infancy
That on the bitter cross
Must redeem our loss,   125
So both himself and us to glorify:
Yet first, to those ychained in sleep,
The wakeful trump of doom must thunder through the
    deep,

With such a horrid clang
As on Mount Sinai rang,   130
While the red fire and smouldering clouds outbrake:
The aged Earth, aghast
With terror of that blast,
Shall from the surface to the center shake,
When, at the world's last session,   135
The dreadful Judge in middle air shall spread his throne.

And then at last our bliss
Full and perfect is,
But now begins; for from this happy day
The Old Dragon under ground,   140
In straiter limits bound,
Not half so far casts his usurpèd sway;
And, wroth to see his Kingdom fail,
Swinges the scaly horror of his folded tail.

The Oracles are dumb;   145
No voice or hideous hum
Runs through the archèd roof in words deceiving.
Apollo from his shrine
Can no more divine,
With hollow shriek the steep of Delphos leaving.   150
No nightly trance, or breathèd spell,
Inspires the pale-eyed priest from the prophetic cell.

The lonely mountains o'er,
And the resounding shore,
A voice of weeping heard, and loud lament;   155
From haunted spring, and dale
Edged with poplar pale,

The parting genius is with sighing sent,
With flower-inwov'n tresses torn
The nymphs in twilight shade of tangled thickets mourn.

    In consecrated earth,   161
      And on the holy hearth,
  The Lars, and Lemurs moan with midnight plaint,
      In urns and altars round,
      A drear and dying sound   165
  Affrights the flamens at their service quaint;
And the chill marble seems to sweat,
While each peculiar power forgoes his wonted seat.

    Peor, and Baalim,
      Forsake their temples dim,   170
  With that twice-battered god of Palestine,
      And mooned Ashtaroth,
      Heav'n's queen and mother both,
  Now sits not girt with tapers' holy shine,
The Lybic Hammon shrinks his horn;   175
In vain the Tyrian maids their wounded Thammuz mourn.

And sullen Moloch, fled,
Hath left in shadows dread
  His burning idol all of blackest hue;
In vain with cymbals' ring   180
They call the grisly king,
  In dismal dance about the furnace blue;
The brutish gods of Nile, as fast,
Isis and Orus and the dog Anubis, haste.

Nor is Osiris seen   185
In Memphian grove or green,
  Trampling the unshowered grass with lowings loud;
Nor can he be at rest
Within his sacred chest;
  Naught but profoundest Hell can be his shroud;   190
In vain, with timbrelled anthems dark,
The sable-stolèd sorcerers bear his worshipped ark.

He feels from Juda's land
The dreaded infant's hand;

   The rays of Bethlehem blind his dusky eyn; 195
Nor all the gods beside
Longer dare abide,
  Not Typhon huge ending in snaky twine:
Our Babe, to show his Godhead true,
Can in his swaddling bands control the damned crew. 200

So when the sun in bed,
Curtained with cloudy red,
  Pillows his chin upon an orient wave,
The flocking shadows pale
Troop to the infernal jail,   205
  Each fettered ghost slips to his several grave,
And the yellow-skirted fays
Fly after the night-steeds, leaving their moon-loved maze.

But see! the Virgin blest
Hath laid her Babe to rest.   210
  Time is our tedious song should here have ending:
Heaven's youngest-teemed star
Hath fixed her polished car,
  Her sleeping Lord with handmaid lamp attending;
And all about the courtly stable   215
Bright-harnessed angels sit in order serviceable.

EXERCISE:

Make a careful comparison of this poem with the preceding
poem with special reference to the handling of imagery.

THE BURNING BABE

ROBERT SOUTHWELL (1561?–1595)

As I in hoary winter's night stood shivering in the snow,
Surprised I was with sudden heat which made my heart to
 glow;
And lifting up a fearful eye to view what fire was near,
A pretty babe, all burning bright, did in the air appear,

Who scorchèd with exceeding heat such floods of tears did
    shed,   5
As though his floods should quench his flames with what his
    tears were fed;
'Alas!' quoth he, 'but newly born in fiery heats I fry,
Yet none approach to warm their hearts or feel my fire but I!
My faultless breast the furnace is, the fuel wounding thorns;
Love is the fire and sighs the smoke, the ashes shame and
    scorns;   10
The fuel Justice layeth on, and Mercy blows the coals;
The metal in this furnace wrought are men's defilèd souls;
For which, as now on fire I am, to work them to their good,
So will I melt into a bath, to wash them in my blood:'
With this he vanished out of sight, and swiftly shrunk away,
And straight I callèd unto mind that it was Christmas-day.   16

EXERCISE:

This poem is a fantasy. The vision outrages our literal-
mindedness, and the allegory may seem to be handled too mechanically. But what means does the poet take to make the
vision acceptable? In this connection discuss the importance
of the first two and the last two lines of the poem.

A VALEDICTION: FORBIDDING MOURNING

JOHN DONNE (1573–1631)

As virtuous men pass mildly away,
    And whisper to their souls, to go,
Whilst some of their sad friends do say,
    The breath goes now, and some say, no:

So let us melt, and make no noise,   5
    No tear-floods, nor sigh-tempests move,
T'were profanation of our joys
    To tell the laity our love.

Moving of th' earth brings harms and fears,
    Men reckon what it did and meant,   10
But trepidation of the spheres,
    Though greater far, is innocent.

Dull sublunary lovers' love
    (Whose soul is sense) cannot admit
Absence, because it doth remove   15
    Those things which elemented it.

But we by a love, so much refined,
    That our selves know not what it is,
Inter-assurèd of the mind,
    Care less, eyes, lips, and hands to miss.   20

Our two souls therefore, which are one,
    Though I must go, endure not yet
A breach, but an expansion,
    Like gold to airy thinness beat.

If they be two, they are two so   25
    As stiff twin compasses are two,
Thy soul the fixed foot, makes no show
    To move, but doth, if th' other do.

And though it in the center sit,
    Yet when the other far doth roam,   30
It leans, and hearkens after it,
    And grows erect, as that comes home.

Such wilt thou be to me, who must
    Like th' other foot, obliquely run;
Thy firmness makes my circle just,   35
    And makes me end, where I begun.

EXERCISE:

Write an analysis of this poem, taking into account the following topics:

1. The tone of the first two stanzas.
2. The implications of the imagery in the last four stanzas.
(For instance, how do the associations one ordinarily has with

compasses tend to give an impression of accuracy and conviction to the conclusion of the poem?)

3. The use of enjambment.
4. The use of alliteration and repetition.
5. The metrical situation in the first line of the seventh stanza.

AFTER GREAT PAIN A FORMAL FEELING COMES

EMILY DICKINSON (1830–1886)

After great pain a formal feeling comes—
The nerves sit ceremonious like tombs;
The stiff Heart questions—was it He that bore?
And yesterday—or centuries before?

The feet mechanical go round   5
A wooden way
Of ground or air or Ought,
Regardless grown,
A quartz contentment like a stone.

This is the hour of lead   10
Remembered if outlived
As freezing persons recollect
The snow—
First chill, then stupor, then
The letting go.   15

In this poem the imagery may seem mixed. (See analysis of "My Springs," pp. 442–45.) The poet uses the figure of the tombs and then immediately drops it to state that the stiff heart questions. Other images like the "hour of lead" are only mentioned, not developed. Indeed, the only rather fully developed figure is that of the person dying in the snow. Are the figures, then, tightly enough related, or are they vague and confused? If they are related, what is it that binds them together? A comparison with the imagery of a poem like "The Definition of Love," for example, sharply emphasizes the questions. Obviously, the figures used by Emily Dickinson here are not related in the same fashion as are those of Marvell's poem. Are they, then, no more unified than those of "My Springs"? Or, are we to conclude that the present poem is successful, but that the figures are related in some other fashion?

The poem is obviously an attempt to communicate to the reader the nature of the experience which comes "after great pain." The poet is using the imagery for this purpose, and the first line of the poem, which states the subject of the poem, is the only abstract statement in the poem. The pain is obviously not a physical pain; it is some great sorrow or mental pain which leaves the mind numbed. The nerves, she says, "sit ceremonious like tombs." The word *sit* is very important here. The nerves, it is implied, are like a group of people after a funeral sitting in the parlor in a formal hush. Then the poet changes the image slightly by adding "like tombs." The nerves are thus compared to two different things, but each of the comparisons contributes to the same effect, and indeed are closely related: people dressed in black sitting around a room after a funeral may be said to be like tombs. And why does the reference to "tombs" seem such a good symbol for a person who has just suffered great pain (whether it be a real person or the nerves of such a person personified)? Because a tomb has to a supreme degree the qualities of deadness (quietness, stillness) and of formality (ceremony, stiffness).

Notice that the imagery (through the first line of the last stanza) is characterized by the possession of a common quality, the quality of *stiff lifelessness*. For instance, the heart is "stiff," the feet walk a "wooden" way, the contentment is a "quartz" contentment, the hour is that of "lead." The insistence on this type of imagery is very important in confirming the sense of numbed consciousness which is made more explicit by the statement that the feet move mechanically and are "regardless" of where they go. Notice too that the lines are bound together, not only by the constant reference of the imagery to the result of grief, but also by the fact that the poet is stating in series what happens to the parts of the body: nerves, heart, feet.

Two special passages in the first two stanzas deserve additional comment before we pass on to the third stanza. The capital letter in the word *He* tells us that Christ is meant. The heart, obsessed with pain and having lost the sense of time and place, asks whether it was Christ who bore the cross. The question is abrupt and elliptic as though uttered at a moment of pain. And the heart asks whether it is not experiencing His pain, and—having lost hold of the real world—whether the crucifixion took place yesterday or centuries before. And behind these questions lies the implication that pain is a constant part of the human lot. The implied figure of a funeral makes the heart's question about the crucifixion come as an appropriate one, and the quality of the suffering makes the connection implied between its own sufferings and that on the cross not violently farfetched.

The line, "A quartz contentment like a stone," is particularly interesting. The comparison involves two things. First, we see an extension of the common association of stoniness with the numbness of grief, as in such phrases as "stony-eyed" or "heart like a stone," etc. But why does the poet use "quartz"? There are several reasons. The name of the stone helps to particularize the figure and prevent the effect of a cliché. Moreover, quartz is a very hard stone. And, for one who knows that quartz is a crystal, a "quartz contentment" is a contentment crystallized, as it were, out of the pain. This brings us to the second general aspect involved by the comparison. This aspect is ironical. The contentment arising after the shock of great pain is a contentment because of the inability to respond any longer, rather than the ability to respond satisfactorily and agreeably.

To summarize for a moment, the poet has developed an effect of inanimate lifelessness, a stony, or wooden, or leaden stiffness; now, she proceeds to use a new figure, that of the freezing person, which epitomizes the effect of those which have preceded it, but which also gives a fresh and powerful statement.

The line, "Remembered if outlived," is particularly forceful. The implication is that few outlive the experience to be able to remember and recount it to others. This experience of grief is like a death by freezing: there is the chill, then the stupor as the body becomes numbed, and then the last state in which the body finally gives up the fight against the cold, and relaxes and dies. The correspondence of the stages of death by freezing to the effect of the shock of deep grief on the mind is close enough to make the passage very powerful. But there is another reason for the effect which this last figure has on us. The imagery of the first two stanzas corresponds to the "stupor." The last line carries a new twist of idea, one which supplies a context for the preceding imagery and which by explaining it, makes it more meaningful. The formality, the stiffness, the numbness of the first two stanzas is accounted for: it is an attempt to hold in, the fight of the mind against letting go; it is a defense of the mind.

MYSTERY

ELIZABETH BARRETT BROWNING (1806–1861)

We sow the glebe, we reap the corn,
   We build the house where we may rest,
And then, at moments, suddenly,
We look up to the great wide sky,
Inquiring wherefore we were born . . .   5
   For earnest, or for jest?

The senses folding thick and dark
   About the stifled soul within,
We guess diviner things beyond,
And yearn to them with yearning fond;   10
We strike out blindly to a mark
   Believed in, but not seen.

We vibrate to the pant and thrill
   Wherewith Eternity has curled
In serpent-twine about God's seat;   15
While, freshening upward to his feet,
In gradual growth his full-leaved will
   Expands from world to world.

And, in the tumult and excess
   Of act and passion under sun,
We sometimes hear—oh, soft and far,   20
As silver star did touch with star,
The kiss of Peace and Righteousness
   Through all things that are done.

God keeps His holy mysteries   25
   Just on the outside of man's dream.
In diapason slow, we think
To hear their pinions rise and sink,
While they float pure beneath His eyes,
   Like swans adown a stream.   30

And, sometimes, horror chills our blood
   To be so near such mystic Things,
And we wrap round us, for defence,
Our purple manners, moods of sense—
As angels, from the face of God,   35
   Stand hidden in their wings.

And, sometimes, through life's heavy swound
   We grope for them!—with strangled breath
We stretch out hands abroad and try
To reach them in our agony,—   40
And widen, so, the broad life-wound
   Which soon is large enough for death.

EXERCISE:

With close attention to the analyses of "The Definition of
Love" (pp. 437–40) and "My Springs" (pp. 442–45), write a comparison of this poem with "The Night" (p. 432), which also treats
the mystery of man's relation to God. In this connection consider the following topics:

   1. The inferiority of the imagery in the first part of the third
stanza to that in the second part.

   2. The confusion of imagery in the fifth stanza.

   3. The credibility of the statement that "horror chills our
blood. . . ." (Does the word *horror* have any accurate applica-

tion here? Or does it merely represent an attempt to gain dramatic force?)

4. The relation of the rhythm to the general intention of the poem.

POOR SOUL, THE CENTER OF MY SINFUL EARTH

WILLIAM SHAKESPEARE (1564–1616)

Poor soul, the center of my sinful earth,
Thrall to these rebel powers that thee array,
Why dost thou pine within and suffer dearth,
Painting thy outward walls so costly gay?
Why so large cost, having so short a lease,   5
Dost thou upon thy fading mansion spend?
Shall worms, inheritors of this excess,
Eat up thy charge? Is this thy body's end?
Then, soul, live thou upon thy servant's loss,
And let that pine to aggravate thy store;   10
Buy terms divine in selling hours of dross;
Within be fed, without be rich no more:
    So shalt thou feed on Death, that feeds on men,
    And Death once dead, there's no more dying then.

EXERCISE:

Comment on the implied images and the relations among them.

CLEOPATRA'S LAMENT

WILLIAM SHAKESPEARE (1564–1616)

Cleopatra. I dreamed there was an Emperor Antony:
O! such another sleep, that I might see
But such another man.
    Dolabella.   If it might please ye,—
    Cleopatra. His face was as the heavens, and therein stuck 5

A sun and moon, which kept their course, and lighted
The little O, the earth.
   Dolabella.   Most sovereign creature,—
   Cleopatra. His legs bestrid the ocean; his reared arm
Crested the world; his voice was propertied   10
As all the tunèd spheres, and that to friends;
But when he meant to quail and shake the orb,
He was as rattling thunder. For his bounty,
There was no winter in 't, an autumn 'twas
That grew the more by reaping; his delights   15
Were dolphin-like, they showed his back above
The element they lived in; in his livery
Walked crowns and crownets, realms and islands were
As plates dropped from his pocket.
   Dolabella.   Cleopatra,—   20
   Cleopatra. Think you there was, or might be, such a man
As this I dreamed of?
   Dolabella.   Gentle madam, no.

(From *Antony and Cleopatra*)

EXERCISE:

This selection is a section of the conversation between Cleopatra and an emissary of Octavius Caesar, who has just defeated the forces of Antony and Cleopatra. Antony is now dead, and Cleopatra is speaking from the memory of his grandeur and generosity. Some of the comparisons here may, at first glance, seem exaggerated and far-fetched. Can they be justified? Furthermore, the relations among the various images are not specifically stated. Is there a confusion on this ground?

TO HIS COY MISTRESS

ANDREW MARVELL (1621–1678)

Had we but world enough, and time,
This coyness, Lady, were no crime.
We would sit down and think which way
To walk and pass our long love's day.

Thou by the Indian Ganges' side   5
Shouldst rubies find; I by the tide
Of Humber would complain. I would
Love you ten years before the Flood,
And you should, if you please, refuse
Till the conversion of the Jews.   10
My vegetable love should grow
Vaster than empires, and more slow;
An hundred years should go to praise
Thine eyes and on thy forehead gaze;
Two hundred to adore each breast,   15
But thirty thousand to the rest;
An age at least to every part,
And the last age should show your heart.
For, Lady, you deserve this state,
Nor would I love at lower rate.   20
    But at my back I always hear
Time's wingèd chariot hurrying near;
And yonder all before us lie
Deserts of vast eternity.
Thy beauty shall no more be found,   25
Nor, in thy marble vault, shall sound
My echoing song; then worms shall try
That long preserved virginity,
And your quaint honor turn to dust,
And into ashes all my lust: 30
The grave's a fine and private place,
But none, I think, do there embrace.
    Now therefore, while the youthful hue
Sits on thy skin like morning dew,
And while thy willing soul transpires   35
At every pore with instant fires,
Now let us sport us while we may,
And now, like amorous birds of prey,
Rather at once our time devour
Than languish in his slow-chapt power.   40
Let us roll all our strength and all
Our sweetness up into one ball,
And tear our pleasures with rough strife
Thorough the iron gates of life:
Thus, though we cannot make our sun   45
Stand still, yet we will make him run.

EXERCISE:

1. Distinguish the three divisions of the logical structure of the poem. Comment upon the changes in tone from division to division and the means used to indicate these changes, especially the use of imagery.

2. Define the attitude of the poet in the section from line 25 to line 33.

FOLLOW THY FAIR SUN, UNHAPPY SHADOW

THOMAS CAMPION (1567–1620)

Follow thy fair sun, unhappy shadow,
Though thou be black as night,
And she made all of light,
Yet follow thy fair sun, unhappy shadow.

Follow her whose light thy light depriveth,   5
Though here thou liv'st disgraced,
And she in heaven is placed,
Yet follow her whose light the world reviveth.

Follow those pure beams whose beauty burneth,
That so have scorchèd thee,   10
As thou still black must be,
Till her kind beams thy black to brightness turneth.

Follow her while yet her glory shineth:
There comes a luckless night,
That will dim all her light;   15
And this the black unhappy shade divineth.

Follow still since so thy fates ordainèd;
The sun must have his shade,
Till both at once do fade,
The sun still proud, the shadow still disdainèd.   20

Exercise:

1. What do the sun and the shadow symbolize?

2. What effect is given by the fact that the poet makes all his statement in terms of this symbolism?

3. What use does the poet make of the short internal couplet of the stanza form?

4. Comment on the use of alliteration and on the *euphonious* effects (*Glossary*) in the poem.

AT MELVILLE'S TOMB

HART CRANE (1899–1932)

Often beneath the wave, wide from this ledge
The dice of drowned men's bones he saw bequeath
An embassy. Their numbers as he watched,
Beat on the dusty shore and were obscured.

And wrecks passed without sound of bells,   5
The calyx of death's bounty giving back
A scattered chapter, livid hieroglyph,
The portent wound in corridors of shells.

Then in the circuit calm of one vast coil,
Its lashings charmed and malice reconciled,   10
Frosted eyes there were that lifted altars;
And silent answers crept across the stars.

Compass, quadrant and sextant contrive
No farther tides—High in the azure steeps
Monody shall not wake the mariner.   15
This fabulous shadow only the sea keeps.

This poem is a little elegy upon Herman Melville, the author of *Moby Dick,* the great American novel of the sea and whaling. The general meaning of the poem is easy enough. The poet says that the spirit of the writer whose imagination was so vividly engaged by the sea, and who saw such grandeur in man's strug-

gle with it, though his body might be buried on land, would find
its real abiding place in the sea:

> This fabulous shadow only the sea keeps.

The imagery of the poem, however, provoked the editor who
first published the poem to write the poet to ask several questions concerning the detailed meanings:

Take me for a hard-boiled unimaginative unpoetic reader, and
tell me how *dice* can *bequeath an embassy* (or anything else);
and how a calyx (*of death's bounty* or anything else) can give
back a *scattered chapter, livid hieroglyph;* and how, if it does,
such a *portent* can be *wound in corridors* (of shells or anything
else).

And so on. I find your image of *frosted eyes lifting altars* difficult to visualize. Nor do compass, quadrant and sextant *contrive*
tides, they merely record them, I believe.

All this may seem impertinent, but is not so intended. Your
ideas and rhythms interest me, and I am wondering by what
process of reasoning you would justify this poem's succession of
champion mixed metaphors, of which you must be conscious.
The packed line should pack its phrases in orderly relation, it
seems to me, in a manner tending to clear confusion instead of
making it worse confounded.

  The first part of the poet's reply to the editor's letter containing these questions was concerned with the general justification of comparisons which are not scientifically and logically
exact. This general consideration has already been raised in
some degree in dealing with various poems analyzed in this
section (pp. 387–91, 442–45, and particularly the analysis of "After
Great Pain," pp. 468–71). The poet then undertook to analyze
the implied points of reference behind his own use of imagery:

. . . I'll . . . come to the explanations you requested on the
Melville poem:

> "The dice of drowned men's bones he saw bequeath
> An embassy."

Dice bequeath an embassy, in the first place, by being ground (in this connection only, of course) in little cubes from the bones of drowned men by the action of the sea, and are finally thrown up on the sand, having "numbers" but no identification. These being the bones of dead men who never completed their voyage, it seems legitimate to refer to them as the only surviving evidence of certain messages undelivered, mute evidence of certain things, experiences that the dead mariners might have had to deliver. Dice as a symbol of chance and circumstance is also implied.

"The calyx of death's bounty giving back," etc.

This calyx refers in the double ironic sense both to a cornucopia and the vortex made by a sinking vessel. As soon as the water has closed over a ship this whirlpool sends up broken spars, wreckage, etc., which can be alluded to as *livid hieroglyphs,* making a *scattered chapter* so far as any complete record of the recent ship and her crew is concerned. In fact, about as much definite knowledge might come from all this as anyone might gain from the roar of his own veins, which is easily heard (haven't you ever done it?) by holding a shell close to one's ear.

"Frosted eyes lift altars."

Refers simply to a conviction that a man, not knowing perhaps a definite god yet being endowed with a reverence for deity— such a man naturally postulates a deity somehow, and the altar of that deity by the very *action* of the eyes *lifted* in searching.

"Compass, quadrant and sextant contrive no farther tides."

Hasn't it often occurred that instruments originally invented for record and computation have inadvertently so extended the concepts of the entity they were invented to measure (concepts of space, etc.) in the mind and imagination that employed them, that they may metaphorically be said to have extended the original boundaries of the entity measured? This little bit of "relativity" ought not to be discredited in poetry now that scientists are proceeding to measure the universe on principles of pure *ratio,* quite as metaphorical, so far as previous standards of scientific methods extended . . .

This correspondence raises in concrete form some very interesting questions that frequently appear in connection not only with the analysis of poems of the type of this one by Hart Crane, but also with the analysis of all other types of poems. People sometimes say: "But the poet couldn't have been thinking of all this when he wrote the poem." And in the sense in which they are using the term "thinking" they are right. The poet certainly did not draw up an analysis of his intention, a kind of blue print, and then write the poem to specification. But it is only a very superficial view of the way the mind works that would cast the question into those terms. Does a finely trained polevaulter in the act of making his leap think specifically of each of the different muscles he is employing; or does a boxer in the middle of a round think of the details of his boxing form? Probably not, even though the vaulter or boxer may have acquired his form by conscious practice which involved detail after detail. Furthermore, at the moment of action, a competent coach would be able to analyze and criticize the performance in detail. In the same way, one might say that a poet, in his role as craftsman in the process of making a poem, does not work by blueprint specifications, but toward a sort of general objective which is conditioned by his "training"—by his previous study of his own responses and by his study of the detailed methods and effects in the work of other poets. The poet, we can say, usually knows what general effect and meaning he intends a poem to have. The process of composing the poem is a process of exploring the full implications of the intended meaning and of finding a suitable structure. The process is probably one of movement by trial and error, governed by self-criticism.

But to say all this is not to deny any of the legitimate meanings of the term "inspiration." One may say that a poet writes something in a mood of happy inspiration, when the work seemed almost effortless. We are told, for instance, that Coleridge composed "Kubla Khan" in a sort of trance.[1] And we know that

[1] In the summer of the year 1797, the author, then in ill health, had retired to a lonely farmhouse between Porlock and Linton, on the Exmoor confines of Somerset and Devonshire. In consequence of a slight indisposition, an anodyne had been prescribed, from the effects of which he fell asleep in his chair at the moment that he was reading the following sentence, or

other poems have been composed with surprising ease. But we can always remember that the moods of happy inspiration never result in the production of good poetry except for people who have submitted themselves to the long preliminary discipline. Or, as Wordsworth puts it in another connection:

For all good poetry is the spontaneous overflow of powerful feelings: and though this be true, poems to which any value can be attached were never produced on any variety of subjects but by a man who, being possessed of more than usual organic sensibility, *had also thought long and deeply* [*editors' italics*].

(Preface to *Lyrical Ballads,* 1800)

But to return to the matter of Crane's analysis of his own poem: in attempting to answer questions about his poem, Crane is obviously acting in the rôle of observer or critic, and one is not to confuse the process of analysis with the process that probably occurred in the actual composition. Moreover, one is not to suppose that the reader necessarily must duplicate the process of analysis in experiencing the force of the poem. Many people who enjoy the work of Emily Dickinson have never, for instance, actually analyzed the meanings of the phrase, "A quartz contentment," but they have felt that the phrase is rich in its mean-

words of the same substance, in *Purchas's Pilgrimage:* "Here the Khan Kubla commanded a palace to be built, and a stately garden thereunto. And thus ten miles of fertile ground were inclosed with a wall." The author continued for about three hours in a profound sleep, at least of the external senses, during which time he has the most vivid confidence, that he could not have composed less than from two to three hundred lines; if that indeed can be called composition in which all the images rose up before him as *things,* with a parallel production of the correspondent expressions, without any sensation or consciousness of effort. On awakening he appeared to himself to have a distinct recollection of the whole, and taking his pen, ink, and paper, instantly and eagerly wrote down the lines that are here preserved. At this moment he was unfortunately called out by a person on business from Porlock, and detained by him above an hour, and on his return to his room, found, to his no small surprise and mortification, that though he still retained some vague and dim recollection of the general purport of the vision, yet, with the exception of some eight or ten scattered lines and images, all the rest had passed away like the images on the surface of a stream into which a stone has been cast, but, alas! without the after restoration of the latter! (Prefatory note to "Kubla Khan," 1798)

ing and "right" in its application. But as the preliminary dis-cipline of the poet extends and enriches his capacity for creation, so the process of analysis extends the reader's capacity for ap-preciation.

AMONG SCHOOL CHILDREN

WILLIAM BUTLER YEATS (1865–   )

I

I walk through the long schoolroom questioning;
A kind old nun in a white hood replies;
The children learn to cipher and to sing,
To study reading-books and history,
To cut and sew, be neat in everything   5
In the best modern way—the children's eyes
In momentary wonder stare upon
A sixty-year-old smiling public man.

II

I dream of a Ledaean body, bent
Above a sinking fire, a tale that she   10
Told of a harsh reproof, or trivial event
That changed some childish day to tragedy—
Told, and it seemed that our two natures blent
Into a sphere from youthful sympathy,
Or else, to alter Plato's parable,   15
Into the yolk and the white of one shell.

III

And thinking of that fit of grief or rage
I look upon one child or t'other there
And wonder if she stood so at that age—
For even daughters of the swan can share   20
Something of every paddler's heritage—
And had that color upon cheek or hair,

And thereupon my heart is driven wild:
She stands before me as a living child.

IV

Her present image floats into the mind—   25
Did Quattrocento finger fashion it
Hollow of cheek as though it drank the wind
And took a mess of shadows for its meat?
And I though never of Ledaean kind
Had pretty plumage once—enough of that,   30
Better to smile on all that smile, and show
There is a comfortable kind of scarecrow.

V

What youthful mother, a shape upon her lap
Honey of generation had betrayed,
And that must sleep, shriek, struggle to escape   35
As recollection or the drug decide,
Would think her son, did she but see that shape
With sixty or more winters on its head,
A compensation for the pang of his birth,
Or the uncertainty of his setting forth?   40

VI

Plato thought nature but a spume that plays
Upon a ghostly paradigm of things;
Solider Aristotle played the taws
Upon the bottom of a king of kings;
World-famous golden-thighed Pythagoras   45
Fingered upon a fiddle-stick or strings
What a star sang and careless Muses heard:
Old clothes upon old sticks to scare a bird.

VII

Both nuns and mothers worship images,
But those the candles light are not as those   50
That animate a mother's reveries,
But keep a marble or a bronze repose.
And yet they too break hearts—O Presences

That passion, piety or affection knows,
And that all heavenly glory symbolize—   55
O self-born mockers of man's enterprise;

VIII

Labor is blossoming or dancing where
The body is not bruised to pleasure soul,
Nor beauty born out of its own despair,
Nor blear-eyed wisdom out of midnight oil.   60
O chestnut tree, great rooted blossomer,
Are you the leaf, the blossom or the bole?
O body swayed to music, O brightening glance,
How can we know the dancer from the dance?

EXERCISE:

1. The structure of the poem may be sketched briefly as follows: Stanza I gives the situation which stimulates the speaker to his reverie. Stanzas II, III, and IV, present the relation of childhood to maturity and of maturity to age with reference to the speaker himself and to the woman he loves. Stanzas V and VI extend the personal comment to a general one: would any mother, if she could see the old age of her child, feel that her own love and sacrifice had been justified, for even the greatest men, Plato, Aristotle, and Pythagoras, were, in old age, little better than scarecrows? Stanza VII goes on to comment that the images which people hold in affection and reverence always mock man's inability to realize them. Stanza VIII presents the idea that when the mind and body are in harmony, there is no distinction between the real and the ideal; the image and the actuality are one. Investigate the ways by which the imagery serves to present these ideas. (Consult the library for information concerning Leda, Quattrocento, Plato, Aristotle, Alexander the Great, who is referred to here as "king of kings," the meaning of the word *taws,* and Pythagoras.)

2. What are the inter-relations among the images? Observe, for instance, that the story of Leda and the swan is alluded to in line 20.

3. In Stanza V, in the first line, why does the poet refer to the "shape" rather than the child upon the mother's lap?

4. Discuss the changes of tone in the poem and indicate some of the ways in which these changes are communicated.

5. What is the function of the image of the chestnut tree?

THE EQUILIBRISTS

JOHN CROWE RANSOM (1888–   )

Full of her long white arms and milky skin
He had a thousand times remembered sin.
Alone in the press of people traveled he,
Minding her jacinth and myrrh and ivory.

Mouth he remembered: the quaint orifice   5
From which came heat that flamed upon the kiss,
Till cold words came down spiral from the head,
Gray doves from the officious tower illsped.

Body: it was a white field ready for love.
On her body's field, with the gaunt tower above,   10
The lilies grew, beseeching him to take,
If he would pluck and wear them, bruise and break.

Eyes talking: Never mind the cruel words,
Embrace my flowers but not embrace the swords.
But what they said, the doves came straightway flying   15
And unsaid: Honor, honor, they came crying.

Importunate her doves. Too pure, too wise,
Clambering on his shoulder, saying, Arise,
Leave me now, and never let us meet,
Eternal distance now command thy feet.   20

Predicament indeed, which thus discovers
Honor among thieves, Honor between lovers.
O such a little word is Honor, they feel!
But the gray word is between them cold as steel.

At length I saw these lovers fully were come   25
Into their torture of equilibrium:
Dreadfully had forsworn each other, and yet
They were bound each to each, and they did not forget.

And rigid as two painful stars, and twirled
About the clustered night their prison world,   30
They burned with fierce love always to come near,
But Honor beat them back and kept them clear.

Ah, the strict lovers, they are ruined now!
I cried in anger. But with puddled brow
Devising for those gibbeted and brave   35
Came I descanting: Man, what would you have?

For spin your period out, and draw your breath,
A kinder saeculum begins with Death.
Would you ascend to Heaven and bodiless dwell?
Or take your bodies honorless to Hell?   40

In Heaven you have heard no marriage is,
No white flesh tinder to your lecheries,
Your male and female tissue sweetly shaped
Sublimed away, and furious blood escaped.

Great lovers lie in Hell, the stubborn ones   45
Infatuate of the flesh upon the bones;
Stuprate, they rend each other when they kiss;
The pieces kiss again—no end to this.

But still I watched them spinning, orbited nice.
Their flames were not more radiant than their ice.   50
I dug in the quiet earth and wrought the tomb
And made these lines to memorize their doom:—

Equilibrists lie here; stranger, tread light;
Close, but untouching in each other's sight;
Mouldered the lips and ashy the tall skull,   55
Let them lie perilous and beautiful.

EXERCISE:

   1. Investigate in detail the way in which the basic comparison
is worked out.
   2. Discuss questions of tone in the poem.

DOOM IS DARK

W. H. AUDEN (1907–   )

Doom is dark and deeper than any sea-dingle.
Upon what man it fall
In spring, day-wishing flowers appearing,
Avalanche sliding, white snow from rock-face,
That he should leave his house,   5
No cloud-soft hand can hold him, restraint by women;
But ever that man goes
Through place-keepers, through forest trees,
A stranger to strangers over undried sea,
Houses for fishes, suffocating water,   10
Or lonely on fell as chat,
By pot-holed becks
A bird stone-haunting, an unquiet bird.

There head falls forward, fatigued at evening,
And dreams of home,   15
Waving from window, spread of welcome,
Kissing of wife under single sheet;
But waking sees
Bird-flocks nameless to him, through doorway voices
Of new men making another love.   20

Save him from hostile capture,
From sudden tiger's spring at corner;
Protect his house,
His anxious house where days are counted
From thunderbolt protect,   25
From gradual ruin spreading like a stain;
Converting number from vague to certain,
Bring joy, bring day of his returning,
Lucky with day approaching, with leaning dawn.

EXERCISE:

1. Discuss the imagery in this poem, relating it to both idea and tone.

2. On what principle, if any, are the lengths of various lines determined in this poem?

TOMORROW AND TOMORROW

I.

WILLIAM SHAKESPEARE (1564–1616)

Tomorrow, and tomorrow, and tomorrow,
Creeps in this petty pace from day to day,
To the last syllable of recorded time;
And all our yesterdays have lighted fools
The way to dusty death. Out, out, brief candle;   5
Life's but a walking shadow; a poor player,
That struts and frets his hour upon the stage,
And then is heard no more: it is a tale
Told by an idiot, full of sound and fury,
Signifying nothing.   10

(From *Macbeth*)

II.

SIR WILLIAM DAVENANT. (1606–1668)

Tomorrow and tomorrow and tomorrow
Creeps in a stealing pace from day to day,
To the last minute of recorded time,
And all our yesterdays have lighted fools
To their eternal homes; out, out, that candle!   5
Life's but a walking shadow, a poor player
That struts and frets his hour upon the stage,
And then is heard no more. It is a tale
Told by an idiot, full of sound and fury,
Signifying nothing.   10

(From *Macbeth*)

EXERCISE:

The second version of this passage is a rewriting of the first.
The intention of Sir William Davenant was to remove certain
defects, offenses against what he considered "correctness" and
"reasonableness."   Write a detailed comparison of the two passages.

VII *theme*

FOREWORD

In examining the poems in this section, the reader will find special opportunities for considering some of the ways in which an idea appears in poetry. But, of course, the idea of any poem, in so far as the poem is being read as poetry, can only be considered in relation to the various other factors which we have previously discussed—narrative, meter, imagery, etc. Just as the student should continually take these factors into account, he should remember that in stressing theme in these poems he is dealing with an aspect of all poetry ("Foreword" to Section III, p. 171) and a topic which has often been discussed in previous pages (pp. 38, 141, 225). That is, every poem involves an idea, for a poem represents an interpretation of its materials. Obviously, the method of presenting theme will vary from poem to poem, as we have already seen. The method will vary according to the special combinations of imagery, rhythm, statement, etc. Each case must be treated on its own merits, for no poem is exactly like any other. But one may, however, offer this basic principle: the real poet in presenting his theme never depends merely on general statement. The poem itself is the dramatizing of the theme in terms of situation, character, imagery, rhythm, tone, etc.

We have said that a theme in poetry manifests itself in constantly varying ways. Among these manifestations, of course, we find the use of explicit statement as a factor in itself. For instance, in the "Ode to a Nightingale," which we have already analyzed (pp. 409–15), Keats makes the explicit statement,

> Now more than ever seems it rich to die,
> To cease upon the midnight with no pain.

Certainly, the theme of the poem, the basic idea, is not the desirability of suicide. The explicit statement is being used here merely as a step in the development of the theme: man's inability to correlate finally the ideal and the actual aspects of his experience.

A further distinction that should be kept in mind is that between the subject of a poem and the theme. For instance, let us compare the following poem with "To an Athlete Dying Young," which has already been discussed (pp. 385–87):

THE LADS IN THEIR HUNDREDS

A. E. HOUSMAN (1859–1936)

The lads in their hundreds to Ludlow come in for the fair,
    There's men from the barn and the forge and the mill and the
      fold,
The lads for the girls and the lads for the liquor are there,
    And there with the rest are the lads that will never be old.

There's chaps from the town and the field and the till and the
      cart,   5
    And many to count are the stalwart, and many the brave,
And many the handsome of face and the handsome of heart,
    And few that will carry their looks or their truth to the grave.

I wish one could know them, I wish there were tokens to tell
    The fortunate fellows that now you can never discern;   10
And then one could talk with them friendly and wish them
      farewell
    And watch them depart on the way that they will not return.

But now you may stare as you like and there's nothing to scan;
    And brushing your elbow unguessed-at and not to be told
They carry back bright to the coiner the mintage of man,   15
    The lads that will die in their glory and never be old.

It should be clear that both of these have the same general theme, but the *subject* of the first, as the title states, is the death of a young athlete, and the subject of the other is a scene at Ludlow Fair. In the same way, a little study of the "Ode to a Grecian Urn," by Keats (p. 626), will show that it has the same basic theme as the "Ode to a Nightingale." The ideal life pictured on the urn, perfect beyond change and time, is brought into contrast with the actual world where desire pushes on to its fulfilment and to the "burning forehead and a parching tongue." But the subjects are very different, one subject being the reactions of a man to the song of the bird, and the other being the reactions of a modern man to an ancient Greek vase.

A further question may have presented itself to the student in this general regard: what is the importance of "truth" in poetry? This question was raised in one way in the *Introduction* (pp. 10–14). It was there pointed out that the goodness of a poem could never be based on the *mere* fact that it said something true or instructive. It was also pointed out that a person can admire poems that contradict each other or express views that are not in agreement with the reader's own views. This general question of the "truth" of poetry is answered if we reflect for a moment on the impulses which take us to poetry. We do not read poetry for the scientific truth of particular statements. We do not read poetry for specific moral instructions. Statements that taken in isolation would seem to raise issues of scientific truth or falsity, and statements that would seem to embody specific moral judgments are not, as we have seen, to be taken by themselves, but as factors contributing to the development of the total experience and the total meaning which the poet is trying to develop for us. A reading which selects such statements out of context for either praise or blame springs from the "message-hunting" impulse (*Introduction,* pp. 10–14). A reader should constantly remember that such detailed statements should be interpreted in the light of the total effect.

But suppose the reader does master the poem as a whole and does see the relation of any detailed statement in the poem to the total intention. There still remains the question of the reader's judgment of the general attitude toward life, the interpretation of life made or implied, in the poem. Suppose the reader does not agree with the interpretation involved? Can he still accept the poem?

Let us approach this question somewhat indirectly. Obviously, a silly or superficial or childish attitude cannot result in a good poem. This is true even if the writer has a skill in the use of certain technical devices. For instance, we can look back to

"The Indian Serenade," by Shelley (p. 319), and see that the rhythms of the poem are not handled crudely and amateurishly. But, as has been pointed out, the poem as a whole is sentimental, and if we care to isolate the conception of love implied in the poem, we can see that it is very superficial and immature when contrasted with that implied in poems like "Rose Aylmer" (p. 270), "A Deep-sworn Vow" (p. 273), "A Litany" (p. 341), or the sonnets of Shakespeare (pp. 325–434). A poem, of course, may also fail because of an inadequate command of poetic skill.

Indeed, any attitude or interpretation, whether or not the reader habitually adopts it himself, will not invalidate a poem, provided that the attitude or interpretation is one that could conceivably be held by a serious and intelligent person in the dramatic situation implied or stated in the poem. (Obviously words like *serious* and *intelligent* do not mean absolutely the same thing to different people, and consequently there is a margin here for disagreement in estimating poetry. But such disagreements, taken by and large over a long period of time, after contemporary prejudices have died, are rather infrequent when really first-rate work is concerned.)

It is easy to see why a considerable difference may exist between the habitual attitudes of a reader and the attitudes inherent in poems which he, nevertheless, appreciates. No matter how strongly a person may hold to certain attitudes and interpretations, he is aware, unless he is fanatical or stupid, that human experience is infinitely complicated and various. Poetry demands, on this ground, to be approached with a certain humility. And human nature is such that the reader will usually approach a poem without raising too immediately the question of his agreement or disagreement in attitude; because poetry is about human experience it appeals to his interests. This postponement of the question of agreement or disagreement—even the reader's feeling that the question may be irrelevant—arises from the fact that the attitude involved in a poem does not come merely as a bare general statement; it comes as part of a complex experience arising from the relation of many different factors to each other. The successful poem is a set of organized and controlled relations.

It is only when the attitude involved in the poem comes as an oversimplified generalization or when the response which the poem insists on seems not warranted by the dramatic situation which is presented or implied—it is only in these cases that the ordinary reader will reject a poem on the basis of his disagreement with its implied "view of life." For in so far as he appreciates the poem he has a sense of the conquest over the disorder and meaninglessness of experience. Perhaps this sense may be the very basis for his exhilaration in the poem—just as it may be the basis for the pleasure one takes in watching the clean drive of an expert golfer or the swoop of a bird in the air, as contrasted with the accidental tumbling of a stone down a hillside. It is this same sense of order and control given by a successful poem that confirms us in the faith that the experiences of life itself may have meaning.

LUCIFER IN STARLIGHT

GEORGE MEREDITH (1828–1909)

On a starred night Prince Lucifer uprose.
Tired of his dark dominion, swung the fiend
Above the rolling ball in cloud part screened,
Where sinners hugged their specter of repose.
Poor prey to his hot fit of pride were those.   5
And now upon his western wing he leaned,
Now his huge bulk o'er Afric's sands careened,
Now the black planet shadowed Arctic snows.
Soaring through wider zones that pricked his scars
With memory of the old revolt from Awe,   10
He reached a middle height, and at the stars,
Which are the brain of heaven, he looked, and sank.
Around the ancient track marched, rank on rank,
The army of unalterable law.

Some of the ways in which an idea finds expression in poetry have been treated more or less fully in many of the earlier discussions, especially in the section dealing with imagery. But the ways in which this process occurs are innumerable and, in fact, vary from poem to poem. In the present instance, "Lucifer in Starlight," the process is a fairly simple one.

An understanding of the poem depends on reference to some specific information that is not given in the poem itself. It presupposes a knowledge and interpretation of the Lucifer myth. Lucifer, the Archangel, rebelled against God, and as a result of his pride, which would not endure the divine dominion over him, was hurled out of heaven. But the subject not only carries with it the bare facts of the myth, but also associations derived from a treatment such as that in Milton's epic, *Paradise Lost,* which involves the rebellion of the angels, and the temptation of Man as a revenge against God. From the myth and its different treatments the reader knows that Lucifer may be taken as the incarnation of pride, and therefore as the principle of anarchy and disorder, in conflict with the principle of order in the universe.

Essentially, Meredith presents this same theme in his poem, but he has put his theme into a new set of terms, and though depending on the body of information and associations which the reader brings to the poem, has succeeded in creating a new poem. Meredith has made, as it were, a new myth, a kind of sequel to the more traditional treatments of the idea. Lucifer, who, as in Milton's *Paradise Lost,* maintains his pride even in the depth of Hell, is shown rising through the starry universe, above the sphere of the earth which is partially concealed from him by clouds. He is not now interested in the sinners on earth through whom, since the Fall of Man, he has been striking at God in revenge; apparently, in his "hot fit of pride" he is aiming at nothing less than a return to his old estate.

Meredith attempts to give as vivid a picture as possible of the enormous bulk of the Fiend, like a planet, flying so near the "rolling ball" of the earth that he shadows it, presumably, from the moon. One may notice that in giving this picture Meredith casts the mythical figure of the Fiend into the universe as we now conceive it, describing the earth revolving in its orbit, and does not use the fixed, central earth of the Ptolemaic conception, which Milton, for instance, used. This detail, though small in itself, gives a certain novelty to Meredith's treatment. It seems to imply, perhaps as a kind of undertone to the poem, that the old force of anarchy is still operating, despite changes in human conceptions, and trying to reach out, even beyond human affairs, to the very center of the universe.

But the real novelty in the new "myth" lies in the reason given by Meredith for Lucifer's failure to proceed with his present rebellion. He does not sink again because he encounters the divine force that once hurled him down. It is definitely stated in the poem that he passes through

> wider zones that pricked his scars
> With memory of the old revolt from Awe.

But this does not deter him, for the reader will observe that he goes on, fearless, to another height, where, simply, he regards the stars, and then quietly sinks to his proper place. The stars, the poet says, are "the brain of heaven." Apparently, the recognition of this fact is what conquers the impulse of the Fiend. The order of the stars demonstrates the reasonable nature of the universe, against which it is useless to rebel. One need not call on an exhibition of the divine powers, the poet is saying, to conquer the impulse of anarchy and rebellion; the slightest understanding of the construction of the universe is enough. The perception of the stars, or of any other item of the ordered universe, not only may comfort man by assuring him that the universe in which he lives is a reasonable one, but may at the same time rebuke his pride, as it rebukes Lucifer, and may teach man humility.

We cannot know very certainly the stages through which the poet's mind passed in writing "Lucifer in Starlight", but we can try to define the logical steps (See "At Melville's Tomb", pp. 477–82). Let us assume that he starts with the general idea, the theme, that rebellion against the reasonable order of the universe is futile. He decides, on reflection, that the orderly procedure of the constellations most majestically exemplifies this order. He might write a poem describing, to a certain extent, the organization of the constellations and pointing his conclusion in general terms.

The chances are strong that such a poem, even if many of the individual lines and passages were beautiful, would be dull. It would have no real principle of poetic organization, would give no device for suspense, and would actually give little scope for the play of the imagination except in so far as the poet might develop details. Presumably, the poet would not long entertain the notion of writing his poem in this way. He would probably want to present his idea more directly, more concretely. It might next occur to him that he could put an observer in the poem, say a man looking at the stars and musing, as in the Bible (Job 38:4-8), on the order of the firmament. In this way the stars might be made to take a symbolic meaning. But such a poem would tend to be undramatic, for not much would happen in it unless the personal situation of the man were so developed that the reader would feel that the fact that he has grasped the meaning of the firmament would have some effect on the man's life. The poet might discard such a solution for his problem on the ground that to build up such a situation for the man would take too much effort and space and would throw the poem out of proportion; in fact, if attempted at all, it would probably develop into a very different piece from the first conception, perhaps a character study. Then the poet might strike upon the subject of Lucifer, who decides on a new revolt and is deterred by a recognition of the meaning of the firmament. This solves the poet's problem. First, it is a dramatic situation. Second, the character of the personage involved, Lucifer, is already established in the reader's mind to give a basis for the poet's new twist of interpretation: that, not the intervention of divine power, but a recognition of the natural order of things, is sufficient to conquer the impulse toward anarchy. Fourth, the use of Lucifer enables the poet to make the same dramatic incident present both of the points involved: the natural order is both a comfort and a rebuke to man.

The process outlined above, as has already been said, is not to be taken as a true account of the working of Meredith's mind in composing the poem. It is far more probable that a poet works from some sudden suggestion of detail, perhaps his stumbling on such a little clause such as "which are the brain of heaven," or his suddenly expressing to himself the idea of the order of the firmament with the line, "the army of unalterable law." Or perhaps he visualized to himself Lucifer moving through the firmament, and asked himself, "Well, what *would* happen?" Almost anything may provide the germ of a poem to the poet, and until he starts developing the poem, exploring in the actual composition the possibilities of the subject, he may not be quite sure where he is going and may not quite know all he intends to say or mean. Writing the poem is for the poet a process of discovery just as reading it is a process of discovery for the reader (See Analysis of "At Melville's Tomb", pp. 477–82).

It is perhaps easier to understand this when one remembers that the total meaning of a poem is not communicated by a single factor of a poem—by the statements, connotations, symbols, or rhythms. We may say that the meaning of a poem is the total result of all of these. We have seen earlier that a poet, for instance, does not merely put an idea into a verse form; he expects the verse to serve as part of the expression of the poem, for, otherwise, there would be no purpose in using verse at all. In this particular poem one can indicate some of the features of the verse that contribute to the total expression of the theme. The poem may be analyzed metrically as follows:

1. On a stárred níght Prince Lúcifér upróse.
2. Tiréd of his dárk domínion swúng the fiénd
3. Abóve the rólling báll in clóud párt screéned,
4. Where sínners húg their spécter óf repóse.
5. Poór préy to his hót fít of príde were thóse.
6. And nów upón his wéstern wing he léaned,
7. Nów his huge búlk o'er Áfric's sánds careéned,
8. Nów the bláck plánet shádowed Árctic snóws.
9. Sóaring through wider zónes that prícked his scárs
10. With mémories óf the old revólt from Áwe,
11. He reáched a míddle héight, and át the stárs,
12. Which áre the brain of heáven, he lóoked, and sánk.
13. Aroúnd the áncient tráck marchéd, ránk on ránk,
14. The ármy óf unálteráble láw.

One can observe that the relatively regular and heavy beat of the verse, the preponderance of monosyllables and hovering accents making for a retarded movement, and the many end-stop lines with light caesura, help give the impression of ponderous, sullen majesty which the image of Lucifer inspires.[1] But there are some more special details that are worthy of notice. The relative absence of heavy internal pauses in the lines makes such pauses come, by comparison, with a special emphasis. The first one appears in line 11 to give an emphatic preparation for the "stars," the word that raises the fundamental idea of the poem. In line 12 the pauses set off "he looked," and "and sank" so that the pauses contribute to the impression of Lucifer's taking a long and thoughtful inspection of the firmament and then slowly descending. In line 13 the fourth foot of the line is composed of the words, *marched, rank,* but the foot gives a spondaic effect, because of the hovering accent, which occurs elsewhere as in the second foot, *black plan* of line 8. This fact, and the preparatory pause before *rank,* give a powerful emphasis. In line 14 the most important idea, in fact, the most important idea of the poem, is contained in the word *unalterable.* This word is composed of five syllables. It is two syllables longer than any other in the poem, standing in contrast to the prevailing use of monosyllables. It is divided *un-al-ter-a-ble.* The accent falls on the second syllable, *al,* and the last three syllables tend to be slurred together. But in the iambic pentameter line in which the word appears in the poem, two of the regular metrical beats fall on syllables of the word: *un-ál-ter-á-ble.* This means that the entire word is given more force than is usual; and this is effective, because of the importance of the word in relation to the subject of the poem.

Concerning another technical factor Chard Powers Smith writes:

Spoken sounds fall naturally into certain groups, the members of each group arising from approximately the same location in the vocal apparatus. In utterance, even in the silent utterance of reading to one's self, the sounds within any one group *feel* alike

---

[1] Of the 111 words in the poem 86 are monosyllables, 3 are trisyllables, and the rest, with the exception of one word, *unalterable,* are disyllables. There are only two run-on lines, and only four cases of internal punctuation.

because the same vocal muscles come into play. It is upon this kinetic basis that assonance rests, quite as much as upon the actual auditory quality of words; it is upon this basis that the sensed similarity of sounds may be most easily explained. Intuitively we feel, for instance, that such a line as this is musically all of a piece:

> The army of unalterable law.
> —*Lucifer in Starlight*—Meredith

The reason is that the principal vowel sounds—the *a* in "army," the first *a* in "unalterable" and the *a* in "law," along with the unimportant vowel sound in "of," all arise in the same region of the throat, while the *u,* second *a* and terminal *e* of "unalterable" arise from an adjoining region; and the dominant consonants— *r, m, n,* and *l*—are likewise all members of a single assonance group.

It will be observed in the line quoted, as in all cases, that it is the stressed syllables that dominate phonetically in any passage, those syllables that receive emphasis in normal prose utterance— quite independent of prosodic scansion. . . . In the line just quoted we may capitalize these stressed syllables, as follows:

> the ARMy of UNALterable LAW.

These are the sounds which, made emphatic by the sense, are most intrusive and which, consequently, give the line its phonetic flavor. According as they do or do not fall into the same assonance group, according, that is, as they are or are not repetitions and variations in the same rhythms of sound, the passage is or is not musical in the present sense. Compared to these syllables, all the rest are of secondary importance.[1]

EXERCISE:

What is the effect of metrical accent on the preposition *at* in line 11?

[1] *Pattern and Variation in Poetry,* New York: Scribner's, pp. 57–58.

THE PALACE OF ART

ALFRED, LORD TENNYSON 1809–1892

I built my soul a lordly pleasure-house,
    Wherein at ease for aye to dwell.
I said, "O Soul, make merry and carouse,
    Dear soul, for all is well."

A huge crag-platform, smooth as burnished brass,   5
    I chose. The rangèd ramparts bright
From level meadow-bases of deep grass
    Suddenly scaled the light.

Thereon I built it firm. Of ledge or shelf
    The rock rose clear, or winding stair,   10
My soul would live alone unto herself
    In her high palace there.

And "while the world runs round and round," I said,
    "Reign thou apart, a quiet king,
Still as, while Saturn whirls, his steadfast shade   15
    Sleeps on his luminous ring."

To which my soul made answer readily:
    "Trust me, in bliss I shall abide
In this great mansion, that is built for me.
    So royal-rich and wide."   20

    .   .   .   .

Four courts I made, East, West, and South and North,
    In each a squarèd lawn, wherefrom
The golden gorge of dragons spouted forth
    A flood of fountain-foam.

And round the cool green courts there ran a row   25
    Of cloisters, branched like mighty woods,
Echoing all night to that sonorous flow
    Of spouted fountain-floods.

And round the roofs a gilded gallery
    That lent broad verge to distant lands,   30
Far as the wild swan wings, to where the sky
    Dipped down to sea and sands.

From those four jets four currents in one swell
  Across the mountain streamed below
In misty folds, that floating as they fell,   35
  Lit up a torrent-bow.

And high on every peak a statue seemed
  To hang on tiptoe, tossing up
A cloud of incense of all odor steamed
  From out a golden cup.   40

So that she thought, "And who shall gaze upon
  My palace with unblinded eyes,
While this great bow will waver in the sun,
  And that sweet incense rise?"

For that sweet incense rose and never failed,   45
  And, while day sank or mounted higher,
The light aerial gallery, golden-railed,
  Burnt like a fringe of fire.

Likewise the deep-set windows, stained and traced,
  Would seem slow-flaming crimson fires   50
From shadowed grots of arches interlaced,
  And tipped with frost-like spires.

        .   .   .   .

Full of long-sounding corridors it was,
  That over-vaulted grateful gloom,
Through which the livelong day my soul did pass,   55
  Well-pleased, from room to room.

Full of great rooms and small the palace stood,
  All various, each a perfect whole
From living Nature, fit for every mood
  And change of my still soul.   60

For some were hung with arras green and blue,
  Showing a gaudy summer-morn,
Where with puffed cheek the belted hunter blew
  His wreathèd bugle-horn.

One seemed all dark and red—a tract of sand,   65
  And some one pacing there alone,
Who paced for ever in a glimmering land,
  Lit with a low large moon.

One showed an iron coast and angry waves,
  You seemed to hear them climb and fall   70
And roar rock-thwarted under bellowing caves,
  Beneath the windy wall.

And one, a full-fed river winding slow
  By herds upon an endless plain,
The ragged rims of thunder brooding low,   75
  With shadow-streaks of rain.

And one, the reapers at their sultry. toil.
  In front they bound the sheaves. Behind
Were realms of upland, prodigal in oil,
  And hoary to the wind.   80

And one a foreground black with stones and slags,
  Beyond, a line of heights, and higher
All barred with long white cloud the scornful crags,
  And highest, snow and fire.

And one, an English home—gray twilight poured   85
  On dewy pastures, dewy trees,
Softer than sleep—all things in order stored,
  A haunt of ancient Peace.

Nor these alone, but every landscape fair,
  As fit for every mood of mind,   90
Or gay, or grave, or sweet, or stern, was there,
  Not less than truth designed.

            .   .   .   .

Or the maid, mother by a crucifix,
  In tracts of pasture sunny-warm,
Beneath branch-work of costly sardonyx,   95
  Sat smiling, babe in arm.

Or in a clear-walled city on the sea,
  Near gilded organ-pipes, her hair
Wound with white roses, slept Saint Cecily;
  An angel looked at her.   100

Or thronging all one porch of Paradise
  A group of Houris bowed to see
The dying Islamite, with hands and eyes
  That said, We wait for thee.

Or mythic Uther's deeply-wounded son   105
  In some fair space of sloping greens
Lay, dozing in the vale of Avalon,
  And watched by weeping queens.

Or hollowing one hand against his ear,
  To list a foot-fall, ere he saw   110
The wood-nymph, stayed the Ausonian king to hear
  Of wisdom and of law.

Or over hills with peaky tops engrailed,
  And many a tract of palm and rice,
The throne of Indian Cama slowly sailed   115
  A summer fanned with spice.

Or sweet Europa's mantle blew unclasped,
  From off her shoulder backward borne,
From one hand drooped a crocus; one hand grasped
  The mild bull's golden horn.   120

Or else flushed Ganymede, his rosy thigh
  Half-buried in the eagle's down,
Sole as a flying star shot through the sky
  Above the pillared town.

Nor these alone; but every legend fair   125
  Which the supreme Caucasian mind
Carved out of Nature for itself, was there,
  Not less than life, designed.

Then in the towers I placed great bells that swung,
  Moved of themselves, with silver sound;   130
And with choice paintings of wise men I hung
  The royal dais round.

For there was Milton like a seraph strong,
  Beside him Shakespeare bland and mild;
And there the world-worn Dante grasped his song,   135
  And somewhat grimly smiled.

And there the Ionian father of the rest;
  A million wrinkles carved his skin;
A hundred winters snowed upon his breast,
  From cheek and throat and chin.   140

Above, the fair hall-ceiling stately-set
  Many an arch high up did lift,
And angels rising and descending met
  With interchange of gift.

Below was all mosaic choicely planned   145
  With cycles of the human tale
Of this wide world, the times of every land
  So wrought, they will not fail.

The people here, a beast of burden slow,
  Toiled onward, pricked with goads and stings;   150
Here played, a tiger, rolling to and fro
  The heads and crowns of kings;

Here rose, an athlete, strong to break or bind
  All force in bonds that might endure,
And here once more like some sick man declined,   155
  And trusted any cure.

But over these she trod; and those great bells
  Began to chime. She took her throne;
She sat betwixt the shining oriels,
  To sing her songs alone.   160

And through the topmost oriels' colored flame
  Two godlike faces gazed below;
Plato the wise, and large-browed Verulam,
    The first of those who know.

And all those names that in their motion were   165
  Full-welling fountain-heads of change,
Betwixt the slender shafts were blazoned fair
    In diverse raiment strange;

Through which the lights, rose, amber, emerald, blue,
  Flushed in her temples and her eyes,   170
And from her lips, as morn from Memnon, drew
    Rivers of melodies.

No nightingale delighteth to prolong
  Her low preamble all alone,
More than my soul to hear her echoed song   175
    Throb through the ribbèd stone;

Singing and murmuring in her feastful mirth,
  Joying to feel herself alive,
Lord over Nature, lord of the visible earth,
    Lord of the senses five;   180

Communing with herself: "All these are mine,
  And let the world have peace or wars,
'T is one to me." She—when young night divine
    Crowned dying day with stars,

Making sweet close of his delicious toils—   185
  Lit light in wreaths and anadems,
And pure quintessences of precious oils
    In hollowed moons of gems,

To mimic heaven; and clapped her hands and cried,
  "I marvel if my still delight   190
In this great house so royal-rich and wide
    Be flattered to the height.

"O all things fair to sate my various eyes!
    O shapes and hues that please me well!
O silent faces of the Great and Wise,   195
    My Gods, with whom I dwell!

"O Godlike isolation which art mine,
    I can but count thee perfect gain,
What time I watch the darkening droves of swine
    That range on yonder plain.   200

"In filthy sloughs they roll a prurient skin,
    They graze and wallow, breed and sleep;
And oft some brainless devil enters in,
    And drives them to the deep."

Then of the moral instinct would she prate   205
    And of the rising from the dead,
As hers by right of full-accomplished Fate;
    And at the last she said:

"I take possession of man's mind and deed.
    I care not what the sects may brawl,   210
I sit as God holding no form of creed,
    But contemplating all."

       .   .   .   .

Full oft the riddle of the painful earth
    Flashed through her as she sat alone,
Yet not the less held she her solemn mirth,   215
    And intellectual throne.

And so she throve and prospered; so three years
    She prospered; on the fourth she fell,
Like Herod, when the shout was in his ears,
    Struck through with pangs of hell.   220

Lest she should fail and perish utterly,
    God, before whom ever lie bare
The abysmal deeps of Personality,
    Plagued her with sore despair.

When she would think, where'er she turned her sight,
   The airy hand confusion wrought,   226
Wrote "Mene, mene," and divided quite
    The kingdom of her thought.

Deep dread and loathing of her solitude
   Fell on her, from which mood was born   230
Scorn of herself; again, from out that mood
    Laughter at her self-scorn.

"What! is not this my place of strength," she said,
   "My spacious mansion built for me,
Whereof the strong foundation-stones were laid   235
    Since my first memory?"

But in dark corners of her palace stood
   Uncertain shapes; and unawares
On white-eyed phantasms weeping tears of blood,
    And horrible nightmares,   240

And hollow shades enclosing hearts of flame,
   And, with dim fretted foreheads all,
On corpses three-months-old at noon she came,
    That stood against the wall.

A spot of dull stagnation, without light   245
   Or power of movement, seemed my soul,
Mid onward-sloping motions infinite
    Making for one sure goal.

A still salt pool, locked in with bars of sand
   Left on the shore, that hears all night   250
The plunging seas draw backward from the land
    Their moon led waters white.

A star that with the choral starry dance
   Joined not, but stood, and standing saw
The hollow orb of moving Circumstance   255
    Rolled round by one fixed law.

Back on herself her serpent pride had curled.
   "No voice," she shrieked in that lone hall,
"No voice breaks through the stillness of this world:
    One deep, deep silence all!"   260

She, moldering with the dull earth's moldering sod,
   Inwrapt tenfold in slothful shame,
Lay there exilèd from eternal God,
    Lost to her place and name;

And death and life she hated equally,   265
   And nothing saw, for her despair,
But dreadful time, dreadful eternity,
    No comfort anywhere;

Remaining utterly confused with fears,
   And ever worse with growing time,   270
And ever unrelieved by dismal tears,
    And all alone in crime:

Shut up as in a crumbling tomb, girt round
   With blackness as a solid wall,
Far off she seemed to hear the dully sound   275
    Of human footsteps fall

As in strange lands a traveler walking slow,
   In doubt and great perplexity,
A little before moonrise hears the low
    Moan of an unknown sea;   280

And knows not if it be thunder, or a sound
   Of rocks thrown down, or one deep cry
Of great wild beasts; then thinketh, "I have found
    A new land, but I die."

She howled aloud, "I am on fire within.   285
   There comes no murmur of reply.
What is it that will take away my sin,
    And save me lest I die?"

So when four years were wholly finishèd,
  She threw her royal robes away.   290
"Make me a cottage in the vale," she said.
  "Where I may mourn and pray.

"Yet pull not down my palace towers that are
  So lightly, beautifully built:
Perchance I may return with others there,   295
  When I have purged my guilt."

EXERCISE:

The general statement about life made by this poem is obvious
and probably presents a reasonable attitude. Moreover, the poem
employs a great deal of imagery. But does the imagery really
bear a close and functional relation to the idea of the poem?

COMPOSED BY THE SEA-SIDE NEAR CALAIS AUGUST 1802

WILLIAM WORDSWORTH (1770–1850)

Fair Star of evening, Splendor of the west,
Star of my Country!—on the horizon's brink
Thou hangest, stooping, as might seem, to sink
On England's bosom: yet well pleased to rest,
Meanwhile, and be to her a glorious crest   5
Conspicuous to the Nations. Thou, I think,
Shouldst be my Country's emblem; and should'st wink,
Bright Star! with laughter on her banners, drest
In thy fresh beauty. There! that dusky spot
Beneath thee that is England; there she lies.   10
Blessings be on you both! one hope, one lot,
One life, one glory! I with many a fear
For my dear Country, many heartfelt sighs,
Among men who do not love her, linger here.

EXERCISE:

What prevents this poem from being merely a general statement of the poet's patriotism?

ELEGY

WRITTEN IN A COUNTRY CHURCHYARD

THOMAS GRAY (1716–1771)

The Curfew tolls the knell of parting day,
  The lowing herd wind slowly o'er the lea,
The plowman homeward plods his weary way,
  And leaves the world to darkness and to me.

Now fades the glimmering landscape on the sight,   5
  And all the air a solemn stillness holds,
Save where the beetle wheels his droning flight,
  And drowsy tinklings lull the distant folds;

Save that from yonder ivy-mantled tower
  The moping owl does to the moon complain   10
Of such, as wandering near her secret bower,
  Molest her ancient solitary reign.

Beneath those rugged elms, that yew-tree's shade,
  Where heaves the turf in many a mouldering heap,
Each in his narrow cell for ever laid,   15
  The rude Forefathers of the hamlet sleep.

The breezy call of incense-breathing Morn,
  The swallow twittering from the straw-built shed,
The cock's shrill clarion, or the echoing horn,
  No more shall rouse them from their lowly bed.   20

For them no more the blazing hearth shall burn,
  Or busy housewife ply her evening care:
No children run to lisp their sire's return,
  Or climb his knees the envied kiss to share.

Oft did the harvest to their sickle yield,   25
  Their furrow oft the stubborn glebe has broke;
How jocund did they drive their team afield!
  How bowed the woods beneath their sturdy stroke!

Let not Ambition mock their useful toil,
  Their homely joys, and destiny obscure;   30
Nor Grandeur hear with a disdainful smile
  The short and simple annals of the poor.

The boast of heraldry, the pomp of power,
  And all that beauty, all that wealth e'er gave,
Awaits alike the inevitable hour.   35
  The paths of glory lead but to the grave.

Nor you, ye Proud, impute to These the fault,
  If Memory o'er their Tomb no Trophies raise,
Where through the long-drawn aisle and fretted vault
  The pealing anthem swells the note of praise.   40

Can storied urn or animated bust
  Back to its mansion call the fleeting breath?
Can Honor's voice provoke the silent dust,
  Or Flattery sooth the dull cold ear of Death?

Perhaps in this neglected spot is laid   45
  Some heart once pregnant with celestial fire;
Hands, that the rod of empire might have swayed,
  Or waked to ecstasy the living lyre.

But Knowledge to their eyes her ample page
  Rich with the spoils of time did ne'er unroll;   50
Chill Penury repressed their noble rage,
  And froze the genial current of the soul.

Full many a gem of purest ray serene,
  The dark unfathomed caves of ocean bear:
Full many a flower is born to blush unseen,   55
  And waste its sweetness on the desert air.

Some village-Hampden, that with dauntless breast
  The little Tyrant of his fields withstood;
Some mute inglorious Milton here may rest,
  Some Cromwell guiltless of his country's blood.   60

The applause of listening senates to command,
  The threats of pain and ruin to despise,
To scatter plenty o'er a smiling land,
  And read their history in a nation's eyes,

Their lot forbade: nor circumscribed alone   65
  Their growing virtues, but their crimes confin'd;
Forbade to wade through slaughter to a throne,
  And shut the gates of mercy on mankind,

The struggling pangs of conscious truth to hide,
  To quench the blushes of ingenuous shame,   70
Or heap the shrine of Luxury and Pride
  With incense kindled at the Muse's flame.

Far from the madding crowd's ignoble strife,
  Their sober wishes never learned to stray;
Along the cool sequestered vale of life   75
  They kept the noiseless tenor of their way.

Yet even these bones from insult to protect,
  Some frail memorial still erected nigh,
With uncouth rhymes and shapeless sculpture decked,
  Implores the passing tribute of a sigh.   80

Their name, their years, spelt by the unlettered muse,
  The place of fame and elegy supply:
And many a holy text around she strews,
  That teach the rustic moralist to die.

For who to dumb Forgetfulness a prey,   85
  This pleasing anxious being e'er resigned,
Left the warm precincts of the cheerful day,
  Nor cast one longing lingering look behind?

On some fond breast the parting soul relies,
  Some pious drops the closing eye requires;   90
Ev'n from the tomb the voice of Nature cries,
  Ev'n in our Ashes live their wonted Fires.

For thee, who mindful of the unhonoured Dead
  Dost in these lines their artless tale relate,
If chance, by lonely contemplation led,   , 95
  Some kindred Spirit shall inquire thy fate,

Haply some hoary-headed Swain may say,
  "Oft have we seen him at the peep of dawn
Brushing with hasty steps the dews away
  To meet the sun upon the upland lawn.   100

"There at the foot of yonder nodding beech
  That wreathes its old fantastic roots so high,
His listless length at noontide would he stretch,
  And pore upon the brook that babbles by.

"Hard by yon wood, now smiling as in scorn,   105
  Muttering his wayward fancies he would rove,
Now drooping, woeful wan, like one forlorn,
  Or crazed with care, or crossed in hopeless love.

"One morn I missed him on the customed hill,
  Along the heath and near his favorite tree;   110
Another came; nor yet beside the rill,
  Nor up the lawn, nor at the wood was he;

"The next with dirges due in sad array
  Slow through the church-way path we saw him borne.
Approach and read (for thou can'st read) the lay,   115
  Graved on the stone beneath yon agèd thorn."

THE EPITAPH

Here rests his head upon the lap of earth
  A youth to fortune and to fame unknown.
Fair Science. frowned not on his humble birth,
  And Melancholy marked him for her own.   120

Large was his bounty, and his soul sincere,
  Heaven did a recompense as largely send:
He gave to Misery all he had, a tear,
  He gained from Heaven ('twas all he wished) a friend.

> *No farther seek his merits to disclose,*   125
>   *Or draw his frailties from their dread abode,*
> (*There they alike in trembling hope repose*)
>   *The bosom of his Father and his God.*

EXERCISE:

1. Are the general statements about life in this poem insisted
upon in isolation, or are they drawn into, and accounted for by,
the body of the poem?
2. Discuss the attitude and tone of the poem.

In connection with this question of the tone and attitude
inherent in the poem, one critic, William Empson, has written:
Gray's *Elegy* is an odd case of poetry with latent political ideas:

> Full many a gem of purest ray serene
> The dark, unfathomed caves of ocean bear;
> Full many a flower is born to blush unseen
> And waste its sweetness on the desert air.

What this means, as the context makes clear, is that eighteenth-
century England had no scholarship system or *carriere ouverte aux
talents*.   This is stated as pathetic, but the reader is put into a
mood in which one would not try to alter it.   (It is true that
Gray's society, unlike a possible machine society, was necessarily
based on manual labor, but it might have used a man of special
ability wherever he was born.)   By comparing the social arrangement to Nature he makes it seem inevitable, which it was not,
and gives it a dignity which was undeserved.   Furthermore, a
gem does not mind being in a cave and a flower prefers not to be
picked; we feel that the man is like the flower, as short-lived,
natural, and valuable, and this tricks us into feeling that he is
better off without opportunities.   The sexual suggestion of *blush*
brings in the Christian idea that virginity is good in itself, and so
that any renunciation is good; this may trick us into feeling
it is lucky for the poor man that society keeps him unspotted
from the world.   The tone of melancholy claims that the poet
understands the considerations opposed to aristocracy, though
he judges against them; the truisms of the reflections in the

churchyard, the universality and impersonality this gives to the style, claim as if by comparison that we ought to accept the injustice of society as we do the inevitability of death.[1]

Criticize Empson's analysis in relation to the entire poem.

ODE TO SIMPLICITY

WILLIAM COLLINS (1721–1759)

O Thou, by nature taught
To breathe her genuine thought,
In numbers warmly pure, and sweetly strong;
    Who first, on mountains wild,
    In fancy, loveliest child,   5
Thy babe, or pleasure's, nursed the powers of song!

    Thou, who, with hermit heart,
    Disdain'st the wealth of art,
And gauds, and pageant weeds, and trailing pall;
    But com'st a decent maid,   10
    In Attic robe arrayed,
O chaste, unboastful nymph, to thee I call;

    By all the honeyed store
    On Hybla's thymy shore;
By all her blooms, and mingled murmurs dear;   15
    By her whose lovelorn woe,
    In evening musings slow,
Soothed sweetly sad Electra's poet's ear:

    By old Cephisus deep,
    Who spread his wavy sweep,   20
In warbled wanderings, round thy green retreat;
    On whose enameled side,
    When holy freedom died,
No equal haunt allured thy future feet.

[1] *English Pastoral Poetry,* New York: Norton, p. 4.

O sister meek of truth,   25
To my admiring youth,
Thy sober aid and native charms infuse!
The flowers that sweetest breathe,
Though beauty culled the wreath,
Still ask thy hand to range their ordered hues.   30

While Rome could none esteem
But virtue's patriot theme,
You loved her hills, and led their laureat band:
But stayed to sing alone
To one distinguished throne;   35
And turned the face, and fled her altered land.

No more, in hall or bower,
The passions own thy power;
Love, only love, her forceless numbers mean:
For thou hast left her shrine;   40
Nor olive more, nor vine,
Shall gain thy feet to bless the servile scene.

Though taste, though genius, bless
To some divine excess,
Faints the cold work till thou inspire the whole;   45
What each, what all supply,
May court, may charm, our eye;
Thou, only thou, cans't raise the meeting soul!

Of these let others ask,
To aid some mighty task,   50
I only seek to find thy temperate vale;
Where oft my reed might sound
To maids and shepherds round,
And all thy sons, O nature, learn my tale.

EXERCISE:

1. The poet here, like Tennyson in "The Palace of Art," is trying to make an abstract idea vivid and forceful by associating it with concrete images and by using the various technical resources of verse. Is Collins more successful than Tennyson?

2. Define the tone and comment upon some of the technical devices used in establishing it.

LEE IN THE MOUNTAINS
1865–1870

DONALD DAVIDSON (1893–   )

Walking into the shadows, walking alone
Where the sun falls through the ruined boughs of locusts
Up to the President's office . . .
                       Hearing the voices
Whisper, *Hush it is General Lee!* And strangely
Hearing my own voice say *Good morning boys.*   5
(*Don't get up. You are early. It is long
Before the bell. You will have long to wait
On these cold steps. . . .*)
                   The young have time to wait.
But the soldiers' faces under the tossing flags
Lift no more by any road or field,   10
And I am spent with old wars and new sorrow.
Walking the rocky path, where the steps decay
And the paint cracks and grass eats on the stone.
It is not General Lee, young men . . .
It is Robert Lee in a dark civilian suit who walks,   15
An outlaw fumbling for the latch, a voice
Commanding in a dream where no flag flies.

My father's house is taken and his hearth
Left to the candle-drippings where the ashes
Whirl at a chimney-breath on the cold stone.   20
I can hardly remember my father's look, I cannot
Answer his voice as he calls farewell in the misty
Mounting where riders gather at gates.
He was old then—I was a child—his hand
Held out for mine, some daybreak snatched away,   25
And he rode out, a broken man. Now let
His lone grave keep, surer than cypress roots,
The vow I made beside him. God too late
Unseals to certain eyes the drift
Of time and the hopes of men and a sacred cause.   30
The fortune of the Lees goes with the land
Whose sons will keep it still. My mother
Told me much. She sat among the candles,
Fingering the *Memoirs,* now so long unread.

And as my pen moves on across the page   35
Her voice comes back, a murmuring distillation
Of old Virginia days now done to death,
The hurt of all that was and cannot be.

Why did my father write? I know he saw
History clutched as a wraith out of blowing mist   40
Where tongues are loud, and a glut of little souls
Laps at the too much blood and the burning house.
He would have his say, but I shall not have mine.
What I do is only a son's devoir
To a lost father. Let him only speak.   45
The rest must pass to men who never knew
(But on a written page) the strike of armies,
And never heard the long Confederate cry
Charge through the muzzling smoke or saw the bright
Eyes of the beardless boys go up to death.   50
It is Robert Lee who writes with his father's hand—
The rest must go unsaid and the lips be locked.

If all were told, as it cannot be told—
If all the dread opinion of the heart
Now could speak, now in the shame and torment   55
Lashing the bound and trampled States—

If a word were said, as it cannot be said—

I see clear waters run in Virginia's Valley
And in the house the weeping of young women
Rises no more. The waves of grain begin.   60
The Shenandoah is golden with new grain.
The Blue Ridge, lapped in a haze of light,
Thunders no more. The horse is at plow. The rifle
Returns to the chimney crotch and the hunter's hand.
And nothing else than this? Was it for this
That on an April day we stacked our arms
Obedient to a soldier's trust—to sink, to lie   65
Ground by heels of little men,
Forever maimed, defeated, lost, impugned?
And was I then betrayed? Did I betray?

If it were said, as still it might be said—
If it were said, and a word should run like fire,   70
Like living fire into the roots of grass,
The sunken flag would kindle on wild hills,
The brooding hearts would waken, and the dream
Stir like a crippled phantom under the pines,
And this torn earth would quicken into shouting   75
Beneath the feet of ragged men—
                                        The quill
Turns to the waiting page, the sword of Lee
Bows to the rust that cankers and the silence.

Among these boys whose eyes lift up to mine
Within gray walls where droning wasps repeat   80
A hollow reveille, I still must face
Day after day, the courier with his summons
Once more to surrender, now to surrender all.
Without arms or men I stand, but with knowledge only
I face what long I saw, before others knew,   85
When Pickett's men streamed back, and I heard the tangled
Cry of the Wilderness wounded, bloody with doom.

The mountains, once I said, in the little room
At Richmond, by the huddled fire, but still
The President shook his head. The mountains wait,   90
I said, in the long beat and rattle of siege
At cratered Petersburg.   Too late
We sought the mountains and those people came.
And Lee is in mountains now, beyond Appomattox,   95
Listening long for voices that never will speak
Again; hearing the hoofbeats come and go and fade
Without a stop, without a brown hand lifting
The tent-flap, or a bugle call at dawn,
Or ever on the long white road the flag   100
Of Jackson's quick brigades. I am alone,
Trapped, consenting, taken at last in mountains.

It is not the bugle now, or the long roll beating.
The simple stroke of a chapel bell forbids
The hurtling dream, recalls the lonely mind.   105
Young men, the God of your father is a just
And merciful God who in this blood once shed

On your green altars measures out all days,
And measures out the grace
Whereby alone we live;   110
And in His might He waits,
Brooding within the certitude of time,
To bring this lost forsaken valour
And the fierce faith undying
And the love quenchless   115
To flower among the hills to which we cleave,
To fruit upon the mountains whither we flee,
Never forsaking, never denying
His children and His children's children forever
Unto all generations of the faithful heart. Amen.   120

EXERCISE:

1. What is the theme of this poem?
2. Account for the poet's method of presenting it in this poem.

IF POISONOUS MINERALS

JOHN DONNE (1573–1631)

If poisonous minerals, and if that tree
Whose fruit threw death on else immortal us,
If lecherous goats, if serpents envious
Cannot be damned, Alas! why should I be?
Why should intent or reason, born in me,   5
Make sins, else equal, in me more heinous?
And mercy being easy, and glorious
To God, in his stern wrath why threatens he?
But who am I, that dare dispute with thee,
O God? O! of thine only worthy blood,   10
And my tears, make a heavenly Lethean flood,
And drown in it my sin's black memory;
That thou remember them, some claim as debt,
I think it mercy, if thou wilt forget.

The theme of this poem may be put as a question: what should
be the attitude of sinful man toward God's justice?   The theme

is presented by a method quite different from that employed in "Lucifer in Starlight," in which the idea appears in terms of an obvious dramatic incident. Here no incident, no narrative element, appears directly. But this poem is, in one sense, dramatic in that, being a prayer, it is addressed by a sin-convicted man to God, and has therefore a special speaker and a special listener and is not merely a general thought or speculation. Being dramatic, it involves a special instance. But the handling of the idea is direct, in the form of argument. The question, then, is: how does the poet invest this argument with the emotional force necessary to poetic effect?

The argument may be briefly summarized as follows: although it appears unjust that man, merely because he possesses the faculty of reason, should be damned for actions common to lower Nature and unpunished there, man should realize that God's treatment is not to be understood by human reason, and should therefore seek the remission of his sins through the double force of Christ's blood and his own repentance. This is a flat prose statement using none of the imaginative resources that can vivify language with poetic force. This statement, as prose, has an interest, not because of the form in which it is put, but because the idea it involves is a serious one in human experience. But as it stands, the reader must supply, by such application as his own imagination affords, the emotional force. One cannot say, however, that the seriousness of the theme of this poem permits the poet to employ successfully a more direct presentation through argument than is characteristic of most poems; for the theme of all effective poetry has, in some degree, a serious reference to human experience. Even such poems as Herrick's "Delight in Disorder" (p. 327), or Corbet's "The Fairies' Farewell" (p. 346), both of which show a playful or fanciful surface effect, have a concealed bearing on important elements of human life. In Donne's poem, then, the success of the more direct presentation of the idea is still dependent upon the way in which it is handled, on the total organization and structure of the poem, and not on the mere seriousness or importance of the idea as such.

We should study, then, the way in which the idea is handled and try to define some of the devices.

In the first paragraph, in comparing the poem with "Lucifer in Starlight," we said that it has a certain dramatic context because of the form of a prayer, an address from man to God. This dramatic effect is heightened in various incidental ways. First, the *octave* (*Glossary*) is composed of three questions, each one leading to the next. A question is more provocative than a statement. This is especially true when the linking, as in this case, creates a kind of suspense, rising to a climax with

> . . . in his stern wrath why threatens he?

Then this is answered in the beginning of the sestet, not by a statement, but by another question:

> But who am I, that dare dispute with thee?

Second, the exclamatory effects, which occur twice in the poem, serve to heighten the dramatic quality. A poet must be very careful in using exclamation, for it frequently strikes the reader as an arbitrary attempt to force him to respond; the poet must, that is, be careful of the context and of preparation for his use of exclamation. But observe in this poem how the preparation has been made. The first case occurs in the fourth line with the word "alas." Let us shift the use to see what change would follow:

> Alas! if poisonous minerals and that tree

Or, perhaps a better version:

> Alas! if poisonous minerals, if that tree

In such cases the exclamation merely serves as a signal to the reader that the poet intends something important, and unless what does follow fulfills that promise the reader feels cheated. Even if the reader feels that the exclamation is justified by what follows, such a use is essentially undramatic because unprepared for. By contrast observe how Donne introduces the exclamatory word just after the idea of damnation has been given, and just before that idea receives a personal application:

> . . . if serpents envious
> Cannot be damned, alas! why should I be?

It is as though the cry were wrung from some one by the sudden full awareness of the meaning of damnation. The same principle is applied in the second instance. The cry "O God, O!" occurs at the point where the thought of the sonnet turns. The first line of the sestet has just stated that human reason cannot question God. It marks the moment when the man ceases to reason about God's justice and question it, and pleads that the memory of his sin be drowned in Christ's blood and the tears of repentance. In both cases, the use of the exclamation is psychologically justified, and is therefore dramatic.

Third, the idea is worked out in a series of contrasts, a device that, as we have seen, is often used to heighten interest. In the first four lines the lower creation is contrasted with man on the grounds of guilt—the mineral, vegetable, and animal kingdoms as distinguished from man. In the fifth and sixth lines the contrast is made on the grounds of the possession of reason. But these lines also imply a paradox: reason, which presumably is given man to raise him from the brute, is the source of his damnation, which even the brute cannot suffer. In the seventh and eighth lines there is the opposition of God's mercy and God's wrath. In the ninth line, human reason is contrasted with divine justice. In the tenth, eleventh, and twelfth lines, the climax, the method of argument is abandoned, and the man throws himself on the promise of redemption. But in the concluding couplet the whole poem is again summarized with a contrast: though some men, the poet says, have hoped for salvation by praying that God remember them, he himself, reflecting on his sinful state, hopes for salvation by a divine forgetfulness.

All of these devices for heightening the effect of the poem depend on the detailed working out of the idea, that is, on the relating of the logical structure to the psychological and emotional effect desired by the poet. (We can see that such devices are somewhat different from devices such as narrative incident, symbol, simile, and metaphor. This poem makes no use, in fact, of narrative incident to embody its theme, as does "Johnie Armstrong" or "Patterns"; and it is peculiarly bare of simile and metaphor, which are so important in most poetry.) But there are still other ways in which the poet has heightened his statement of the idea. He does not give his contrast between man and the lower creation in general terms, but introduces the idea with concrete instances, "poisonous minerals," "that tree whose fruit threw death," "lecherous goats," and "serpents envious." By taking this approach he has put the reader's imagination to work; the objects named serve to symbolize the idea to a certain extent. Though, as we have said, the poem is peculiarly bare of simile and metaphor, the major one in the poem is very violent and powerful. It seems that the poet, feeling the effectiveness of such a device, has reserved it for his climax, introducing it to focus the idea just stated. The image of the blood of Christ and the tears of the penitent combining to make a flood is very bold, and especially bold in contrast with the more direct method characteristic of the octave.

EXERCISE:

Investigate the relation of the *forced pauses* (p. 280 and *Glossary*) in the second line to the intention of the poem.

DEATH

JOHN DONNE (1573–1631)

Death, be not proud, though some have callèd thee
Mighty and dreadful, for thou art not so;
For those whom thou think'st thou dost overthrow
Die not, poor Death; nor yet canst thou kill me.
From rest and sleep, which but thy picture be,   5
Much pleasure, then from thee much more must flow;
And soonest our best men with thee do go—
Rest of their bones and souls' delivery!
Thou'rt slave to Fate, chance, kings and desperate men,
And dost with poison, war, and sickness dwell,   10
And poppy or charms can make us sleep as well,
And better than thy stroke; why swell'st thou then?
One short sleep past, we wake eternally,
And death shall be no more: Death, thou shalt die!

EXERCISE:

Using the analysis of "If Poisonous Minerals" for a model, write an analysis of this poem.

THANATOPSIS

WILLIAM CULLEN BRYANT (1794–1878)

To him who in the love of Nature holds
Communion with her visible forms, she speaks
A various language; for his gayer hours
She has a voice of gladness, and a smile
And eloquence of beauty, and she glides   5
Into his darker musings, with a mild
And healing sympathy, that steals away
Their sharpness, ere he is aware. When thoughts
Of the last bitter hour come like a blight
Over thy spirit, and sad images   10
Of the stern agony, and shroud, and pall,
And breathless darkness, and the narrow house,
Make thee to shudder, and grow sick at heart;—
Go forth, under the open sky, and list
To Nature's teachings, while from all around—   15
Earth and her waters, and the depths of air—
Comes a still voice—Yet a few days, and thee
The all-beholding sun shall see no more
In all his course; nor yet in the cold ground,
Where thy pale form was laid, with many tears,   20
Nor in the embrace of ocean, shall exist
Thy image. Earth, that nourished thee, shall claim
Thy growth, to be resolved to earth again,
And, lost each human trace, surrendering up
Thine individual being, shalt thou go   25
To mix forever with the elements,
To be a brother to the insensible rock
And to the sluggish clod, which the rude swain
Turns with his share, and treads upon. The oak
Shall send his roots abroad, and pierce thy mould.   30

  Yet not to thine eternal resting place
Shalt thou retire alone, nor couldst thou wish
Couch more magnificent. Thou shalt lie down
With patriarchs of the infant world—with kings,
The powerful of the earth—the wise, the good,   35
Fair forms, and hoary seers of ages past,
All in one mighty sepulchre. The hills

Rock-ribbed and ancient as the sun,—the vales
Stretching in pensive quietness between;
The venerable woods—rivers that move   40
In majesty, and the complaining brooks
That make the meadows green; and, poured round all,
Old Ocean's gray and melancholy waste,—
Are but the decorations all
Of the great tomb of man. The golden sun,   45
The planets, all the infinite host of heaven,
Are shining on the sad abodes of death,
Through the still lapse of ages. All that tread
The globe are but a handful to the tribes
That slumber in its bosom.—Take the wings   50
Of morning, pierce the Barcan wilderness,
Or lose thyself in the continuous woods
Where rolls the Oregon, and hears no sound,
Save his own dashings—yet the dead are there:
And millions in those solitudes, since first   55
The flight of years began, have laid them down
In their last sleep—the dead reign there alone.
So shalt thou rest, and what if thou withdraw
In silence from the living, and no friend
Take note of thy departure? All that breathe   60
Will share thy destiny. The gay will laugh
When thou art gone, the solemn brood of care
Plod on, and each one as before will chase
His favorite phantom; yet all these shall leave
Their mirth and their employments, and shall come   65
And make their bed with thee. As the long train
Of ages glide away, the sons of men,
The youth in life's green spring, and he who goes
In the full strength of years, matron and maid,
The speechless babe, and the gray-headed man—   70
Shall one by one be gathered to thy side,
By those who in their turn shall follow them.

    So live that when thy summons comes to join
The innumerable caravan, which moves
To that mysterious realm, where each shall take   75
His chamber in the silent halls of death,
Thou go not, like the quarry-slave at night,

Scourged to his dungeon, but, sustained and soothed
By an unfaltering trust, approach thy grave,
Like one who wraps the drapery of his couch   80
About him, and lies down to pleasant dreams.

LIFE AND DEATH

WILLIAM SHAKESPEARE (1564–1616)

I

Reason thus with life:
If I do lose thee, I do lose a thing
That none but fools would keep: a breath thou art,
Servile to all the skyey influences,
That dost this habitation, where thou keep'st,   5
Hourly afflict. Merely, thou art death's fool;
For him thou labor'st by thy flight to shun,
And yet runn'st toward him still. Thou art not noble:
For all the accommodations that thou bearest
Are nursed by baseness. Thou art by no means valiant;   10
For thou dost fear the soft and tender fork
Of a poor worm. Thy best of rest is sleep,
And that thou oft provok'st; yet grossly fear'st
Thy death, which is no more. Thou art not thyself;
For thou exist'st on many a thousand grains   15
That issue out of dust. Happy thou art not;
For what thou hast not, still thou striv'st to get,
And what thou hast, forget'st. Thou art not certain;
For thy complexion shifts to strange effects,
After the moon. If thou art rich, thou'rt poor;   20
For, like an ass whose back with ingots bows,
Thou bear'st thy heavy riches but a journey,
And death unloads thee. Friend hast thou none;
For thine own bowels, which do call thee sire,
The mere effusion of thy proper loins,   25
Do curse the gout, serpigo, and the rheum,
For ending thee no sooner. Thou hast nor youth nor age;
But, as it were, an after-dinner's sleep,
Dreaming on both; for all thy blessed youth

Becomes as agèd, and doth beg the alms   30
Of palsied eld; and when thou art old and rich,
Thou hast neither heat, affection, limb, nor beauty,
To make thy riches pleasant. What's yet in this
That bears the name of life? Yet in this life
Lie hid moe thousand deaths: yet death we fear,   35
That makes these odds all even.

                              II

Ay, but to die, and go we know not where;
To lie in cold obstruction and to rot;
This sensible warm motion to become
A kneaded clod; and the delighted spirit
To bathe in fiery floods, or to reside   5
In thrilling region of thick-ribbèd ice;
To be imprisoned in the viewless winds,
And blown with restless violence round about
The pendant world; or to be worse than worst
Of those that lawless and incertain thoughts   10
Imagine howling: 'tis too horrible!
The weariest and most loathèd worldly life
That age, ache, penury and imprisonment
Can lay on nature is a paradise
To what we fear of death.   15
                        (From *Measure for Measure*)

EXERCISE:

   It would be almost universally agreed that the poem by Bryant
is inferior to the passage from Shakespeare or the sonnet by Donne.
Discuss this question in detail.

                          PROSPICE

                ROBERT BROWNING (1812–1889)

   Fear death? to feel the fog in my throat,
        The mist in my face,
   When the snows begin, and the blasts denote
        I am nearing the place,

The power of the night, the press of the storm,   5
   The post of the foe;
Where he stands, the Arch Fear in a visible form,
   Yet the strong man must go:
For the journey is done and the summit attained,
   And the barriers fall,   10
Though a battle's to fight ere the guerdon be gained,
   The reward of it all.
I was ever a fighter, so—one fight more,
   The best and the last!
I would hate that death bandaged my eyes, and forbore,
   And bade me creep past.   16
No! let me taste the whole of it, fare like my peers
   The heroes of old,
Bear the brunt, in a minute pay glad life's arrears
   Of pain, darkness and cold.   20
For sudden the worst turns the best to the brave,
   The black minute's at end,
And the elements' rage, the fiend-voices that rave,
   Shall dwindle, shall blend,
Shall change, shall become first a peace out of pain,   25
   Then a light, then thy breast,
O thou soul of my soul! I shall clasp thee again,
   And with God be the rest!

EXERCISE:
   Discuss this poem in relation to the three preceding selections.

1887

A. E. HOUSMAN (1859–1936)

From Clee to heaven the beacon burns,
   The shires have seen it plain,
From north and south the sign returns
   And beacons burn again.

Look left, look right, the hills are bright,   5
   The dales are light between,
Because 'tis fifty years tonight
   That God has saved the Queen.

Now, when the flame they watch not towers
  About the soil they trod,   10
Lads, we'll remember friends of ours
  Who shared the work with God.

To skies that knit their heartstrings right,
  To fields that bred them brave,
The saviors come not home tonight: 15
  Themselves they could not save.

It dawns in Asia, tombstones show
  And Shropshire names are read;
And the Nile spills his overflow
  Beside the Severn's dead.   20

We pledge in peace by farm and town
  The Queen they served in war,
And fire the beacons up and down
  The land they perished for.

"God save the Queen" we living sing,   25
  From height to height 'tis heard;
And with the rest your voices ring,
  Lads of the Fifty-third.

Oh, God will save her, fear you not:
  Be you the men you've been,   30
Get you the sons your fathers got,
  And God will save the Queen.

EXERCISE:

1. This poem concerns the celebration of the fiftieth year of
Queen Victoria's reign. How does the poet develop his attitude
toward the patriotic occasion?

2. In the foregoing connection notice the shift in tone at the
beginning of the third stanza, and discuss the technical features
involved in this shift.

3. Notice the biblical allusion in the fourth stanza. What is
its effect?

4. How does the last stanza serve to summarize the effect of
the poem? How has it been prepared for?

AN HORATIAN ODE UPON CROMWELL'S RETURN FROM IRELAND

ANDREW MARVELL (1621–1678)

The forward youth that would appear
Must now forsake his muses dear,
  Nor in the shadows sing
  His numbers languishing:

'Tis time to leave the books in dust,   5
And oil the unused armor's rust,
  Removing from the wall
  The corselet of the hall.

So restless Cromwell would not cease
In the inglorious arts of peace,   10
  But through adventurous war
  Urgèd his active star;

And, like the three-forked lightning, first
Breaking the clouds where it was nursed,
  Did thorough his own side   15
  His fiery way divide;

For 'tis all one to courage high,
The emulous, or enemy,
  And with such to inclose,
  Is more than to oppose.   20

Then burning through the air he went,
And palaces and temples rent;
  And Caesar's head at last
  Did through his laurels blast.

'Tis madness to resist or blame   25
The face of angry heaven's flame;
  And if we would speak true,
  Much to the man is due,

Who from his private gardens, where
He lived reservèd and austere,   30
  As if his highest plot
  To plant the bergamot,

Could by industrious valor climb
To ruin the great work of Time,
   And cast the kingdoms old,   35
   Into another mould,

Though Justice against Fate complain,
And plead the ancient rights in vain;
   But those do hold or break,
   As men are strong or weak.   40

Nature, that hateth emptiness,
Allows of penetration less,
   And therefore must make room
   Where greater spirits come.

What field of all the civil war,   45
Where his were not the deepest scar?
   And Hampton shows what part
   He had of wiser art;

Where, twining subtle fears with hope,
He wove a net of such a scope   50
   That Charles himself might chase
   To Caresbrooke's narrow case.

That thence the royal actor borne
The tragic scaffold might adorn:
   While round the armèd bands   55
   Did clap their bloody hands.

He nothing common did or mean
Upon that memorable scene:
   But with his keener eye
   The ax's edge did try: 60

Nor called the gods with vulgar spite
To vindicate his helpless right,
   But bowed his comely head,
   Down as upon a bed.

This was that memorable hour   65
Which first assured the forcèd power.
   So when they did design
   The Capitol's first line,

A bleeding head where they begun,
Did fright the architects to run;   70
   And yet in that the state
   Foresaw its happy fate.

And now the Irish are ashamed
To see themselves in one year tamed:
   So much one man can do,   75
   That does both act and know.

They can affirm his praises best,
And have, though overcome, confessed
   How good he is, how just,
   And fit for highest trust: 80

Nor yet grown stiffer with command,
But still in the Republic's hand:
   How fit he is to sway
   That can so well obey.

He to the Commons' feet presents   85
A kingdom, for his first year's rents;
   And what he may, forbears
   His fame to make it theirs:

And has his sword and spoils ungirt,
To lay them at the public's skirt.   90
   So when the falcon high
   Falls heavy from the sky,

She, having killed, no more does search,
But on the next green bough to perch;
   Where, when he first does lure,   95
   The falconer has her sure.

What may not then our isle presume
While victory his crest does plume!
   What may not others fear
   If thus he crown each year!   100

A Caesar he ere long to Gaul,
To Italy a Hannibal,
   And to all states not free
   Shall climacteric be.

The Pict no shelter now shall find   105
Within his parti-colored mind;
    But from this valor sad
    Shrink underneath the plaid:

Happy if in the tufted brake
The English hunter him mistake;   110
    Nor lay his hounds in near
    The Caledonian deer.

But thou the Wars' and Fortune's son
March indefatigably on;
    And for the last effect   115
    Still keep thy sword erect:

Besides the force it has to fright
The spirits of the shady night,
    The same arts that did gain
    A power must it maintain.   120

EXERCISE:

1. For the general historical background of this poem consult
the library. Compare the attitude toward the historical situation
in this poem with that in "The Fairies' Farewell" (p. 346) and
"The Bad Season Makes the Poet Sad" (p. 347).

2. What is the tone of the poem? How is it established?

A FAREWELL

SIR PHILIP SIDNEY (1554–1586)

Leave me, O Love! which reachest but to dust;
And thou, my mind, aspire to higher things:
Grow rich in that which never taketh rust;
Whatever fades, but fading pleasure brings.
Draw in thy beams, and humble all thy might   5
To that sweet yoke, where lasting freedoms be,
Which breaks the clouds, and opens forth the light,
That doth both shine, and give us sight to see.

O take fast hold! let that light be thy guide,
In this small course, which birth draws out to death,   10
And think how evil becometh him to slide,
Who seeketh heav'n, and comes of heav'nly breath.
Then farewell, World, thy uttermost I see;
Eternal Love, maintain thy life in Me!

EXERCISE:

How is the poet's statement here given authority and force
through his control of the tone?   In this connection compare the
poem to "If Poisonous Minerals" (p. 520) and "Poor Soul"
(p. 473).

THE VANITY OF HUMAN WISHES

THE TENTH SATIRE OF JUVENAL IMITATED

SAMUEL JOHNSON (1709-1784)

Let observation with extensive view,
Survey mankind, from China to Peru;
Remark each anxious toil, each eager strife,
And watch the busy scenes of crowded life;
Then say how hope and fear, desire and hate,   5
O'erspread with snares the clouded maze of fate,
Where wav'ring man, betrayed by vent'rous pride,
To tread the dreary paths without a guide;
As treach'rous phantoms in the mist delude,
Shuns fancied ills, or chases airy good.   10
How rarely reason guides the stubborn choice,
Rules the bold hand, or promps the suppliant voice,
How nations sink, by darling schemes oppressed,
When vengeance listens to the fool's request.
Fate wings with ev'ry wish th' afflictive dart,   15
Each gift of nature, and each grace of art,
With fatal heat impetuous courage glows,
With fatal sweetness elocution flows,
Impeachment stops the speaker's pow'rful breath,

And restless fire precipitates on death. . . .   20
    On what foundation stands the warrior's pride,
How just his hopes let Swedish Charles decide;
A frame of adamant, a soul of fire,
No dangers fright him, and no labors tire;
O'er love, o'er fear extends his wide domain,   25
Unconquered lord of pleasure and of pain;
No joys to him pacific scepters yield,
War sounds the trump, he rushes to the field;
Behold surrounding kings their pow'r combine,
And one capitulate, and one resign;   30
Peace courts his hand, but spreads her charm in vain;
"Think nothing gained," he cries, "till nought remain,
On Moscow's walls till Gothic standards fly,
And all be mine beneath the polar sky."
The march begins in military state,   35
And nations on his eye suspended wait;
Stern Famine guards the solitary coast,
And Winter barricades the realms of Frost;
He comes, not want and cold his course delay;—
Hide, blushing Glory, hide Pultowa's day: 40
The vanquished hero leaves his broken bands,
And shews his miseries in distant lands;
Condemned a needy supplicant to wait,
While ladies interpose, and slaves debate.
But did not Chance at length her error mend?   45
Did no subverted empire mark his end?
Did rival monarchs give the fatal wound?
Or hostile millions press him to the ground?
His fall was destined to a barren strand,
A petty fortress, and a dubious hand;   50
He left the name, at which the world grew pale,
To point a moral, or adorn a tale. . . .
    Enlarge my life with multitude of days,
In health, in sickness, thus the suppliant prays;
Hides from himself his state, and shuns to know,   55
That life protracted is protracted woe.
Time hovers o'er, impatient to destroy,
And shuts up all the passages of joy:
In vain their gifts the bounteous seasons pour,
The fruit autumnal, and the vernal flow'r,   60
With listless eyes the dotard views the store,

He views, and wonders that they please no more;
Now pall the tasteless meats, and joyless wines,
And Luxury with sighs her slave resigns.
Approach, ye minstrels, try the soothing strain,   65
And yield the tuneful lenitives of pain:
No sounds alas would touch th' impervious ear,
Though dancing mountains witnessed Orpheus near;
Nor lute nor lyre his feeble pow'rs attend,
Nor sweeter music of a virtuous friend,   70
But everlasting dictates crowd his tongue,
Perversely grave, or positively wrong.
The still returning tale, and ling'ring jest,
Perplex the fawning niece and pampered guest,
While growing hopes scarce awe the gath'ring sneer,   75
And scarce a legacy can bribe to hear;
The watchful guests still hint the last offense,
The daughter's petulance, the son's expense,
Improve his heady rage with treach'rous skill,
And mould his passions till they make his will. . . .   80
    Where then shall Hope and Fear their objects find?
Must dull Suspense corrupt the stagnant mind?
Must helpless man, in ignorance sedate,
Roll darkling down the torrent of his fate?
Must no dislike alarm, no wishes rise,   85
No cries attempt the mercies of the skies?
Enquirer, cease, petitions yet remain,
Which heav'n may hear, nor deem religion vain.
Still raise for good the supplicating voice,
But leave to heav'n the measure and the choice.   90
Safe in his pow'r, whose eyes discern afar
The secret ambush of a specious pray'r.
Implore his aid, in his decisions rest,
Secure whate'er he gives, he gives the best.
Yet when the sense of sacred presence fires,   95
And strong devotion to the skies aspires,
Pour forth thy fervors for a healthful mind,
Obedient passions, and a will resigned;
For love, which scarce collective man can fill;
For patient sov'reign o'er transmuted ill;   100
For faith, that panting for a happier seat,
Counts death kind Nature's signal of retreat:
These goods for man the laws of heav'n ordain,

These goods he grants, who grants the pow'r to gain;
With these celestial Wisdom calms the mind,   105
And makes the happiness she does not find.

EXERCISE:

1. Try to define the intention of the irony in this poem, and
compare it with that in "1887."

2. Try to define the tone of the poem. In this connection
discuss the use of paradox, alliteration, antithesis, and imagery.

THE SCHOLAR GIPSY

MATTHEW ARNOLD (1822–1888)

"There was very lately a lad in the University of Oxford, who
was by his poverty forced to leave his studies there; and at
last to join himself to a company of vagabond gipsies. Among
these extravagant people, by the insinuating subtilty of his car-
riage, he quickly got so much of their love and esteem as that
they discovered to him their mystery. After he had been a
pretty while well exercised in the trade, there chanced to ride
by a couple of scholars, who had formerly been of his acquaintance. They quickly spied out their old friend among the gipsies;
and he gave them an account of the necessity which drove him
to that kind of life, and told them that the people he went with
were not such impostors as they were taken for, but that they
had a traditional kind of learning among them, and could do
wonders by the power of imagination, their fancy binding that
of others: that himself had learned much of their art, and when
he had compassed the whole secret, he intended, he said, to leave
their company, and give the world an account of what he had
learned."—Glanvil's *Vanity of Dogmatising,* 1661.

Go, for they call you, Shepherd, from the hill;
    Go, Shepherd, and untie the wattled cotes:
        No longer leave thy wistful flock unfed,
    Nor let thy bawling fellows rack their throats,
        Nor the cropped grasses shoot another head.   5

But when the fields are still,
And the tired men and dogs all gone to rest,
  And only the white sheep are sometimes seen
  Cross and recross the strips of moon-blanched green;
    Come, Shepherd, and again renew the quest.   10

Here, where the reaper was at work of late,
  In this high field's dark corner, where he leaves
  His coat, his basket, and his earthen cruse,
  And in the sun all morning binds the sheaves,
    Then here, at noon, comes back his stores to use;   15
    Here will I sit and wait,
While to my ear from uplands far away
  The bleating of the folded flocks is borne,
  With distant cries of reapers in the corn—
    All the live murmur of a summer's day.   20

Screened in this nook o'er the high, half-reaped field,
  And here till sun-down, Shepherd, will I be.
    Through the thick corn the scarlet poppies peep,
  And round green roots and yellowing stalks I see
    Pale blue convolvulus in tendrils creep: 25
    And air-swept lindens yield
Their scent, and rustle down their perfumed showers
  Of bloom on the bent grass where I am laid,
  And bower me from the August sun with shade;
    And the eye travels down to Oxford's towers: 30

And near me on the grass lies Glanvil's book—
  Come, let me read the oft-read tale again,
  The story of that Oxford scholar poor
  Of pregnant parts and quick inventive brain,
    Who, tired of knocking at Preferment's door,   35
    One summer morn forsook
His friends, and went to learn the Gipsy lore,
  And roamed the world with that wild brotherhood,
  And came, as most men deemed, to little good,
    But came to Oxford and his friends no more.   40

But once, years after, in the country lanes,
  Two scholars whom at college erst he knew
  Met him, and of his way of life enquired.

Whereat he answered, that the Gipsy crew,
  His mates, had arts to rule as they desired   45
    The workings of men's brains;
And they can bind them to what thoughts they will:
  "And I," he said, "the secret of their art,
    When fully learned, will to the world impart:
      But it needs heaven-sent moments for this skill." 50

This said, he left them, and returned no more,
  But rumors hung about the country side
    That the lost Scholar long was seen to stray,
  Seen by rare glimpses, pensive and tongue-tied,
    In hat of antique shape, and cloak of gray,   55
      The same the Gipsies wore.
  Shepherds had met him on the Hurst in spring;
    At some lone alehouse in the Berkshire moors,
      On the warm ingle bench, the smock-frocked boors
        Had found him seated at their entering.   60

But, mid their drink and clatter, he would fly:
  And I myself seem half to know thy looks,
    And put the shepherds, Wanderer, on thy trace;
  And boys who in lone wheatfields scare the rooks
    I ask if thou hast passed their quiet place;   65
      Or in my boat I lie
  Moored to the cool bank in the summer heats,
    Mid wide grass meadows which the sunshine fills,
      And watch the warm green-muffled Cumner hills,
        And wonder if thou haunt'st their shy retreats.   70

For most, I know, thou lov'st retired ground.
  Thee, at the ferry, Oxford riders blithe
    Returning home on summer nights have met
  Crossing the stripling Thames at Bab-lock-hithe,
    Trailing in the cool stream thy fingers wet,   75
      As the slow punt swings round:
  And leaning backwards in a pensive dream,
    And fostering in thy lap a heap of flowers
      Plucked in shy fields distant and Wychwood bowers,
        And thine eyes resting on the moonlit stream: 80

And then they land, and thou art seen no more.
  Maidens who from the distant hamlets come

To dance around the Fyfield elm in May,
Oft through the darkening fields have seen thee roam,
  Or cross a stile into the public way.   85
    Oft thou hast given them store
Of flowers—the frail-leafed, white anemone—
  Dark bluebells drenched with dews of summer eves—
  And purple orchises with spotted leaves—
    But none has words she can report of thee.   90

And, above Godstow Bridge, when hay-time's here
  In June, and many a scythe in sunshine flames,
Men who through those wide fields of breezy grass
Where black-winged swallows haunt the glittering Thames,
  To bathe in the abandoned lasher pass,   95
    Have often passed thee near
Sitting upon the river bank o'ergrown:
  Marked thy outlandish garb, thy figure spare,
  Thy dark vague eyes, and soft abstracted air;
    But, when they came from bathing, thou wert gone.

At some lone homestead in the Cumner hills,   101
  Where at her open door the housewife darns,
    Thou hast been seen, or hanging on a gate
To watch the threshers in the mossy barns.
  Children, who early range these slopes and late   105
    For cresses from the rills,
Have known thee watching, all an April day,
  The springing pastures and the feeding kine;
  And marked thee, when the stars come out and shine,
    Through the long dewy grass move slow away.   110

In Autumn, on the skirts of Bagley wood,
  Where most the gipsies by the turf-edged way
    Pitch their smoked tents, and every bush you see
With scarlet patches tagged and shreds of gray,
  Above the forest ground called Thessaly—   115
    The blackbird picking food
Sees thee, nor stops his meal, nor fears at all;
  So often has he known thee past him stray
  Rapt, twirling in thy hand a withered spray,
    And waiting for the spark from Heaven to fall.   120

And once, in winter, on the causeway chill
  Where home through flooded fields foot-travellers go,
    Have I not passed thee on the wooden bridge
  Wrapt in thy cloak and battling with the snow,
    Thy face towards Hinksey and its wintry ridge?   125
      And thou hast climbed the hill
  And gained the white brow of the Cumner range,
    Turned once to watch, while thick the snow-flakes fall,
    The line of festal light in Christ-Church hall—
      Then sought thy straw in some sequestered grange.

But what—I dream! Two hundred years are flown   131
  Since first thy story ran through Oxford halls,
    And the grave Glanvil did the tale inscribe
  That thou wert wandered from the studious walls
    To learn strange arts, and join a Gipsy tribe: 135
      And thou from earth art gone
  Long since, and in some quiet churchyard laid;
    Some country nook, where o'er thy unknown grave
    Tall grasses and white flowering nettles wave—
      Under a dark red-fruited yew-tree's shade.   140

—No, no, thou hast not felt the lapse of hours.
  For what wears out the life of mortal men?
    'Tis that from change to change their being rolls:
  'Tis that repeated shocks, again, again,
    Exhaust the energy of strongest souls,   145
      And numb the elastic powers.
  Till having used our nerves with bliss and teen,
    And tired upon a thousand schemes our wit,
    To the just-pausing Genius we remit
      Our worn-out life, and are—what we have been.   150

Thou hast not lived, why should'st thou perish, so?
  Thou hadst *one* aim, *one* business, *one* desire:
    Else wert thou long since numbered with the dead—
  Else hadst thou spent, like other men, thy fire.
    The generations of thy peers are fled,   155
      And we ourselves shall go;
  But thou possessest an immortal lot,
    And we imagine thee exempt from age
    And living as thou liv'st on Glanvil's page,
      Because thou hadst—what we, alas, have not!   160

For early didst thou leave the world, with powers
  Fresh, undiverted to the world without,
    Firm to their mark, not spent on other things;
  Free from the sick fatigue, the languid doubt,
    Which much to have tried, in much been baffled, brings.
      O Life unlike to ours!   166
  Who fluctuate idly without term or scope,
    Of whom each strives, nor knows for what he strives,
    And each half lives a hundred different lives;
      Who wait like thee, but not, like thee, in hope.   170

Thou waitest for the spark from Heaven: and we,
  Vague half-believers of our casual creeds,
    Who never deeply felt, nor clearly will'd,
  Whose insight never has borne fruit in deeds,
    Whose weak resolves never have been fulfilled;   175
      For whom each year we see
  Breeds new beginnings, disappointments new;
    Who hesitate and falter life away,
    And lose to-morrow the ground won to-day—
      Ah, do not we, Wanderer, await it too?   180

Yes, we await it, but it still delays,
  And then we suffer; and amongst us One,
    Who most has suffered, takes dejectedly
  His seat upon the intellectual throne;
    And all his store of sad experience he   185
      Lays bare of wretched days;
  Tells us his misery's birth and growth and signs,
    And how the dying spark of hope was fed,
    And how the breast was sooth'd, and how the head,
      And all his hourly varied anodynes.   190

This for our wisest: and we others pine,
  And wish the long unhappy dream would end,
    And waive all claim to bliss, and try to bear,
  With close-lipped Patience for our only friend,
    Sad Patience, too near neighbor to Despair: 195
      But none has hope like thine.
  Thou through the fields and through the woods dost stray,
    Roaming the country side, a truant boy,
    Nursing thy project in unclouded joy,
      And every doubt long blown by time away.   200

O born in days when wits were fresh and clear,
  And life ran gaily as the sparkling Thames;
    Before this strange disease of modern life,
  With its sick hurry, its divided aims,
    Its heads o'ertaxed, its palsied hearts, was rife—   205
      Fly hence, our contact fear!
  Still fly, plunge deeper in the bowering wood!
    Averse, as Dido did with gesture stern
    From her false friend's approach in Hades turn,
      Wave us away, and keep thy solitude.   210

Still nursing the unconquerable hope,
  Still clutching the inviolable shade,
    With a free onward impulse brushing through,
  By night, the silvered branches of the glade—
    Far on the forest skirts, where none pursue,   215
      On some mild pastoral slope
  Emerge, and resting on the moonlit pales,
    Freshen thy flowers, as in former years,
    With dew, or listen with enchanted ears,
      From the dark dingles, to the nightingales.   220

But fly our paths, our feverish contact fly!
  For strong the infection of our mental strife,
    Which, though it gives no bliss, yet spoils for rest;
  And we should win thee from thy own fair life,
    Like us distracted, and like us unblest.   225
      Soon, soon thy cheer would die,
  Thy hopes grow timorous, and unfixed thy powers,
    And thy clear aims be cross and shifting made:
    And then thy glad perennial youth would fade,
      Fade, and grow old at last, and die like ours.   230

Then fly our greetings, fly our speech and smiles!
  —As some grave Tyrian trader, from the sea,
    Descried at sunrise an emerging prow
  Lifting the cool-haired creepers stealthily,
    The fringes of a southward-facing brow   235
      Among the Aegean isles;
  And saw the merry Grecian coaster come,
    Freighted with amber grapes, and Chian wine,
    Green bursting figs, and tunnies steeped in brine;
      And knew the intruders on his ancient home,   240

The young light-hearted Masters of the waves;
  And snatched his rudder, and shook out more sail,
    And day and night held on indignantly
O'er the blue Midland waters with the gale,
  Betwixt the Syrtes and soft Sicily,   245
    To where the Atlantic raves
Outside the Western Straits, and unbent sails
  There, where down cloudy cliffs, through sheets of foam,
  Shy traffickers, the dark Iberians come;
    And on the beach undid his corded bales.   250

This poem has four sections. The first ends with the third
stanza of the poem. The second may be said, perhaps arbitrarily,
to end with the fourteenth stanza (line 140). The third section
ends with the twenty-third stanza (line 230). The last two
stanzas of the poem compose the fourth section. The first of
these sections gives a kind of setting, or frame, for the poem.
The second section gives the story of the scholar. The third
section contrasts the faith and simplicity of the scholar with the
doubts and divided aims of Arnold and his age. The fourth
summarizes this contrast by an image of the Tyrian and Grecian
traders.

In some discussions of this poem the third section (or some
part of the third section, for these divisions are somewhat arbitrary) is said to give the "heart of the poem" or to make the
"point of the poem." It is perfectly true that in the third section
one finds the most explicit statement of the theme of the poem.
The poet says that his own age is confused by doubts and lacks
the powers which are, like those of the scholar, "fresh, undiverted
to the world without," that it suffers from the "strange disease
of modern life," which is full of "sick hurry and divided aims."
He says that the scholar, as contrasted with the modern world,
at least has the "unconquerable hope" of a fulfillment, and should
avoid contact with the "strong infection of our mental strife,"
which destroys faith and purpose. In these matters the statement is absolutely definite, and although the poem does not,
appropriately enough, support the statement by a series of

arguments, the opinion is as definitely put as in Arnold's various prose statements on the same general subject.

But in comparing any general prose statement of this view with the third section of this poem, we may see certain matters that make for decided differences of effect, meter, rime, the dramatic framework, and the use of incidental comparisons, such as the reference to Dido and Aeneas. These factors tend to make the statement from the poem more imaginatively compelling, and perhaps more memorable, than the prose statement. But these factors do not differentiate the third section of the poem from other sections; what differentiates it from those sections, and gives rise to the statement that it is the "heart of the poem," is the explicitness of statement. But if this explicitness of statement is taken in itself to be the central poetic fact, a great error has been made. If that were true, then a prose paraphrase would have a similar poetic effect.

The question, then, is how the third section is related to the other sections. How do the other sections affect this one and how does this one affect the others in the reader's mind?

Let us assume that the poem were treated entirely in the explicit method characteristic of the following stanzas, with such references as appear even here to the scholar replaced by definite elaboration of the idea:

> Thou waitest for the spark from heaven! and we,
> Light half-believers of our casual creeds,
> Who never deeply felt, nor clearly willed,
> Whose insight never has borne fruit in deeds,
> Whose vague resolves never have been fulfilled;   5
>   For whom each year we see
> Breeds new beginnings, disappointments new;
> Who hesitate and falter life away,
> And lose tomorrow the ground won today:
> Ah! do not we, wanderer, await it too?   10
>
> Yes, we await it! but it still delays,
> And then we suffer! and amongst us, one
> Who most has suffered, takes dejectedly
> His seat upon the intellectual throne;

And all his store of said experience he   15
    Lays bare of wretched days;
Tells us his misery's birth and growth and signs,
And how the dying spark of hope was fed,
And how the breast was soothed, and how the head,
And all his hourly varied anodynes.   20

This for our wisest: and we others pine,
And wish the long unhappy dream would end,
And waive all claim to bliss, and try to bear,
With close-lipped patience for our only friend,
Sad patience, too near neighbor to despair.   25
    But none has hope like thine!
Thou through the fields and through the woods dost
    stray,
Roaming the country-side, a truant boy,
Nursing thy project in unclouded joy,
And every doubt long blown by time away.   30

If references to the scholar, and the dramatic framework depending on them, were eliminated, even these stanzas would be
considerably weakened, for there would be no point of focus for
the indictment the poet is making, and no symbol or object on
which the imagination of the reader could seize. That is, the
element of statement is only one factor in giving the effect, even
in this section that seems to contain the most explicit statement;
only in so far as the statement acts on, and is acted on by, the
preceding section, the section of the poem which makes us accept
the scholar imaginatively, do we get the full force of the poem.
The statement, as a statement, lacks a context until we discover a
dramatic form for it: the poet's musing over Glanvil's book that
contains the story of the scholar, the series of imagined meetings
with the scholar, the address to the scholar and the warning to
him to fly, etc. These elements prevent the idea from coming to
us as an abstraction. But at the same time, the preceding section
has been prevented from being merely a presentation of a quaint
character and a curious incident. The character of the gipsy
and the incidents woven about him by the poet are interesting,
but if the poem should end with that, we would probably have
some confusion of mind mixed with our pleasure in Arnold's

method of presentation. *The basic imaginative fact of the poem is the making of the scholar into a symbol of a way of life.* Therefore, either the second or the third section of the poem would be greatly impoverished if the other were omitted.

But what of the last section of the poem, the concluding two stanzas? The point, as it were, of the poem has already been made, and made, as we have said, in terms of the symbolic and dramatic reference to the scholar. What, then, does the last section add? The poem could end, and remain a very good poem, with the third stanza from the end, with

> And then thy glad perennial youth would fade,
> Fade, and grow old as last, and die like ours.

But if the poem should end there, it would tend to fall into two long sections (exclusive of the short introductory section) that are closely related poetically, each supporting the other, but that, nevertheless, do not give the poem a final effect of unity. To give the poem this unity the poet has concluded with a rather short, brilliantly presented image that serves as a symbolic summary of the entire poem. This image is introduced by a repetition of the injunction to the scholar to flee contact with modern men: The Tyrian trader, because of the coming of the "merry Grecian coaster," leaves the small and safe Aegean Sea and ventures out into the open Atlantic. So the scholar should avoid the trivial contact and pursue independently his own lonely attempt at truth.

The poet, one might suspect, felt that the poem without these last two stanzas concluded too flatly, with too great a proportion of generalization and statement, and wanted, instead, to leave the reader with a symbol that had absorbed the meaning of these generalizations but, at the same time, directly stimulated the imagination. Many excellent poems do conclude with general statements, for instance Keats' "Ode on a Grecian Urn" and many of Shakespeare's sonnets. But one can observe that in these cases the general statement grows intimately out of a special context, Keats' description of the urn, for instance, and does not come merely as a kind of disconnected comment on life or as an adage. We accept such a general statement, not because we promptly decide that it is true or false, but because we feel that it is justified and interpreted by the more directly imaginative elements of the rest of the poem in question. A poem, then, may give very good advice to us, or may state what we regard as important truths, but may remain a very bad poem because the writer has been unable to give his statement any imaginative appeal—because, for example, he lacks dramatic force, a strong sense of imagery, or a good ear for the rhythm of verse (pp. 334–36). The mere fact of the abstract truth of a poem, does not make it a good poem, any more surely than does the fact of the writer's personal sincerity (pp. 442–45, 611–12). An example of a poor poem that we know was composed in full personal sincerity is Lowell's "After the Burial" (p. 337).

The opposite line of reasoning may also be taken. It is possible for a reader to derive great pleasure from a poem that does not conform in the opinions stated with the reader's own view. For example, it would be possible for a person who did not share the opinion expressed in Arnold's poem that the nineteenth century was spiritually poorer than the seventeenth century to appreciate "The Scholar Gipsy." He could do this because Arnold has dramatized the poem so that it strikes us as more than a mere general commentary.

ODE TO THE SEA

HOWARD BAKER (1906–   )

O first created and creating source,
Beloved rib of elemental force;
    Being, in whose deep thighs
    Nascence remotely lies,
Whose golden arms still dripping of the stream   5
And liquid eyes inform my deepest dream—
    Spotless daughter of Time,
    Teach me his paradigm!
Patient and perfect literate, say how
I may conciliate the Then and Now!   10

What is the now?   Is it my present glance
Drifting upon this shaken blue expanse?
    The showering sun upon my face,
    My breath inhaling salty space?
Time seems to focus on this lonely beach;   15
It crowds my taste and sight, and pours the speech
    Of living Sea into my ear
    So that naught is, but what I hear:
Behind me but a silent mesa land
Recessive from this fragrant step of sand,   20
    Only the shelving gulf before,
    Lifting a low deep-structured roar!

Yet listen, for there towers in that roar
Much more than washes on the sensuous shore:
    —One standing off may mark   25
    A glowing in the dark
Regions of space, and coming closer see
That Earth is clouded like an April tree
    With green beneath the spray.
    This river, he may say,   30
Is Danube, where our race made dusky stage;
There sleeps pale Crete, there northern forges rage.

The present time is not so small nor dense
That it lies here encompassed by my sense;
    And past and future times are naught   35
    But modes of individual thought.
Pondering this, I watch the balanced sea—
How from the surf the smooth blue arches flee
    Out, out upon the globe's cold side
    Where purest magnitudes abide,   40
Where time, eventless, melts away, and then
Grows absolute, devoid of deeds of men!
    Devoid of pride, of shame and crime,
    And time itself devoid of time!

Deep hollow Sea, I am but human kind!   45
Your sloping azure dales dismay my mind;
    I see your mantle swirled
    Along an empty world
Beckoning where I cannot come, and live.

And live!—Ask, Sea, no more than I can give!   50
    Love with the lover dies;
    With drowned and bleaching thighs,
Clutching your gift of seaweed in my hand,
I should return still undissolved to land!

Man lives with shadeless meadows at his side;   55
He reckons that his earthly deeds provide
    Fruits for a shading temporal vine,
    Gourds for the well, cool, green, and fine;
The shaggy vine in multiplicity
Matches the pale perfections of the sea,   60
    But the clear modes of Sea prevail
    Over the vine's complex detail.
Up from the bright sea-coasts his history twines;
Sensitive, frail,—uncared for it declines.
    Man knows the grip of long sea-hours,   65
    But counts his days by drouths and showers.

In modes of specious presentness, what store,
O Sea, of past events, endows this shore?
    What was the quick gaunt ring
    Of voices by the spring;   70
And what the silent gazing wonderment
Of eyes, on nameless trees and creatures bent?
    Where wept the old grandee
    Recurrent harms of Sea?
And where emerged from waves upon these sands   75
That priest who carried God in drenchèd hands?

Fragments!—From fragments history here descends
Onto a bare mud house where seaward bends
    A river-bed. The folk are poor,
    The mesa silent as the spoor   80
Of the coyote; mongrels hold the wall
For shade and roam at night; and prayers recall
    Stanchioning names to tongues inside—
    Names like the ruined spars the tide
Casts up, the craft's homeport and form unknown.   85
Sometimes the folk, when dry east winds have blown,
    Stooping for shells along the beach,
    With sea-roar blend a bird-like speech.

Evenings with desert glooms enclose their days.
Westward each night the sea's low radiance strays   90
    Into a brilliant sky.
    So institutions die.
Conserving Sea! To what auroral plains
Have you consigned the meaning of the names
        Augustine, Abelard,   95
        Aquinas, Bede, Bernard?
Permanent, lossless, undiminished Sea,
Change is the law of your stability!

Swift from the sea comes change, and Christendom—
Like childhood gardens echoing the hum   100
    Of words from the parental lip—
    Vanishes with the rising ship.
The liner slanting southward changes place
Mysteriously, as if both sea and space,
        Under compulsions of its will,   105
        Retreat from it while it stands still:
It rends perspectives, it commands the Now!
I with the sea's low eyes inspect its bow,
        Its funnels, inset decks and bridge—
        Steadily from my splashèd ridge.   110

How well I know the structures of my age!
This long, compact, careering ship is gauge
        An archetype of them all:
        Here man's import is small
Beside the turbine, his rewards are slight;   115
And yet for some the engines spin delight.
        The ship has rich cuisine,
        Damasks of frosty sheen,
Flowers and wine, with music brass and bold;
And tools, to flay the heathen, in the hold.   120

Wreathed with horizons momentarily green,
Drunk as a caesar who has lately seen
        Auspice in birds' fastidious flight,
        The ship assails the casual night.
Think that this Leviathan of Ocean,   125
This swimmer seeming urged by lust for motion,
        Moves only under someone's hand,

Labors, and answers his command;
Whatever weaker nations it offends,
However it disrupts their codes for ends   130
        Potentially both good and ill,
        It shapes the world to someone's will.

Men and not monsters warp the bounds of Sea—
But who provides responsibility?
        Not fate but men unlock   135
        The energies of rock,
And to what end?   Ah, guileful Sea, they ask
Only in your false presentness to bask,
        And recklessly to throw
        Their navies on those slow   140
Confounding graveyards, where dank weeds enchain
The junks of China and the fleets of Spain!

Nations, beguiled like dim Narcissus, drown
Amidst their shattered triumph, and go down
        Gasping a pledge still to restore   145
        What time has riven from their shore!
I, on my coppery beach, regret the falls
Not of brash banners but of sober halls.
        —And suddenly there blows on me
        The sterner discipline of Sea: 150
History is long.   Nor men nor nations bear
Lasting degrees of value.   They who stare
        Backwards see but themselves impure.
        Man is collective.   Change is sure.

The surf is brushing at my steps; I seek   155
An aged cliff that stands among the sleek
        Young chargers of the sea.
        Bounds of anemone
And areas by sea-urchins held devise
The narrow range in which the tides will rise   160
        And fall, though cliffs themselves
        And all the earth's vast shelves
Crumble.   And there the mode of permanence
Is framed in the sea-tide's changeful cadence.

Sibilant, whispering Sea, beyond the steep   165
And thorny reach of doubt, your peace hangs deep;

In its abundant room
One views the ways of doom,
And viewing may withhold the part of fear.
O steady in your variance, appear   170
Unceasing in my eye,
And let me now descry
My course, for I return to inland ground
Burdened, yet to the nascent future bound!

EXERCISE:

Compare the way in which the poet uses the image of the sea as a means of expressing his idea with the way in which Arnold uses the gipsy.

DOVER BEACH

MATTHEW ARNOLD (1822–1888)

The sea is calm tonight,
The tide is full, the moon lies fair
Upon the straits;—on the French coast the light
Gleams and is gone; the cliffs of England stand,
Glimmering and vast, out in the tranquil bay.   5
Come to the window, sweet is the night-air!
Only, from the long line of spray
Where the sea meets the moon-blanched land,
Listen! you hear the grating roar
Of pebbles which the waves draw back, and fling,   10
At their return, up the high strand,
Begin, and cease, and then again begin,
With tremulous cadence slow, and bring
The eternal note of sadness in.

Sophocles long ago   15
Heard it on the Aegean, and it brought
Into his mind the turbid ebb and flow
Of human misery; we
Find also in the sound a thought,
Hearing it by this distant northern sea.   20

The Sea of Faith
Was once, too, at the full, and round earth's shore
Lay like the folds of a bright girdle furled.
But now I only hear
Its melancholy, long, withdrawing roar,   25
Retreating, to the breath
Of the night-wind, down the vast edges drear
And naked shingles of the world.

Ah, love, let us be true
To one another! for the world, which seems   30
To lie before us like a land of dreams,
So various, so beautiful, so new,
Hath really neither joy, nor love, nor light,
Nor certitude, nor peace, nor help for pain;
And we are here as on a darkling plain   35
Swept with confused alarms of struggle and flight,
Where ignorant armies clash by night.

EXERCISE:

1. Write an analysis of this poem, discussing the similarity
of the basic theme to that of "The Scholar Gipsy."
2. Investigate the similarity in structure of the two poems.

IN MEMORIAM A. H. H.

OBIIT MDCCCXXXIII

ALFRED, LORD TENNYSON (1809–1893)

Strong Son of God, immortal Love,
    Whom we, that have not seen thy face,
    By faith, and faith alone, embrace,
Believing where we cannot prove;

Thine are these orbs of light and shade;   5
    Thou madest Life in man and brute;
    Thou madest Death; and lo, thy foot
Is on the skull which thou hast made.

Thou wilt not leave us in the dust;
   Thou madest man, he knows not why,   10
   He thinks he was not made to die;
And thou hast made him: thou art just.

Thou seemest human and divine,
   The highest, holiest manhood, thou:
   Our wills are ours, we know not how;   15
Our wills are ours, to make them thine.

Our little systems have their day,
   They have their day and cease to be;
   They are but broken lights of thee,
And thou, O Lord, art more than they.   20

We have but faith: we cannot know;
   For knowledge is of things we see;
   And yet we trust it comes from thee,
A beam in darkness: let it grow. . . .

VII

Dark house, by which once more I stand   25
   Here in the long unlovely street,
   Doors, where my heart was used to beat
So quickly, waiting for a hand,

A hand that can be clasped no more—
   Behold me, for I cannot sleep,   30
   And like a guilty thing I creep
At earliest morning to the door.

He is not here; but far away
   The noise of life begins again,
   And ghastly thro' the drizzling rain   35
On the bald street breaks the blank day.

L

Be near me when my light is low,
   When the blood creeps, and the nerves prick
   And tingle; and the heart is sick,
And all the wheels of Being slow.   40

Be near me when the sensuous frame
  Is racked with pangs that conquer trust;
  And Time, a maniac scattering dust,
And Life, a Fury slinging flame.

Be near me when my faith is dry,   45
  And men the flies of latter spring,
  That lay their eggs, and sting and sing
And weave their petty cells and die.

Be near me when I fade away,
  To point the term of human strife,   50
  And on the low dark verge of life
The twilight of eternal day.

LIV

Oh yet we trust that somehow good
  Will be the final goal of ill,
  To pangs of nature, sins of will,   55
Defects of doubt, and taints of blood;

That nothing walks with aimless feet;
  That not one life shall be destroyed,
  Or cast as rubbish to the void,
When God hath made the pile complete;   60

That not a worm is cloven in vain;
  That not a moth with vain desire
  Is shriveled in a fruitless fire,
Or but subserves another's gain.

Behold, we know not anything;   65
  I can but trust that good shall fall
  At last—far off—at last, to all,
And every winter change to spring.

So runs my dream: but what am I?
  An infant crying in the night: 70
  An infant crying for the light:
And with no language but a cry.

LV

The wish, that of the living whole
  No life may fail beyond the grave,
  Derives it not from what we have   75
The likest God within the soul?

Are God and Nature then at strife,
  That Nature lends such evil dreams?
  So careful of the type she seems,
So careless of the single life.   80

That I, considering everywhere
  Her secret meaning in her deeds,
  And finding that of fifty seeds
She often brings but one to bear,

I falter where I firmly trod,   85
  And falling with my weight of cares
  Upon the great world's altar-stairs
That slope thro' darkness up to God,

I stretch lame hands of faith, and grope,
  And gather dust and chaff, and call   90
  To what I feel is Lord of all,
And faintly trust the larger hope. . . .

CVI

Ring out, wild bells, to the wild sky,
  The flying cloud, the frosty light: ·
  The year is dying in the night;   95
Ring out, wild bells, and let him die.

Ring out the old, ring in the new,
  Ring, happy bells, across the snow:
  The year is going, let him go;
Ring out the false, ring in the true.   100

Ring out the grief that saps the mind,
  For those that here we see no more;
  Ring out the feud of rich and poor;
Ring in redress to all mankind.

Ring out a slowly dying cause, 105
   And ancient forms of party strife;
   Ring in the nobler modes of life,
With sweeter manners, purer laws.

Ring out the want, the care, the sin,
   The faithless coldness of the times;
   Ring out, ring out my mournful rhymes, 110
But ring the fuller minstrel in.

Ring out false pride in place and blood,
   The civic slander and the spite;
   Ring in the love of truth and right, 115
Ring in the common love of good.

Ring out old shapes of foul disease;
   Ring out the narrowing lust of gold;
   Ring out the thousand wars of old,
Ring in the thousand years of peace. 120

Ring in the valiant man and free,
   The larger heart, the kindlier hand;
   Ring out the darkness of the land,
Ring in the Christ that is to be.

CXVIII

Contemplate all this work of Time. 125
   The giant laboring in his youth;
   Nor dream of human love and truth,
As dying Nature's earth and lime;

But trust that those we call the dead
   Are breathers of an ampler day 130
   For ever nobler ends. They say,
The solid earth whereon we tread

In tracts of fluent heat began,
   And grew to seeming-random forms,
   The seeming prey of cyclic storms, 135
Till at the last arose the man;

Who throve and branched from clime to clime,
  The herald of a higher race,
  And of himself in higher place,
If so he type this work of time   140

Within himself, from more to more;
  Or, crowned with attributes of woe
  Like glories, move his course, and show
That life is not as idle ore,

But iron dug from central gloom,   145
  And heated hot with burning fears,
  And dipped in baths of hissing tears,
And battered with the shocks of doom

To shape and use. Arise and fly
  The reeling Faun, the sensual feast;   150
  Move upward, working out the beast,
And let the ape and tiger die. . . .

CXXX

Thy voice is on the rolling air;
  I hear thee where the waters run;
  Thou standest in the rising sun,   155
And in the setting thou art fair.

What art thou then? I cannot guess;
  But though I seem in star and flower,
  To feel thee some diffusive power,
I do not therefore love thee less.   160

My love involves the love before;
  My love is vaster passion now;
  Though mixed with God and Nature thou,
I seem to love thee more and more.

Far off thou art, but ever nigh;   165
  I have thee still, and I rejoice;
  I prosper, circled with thy voice;
I shall not lose thee though I die. . . .

Exercise:

1. This poem was written in memory of Arthur Hallam, a close personal friend of Tennyson. (Consult the library for further information concerning the circumstances of its composition.) The poem is not only concerned with the writer's personal grief. The sudden death of his friend prompts the poet to speculation on the meaning of life. How are these two elements related in the sections of the poem given here? Is the poem unified?

2. Discuss the relation of the theme of this poem to that of "The Scholar Gipsy," and of "Dover Beach." Compare and contrast the treatment of the theme in the various poems.

3. Is this stanza form suitable to a long poem? Discuss the technical devices which the poet employs to avoid monotony of effect.

THE LAST DAYS OF ALICE

ALLEN TATE (1899–   )

Alice grown lazy, mammoth but not fat,
Declines upon her lost and twilit age,
Above in the dozing leaves the grinning cat
Quivers forever with his abstract rage;

Whatever light swayed on the perilous gate   5
Forever sways, nor will the arching grass
Caught when the world clattered undulate
In the deep suspension of the looking-glass.

Bright Alice! always pondering to gloze
The spoiled cruelty she had meant to say   10
Gazes learnedly down her airy nose
At nothing, nothing thinking all the day:

Turned absent minded by infinity
She cannot move unless her double move,
The All-Alice of the world's entity   15
Smashed in the anger of her hopeless love.

Love for herself who as an earthly twain
Pouted to join her two in a sweet one:
No more the second lips to kiss in vain
The first she broke, plunged in the glass alone—   20

Alone to the weight of impassivity
Incest of spirit, theorem of desire
Without will as chalky cliffs by the sea
Empty as the bodiless flesh of fire;

All space that heaven is a dayless night   25
A nightless day driven by perfect lust
For vacancy, in which her frail eyesight
Stares at the drowsy cubes of human dust.

We, too, back to the world shall never pass
Through the splintered door, a dumb shade-harried
   crowd,   30
Being all infinite, function, depth and mass
Without figure; a mathematical shroud.

Hurled at the air; blessèd without sin:
O god of our flesh, return to us your wrath
Let us be evil could we enter in   35
Your grace, and falter on the stony path!

EXERCISE:

1. In general idea this poem is very similar to "The Scholar Gipsy," "Dover Beach," and "In Memoriam." Each of these poems makes specific or implied reference to the decay of religious faith under the impact of modern science; and furthermore, each poem implies that man cannot consider life merely in abstract and quantitative terms, such as pure science dictates. "The Last Days of Alice" makes an indirect and ironical approach to the matter, using the figure of the Alice of *Alice in Wonderland* and *Through the Looking Glass*. Is this an appropriate basic symbol?

2. What is the meaning of the phrase "incest of spirit"?

3. What is the relation to the rest of the poem of the paradox in the last stanza?

FRESCOES FOR MR. ROCKEFELLER'S CITY

ARCHIBALD MACLEISH (1892–   )

I.

Landscape as a Nude

She lies on her left side her flank golden:
Her hair is burned black with the strong sun:
The scent of her hair is of rain in the dust on her shoulders:
She has brown breasts and the mouth of no other country:

Ah she is beautiful here in the sun where she lies: 5
She is not like the soft girls naked in vineyards
Nor the soft naked girls of the English islands
Where the rain comes in with the surf on an east wind:

Hers is the west wind and the sunlight: the west
Wind is the long clean wind of the continents—   10
The wind turning with earth: the wind descending
Steadily out of the evening and following on:

The wind here where she lies is west: the trees
Oak ironwood cottonwood hickory: standing in
Great groves they roll on the wind as the sea would: 15
The grasses of Iowa Illinois Indiana.

Run with the plunge of the wind as a wave tumbling:

Under her knees there is no green lawn of the Florentines:
Under her dusty knees is the corn stubble:
Her belly is flecked with the flickering light of the corn: 20

She lies on her left side her flank golden:
Her hair is burned black with the strong sun:
The scent of her hair is of dust and of smoke on her
    shoulders:
She has brown breasts and the mouth of no other country:

2.

Wildwest

There were none of my blood in this battle: 25
There were Minneconjous: Sans Arcs: Brules:
Many nations of Sioux: they were few men galloping:

This would have been in the long days in June:
They were galloping well deployed under the plum-trees:
They were driving riderless horses: themselves they were
    few: 30

Crazy Horse had done it with few numbers:
Crazy Horse was small for a Lakota:
He was riding always alone thinking of something:

He was standing alone by the picket lines by the ropes:
He was young then: he was thirty when he died: 35
Unless there were children to talk he took no notice:

When the soldiers came for him there on the other side
On the Greasy Grass in the villages we were shouting
"Hoka Hey! Crazy Horse will be riding!"

They fought in the water: horses and men were drowning:
They rode on the butte: dust settled in sunlight: 41
Hoka Hey! they lay on the bloody ground:

No one could tell of the dead which man was Custer . . .
That was the end of his luck: by that river:
The soldiers beat him at Slim Buttes once: 45

They beat him at Willow Creek when the snow lifted:
The last time they beat him was the Tongue:
He had only the meat he had made and of that little:

Do you ask why he should fight? It was his country:
My God should he not fight? It was his: 50
But after the Tongue there were no herds to be hunting:

He cut the knots of the tails and he led them in:
He cried out "I am Crazy Horse! Do not touch me!"
There were many soldiers between and the gun glinting. . . .

And a Mister Josiah Perham of Maine had much of the   55
land Mister Perham was building the Northern Pacific
railroad that is Mister Perham was saying at lunch that

forty say fifty millions of acres in gift and
government grant outright ought to be worth a
wide price on the Board at two-fifty and   60

later a Mister Cooke had relieved Mister Perham and
later a Mister Morgan relieved Mister Cooke:
Mister Morgan converted at prices current:

It was all prices to them: they never looked at it:
why should they look at the land: they were Empire Build-
    ers: 65
it was all in the bid and the asked and the ink on their
    books . . .

When Crazy Horse was there by the Black Hills
His heart would be big with the love he had for that country
And all the game he had seen and the mares he had ridden

And how it went out from you wide and clean in the sun-
    light   70

3.

Burying Ground by the Ties

Ayee! Ai! This is heavy earth on our shoulders:
There were none of us born to be buried in this earth:
Niggers we were Portuguese Magyars Polacks:

We were born to another look of the sky certainly:
Now we lie here in the river pastures: 75
We lie in the mowings under the thick turf:

We hear the earth and the all-day rasp of the grasshoppers:
It was we laid the steel on this land from ocean to ocean:
It was we (if you know) put the U. P. through the passes

Bringing her down into Laramie full load   80
Eighteen mile on the granite anticlinal
Forty-three foot to the mile and the grade holding:

It was we did it: hunkies of our kind:
It was we dug the caved-in holes for the cold water:
It was we built the gully spurs and the freight sidings: 85

Who would do it but we and the Irishmen bossing us?
It was all foreign-born men there were in this country:
It was Scotsmen Englishmen Chinese Squareheads Aus-
    trians. . . .

Ayee! but there's weight to the earth under it:
Not for this did we come out—to be lying here   90
Nameless under the ties in the clay cuts:

There's nothing good in the world but the rich will buy it:
Everything sticks to the grease of a gold note—
Even a continent—even a new sky!

Do not pity us much for the strange grass over us: 95
We laid the steel to the stone stock of these mountains:
The place of our graves is marked by the telegraph poles!

It was not to lie in the bottoms we came out
And the trains going over us here in the dry hollows. . . .

4.
Oil Painting of the Artist as the Artist

The plump Mr. Pl'f is washing his hands of America: 100
The plump Mr. Pl'f is in ochre with such hair:

America is in blue-black-grey-green-sandcolor:
America is a continent—many lands:

The plump Mr. Pl'f is washing his hands of America:
He is pictured at Pau on the *place* and his eyes glaring: 105

He thinks of himself as an exile from all this:
As an émigré from his own time into history—

(History being an empty house without owners
A practical man may get in by the privy stones—

The dead are excellent hosts: they have no objections—   110
And once in he can nail the knob on the next one

Living the life of a classic in bad air with
Himself for the Past and his face in the glass for Posterity)

The Cinquecento is nothing at all like Nome
Or Natchez or Wounded Knee or the Shenandoah: 115

Your vulgarity Tennessee: your violence Texas:
The rocks under your fields Ohio Connecticut:

Your clay Missouri your clay: you have driven him out:
You have shadowed his life Appalachians purple mountains:

There is much too much of your flowing Mississippi: 120
He prefers a tidier stream with a terrace for trippers and

Cypresses mentioned in Horace or Henry James:
He prefers a country where everything carries the name of a

Countess or real king or an actual palace or
Something in Prose and the stock prices all in Italian: 125

There is more shade for an artist under a fig
Than under the whole damn range (he finds) of the Big
    Horns.

5.

Empire Builders

The Museum Attendant:

This is *The Making of America in Five Panels:*

This is Mister Harriman making America:
Mister-Harriman-is-buying-the-Union-Pacific-at-Seventy:
The Sante Fe is shining on his hair: 130

This is Commodore Vanderbilt making America:
Mister-Vanderbilt-is-eliminating-the-short-interest-in-Hudson:
Observe the carving on the rocking chair:

This is J. P. Morgan making America:
(The Tennessee Coal is behind to the left of the Steel Com-
     pany:)   135
Those in mauve are braces he is wearing:

This is Mister Mellon making America:
Mister-Mellon-is-represented-as-a-symbolical-figure-in-alumi-
     num-
Strewing-bank-stocks-on-a-burnished-stair:

This is the Bruce is the Barton making America: 140
Mister-Barton-is-selling-us-Doctor's-Deliciousest-Dentifrice:
This is he in beige with the canary:

You have just beheld the Makers making America:
This is *The Making of America in Five Panels:*
America lies to the west-southwest of the Switch-Tower:
There is nothing to see of America but land: 146

The Original Document
under the Panel Paint:
     "To Thos. Jefferson Esq. his obd't serv't
     M. Lewis: captain: detached:
                              Sir: 149
Having in mind your repeated commands in this matter:
And the worst half of it done and the streams mapped:

And we here on the back of this beach beholding the
Other ocean—two years gone and the cold

Breaking with rain for the third spring since St. Louis:
The crows at the fishbones on the frozen dunes: 155

The first cranes going over from south north:
And the river down by a mark of the pole since the morning:

And time near to return, and a ship (Spanish)
Lying in for the salmon: and fearing chance or the

Drought or the Sioux should deprive you of these discoveries—   160
Therefore we send by sea in this writing:

                                              Above the
Platte there were long plains and a clay country:
Rim of the sky far off: grass under it:

Dung for the cook fires by the sulphur licks:
After that there were low hills and the sycamores: 165

And we poled up by the Great Bend in the skiffs:
The honey bees left us after the Osage River:

The wind was west in the evenings and no dew and the
Morning Star larger and whiter than usual—

The winter rattling in the brittle haws: 170
The second year there was sage and the quail calling:

All that valley is good land by the river:
Three thousand miles and the clay cliffs and

Rue and beargrass by the water banks
And many birds and the brant going over and tracks of   175

Bear elk wolves marten: the buffalo
Numberless so that the cloud of their dust covers them:

The antelope fording the fall creeks: and the mountains and
Grazing lands and the meadow lands and the ground

Sweet and open and well-drained:
                                 We advise you to   180
Settle troops at the forks and to issue licenses:

Many men will have living on these lands:
There is wealth in the earth for them all and the wood
  standing

And wild birds on the water where they sleep:
There is stone in the hills for the towns of a great
    people . ."   185

You have just beheld the Makers making America:

They screwed her scrawny and gaunt with their seven-year
    panics:
They bought her back on their mortgages old-whore-cheap:
They fattened their bonds at her breasts till the thin blood
    ran from them:

Men have forgotten how full clear and deep   190
The Yellowstone moved on the gravel and grass grew
When the land lay waiting for her westward people!

6.

Background with Revolutionaries

And the corn singing Millennium!
Lenin! Millennium! Lennium!

When they're shunting the cars on the Katy a mile off 195
When they're shunting the cars when they're shunting the
*   cars on the Katy*
You can hear the clank of the couplings riding away

Also Comrade Devine who writes of America
Most instructively having in 'Seventy-four   200
Crossed to the Hoboken side on the Barclay Street Ferry

She sits on a settle in the State of North Dakota
O she sits on a settle in the State of North Dakota
She can hear the engines whistle over Iowa and Idaho

Also Comrade Edward Remington Ridge   205
Who has prayed God since the April of 'Seventeen
To replace in his life his lost (M.E.) religion.

And The New York Daily Worker *goes a'blowing over*
   Arkansas
The New York Daily Worker *goes a'blowing over Arkansas*
The grasses let it go along the Ozarks over Arkansas   210

Even Comrade Grenadine Grilt who has tried since
August tenth for something to feel about strongly in
Verses—his personal passions having tired

I can tell my land by the jays in the apple-trees
Tell my land by the jays in the apple-trees   215
I can tell my people by the blue-jays in the apple-trees

Aindt you read in d'books you are all brudders?
D' glassic historic objective broves you are brudders!
You and d'Wops and d'Chinks you are all brudders!
Havend't you got it d' same ideology? Havend't you?   220

When it's yesterday in Oregon it's one A M in Maine
And she slides: and the day slides: and it runs: runs over us:
And the bells strike twelve strike twelve strike twelve
In Marblehead in Buffalo in Cheyenne in Cherokee
Yesterday runs on the states like a crow's shadow   225

For Marx has said to us Workers what do you need?
And Stalin has said to us Starvers what do you need?
You need the Dialectical Materialism!

She's a tough land under the corn mister:
She has changed the bone in the cheeks of many races: 230
She has winced the eyes of the soft Slavs with her sun on
   them:
She has tried the fat from the round rumps of Italians:
Even the voice of the English has gone dry
And hard on the tongue and alive in the throat speaking:

She's a tough land under the oak-trees mister: 235
It may be she can change the word in the book
As she changes the bone of a man's head in his children:
It may be that the earth and the men remain. . . .

There is too much sun on the lids of my eyes to be listening

EXERCISE:

1. What is the theme of this long poem? What is the function of each of the various sections of the poem in developing this theme? Is the poem unified?

2. Discuss in relation to tone the verse form used. Discuss shifts of tone, considering the use of satirical and realistic elements.

LINES

COMPOSED A FEW MILES ABOVE TINTERN ABBEY, ON REVISITING THE BANKS OF THE WYE DURING A TOUR, JULY 13, 1798

WILLIAM WORDSWORTH (1770–1850)

Five years have past; five summers, with the length
Of five long winters! and again I hear
These waters, rolling from their mountain-springs
With a soft inland murmur.—Once again
Do I behold these steep and lofty cliffs,   5
That on a wild secluded scene impress
Thoughts of more deep seclusion; and connect
The landscape with the quiet of the sky.
The day is come when I again repose
Here, under this dark sycamore, and view   10
These plots of cottage-ground, these orchard-tufts,
Which at this season, with their unripe fruits,
Are clad in one green hue, and lose themselves
'Mid groves and copses. Once again I see
These hedge-rows, hardly hedge-rows, little lines   15
Of sportive wood run wild; these pastoral farms,
Green to the very door; and wreaths of smoke
Sent up, in silence, from among the trees!
With some uncertain notice, as might seem
Of vagrant dwellers in the houseless woods,   20
Or of some hermit's cave, where by his fire
The hermit sits alone.

These beauteous forms,
Through a long absence, have not been to me
As is a landscape to a blind man's eye:
But oft, in lonely rooms, and 'mid the din   25
Of towns and cities, I have owed to them,
In hours of weariness, sensations sweet,
Felt in the blood, and felt along the heart;
And passing even into my purer mind,
With tranquil restoration:—feelings too   30
Of unremembered pleasure: such, perhaps,
As have no slight or trivial influence
On that best portion of a good man's life,
His little, nameless, unremembered, acts
Of kindness and of love. Nor less, I trust,   35
To them I may have owed another gift,
Of aspect more sublime; that blessed mood,
In which the burden of the mystery,
In which the heavy and the weary weight
Of all this unintelligible world,   40
Is lightened:—that serene and blessèd mood,
In which the affections gently lead us on,—
Until, the breath of this corporeal frame
And even the motion of our human blood
Almost suspended, we are laid asleep   45
In body, and become a living soul;
While with an eye made quiet by the power
Of harmony, and the deep power of joy,
We see into the life of things.
                                        If this
Be but a vain belief, yet, oh! how oft—   50
In darkness and amid the many shapes
Of joyless daylight; when the fretful stir
Unprofitable, and the fever of the world,
Have hung upon the beatings of my heart—
How oft, in spirit, have I turned to thee,   55
O sylvan Wye! Thou wanderer through the woods,
How often has my spirit turned to thee!

And now, with gleams of half-extinguished thought,
With many recognitions dim and faint,
And somewhat of a sad perplexity,   60
The picture of the mind revives again:

While here I stand, not only with the sense
Of present pleasure, but with pleasing thoughts
That in this moment there is life and food
For future years.   And so I dare to hope,   65
Though changed, no doubt, from what I was when first
I came among these hills; when like a roe
I bounded o'er the mountains, by the sides
Of the deep rivers and the lonely streams,
Wherever nature led: more like a man   70
Flying from something that he dreads, than one
Who sought the thing he loved.   For Nature then
(The coarser pleasures of my boyish days,
And their glad animal movements all gone by)
To me was all in all.—I cannot paint   75
What then I was.   The sounding cataract
Haunted me like a passion: the tall rock,
The mountain, and the deep and gloomy wood,
Their colors and their forms, were then to me
An appetite; a feeling and a love,   80
That had no need of a remoter charm,
By thought supplied, nor any interest
Unborrowed from the eye.—That time is past,
And all its aching joys are now no more,
And all its dizzy raptures.   Not for this   85
Faint I, nor mourn, nor murmur; other gifts
Have followed; for such loss, I would believe,
Abundant recompense.   For I have learned
To look on nature, not as in the hour
Of thoughtless youth; but hearing oftentimes   90
The still, sad music of humanity,
Nor harsh nor grating, though of ample power
To chasten and subdue.   And I have felt
A presence that disturbs me with the joy
Of elevated thoughts; a sense sublime   95
Of something far more deeply interfused,
Whose dwelling is the light of setting suns,
And the round ocean and the living air,
And the blue sky, and in the mind of man;
A motion and a spirit, that impels   100
All thinking things, all objects of all thought,
And rolls through all things.   Therefore am I still
A lover of the meadows and the woods,

And mountains; and of all that we behold
From this green earth; of all the mighty world   105
Of eye, and ear,—both what they half create,
And what perceive; well pleased to recognize
In nature and the language of the sense,
The anchor of my purest thoughts, the nurse,
The guide, the guardian of my heart, and soul   110
Of all my moral being.

                Nor perchance,
If I were not thus taught, should I the more
Suffer my genial spirits to decay:
For thou art with me here upon the banks
Of this fair river; thou, my dearest Friend,   115
My dear, dear Friend; and in thy voice I catch
The language of my former heart, and read
My former pleasures in the shooting lights
Of thy wild eyes. Oh! yet a little while
May I behold in thee what I was once,   120
My dear, dear Sister! and this prayer I make,
Knowing that Nature never did betray
The heart that loved her; 'tis her privilege
Through all the years of this our life, to lead
From joy to joy: for she can so inform   125
The mind that is within us, so impress
With quietness and beauty, and so feed
With lofty thoughts, that neither evil tongues,
Rash judgments, nor the sneers of selfish men,
Nor greetings where no kindness is, nor all   130
The dreary intercourse of daily life,
Shall e'er prevail against us, or disturb
Our cheerful faith, that all which we behold
Is full of blessings. Therefore let the moon
Shine on thee in thy solitary walk;   135
And let the misty mountain-winds be free
To blow against thee: and, in after years,
When these wild ecstasies shall be matured
Into a sober pleasure; when thy mind
Shall be a mansion for all lovely forms,   140
Thy memory be as a dwelling-place
For all sweet sounds and harmonies; oh! then,
If solitude, or fear, or pain, or grief,

Should be thy portion, with what healing thoughts
Of tender joy wilt thou remember me,   145
And these my exhortations! Nor, perchance—
If I should be where I no more can hear
Thy voice, nor catch from thy wild eyes these gleams
Of past existence—wilt thou then forget
That on the banks of this delightful stream   150
We stood together; and that I, so long
A worshipper of Nature, hither came
Unwearied in that service: rather say
With warmer love—oh! with far deeper zeal
Of holier love. Nor will thou then forget,   155
That after many wanderings, many years
Of absence, these steep woods and lofty cliffs,
And this green pastoral landscape, were to me
More dear, both for themselves and for thy sake!

EXERCISE:

  1. Work out the logical structure of the poem.
  2. What means has the poet taken to dramatize his idea?
  3. Discuss the dramatic function of the rhythms in the passage
from line 75 to line 88.

A POET'S EPITAPH

WILLIAM WORDSWORTH (1770–1850)

Art thou a Statist in the van
Of public conflicts trained and bred?
—First learn to love one living man;
Then may'st thou think upon the dead.

A lawyer art thou?—draw not nigh!   5
Go, carry to some fitter place
The keenness of that practiced eye,
The hardness of that sallow face.

Art thou a man of purple cheer?
A rosy man, right plump to see?   10
Approach; yet, doctor, not too near,
This grave no cushion is for thee.

Or art thou one of gallant pride,
A soldier and no man of chaff?
Welcome!—but lay thy sword aside,   15
And lean upon a peasant's staff.

Physician art thou?—one, all eyes,
Philosopher!—a fingering slave,
One that would peep and botanize
Upon his mother's grave?   20

Wrapped closely in thy sensual fleece,
O turn aside,—and take, I pray,
That he below may rest in peace,
Thy ever-dwindling soul, away!

A moralist perchance appears;   25
Led, Heaven knows how! to this poor sod:
And he has neither eyes nor ears;
Himself his world, and his own God;

One to whose smooth-rubbed soul can cling
Nor form, nor feeling great or small;   30
A reasoning, self-sufficing thing,
An intellectual all-in-all!

Shut close the door; press down the latch;
Sleep in thy intellectual crust;
Nor lose ten tickings of thy watch   35
Near this unprofitable dust.

But who is he, with modest looks,
And clad in homely russet brown?
He murmurs near the running brooks
A music sweeter than their own.   40

He is retired as noontide dew,
Or fountain in a noon-day grove;
And you must love him ere to you
He will seem worthy of your love.

The outward shows of sky and earth,   45
Of hill and valley, he has viewed;
And impulses of deeper birth
Have come to him in solitude.

In common things that round us lie
Some random truths he can impart,—   50
The harvest of a quiet eye
That broods and sleeps on his own heart.

But he is weak; both man and boy,
Hath been an idler in the land;
Contented if he might enjoy   55
The things which others understand.

—Come hither in thy hour of strength;
Come, weak as is a breaking wave!
Here stretch thy body at full length;
Or build thy house upon this grave.   60

THE SCOFFERS

WILLIAM BLAKE (1757–1827)

Mock on, mock on, Voltaire, Rousseau,
   Mock on, mock on; 'tis all in vain;
You throw but dust against the wind
   And the wind blows it back again.

And every stone becomes a gem   5
   Reflected in the beams divine;
Blown back, they blind the mocking eye,
   But still in Israel's paths they shine.

The atoms of Democritus
   And Newton's particles of light   10
Are sands upon the Red Sea shore,
   Where Israel's tents do shine so bright.

Blake's "Scoffers" and Wordsworth's "A Poet's Epitaph" have similar themes. Both poets are protesting against the supremacy of intellectual abstraction, and place over against it, what is usually referred to as "appreciation of spiritual values." They are protesting against the habit of breaking life up into neat and unrelated fragments instead of perceiving it as a whole, and against the habit of conceiving of it exclusively in terms of the intellect rather than in terms of the imagination.

The theme is one on which a good poem may be based, and the theme emerges with sufficient clarity in both poems. A comparison of the two poems, however, will remind us that poems with similar themes may be vastly different.

How does Wordsworth go about making us share with him the theme, not as mere intellectual statement, but as an imaginative experience? He constructs a little framework into which to cast his statement. He states what he has to say as a poet might state it in his epitaph, warning away from his grave those who lack interest in spiritual qualities: thus he warns away the statesman, the lawyer, the scholar, the physician, and the moralist. On the other hand, he welcomes the soldier, a man of honor and warm feeling, provided he exchanges his sword for a peasant's staff and lays aside his pride; and most of all he welcomes the person who has lived simply and close to nature and who is content if he may enjoy "the things which others understand." Indeed, in his adverse characterizations of the men of intellect and in his favorable description of the lover of nature, he states the basic theme of the poem. With the first class, the poet can feel no kinship; to the second class, he wishes to bequeath his strength and help. And from the form which the statement of the theme takes, there results a subsidiary theme: namely, that poetry is based not on the observation of rules—not on nice calculations—but on warm and loving appreciation of nature.

Now such a framework *may* support a very fine poem; the framework at least indicates an attempt to make an otherwise abstract point concretely and with some dramatic force. Is this particular poem successful? It may be best to defer a consideration of this point until we have examined the structure of Blake's "Scoffers."

Blake also has constructed a dramatic framework to support his theme, and it seems, at least at first glance, to be a far less elaborate and dramatic framework than that which Wordsworth uses. Blake begins abruptly by addressing two of the Scoffers, Voltaire and Rousseau. (It does not matter, in so far as the poem is concerned, whether or not we think that the historical Voltaire and Rousseau, or for that matter Newton and Democritus, are really scoffers against the things of the spirit. The important thing is that Blake felt them so, and should have made out of his indignation against them a fine poem. The poem is to be judged good or bad in terms of itself—not in terms of what we think today is the essential truth with regard to either Voltaire or Rousseau. "Foreword," Section VII, pp. 491–93 and analysis of "The Scholar Gipsy," p. 549.)

Blake taunts the Scoffers with the futility of their mockery. He uses a vivid figure to make this point: they are throwing dust against the wind. But this figure is a development of a merely conventional one: "To throw dust into a person's eyes" is a proverbial figure for an attempt at deception. Blake freshens and sharpens the conventional figure by having the wind blow the dust back into the eyes of the would-be deceivers.

The second stanza gives an extension of the same image of one throwing dust against the wind. And the development of the idea is made in terms of the development of the figure. Blake amplifies the meaning of the dust, stating that every mote (we shall see in a few moments why he calls the motes *stones*) becomes a gem. He also amplifies it by making the apparently puzzling statement that the motes of dust shine in *Israel's* path.

The third stanza is connected to the second largely in terms of the reference to Israel. Here the dust is compared to the sands along the Red Sea shore where Israel camped on the way out of Egypt.

Blake, one sees at once, is not building his poem in terms of a logical chain of ideas as Wordsworth does. And for this reason, Wordsworth's poem is much clearer for the casual reader. One gets the "prose" meaning of Wordsworth's poem almost at once. But Blake's poem contributes a much sharper shock of emotion, even at a first reading. He gains in force and intensity by pointing to some real people as mockers, Voltaire and Rousseau (though he may lose in clarity, since his reader is compelled to know these characters and to define their meaning in this context). Consider also the opening of the poem. The statement, "Mock on, mock on," is much more powerful than Wordsworth's question, "Art thou a Statist. . . ?" The fact that the various persons in Wordsworth's poem are, after all, only general types and not particular people, makes the irony diffuse and weakens the dramatic effect of the poet's indignation.

Wordsworth's poem, then, is less concentrated in effect than Blake's, though his theme *as a statement* is more easily found. We have then what may seem an odd contrast: at a first reading we understand Wordsworth's poem more easily, but we feel Blake's more intensely. We have already found that poetry insists on more than abstract statement. Blake's poem, if we accept this view of poetry, scores higher than Wordsworth's even on a first reading. But a closer examination will reveal that Blake's poem makes an even more intricate and rich statement than does Wordsworth's.

We have already remarked on the fact that Blake's poem is knit together by its *imagery,* and we have already noted that the image of throwing dust has been made to carry a complex idea.

It is important to notice that the development of the theme is made *through a development of the figure.* The poet implies that nature itself opposes the mocker: the dust blown back, ironically enough, blinds the "mocking eye." And since the dust in reality is performing the service of nature ("Reflected in the beams *divine*"), the poet says that the grains of dust shine like gems. Here, one may notice that Blake keeps hold on the concrete figure. Motes of dust shining in the light do seem to gleam like points of light, and thus give the poet some sort of physical basis for his characterization of the motes as *gems.* This makes his treatment of them as "Reflected in the beams divine" not a mere extravagance of statement, but a definite symbolism.

The last stanza picks up and summarizes the meanings already developed. The analytic attitude, the exclusive preoccupation with abstractions, which Blake is protesting against, is represented

by the various atomic theories which seem to break up the
universe into little separate entities—separate entities which are
like the small particles of dust. Blake refers to the founder of
the atomic theory in ancient time, Democritus, and to an exponent
of the theory in modern times, Newton. Democritus's atoms
and Newton's particles of light, in reality, are nothing more than
grains of sand on the seashore by which God's chosen people
encamp in triumph on their way to the Land of Promise. The
sands lying on the shore are a strong image of the inert and
worthless and meaningless matter in contrast to Israel's tents
shining with God's favoring light. Moreover, far from being a
stop or impediment, the sands form the roadway across which they
will travel.

Blake has done his thinking in terms of his concrete images;
and yet his thinking is much more intricate than is Wordsworth's;
but it is also more concentrated and gives a sharper and more
forceful experience.

LONDON

WILLIAM BLAKE (1757–1827)

I wander through each chartered street,
Near where the chartered Thames does flow
And mark in every face I meet
Marks of weakness, marks of woe.

In every cry of every man,   5
In every infant's cry of fear,
In every voice; in every ban,
The mind-forged manacles I hear:

How the chimney-sweeper's cry
Every blackening church appalls,   10
And the hapless soldier's sigh
Runs in blood down palace-walls.

But most, through midnight streets I hear
How the youthful harlot's curse
Blasts the new-born infant's tear,   15
And blights with plagues the marriage-hearse.

EXERCISE:

Write an analysis of this poem.

HYMN TO INTELLECTUAL BEAUTY

PERCY BYSSHE SHELLEY (1792–1822)

The awful shadow of some unseen Power
  Floats though unseen amongst us,—visiting
  This various world with as inconstant wing
As summer winds that creep from flower to flower;—
Like moonbeams that behind some piny mountain shower,
    It visits with inconstant glance   6
    Each human heart and countenance;
Like hues and harmonies of evening,—
    Like clouds in starlight widely spread,—
    Like memory of music fled,—   10
    Like aught that for its grace may be
Dear, and yet dearer for its mystery.

Spirit of Beauty, that dost consecrate
  With thine own hues all thou dost shine upon
  Of human thought or form,—where art thou gone?   15
Why dost thou pass away and leave our state,
This dim vast vale of tears, vacant and desolate?
    Ask why the sunlight not forever
    Weaves rainbows o'er yon mountain river,
Why aught should fail and fade that once is shown,   20
    Why fear and dream and death and birth
    Cast on the daylight of this earth
    Such gloom,—why man has such a scope
For love and hate, despondency and hope?

No voice from some sublimer world hath ever   25
    To sage or poet these responses given—
    Therefore the names of Dæmon, Ghost, and Heaven,
Remain the records of their vain endeavor,
Frail spells—whose uttered charm might not avail to sever,
        From all we hear and all we see,   30
        Doubt, chance, and mutability.
Thy light alone—like mist o'er mountains driven,
        Or music by the night wind sent,
        Through strings of some still instrument,
        Or moonlight on a midnight stream,   35
Gives grace and truth to life's unquiet dream.

Love, Hope, and Self-esteem, like clouds depart
    And come, for some uncertain moments lent.
    Man were immortal, and omnipotent,
Didst thou, unknown and awful as thou art,   40
Keep with thy glorious train firm state within his heart.
        Thou messenger of sympathies,
        That wax and wane in lovers' eyes—
Thou—that to human thought art nourishment,
        Like darkness to a dying flame!   45
        Depart not as thy shadow came,
        Depart not—lest the grave should be,
Like life and fear, a dark reality.

While yet a boy I sought for ghosts, and sped
    Through many a listening chamber, cave and ruin,   50
    And starlight wood, with fearful steps pursuing
Hopes of high talk with the departed dead.
I called on poisonous names with which our youth is fed;
        I was not heard—I saw them not—
        When musing deeply on the lot   55
Of life, at the sweet time when winds are wooing
        All vital things that wake to bring
        News of birds and blossoming,—
        Sudden, thy shadow fell on me;
I shrieked, and clasped my hands in ecstasy!   60

I vowed that I would dedicate my powers
    To thee and thine—have I not kept the vow?
    With beating heart and streaming eyes, even now

I call the phantoms of a thousand hours
Each from his voiceless grave: they have in visioned bowers
    Of studious zeal or love's delight   66
    Outwatched with me the envious night—
They know that never joy illumed my brow
    Unlinked with hope that thou wouldst free
    This world from its dark slavery,   70
    That thou—O awful Loveliness,
Wouldst give whate'er these words cannot express.

The day becomes more solemn and serene
    When noon is past—there is a harmony
    In autumn, and a luster in its sky,   75
Which through the summer is not heard or seen,
As if it could not be, as if it had not been!
    Thus let thy power, which like the truth
    Of nature on my passive youth
Descended, to my onward life supply   80
    Its calm—to one who worships thee,
    And every form containing thee,
    Whom, Spirit fair, thy spells did bind
To fear himself, and love all human kind.

EXERCISE:

The poet here is attempting to present an abstract and intangible quality. What means does he use for accomplishing this purpose? Is he successful? Compare this poem with "Ode to Simplicity" (p. 515).

THE LOVE SONG OF J. ALFRED PRUFROCK

T. S. ELIOT (1888–   )

Let us go then, you and I,
When the evening is spread out against the sky
Like a patient etherized upon a table;
Let us go, through certain half-deserted streets,
The muttering retreats   5

Of restless nights in one-night cheap hotels
And sawdust restaurants with oyster-shells:
Streets that follow like a tedious argument
Of insidious intent
To lead you to an overwhelming question. . . .   10
Oh, do not ask, "What is it?"
Let us go and make our visit.

In the room the women come and go
Talking of Michelangelo.

The yellow fog that rubs its back upon the windowpanes,   15
The yellow smoke that rubs its muzzle on the windowpanes
Licked its tongue into the corners of the evening,
Lingered upon the pools that stand in drains,
Let fall upon its back the soot that falls from chimneys,
Slipped by the terrace, made a sudden leap,   20
And seeing that it was a soft October night,
Curled once about the house, and fell asleep.

And indeed there will be time
For the yellow smoke that slides along the street,
Rubbing its back upon the windowpanes;   25
There will be time, there will be time
To prepare a face to meet the faces that you meet;
There will be time to murder and create,
And time for all the works and days of hands
That lift and drop a question on your plate;   30
Time for you and time for me,
And time yet for a hundred indecisions,
And for a hundred visions and revisions,
Before the taking of a toast and tea.

In the room the women come and go   35
Talking of Michelangelo.

And indeed there will be time
To wonder, "Do I dare?" and, "Do I dare?"
Time to turn back and descend the stair,
With a bald spot in the middle of my hair—   40
(They will say: "How his hair is growing thin!")
My morning coat, my collar mounting firmly to the chin,

My necktie rich and modest, but asserted by a simple pin—
(They will say: "But how his arms and legs are thin!")
Do I dare   45
Disturb the universe?
In a minute there is time
For decisions and revisions which a minute will reverse.

For I have known them all already, known them all:
Have known the evenings, mornings, afternoons,   50
I have measured out my life with coffee spoons;
I know the voices dying with a dying fall
Beneath the music from a farther room.
    So how should I presume?

And I have known the eyes already, known them all—   55
The eyes that fix you in a formulated phrase,
And when I am formulated, sprawling on a pin,
When I am pinned and wriggling on the wall,
Then how should I begin
To spit out all the butt-ends of my days and ways?   60
    And how should I presume?

And I have known the arms already, known them all—
Arms that are braceleted and white and bare
(But in the lamplight, downed with light brown hair)
Is it perfume from a dress   65
That makes me so digress?
Arms that lie along a table, or wrap about a shawl.
    And should I then presume?
    And how should I begin?

           .   , ...

Shall I say, I have gone at dusk through narrow streets   70
And watched the smoke that rises from the pipes
Of lonely men in shirt-sleeves, leaning out of windows? . . .

I should have been a pair of ragged claws
Scuttling across the floors of silent seas.

           .   .   .   .

And the afternoon, the evening, sleeps so peacefully!   75

Smoothed by long fingers,
Asleep . . . tired . . . or it malingers,
Stretched on the floor, here beside you and me.
Should I, after tea and cakes and ices,
Have the strength to force the moment to its crisis?   80
But though I have wept and fasted, wept and prayed,
Though I have seen my head (grown slightly bald) brought
        in upon a platter,
I am no prophet—and here's no great matter;
I have seen the moment of my greatness flicker,
And I have seen the eternal Footman hold my coat, and snicker,
And in short, I was afraid.   86

And would it have been worth it, after all,
After the cups, the marmalade, the tea,
Among the porcelain, among some talk of you and me,
Would it have been worth while,   90
To have bitten off the matter with a smile,
To have squeezed the universe into a ball
To roll it toward some overwhelming question,
To say: "I am Lazarus, come from the dead,
Come back to tell you all, I shall tell you all"—   95
If one, settling a pillow by her head,
      Should say: "That is not what I meant at all;
      That is not it, at all."

And would it have been worth it, after all,
Would it have been worth while,   99
After the sunsets and the dooryards and the sprinkled streets,
After the novels, after the teacups, after the skirts that trail
        along the floor—
And this, and so much more?—
It is impossible to say just what I mean!
But as if a magic lantern threw the nerves in patterns on a
        screen:
Would it have been worth while   105
If one, settling a pillow or throwing off a shawl,
And turning toward the window, should say:
      "That is not it at all,
      That is not what I meant, at all."

No! I am not Prince Hamlet, nor was meant to be;   110
Am an attendant lord, one that will do
To swell a progress, start a scene or two,
Advise the prince; no doubt, an easy tool,
Deferential, glad to be of use,
Politic, cautious, and meticulous;   115
Full of high sentence, but a bit obtuse;
At times, indeed, almost ridiculous—
Almost, at times, the Fool.

I grow old . . . I grow old . . .
I shall wear the bottoms of my trousers rolled.   120

Shall I part my hair behind? Do I dare to eat a peach?
I shall wear white flannel trousers, and walk upon the beach.
I have heard the mermaids singing, each to each.

I do not think that they will sing to me.

I have seen them riding seaward on the waves   125
Combing the white hair of the waves blown back
When the wind blows the water white and black.

We have lingered in the chambers of the sea
By sea-girls wreathed with seaweed red and brown
Till human voices wake us, and we drown.   130

The character of Prufrock, as we shall see, is really very much like that of Hamlet—a man who is apparently betrayed by his possession of such qualities as intellect and imagination. But it is particularly dangerous to attempt to portray, and make the audience believe in and take seriously, such a person as Prufrock. We are inclined to laugh at the person who is really so painfully self-conscious that he is inhibited from all action. Moreover, in so far as the poet is using Prufrock as a character typical of our age, he must in fairness to truth avoid treating him quite so heroically as a Hamlet. At the very beginning, therefore, the poet faces a difficult problem. In using the materials of the present, the desire to be accurate, to be thoroughly truthful, forces him to exhibit the character as not purely romantic or tragic. And yet there is in such a person as he describes a very real tragedy. How shall he treat him? To attempt to treat Prufrock in full seriousness is doomed to failure; on the other hand, to make him purely comic is to falsify matters too.

Faced with this problem, the poet resorts to irony, and by employing varying shades of irony he is able to do justice to the ludicrous elements in the situation and yet do justice to the serious ones also. The casual and careless reader will probably see only the comic aspects: he will be likely to fail to appreciate the underlying seriousness of the whole poem.

The title itself gives us the first clue to the fact that the poem is ironical. We think of a love song as simple and full of warm emotion. But this poem opens on a scene where the streets

> . . . follow like an argument
> Of insidious intent
> To lead you to an overwhelming question. . . .

One notices also that the character Prufrock is continually interested in stating that "there will be time" to make up his mind. But in saying that there will be time for this, he is so hopelessly unable to act that he continues in a sort of abstracted and unconscious patter to state that there will be time

> For the yellow smoke that slides along the street,
> Rubbing its back upon the windowpanes;
> There will be time, there will be time
> To prepare a face to meet the faces that you meet;
> There will be time to murder and create,
> And time for all the works and days of hands
> That lift and drop a question on your plate.

Then, caught up by the irrelevance of his patter, he goes on to say that there will be time—not for decisions—but, ironically, for a "hundred indecisions," and for a "hundred visions and revisions."

The first part of the poem, then, can be imagined as the monologue of Prufrock himself as he finds his indecisiveness reflected in the apparently aimless streets of the city and in the fog which hangs over the city. It is filled with a rather bitter self-irony, a self-irony which is reflected in some of the abrupt transitions. But in observing this ironical monologue which illuminates the character, one has missed the point entirely if he has failed to see the psychological penetration in it. Take, for example, the tone and associations of the comparison of the evening to a "patient etherized upon a table." This comparison is "in character." It is an appropriate observation for Prufrock, being what he is, though it might not be very appropriate for an entirely different character or in a poem of entirely different tone. The evening—not any evening, but this particular evening, as seen by this particular observer—does seem to have the hushed quiet of the perfectly, and yet fatally relaxed, body of a person under ether.

Or notice also the psychological penetration of the remark, "To prepare a face to meet the faces that you meet." Again, the remark must be taken in character. Yet it is possible to observe, as a general truth, that we do prepare a face, an expression, a look, to meet the various "faces" that we meet— faces which have duly undergone a like preparation. A poorer poet would have written "To put on a mask to meet the people that you meet." Eliot's line with its concentration and its slight ironical shock is far superior.

The structure of the poem is similar to that which we observed in the poem "Patterns" (p. 136). But the transitions here appear, at first glance, more violent. This apparent violence disappears, however, as soon as we realize that the relations between the various scenes, ideas, and observations in the poem are determined by a kind of flow of associations which are really based on the fact that they develop and illustrate the fundamental character and situation of Prufrock.

After the opening sections in which the character of the speaker is to some extent established for the reader, Prufrock describes a scene in which overcultured, bored women sip tea and discuss art. It is as though he had just stepped inside after wandering alone in the streets. Here are the people of whose criticism Prufrock is most afraid, and yet, as his characterization of them abundantly shows, he sees their shallowness. But Prufrock does not attempt to treat romantically or heroically his own character: he is able to see the ludicrous aspect of himself, his timid preciseness and vanity.

> With a bald spot in the middle of my hair—
> (They will say: "How his hair is growing thin.")
> My necktie rich and modest, but asserted by a simple pin.

But what is the function of a statement so abrupt as "I have measured out my life with coffee spoons?" Here again, the line must be taken in character. But if we are willing to take it in character, we shall be able to see that it is brilliantly ironical. It would mean literally, one supposes, that he has measured out his life in little driblets, coffee spoons being tiny in size. But it carries another and more concrete meaning: namely, that he has spent his life in just such an environment as this drawing room which he is describing. The comparison makes the same ironical point, therefore, as the lines

> And time yet for a hundred indecisions,
> And for a hundred visions and revisions,
> Before the taking of a toast and tea.

The poem's sense of fidelity to the whole situation—its willingness to take into account so many apparently discordant views and points of view—is shown in the lines

> Arms that are braceleted and white and bare
> (But in the lamplight, downed with light brown hair!)

These lines give us a contrast between what might be termed loosely the romantic and the realistic attitude. The ironical comment here parallels exactly the reference to his own bald head.

The structure of the poem is, as we have noticed, that of a sort of monologue in which the poet describes this scene or that and comments on them, and, by means of them, on himself. The irrelevance, or apparent irrelevance, is exactly the sort of irrelevance and abrupt transition which is often admired in a personal essay by a writer like Charles Lamb. The structure is essentially the same here (though of course with an entirely different tone and for a different effect). But having seen what the structure is—not a logical structure, or one following the lines of a narrative, or one based on the description of a scene, but the structure of the flow of ideas—the reader is not puzzled at the rather abrupt transition from the stanza about the arms to

> Shall I say, I have gone at dusk through narrow streets,

etc. It is a scene from the beginning of the poem—or perhaps it is a scene viewed earlier and brought back to memory by the statement about the streets and the smoke in the opening lines of the poem. It is the sort of scene which has a very real poignance about it. Prufrock feels that it meant something. But he is utterly incapable of stating the meaning before the bored and sophisticated audience of the world to which he belongs. He would be laughed at as a fool. And then comes the thought— apparently irrelevant, but the sort of thought which might easily occur in such a monologue:

> I should have been a pair of ragged claws
> Scuttling across the floors of silent seas.

A crab is about as vivid a symbol as one might find, for a person who is completely self-sufficing and cannot be, and does not need to be, sociable. And there is, moreover, a secondary implication of irony here growing out of Prufrock's disgust with these people about him and with himself: the crab is at least "alive" and has, as Prufrock does not have, a meaning and a place in its world. (Observe that the poet does not use the word *crab*. Why? Because in mentioning the most prominent feature of the crab, the claws, and with the vivid description of the effect of the crab's swimming, "scuttling," he makes the point more sharply.)

There are several literary allusions in the latter part of the poem, allusions which we must know in order to understand the poem just as one must know the various allusions in Blake's "The Scoffers" (p. 578). Can they be justified? And if so, how? In the first place, they are fairly commonly known: an allusion to John the Baptist's head having been cut off at Herod's orders and brought in on a platter; an allusion to the raising of Lazarus from the dead; and a reference to Shakespeare's *Hamlet*. The poet has not imposed a very heavy burden on us, therefore, in expecting that we shall know these references. But what can be said by way of justification? In the first place, all the allusions are "in character." They are comparisons which would normally occur to such a person as Prufrock, and they would naturally occur in the sort of meditation in which he indulges in this poem. In the second place, they do a great deal to sharpen the irony in the poem. Prufrock is vividly conscious of the sorry figure which he cuts in comparison with the various great figures from the past or from literature whom, in a far-off sense, he resembles. He has seen his reputation picked to pieces— his head, a slightly bald head, brought in on a platter like that of John the Baptist. But *he* is no prophet—nothing is lost. Death itself in this society can be regarded as nothing more than a liveried footman, putting on the coats of the departing, and death, like the knowing and insolent footman, is quite capable, he believes, of snickering behind his back.

Prufrock is also conscious of his own remote resemblance to Hamlet, but he is honest enough to repudiate the comparison, even to himself. He is merely (and he thinks here of the whole play) one of the minor figures used to begin a scene; a sort of Polonius or Rosenkrantz or Osric,

> Politic, cautious, and meticulous;
> Full of high sentence, but a bit obtuse;

Or worse, he is, he has to admit to himself, almost the stock character of the fool with which each Elizabethan tragedy is equipped.

At first glance one may wonder about the relevance of the mermaids. What do they represent? What do they mean? For the first time in the poem we leave the twisting streets and the fog-hung town and the desiccated drawing rooms where people prattle of inanities. It is the first vision of "beauty" in the poem—and the first dynamic passage. The mermaids represent, presumably, just the opposite of what the women in the drawing rooms represent. They stand for life and vitality—completely opposed to the dried out and over-refined life which the poet has been describing. It is the *human* voices which "wake us and we drown." And this paradox sums up the theme of the whole poem. We are better able now to appreciate the reference to Lazarus. The people in the drawing rooms have lost hold of the real meaning of life; they are drowned, are dead, the implication is; and if he, as one who has glimpsed something of another world were to come to them, like Lazarus arisen from the dead, he would not be able to make himself understood.

But there is another aspect of the paradox here which makes the poem very rich and meaningful. Life on the sea bed, we ordinarily think of as death—yet the poet is seeming to say that death is really life, and what people think of as life may be really death. And how does this relate to his theme of indecision? Prufrock is really living a kind of death.

The poem has some complication, of course, but its primary difficulty for the reader is the apparent lack of logical transitions—a lack of which, by seeming to give something of the natural sequence of ideas in a person's mind, allows the poet to leap from one scene to another and from one idea to another. Moreover, these abrupt transitions and paradoxes and strange juxtapositions, as we have already seen, are used for an ironical effect. This same general method of organization appears, for instance, in the "Ode to a Nightingale," by Keats, though there the irony is much more diffuse and subdued. But we can really understand neither poem unless we appreciate the various functions of the irony involved.

What is the essential function of irony? Its primary function is to let the reader know that the poet is not really oversimplifying the material of the poem. The poet is stating his attitude by *apparently* expressing an opposed attitude. We rarely find the ironical poet therefore falling into sentimentality; other faults he may have, but this fault his irony usually protects him against. It is easy to see why. The sentimental poet is nearly always straightforward and direct. When we feel that he is caught off guard and that he takes his subject or himself too seriously without previous consideration—when we feel that he is "carried away" by his own enthusiasm, we say that he is sentimental. Apparently he does not see the full context of what he is saying. Thus when Shelley, in pouring out his love, says, "I faint, I die, I fail," we feel that he has been caught off balance.

Now the poet who is ironical at least does not suffer this fault, and he does not, because we feel that he has already perceived what is essentially ludicrous in his situation and has already done justice to it: he has already, in one sense, laughed at himself. But the question is not so simple as even this. There are many shades of irony. A statement may be rather direct, and there may be only a flicker of irony indicating that the poet, in making his direct statement of attitude, is still aware of other possible attitudes toward the situation. Or the weight may be shifted heavily toward the negative aspect of the statement, so that we feel it as only a bitter, sardonic jest. And between these extremes there are all sorts of intermediate shades. Irony, therefore in skillful hands, is a very delicate and accurate instrument. This is not to say of course that all poetry must be ironical, though there is a large number of good poems of all periods in which the ironical function is represented. Certainly, it is not to say that irony is a recent invention. We shall be able to find ironical contrasts at the very root of the works of such poets as Chaucer and Shakespeare.

RABBI BEN EZRA

ROBERT BROWNING (1812–1889)

I

Grow old along with me!
The best is yet to be,
The last of life, for which the first was made:
Our times are in His hand
Who saith, "A whole I planned,   5
Youth shows but half; trust God: see all, nor be afraid!"

II

Not that, amassing flowers,
Youth sighed, "Which rose make ours,
Which lily leave and then as best recall?"
Not that, admiring stars,   10
It yearned, "Nor Jove, nor Mars;
Mine be some figured flame which blends, transcends them
    all!"

III

Not for such hopes and fears
Annulling youth's brief years,
Do I remonstrate; folly wide the mark!   15
Rather I prize the doubt
Low kinds exist without,
Finished and finite clods, untroubled by a spark.

IV

Poor vaunt of life indeed,
Were man but formed to feed   20
On joy, to solely seek and find and feast;
Such feasting ended, then
As sure an end to men;
Irks care the crop-full bird?   Frets doubt the maw-
    crammed beast?

V

Rejoice we are allied   25
To That which doth provide
And not partake, effect and not receive!
A spark disturbs our clod;
Nearer we hold of God
Who gives, than of His tribes that take, I must believe. 30

VI

Then, welcome each rebuff
That turns earth's smoothness rough,
Each sting that bids nor sit nor stand but go!
Be our joys three-parts pain!
Strive, and hold cheap the strain;   35
Learn, nor account the pang; dare, never grudge the throe!

VII

For thence,—a paradox
Which comforts while it mocks,—
Shall life succeed in that it seems to fail:
What I aspired to be,   40
And was not, comforts me:
A brute I might have been, but would not sink i' the scale.

VIII

What is he but a brute
Whose flesh hath soul to suit,
Whose spirit works lest arms and legs want play?   45
To man, propose this test—
Thy body at its best,
How far can that project thy soul on its lone way?

IX

Yet gifts should prove their use:
I own the Past profuse   50
Of power each side, perfection every turn:
Eyes, ears took in their dole,
Brain treasured up the whole;
Should not the heart beat once "How good to live and
      learn?"

X

Not once beat "Praise be Thine!   55
I see the whole design,
I, who saw Power, see now Love perfect too:
Perfect I call Thy plan:
Thanks that I was a man!
Maker, remake, complete,—I trust what Thou shalt do!" 60

XI

For pleasant is this flesh;
Our soul, in its rose-mesh
Pulled ever to the earth, still yearns for rest:
Would we some prize might hold
To match those manifold   65
Possessions of the brute,—gain most, as we did best!

XII

Let us not always say,
"Spite of this flesh today
I strove, made head, gained ground upon the whole!"
As the bird wings and sings,   70
Let us cry "All good things
Are ours, nor soul helps flesh more, now, than flesh helps
    soul!"

XIII

Therefore I summon age
To grant youth's heritage,
Life's struggle having so far reached its term: 75
Thence shall I pass, approved
A man, for aye removed
From the developed brute; a God though in the germ.

XIV

And I shall thereupon
Take rest, ere I be gone   80
Once more on my adventure brave and new:
Fearless and unperplexed,
When I wage battle next,
What weapons to select, what armor to indue.

XV

Youth ended, I shall try   85
My gain or loss thereby;
Leave the fire-ashes, what survives is gold:
And I shall weigh the same,
Give life its praise or blame:
Young, all lay in dispute; I shall know, being old.   90

XVI

For note, when evening shuts,
A certain moment cuts
The deed off, calls the glory from the gray:
A whisper from the west
Shoots—"Add this to the rest,   95
Take it and try its worth: here dies another day."

XVII

So, still within this life,
Though lifted o'er its strife
Let me discern, compare, pronounce at last,
"This rage was right i' the main,   100
That acquiescence vain:
The Future I may face now I have proved the Past."

XVIII

For more is not reserved
To man with soul just nerved
To act tomorrow what he learns today: 105
Here, work enough to watch
The Master work, and catch
Hints of the proper craft, tricks of the tool's true play.

XIX

As it was better, youth
Should strive, through acts uncouth,   110
Toward making, than repose on aught found made:
So, better, age, exempt
From strife, should know, than tempt
Further. Thou waitedst age: wait death, nor be afraid!

XX

Enough now, if the Right   115
And Good and Infinite
Be named here, as thou callest thy hand thine own,
With knowledge absolute,
Subject to no dispute
From fools that crowded youth, nor let thee feel alone. 120

XXI

Be there, for once and all,
Severed great minds from small,
Announced to each his station in the Past!
Was I, the world arraigned,
Were they, my soul disdained,   125
Right? Let age speak the truth and give us peace at last!

XXII

Now, who shall arbitrate?
Ten men love what I hate,
Shun what I follow, slight what I receive;
Ten, who in ears and eyes   130
Match me: we all surmise,
They this thing, and I that: whom shall my soul believe?

XXIII

Not on the vulgar mass
Called "work," must sentence pass,
Things done, that took the eye and had the price;   135
O'er which, from level stand,
The low world laid its hand,
Found straightway to its mind, could value in a trice:

XXIV

But all, the world's coarse thumb
And finger failed to plumb,   140
So passed in making up the main account;
All instincts immature,
All purposes unsure,
That weighed not as his work, yet swelled the man's
        amount:

XXV

Thoughts hardly to be packed   145
Into a narrow act,
Fancies that broke through language and escaped;
All I could never be,
All, men ignored in me,   149
This, I was worth to God, whose wheel the pitcher shaped.

XXVI

Ay, note that Potter's wheel,
That metaphor! and feel
Why time spins fast, why passive lies our clay,—
Thou, to whom fools propound,
When the wine makes its round,   155
"Since life fleets, all is change; the Past gone, seize today!"

XXVII

Fool! All that is, at all,
Lasts ever, past recall;
Earth changes, but thy soul and God stand sure:
What entered into thee,   160
That was, is, and shall be:
Time's wheel runs back or stops: Potter and clay endure.

XXVIII

He fixed thee mid this dance
Of plastic circumstance,
This Present, thou, forsooth, wouldst fain arrest: 165
Machinery just meant
To give thy soul its bent,
Try thee and turn thee forth, sufficiently impressed.

XXIX

What though the earlier grooves,
Which ran the laughing loves,   170
Around thy base, no longer pause and press?
What though, about thy rim,
Skull-things in order grim
Grow out, in graver mood, obey the sterner stress?

XXX

Look not thou down but up!   175
To uses of a cup,
The festal board, lamp's flash and trumpet's peal,
The new wine's foaming flow,
The Master's lips aglow!
Thou, heaven's consummate cup, what needst thou with
          earth's wheel?   180

XXXI

But I need, now as then,
Thee, God, who mouldest men;
And since, not even while the whirl was worst,
Did I—to the wheel of life
With shapes and colors rife,   185
Bound dizzily—mistake my end, to slake Thy thirst:

XXXII

So, take and use Thy work:
Amend what flaws may lurk,
What strain o' the stuff, what warpings past the aim!
My times be in Thy hand!   190
Perfect the cup as planned!
Let age approve of youth, and death complete the same!

EXERCISE:

1. In relation to the tone of the poem discuss the stanza form
and the use of direct statement.

2. Discuss metrical and other technical factors involved in the
last line of Stanza IV.

3. Discuss the relation of imagery to statement.

RUBAIYAT OF OMAR KHAYYAM

EDWARD FITZGERALD (1809–1883)

Wake! For the Sun, who scattered into flight
The Stars before him from the Field of Night,
    Drives Night along with them from Heav'n, and
    strikes
The Sultán's Turret with a Shaft of Light.

Before the phantom of False morning died   5
Methought a Voice within the Tavern cried,
    "When all the Temple is prepared within,
Why nods the drowsy Worshipper outside?"

And, as the Cock crew, those who stood before
The Tavern shouted—"Open then the Door!   10
    You know how little while we have to stay,
And, once departed, may return no more."

            .   .   .   .

Come, fill the Cup, and in the fire of Spring
Your Winter-garment of Repentance fling:
    The Bird of Time has but a little way   15
To flutter—and the Bird is on the Wing.

Whether at Naishápúr or Babylon,
Whether the Cup with sweet or bitter run,
 The Wine of Life keeps oozing drop by drop,
The Leaves of Life keep falling one by one.   20

 .   .   .   .   .   .

Think, in this battered Caravanserai
Whose Portals are alternate Night and Day,
 How Sultán after Sultán with his Pomp
Abode his destined Hour, and went his way.

They say the Lion and the Lizard keep   25
The Courts where Jamshyd gloried and drank deep:
 And Bahrám, that great Hunter—the Wild Ass
Stamps o'er his Head, but cannot break his Sleep.

I sometimes think that never blows so red
The Rose as where some buried Caesar bled;   30
 That every Hyacinth the Garden wears
Dropt in her Lap from some once lovely Head.

And this reviving Herb whose tender Green
Fledges the River-Lip on which we lean—
 Ah, lean upon it lightly! for who knows   35
From what once lovely Lip it springs unseen!

Ah, my Beloved, fill the Cup that clears
TODAY of past Regrets and future Fears:
 Tomorrow!—Why, Tomorrow I may be
Myself with Yesterday's Sev'n thousand Years.   40

For some we loved, the loveliest and the best
That from his Vintage rolling Time hath prest,
 Have drunk their Cup a Round or two before,
And one by one crept silently to rest.

And we that now make merry in the Room   45
They left, and Summer dresses in new bloom,
 Ourselves must we beneath the Couch of Earth
Descend—ourselves to make a couch—for whom?

Ah, make the most of what we yet may spend,
Before we too into the Dust descend;   50
 Dust into Dust, and under Dust to lie,
Sans Wine, sans Song, sans Singer, and—sans End!

  . . . . . .

Myself when young did eagerly frequent
Doctor and Saint, and heard great argument
 About it and about: but evermore   55
Came out by the same door where in I went.

With them the seed of Wisdom did I sow,
And with mine own hand wrought to make it grow;
 And this was all the Harvest that I reaped—
"I came like Water, and like Wind I go."   60

  . . . . . .

So when the Angel of the darker Drink
At last shall find you by the river-brink,
 And, offering his Cup, invite your Soul
Forth to your Lips to quaff—you shall not shrink.

Why, if the Soul can fling the Dust aside,   65
And naked on the Air of Heaven ride,
 Were't not a Shame—were't not a Shame for him
In this clay carcase crippled to abide?

'Tis but a Tent where takes his one day's rest
A Sultán to the realm of Death addressed;   70
 The Sultán rises, and the dark Ferrásh
Strikes, and prepares it for another Guest.

And fear not lest Existence closing your
Account, and mine, should know the like no more;
 The Eternal Sáki from that Bowl has poured   75
Millions of Bubbles like us, and will pour.

  . . . . . .

Ah Love! could you and I with Him conspire
To grasp this sorry Scheme of Things Entire,
 Would not we shatter it to bits—and then
Remould it nearer to the Heart's desire!   80

Yon rising Moon that looks for us again—
How oft hereafter will she wax and wane;
   How oft hereafter rising look for us
Through this same Garden—and for *one* in vain!

And when like her, oh Sákí, you shall pass   85
Among the Guests Star-scattered on the Grass,
   And in your joyous errand reach the spot
Where I made One—turn down an empty Glass!

EXERCISE:

   1. Compare this poem with "The Vanity of Human Wishes"
(p. 535) on the basis of theme and tone.
   2. Compare and contrast this poem with "Rabbi Ben Ezra"
(p. 596) with regard to the fitness of stanza form in each case
and with regard to the relation of statement to imagery.
   3. Discuss the technical factors involved in the fourth stanza
of this selection.

LYCIDAS

JOHN MILTON (1608–1674)

Yet once more, O ye Laurels, and once more,
Ye Myrtles brown, with Ivy never sear,
I come to pluck your berries harsh and crude,
And with forced fingers rude
Shatter your leaves before the mellowing year.   5
Bitter constraint and sad occasion dear
Compels me to disturb your season due;
For Lycidas is dead, dead ere his prime,
Young Lycidas, and hath not left his peer.
Who would not sing for Lycidas? he knew   10
Himself to sing, and build the lofty rhyme.
He must not float upon his wat'ry bier
Unwept, and welter to the parching wind,
Without the meed of some melodious tear.
   Begin, then, Sisters of the Sacred Well   15

That from beneath the seat of Jove doth spring,
Begin, and somewhat loudly sweep the string.
Hence with denial vain and coy excuse:
So may some gentle Muse
With lucky words favor my destined urn,   20
And, as he passes, turn,
And bid fair peace be to my sable shroud!
For we were nursed upon the self-same hill,
Fed the same flock, by fountain, shade, and rill;
  Together both, ere the high lawns appeared   25
Under the opening eyelids of the Morn,
We drove a-field, and both together heard
What time the gray-fly winds her sultry horn,
Battening our flocks with the fresh dews of night,
Oft till the star that rose at evening bright   /   30
Towards Heaven's descent had sloped his westering wheel.
Meanwhile the rural ditties were not mute,
Tempered to the oaten flute,
Rough Satyrs danced, and Fauns with cloven heel
From the glad sound would not be absent long;   35
And old Damætas loved to hear our song.
  But, O the heavy change, now thou art gone,
Now thou art gone, and never must return!
Thee, Shepherd, thee the woods and desert caves,
With wild thyme and the gadding vine o'ergrown,   40
And all their echoes mourn.
The willows, and the hazel copses green,
Shall now no more be seen
Fanning their joyous leaves to thy soft lays.
As killing as the canker to the rose,   45
Or taint-worm to the weanling herds that graze,
Or frost to flowers, that their gay wardrobe wear
When first the white thorn blows;
Such, Lycidas, thy loss to shepherd's ear.
  Where were ye, Nymphs, when the remorseless deep 50
Closed o'er the head of your loved Lycidas?
For neither were ye playing on the steep
Where your old bards, the famous Druids, lie,
Nor on the shaggy top of Mona high,
Nor yet where Deva spreads her wizard stream.   55
Ay me! I fondly dream
"Had ye been there". . . for what could that have done?

What could the Muse herself that Orpheus bore,
The Muse herself, for her enchanting son,
Whom universal Nature did lament,   60
When, by the rout that made the hideous roar,
His gory visage down the stream was sent,
Down the swift Hebrus to the Lesbian shore?
    Alas! what boots it with uncessant care
To tend the homely, slighted, shepherd's trade,   65
And strictly meditate the thankless Muse?
Were it not better done, as others use,
To sport with Amaryllis in the shade,
Or with the tangles of Neæra's hair?
Fame is the spur that the clear spirit doth raise   70
(That last infirmity of noble mind)
To scorn delights and live laborious days;
But the fair guerdon when we hope to find,
And think to burst out into sudden blaze,
Comes the blind Fury with the abhorrèd shears,   75
And slits the thin-spun life. "But not the praise,"
Phœbus replied, and touched my trembling ears:
"Fame is no plant that grows on mortal soil,
Nor in the glistering foil
Set off to the world, nor in broad Rumor lies,   80
But lives and spreads aloft by those pure eyes
And perfect witness of all-judging Jove;
As he pronounces lastly on each deed,
Of so much fame in Heav'n expect thy meed."
    O fountain Arethuse, and thou honored flood,   85
Smooth-sliding Mincius, crowned with vocal reeds,
That strain I heard was of a higher mood:
But now my oat proceeds,
And listens to the Herald of the Sea,
That came in Neptune's plea.   90
He asked the waves, and asked the felon winds,
What hard mishap hath doomed this gentle swain?
And questioned every gust of rugged wings
That blows from off each beakèd promontory:
They knew not of his story;   95
And sage Hippotadès their answer brings,
That not a blast was from his dungeon strayed:
The air was calm, and on the level brine
Sleek Panopè with all her sisters played.

It was that fatal and perfidious bark,   100
Built in the eclipse, and rigged with curses dark,
That sunk so low that sacred head of thine.
　　Next, Camus, reverend sire, went footing slow,
His mantle hairy, and his bonnet sedge,
Inwrought with figures dim, and on the edge   105
Like to that sanguine flower inscribed with woe.
"Ah! who hath reft," quoth he, "my dearest pledge?"
Last came, and last did go,
The pilot of the Galilean lake;
Two massy keys he bore of metals twain   110
(The golden opes, the iron shuts amain).
He shook his mitered locks, and stern bespake:—
"How well could I have spared for thee, young Swain,
Enow of such, as for their bellies' sake,
Creep, and intrude, and climb into the fold!   115
Of other care they little reckoning make
Than how to scramble at the shearers' feast,
And shove away the worthy bidden guest.
Blind mouths! that scarce themselves know how to hold
A sheep-hook, or have learned aught else the least   120
That to the faithful herdsman's art belongs!
What recks it them? What need they? they are sped;
And, when they list, their lean and flashy songs
Grate on their scrannel pipes of wretched straw;
The hungry sheep look up, and are not fed,   125
But, swollen with wind and the rank mist they draw,
Rot inwardly, and foul contagion spread;
Besides what the grim wolf with privy paw
Daily devours apace, and nothing said;
But that two-handed engine at the door   130
Stands ready to smite once, and smite no more."
　　Return, Alphéus; the dread voice is past
That shrunk thy streams; return, Sicilian Muse,
And call the vales, and bid them hither cast
Their bells and flowerets of a thousand hues.   135
Ye valleys low, where the mild whispers use
Of shades, and wanton winds, and gushing brooks,
On whose fresh lap the swart star sparely looks,
Throw hither all your quaint enameled eyes,
That on the green turf suck the honied showers,   140
And purple all the ground with vernal flowers.

Bring the rathe primrose that forsaken dies,
The tufted crow-toe, and pale jessamine,
The white pink, and the pansy freaked with jet,
The glowing violet,   145
The musk-rose, and the well-attired woodbine,
With cowslips wan that hang the pensive head,
And every flower that sad embroidery wears;
Bid Amaranthus all his beauty shed,
And daffadillies fill their cups with tears,   150
To strew the laureate hearse where Lycid lies.
For so, to interpose a little ease,
Let our frail thoughts dally with false surmise,
Ay me! whilst thee the shores and sounding seas
Wash far away, where'er thy bones are hurled;   155
Whether beyond the stormy Hebrides,
Where thou, perhaps, under the whelming tide
Visit'st the bottom of the monstrous world;
Or whether thou, to our moist vows denied,
Sleep'st by the fable of Bellerus old,   160
Where the great Vision of the guarded mount
Looks toward Namancos and Bayona's hold:
Look homeward, angel, now, and melt with ruth;
And, O ye Dolphins, waft the hapless youth.
    Weep no more, woeful shepherds, weep no more,   165
For Lycidas, your sorrow, is not dead,
Sunk though he be beneath the watery floor:
So sinks the day-star in the ocean bed,
And yet anon repairs his drooping head,
And tricks his beams, and with new-spangled ore   170
Flames in the forehead of the morning sky:
So Lycidas sunk low, but mounted high,
Through the dear might of Him that walked the waves,
Where, other groves and other streams along,
With nectar pure his oozy locks he laves,   175
And hears the unexpressive nuptial song,
In the blest kingdoms meek of Joy and Love.
There entertain him all the Saints above,
In solemn troops, and sweet societies,
That sing, and singing in their glory move,   180
And wipe the tears forever from his eyes.
Now, Lycidas, the shepherds weep no more;
Henceforth thou art the Genius of the shore,

In thy large recompense, and shalt be good
To all that wander in that perilous flood.   185

Thus sang the uncouth swain to the oaks and rills,
While the still Morn went out with sandals grey;
He touched the tender stops of various quills,
With eager thought warbling his Doric lay:
And now the sun had stretched out all the hills,   190
And now was dropped into the western bay.
At last he rose, and twitched his mantle blue:
Tomorrow to fresh woods and pastures new.

EXERCISE:

1. This is a pastoral elegy written at the death of one of
Milton's friends, Edward King, a young scholar who was
drowned in the Irish Sea. At this time Milton was a relatively
young man already engaged in his pursuit of literary fame. Is
the poem a mere compliment to King and a mere expression
of grief at his death? What is the real theme of the poem?
How is the theme related to the fact of the death of King? What
is the relation of the apparently irrelevant passages (line 63
to line 84, line 103 to line 131) to the theme?

2. Dr. Samuel Johnson criticized this poem adversely in the
following terms:

One of the poems on which much praise has been bestowed is
Lycidas of which the diction is harsh, the rhymes uncertain, and
the numbers unpleasing. What beauty there is we must therefore seek in the sentiments and images. It is not to be considered as the effusion of real passion; for passion runs not after
remote allusions and obscure opinions. Passion plucks no berries
from the myrtle and ivy, nor calls upon Arethuse and Mincius,
nor tells of rough *satyrs* and *fauns with cloven heel*. Where
there is leisure for fiction there is little grief.

In this poem there is no nature, for there is nothing new. Its
form is that of a pastoral, easy, vulgar, and therefore disgusting;
whatever images it can supply are long ago exhausted, and its
inherent improbability always forces dissatisfaction on the mind

When Cowley [a poet who was the contemporary of Milton and who wrote a poem on Hervey] tells of Hervey, that they studied together, it is easy to suppose how much he must miss the companion of his labors, and the partner of his discoveries; but what image of tenderness can be excited by these lines?—

> We drove a-field, and both together heard
> What time the gray fly winds her sultry horn,
> Battening our flocks with the fresh dews of night.

We know that they never drove a-field, and that they had no flocks to batten; and though it be allowed that the representation may be allegorical, the true meaning is so uncertain and remote that it is never sought because it cannot be known when found. . . . He who thus grieves will excite no sympathy; he who thus praises will confer no honor.

("John Milton," in *Lives of the English Poets*)

In this book there is a selection from the poetry of Dr. Johnson himself. Judging from a comparison of "The Vanity of Human Wishes" (p. 535) with "Lycidas," try to determine why Dr. Johnson did not approve of the versification of "Lycidas." How could the versification of "Lycidas," although it is not as regular as that of "The Vanity of Human Wishes," be justified? Dr. Johnson also attacked "Lycidas," because the pastoral imagery, having no basis in biographical fact, indicates insincerity on the part of the poet. Would this attack also apply to "Adonais"? Is not the question of insincerity approached by Johnson on false terms? For instance, does a poet in writing a poem about grief ever try to make the reader have an experience identical with that caused by a bereavement (*Introduction*, pp. 14–16)? Is the pastoral machinery in itself any more artificial than the fiction indulged in by Browning that his loved one is a "star" (p. 392)?

3. Discuss the shifts of tone in this poem.

4. Compare the relation of occasion to theme in this poem with the relation of occasion to theme in "In Memoriam" (p. 555).

THE ANNIVERSARY

JOHN DONNE (1573–1631)

All kings, and all their favorites,
  All glory of honors, beauties, wits,
The sun itself, which makes times, as they pass,
Is elder by a year, now, than it was
When thou and I first one another saw: 5
All other things, to their destruction draw,
  Only our love hath no decay;
This, no tomorrow hath, nor yesterday,
Running it never runs from us away,
But truly keeps his first, last, everlasting day.   10

Two graves must hide thine and my corse,
  If one might, death were no divorce.
Alas, as well as other princes, we,
(Who prince enough in one another be,)
Must leave at last in death, these eyes, and ears,   15
Oft fed with true oaths, and with sweet salt tears;
  But souls where nothing dwells but love
(All other thoughts being inmates) then shall prove
This, or a love increasèd there above,
When bodies to their graves, souls from their graves remove.

And then we shall be throughly blest,   21
  But we no more, than all the rest;
Here upon earth, we are kings, and none but we
Can be such kings, nor of such subjects be.
Who is so safe as we? where none can do   25
Treason to us, except one of us two.
  True and false fears let us refrain,
Let us love nobly, and live, and add again
Years and years unto years, till we attain
To write three score: this is the second of our reign.   30

EXERCISE:

  Examine the relation of the imagery to the theme and tone
in this poem.

TWO SONGS FROM A PLAY

WILLIAM BUTLER YEATS (1865–   )

I

I saw a staring virgin stand
Where holy Dionysus died,
And tear the heart out of his side,
And lay the heart upon her hand
And bear that beating heart away;   5
And then did all the Muses sing
Of Magnus Annus at the spring,
As though God's death were but a play.

Another Troy must rise and set,
Another lineage feed the crow,   10
Another Argo's painted prow
Drive to a flashier bauble yet.
The Roman Empire stood appalled:
It dropped the reins of peace and war
When that fierce virgin and her Star   15
Out of the fabulous darkness called.

II

In pity for man's darkening thought
He walked that room and issued thence
In Galilean turbulence;
The Babylonian starlight brought   20
A fabulous, formless darkness in;
Odor of blood when Christ was slain
Made all Platonic tolerance vain
And vain all Doric discipline.

Everything that man esteems   25
Endures a moment or a day.
Love's pleasure drives his love away,
The painter's brush consumes his dreams;
The herald's cry, the soldier's tread
Exhaust his glory and his might: 30
Whatever flames upon the night
Man's own resinous heart has fed.

These may be considered as separate poems, although they have certain definite connections; and though they form the prologue and epilogue of a play, they are not integral parts of that play. Their obscurity, in so far as they are obscure poems, is not occasioned by their having been removed from the play.

Most readers would, in fact, admit to finding a certain obscurity in these poems. There are really two types of obscurity involved. One type has been touched on in various connections in the discussion of previous poems, especially "The Scoffers," by Blake, and "The Love Song of J. Alfred Prufrock," by Eliot. This type of obscurity comes from the poet's allusions to matters taken from history, literature, etc. The reader may miss part, or all, of the meaning of such a poet because he simply does not have the knowledge which the poet expects from his audience. The reader of the present poems, for example, must be able to grasp the references to Dionysus, Magnus Annus, Troy, the Argo, the Roman Empire, Galilee, Babylon, Plato, and the Dorians. Information of this sort may be said to belong to the common heritage of our civilization, and a poet who makes such general references assumes that he is addressing readers of a certain degree of education. No one reader, of course, possesses a complete body of information of this sort, but he knows that the information is available to him for the interpretation of any particular poem.

The second type of obscurity in these poems springs from a private system of references used by the poet. For instance, the phrase "Babylonian starlight" means for Yeats something much more special than "the starlight in Babylon." It has, in addition to that simple surface meaning, a symbolic meaning for the poet which is not stated in these poems. The reader who does not have an acquaintance with the details of these more personally symbolic meanings may nevertheless have a keen appreciation of the effect of the poem. He may get the surface excitement, and, as a matter of fact, he may grasp the basic theme; but the poem as the poet conceived it is not finally communicated to him. (*It is probably true that no reader ever receives any poem precisely as the poet conceived it;* but the discrepancy is, in such cases as the present one, relatively greater unless the reader will make the effort to acquaint himself with the poet's particular symbols.)

The "Two Songs from a Play" are very fine poems and have appealed to many readers who have no specific information concerning Yeats' system of symbolism; on their own account they are worth examining as fully as possible. But an analysis of them may be further justified in so far as it exhibits the ramifications of a symbolism which underlies the surface effect of a poem.

The poems deal with the moment of transition from the classical civilization to the Christian. In the first poem, the poet represents the birth of Christ, not only as marking a date in history, but as offering a new principle that was to change the nature of all human activity. But though emphasizing the contrast between the two civilizations ("The Roman Empire stood appalled"), the poet establishes, paradoxically, the continuity between them. The Virgin tears the heart from the slain Dionysus. (According to the rites of the Dionysiac cult, those who tasted sacramentally of the flesh of Dionysus might live again.) With her child (the "Star," which we may take as expressing the same principle as Dionysus) she then utters her challenge to the older civilization. The poet implies further that one cycle (of roughly 2000 years) is merely ended and another is begun. (The Great Year, the period in which twelve such cycles run their course, begins, according to Yeats' system, approximately at the birth of Christ.) But this new cycle, the poet implies, will merely recapitulate that which has preceded it: it too will have Troys that rise to power and fall, races of heroes who feed the crows, and Argonauts who search for a Golden Fleece.

A reader unacquainted with Yeats' special symbols and his special way of treating them might infer from the poem much of the foregoing account, but how would he explain the last two lines? If he takes the "Star" merely to be a vague poetic epithet for *child,* or the "Star" to be the Star of Bethlehem, and the "fabulous darkness" the night through which it shone, he has actually missed a great deal of the poet's intention.

As a matter of fact, we can find almost all the imagery of the first "Song," including the "Star" in a passage which Yeats has written in another connection. The poet, contemplating the positions of the heavenly bodies as they were at the birth of Christ, comments as follows:

Three hundred years, two degrees of the Great Year, would but correspond to two days of the Sun's annual journey, and his transition from Pisces to Aries had for generations been associated with the ceremonial death and resurrection of Dionysus. Near that transition the women wailed him, and night showed the full moon separating from the constellation Virgo, with the star in the wheatsheaf, or in the child, for in the old maps she is represented carrying now one now the other. (*A Vision,* [Privately printed] London: Werner Laurie, Ltd., pp. 156.)

Moreover, in another passage of the same work (p. 190), Yeats mentions the fact that a Roman philosopher of the fourth century described Christianity as "a fabulous formless darkness" which blotted out "every beautiful thing." To the reasonable, ordered thought of the Graeco-Roman civilization this new religion seemed to be a superstitious, irrational belief inimical to all clarity and good order and to all its achievements:

Meanwhile the irrational force that would create confusion and uproar as with the cry "The Babe, the Babe, is born"—the women speaking unknown tongues, the barbers and weavers expounding Divine revelation with all the vulgarity of their servitude, the tables that move or resound with raps—still but creates a negligible sect. (*A Vision,* pp. 188–189)

This points the paradox of the antagonism and continuity of the two cycles. Furthermore, it helps explain why the Virgin, usually portrayed as meek, appears here as a fierce, pitiless force at which the Roman Empire stands appalled.

In the second poem we find even more need for special information than in the first. The first stanza of the second poem defines the meaning of Christ as a destroying force. Something of this may be grasped from the last three lines of the first stanza by a person without special information about Yeats' symbolism if that person has adequate historical information. But even such a person would not understand why it is "Babylonian starlight" that is said to usher in the new force, or why this new force is called the "fabulous formless darkness," or why the "odor of blood" is said to destroy the tolerance of the Platonic philosophies.

In dealing with the first "Song" we have already stated that Yeats believes in a cyclic theory of history. He has a particular set of symbols for describing stages in these cycles through which human events move. The beginning of such a cycle he compares in his system of symbols to the new moon, or the dark of the moon; the height of the civilization of such a cycle he compares to the full moon; and the various stages from full back to dark he compares to the gradual decay of the civilization of such a cycle. Thus, the moment of transition from the classical to the Christian civilization he compares to the dark of the moon; and when the moon is dark one sees only the starlight. But why does he call it "Babylonian starlight"?

First, the Babylonians, from remote antiquity, have been associated with the study of the stars. Second, Yeats conceives of the motive power for the new Christian cycle as coming from Asia Minor, where, of course, Babylon had been situated. Yeats conceives of Christ as representing a "primary" force; by "primary"[1] he means objective as opposed to subjective, physical as opposed to intellectual and rational, preoccupation with the mass as

---

[1] When one uses the phases, in popular exposition or for certain symbolic purposes, one considers full Sun as merely the night when there is no moon, and in representing any phase visibly one makes the part which is not lunar dark. The Sun is objective man and the Moon subjective man, or more properly the Sun is *primary* man and the Moon *antithetical* man—terms that will be explained later. Objective and Subjective are not used in their metaphysical but in their colloquial sense. Murray's dictionary describes the colloquial use of the word "objective" thus. All that "is presented to consciousness as opposed to consciousness of self, that is the object of perception or thought, the non-ego." And again, objective when used in describing works of art means "dealing with or laying stress upon that which is external to the mind, treating of outward things and events rather than inward thought," "treating a subject so as to exhibit the actual facts, not colored by the opinions or feelings of the writer." The volume of Murray's dictionary containing the letter S is not yet published, but as "subjective" is the contrary to "objective" it needs no further definition. Under the Sun's light we see things as they are, and go about our day's work, while under that of the Moon, we see things dimly, mysteriously, all is sleep and dream. All men are characterised upon a first analysis by the proportion in which these two characters or *Tinctures*, the objective or *primary*, the subjective or *antithetical*, are combined. (*A Vision*, pp. 12–14)

opposed to preoccupation with the individual and aristocratic. All of these "primary" attributes are associated with the dark of the moon as opposed to the full moon, which symbolizes the intellectual, the rational, the individual, the ordered. Moreover, Yeats associates the East with the "primary" and the West with its opposite, which he calls the "antithetical." Thus the lines

> The Babylonian starlight brought
> A fabulous, formless darkness in

indicate the impingement of a "primary" elemental force coming in from the East to put a close to the ordered, rational "antithetical" cycle of Greek civilization. Further, the two lines suggest a very powerful concrete image—a dark, mysterious cloud boiling up out of the ancient East to obscure all the distinctions that the rational Western mind had made.

We must not understand these opposed aspects, "primary" and "antithetical" to be absolute. They represent an emphasis in the temper of a civilization—not attitudes complete in themselves. The Greeks, for instance, had not been unaware of the supernatural and irrational aspect of life, but the temper of the Greek or Western mind had emphasized the search for rational explanations and systematic ordering, and the gradual development of Greek philosophy up through Aristotle was in the direction of rational explanation.

But the "odor of blood"—blood is another symbol Yeats uses in many of his poems for the "primary" force—renders vain the achievements of the "antithetical" civilization as represented here by Platonic tolerance and Doric discipline. Yeats, then, has used here three different symbols of the general "primary" force; first, "Babylonian starlight," as the symbol which indicates the history and the basic continuity of the force; second, the "fabulous formless darkness" as the force as it appeared to men of the antithetical civilization; and third, blood as symbolizing the violent fact of the transition itself.

The last stanza of the second song seems to abandon the consideration of the particular matters involved in the first stanza of the second song, and, indeed the matters involved in the whole of the first song. It makes a statement about the relation of a man to his various activities—love, art, politics, war. But we must assume that the content of this last stanza is determined by the content of the three preceding stanzas. The problem here is to define the particular nature of the relationship involved.

After presenting, in terms of his symbols, the recurrent cycles of history, the poet sums up by saying that

> Everything that man esteems
> Endures a moment or a day.

But by this he does not mean to imply merely the pathos of the transience of human achievements. Their very meaning, he seems to say, lies in the fact they express man's deepest nature, that in expressing this nature they fulfill man's creative impulse in the act of consuming it. The poet does not intend the same thing by these lines as does the author of the "Rubaiyat of Omar Khayyam" in such a passage as

> They say the lion and the lizard keep
> The courts where Jamshyd gloried and drank deep.

Instead of the static idea of the vanity of all human glory— the fall of the mighty, the feebleness of man's might—Yeats intends a dynamic idea, an idea of development and fulfillment in this process. Most of all, he intends for us to see the varied and constant pageant of man's life, either primary or antithetical in emphasis, as springing from man's own creative and imaginative force. This ties back to the idea of the repetition of the cycles as given in the first song—

> Another Troy must rise and set,
> Another lineage feed the crow.

The whole idea is brought to a climactic summary in the last figure which the poet uses, the figure of man's "resinous heart" feeding the flame, just as, on a larger scale, the last figure of "The Scholar Gipsy" summarizes the poem.

The two songs, as we have seen, involve for their full meaning some knowledge of the poet's personal system of references

But the appreciation of these poems does not require our literal belief in Yeats' system. (*Introduction,* p. 14.) As a matter of fact, the use we have made of the system in connection with these poems has been to throw more light on the meaning of the symbols used here. In a sense, then, the question of the relation of the poet's personal system to these poems is simply an aspect of the question of the relation between a single poem and the complete context of the poet's work. For the reader who had never seen Yeats' *A Vision* might by a careful reading of a large part of his poetry come to an adequate understanding of the symbols. Any one of the odes of Keats, for example, requires, for full appreciation, a knowledge of his other poetry. There is an approach to the body of a man's work as well as to single examples.

BRAHMA

RALPH WALDO EMERSON (1803–1882)

If the red slayer think he slays,
  Or if the slain think he is slain,
They know not well the subtle ways
  I keep, and pass, and turn again.

Far or forgot to me is near;   5
  Shadow and sunlight are the same;
The vanished gods to me appear;
  And one to me are shame and fame.

They reckon ill who leave me out;
  When me they fly, I am the wings; ·   10
I am the doubter and the doubt,
  And I the hymn the Brahmin sings.

The strong gods pine for my abode,
  And pine in vain the sacred Seven;
But thou, meek lover of the good!   15
  Find me, and turn thy back on heaven.

622

TO THE ACCUSER, WHO IS THE GOD
OF THIS WORLD

WILLIAM BLAKE (1757–1827)

Truly, my Satan, thou art but a dunce,
  And dost not know the garment from the man:
Every harlot was a virgin once,
  Nor canst thou ever change Kate into Nan.

Though thou art worshipped by the names divine   5
  Of Jesus and Jehovah, thou art still
The son of morn in weary night's decline,
  The lost traveler's dream under the hill.

EXERCISE:

1. Compare this poem with "Brahma" on the basis of theme.
2. Discuss these two poems on the basis of tone and complications of tone; and compare "To the Accuser" with "Address to the Deil," by Burns (p. 299).
3. Discuss the function of enjambment and pauses in the second stanza of "To the Accuser."

AND DID THOSE FEET

WILLIAM BLAKE (1757–1827)

And did those feet in ancient time
  Walk upon England's mountains green?
And was the holy Lamb of God
  On England's pleasant pastures seen?

And did the countenance divine   5
  Shine forth upon our clouded hills?
And was Jerusalem builded here
  Among these dark Satanic mills?

Bring me my bow of burning gold!
  Bring me my arrows of desire!   10
Bring me my spear! O clouds, unfold!
  Bring me my chariot of fire!

I will not cease from mental fight,
  Nor shall my sword sleep in my hand,
Till we have built Jerusalem   15
  In England's green and pleasant land.

(From Milton)

EXERCISE:

Discuss in detail the means the poet has used to dramatize his theme.

ODE TO THE CONFEDERATE DEAD

ALLEN TATE (1899–   )

Row after row with strict impunity
The headstones yield their names to the element,
The wind whirrs without recollection;
In the riven troughs the splayed leaves
Pile up, of nature the casual sacrament   5
To the seasonal eternity of death;
Then driven by the fierce scrutiny
Of heaven to their election in the vast breath,
They sough the rumor of mortality.

Autumn is desolation in the plot   10
Of a thousand acres where these memories grow
From the inexhaustible bodies that are not
Dead, but feed the grass row after rich row.
Think of the autumns that have come and gone!—
Ambitious November with the humors of the year,   15
With a particular zeal for every slab,
Staining the uncomfortable angels that rot
On the slabs, a wing chipped here, an arm there:

The brute curiosity of an angel's stare
Turns you, like them, to stone,   20
Transforms the heaving air
Till plunged to a heavier world below
You shift your sea-space blindly
Heaving, turning like the blind crab.

       Dazed by the wind, only the wind   25
       The leaves flying, plunge

You know who have waited by the wall
The twilight certainty of an animal,
Those midnight restitutions of the blood
You know—the immitigable pines, the smoky frieze   30
Of the sky, the sudden call: you know the rage,
The cold pool left by the mounting flood,
Of muted Zeno and Parmenides.
You who have waited for the angry resolution
Of those desires that should be yours tomorrow,   35
You know the unimportant shrift of death
And praise the vision
And praise the arrogant circumstance
Of those who fall
Rank upon rank, hurried beyond decision—   40
Here by the sagging gate, stopped by the wall.

       Seeing, seeing only the leaves
       Flying, plunge and expire

Turn your eyes to the immoderate past,
Turn to the inscrutable infantry rising   45
Demons out of the earth—they will not last.
Stonewall, Stonewall, and the sunken fields of hemp,
Shiloh, Antietam, Malvern Hill, Bull Run.
Lost in that orient of the thick and fast
You will curse the setting sun.   50

       Cursing only the leaves crying
       Like an old man in a storm

You hear the shout, the crazy hemlocks point
With troubled fingers to the silence which
Smothers you, a mummy, in time.   55

                    The hound bitch
Toothless and dying, in a musty cellar
Hears the wind only.

                    Now that the salt of their blood
Stiffens the saltier oblivion of the sea,   60
Seals the malignant purity of the flood,
What shall we who count our days and bow
Our heads with a commemorial woe
In the ribboned coats of grim felicity,
What shall we say of the bones, unclean,   65
Whose verdurous anonymity will grow?
The ragged arms, the ragged heads and eyes
Lost in these acres of the insane green?
The gray lean spiders come, they come and go;
In a tangle of willows without light   70
The singular screech-owl's tight
Invisible lyric seeds the mind
With the furious murmur of their chivalry.

            We shall say only the leaves
            Flying, plunge and expire   75

We shall say only the leaves whispering
In the improbable mist of nightfall
That flies on multiple wing:
Night is the beginning and the end
And in between the ends of distraction   80
Waits mute speculation, the patient curse
That stones the eyes, or like the jaguar leaps
For his own image in a jungle pool, his victim.

What shall we say who have knowledge
Carried to the heart?   Shall we take the act   85
To the grave?   Shall we, more hopeful, set up the grave
In the house?   The ravenous grave?

                    Leave now
The shut gate and the decomposing wall:
The gentle serpent, green in the mulberry bush,   90
Riots with his tongue through the hush—
Sentinel of the grave who counts us all!

EXERCISE:

The poet himself has written an account of the composition of this poem (See "Narcissus as Narcissus," *The Virginia Quarterly Review,* Vol. 14, No. 1, pp. 108–122). Study this account, especially sections II, III, and IV, in connection with the poem, as a preparation for writing an analysis.

[handwritten annotations: "iambic pentameter", "form", "a b a b c d e c d e", "varied"]

ODE ON A GRECIAN URN

JOHN KEATS (1795–1821)

Thou still unravished bride of quietness,
   Thou foster-child of silence and slow time,
Sylvan historian, who canst thus express
   A flowery tale more sweetly than our rime:
What leaf-fringed legend haunts about thy shape   5
   Of deities or mortals, or of both,
     In Tempe or the dales of Arcady?
What men or gods are these?   What maidens loth?
   What mad pursuit?   What struggle to escape?
     What pipes and timbrels?   What wild ecstasy?   10

Heard melodies are sweet, but those unheard
   Are sweeter; therefore, ye soft pipes, play on;
Not to the sensual ear, but, more endeared,
   Pipe to the spirit ditties of no tone:
Fair youth, beneath the trees, thou canst not leave   15
   Thy song, nor ever can those trees be bare;
     Bold Lover, never, never canst thou kiss,
Though winning near the goal—yet, do not grieve;
   She cannot fade, though thou hast not thy bliss,
     Forever wilt thou love, and she be fair!   20

Ah, happy, happy boughs!   That cannot shed
   Your leaves, nor ever bid the Spring adieu:
And, happy melodist, unwearièd,
   Forever piping songs forever new;
More happy love! more happy, happy love!   25

Forever warm and still to be enjoy'd,
   Forever panting, and forever young;
All breathing human passion far above,
   That leaves a heart high-sorrowful and cloyed,
      A burning forehead, and a parching tongue.   30

Who are these coming to the sacrifice?
   To what green altar, O mysterious priest,
Lead'st thou that heifer lowing at the skies,
   And all her silken flanks with garlands drest?
What little town by river or sea shore,   35
   Or mountain-built with peaceful citadel,
      Is emptied of this folk, this pious morn?
And, little town, thy streets for evermore
   Will silent be; and not a soul to tell
      Why thou art desolate, can e'er return.   40

O Attic shape! Fair Attitude! with brede
   Of marble men and maidens overwrought,
With forest branches and the trodden weed;
   Thou, silent form, dost tease us out of thought
As doth eternity: Cold Pastoral!   45
   When old age shall this generation waste,
      Thou shalt remain, in midst of other woe
Than ours, a friend to man, to whom thou sayst,
   "Beauty is truth, truth beauty,"—that is all,
      Ye know on earth, and all ye need to know.   50

EXERCISE:

1. Discuss the function in the poem of the statement in the last two lines.

2. Compare this poem with "Among School Children," by Yeats (p. 482), on the basis of theme and the method of presenting the theme.

APPENDIX I

GLOSSARY

ABSTRACT: General statements, or purely theoretical statements, are called abstract. The fundamental method of literature is to present a subject concretely. For instance, a novel or a play tells a particular story of particular people and does not merely give general comments on human nature. It presents individual human beings, directly, in action (p. 38). Poetry, even more than other literary forms, makes use of particular images and incidents for communicating its ideas (p. 43).

ACCENT: See Verse, pp. 642, 643, and p. 212.

ALEXANDRINE: See Verse, p. 642.

ALLEGORY: See Imagery, p. 634.

ALLITERATION: See Verse, pp. 646, 651, and pp. 249–50, 290.

ALLUSION: a reference to some event, person, or place of literary or historical significance. For example, Keats in his "Ode to a Nightingale" alludes to Bacchus, to Provençe, to an incident related in the Book of Ruth in the Bible, etc.

ANAPAEST: See Verse, p. 642.

ARCHAIC DICTION: See Diction, p. 631.

ASSONANCE: See Verse, p. 646, and p. 250.

ATMOSPHERE: This term is obviously a metaphor in itself. It may be taken to mean the general pervasive feeling which may be said to condition the treatment of the subject of any literary work. It is a mistake to connect it exclusively with the setting or background, even though this factor usually does contribute heavily to the establishing of the atmosphere of a particular piece. Rhythm and imagery, for instance, may also contribute to the establishing of the atmosphere (pp. 37, 45, 320, 322, 359–61).

BALLAD: 1. Folk ballad (pp. 32, 34). 2. Literary ballad (pp. 32, 68).

BALLAD STANZA: See Verse, p. 647.

BLANK VERSE: See Verse, p. 648, and pp. 260–62.

CACOPHONY: See Verse, p. 645, and p. 280.

CAESURA: See Verse, p. 644, and p. 241.

CLICHÉ: This term is really a metaphor, for, in French, a "cliché" is a stereotype plate. It is applied to any expression which has lost all freshness and vitality because of continued use—that is, an expression which has become trite (pp. 335, 344, 442).

CLIMAX: The peak of interest or intensity (p. 119).

CLOSED COUPLET: See Verse, p. 647, and p. 257.

COMPENSATION: See Verse, p. 644.

CONCENTRATION: In addition to what has already been said on this topic (p. 167), it may be pointed out that the concentration characteristic of poetry is a result of its highly organized form. This concentration does not depend on logical succinctness or on simplicity. Rather, it depends on the functional relationships existing among a number of complex factors, rhythm, imagery, theme, etc.

CONCRETE: See Abstract, p. 629.

CONNOTATION: See Denotation, p. 630.

CONSONANCE: See Verse, p. 646, and pp. 250–51.

CONVENTIONAL: See Form, p. 632.

COUPLET: See Verse, p. 647, and pp. 254–59.

DACTYL: See Verse, p. 642.

DENOTATION: The denotation of a word is its specific signification. For instance, the denotation of the word *hound* is "one of a class of carnivorous mammals (*Canis familiaris*) of the family *Canidae*, etc." But the word also has a large number of CONNOTATIONS, or implied meanings and associations. The connotations of a word may vary considerably, from person to person and from context to context. For instance, in the discussion of the poem "The Three Ravens" (p. 119) it is pointed out that the hounds symbolize fidelity. That is, certain connotations of the word *hound* are emphasized in the poem. But the word also has other connotations which, in another context, might appear. For instance, the word can be used as an insult. (For another discussion of connotation see p. 194.)

DICTION: Diction is simply the choice of words in poetry or in any other form of discourse. Critics sometimes refer to POETIC DICTION as if certain words were especially poetic without regard to context. But it has been argued that the choice of words in any given poem must be determined by the intention in that particular case (pp. 18–23). The term ARCHAIC DICTION is used to indicate the use of words which are no longer current. For example, some of the words which Coleridge used in "The Rime of the Ancient Mariner" were no longer current in his day (p. 68).

DIMETER: See Verse, p. 642.

DOUBLE RIME: See Verse, p. 646.

DRAMATIC: In earlier discussions frequent reference has been made to the means by which a poet may dramatize his theme. This term is, of course, metaphorical. It must not be taken to mean that a given poem represents in any detail the structure and circumstance of a play except in the sense which has been discussed (p. 23). But the fact that a drama presents its materials directly, concretely, and actively, justifies the use of the term, for poetry tends to present its themes in the same manner, not abstractly.

ELEGY: The term is used loosely for any poem of subjective and meditative nature, but more specially for a poem of grief, such as "Adonais" (p. 417) or "Lycidas" (p. 606).

END-STOPPED LINES: See Verse, p. 645, and pp. 253–54.

ENJAMBMENT: See RUN ON under Verse, p. 645, and pp. 253–54.

EPIC: An epic is a long narrative poem dealing with persons of heroic proportions and actions of great significance. The general type includes poems as different as The Iliad, The Faerie Queene, and Paradise Lost. The MOCK EPIC, or the MOCK HEROIC poem, adopts for ironical or comic purposes the manner of the true epic. It presents trivial materials in a grandiose style.

EUPHONY: See Verse, p. 645.

EXPOSITION: The process of giving the information necessary for the understanding of an action (p. 36).

FEMININE ENDING: See Verse, p. 646.

FEMININE RIME: See Verse, p. 646.

FIGURATIVE LANGUAGE: See Imagery, p. 633.

FOCUS: This term, too, is metaphorical. Just as a burning glass concentrates and unifies the rays of the sun, so a poet may, by various means, concentrate and unify various elements of a poem. This may be accomplished in many different ways. For instance, the farewell spoken by the youngest brother in "The Wife of Usher's Well" may be said to provide a focus for the poem (p. 44). Or the image developed in the last two stanzas of "The Scholar Gypsy" may be said to serve the same purpose (p. 548).

FOOT: See Verse, pp. 642, 643.

FORM: This term is used in various senses. Usually when people use the term they mean METRICAL FORM or STANZA FORM (see Verse, p. 647, and pp. 251–53). But since metrical form, or stanza form, describes an organization of the rhythm of a poem, and since rhythm is only one factor contributing to the poetic effect, it is obvious that the consideration of the form of a poem must, finally, involve the discussion of the organization of other factors in relation to the total effect. In "Lord Randall," for example, both the sequence of questions and answers and the use of refrain build toward the effect in the last stanza (p. 123). In the same way, the use of imagery contributes to the forming of a poem. For example, one may consider the functional interrelations among the images in "The Definition of Love" (pp. 438–40), or in "After Great Pain" (pp. 468–71). In brief, the form of a poem is the organization of the material (rhythm, imagery, idea, etc.) for the creation of its particular effect. Though the poet must finally work out a form for each particular poem, this does not mean that he may not make use of elements of form handed down from other poets—elements such as metrical patterns, symbols, and ways of relating images to a theme, etc. Such elements, when their use has become fixed and recognized, are called CONVENTIONS. For instance, the sonnet in respect to its stanza pattern is a conventional form; or the pastoral elegy, such as "Lycidas," is a conventional form in regard to the "fictions" and symbols it employs in treating the subject of bereavement. A poet may properly make use of conventional patterns of all sorts, but, in so far as he is successful, he must relate the conventional elements to the total form of the individual poem. In this connection one might compare the use made of conventions in "Lycidas" and in "Adonais." But the term *conventional* is sometimes used in an adverse sense to indicate that the poet has merely imitated his models and has failed to adapt the conventional elements to the general form of the individual poem (pp. 335, 343).

FREE VERSE: See Verse, p. 651, and pp. 212–13.

HEPTAMETER: See Verse, p. 642.

HEROIC COUPLET: See Verse, p. 647, and pp. 254–56.

HEXAMETER: See Verse, p. 642.

IAMBIC: See Verse, p. 642.

IMAGERY: The representation in poetry of any sense experience is called imagery. Imagery does not consist merely of "mental pictures," but may make an appeal to any of the senses. Poetry characteristically appeals continually to the senses; this is another way of saying that poetry is concrete. But frequently the poet does not use imagery merely in an obviously descriptive fashion; the poet characteristically makes his statements and conveys his ideas through comparisons, that is, through what is called FIGURATIVE LANGUAGE. The most common types of figurative language are SIMILE and METAPHOR. The first is usually defined as a stated comparison (generally announced by *like* or *as*); the second as an implied comparison (in which the two things compared are identified with each other). The following comparison is a simile:

> The city now doth like a garment wear
> The beauty of the morning. . . .

The following comparison is a metaphor:

> So the soul, that drop, that ray
> Of the clear fountain of eternal day

As for the functions of imagery, it has already been argued (pp. 17–18) that imagery is important, not as decoration but as a means of communication. The particular ways in which imagery functions are too numerous to be dealt with summarily here; indeed, every poem involves imagery in some respect, and, in this book, two sections (Section III and Section VI) have been devoted to studying a number of special instances. Even in so brief a statement as this, however, one fact should be insisted upon: *the function of imagery in poetic communication is never, as is sometimes said, that of mere illustration.* Closely related to the metaphorical process is the process by which a poet creates or makes use of a SYMBOL. The symbol may be regarded, as a matter of fact, as a metaphor from which the first term has been omitted. For example,

> Queen rose of the rosebud garden of girls

is a metaphor, but, if the poet simply refers to the rose to suggest the qualities of love which he is treating and does not indicate the metaphorical framework, he has turned the rose into a symbol. To take another example, the poet in "Patterns" does not say, "Life is a cruel pattern," but deals successively with various sorts of patterns—those of the woman's dress, of the beds of flowers and formal walks in the garden, of social codes and manners—so that the theme may be stated dramatically in terms of a symbol at the end of the poem:

> Christ, what are patterns for!

Obviously, certain symbols are conventional, that is, are commonly accepted as standing for a certain thing. For instance, the cross is by convention a symbol of the Christian religion or the flag is a symbol of a nation. The important use of symbol which the poet makes, however, is not merely a conventional one: he must frequently create his own symbols (pp. 19–21). The poems toward the end of Section III will indicate instances of objects which have been given symbolic force. More specialized instances appear later in the book (Section VI and Section VII).

ALLEGORY, also, is a development of the metaphorical process. Allegory is often defined as an extended metaphor, and, in regard to the matter of structure, this is an adequate description, for an allegory, strictly speaking, is a narrative in which the objects and persons are equated with meanings lying outside the narrative itself. For example, *The Pilgrim's Progress* is on the surface the story of the journey which one of the characters, Christian, makes from his home to the Heavenly City; but, as the name implies, Christian really stands for any Christian man, and the various adventures which befall him stand for the perils and temptation which beset any Christian man in his progress through life. But most allegories are much less obvious than this. Allegory is bad when the system of equivalents involved seems to be mechanical and arbitrary, or seems to be confused (pp. 442–445).

Allegorical personages are frequently PERSONIFICATIONS, that is, abstract qualities treated in the narrative as though they are real persons. For instance, the Giant Despair in *The Pilgrim's Progress* is a personification. But the device of personification is not confined to formal allegory. "An Elegy Written in a Country Churchyard" (p. 510) is not an allegory, yet in such a line as the following it employs personification:

> Let not ambition mock their useful toil.

IMAGIST: A group of poets in England and America, who about 1912 attempted to re-emphasize certain qualities of poetry which they felt had been ignored in the work of their immediate predecessors. Their manifesto reads as follows:

1. To use the language of common speech, but to employ always the *exact word*, not the merely decorative word.
2. To create new rhythms—as the expression of new moods. We do not insist upon "free-verse" as the only method of writing poetry. . . . We do believe that the individuality of a poet may often be better expressed in free verse than in conventional forms.
3. To allow absolute freedom in the choice of subject.
4. To present an image (hence the name: "Imagist"). We are not a school of painters, but we believe that poetry should render particulars exactly and not deal in vague generalities, however magnificent and sonorous.
5. To produce poetry that is hard and clear, never blurred or indefinite.

6. Finally, most of us believe that concentration is the very essence of poetry.

To sum up, one may say that they revolted against the tendency toward vague abstractions and preachments in much nineteenth century poetry (p. 174).

INDIRECT METHOD: See Irony, p. 636.

INTENSITY: It has been said previously (p. 167) that intensity is a result of the highly organized form of poetry. This implies, not simply a loose emotionalism or a preoccupation with thrilling subject matter (pp. 14–16, 320–23), but a meaningful relationship among all the factors involved in a poem.

INTERNAL RIME: Rime occurring within a line unit.

INTERPRETATION: See pp. 5–6, 38–39, 170–71, 175.

IRONY: An ironical statement indicates a meaning contrary to the one it professes to give; an ironical event or situation is one in which there is a contrast between expectation and fulfilment or desert and reward. In the irony of both statement and event there is an element of contrast. Either form of irony, or both, may appear in a poem. For instance, the irony of situation appears in "Johnie Armstrong" (p. 37). But the irony of statement, and of tone and attitude, are more important for poetry. The successful management of ironical effects is one of the most difficult problems of a poet. In actual speech, gesture, tone of voice, and expression all play their part to indicate an ironical intention, but poetry must indicate an ironical interpretation in other ways (p. 295). There are many shades of irony and many functions which irony may perform. Certainly, it is not to be limited to an obvious and heavy sarcasm. For instance, one may observe the different uses of irony in "Portrait" (pp. 296–98), "Channel Firing" (pp. 309–11), "A Litany" (pp. 342–45), "The Blossom" (pp. 372–74), "Ode to a Nightingale" (pp. 412–13), and "The Love Song of J. Alfred Prufrock" (pp. 589–96).

Obviously, irony, along with UNDERSTATEMENT (in which there is a discrepancy, great or small, between what is *actually* said and what *might* be said), is a device of INDIRECTION. That is, the poet does not present his meaning directly, but depends on the reader's capacity to develop implications imaginatively.

ITALIAN SONNET: See Verse, p. 648.

LYRIC: Originally a poem to be sung, but now much more loosely applied to any short poem of which the verse seems to be especially musical, for instance, "Slow, Slow, Fresh Fount," by Ben Jonson (p. 245). In a more special sense, the term is applied to poems having a marked subjective element, for instance, "Tears, Idle Tears," by Tennyson (p. 365), "In Tenebris, I," by Hardy (p. 280), or "Rose Aylmer," by Landor (p. 270).

MASCULINE ENDING: See Verse, p. 646.

MASCULINE RIME: See Verse, p. 646.

METAPHOR: See Imagery, p. 633.

METER: See Verse, p. 641, and pp. 213–16.

MOCK EPIC: See Epic, p. 631.

MOCK HEROIC: See Epic, p. 631.

MONOMETER: See Verse, p. 642.

OBJECTIVE: See Subjective, p. 640, and pp. 169–73.

OCTAVE: See Verse, p. 648.

ODE: A rather extended poem, usually complicated in metrical and stanzaic form, dealing with a serious theme.

ONOMATOPOEIA: See Verse, p. 646, and pp. 242–45.

OTTAVA RIMA: See Verse, p. 648.

PARADOX: A statement which seems on the surface contradictory, but which involves an element of truth. Because of the element of contrast between the form of the statement and its true implications, paradox is closely related to irony (pp. 437–40).

PASTORAL: Loosely used in application to any sympathetic literary treatment of simple rural life. In this sense, "Michael," is a pastoral poem (p. 71). But more specially used, the term applies to a poetry which is based on the conventions descended from the classic poetry of shepherd life. The persons involved are presented as shepherds, although, as in "Lycidas" (p. 606), they may be poets, scholars, and churchmen; and the subjects treated, such as ecclesiastical abuses, in "Lycidas," may have no reference to rural life.

PENTAMETER: See Verse, p. 642.

PERSONIFICATION: See Imagery, p. 635.

PETRARCHAN: The Petrarchan conventions stem from the love sonnets of the Italian poet Petrarch. His sonnets represented his mistress as more than humanly beautiful and as cold and disdainful, and himself as completely abased before her. The imagery is sometimes elaborate and far-fetched (pp. 343–44, 373).

POETIC DICTION: See Diction, p. 631.

QUANTITY: See Verse, p. 644, and pp. 242–45.

QUATRAIN: See Verse, p. 647.

REALISTIC: The term is used throughout this book with reference to the presentation of ordinary, easily observable details, which give an impression of fidelity to the facts of ordinary life (pp. 43, 83). It is to be contrasted with ROMANTIC, which implies the remote, the exotic, the uncontrolled, and the exaggerated. The special senses in which such terms as *realistic*, *romantic*, and *classic* are used by many critics, do not appear in this book.

RHYTHM: See Verse, p. 642, and pp. 209–11.

RIME: See Verse, p. 646, and pp. 249, 251–52.

RIME ROYAL: See Verse, p. 648.

RIME SCHEME: See Verse, p. 647.

ROMANTIC: See Realistic, p. 638.

RUN-ON LINE: See Verse, p. 645, and pp. 253–54.

SENTIMENTALITY: Emotional response in excess of the occasion (pp. 84, 272–73, 320–23, 334–36, 345, 373–74, 437).

SESTET: See Verse, p. 648.

SHAKESPERIAN SONNET: See Verse, p. 648.

SIMILE: See Imagery, p. 633.

SINCERITY: This term is often used in two senses, which are not clearly discriminated. The first sense refers to the poet's attitude, in his private life, toward a subject which he treats in a poem. This sense *may* have no reference to the critical judgment to be passed on a poem. A poet may be thoroughly sincere in this personal sense and yet produce a very bad and sentimental piece of work (pp. 334–36, 339, 442). The second sense in which the term is used really refers to the degree of success which the poet has achieved in integrating the various elements of a poem. When one says that a poem is "sincere," one is actually saying, consciously or unconsciously, that it does not over-reach itself, is not sentimental. Such a judgment is irrelevant to any biographical information concerning the poet.

SONNET: See Verse, p. 648, and pp. 252–53.

SPENSERIAN STANZA: See Verse, p. 648, and pp. 252, 263–65.

SPONDEE: See Verse, p. 644.

STANZA: See Verse, p. 647, and pp. 251–54.

STOCK RESPONSE: The general uncritical response made on conventional or habitual grounds to a situation, subject, phrase, or word in literature. Advertisers frequently attempt to appeal to stock responses by arbitrarily associating a product with patriotism, mother love, etc. (pp. 9–10). The good poet tries to provide in his work the grounds for the responses he seeks from his audience, but the bad poet, like the writer of advertising copy, merely appeals to the already established attitudes, however crude or general they may be (pp. 335, 360).

STREAM OF CONSCIOUSNESS: When a writer presents his material, not in the systematic order of narrative or logical argument, but in an apparently unorganized succession of items connected on grounds of association, he is said to employ the stream-of-consciousness method. In other words, he is imitating the sequence of idea and image in the mind (pp. 412, 592–93).

STRUCTURE: In its fullest sense the structure of a poem may be said to be synonymous with the form, but in practice there is a tendency to use the term with special reference to the arrangement of, and the relationships among, episodes, statements, scenes, and details of action, as contrasted with the arrangement of words, for which the term *style* is usually employed (p. 45).

STYLE: This term is usually used with reference to the poet's manner of choosing, ordering, and arranging his words. But, of course, when one asks on what grounds certain words are chosen and ordered, one is raising the whole problem of form. Style, in its larger sense, is essentially the same thing as form (see Form, p. 632, and Structure, p. 639).

SUBJECTIVE: The ordinary terms applied to the person who perceives or experiences a thing, and the thing perceived or experienced, are *subject* and *object*. Of course, all poetry, since it involves the communication of attitudes, feelings, and interpretations, is subjective; that is, it represents the response of a person, the poet, to an object or to a body of objects (p. 171). But there are, nevertheless, distinctions of degree. One may properly say, for example, that the "Ode to a Nightingale" (p. 412), or "The Love Song of J. Alfred Prufrock" (pp. 592–93), is highly subjective, and that "The Main-Deep" (p. 171), or "The Pear Tree" (p. 173), is objective.

SUBSTITUTION: See Verse, p. 643.

SYMBOL: See Imagery, p. 634.

TERZA RIMA: See Verse, p. 647.

TETRAMETER: See Verse, p. 642.

THEMATIC DEVELOPMENT: The structure of a poem as related to the presentation of the theme.

THEME: The basic idea or attitude which is presented in a poem (pp. 38, 121, 295–96, 489–93. See Interpretation, p. 636).

TONE: Foreword (pp. 295–96) and all Analyses in Section V.

TRIMETER: See Verse, p. 642.

TRIPLE RIME: See Verse, p. 646.

TROCHEE: See Verse, p. 642.

UNDERSTATEMENT: See Irony, p. 636.

UNITY: The unity of a poem, like that of any work of art, is a unity of final meaning, or total impression. This does not imply simplicity, or merely logical congruity or sequence. Poetry that is *merely* simple achieves its effect by eliminating all elements that might prove discordant, but all really good poetry attains its unity by establishing meaningful relationships among its apparently discordant elements. This is why critics sometimes say of a successful poem that it gives a sense of revelation, or gives a new insight. For—far from trimming our view of a subject down to a single, neatly ordered category —the poet ties together the items of ordinarily disordered experience into a new, and unsuspected, pattern. For example, the sort of imaginative unity which is analyzed in Coleridge's discussion of Shakespeare's *Venus and Adonis* (pp. 383–84). Poems like "Lycidas" (p. 606), "Among School Children" (p. 482), "Frescoes for Mr. Rockefeller's City" (p. 563), and "Ode to a Nightingale" (p. 407) offer examples of the unification of apparently discordant materials. Moreover, many poems, like some of the folk ballads or "The Ancient Mariner" (p. 49), which are praised for their "fine simplicity" reveal, on examination, a very complicated structure underlying the effect of simplicity which they achieve. A student should be careful to make the distinction between poems that are *apparently* simple because the poet has unified his materials, and poems that are simple because the poet has avoided using all materials with which he was afraid to deal.

VARIATION: See Verse, p. 643, and pp. 239–42, 242–45.

VERS DE SOCIÉTÉ: a term applied to light verse, usually occasional and complimentary, which deals in a witty and polished fashion with subjects that, on the surface at least, are not very serious. But there is no sharp line of demarcation between *vers de société* and serious poetry. For instance, "To His Coy Mistress," by Andrew Marvell (p. 474), opens with the tone and manner of *vers de société*.

VERSE: This term is sometimes used to mean a single line of a poem. But the more usual, and more important, meaning of the term, and the one which will be discussed here, is that form of literary composition in which the rhythms are regularized and systematized. All language, as has been pointed out, has the quality of rhythm (p. 209). It has also been pointed out that there are varying degrees of formalization of rhythm and that between the clear extremes of ordinary prose and strict verse there are many intermediary types (pp. 210–11).

METER, in English verse, is the systematization of rhythm in so far as this systematization is determined by the relationships between ACCENTED or stressed, and UNACCENTED or unstressed, syllables. (This relationship between accented and unaccented syllables is a fundamental factor, but not the only factor, in determining the RHYTHM. Other factors involved—pause and emphasis conditioned by the length of syllables, consideration of sense, rime, etc., which will be treated below—contribute to the total rhythmical effect.) The following set of terms is conventionally accepted to describe meter:

> FOOT: The metrical unit, a combination of one accented and one or more unaccented syllables.

> The following types of feet will describe most metrical situations which occur in English verse:

>> IAMB: An unaccented followed by an accented syllable (ăvóid).

>> ANAPAEST: Two unaccented syllables followed by an accented syllable (ĭntĕrvéne).

>> TROCHEE: One accented followed by one unaccented syllable (ónlў).

>> DACTYL: One accented syllable followed by two un-accented syllables (háppĭlў).

The LINE of verse is composed of one or more feet. The following names are used to denominate various line lengths:

> MONOMETER: One foot
> DIMETER: Two feet
> TRIMETER: Three feet
> TETRAMETER: Four feet
> PENTAMETER: Five feet
> HEXAMETER: Six feet (or ALEXANDRINE)
> HEPTAMETER: Seven feet

(Since a line is really a unit of attention, lines composed of more than six feet tend to break up into smaller units. Thus a heptameter line tends to break up into a tetrameter and a trimeter line.) There are two items involved in the metrical description of a line: the kind of foot and the number of feet. Thus, a line containing five iambic feet would be described as *iambic pentameter*.

Even in a single poem a poet does not necessarily adhere to a single type of foot. For various reasons, he may make a SUBSTITUTION of one type of foot for another (p. 226). For instance, in the opening of the following line a trochaic foot has been substituted for an iambic foot:

$$\overset{/}{}\qquad\qquad\overset{/}{}\quad\overset{/}{}\qquad\overset{/}{}$$

Crowned from some sing-le herb/or tree

Thus far in discussing a scheme for indicating the scansion of verse, all accented syllables have been assumed to have equal value; and in an abstract schematic sense this is true. But obviously, in the rhythm as one actually experiences it in a particular line, accented syllables may be of very unequal emphasis (pp. 239–40). By the same token, unaccented syllables are not on the level an abstract scheme would seem to indicate (pp. 239–40). Sometimes, a syllable which, according to the abstract metrical pattern, would be unaccented, receives, because of rhetorical considerations, what appears to be an additional accent in its own right. For instance, consider the first foot of the following line:

$$\overset{//}{}\quad\overset{/}{}\quad\overset{/}{}\qquad\overset{/}{}\qquad\overset{/}{}$$

Ah, what avails the sceptered race (p. 271)

The syllable *ah* may be said to receive a SECONDARY ACCENT (indicated as above). When we consider the relationship between the two syllables of such a foot as *ah, what*, we may describe the situation by saying that there is a HOVERING EFFECT, or a HOVERING ACCENT (indicated as follows: *ah, what*). A similar situation is created when by substitution, or by the use of an IMPERFECT FOOT (a foot from which the unaccented syllable is missing [1]), two regularly accented syllables are thrown into juxtaposition (p. 228). When a hovering accent occurs, or when two regular accents are forced together, there may be said to exist a SPONDAIC MOVEMENT. (This term is derived from one of the feet in classical metrics, the SPONDEE, which is composed of two long syllables, for classical verse is founded on QUANTITY. But the term is frequently used in reference to English verse, which is founded on accent, to describe any situation in which two accents, either when the two accents are not in the same foot, or when one is a secondary accent, appear in succession.)

Though English metrics is founded on accent, the factor of quantity has an importance in determining the final rhythmical result of a piece of verse as actually experienced. But this factor never appears in systematic form; it works, merely, to condition and modify the rhythmical pattern defined by accent (pp. 242–43).

Another factor which influences the total rhythmical effect of a particular line is the location of pauses defined by sense units. Although the line may be abstractly considered as a metrical unit, it is obvious that the sense unit does not always coincide with the line unit. In practice, sense divisions— phrase, clause, sentence, etc.—often terminate within the line; and conversely, the end of a line unit may divide a sense unit. The pauses within the line, their number and their emphasis, are extremely important in determining the tempo of the rhythm. The main pause is called the CAESURA, but there may be, obviously, other pauses, which may be called SECOND- ARY PAUSES. Variety, from line to line, in the location of the

---

[1] Such a defect may be COMPENSATED for in either or both of two ways. First, by a pause before the accented syllable, or second, by the addition of an unaccented syllable elsewhere in the line. As an example of the first:

Speech after long silence; *it* is right (p. 227)

Of the second:

Upon the supreme *theme* of Art and Song (p. 228)

In the first instance, there is COMPENSATION for the imperfect foot *it* by the caesaural pause; in the second there is compensation for the imperfect foot *theme* by the preceding anapaest, *the supreme.*

caesura, and of secondary pauses, is extremely important in versification.   But mere variety is not the only consideration, for in good verse there is usually a connection between the handling of pauses and the total intention of the poet (pp. 241-42, 253-54). Just as sense units may divide a line, so the end of a line, conversely, may divide sense units. This factor becomes extremely important when considered not in relation to a single line, but in relation to a group of lines. When the end of the line does not coincide with a normal speech pause of any kind, it is called RUN-ON; when it does coincide with such a pause, the line is said to be END-STOPPED.

The factor of sound, as well as that of sense, may condition the rhythm of verse.   For example, the presence of certain groups of consonants may create a FORCED PAUSE.   Such combinations, which cause a sense of strain in pronunciation and a slowing of rhythmical tempo, are said to be CACOPHONOUS (p. 280).   Conversely, consonant combinations easily pronounced give a sense of ease and tend to speed up the rhythmical tempo.   Such combinations are said to be EUPHONIOUS. Euphonious effects are pleasant in themselves, but euphony in itself is never a primary objective of any good poem—that is, poetry, even lyrical poetry, is not *merely* "verbal music." Thus far we have spoken of relationships among consonants. The term euphony in its largest sense is used also to designate agreeable relationships among vowel sounds.   Obviously, some vowels are closely related to each; others much more distantly related.   For example, the vowel sounds *oh* and *ah* are formed far back in the voice chamber; the vowel sounds *ee* and *ay* far to the front.   Obviously, a line dominated by closely related vowels gives—provided other factors support this effect—a sense of ease and fluency.   Some lines may achieve a sense of vitality by the fact that the vowels in them are not closely related—involve shifts in position.   There may be shifts in position, either violent or modulated.   The combinations, in this matter, are, of course, infinite.   One may associate certain effects with certain vowels—an effect of heaviness with the sonority of the long back vowel sounds (*oh*, *ah*, *aw*, *oo*), but this factor is only effective in so far as it operates in conjunction with other factors.

Certain words have been developed, as a matter of fact, in imitation of the sounds which they designate. Words like *hiss* and *bang* are called ONOMATOPOEIC words. But the relation of sound to sense, in onomatopeia, and the relation of mood to specific vowel sounds, are not fundamental factors in poetic effects (p. 243).

Euphony, like cacophony, is to be considered in its functional relation to the total effect of a poem. This general relationship among the sounds in verse, of which cacophony, euphony, and onomatopeia are aspects, is sometimes called VERSE TEXTURE. Other aspects of this relationship are ASSONANCE, CONSONANCE, and ALLITERATION. Assonance may be defined as identity of vowel sounds, as in the words *scream* and *beach* (p. 250); consonance as the mere identity of the pattern of consonants, as in the words *leaves* and *lives* (pp. 250–51); alliteration as the repetition of consonants, particularly initial consonants, as in the words *lovely* and *lullaby* (pp. 249–50). But assonance, consonance, and alliteration may also be considered as forms of RIME because they involve degrees of identity of sound combinations. The term *rime*, however, is ordinarily used in the sense of END RIME, which is the identity in the riming words of the accented *vowels* and of all consonants and vowels following. (This is sometimes called *rime suffisante* in distinction from *rime riche*, or identical rime, in which there is identity of the accented *syllables* of the words rimed. For instance: *incline* and *decline*.) The forms of end rime may be classified as follows:

MASCULINE RIME: the rimed syllables are the last syllables of the words in question, as in *surmount* and *discount*.

FEMININE RIME: the rimed syllables are followed by identical unaccented syllables, as in *delightful* and *frightful*. When only one unaccented syllable occurs after the accented syllable, there is an instance of DOUBLE RIME, as in the above example. When two unaccented syllables, identical in the rimed words, follow the accented syllable, there is an instance of TRIPLE RIME. For example: *regretfully* and *forgetfully*.

In addition to the above forms of rime there are approximate rimes, sometimes called SLANT RIMES. For instance, *rover* and *lover*, or *steel* and *chill*. Such rimes are not necessarily indications of a poet's carelessness, but may be used for various special effects. When the student discovers examples of slant rime, he should try to determine what the effect would have been with the emphasis of full rime. Many rimes that now are apparently slant rimes were, of course, in the past full rimes; therefore, a student should try to determine the pronunciation used by the poet before passing judgment on a poem of the past.

Although there is a pleasure in rime in itself, and rime may serve as a decoration to verse, the fundamental function of rime is that of a binder. It is this function which makes rime so important as a device of emphasis and as a means of defining a pattern of lines, or a STANZA. Indeed, most stanzas involve not only a fixed pattern of lines, but also a pattern of rimes, or a RIME SCHEME. An unrimed stanza is to be defined by the prevailing type of foot, the number of feet in each line, and the number of lines. That is, a poem might be written in iambic tetrameter quatrains. The definition of a rimed stanza would add to such items the description of the rime scheme. For instance, the rime scheme of the envelope quatrain in which the first and fourth lines and the second and third lines rime, would be described as follows: *abba*. The most ordinary stanzas and line patterns are:

COUPLET: (1) TETRAMETER couplet, sometimes called the octosyllabic couplet; iambic tetrameter, *aa*. (2) HEROIC couplet; iambic pentameter, *aa*. (A couplet is CLOSED when the sense is completed within its compass.)

TERZA RIMA: iambic pentameter TERCETS in LINKED rime: *aba-bcb-cdc*, etc. *Ode to the West Wind*

QUATRAIN: (1) BALLAD MEASURE, or quatrain; iambic, first and ~~fourth~~ lines tetrameter, second and fourth lines trimeter, with second and fourth lines riming. (This may be indicated as follows: iambic, *4-3-4-3*, *xaxa*.) A very common variant of this pattern rimes *abab*. (2) ENVELOPE, or "IN MEMORIAM" quatrain; iambic tetrameter, *abba*. (3) "RUBAIYAT" quatrain; iambic pentameter, *aaxa*. (4) Several other types of quatrains are commonly used but have no name (see Index of Stanza Forms, p. 674).

RIME ROYAL: iambic pentameter, *ababbcc*.

OTTAVA RIMA: iambic pentameter, *abababcc*.

SPENSERIAN STANZA: iambic pentameter, *ababbcbcc*. The last line is an alexandrine.

SONNET: An iambic pentameter poem in fourteen lines. There are two general types: (1) ITALIAN sonnet: iambic pentameter, *abbaabba-cdecde*. The first eight lines, in which the general theme of the sonnet is usually presented, is called the OCTAVE. The last six lines, in which the poet presents the conclusion he has drawn from the theme, is called the SESTET. Common variants on the rime scheme of the sestet are *cdeedc*, *cdedce*. (2) SHAKESPEARIAN sonnet: iambic pentameter, *ababcdcdefefgg*. In its typical form this sonnet presents and develops its theme in the three quatrains, and states a conclusion in the couplet. But there are many variations of this method of handling the idea. For instance, the first two quatrains may be used as the octave of the Italian sonnet is used and the last quatrain and couplet as the sestet. (3) Irregular sonnets: in addition to various slight departures from the strict rime scheme of the Italian and Shakespearian sonnet, there occur rime schemes which are highly irregular (Index of Stanza Forms, p. 679).

Although BLANK VERSE is not a form of stanza it may be considered here. Blank verse is unrimed iambic pentameter, not broken into formal units. This is not to say that in the case of blank verse, and for that matter in the case of other verse forms not employing the stanza (for instance, the couplet) a poem may not be broken up into VERSE PARAGRAPHS, which may be defined as large rhetorical units. For instance, "Lycidas," is divided into verse paragraphs (p. 606).

The definitions given above present various elements of VERSIFICATION in an abstract and schematic form. In studying such definitions one should realize that they are merely terms conventionally accepted to describe certain verbal situations which occur in poetry and are not to be taken as "laws" for the making of poetry. When they are applied to the criticism of particular poems, it should be remembered that the degree of excellence achieved by any poet in his management of such technical factors is to be determined by answering the following questions: *how has he adapted these technical factors to his total intention?* As has been pointed out earlier, there are two general types of such adaptation. First, these technical factors bear a general relation to the other factors of a poem. Second, these technical factors may be adapted to specific dramatic effects. The function of meter in these connections has already been discussed (pp. 215-20). And the function of alliteration, assonance, and consonance, as devices for binding and for emphasis, has received some treatment (pp. 248-51). All the principles which have been mentioned in reference to meter will apply, with appropriate modifications, to the various factors grouped together under the term *verse texture*. To sum up with a vivid instance which will illustrate the use and the misuse of these various technical factors, consider the following comments by Aldous Huxley on the first two stanzas of "Ulalume" (p. 355).

These lines protest too much (and with what a variety of voices!) that they are poetical, and, protesting, are therefore vulgar. To start with, the walloping dactylic meter is all too musical. Poetry ought to be musical, but musical with tact, subtly and variously. Meters whose rhythms, as in this case, are strong, insistent and practically invariable offer the poet a kind of short cut to musicality. They provide him (my subject calls for a mixture of metaphors) with a ready-made, reach-me-down music. He does not have to create a music appropriately modulated to his meaning; all he has to do is to shovel the meaning into the moving stream of the meter and allow the current to carry it along on waves that, like those of the best hairdressers, are guaranteed permanent. . . . A quotation and a parody will illustrate the difference between ready-made music and music made to measure. I remember (I trust correctly) a simile of Milton's:—

> Like that fair field
> Of Enna, where Proserpine gathering flowers,
> Herself a fairer flower, by gloomy Dis
> Was gathered, which cost Ceres all that pain
> To seek her through the world.

Rearranged according to their musical phrasing, these lines would have to be written thus:—

> Like that fair field of Enna,
>   where Proserpine gathering flowers,
> Herself a fairer flower,
>   by gloomy Dis was gathered,
> Which cost Ceres all that pain
> To seek her through the world.

The contrast between the lyrical swiftness of the first four phrases, with that row of limping spondees which tells of Ceres' pain, is thrillingly appropriate. Bespoke, the music fits the sense like a glove.

How would Poe have written on the same theme? I have ventured to invent his opening stanza.

> It was noon in the fair field of Enna,
>   When Proserpina gathering flowers—
>   Herself the most fragrant of flowers,
> Was gathered away to Gehenna
>   By the Prince of Plutonian powers;
> Was borne down the windings of Brenner
>   To the gloom of his amorous bowers—
> Down the tortuous highway of Brenner
>   To the god's agapemonous bowers.

The parody is not too outrageous to be critically beside the point; and anyhow the music is genuine Poe. That permanent wave is unquestionably an *ondulation de chez Edgar*. The much too musical meter is (to change the metaphor once more) like a rich chasuble, so stiff with gold and gems that it stands unsupported, a carapace of jewelled sound, into which the sense, like some snotty little seminarist, irrelevantly creeps and is lost. This music of Poe's—how much less really musical it is than that which, out of his nearly neutral decasyllables, Milton fashioned on purpose to fit the slender beauty of Proserpine, the strength and swiftness of the ravisher and her mother's heavy, despairing sorrow!

We have given above in schematic form the conventions which apply to most modern English verse, a verse which is based on the patterned relationship between the number of syllables in a line and the disposition of accents. But there are two general types of verse represented in this book to which these conventions do not apply.

The first is FREE VERSE. Free verse, as the term implies, does not conform to any pattern. This is not to say, of course, that none of the individual metrical situations previously discussed here may not appear, incidentally, in a free verse poem. But it is to say that such situations occur only incidentally. There is, obviously, in free verse a much looser organization of rhythm than there is in ordinary accentual-syllabic verse. In reading a free verse poem, the student should ask himself whether there is an appropriate relationship between the rhythmical factor and the other factors involved.

The second is a verse derived originally from the Old English four-beat alliterative verse (p. 249). In the modern survivals of this verse, the alliteration may or may not appear, but the verse is still characterized by the presence of four heavily accented syllables and a varying number of unaccented syllables, the line usually being broken between the second and third accents by an emphatic caesura.[1] For example:

<pre>
    /   /   /   /
Sing a song of sixpence, pocketful of rye,
    /   /   /   /
Four and twenty blackbirds baked within a pie
</pre>

or:

[1] For a detailed discussion of this point see Jakob Schipper, *A History of English Versification,* Oxford: Oxford University Press, pp. 85–125.

      /   /   /   /

My heart's in the Highlands, my heart is not here;

      /   /   /   /

My heart's in the Highlands, a-chasing the deer

                                          (Robert Burns)

or:

         /   /   /   /

For our hearts are grown heavy, and where shall we turn to,

   /   /   /   /

If thus the king's glory, our gain and salvation

                                          (William Morris)

There are two poems in this book which seem to fall into this class, "Upon a Dead Man's Head," by John Skelton (p. 375), and "The Revenge," by Tennyson (p. 91). The two-beat line of the poem by Skelton may be taken as representing a half of the normal four-beat line of this tradition.[1] Although a number of the lines of "The Revenge" may be scanned in terms of the conventions of accentual-syllabic verse, many other lines cannot be so scanned, and the least arbitrary approach to the metrics of the poem is that of regarding it as developed from a norm of four heavy beats with clusters of varying numbers of unaccented syllables or syllables with secondary accents. For example:

       /   /   /   /

  But I cannot meet them here, for my ships are out of gear

or:

      /   /   /   /

Then spake Sir Richard Grenville: "I know you are no coward

In the shorter lines of the poem the same principle holds, although there may be only two beats in a line.

VERSE TEXTURE: See Verse, p. 646.

  [1] But other factors perhaps modified the development of this form.

INDEX OF AUTHORS, TITLES, AND FIRST LINES [1]

[1] Authors are in small capital letters, titles in italics, and first lines in Roman type. An asterisk indicates that the poem has been analyzed.

INDEX OF STANZA FORMS

This index is, as every such index must be, somewhat arbitrary at certain points. For instance, some poems which might be regarded as written in couplets or as written in an irregular form, have been classed under stanzas. All poems are in iambic meter unless otherwise noted. Variations are not specified unless very numerous. The use of repetition is not necessarily indicated, but in some cases, where it seems particularly important, it is marked as follows: a¹, a1.

[1] The meter is highly irregular and *may* be resolved in terms of a four-beat line (See *Glossary*, under Verse, p. 651).